SCOUNDREL'S TALE

SAMUEL BRANNAN, CIRCA 1860.
This image shows Brannan at the height of his influence in California.
Courtesy, California Historical Society.

SCOUNDREL'S TALE

The Samuel Brannan Papers

by
Will Bagley

UTAH STATE UNIVERSITY PRESS
Logan, Utah
1999

Copyright © 1999 Will Bagley
All rights reserved

LIBRARY OF CONGRESS CATALOG CARD NUMBER 99-12606
ISBN -0-87421-273-1

published by
Utah State University Press
Logan, Utah 84322-7800

This book was first published by the
Arthur H. Clark Company
as Volume 3 in the series
KINGDOM IN THE WEST:
The Mormons and the American Frontier

Brannan, Sam 1819–1889.
  Scoundrel's tale : the Samuel Brannan papers / edited by Will Bagley,
  480 p. cm.
  Originally published : Spokane, Wash. : A. H. Clark, 1999, in series :
Kingdom in the West.
  Includes Bibliographical references and index.
  ISBN 0-87421-273-1
  1. Brannan, Sam 1819–1889–Archives. 2. California—History—
1846–1850—Sources.   3. California—History—1850–1950—
History—Sources.   4. West (U.S.)—History—1848–1860—Sources.
5. West (U.S.)–History— 1860–1890 —Sources. 6. Pioneers—
California—Archives. 7. Mormons—California—Archives. 8. Business-
men—West (U.S.) —Archives.   9. Rogues and vagabonds—West (U.S.)—
Archives.   I. Bagley, Will, 1950-   .   II. Title
F 865.B83B73 1999
978–dc21
                                              99-12606
                                              CIP

FOR MY FATHER

Who inspired my love of History and California

Contents

ILLUSTRATIONS

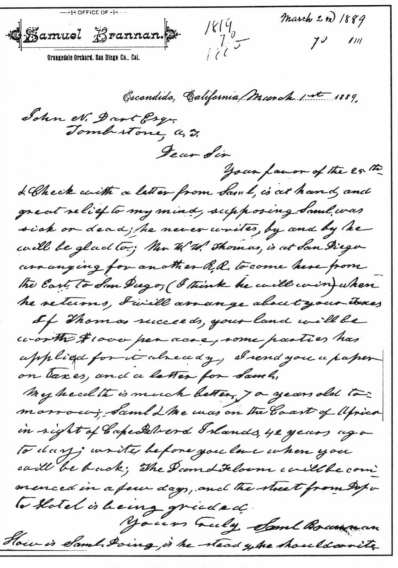

SAMUEL BRANNAN'S LAST LETTER.
This 1 March 1889 note to John N. Dart from the Herbert S. Auerbach Collection
is the last known Brannan letter, and provides a good example of his handwriting.
At the top of the page, someone has calculated Brannan's age on the eve of his
seventieth birthday, but it had actually been forty-three years since Brannan was
off the coast of Africa on the *Brooklyn*. For the transcription, see page 420.
Courtesy, Special Collections and Manuscripts, Harold B. Lee Library, Brigham Young University.

ACKNOWLEDGMENTS

I can only begin to recognize a few of the many people who assisted my decade-long search for the papers of Samuel Brannan and contributed to the writing of this book. The staffs of the Bancroft Library, the California State Library, the California Historical Society, the Nevada Historical Society, the Utah State Historical Society, the Society of California Pioneers, Special Collections and Manuscripts at the Harold B. Lee Library at Brigham Young University, Special Collections at the University of Utah's Marriott Library, the Daughters of Utah Pioneers' Pioneer Memorial Museum, the Henry E. Huntington Library, the Library & Archives of the Reorganized Church of Jesus Christ of Latter Day Saints, the National Archives, and the Library of Congress helped locate many of the original manuscripts presented in this volume. Once again I owe a great debt to the staff of the Historical Department and Library of the Church of Jesus Christ of Latter-day Saints, whose untiring assistance has opened new windows into the life of Samuel Brannan and the history of the American West. I would like to acknowledge the special help of librarians and archivists Barbara Bernauer, Peter J. Blodgett, Kelly Bullock, Bonnie Hardwick, Walter Jones, Patricia Keats, Michael N. Landon, Sue McDonald, Ronald E. Romig, William W. Slaughter, Teena Stern, Gregory C. Thompson, Ronald G. Watt, Bradford Westwood, David Whittaker, and Sibylle Zemitis.

Editor Ron Priddis first inspired my search for the historical Samuel Brannan more than a decade ago, and my brother, Patrick Francis Bagley, did much of the initial archival research. Historians Gordon Morris Bakken, Lyndia Carter, D. Robert Carter, Richard O. Cowan, Peter DeLafosse, Richard Etulain, George Hesse, Robert Hoshide, Myrtle S. Hyde, Kristin Johnson, Gary F. Kurutz, Ben Lofgren, Edward Leo Lyman, Brigham D. Madsen, Tom Mahach, Floyd A. O'Neil, Stanley W. Paher, D. Michael Quinn, Wil "Bud" Rusho, Terry L. Shoptaugh, and Harold Schindler extended my understanding of Brannan and his times.

G. Ralph Bailey, Robert J. Chandler, H. Michael Marquardt, Albert Shumate, and Norma B. Ricketts graciously shared their extensive private Brannan archives.

Pat and Ray Branstetter, Wade W. Fillmore, Dale Goodwin, Floyd Garn Hatch, Lilian Kelly, Jack Lambrecht, Carolyn McDonald, Carol Osburn, and Stewart R. Wyatt share family ties to Brannan's story. They provided me a wealth of information that otherwise would have been unavailable.

David L. Bigler, Lorin K. Hansen, William P. MacKinnon, Kevin J. Mullen, and Kenneth N. Owens have reviewed all or parts of this book. Newell G. Bringhurst and Malcolm E. Barker, who have made their own scholarly pursuits of Sam Brannan, deserve special thanks for sharing their time, sources, transcriptions, suggestions, and insights.

The mistakes that remain in this work are, of course, solely my own.

EDITORIAL PROCEDURES

This collection of Samuel Brannan's papers seeks to represent faithfully the original records in a readable format. With the noted exceptions, these transcriptions preserve the grammar, spelling, and diction of the original documents. Capitalization follows the source except that the first letters of sentences and of personal names are capitalized; where the case used in the manuscript is ambiguous, I follow standard capitalization. Where a writer employed commas in the place of periods, I have converted them to periods, but otherwise I maintained the punctuation (or its absence) of the original, except to add periods to the ends of sentences.

The material is organized into chapters, sections, and documents. Each document contains an abbreviated heading identifying the source and its location. Full citations for these items, including manuscript numbers, are found in the bibliography.

I use *sic* sparingly, where the word or phrase in question is especially significant or could be mistaken for a typo. Brackets enclose added letters, missing words, and conjectural readings. [Blank] indicates a blank space, while other bracketed comments, such as [*tear*], note physical defects in the manuscript. I have dropped most superscripts and placed interlined insertions in their logical location in the text. Long, unbroken text is sometimes divided into paragraphs, while single-sentence paragraphs are occasionally combined. Underlined text is italicized, while crossed-out text is rendered as ~~strikethroughs~~.

Footnotes cite published sources by author, title, and page number. Where available, newspaper citations are to page/column: 2/3. The bibliography contains a complete listing of all the books, articles, newspapers, journals, and manuscripts referenced in annotations. I italicize book titles and put article and thesis titles in quotation marks. Manuscript citations appear in plain text without quotation marks. Quoted material from the sources reproduced in this volume book is not footnoted, though it is sometimes cross-referenced.

SAMUEL BRANNAN, CIRCa 1853.
Herbert S. Auerbach, whose father knew Sam Brannan in
California, collected material for an unfinished Brannan
biography over many decades. Auerbach attributed this
image from his famous Western history collection to
noted photographer Matthew Brady.
Courtesy, G. Ralph Bailey.

PREFACE

Few nineteenth-century Americans were more representative of the spirit of their times than the mercurial Samuel Brannan (1819–1889). His career as a preacher, newspaper publisher, California and Arizona pioneer, vigilante, filibuster, politician, philanthropist, railroad developer, and land speculator spanned all but the first and last decades of the century. More than simply a child of his times, Brannan was an archetype of his gilded age. Raised in New England and always a proud Yankee (who never made a surviving mention of his Irish heritage), Brannan caught the visionary fever of the Church of Jesus Christ of Latter-day Saints (abbreviated as LDS, and popularly known as the Mormons), falling under the spell of its founding prophet, Joseph Smith. While still in his teens, the Panic of 1837 wiped out his first real-estate ventures and for several years he wandered the country as an itinerant printer. Brannan rejoined the Saints, as they still like to be called, as a missionary who became one of the "Young Lions of Mormonism" in the city of New York, publishing two of the church's newspapers. Beguiled by tales of the West—and envisioning a Mormon kingdom on its shores—Brannan led the first shipload of American emigrants to California in 1846. They arrived in Yerba Buena, today's San Francisco, just weeks after it was seized by the American navy. Poised on the cutting edge of Manifest Destiny, Brannan made the most of opportunities as they arose. As "the herald of the gold rush," he spread the news of the 1848 gold discovery to California and the world, building a legendary fortune in the process.

Always a dreamer, Brannan rejected the Mormon kingdom when Brigham Young refused to follow him to California. After his many schemes made him one of the richest men in the West, Brannan pursued an empire of his own in Hawaii. His taste for violence drove him to pull the rope that hanged the first victim of San Francisco's vigilantes—and his love of street fighting eventually nearly killed him. Brannan's "flaming devotion to the tender passion" and "his dissolute habits and drunken freaks" were notorious, but his philanthropies were more publicly celebrated. He founded newspapers, schools, fraternal and political organizations, banks, resorts, ranches, and railroads. As perhaps the state's first real-estate agent and commercial vintner, he helped define the American vision of the California dream. For decades Brannan personified the spirit of the young West—and his early visits to Europe may have helped create the stereotype of the crude and acquisitive Yankee millionaire. The highs and lows of his colorful life traced the trajectory of the history of California. In an old age of financial ruin, Brannan never quit looking for El Dorado, and never gave up.

"Sam" Brannan was a man of many contradictions and a puzzle to his contemporaries. They spoke of him with both admiration and approbation. Listen to the chroniclers of *The Annals of San Francisco*, written by Brannan's friends in 1854: "His energy, abilities, force of character and courage, are very great, and have only the more conspicuously shown in the face of those obstacles and dangers that would have hampered and filled with dread less bold and talented men." Yet H. H. Bancroft could call him "odious, soul-bespattered, spiteful," and William White denounced his "tyrannical, overbearing and grasping disposition." Brannan, wrote Asbury Harpending, "had a history of thrills and adventures which, if gathered into book form, would make the heroes of Dumas look cheap and commonplace . . . he was of a coarse-fibered nature, with a rather forbidding, saturnine face, but singularly keen witted, resolute, and fearing neither man nor the devil."

I have spent the last ten years trying to separate the historical Samuel Brannan from the legendary Sam. I initially hoped merely to identify his companions on the trip to Green River in 1847, a mystery that remains unsolved. My search for Sam Brannan has taken many detours, including an adventure with his trail companion, Abner Blackburn, but chasing his shadow through the archives of the West has been a singular pleasure and has, perhaps, made me a better historian. As a native Utahn who was educated in California, I found Brannan's story fascinating and sadly forgotten. His status as Mormonism's most notorious apostate—and as the man who most publicly challenged the power of Brigham Young—still makes Brannan a comforting figure to many dissenting

Latter-day Saints. Mormon Utah better remembers the man who spent less than two weeks in the state than does California, where Brannan contributed substantial color to the state's legend and much to its culture. It is unfortunate that California appears to have so little appreciation of its past, even as it celebrates the sesquicentennial of the gold rush Samuel Brannan set in motion.

Was Brannan a scoundrel? His papers usually portray him as a hero, but the title of this collection reflects my judgment that it is impossible to chart this rake's progress without concluding that he was, even by the standards of his time, a scoundrel. This conclusion is not meant as condemnation: even as a scoundrel I find him more entertaining than evil. The rascal interpretation of scoundrel is much more applicable to Brannan's case than the villain definition. I admit to a great affection for the scoundrels who played such a significant role in the story of the American West. It is hard to tell the rags-to-riches-to-rags story of Brannan's life—with his forays into alcoholism, gambling, political corruption, and adultery—without turning the story into an object lesson, but Brannan himself never expressed remorse for any of his actions. While it is fashionable to picture Brannan and his counterparts as robber barons, their own generation placed more value on their contributions than on their crimes. Many of Brannan's enterprises might not meet the ethical standards of modern scholars, but among his contemporaries, he "was generally considered honest." My belief that Brannan was a scoundrel is based on his involvement in the vigilante movement, the dishonesty that surrounded his many filibustering schemes, and the scandalous conduct of his personal life rather than on his actions as a businessman or religious leader. Like many of his compatriots, he was fiercely committed to his principles—and however problematic those principles may appear from the perspective of the late twentieth century, Brannan regarded himself a man of honor and integrity to his dying day. I am confidant that the man I have come to know would not give a damn about my assessment of his character.

Brannan's story is encrusted with legend. The blame for many of the tall tales that surround his flamboyant life must be laid at his own door, for as a master of self-promotion he repeatedly recreated his past to fit his current needs, so many of the facts of his career have vanished behind a veil of myth. He successfully obscured his early connection with the Mormons, and no one has ever puzzled out Sam Brannan's true relationship with the LDS church—a complex web of religious fervor, personal belief and ambition, and sectarian politics. His papers provide many insights into his true commitment to Mormonism.

Historians have generally accepted Brannan's misrepresentations of his personal history and of his relations with the Latter-day Saints. Few scholars have examined the original sources, relying instead on the heavily edited versions of Brannan's correspondence that appeared in B. H. Roberts' official annals of the LDS church or in the Journal History, a daily "scrapbook" of Mormon history consisting of journals, minutes, letters, and articles extracted (and expurgated) from church records by Andrew Jenson. These works had a clear agenda: to align the contentious history of "primitive" Mormonism with the triumphant story of the American republic popular in the early twentieth century. To do this, the institution's official historians created a record that often ignored and sometimes misrepresented the controversial elements of its past. A more open approach by the modern church archives lets us look at the missing pieces that better tell the complex story of Mormonism's role in the American West of the 1840s.

Ideas may be more interesting than facts, but a documentary historian's task is to present the sources containing the empirical facts necessary to create accurate interpretations of history. I have tried to put Brannan's life in context and note the wider issues reflected in his story, but my job is basically prosaic: to present previously unavailable historical evidence. Such work may be professionally unfashionable, but the documentary record is essential to our understanding of the past. Without a solid basis in fact, the most imaginative and inventive interpretations of the past are not history, but myth.

Brannan's life presents a singular challenge to a biographer, which helps explain why no reliable Brannan biography exists. Invented conversations and misguided attempts to apply fictional techniques to history marred the several popular biographies published before 1960, and no one has subsequently tackled the subject. A number of competent historians have attempted Brannan biographies but failed to complete them, probably defeated by the elusive subject himself. Sorting out the facts of Brannan's life from the myths he created would challenge the devil himself.

Embedded in the documents that make up this collection is a tremendous amount of misinformation. If one counted up the sources that repeat Brannan's story that he joined the Mormon church in 1842, the evidence might seem to overwhelm the fact that he converted in 1833, if not earlier. The narrative text is as accurate as I can make it, but readers should treat the information in the source material with caution—and some skepticism. This book is not for the faint-hearted, but is intended for those with a love for the raw materials from which history is written. Anyone assembling a documentary history can only speculate on the usefulness of their work, but I have tried to arrange and connect the material so that it tells its many stories—of Mormonism, Manifest Destiny and the conquest of California, Western exploration and settlement, the gold rush, vigilantism, and the Gilded Age—as part of the central story of Brannan's life. These voices tell an amazing tale.

SOURCES

Samuel Brannan's collection of his personal papers did not survive the nineteenth century, so I have assembled this book from a variety of sources. Like his fortune, Brannan's papers were scattered to the four winds, so gathering this material has been no easy task. Surprisingly, my quest turned up enough material to fill two volumes. While this book contains most of Brannan's surviving correspondence and original writing, I have only summarized his extensive correspondence with Jesse Carter Little. The appendix provides a calendar of Brannan letters not included in this volume. I selected the documents presented here not only for the insights they give into the life of Samuel Brannan, but especially for the light they shed on early Mormonism and its role in the American West. As the third volume in the Arthur H. Clark Company series KINGDOM IN THE WEST: *The Mormons and the American Frontier*, it gives preference to materials related to LDS history.

This book applies a broad definition to what constitutes Samuel Brannan's papers. The scattered condition of his surviving papers—and the odd circumstances that led to the survival of some materials and the disappearance of others—makes this is an eclectic collection. In addition to documents, letters, and published records that can be definitely attributed to Brannan or his intimate associates, it includes contemporary biographies, newspaper articles, and documents that used Brannan as a primary source. Brannan's activities in the 1840s and 1880s are well documented, but for the critical decades at the peak of his career in California, practically nothing survives from his personal record. To supplement Brannan's own writings from these years, I have relied on contemporary memoirs, newspaper articles, and official documents. The chronological arrangement and the connecting narrative attempt to shape these sources into a life history that reflects the dazzling complexity of the times. Yet broad fields of Brannan's activities—his role in the political wars of early San Francisco, his acquisition of much of John Sutter's empire and his subsequent battle with the Sacramento "squatters," and the litigation surrounding his land claims and railroad investments—remain largely unexplored.

Brannan's papers are remarkable for their historical, not their literary, value. As C. V. Gillespie told H. H. Bancroft, Brannan "appeared to have the Bible at his tongue's end, but when he came to write the words he couldn't spell two lines correctly." His handwriting was so poor that he asked Brigham Young to "Excuse my bad writing, if I should write from now till dooms day I should ~~write~~ wright no better, it is not because I am too lazy to learn, but as the Hoosier said it is not in me." He admitted, "I have writen all my lifetime and yet I can hardly read my own handwriting so you must excuse me." Brannan told C. F. McGlashan in 1879 that writing was "never an agreeable occupation to me." Still, Brannan was a better writer than he realized—and he had a great story to tell. "You will here the history of the whole when I write the History of California next year and a good many other things," he told Jesse Little. "I am the only man living that can write it correctly."

The most significant concentration of Brannan material is in the Brigham Young Collection at the Archives of the Historical Department of the Church of Jesus Christ of Latter-day Saints (referred to hereafter as LDS Archives) in Salt Lake City, Utah. Originally located in a "Samuel Brannan File," the documents have been reorganized based on current archival procedures. The archive's staff has graciously given me much help tracking down Brannaniana in their collection.

The Samuel Brannan Papers (cited hereafter as BYU Brannan Papers) at Special Collections and Manuscripts, Harold B. Lee Library, Brigham Young University, Provo, Utah (cited as BYU Library), contain Brannan's correspondence with his old friend Jesse C. Little. They constitute the largest collection of Brannan manuscript material. Only a few examples of this large correspondence are printed in full. The Bancroft Library, University of California, Berkeley (cited as Bancroft Library), the Society of California Pioneers, the California Historical Society, and the Huntington Library also possess smatterings of Brannan's correspondence, as do several individuals. During the early 1940s Virginia and Dr. Frederick Sorensen conducted extensive research for a Brannan biography that was, unfortunately, never published. Their extensive notes and a rough draft of Dr. Sorensen's excellent work are now in the Virginia Sorensen Papers at Boston University (cited as Sorensen Papers). This material includes typescripts of Brannan's letters to his nephew and business manager, Alexander Badlam, Jr. Many of the originals owned by Badlam's daughter, Maude Pettus, are now in the California State Library, but some of the items viewed by scholars in the 1940s, including letters owned by Pettus' daughter, Mrs. W. F. Mitchell, have vanished. For these items and for the text of some illusive newspaper articles, I have relied on Frederick Sorensen's excellent transcriptions, which Newell Bringhurst generously shared with me.

Although this collection favors Brannan's Mormon papers, it contains much material about California, Hawaii, Arizona, and Mexico. It should be a useful source book on the role of Indians, religion, violence, expansionism, politics, racial conflict, women, and business in the American West. Perhaps it will contribute our knowledge of the Latter-day Saints' part in Manifest Destiny. I hope that this study will provide a better understanding of the life and times of Samuel Brannan, replacing a few of the myths embedded in this forgotten American story with the much more interesting truth.

WILL BAGLEY
Salt Lake City
August 1998

SAMUEL BRANNAN, CIRCA 1854.
From Soulé, Gihon, and Nisbet, *The Annals of San Francisco . . . To Which are Added,*
Biographical Memoirs of Some Prominent Citizens.

Chapter I

"A MAN BY THE NAME OF BRANNAN"

"I was born in 1819 on the 2 day of March," Samuel Brannan recalled in his old age.[1] He came into the world in Saco, Maine, a thriving coastal village fourteen miles southwest of Portland, the fifth and last child of Thomas and Sarah Knox Emery Brannan.[2] His father was an emigrant from Waterford, Ireland, who had worked in a whiskey distillery to earn his passage to America in 1775. A widower himself, Thomas Brannan filed his intention to marry the widow Sarah Emery, the niece of Henry Knox, George Washington's secretary of war, in September 1805.[3]

Thomas Brannan was sixty-three when his youngest son was born. He appears to have been a reasonably prosperous farmer with an interest in progressive religion. No facts survive about his son's childhood, but Thomas Brannan took pains to educate his other children and enrolled himself at the age of fifty-nine in the Thornton Academy. Dubious family traditions picture him as "irritable, and hard drinking," and a victim of "bone fever"—rheumatism.[4] The same traditions claim that he beat his wife and children, but in his own old age Samuel Brannan wrote that

---

[1]Brannan to Little, 11 February 1885, Folder 2, BYU Brannan Papers.

[2]Brannan had a middle initial, variously identified as S, E, K, or L, letters that are easily confused in manuscript sources. The Kirtland High Council minutes and the *Millennial Star*, 1 September 1848, 317, referred to "Samuel S. Brannan," as did Smith, Jr., *History of the Church*, 2:206, 208. In Willard Richard's 23 May 1845 diary entry, the initial "S" is identical with the "S" in "Samuel." The obituaries of Samuel L. Brannan, Jr., may use the correct initial; see Brannan, Memorabilia, 1924–1979, LDS Archives. What name the initial stood for is unknown, but Brannan seldom used it in California.

[3]Stellman, *Sam Brannan*, 13–15. See also Brannan Family Group Record in the Paul Bailey Papers; and *Record Book of the Town of Saco*, 20.

[4]Bailey, *Sam Brannan and the California Mormons*, 17; and Stellman, *Sam Brannan*, 13–16. Death dates for Thomas and Sarah Brannan are unknown, but their great-granddaughter, Maude Pettus, thought that "Patrick" Brannan "lived to be over—well over—100." See Pettus to Virginia Sorensen, 13 July 1942, Sorensen Papers.

his father "was natures nobleman and his wife also." Sarah Brannan was said to be frail, so there may be something to the stories that the care of her youngest child fell largely to her daughter, Mary Ann. Samuel Brannan was undoubtedly close to his older sister, who by 1832 had married a carriage maker named Alexander Badlam and moved to Boston.

Since 1830 representatives of a new religion born in the heated revivalism of upstate New York's "Burnt-over District" had scoured New England for converts to their millennial beliefs. Founded in 1830 by Joseph Smith, Jr., the visionary son of a poor farmer, the church based its doctrines on *The Book of Mormon*, which Smith claimed was holy scripture he had translated from an ancient record engraved on gold plates. His followers in the Church of Christ (as it was first named) were already popularly known as Mormons, but would soon take the name Latter-day Saints. Smith's reputation as a necromancer and n'er-do-well soon started his young religion on a western pilgrimage that would ultimately take it to the Rocky Mountains. By 1832 the Brannan family had established connections with the religion that would forever shape the life of Samuel Brannan.

He Could Touch Nothing that Did Not Turn to Gold: Brannan in *The Annals*, 1854

The following biographical sketches provide an overview of Samuel Brannan's remarkable life. Three are well-known reports published during his lifetime that were clearly based on information provided by the subject himself. The first, written early in 1854, reveals that Brannan was already recasting his personal history to distance himself from the Mormon church. Most biographers accepted the information in this "biographical memoir" from *The Annals of San Francisco* without reservation, but it contains several errors worth noting. The author, certainly one of Brannan's friends, admitted his connection to the Latter-day Saints, but post-dated his actual conversion by almost a decade, masking the years Brannan spent at the fledgling faith's Kirtland headquarters. The sketch claimed that Brannan conceived and financed the *Brooklyn* expedition, both possible but dubious propositions. It conceded that this "band of American pioneers" consisted of "mostly Mormons," but downplayed their religious affiliation, and presented Brannan's 1851 filibustering expedition to Hawaii, the most embarrassing episode of his early career, as a real-estate venture. Still, this earliest account of Brannan's life was filled with wonderful detail and pictured him at the height of his power and influence.

"SAMUEL BRANNAN," IN SOULÉ ET AL, THE ANNALS OF SAN FRANCISCO, 748–53.

This gentleman was born at Saco, State of Maine, on the 2d of March, 1819, at which town he was educated, and passed his earlier years. In 1833, he removed, accompanied by his sister, to Lake County, Ohio, where he entered upon an apprenticeship to letter-press printing. Before the term of his indenture was completed, in 1836, he bought up the remainder of his time. He next entered into the great land speculations of the memorable years 1836 and 1837, when the whole Union was seized with the mania of making fortunes without the worrying need of time, trouble or capital. It was rather an early age at which to become a land-jobber, but Mr. Brannan had a deal to do in the world, and pretty soon began his eventful career. He came out of his speculations nearly as he went into them—without a cent. In 1837, he turned again to the press, and travelled the country as a journeyman printer. In the course of the five following years he visited most of the States in the Union, staying a month in one town, two months in another, and perhaps half a year in some more important place, [during] all [of] which time he was regularly pursuing his profession. In 1842, he connected himself with the religious body of Mormons, and for several years advocated their principles, and published for them in New York a weekly newspaper, styled the "New York Messenger."

In 1846, he conceived the idea of leading a band of American pioneers to the shores of the Pacific, to settle and grow into greatness among the Mexicans of California. At his own risk and expense, he chartered the ship "Brooklyn," of three hundred and seventy tons, fitted it up with state-rooms and cabins, supplied it amply with provisions and all necessaries for the voyage, and invited intending emigrants to take passages for California. Two hundred and thirty-six passengers embarked (mostly Mormons), of which number, upwards of sixty were adult females, and about forty children of both sexes. With the foresight that distinguishes him, Mr. Brannan provided a printing-press, types, and a stock of paper, flour-mill machinery, ploughs and other agricultural implements, and a great variety of such scientific apparatus as would likely be of service in the new country.

On the 4th of February, 1846, the "Brooklyn" sailed from New York; and about five months afterwards, touched at the Sandwich Islands for refreshments. Here Mr. Brannan landed all the passengers, provided them with lodgings on shore, and was at the whole expense of maintaining them while there. Previously and during the voyage, many of the passengers, considering the uncertain character of the country they were proceeding to, and the probable chances of a war between the United States and Mexico at the time when they would likely reach California, had formed themselves into an association for mutual support and protection, whereby they were to work in common and share together the proceeds of their labor. Mr. Brannan was chosen president of this association. The other members had nothing which they could put into the common stock but their labor; while the president, patron, projector and leader of the party contributed every thing he possessed—agricultural implements, machinery, tools, provisions and all. There were then only twenty-four muskets on board; but Mr. Brannan purchased at the Sandwich Islands, in addition, one hundred and fifty stand of arms.

Here, a person by the name of Henry Harris, residing in Honolulu, became enamored with a pretty girl among the passengers, and wished to join the association, so that he might follow and marry her, which he afterwards did. The proposal of Harris, however, to become one of the party, was at first opposed by Mr. Brannan, who foresaw difficulties and future contention in the scheme; but when much intercession was used by influential people, whom he regarded, that Harris should join the expedition, he consented. Harris paid accordingly his fifty dollars for a passage, and no more. It is from these circumstances, that afterwards arose a great scandal and much foolish clamor against Mr. Brannan; and as the subject has been little understood, and never before properly explained, we think it right to enter a little upon it.

On the 31st of July the Brooklyn reached San Francisco, then called Yerba Buena, and the passengers immediately landed and squatted among the sand-hills of the beach. At first, there was but trifling work for them to do, save to erect adobe or frame buildings for the former inhabitants or themselves. There was little or no money to be had, in those days, in the country; but their services were paid mostly in provisions or goods, which were consumed almost as soon as received.

Harris, after three months' connection with the association, grew tired of it, and wished to separate. He therefore asked the directors to let him go, and pay him the share of the common stock to which he thought he was entitled. His application was refused on many plausible grounds; and, particularly, in regard to the payment of any thing, for this very good reason, that the association, after paying its debts, had nothing to divide—neither money nor goods, that could be shared. They further urged, that Harris himself had been all along supported out of the common stock of provisions, and had received in that way a great deal more than his services were

worth. Still dissatisfied, Harris raised an action, not against the whole association nor the directors conjointly, but against Mr. Brannan himself, as an
individual.

The suit terminated in a formal jury trial, the first that ever took place in
California. The alcalde[5] of the day, Washington A. Bartlett, presided as
judge; and Colonel W. H. Russell acted as counsel for the defendant. The
jury found for Mr. Brannan. Upon these simple circumstances, and the subsequent dissolution of the association, people have raised calumnies against
the subject of our sketch, and have pretended to consider him indebted for
his present position and wealth to the money he wrongfully withheld from
his fellow-partners in the firm of "S. Brannan & Co.," under which name the
association had conducted its business transactions. The fact was, that Mr.
Brannan had supplied every thing to that association, and received nothing
from them but the original moderate passage-money; that being only from
fifty to seventy-five dollars for each passenger. At the dissolution of the
concern, in 1847, its property was sold, its debts were paid, and the balance
of the funds properly divided among the remaining partners.

Mr. Brannan, meanwhile, both as a partner and president of the associated immigrants, and as an individual on his own account, was interested in
a number of speculations. In 1846, he erected the machinery of two flour-
mills in the existing Clay street, which were the first introduced into the
country. He also, in January, 1847, projected and published a weekly newspaper called the "California Star," which was the first journal that appeared
in San Francisco, and is the parent of the present "Alta California." In the
fall of 1846, he had likewise commenced a farm at the junction of the San
Joaquin and Stanislaus rivers; but, whether this was too slow a business for
him, or that Providence had simply willed it otherwise, his farming operations were failures, and he abruptly abandoned them.

In the fall of 1847, Mr. Brannan started a store at Sutter's Fort, under
the name of C. C. Smith & Co. This was the first establishment of the kind
formed in Sacramento Valley. In the spring of 1848, he bought out Mr.
Smith, who shortly afterwards returned to the Atlantic States, possessed of
a handsome fortune. The business was subsequently conducted under the
firm of S. Brannan & Co. The discovery of gold had in the mean while
attracted a great crowd to the neighborhood, and the demands and riches of
the miners speedily enhanced prices to a wonderful degree. During 1848
and 1849, sales were made at this store to the extent of $150,000, on an
average, *per month*. But, by and by, competition began to appear, and the first
enormous profits to become less. Many other stores were established in the
mining districts, and great importations of goods arrived. Mr. Brannan then

---

[5]The alcalde was a Mexican office combining the functions of mayor and justice of the peace.

withdrew from the new City of Sacramento, which had suddenly grown up around him. While there he had speculated in the town allotments like every other person, and like every body else, in the beginning, made much money by his ventures. Indeed it seemed at this period, that, like Midas, he could touch nothing that did not turn to gold in his hands.

In 1849, Mr. Brannan returned to San Francisco, where he had still preserved a residence and citizenship, and under the firm of Osborn & Brannan carried on an extensive business for nearly a year in China merchandise. In the noted affair of the "hounds" about midsummer of 1849, he took an active part, and mainly helped to extirpate that society of rascals from the town. In August following, he was elected a member of the first regular town-council; and in 1851 was chosen president of the famous "Vigilance Committee."

Since the beginning of 1850, Mr. Brannan has chiefly confined his business operations to dealings in real estate, both in San Francisco and Sacramento, in which he has been so successful that he is, at this moment, reported to be the wealthiest man in either city, and perhaps in all California. The many buildings which he has bought or erected are distinguished by their strength and magnificence; and form some of the most striking and beautiful features of the city. Montgomery street is particularly remarkable for several of these substantial and elegant structures.

About the end of 1851, Mr. Brannan visited the Sandwich Islands, where he bought extensive properties, farming land, and building lots and houses at Honolulu. In 1853 he was elected a senator of California. Business and private engagements, however, calling him to the Atlantic States, he was compelled to relinquish the high honor and resign the office.

It is impossible, in our narrow limits, even to allude to the numberless public affairs in which this gentleman has been engaged in California. From the earliest to the latest records of San Francisco, we discover him appearing at every public meeting, and taking a prominent part in municipal business. At one time he is encouraging the establishment of the first school, and offering handsome contributions to the building; at another he is haranguing the people on the subject of the "hounds;" now, he takes on himself the responsibility of hanging a rogue by Lynch law for the benefit of the citizens; now, he charitably bestows sufficient land for a cemetery to the Odd-Fellows, of which Order he is an active member; now, he bullies, reasons, and conquers in some purely municipal matters, urging a local improvement, or where jobbing officials seek to line their pockets at the expense of the community. His energy, abilities, force of character and courage, are very great, and have been only the more conspicuously shown in face of those obstacles and dangers that would have hampered and filled with dread less bold and talented men. He is but young still, yet years have passed since he was first noted for consummate skill and daring. No man has been better abused than himself, and yet to no man, perhaps, would the community sooner turn to find a leader who would not scruple to act determinedly upon principles which he thought right in themselves, however strange and obnoxious they might appear at first sight, or to commonplace, feeble minds. Such a man was needed in the early days of San Francisco, when vice and crime overshadowed law and justice. All honor and praise should therefore be freely given to him who did his duty at that perilous period. On other accounts, Mr. Brannan is entitled to notice and commendation;—as a citizen whose great private fortune has been invested in bestowing beauty and grandeur on the town, as well as for his well known public services on very many occasions.

Mr. Brannan married in 1844, and has now a family of four children. He is slightly above the middle stature, and well-proportioned. His features are agreeable and intelligent, while beautiful dark eyes give increased animation to his face. He dresses somewhat richly, as is the fashion in San Francisco; and, in fine, wears a modest "imperial."

WILLIAM V. WELLS: SAMUEL BRANNAN, 1870

William V. Wells' 1870 sketch derived Brannan's early life from *The Annals of San Francisco*, with one interesting alteration: it made no mention of Mormonism. Published in the year of the divorce that would wreck his fortunes, it contained not a hint of Brannan's already legendary drinking and womanizing. Wells' biography is primarily useful for its listing of his subject's "curious variety of enterprises" in the 1860s, including many business ventures and philanthropies. It provided some of the only information about Brannan's investments in southern California and the Comstock, his contributions to the Union cause in California, and his support of Benito Juarez in Mexico.

WILLIAM V. WELLS, "SAMUEL BRANNAN,"
IN SHUCK, ED., *REPRESENTATIVE AND LEADING MEN OF THE PACIFIC COAST*, 454–59.

Few names among the prominent pioneers of California have been more intimately associated with the history of the State than that of Mr. Brannan. A review of many of the principal enterprises for internal or metropolitan improvement during the last twenty years, would reveal him as their zealous advocate and master mind, either as the originator or the active promoter;

and it may be truly said of him that he has not been surpassed by any individual in the State in his encouragement of industrial progress . . .[6]

It is impossible in our narrow limits even to allude to the numberless public affairs in which this gentleman has been engaged. The cause of education always found in him an ardent supporter. He was one of the founders of the first school in San Francisco, and contributed liberally to the edifice. Many of the most elegant structures in the city were built by him, and there is scarcely an institution of public usefulness that has not experienced the benefits of his impulsive generosity. Libraries; institutes; lectures for charitable purposes; churches; Sunday schools; works of art; literary societies; military companies; hospitals; poor artists, authors, and editors; needy inventors, and suffering humanity generally, of whatever religion or nationality, have had cause gratefully to remember his liberality. Not only associations of public beneficence have found a friend in Mr. Brannan, but he has been a pioneer in, and a liberal encourager of, a curious variety of enterprises, embracing some of the most useful branches of California industry. The importation, *via* Panama, of rare breeds of French and Spanish merino sheep, at a time when the success of such investment was problematical; the collection throughout France, Spain, and Italy, of choice varieties of grape cuttings, he having visited Europe in 1857 for that and other purposes; the reclaiming of tule-land along the San Joaquin river, thus setting the example to others; the raising of blood stock, and the improvement of his extensive farming lands in various parts of the State, have divided his attention with the management of his real estate in San Francisco. The Pacific Railroad, Overland Telegraph, Express Companies, banking and insurance and loan associations, enterprises connected with and forming the very essence of the prosperity of California—all of these have found in Mr. Brannan one of their most ready and intelligent cooperators.

In 1868, he purchased the entire landed estates of Abel Stearns in Los Angeles county, embracing an area of about one hundred and seventy thousand acres, which resulted in the opening of those extensive tracts to settlement by small farmers, thus greatly stimulating the industry of that portion of the State.[7] In the silver mining regions of Eastern Nevada, Mr. Brannan's restless business talents have also been exerted, in the erection at Robinson District[8] of saw mills, quartz mills, and smelting works, the building of toll

---

[6]The three paragraphs omitted here that summarize Brannan's early life are glosses of the information in the biographical sketch from *The Annals of San Francisco*.

[7]Brannan was actually part of a syndicate led by Alfred Robinson. For details, see Cleland, *The Cattle on a Thousand Hills*, 203–07.

[8]Copper deposits in the Robinson District, in eastern Nevada's White Pine County, eventually resulted in "mineral production destined to eclipse that from the great Comstock Lode." See Elliot, *History of Nevada*, 224.

SAMUEL BRANNAN, CIRCA 1870.
From Shuck, ed., *Representative and Leading Men of the Pacific Coast.*

roads, and development of one of the richest mineral districts in that State; together with the location of valuable tracts of timber and agricultural lands near Mineral City and in Steptoe Valley.

From among his numerous enterprises, we may particularize the instance of Napa Valley, where he is the proprietor of the Calistoga Hot Springs, and a valuable estate of three thousand acres surrounding them. Here, his all-pervading activity has created out of bare nature the principal watering place in California, not inaptly termed the "Saratoga of the Pacific Coast." This famous place of fashionable resort is too well known in California to require any extended description at our hands. Its climate, rivaling the most celebrated localities of Italy or the south of France, and the scenery, uniting the grandeur of the loftiest summits of the coast range with the pastoral features of the adjacent rich farming country, have made Calistoga the favorite resort of tourists and invalids from all parts of the country. This costly scene of comfort and healthful recreation Mr. Brannan has reared by his own unaided resources, and the effect of his far-reaching enterprise is felt in the impetus he has given to the prosperity of all that section of the State. The Napa Valley Railroad, connecting Calistoga with tide water at Vallejo, is especially due to his persistent energy.

We cannot close this imperfect sketch without recording the unwavering and outspoken loyalty of Mr. Brannan to the cause of the Union in the darkest periods of its trial by fire and sword. On the stump, in the press, among the people, his voice has been heard in emphatic denunciation of the rebellion, and his contributions in aid of the cause he espoused were unstinted in fitting out officers for the war, in printing and disseminating loyal documents, and in every way strengthening the hands of the Government. In the second Lincoln campaign, Mr. Brannan was chosen as one of the Presidential Electors from California. During that memorable contest he canvassed the northern part of the State, and aided materially in carrying the Union ticket. His generous sympathies were not confined to his native land. The cause of freedom in Mexico, menaced by the French intervention, received his substantial aid. In 1866, he armed and equipped at his own expense a company to join President Juarez, and these recruits, composed of hardy and experienced frontiersmen, rendered important services in expelling the foreign invaders.

Mr. Brannan is a signal example of the American self-made man. Starting in life a poor boy, thrown early on his own resources, and with few of the advantages possessed by the youth of the succeeding generation, he had the sagacity to foresee the mighty future of the Pacific coast, and the pluck and energy to avail himself of the circumstances of the times. As his influence in the community has thus far been beneficial to the welfare of California, so it is equally certain that it will continue to be exerted for the best interests of his adopted State.

H. H. Bancroft: This Erratic Genius, 1885

After 1870 Brannan's life quickly diverged from the bright future predicted in William Wells' sketch. Brannan's entry in Hubert Howe Bancroft's "Pioneer Register and Index, 1542–1848," found in volume 2 of Bancroft's seven-volume *History of California*, was his first encounter with a serious historian. Bancroft explored elements of his career that Brannan preferred to forget and did not hesitate to examine the darker side of the man's character and career.[9]

"SAMUEL BRANNAN,"

IN BANCROFT, *HISTORY OF CALIFORNIA*, 2:728.

Mormon elder and chief of the colony sent from New York on the *Brooklyn* [in 1846] . . . Brannan was born at Saco, Maine, in 1819; learned the printer's trade in Ohio from 1833; travelled as a printer through many parts of the country; and from 1842 published the *New York Messenger* and later the *Prophet*, as organs of the Mormon church.[10] Of his conversion and early experience as a latter-day saint not much is known, the subject being avoided both by himself and his old associates; but he was clearly a leading spirit in the church, and was just the man to take charge of the California scheme. There is no good reason to doubt his devotion to the cause, but it was his firm intention to build up his own fortunes with those of his sect; he was greatly displeased with President Young's change of plans respecting California; and having failed during a visit to Salt Lake to modify the president's views, it required but few years to divest himself entirely of his old-time religious fervor and become an apostate.

Meanwhile, at San Francisco he was a leading spirit from the first, preaching eloquently on Sundays, publishing the *Star*, buying town lots, taking part in political controversies, working zealously for the advancement of the town's educational and other interests, always aggressive but liberal in his views, showing no signs of sectarianism. . . . In 1847 he established the firm of C. C. Smith & Co. at Sacramento, later Brannan & Co., in which Mellus & Howard and William Stout were partners. The immense profits of his store after the discovery of gold in 1848–1849, with his mining operations at Mormon Island, and the increase in San Francisco real estate, made him a little later the richest man in California. Of his career after 1848 something will be found in volume VI of this work; also in my *Popular Tribunals* [see below], Brannan having been prominent in connection with the vigilance committees. I do not attempt even to outline his most remarkable career as capitalist and speculator. In many parts of the state and even beyond its limits he acquired immense interests, showing in their management the ability and energy so characteristic of the man. He probably did

---

[9]Bancroft's thirty-nine-volume masterpiece was the work of many authors, and the ambivalence about Brannan apparent in Bancroft's *Works* reflected their varying opinions of the man. Henry L. Oak wrote the first five volumes of the history of California, while Bancroft, William Nemos, and Mrs. Frances Victor wrote the last two. Bancroft wrote *Popular Tribunals* and *California Inter Pocula* with assistance from Victor. See Caughey, *Hubert Howe Bancroft*, 257–58, 261–62; and Clark, *A Venture in History*, 24–36. In this selection, abbreviations are expanded and ellipses replace internal references.

[10] Bancroft reversed the sequence of the newspapers; *The Prophet* preceded the *Messenger*.

more for San Francisco and for other places than was effected by the combined dealings of scores of better men; and indeed, in many respects he was not a bad man, being as a rule straightforward as well as shrewd in his business dealings, as famous for his acts of charity and open-handed liberality as for his enterprise, giving also frequent proofs of personal bravery. In 1859 he purchased the Calistoga estate, in connection with the improvement of which his name is perhaps most widely known. Here he established a distillery on a grand scale, and here in 1868 he received eight bullets and nearly lost his life in a quarrel for possession of a mill. Meanwhile he had given himself up to strong drink; for 20 years or more he was rarely sober after noon; and he became as well known for his dissolute habits and drunken freaks as he had been for his wealth and ability.

Domestic troubles led to divorce from the wife married in 1844, who with their child had come with him in 1846 and borne him other children in California; division of the estate was followed by unlucky speculations, and Brannan's vast wealth melted gradually away. In the days of his prosperity he had liberally supported the cause of Mexico against the French invasion and its tool Maximilian, and just before 1880 he obtained in return a grant of lands in Sonora, embarking with somewhat of his old energy in a grand scheme of colonization, which has thus far proved a total failure. For the last year or two down to 1885 Brannan has lived at Guaymas or on the frontier, remarried to a Mexican woman, a sorry wreck physically and financially, yet clear-headed as ever and full of courage for the future.

Thousands of pioneers in California remember this erratic genius with the kindliest of feelings, and hope that he may yet add a brilliant closing chapter to the record of one of the most remarkable characters in Californian annals.

In a much more pointed statement in his 1887 history of vigilantism, Bancroft compared Brannan's character with that of William Coleman, president of San Francisco's second vigilance committee. Bancroft observed that both men were "strikingly representative each of his associates and the general temper of the times."

Sam Brannan, men called the first [president of the Vigilance Committee], and sometimes plain Sam. There is no little significance in the name one goes by among one's associates. It implies dignity or the lack of it; morality or the lack of it; hearty fellowship, wit, learning, modesty, refinement, or the absence of these qualities. In this instance to have employed the term Mister, or Samuel, or Reverend, or Esquire, would have seemed as malapropos in a friend or companion as to have applied the same expressions of courtesy or respect to a circus clown or to a watch-dog. Though for a time one of the most prominent men in California, one of the wealthiest— I do not say one of the most highly esteemed—the sobriquet Sam was used instinctively as the synonym of the individual. It was only once, within my recollection, when he assumed the *rôle* of banker, that these titles of respectability were affected, and then the sensitive public seemed shy of him, and the project was abandoned. Sam Brannan, banker, would have been a tangible reality, however hirsute or churlish he may have been, but Samuel Brannan, Esquire, was a social myth, a far-away incorporeal thing.

When Sam was a saint appellations of reverence were not out of place; but saturated with the avarice and strong drink incident to California, since his arrival here Sam has been no saint. It is true he followed preaching as a Mormon leader, priest, or prophet, for a short time after landing at San Francisco; but when the enlightened brethren declined the payment of further tithes he cursed them, told them to go to hell, while he went—his way. Monogamous or polygamous doctrines never troubled him much, judging from his flaming devotion to the tender passion; in fact, the not wholly pleasurable scrutiny of his life and character my labors have forced upon me, judging from the record since 1848 and from practices notorious for more than a quarter of a century, I have often wondered what Sam really did preach when he was a Mormon elder.

But as Casey said of his Sing Sing experiences, Sam's early piety should not now be raked up against him.[11] He was a leader in Israel as long as it paid; and all wise leaders lay down their arms when the remuneration fails, for in religion as in war money is half the battle.

Yet with all these repulsive qualities flung in with other scarcely more palatable ingredients to the composition of his character, the occasion of 1851, as I have before remarked, needed just such an instrument. Analyze still closer the qualities here present, and see how well they fit the exigency. Principle we regard as a nobler and more desirable quality than unbridled passion; yet principle alone would not have struck the sudden blow that stunned the monster of 1851. An evenly balanced mind wherein justice calmly sits, and soothing piety and all the sweet amenities of life find welcome, we look upon as more lovely than the ruling power of man roused to vindictive hate and bloody revenge; and yet neither justice, piety, nor civility would have delivered the city in 1851. The disease was passionate, hateful, bloody; so were the times, and bloody, hateful, passionate must be the cure. To odious, soul-bespattered, spiteful Sam, the commonwealth of California owes much.[12]

---

[11]San Francisco supervisor and former convict James P. Casey shot editor James King of William for publicizing his unsavory past in 1856, sparking the second vigilante movement.

[12]Bancroft, *Popular Tribunals*, 2:115–17.

BRANNAN ON BRANNAN: THE HON. SAMUEL BRANNAN

In his later years, Brannan often spoke of writing a "true" history of California. He may have actually put words to paper, but no trace of any such effort survives. This thirteen-page manuscript was apparently written in 1882 and is probably as close as historians will ever come to a Brannan autobiography. The document appears to be based on an interview conducted by a member of H. H. Bancroft's staff, but may have been written in the third person by Brannan himself. It retold the story of his early wanderings and provided an interesting summary of the *Brooklyn* adventure, again without mentioning Mormons. The description of Brannan's "colossal" gold rush enterprises is reinforced with wonderful detail, such as the story that he kept a barrel in his cellar "filled with gold Coin and solid gold ingots." The manuscript painted a much more favorable portrait of Brannan than that incorporated into Bancroft's *History*, and Brannan's decline was far enough advanced by 1882 to cast considerable doubt on its claim that he was "one of California's first and most highly respected pioneers." But it is hard to dispute the claim that "his history is a part of California's history."

THE HONORABLE SAMUEL BRANNAN: A BIOGRAPHICAL SKETCH,
BANCROFT LIBRARY.

HON. SAMUEL BRANNAN

On the first publication of his (Duke of Wellingtons) "Despatches", one of his friends said to him, on reading of his Indian Campaigns: "It seems to me Duke, that your chief business in India was to procure rice and bullocks." "And so it was," replied Wellington, "for if I had rice and bullocks, I had men; and if I had men I knew I could beat the enemy."

Character by Samuel Smiles[13]

And he did beat the enemy and beat him badly whenever he met him. So with the subject of this sketch also but in a different field. Follow the writer but a few moments and we shall soon learn how truly the above quotation applies to the gentleman whose name heads these comments. Born in Saco, State of Maine ~~and like most~~ on the second day of March 1819; he is now

---

[13]Samuel Smiles (1812–1904), author of the work quoted here, *Character*, was the "pious chronicler of the men who founded the industrial greatness of England." This quotation reflected Brannan's great concern in 1882: finding colonists for his new empire in Sonora.

in his 63rd year. He was educated in the public schools of his native place but being endowed with a spirit of adventure he left his associates behind him and in company with his sister arrived in Lake County Ohio in the Spring of 1833. There he undertook to learn the printing trade. So assiduously did he apply himself and so industriously did he labor that in three years after [its start] he was released from his five years apprenticeship. Being armed with a load easy to carry and very advantageous to possess [he] added to the money the husbanding of his resources enabled him to acquire [and] he cast his eyes about him for "Fields green and pastures new." He was not long in deciding. The great excitement in Land Speculation then prevailed, in 1836–37; and betook himself to the scene of action; but the great crash came and like many other enterprising young men he too sustained a temporary loss. He saw at once that there were other avenues open to him where fortune was waiting to meet with the brave and heroic young men of that day.

The knowledge he had acquired of the printing business proved a great lever for his advancement and enabled him to travel as an independent man only can. To gratify his tastes he visited every state in the Union. He identified himself with various enterprise[s] during his peregrinations and in 1842, then but 23 years of age, we find him in the possession of considerable wealth. His fondness for his business led him to New York City where he started the New York "Messenger." Out of this undertaking in a few years he realized far more prophet [sic] than he ever anticipated so that in 1846 he conceived the idea of visiting, with the avowed purpose of remaining, the Pacific Coast. That he knew what he was about subsequent facts will fully demonstrate. He fitted out a vessel of 370 tons at his own expense and called her the "Brooklyn." The ship was well and strongly built: with all the modern improvements of the day. On the 4th day of February 1846 with 236 passengers ~~consisting of the crew~~ of whom 60 were females and 40 children of both sexes.

He supplied the vessel with ample provisions for a long voyage and added to the necessaries of a vast quantity of household and farming implements—Etc. but what seemed to him most important was that he brought with him an improved printing press, paper, type and all that was needed to start a newspaper on the shores of the Western World. He carefully stored away also a large amount of machinery for the erection of a Flour Mill. Thus equipped and after being 5 months at sea he landed at the Sandwich Islands with his heroic followers. They did not tarry long but long enough to learn that war was anticipated between the United States and Mexico. For self-protection they formed themselves into an Association and elected Mr. Brannan President thereof. Having considerable money and being a very cautious far seeing man he purchased 174 stand of arms; plenty of ammunition, replenished his ship with provisions and on the 31st day of July 1846 he land[ed] his party at *Yerba Buena* as San Francisco was then called.

They camped among the sand hills, which were then very numerous indeed until such times as they could erect Adobe buildings. Their finances began to grow short so that men worked for pay in provisions and to appropriate the labor which was at his disposal, knowing many of the men had families, he put them to work the same year and erected the first flour mill ever built in California. This was followed immediately with another. They both stood, as many an early settler will well remember, where Clay St now is. In the following year he put up his printing press and issued the "California Star," the parent of the "Alta" California. A newspaper in those days was quite an interesting medium of exchange of thought among the pioneers. Things began to look well and times men to prosper. Mr. Brannan kept a keen watch look out for business chances and in the summer of 1847 he opened a general merchandising store at Sutters Creek [*sic*] under the name of C. C. Smith & Co. which being the first of the kind established in the Sacramento Valley success crowned their efforts and in 1848 Mr. Brannan bought out the interest of Mr. Smith, the firm being henceforth known as that of S. Brannan & Co.

Shortly after he made this purchase gold was discovered in the neighborhood and then the great feverish excitement set in. Again trade grew so prosperous all through the remainder of '48 and '49 that the receipts from his business transactions alone—notwithstanding his connection with mining interprises—aggregated monthly something in the neighborhood of $150,000.[14] Such mammoth receipts naturally gave him great influence among the people and as is often said of him even to this day, "*I wish I was as rich as Samuel Brannan.*"

The later part of '49 found him in San Francisco with a large fortune but still eager to be up and doing as such spirits as his can never rest while opportunity is wrapping [*sic*] at their doors. So he, of the firm of Osborne and Brannan again returned to make money out of China Merchandise which was then a scarce commodity and it is needless to add again was he made rich. His popularity now began to become widespread and the presence of a very numerous class and dangerous class of men began to infest the City and Surrounding business centers who were commonly known as "The Hounds"

---

[14]This figure may be exaggerated. Governor Richard Mason reported on 17 August 1848 that Brannan & Co. "had received in payment for its goods $36,000 (worth of this gold) from the 1st of May to the 10th of July." See Browning, *To the Golden Shore*, 41. Brannan's clerk, R. F. Peckham, recalled he shipped "about twenty-five thousand dollars weekly" to San Francisco. Writing to his sister on 13 March 1849, Brannan estimated, "With in the Last year I have Cleard over a Hundred Thousand Dollars."

and for whose overthrow the better class of citizens organized together. During this period our subject was elected Town Councillor and in a little over a year following when the disreputable element above referrd [to] grew still more bold and insolent Mr Brannan (who was then regarded as being the wealthiest man in California,) was elected President of the Vigilance Committee—1851.— It should be borne in mind that all this time, by a liberal use of his fabulous wealth he was adding to the credit beauty and desirability of the City by Erecting magnificent buildings throughout the City, but particularly along Montgomery Street. Many of them Even at this late date are remarkable for their strength and magnificence.

Having large interests at stake in the Sandwich Islands after a short stay he returned to this City in 1853 and was almost unanimously elected State Senator. The rapid increase in the multitudinous amount of labor that his many enterprises pressed upon him he at once resigned the preferred honor. It was just such men as he who were instrumental in moulding public opinion and giving character to the new country. He was married as early as 1844 and became the Father of four children. His Character is indeed one that should receive more space than we can afford to give it but no doubt it will be at some future day figure more conspicuously in California's strange history. He is a man unquestionably of large ideas and in force of will, energy and enterprise he was unrivalled. He associated with Hon. Hall McAllister.[15] and men of that calibre from the earliest days. The enterprises in which he was engaged were colossal. They involved great expenditures of Capital—but Capital always seemed to be at his command. It is said of him that so great was the amount of wealth he possessed that at one time he had in his cellar a Barrell filled with gold Coin and solid gold ingots while as to the amount of valuable Bonds and rich lands it is almost impossible to determine.

He purchased a tract of land in Napa County and called it Calistoga. It was unimproved; of little value and had no repute but for the presence of the hot Sulpher Springs. He immediately entered upon the work of giving it a character and a value. The improvements which he made involved an expenditure of about $200,000. He erected handsome cottages and introduced every variety of ornamental trees, flowers and vegetation. At that period the telegraph was in its infancy; yet he procured a telegraphic construction to be made connecting it with San Francisco. He also procured a RailRoad to be built and at great expense and in the face of almost insurmountable obstacles, which extended from Calistoga to Napa Junction and then connected with the Vallejo RailRoad and thus establishing a direct

---

[15]Matthew Hall McAllister (1800–65), or his son, Hall McAllister (1832–88). This was not an amiable association. For Brannan's denial that he had accused McAllister of swindling a mutual acquaintance, see *San Francisco Daily Herald*, "Personal," 2 August 1851; and "A Card," 5 August 1851.

communication by RailRoad and Steamer with San Francisco. He erected a large Distillery where he manufactured Brandy in ~~large~~ great quantities and shipped it to New York for a market.

As an incident of his intrepidity and daring we may mention that on one occasion when a band of outlaws had taken possession of his Saw Mill at Calistoga he determined to recapture it. To this end he gathered together a company of men from among ~~whom~~ the residents of the vicinity and having armed them placing himself at their head set forth to regain the Mill.

It was a very bright moonlight night and when the party reached the vicinity of the Mill, when they were actually in open view, while those who had held the Mill were in deep shadow, they were ordered from the mill to halt, with the additional announcement that if they advanced any further the party in the Mill would fire upon them. Unwilling to sacrifice their lives they therefore did halt, while Mr Brannan vainly urged them to advance and finding himself unable to control them marched on alone towards the Mill. In a few minutes a volley was fired from the firearms in the Mill and he fell, apparently almost riddled with bullets. Not less than thirty of them were found to have either pierced his clothing or punctured his body. Some of them were extricated by surgical skill while others remain within his person to this day. ~~Many stories of this kind can be heard of him from old residents of this Coast. Some one of them will bear repetition as we are convinced that his history is a part of California's history~~

In 1865 General Ochoa in company with another Mexican officer named Placido Vaga came here to San Francisco for the purpose of raising money to fight against Maximillian. Mr. Brannan who was then exceedingly rich and in his characteristic manner advanced them $80,000 on their Bonds.[16] With this money they purchased arms and ammunition and under the command of Col. George Green—a gentleman well known in both American and Mexican circles for his courage—equipped over one hundred men to be accompanied and officered as well by Harvey Lake. This troop went overland and did good service for the Republic under the title of the American Legion. In 1878 ~~and~~ being still in possession of the Bonds referred to, which he hunted up and obtained from a bankers vault in N. Y. where they had laid [in a] neglected and ignored [?] condition to Exist for nearly 15 years. He took them to the City of Mexico and by dint of his energy & perseverance induced the Mexican Government to give him in payment thereof a large grant of land in Sonora. There he established a colony there calling it Sonora Colonization Society, and had 800 men with their families ready and willing to follow him to Mexico [should he] acquire a

[16]Frazer, "The Ochoa Bond Negotiations of 1865–1867," 398, put the actual sum at "thirty thousand dollars in gold coin," but *New York Times*, 3 February 1880, reported that the mortgage held in New York set the amount of Brannan's original loan at $43,478.26. See Chapter 13.

grant and Rail Road Franchise in Sonora, commencing at the head waters of the Yaqy River. At Guaymas he became well acquainted during his many trips and while attending to his enterprises, with a prominent Mexican family. Having ~~lost~~ been divorced from his first wife some years ago, this acquaintanceship led to match making and he married the young lady the daughter of the family mentioned who is spoken of as one of the fairest daughters of Sonora.

He is now happy and contented living in Sonora and in business associated with a Mr. Ricketson in making Surveys for Rail Roads for the Colonists calculated to connect that rich inland country with the sea and with the Achison Topeka & San[ta] Fe and thereby bring San Francisco in close communication with one of the richest though yet undeveloped countries on Earth much of the future success of which one can vouchsafe to say will depend upon the energy good judgment foresight and perseverance of one of California's first and most highly respected pioneers Mr. Samuel Brannan who as it was said of Hercules: "that whether he stood, and walked, or sat, or whatever thing he did, he conquered."

An Aged Man and Poor:
Early Encounters with Mormonism

If the preceding accounts read more like a romantic adventure than honest history, they give some hint of the problem of separating truth from fiction in telling Brannan's story. The documentary record of his early life is practically non-existent, but the first surviving records show that his family had a much earlier and more intimate association with Mormonism than he would later admit.

The Brannan family's life changed forever in the fall of 1832 when the younger brother of Mormon prophet Joseph Smith stopped in Saco. *Maine* Samuel Harrison Smith and his missionary companion, Orson Hyde, represented one of the many religious movements born in upstate New York during the revival known as the Second Great Awakening. Mormon missionaries experienced some success in New England, and one of their Boston converts, Alexander Badlam, directed Smith and Hyde to the home of his father-in-law. (Smith recorded on 26 June 1832 that he had "Baptized four, names: Alexander Badlam and his wife, Maryan, Sabre Grainger, Mary Bailey; and in the evening confirmed them by the laying on of hands.") Samuel Smith painted a very different picture of the family's condition than that presented in Brannan's novelized biographies, revealing that Thomas Brannan was a Unitarian who maintained an open mind about Mormonism.

> 29th [September 1832] left Kenebunk & went on to Saco. Stop[p]ed to visit one House on the way. Came into Saco & [met a] man by the name of brannan. He was father-in-law to Brother Elaxander Badlam. He was an aged man abo[ut] 86 years old his daughter having sent a letter to him by us from Boston & She desired him to get a place for us to preach in. He was a universales in belief & he obtained the hall that the universallers preached in & the next day on Sunday the 30th we preached in the forenoon & afternoon. . .
>
> October 1st, 1832 . . . stayed part of the day at the Brannards
>
> Oct 3rd . . . Went into Saco village. Bought a pair of shows [shoes] and then I went to Mr Brennerds and Brother Orson went around the village to get subscriptions for the Star, but did not get any. The people appeared thoughtless concerning these things.[17]

The second missionary, Orson Hyde, later became a Mormon apostle and a confidant of Brannan. Nothing confirms that the thirteen-year-old Samuel was present during the missionaries' visit, but his sister's marriage to "Brother" Badlam suggests that the young man had already heard of the new religion that would shape the course of his life. Hyde's comments indicate that the family had fallen on hard times as Thomas Brannan grew old.

> 29th [September 1832] Left Kenebunk and went on to Saco ten miles . . . called in Sauco [sic] in the afternoon on an old gentleman by the name of Brannen whose daughter we saw in Boston and he received us kindly; tarried with him during the day and night; he was an aged man and poor, but the Lord will bless him.
>
> October 1st, 1832: Rained incessantly all day long; tarried part of the day at Mr Brannen's, then left.[18]

In the spring of 1833 Samuel Brannan moved with the Badlams to Kirtland, Ohio, site of the first Mormon gathering. No baptismal records survive to confirm exactly when he joined the LDS church, but a knowledgeable early source reported that Brannan "united with the

---

[17]Samuel Harrison Smith, Diary 1832 Feb.–1833 May, LDS Archives. "Star" referred to the Kirtland, Ohio, *The Evening and Morning Star;* Star was a popular name for early Mormon newspapers, including the *Millennial Star* and Brannan's own *California Star.*

[18]Orson Hyde, Journal, 1832, LDS Archives.

church at Kirtland, Ohio, when he was but a boy."[19] He apprenticed in the LDS church's printing office, which published *The Evening and Morning Star* and the *Messenger and Advocate.* Ebenezer Robinson recalled that foreman James Carrell directed the operation, which employed another of the prophet's brothers, Don Carlos Smith, in addition to Brannan.[20] Editor Oliver Cowdery later remembered Brannan as "my old apprentice."[21]

The Badlams, along with the rest of the Mormon community, were not welcomed by the older settlers. The "overseers of the Poor of the Township of Kirtland" ordered Constable William Crary on 31 January 1834 "to warn the following persons to depart the township immediately." Crary served the order (which failed to have its desired effect) on Joseph Smith and most of his immediate family, and also on "Alexander Badalon & family."[22] The printer's apprentice was among the Kirtland temple builders who received blessings from the prophet in March 1835.[23]

Brannan told an editor in Hawaii in 1846 that he had "resided for nearly three years in the family of Joseph Smith, Jr." The earliest recollections of Joseph Smith III of "men, things, and events" at Kirtland included two young printers, Samuel Brannan and Ebenezer Robinson. "Brannan and Robinson were young men," recalled the prophet's son, "and were either inmates of my Father's house or frequent visitors therein." The Badlams' house was located "not far from our house, up on the hillside," and he remembered peering through a crack in Alexander Badlam's coach shop to view "a nicely painted" red wagon Badlam had built for him.[24]

Joseph Smith's journal noted on 14 December 1835: "To day Samuel Branum came to my house much afflicted with a swelling on his left arm which was occasioned by a bruise on his elbow. We had been called to

---

[19]"Samuel Brannan," *The Saints' Herald,* 25 May 1889, 323/3. Joseph Smith III, who knew Brannan in Kirtland, probably wrote this part of Brannan's obituary.

[20]Robinson, "Items of Personal History of the Editor," 104.

[21]Cowdery to Phinehas Young, 14 February 1847 in Gunn, *Oliver Cowdery,* 253.

[22]Kirtland, Ohio, Township Record, 1817–1846, LDS Archives.

[23]The 8 March 1835 Kirtland High Council Minutes, 1832–1837, LDS Archives, 150, included "Samuel S. Branan" in a list of blessings and ordinations, indicating that he was an official church member.

[24]Anderson, ed., "The Memoirs of President Joseph Smith (1832–1914)," 1,414.

pray for him and anoint him with oil, but his faith was not sufficient to effect a cure. My wife prepared a poultice of herbs and applyed to it and he tarryed with me over night."[25] Samuel Brannan's first appearance in Mormon annals reported that "his faith was not sufficient," but such scraps of information demonstrate that he had an earlier and much more intimate association with Mormonism and Joseph Smith than he would later admit. Brannan's real-estate speculations, speaking style, and extravagant ambitions suggest that Smith continued to influence his young disciple long after the prophet's martyrdom. Brannan enjoyed immense success in many of the enterprises that ended disastrously for Joseph Smith, but the young printer shared in the consequences of the prophet's early financial enterprises. Brannan participated in Smith's questionable Ohio land and banking enterprises. He joined "the mania of making fortunes" without "time, trouble or capital" that swept Kirtland and the United States, for records confirm that he bought fifteen acres of land in Kirtland with L. Robbins for $600 on 17 May 1837.[26] These speculations ended in disaster when the national economy collapsed in the Panic of 1837.

Promise to the Inhabitants of the Town of Saco, 1837

Brannan left Ohio to appear again in his home town in search of a loan. The following document is from the Herbert S. Auerbach collection, now in the possession of Dr. G. Ralph Bailey of Bountiful, Utah. The original is on a single sheet and may be in Brannan's hand.

(Copy)

Saco July 5th 1837. For value received, I, Samuel Brannan, of Kirtland, County of Geauaga, State of Ohio, promise to pay the Inhabitants of the Town of Saco or Cotton Bradbury, Jonathan King, & Tristram Jordan Jr. in their capacity as Selectmen of the town of Saco, County of York & State of Maine, or their successors in office, on Order, Thirty Five Dollars on demand with interest semi annually.

Samuel Brannan

Witness
John T. Scamman

---

[25]Faulring, *An American Prophet's Record*, 77.
[26]Backman, *A Profile of Latter-day Saints of Kirtland*, 121, 133, 135.

(Copy)

I, Samuel Brannan, agree that a letter from the Selectmen of Saco for the time being, demanding payment of the above note, or interest that may be due them transmitted by mail or otherwise, to me at Kirtland, mentioned in the above note—and evidence being adduced that such a letter was deposited in the Post Office at Saco, or any neighboring Post Office or otherwise transmitted shall be sufficient notice for the payment of said note or interest. Saco July 5th 1837.

Witness   Samuel Brannan
John T. Scamman[27]

Tradition holds that soon after this Brannan went by sea to New Orleans to join his older brother, Thomas. They purchased an ancient printing press and started a weekly literary journal that met with little success. Disaster struck when Thomas Brannan, Jr., "died at New Orleans of Yellow Fever" on 13 September 1837.[28] Nothing is known of Samuel Brannan's subsequent southern sojourn, but at this time he probably developed his enduring hatred for the South and its peculiar institution, slavery.

Brannan left New Orleans after a stay of perhaps a year and worked his way up the Mississippi and Ohio valleys, finally landing in Indianapolis. On 1 March 1839 his half-sister Nancy wrote to her brother, John Brannan, a mate on the brig *Cronstadt*. Nancy reported, "I have written to Samuel at New-Orleans, no answer since that i have Heard he was at India-Anna."[29] Brannan later claimed he worked in Indianapolis at the anti-slavery *Gazette*.[30] Some claim he published and edited the newspaper, using the press he had purchased in New Orleans, but the

---

[27]For an alternate transcription, see the typescript in the Herbert S. Auerbach Collection, Box B, 4–5, BYU Library, cited hereafter as Auerbach Collection.

[28]*Record Book of the Town of Saco*, 244. Existing accounts of Brannan's stay in New Orleans are difficult to link to documented facts. Bailey, *Sam Brannan and the California Mormons*, 30, wrote that Thomas Brannan was a clerk, while Stellman, *Sam Brannan*, 16, had him working on a riverboat. Scott, *Samuel Brannan and the Golden Fleece*, 32–36, ignored the existence of Thomas completely, but had a romantic Brannan stay in New Orleans until 1841.

[29]Nancy Brannan to John Brannan, 1 March 1839, Auerbach Collection, 8. The preceding sentence, "i have not heard any thing from Father, or Mother, i shall try to hear from them," suggests that Thomas and Sarah Brannan were still alive.

[30]Brannan told a reporter in the late 1880s that "During several years succeeding 1841 he published a literary journal at New Orleans, a paper called the *Gazette* at Indianapolis, and the *Messenger* at New York." See "A Strange Career" in Chapter 14. Brannan was in New Orleans *before* 1841. He might have worked for the *Indianapolis Gazette*, which was founded in 1822, but he probably was not its publisher.

MARY ANN BRANNAN BADLAM,
CIRCA 1860.
Brannan's older sister, pictured
here in California, is often cred-
ited with raising him.
Courtesy, California State Library.

enterprise failed after six months.[31] The newspaper business introduced Brannan to Jacksonian politics and it appears he established his remarkable connections to "the democracy" during this time, for he demonstrated extraordinary influence in Democratic party circles after his move to New York in 1844.

Brannan may have visited his relatives in Missouri or Illinois during his sojourn in the Midwest. Alexander Badlam moved his family to the Mormon settlements in Daviess County, Missouri, where they were caught up in the "Mormon War" that swept the state in 1838. Badlam testified that he was forced to move "to Caldwell County in a Severe Snow Storm Myself Sick and a part of my family also." Badlam stated, "I feel My Loss is very great because it was all I had."[32] He was one of the men at Far West in January 1839 who pooled their resources to assist in the evacuation of Mormons from the state.[33] The Badlams had

---

[31]Bailey, *Sam Brannan and the California Mormons,* 31; and Stellman, *Sam Brannan,* 18. Scott, *Samuel Brannan and the Golden Fleece,* 37, told much the same story.

[32]Johnson, *Mormon Redress Petitions,* 129.

[33]Smith, Jr., *History of the Church,* 3:251–53.

settled in Nauvoo by February 1840. Mary Ann Badlam was now the mother of five children: Alexander, Jr., Mary Ann, Sarah, and twins Ezra and Emma. Emma died "aged one year" in Nauvoo on 24 November 1841.[34] No evidence places Brannan in Nauvoo before 1845, but he may have renewed his relationship with the LDS church while visiting the Badlams in Illinois.

The Onward Progress of This Glorious Kingdom

Alexander Badlam received a mission call in 1842 to preach in Ohio and returned to Kirtland with the eloquent and erratic Apostle Lyman Wight. They hoped "to purchase a steamboat to convey the Kirtland Saints to Nauvoo," but Wight's drinking scuttled the venture.[35] Brannan returned to the LDS faith about this time, perhaps joining his brother-in-law as a missionary in Ohio. Brannan reported to Apostle Wilford Woodruff from Waynesville, near Dayton, in a letter that captures his early devotion to Mormonism.

"COMMUNICATIONS,"
Times and Seasons, 1 JANUARY 1844, 5:388/1–2.

Waynerville [*sic*], Dec. 5th, 1843.

Dear Brother Woodruff,—My ears being constantly saluted with the onward progress of this glorious kingdom of the "eleventh hour dispensation," through the untiring struggles, and faithful perseverance of the servants of God, in Europe, as well as in America, and that too, through the medium of your respectably conducted periodical, that comes, as it were like a heavenly messenger, holding upon its pages the intelligence of the future glory and reward of that servant, that shall be found laboring when the Lord again shall visit his vineyard, induces me at this time to trouble you with a short sketch of the increase and prosperity of the kingdom of our God, in this part of his vineyard.

On my arrival at Clinton Co., the adjoining one to this, I had the happy fortune of meeting with Elder Ball,[36] who was lifting up a warning voice to the inhabitants of that region, which induced many to come forward and

---

[34]Memorandum of Agreement 1840, LDS Archives; and *Times and Seasons*, 1 December 1841, 3:622.

[35]Manuscript History of Kirtland, Ohio, LDS Archives.

[36]This was perhaps the Joseph Ball who was later accused of seducing the girls of Lowell, Massachusetts, but Brannan's New York newspapers reported on the activities of Joseph T. Ball and the LDS church in Waynesville. See *The Prophet*, 2 November 1844.

renounce the world, and be buried with Christ by baptism for the remission of sins. They now number between 60 and 70 in good standing. Elder Ball and myself commenced laboring together, in the adjoining region of country, and, "God giving the increase," 12 more were immersed for the remission of sins, and are now rejoicing in the truth, with their faces Zion-ward.

There being quite a manifestation of feeling in this place by some of the citizens, and having received a special invitation from them, I came to this place and commenced preaching the word, and soon the seed sprouted and needed watering. I was joined by Elder Elliot, from Cincinnatti, who laid hold of the work with undaunted courage, and through many struggles of debate and refutation of lies and slanders, we have been enabled, through the grace of God to plant the standard of truth, in defiance of all the opposition of men and devils—for truly we have been visited by both. The faithful in this region numbers about 22, and there are many more that will obey from the heart that form of doctrine which we have delivered unto them.

I remain yours truly,
S. BRAMAN.[37]

With this letter, Elder Samuel Brannan stepped into history.

---

[37]"S. BRAMAN" was a typo, for the newspaper's contents spelled Brannan's name correctly.

Chapter 2

"In the Vortex of Recklessness"
Brannan in New York

An attack of malaria cut short Samuel Brannan's mission in Ohio early in 1844 and the sickness may have caused him to visit the Badlam home in Nauvoo. Brannan was soon called on another mission to New England and New York, where he would advance rapidly in the Mormon hierarchy, marry, work for the presidential campaigns of Joseph Smith and James K. Polk, take control of the leading LDS publication in the East, marry again, and launch a surprising number of business ventures. He naturally found himself deeply embroiled in Mormon scandals and national politics.

"A poor and penniless printer," Brannan arrived in New York with only a "crownless hat and a shabby suit of clothes."[1] For the next two years this "young Lion of Mormonism" roared through the East, spreading the gospel to the generally indifferent citizens of the city of New York.[2] Brannan met the attractive twenty-two year old Ann Eliza Corwin, daughter of the widow Fanny M. Corwin, a Mormon convert, and married her after a short courtship.[3] Fanny Corwin seems to have been a woman of substance, and Brannan's new bride and her mother settled with him in New York.

Turning the World Upside Down

In early April 1844 several New York elders proposed that the LDS

---

[1] "Change of Fortune," *Alta California*, 12 December 1853, 1/7, citing *N. Y. Pick.*

[2] I. Drew used this phrase to describe Brannan in an 8 October 1844 letter to *The Prophet.*

[3] According to Carter, *Treasures of Pioneer History*, 3:485, "Anna Elizabeth Corwin was born 1 April 1823 at Litchfield, Connecticut, the daughter of Fanny Corwin who kept the village boarding house." Bailey, Stellman, and Scott all tell different stories about the Corwins.

church launch "a weekly paper for the dispensation of our principles." The first issue of *The Prophet* came off the press on 18 May 1844 at its offices at 7 Spruce Street, near the headquarters of several of New York's leading newspapers, including Horace Greeley's *Tribune*. The 29 June issue listed William Smith, soon to be the sole surviving brother of Mormonism's founding prophet, as editor. Throughout June *The Prophet* reported the varied activities of "our indefatigable young friend, Elder Samuel Brannan." Brannan was a busy man as the spring of 1844 came to a close. In early June he lectured at Williamsburg (part of today's Brooklyn) in the morning and in Brooklyn in the afternoon. The paper invited "the friends of Gen. Joseph Smith" to meet at the Military Hall in the Bowery on 11 June "to select delegates to the great State Convention at Utica . . . and take such other measures as will secure his election to the highest office in the gift of a free and enlightened people." The notice, "Jeffersonians Attend!!" was signed by "Sam'l. Brannan, Sec'y."[4]

The Prophet's black-bordered columns announced on 20 July 1844 stunning news: Joseph Smith was dead, martyred at the Carthage jail by a painted mob. Mormon critics assumed that the prophet's murder sounded the death-knell of his young religion, but they had underestimated the talent and devotion of his followers. Brannan's faith was unshaken, and *The Prophet* reported his numerous sermons throughout New York and New England during the last half of 1844. In late summer the paper described Brannan's busy schedule.

"ELDER S. BRANNAN,"
THE PROPHET, 31 AUGUST 1844.

On the coming week our beloved brother Elder Brannan (whose hand is never slack in finding something to do in this last dispensation,) will take his leave of us again, on another mission to the east by the way of Westfield, Mas, Boston, Lowell, Peterboro, Salem, and New Bedford; he will be at Westfield on the 8th of September next, and will proceed from thence to the above mentioned places; may the Angel of the Covenant go before him; he is another of those that "go turning the world upside down."

The Prophet reported on 28 September that Brannan had given "a course of lectures" at Westfield and then went to Boston "to continue

---

[4]*The Prophet*, 8 June 1844.

the protracted meeting commenced by Elders Smith and Adams some ten days since." Brannan impressed one I. Drew, whose admiring letter appeared on 12 October. Drew was "astounded at the arguments hurled forth from this youth from half past ten o'clock in the morning until nine in the evening." Part of Drew's astonishment was that "this rising witness of Mormonism" appeared to be "not more than twenty three years of age." Young Henry Southworth of Boston was also dazzled. The editor of *The Prophet* "gave one of the most eloquent sermons I ever heard of any denominations. [It was some] 2 hours long. Called upon the different saints to go up to Nauvoo. The devil was using all his powers to overthrow." Southworth rated Brannan "one of the best preachers in the Mormon church." Brannan did not confine himself to religion, for in April 1845 Southworth "Heard a lecture on politics from Elder B. [and] heard of great deal of the principles which govern Judicial men."[5]

Edward Kemble, the young printer from upstate New York Brannan hired to help produce *The Prophet*, recalled him as "a sallow, cadaverous, hard-featured man, debilitated by a long attack of Western fever." Brannan was still so feeble from malaria "as scarcely to be able to stand at 'case' or perform an ordinary day's work." Despite Brannan's illness, Kemble marked him as a "coming man," and noted that "the vigor, boldness and ability with which he went straight to work were irresistible, and very soon he had placed himself at the head" of the Saints in New York, "preaching on Sundays and quite carrying captive his hearers with his nervous, impassioned declamation." Brannan was "a power among the dull, pliant minds about him."[6]

GO AHEAD & RIP IT UP

On his way to a mission in England that fall, Wilford Woodruff described the firestorm generated by the polygamous adventures of his fellow apostle, William Smith. In this "vortex of recklessness," Woodruff found that Smith and George J. Adams had "spent hundreds

[5]Henry Larkin Southworth, Journal, 9 March 1845, 6 and 8 April 1845, LDS Archives.
[6]Rogers, ed., *A Kemble Reader*, 14.

of dollars of Temple money for their own use" and accused them of employing *The Prophet* as "an engine in their hands to accomplish the same end." To Woodruff's horror they were preaching "a principal they call the spiritual wife doctrine," winning enthusiastic converts who found any opponent of the practice "an old granny and weak in the faith." Joseph Smith had personally introduced Woodruff to the "doctrine of the plurality of wives," but Smith had kept the revelation and practice of polygamy a closely guarded if poorly held secret. Under the leadership of Brigham Young, the Quorum of Twelve tried to continue this delicate balancing act between private practice and public denial. Woodruff feared that the exposure of "such an order of things will explode any society to the four winds."[7]

Woodruff's confidential report to Brigham Young revealed the controversies that swirled through the eastern Mormon congregations and the serious problems William Smith had created for his fellow apostles. Woodruff's long letter, composed over several days, illustrated the dilemmas the secret doctrine of polygamy presented to LDS authorities. Woodruff was especially dismayed to learn that Brannan and his colleagues had been "sealing a man to his wife for Eternity" without the proper authority, performing rituals that are now restricted to temples and are only available to the most devoted members. Woodruff also revealed that Brannan had secured Democratic financial aid for *The Prophet*, for "the Polk parties are supporting the paper some untill after the election."

WOODRUFF TO YOUNG, 9 AND 14 OCTOBER 1844,
BRIGHAM YOUNG COLLECTION, LDS ARCHIVES.

Boston Oct 9th 1844
President Brigham Young
    Beloved Brother
    While the Sable shades of night has drawn its dark curtains over the Earth, I seat myself by the side of Brother Phelps table in the City of Boston to spread some of the cogitations of my mind before you. . . . On my arrival at the Westfield Branch of the Church, An Elder informed me that he attended the New York conference, & their appeared much difficulty arising in that quarter upon a variety of subjects, but [the] Kissing Women spiritual wife [doctrine] being the most prominent one. One was turned out of the Church

---

[7]Journal History, 3 December 1844.

for calling Adams or Wm Smith a raskall; much difficulty appeared to be brewing in New York & Philadelphia; I visited a sick woman in the Westfield Branch. For some reason the subject of marriage for eternity rested with wait upon my mind [and] to introduce the subject I enquired of Br. Sparks[8] if their had been any thing said upon the subject; he informed me she had been sealed to her husband. I asked who by. He said Elder Brannan, Elder of the prophet. I was a little surprised at this. He one informed me that Elder Brannan had been through the churchs, calling collections for the prophet[9] [and] got considerable in the Small Cash. Wm Smith was with him gathering funds at the same time for the Temple. This Brother paid him over $20 or $25 dollars for the Temple as he [Smith] was one of the Twelve, the tale to me is that Elders Smith Adams & Brannan are leagued together in all things. [They] visit the Churches constantly & beg together one for the prophet, one for the Temple & Adams to pay a debt that he had borrowed in Nauvoo or he had lent so much to the Saints. And preaching the spiritual wife doctrine (as they call it) to perfection. After getting through with this Branch I took cars[10] for Boston [where Woodruff attended an LDS meeting]. Elder Smith asked what the feelings of the Twelve was towards him in Nauvoo, spoke of the office of patriarch [and] said it was his right, should contend for it through death & the grave &c.[11] The first business I saw was John Hardy resign his Office as president, and another appointed in his stead, which was Joseph Ball who was contended for strenuously by Brannan & Wm Smith. I will confess that some feeling came across me that made me squirm all over, [when] I saw their was wrong spirits, conflicting spirits. Elder Phelps was the ownly man that opposed openly Elder Balls appointment . . . I sat by the side of Wm Smith . . . I asked how Br Brannan came to be marrying people for Eternity. He Says I appointed him to do it. [Woodruff objected,] His Administrations are not legal. "Yes they are any Elder can do it that has power to marry at all," [said Smith. Woodruff replied,] "It is a right Exclusively belonging to the quorum of the Twelve or the president of the Quorum [and is] not legal with those who are not Endowed." [Smith answered,] "That has reference to exclusive privileges, & not to sealing a man to his wife for Eternity for any Elder can do that." Here the conversations ended. . .

I soon discovered from various sources that the conduct of Wm Smith, Adams, Brannan, Ball, &c had been such in crowding their spiritual wife

[8]Quartus S. Sparks and his wife Mary Hamilton Sparks accompanied Brannan to California and later settled at San Bernardino, where he served on the city council. Sparks had violently apostatized from the LDS church by 1857.

[9]This, of course, referred to Brannan's newspaper.

[10]"Taking the cars" was an early phrase for traveling by railroad.

[11]During the struggle to control the LDS church, the apostles conceded William Smith's point and appointed him presiding patriarch on 24 May 1845. See Quinn, *The Mormon Hierarchy: Origins of Power*, 215.

claims, visiting the Churchs, Uniting together in Begging money, running all
over the rights of presiding Elders, on the Claim that Wm Smith was one of
the Twelve, the prophets Brother, & Adams was the great Apostle to the gentiles as Paul even was the 13th Apostle (which claim Wm Held up to me) . . .
Adams Smith [and] Brannan was combining with the press to do any thing to
carry out their designs, preach polaticks & voting for Polk for a little gold . . .
Elder Ball has taught as well as Wm Smith the Lowell girls that [it] is not
wrong to have intercourse with the men what they please & Elder Ball tries to
sleep with them when he can. They have tried to remove a good presiding
Elder in Lowell to put in Br Rolins who is in their company. . . .

If I had not come . . . all the Eastern churches would quickly go to the
devil. I can say my spirit is not congenial with Adams, Williams & Brannan.
I should take a different course from what they are taking. I have been with
them a little while to day. Our spirits dont gibe, they keep together in a clus-
ter. They don't visit the afflicted ones much . . . I inquired to day why they
were pressing the cause they are on the subject of political affairs. "Because
the Polk parties are supporting the paper some untill after the election." I
told them if they would fill my hat with gold I would not do it . . . Would
advice not to mingle with politicks or the election this fall.

Boston Monday Morning Oct 14th

Elder Young . . .

When I closed my meeting Elder Brannan prefered a charge against Elder
John Hardy for Slander for saying they had been engaged in the Spiritual wife
business & I immediately advised Br. Adams & Brannan to let it alone at present & not stir it up as Hardy had withdrawn from the presidency & stood as
a private member on purpose to let it alone. But Br Brannan said he was asked
by Br Adams & Smith to go ahead & rip it up & he should do so. The trial
comes on to morrow night before the whole Church & not a council of
Elders. The object on one side is [to] crush Hardy, & on the other to make all
Hell over for certainly a stinking mess it will be, you may look out for a storm
in Boston . . .

W. Woodruff

John Hardy subsequently published an account of his church trial
"for slander, in saying that G. J. Adams, S. Brannan, and Wm. Smith
were licentious characters." Brannan read the charge in a meeting in Suf-
folk Hall on 12 October 1844, and stood accused at the trial held on
15 October of "whoremongery"—though Hardy "denied using Brannan's name in the matter."[12] At a conference in Boston a week later, Bran-

---

[12]Hardy, "History of the Trials of Elder John Hardy," 4.

nan charged Hardy "with having unrighteously assailed and slandered him." Brannan persuaded the congregation to excommunicate Hardy the next day.[13]

The Prophet and its principal men became entangled in a slander lawsuit with a young Mormon writer, Benjamin Winchester, after William Smith accused Winchester in the pages of *The Prophet* of complicity in the death of Joseph Smith.[14] Brannan explained that the Winchester trouble began because "the proof of the article at the time of its publication was not read by myself, having been up all the night previous to the paper going to press, I left that with one or two other articles to be read by one of the hands in the office, and retired to rest and did not notice the article again until some one made mention of it and wished to konw [sic] if it was true."[15] Winchester had a warrant issued against Brannan for slander.

William Smith left New York by early November 1844, to "remain during the winter in Burdentown, N. J." Prior to his departure, the congregation at the New York conference on 26 October unanimously approved a motion "That Elder Brannan be appointed Presiding Elder of the New York Branch."[16] Aside from visiting apostles, Brannan was now the ranking Mormon authority in America's largest city. Smith also introduced Brannan to Jesse Carter Little of Peterborough, New Hampshire, launching a friendship that would last until Brannan's death. Smith recommended Little as "a man of interesting spirit, and qualifications, and good company," who had "an interesting little family."[17]

Wilford Woodruff again wrote to Brigham Young expressing his despair over the condition of affairs in the East. He asked Young to send someone to take control and pointedly told him that Brannan was not the man to run the Mormon paper in New York, warning him to beware of Brannan's self-interest.

---

[13]"Boston Conference," *The Prophet*, 2 November 1844.

[14]*The Prophet*, 23 November 1844. Smith said Winchester "would or has stole a horse, or slept with bad women," and charged that he was "more or less engaged in the Law infraction at Nauvoo." William Law, Joseph Smith's former counselor, published an exposé of polygamy and started the chain of events that led to Smith's murder.

[15]*The Prophet*, 28 December 1844. For details of this case, see Whittaker, "East of Nauvoo: Benjamin Winchester and the Early Mormon Church," 70–74.

[16]Untitled notice; and "New York Conference," *The Prophet*, 2 November 1844.

[17]William Smith to Brannan, 1 November 1844, in *The Prophet*, 16 November 1844.

WOODRUFF TO YOUNG, 3 DECEMBER 1844,
BRIGHAM YOUNG COLLECTION, LDS ARCHIVES.

Philadelphia Pa Dec 3d 1844

President Brigham Young
Beloved Brother . . .

I feel bad about the eastern Churches [for] they are not out of Danger. The New York Church is in a bad situation, & to cap the climax, Wm [Smith] wrote a peace accusing Winchester of having a hand in the murdering of his brothers, & he [Winchester] has got out warrants for him, one about to take Brannan for printing it & [the authorities] have taken Elder [Jedediah] Grant for selling the papers & he has been bound over to appear at Court under $1000 dollars bond,[18] & Adams has taken Winchester for Slander & all these cases will come up & be investigated to the fullest extent. The character of Joseph and Hiram & the Twelve will be made as black through falsehood as the Lawyers can make them & all Hell is [to be] raked over to get testimony against the Twelve, & others Especially Wm Smith & Adams, & any imprudence that these men have been guilty of . . .

[Postscript] The New York Prophet might do the church much good if it was in the hands of the right kind of man. But I dont believe Brannan to be such an one. Their is two much of an exertions to build himself & Adams & Wm up instead of the Temple, the Twelve, & Nauvoo. He asked me if the copy right of the Covenants was secured. Keep an eye on these doings, he may take council. I wish Wm would go to Nauvoo & stay there & Adams to[o]. I don't feel like sustaining them in their practice until they reform.

Woodruff went on to England, but the trouble he described continued. Brannan reported, "As our paper was going to press we were arrested by the prosecution of B. Winchester, gave bail for appearance on the first Monday in January for $500—This, in connection with other things, occasions the delay of our paper."[19] Such contention appeared to be endemic in the little Mormon outpost, but late in December, Apostle Parley P. Pratt arrived to take over the quarrelsome New York branch. Soon after another missionary, William I. Appleby of New Jersey, visited the city. This passage from Appleby's journal paints a vivid picture of a fire on newspaper row that threatened to put *The Prophet* out of business.

---

[18]"Arrests," *The Prophet*, 21 December 1844, announced Grant's arrest "by the prosecution of Benj. Winchester" for distributing the paper that charged Winchester was involved in Joseph Smith's death. Brannan wrote, "We are sorry that Elder Grant has been called to suffer for any thing we have published."

[19] *The Prophet*, 14 December 1844.

WILLIAM I. APPLEBY, AUTOBIOGRAPHY AND JOURNAL 1841–1856,
LDS ARCHIVES, 125.

3 February 1845

Took passage in the Steamer "Croton" for New York, arrived there in the afternoon.—Ice very bad in the rivers, and along the [Long Island] "Sound." Attended a prayer meeting in the Evening. The next day it snowed and blowed severely and continued on through the night. Staid with Elders Brannan, Miles and Willie at the "Prophet Office."—Occupied by the Church for the Publication of a weekly Paper, Called the "Prophet" No. 7. Spruce St. Slept in the office the same night with Br. John Edgar [Eagar], until about 4 o'clock the next morning. I was awoke by a light shining in the Room. The offices of the "Tribune" & "Sun" two or three doors above were on fire, and destroyed. We expected the Prophet office to go together with the whole Block, But our prayers were offered up for the protection of the office and the support of the cause,—although the flames were crack[l]ing around it, yet it was preserved with all the Materials. Br. Edgar and myself had removed the most valuable [items] into the Street. I watched them, although it was snowing and blowing severely. Snow in the Streets, two feet deep. The walls of the buildings on fire soon fell in, and the flames were soon over come. Engines were not used as they could not get them through the Snow in the Streets—only Hoses. About 6 O'clock we carried the Books, &c back into the office, Feeling thankful to our Heavenly Father for his preservation, &c. Saw Elder P. P. Pratt of the "twelve" there, who gave me a Mission to Delaware &c.

Preaching, politicking, and publishing were not enough to keep Brannan fully occupied. *The Prophet* announced on 22 February 1845 that the young entrepreneur's new land-office would open for business on 1 May. The article carried an unintentionally prophetic headline, "Latter Day Saints, Look out!" Brannan offered to advertise property "in all the principle [*sic*] cities in the United States and Great Britain," in return for "six per cent on the dollar, and the expenses of advertizing, which will be but very small" on any property sold. This establishment would "become a regular depot for land seekers." Brannan started a travel agency to help Mormons bound for Nauvoo, "Owing to the many impositions that have been practiced upon emigrants journeying westward, and feeling it our duty to look well to the interests of the household of faith." He offered railroad tickets to Pittsburgh at a reduced price and promised his clients "a card that will prevent them from falling into the many snares laid to rob them of their money."[20] Brannan also

[20]"Take Notice," *The Prophet*, 5 April 1845.

worked on a deal with Pratt to purchase land for the LDS church on Lake Superior for five dollars an acre from a "Gentleman who . . . lives in N. Jersey," but nothing came of the venture.[21]

DISFELLOWSHIPPED AND CUT OFF

Brannan attended the inauguration of James K. Polk in March 1845, and *The Prophet* casually mentioned his cordial relations with the new administration. "Our visit to the President was decidedly satisfactory and quite interesting," he wrote. "You may rely that he was not taken from the same piece of cloth, neither of the same stripe of Martin Van Buren, but carries the very appearance of a nobleman. So much for appearance and expression."[22] Brannan's political connections to the Democratic party are obscure, but he participated in the spoils system, for he told Brigham Young in July 1845 that he had secured "a situation in the Custom House" for Elder Elijah R. Schwackhamer that paid $1,100 a year. When Brannan joined Elijah Fordham and Parley Pratt in sending a letter to Wilford Woodruff in England, he could not resist boasting of his political connections with the Democratic party—and the rewards he was now collecting as part of its political machine.

> BRANNAN TO WOODRUFF, 13 MARCH 1845,
> LDS ARCHIVES.
> Prophet Office New York March 13th 1845
> [Heading on Elijah Fordham letter]
> Brother Woodruff—Knowing the anxiety you must feel for the cause of God in America, I imbrace the present to drop you a line by permision of Elder Fordham who leaves this place to remove with many others for Nauvoo. They carry up much money & goods for the Temple. All the Elders have been called in this Summer to labor on the temple, the brethren are resolved to have the endowment this fall. Our enemies say if we are not exterminated before the Temple is finished, it never can be done—so you may depend on a decisive blow being struck for its completion, I mean the completion of the Temple. I would inform you that we now as a people stand in relationship to this country [better] than we stood before. I have succeeded in obtaining an appointment for one of our brethren in the Custom House in this city and have the promise of some more in other ports of the country

---

[21]P. P. Pratt to Young and Council, 9 April 1845, Brigham Young Collection, LDS Archives.
[22]"Washington," *The Prophet*, 5 April 1845.

or in other cities. I have also obtained quite an influence on the part of the executive of the General Government in our behalf. Governor Ford will have to give us protection during his administration or he will lose his influence with the General Government, to whom he will be looking for an appointment in the cabinet after he has left the executive chair in Illinois, and he will lose it if he is not our friend. I have much I would like to tell you but I have not the roome. I close for Elder Pratt.

yours truly S. Brannan

Brigham Young and the apostles "disfellowshipped and cut off" Brannan from the LDS church on 10 April 1845 for a polygamous marriage performed by William Smith.[23] The "most disgraceful and diabolical conduct" Young denounced was simply Brannan's attempt to participate in the doctrine of plural marriage that was among the most troublesome of Joseph Smith's legacies. For Parley Pratt, Young enlarged on the printed "Notice" and outlined a course of action regarding Brannan, whose political connections Young still valued.

NOTICE TO THE CHURCHES ABROAD, 10 APRIL 1845,
BRIGHAM YOUNG COLLECTION, LDS ARCHIVES.

This may certify, that Elder George J Adams and Elder *Samuel Brannan*, are disfellowshipped and cut off from the Church of Jesus Christ of Latter Day Saints. Their conduct has been such as to disgrace them in the eyes of justice and virtue, and we cannot, and will not sanction men who are guilty of such things as we have every reason to believe that *they* have been, from the most inscrutible testimony. We have for some time been unwilling to believe the foul statements made concerning them, but the nature of the testimony now adduced, compels us to believe that the statements are but too true: and that under the sacred garb of religion, they have been practicing the most disgraceful and diabolical conduct.

We think it just to the saints at large to make this statement. And, Elder Brannan will no longer be supported as an editor, by us, nor any land agency of his be sustained by us.

And let this be a warning to other elders, if there are any guilty of like conduct.

Done by order of the council,

Brigham Young President
Willard Richards Clerk
April 10 1845[24]

[23]Quinn, *The Mormon Hierarchy: Origins of Power*, 214, 426n156.

[24]See "Notice to the Churches Abroad," *The Prophet*, 10 May 1845, for the published version.

YOUNG TO P. P. PRATT, 10 APRIL 1845,
BRIGHAM YOUNG COLLECTION, LDS ARCHIVES.

Nauvoo April 10, 1845

Dear Bro. Pratt,

We have this day excommunicated George J. Adams, and Samuel Brannan, for abominations that are not necessary to mention now. They will be published in our next paper. This is, therefore, to notify you beforehand of the fact, that you may have the advantage in negotiating any necessary business. Take into your hands immediately, the Prophet and all things appertaining thereto. Or you may let Brannan keep the Prophet, and devote it altogether to political matters; and let Mormonism never be named in it any more than in any other worldly, political paper. And you can start a religious periodical according as you have been previously counselled, and you can employ Brannan to print your paper if you choose, and support him as a democrat, and let him support us as a democratic community.

There are other Elders in the East, that have reason to beware, for we are resolved that if men will not be wise and virtuous, they shall not have our confidence or fellowship.

May God bless you and prosper your labors.

Brigham Young Prst
Willard Richards, clerk

William Smith returned to Nauvoo shortly afterward. In a meeting on 5 May, Smith persuaded his fellow apostles to restore Brannan "to church fellowship immediately," though they delayed an official announcement of the action until Brannan could appear before them.[25]

"NOTICE,"
TIMES AND SEASONS, 15 APRIL 1845.

Some few weeks ago an article appeared in the "Neighbor," wherein it was stated that Elder Samuel Brannan was cut off from the church. From representations made by Elder William Smith, who has since returned home and is personally acquainted with him, the order is reversed, and Elder Brannan restored to his former standing.[26]

Unaware that he had been "cut off," Brannan wrote his first letter to Brigham Young in late April. It concerned personal issues that came to a head when his sister, Mary Ann Badlam, arrived from the West, "entirely disheartened and discouraged." Perhaps it was not just the uncertainties

---

[25]Quinn, *The Mormon Hierarchy: Origins of Power*, 214.

[26]The date on the notice was an anachronism, since "the actual publishing date of *Times and Seasons* was several weeks behind the date of each issue at this time." See Ibid., 426n157.

of frontier life that brought Mrs. Badlam to New York, for years later Benjamin Winchester recalled that Mr. Badlam of Old Nauvoo was a wife-beater. Winchester claimed a "very bitter" Joseph Smith had complained about "the talk among people about his lewdness, especially [among] the women gossipers," and told his audience, "those women deserved to be threshed . . . One of the brethren, Badlam by name, took his suggestion in a literal sense; he went home and gave his wife a severe whipping, which circumstance became the talk of the town."[27]

BRANNAN TO YOUNG, 26 APRIL 1845,
BRIGHAM YOUNG COLLECTION, LDS ARCHIVES.

New York, April 26 [1845]

Elder Young
     Dear Sir—My principle reason for introducing myself upon your notice at this time, is a matter connected with my Brother in Law Elexander Badlam— Owing to the many privations and sufferings that his wife and family have had to pass through, by hunger and sickness, from the time they emigrated West 12 years ago, has entirely disheartened and discouraged his wife of thinking to live in the West and five weeks ago today she started from Galena, Ill. with her children, determined that she would remain in that country no longer, but would join her friends and relatives in the east, and leave her husband behind, to attend the Conference and receive council from the Twelve, for he was resolved to make no move in so important a matter as going east without instructions from head quarters to that effect, but his wife took the briches and the children and her own council and in five weeks today landed in New York. She had a pleasant journey and met no difficulty in getting here. She will be attended to and taken care off [sic] ~~which is true~~ (but then she wants some person besides the attention of ~~strangers~~ friends and her husband is needed to rapevertenel [?] his own family. And I have dropped you this line, ~~and would [ask] you to council him accordingly~~ in order that when he applies to you for council you may be acquainted with the circumstances, and will know what council he needs. If he is sent east and that to[o] as soon as you can spare him, it will take a burthen from me, which the Lord knows I have as much as I can clearly walk under, and [this] is likely to continue for the coming season.

     P.S.
     I am now gathering up documents from the leading Democracy east of the Mountains to stimulate that Democracy and executive of Illinois, to move promptly against any mob that may be got up in that state against

---

[27]"Primitive Mormonism: A Personal Narrative of it by Mr. Benjamin Winchester," *Salt Lake Tribune*, 22 September 1889. In his memoir, Winchester remained bitter about his experiences with Mormonism in the 1840s.

Nauvoo. I am holding myself ready to start any moment or as soon as it is actually required. If I visit the west my business will be confidential to the Executive and the bablic [*sic*] must be kept ignorant, [for] if the Rigdonites should get hold of the matter they would commute with [anti-Mormon newspaper editor] Tom Sharp and he would blow it all over the State to our disadvantage. No more at present

    My love to God's people Amen

S. Brannan

    N.P. I learn that A. Badlam is thinking about starting a paper in Galena. I wish you would council him to abandon such an idea, for it cant succeed, and send him to his family as soon as he can come.

Brannan hinted that his recent political machinations would send him to Illinois, but news of his excommunication probably expedited the trip. His strong ties to both William Smith and Parley P. Pratt saved Brannan's career in the LDS church, and Pratt sent Brigham Young a forceful appeal for Brannan's reinstatement. He praised Brannan's humility, obedience, diligence, zeal, perseverance, and industry, and blamed "whatever errors or faults he may have been led into" on "older and higher authority"—meaning William Smith. Pratt assumed his "editorial and public duties" while Brannan would "repair to the west, on this and other business," to "obtain a fair trial, and a chance to defend his own cause."[28]

Brannan's humble *mea culpa* followed Pratt's letter. That Brannan would endure such humiliation indicates the depth of his devotion to the Mormon cause. The phrase "I have had a knowledge of the existence of his kingdom on the earth" suggests that he had learned some of the secrets of the Council of Fifty, also called the Kingdom of God and the Living Constitution, the secret organization Joseph Smith had created before his death to govern the earth after the return of Christ. Only a month earlier, on Mormonism's fifteenth anniversary, Pratt and Brannan had published a proclamation "to All the Kings of the World, to the President of the United States of America; to the Governors of the Several States, and to the Rules and People of All Nations" that outlined the goals of the Kingdom.[29] Alexander Badlam or Parley P. Pratt, char-

---

[28]P. P. Pratt to Young and Council, 7 May 1845, LDS Archives.

[29]Pratt, "Proclamation of the Twelve Apostles of the Church of Jesus Christ of Latter-day Saints . . . " (N.Y: Pratt and Brannan, 6 April 1845). This remarkable record was republished as the keepsake issued with the collector's edition of David L. Bigler's *Forgotten Kingdom*, the second volume of the KINGDOM IN THE WEST series.

BRIGHAM YOUNG, CIRCA 1845.
Pictured as president of the
Quorum of the Twelve Apostles,
this youthful image captures
the Mormon leader during
one of the most difficult
periods in his career.
Courtesy, LDS Archives.

ter members of the Council of Fifty, probably contributed to Brannan's growing awareness of Mormonism's worldly ambitions.

"BRETHREN AND FRIENDS,"
THE PROPHET, 10 MAY 1845, 2/1–2.

In this number of the Prophet, you will learn that charges have been preferred against me, and the testimony has been deemed sufficien[t] by the Presidency of the church, for my excommunication. The blow is truly a severe one, but I feel to bear it patiently, and even more if required. If I have deviated from the path of rectitude—violated the commandments of God, or been the means of bringing reproach upon his cause, I look upon myself as being bound to make restitution for the same. It has ever been during my ministry in the church, my desire to do the will of my God, and heavenly Father, and inasmuch as I have had a knowledge of the existence of his kingdom on the earth, I have been willing to yield obedience to the authorities of the same, and pray my heavenly Father, that [all] the time in the future, my mind and heart may not be guided otherwise. On to-morrow I shall start for Nauvoo, there to meet my accusers face to face, and abide the decision of the council of God. I cannot say that I am sorry for what has transpired, I mean in relation to the course my brethren have taken in the west in regard to myself, for I am in hope some good may grow out of it, if nothing more, it may be a terror to evil doers hereafter. And when I come to reflect on the responsibility resting upon the elders of this church, and at the same time see the carelessness that is in existance, I am left to conclude without any hesitation, of the necessity for a prompt and decided course to be taken, in pruning the tree.

Brethren I desire your prayers during my absence, that God may guide me by his spirit into all truth.

S. BRANNAN.

Immediately following Brannan's humble letter, *The Prophet* reported a rumor (not true, as it turned out) that reflected its long-standing interest in the West: "A rumor is now in circulation, that Sir George Simpson has been appointed by the British Government, governor of Oregon." It also contained an interesting look at "The Science of Anti-Mormon Suckerology—Its Learned Terms, and their Significance."

Brannan left for Nauvoo after 7 May, though hardly under the conditions he had imagined. Young had already written Parley Pratt on 4 May, "Concerning Samuel Brannan if he is humble & receives his chastisement as becomes him it may yet be well with him, if he repents he might then continue a *political* paper as specified in another letter which ought to have been forwarded to you some time since."[30]

P. P. PRATT TO YOUNG, 7 MAY 1845,
BRIGHAM YOUNG COLLECTION, LDS ARCHIVES.

N.Y., May 7th '45

Dear Br. Young, and the twelve

Elder Brannan, the bearer of this, will appear before your Honorable Council, to learn the nature of the charges prefered against him, and if necessary, to demand a fair trial with a chance to answer for him self. This of course he is entitled to do by the Laws of God, and cannot be denied him.

---

[30]Council of the Twelve to Parley P. Pratt, 4 May 1845, LDS Archives.

I also wish to say that he has laboured faithfully and diligently, since I came here last winter, and has set a good example, in all things as far as I know, and veryly believe, and has at all times possessed a Spirit of willingness to hearken to Council.

When I first came in [to New York], I had reason to believe he had been led by others into some gross errors and misconduct; I therefore told him in the name of the Lord that he must repent, with all his heart, and do so no more, if he had been guilty of acting upon, or holding to certain principles, or he could no longer stand in his place. He promised me faithfully that he would, and I do believe he has fulfilled [this charge] thus far. And he said he is now willing to repent and give any Satisfaction against him. On this ground I am confident he must and will obtain a restoration to his standing in the Church, and priesthood, and also in the Caracter, among all Good men.

Should this be the case, I wish you to sanction his immediate return to this place as his family and buisiness will make it indispensably necessary for him to return. He owes several sums of money, and has business of several kinds to settle. And he has experience as a printer, and in the mailing and publishing of the paper, etc., that I have not, and devotes his time night and day in that department in a way that I cannot do, consistent with my other duties. If therefore, I edit the Prophet or publish any periodical I need his services. And besides this he has a run of Politicks, and an acquaintance, and Influence, which I neither have nor want, but which will command some means to publish, and some influence on our behalf, if carried out.

I hope that your honorable body will strike at the root of the evils which may have entangled him; for I consider him at worst, as only one of the Branches. That is I consider that he may have been led, or influenced by Others, on whom justice ought to rest with greater weight and severity. This I do not learn from him but from facts which I would Lay before you if I were present, and facts too, which would astonish you and make all heaven weep.

I had thought of prefering charges against some persons—but I forbear, and leave them in the hands of God.

Dear Brethren of the Council, I have written to you here before on several important subjects, but have recieved no decisive answer.

Do you approve of the proclamation of the twelve and wish it published?[31] Can we have some Doctrine and Cove[nant]s and some Hymn Books? If so where and how? Mr. [Sidney] Rigdon is publishing the

[31]This is a reference to Pratt's "Proclamation of the Twelve Apostles," which bore the date of 6 April 1845. Parley Pratt apparently waited for Young's permission before he actually published the piece, for it was October before Wilford Woodruff wrote from Liverpool, "I have received a copy of 'The Proclamation of the Twelve' and ordered 20,000 of them to be printed in English which I shall cause to be circulated as widely as possible through the British Mission, and as soon as an opportunity affords they will be published in Welsh." See Woodruff to O. Pratt and Brannan, 17 October 1845, LDS Archives.

D[octrine and] C[ovenants] and I think some of the Saints will buy of him rather than be without them, if we don't supply them. I could supply them in two weeks if the plates were here . . .

I remain your affectionate Brother and fellow labourer,

P. P. Pratt

PRES'T YOUNG AND THE QUORUM TO P. P. PRATT, 10 MAY 1845,
BRIGHAM YOUNG COLLECTION, LDS ARCHIVES.

Nauvoo May 10, 1845

Elder P. P. Pratt

Dear Brother

Since our last we have had an interview with Bro. Wm Smith and concluded if Samuel Brannon has borne his chastisement like a Saint that he will be restored to fellowship.

We think it would be best for him for you to lead him into the water and admit him through the door, no one but yourself knowing it, but we leave this with you.

We had no *personal feelings* against Brannan which caused us to cut him off. It was all done on testimony.

You will do well to continue the Prophet, and keep up an influence which you will understand.

Brigham Young, Prst
Willard Richards clerk

Brannan arrived in Nauvoo on 23 May and immediately met with William Smith and the apostles. The next afternoon, the ruling body of the LDS church again met "in council with Samuel S. Brannan." After a "long investigation," Brannan "was restored, to full fellowship in good standing" and William Smith "was ordained Patriarch to the whole church." To celebrate, one of the sisters "sent a bottle of wine by Sis Young—which the Twelve drunk." There was "a warm interchange of good feeling between Wm Smith and the Quorum"—but the minutes of this meeting suggest the "good feeling" was conditional at best.[32]

BRANNAN ACCOMPLISHED HIS DESIRE

Mormon accounts have never reported the true cause of Brannan's chastisement—his polygamous sealing by William Smith to Sarah E.

---

[32]Willard Richards, Journal, 5, 23, and 24 May 1845, LDS Archives.

Wallace, the sister of G. B. Wallace, a church leader in New England and by 1845 Nauvoo's undertaker. This early and unhappy example of "spiritual wifery" apparently began in the fall of 1844, only months after Brannan's legal marriage to Ann Eliza Corwin. The apostles present at Brannan's hearing on 24 May 1845 had all learned the secret doctrine of celestial marriage directly from Joseph Smith. Only radicals such as William Smith and George J. Adams seem to have shared the doctrine beyond the tight and trusted circle who learned it from the prophet, and the consequences were both disastrous and comical.

The minutes of the 24 May 1845 meeting of the apostles describe a seduction made under religious pretenses, but also cast light on relations between William Smith and his fellow church leaders. The apostles at the hearing could hardly have ignored Wallace's charge that Brannan had seduced his sister and then covered up "the humbug," but they chose to follow Brigham Young's advice to "throw the mantle" over the whole sorry affair. These men—all polygamists—may have wondered how their own polygamous courtships would stand up to similar scrutiny.[33] Young accepted Smith's unauthorized sealing and did not deny that he had authority to perform polygamous marriages outside the carefully controlled setting of the Mormon temple endowment—but only in this specific case. The quorum would finally excommunicate the troublesome Smith in October 1845.

D. MICHAEL QUINN, MINUTES OF QUORUM OF TWELVE APOSTLES, 24 MAY 1845.

24 May 1845, Nauvoo meeting of Apostles with Samuel E. Brannan:

Bro. [George B.] Wallace said, his sister came to his house in New Bedford, [Massachusetts, and] told him Bro Brannan had waited on some, one Sunday [when] she staid at home. Bro Brannan staid at home [too]. On the edge of the [bed?] Brannan accomplished his desire, & went into the kitchen. Messeur [my sister?] came in & after reported She was dissatisfied. Wm [Smith] sealed them up. It worried her to think she must be Brannans. Bro [Parley P.] Pratt told her the sealing was not according to the Law of

---

[33]Despite repeated written requests to the LDS Historical Department, the original minutes are not available to scholars. Historian D. Michael Quinn provided these transcriptions from the Minutes of the Quorum of Twelve Apostles made while he was employed by the LDS church. Quinn's transcripts are in his papers in the Yale Collection of Western Americana and will eventually be opened to researchers. Quinn's notes are the only source to give "E" as Brannan's middle initial.

God. [She] went into consumption & died.[34] Wallace wrote Br Pratt, about Brannan, that unless he repented he could not be crowned in the celestial kingdom. She said her sickness was occasioned by what had passed.

Wm Smith, acquainted with Sis Wallace at Low[el]l, [said she was] of poor health. Brannan asked Smith if he had any objection to mary them. She manifested [a] strong attachment for Brannan. I married them[—]did not consider he had was under any obligation to any one else. Married them by all the authority he possessd for time & Eternity, and had a right &c to do as an apostle of J Christ. Father [Freeman] Nickerson preached that if anyone should get hold of his skirts or any else, on the spiritual wife system, they would go to hell. & she believed it. Sis Wallace wrote Brannan upbraiding him with the humbug & charging me with assisting Brannan.

Prest Young, said since Sis Wallace had gone home, we could throw the mantle over the whole & shuter the subject.

Wm. Smith said he felt interested in the subject & wished the council if they chose to say whether he had a right so to do.—whether he [had] a right to mary Brannan & do what he had done. Or whether [he] was to be rode on a rail, & put down, or not. Quite a time for him.

Prest Young.—said he was satisfied with what Wm Smith did in the case of Brannan in marrying him to Sis Wallace. [Young] did not couple any other of Wms acts, in this decision.—

Wm Supposed that P. P. Pratt supposed that Brannan was married to two, at once. Brannan walked with Sis Wallace in public &c. She had discovered that the time would come when men would have more wives than one==made arrangements to take her to N. York in the spring.—Told her I should be master.—Would correspond with her. But [he] did not write for fear some one would get the letter. Father Nickerson went to Lowell & disaffected the minds of the sisters.

Wallace was in N. York when Brannan received his sisters letter, but did not talk with him about it as freely as with other women.

Brigham Young's decision to "throw the mantle" over the matter reflected a strategy he would employ to deal with later problems. He immediately reported the council's decision to Parley Pratt, with a note on how to deal with the troublesome Alexander Badlam.

YOUNG TO P. P. PRATT, 26 MAY 1845,
SPECIAL COLLECTIONS, BYU LIBRARY.

Dr Brother Pratt.

A few of the Twelve and the Trustees have been in council together this

---

[34]Sarah E. Wallace, born 12 July 1825, died on 17 March 1845. See her entry in the Ancestral File, LDS Family History Library.

morning in brother [George] Millers upper room and we have concluded we would write to you giving you a short sketch of the prospect and situation of things as they now exist among us.

Brother Samuel Brannan arrived here on friday last and immediately reported himself to us. We held a council on his case and called brothers Wm Smith and [George B.] Wallace into the council. The whole matter was thoroughly investigated and the facts related by the brethren. On the whole we did not find matters in relation to brother Brannans conduct so bad as had been reported. The difficulty between him and brother Wallace was sat-isfactorally adjusted and inasmuch as the principal accuser is now dead we have con[clud]ed to let it rest and have restored brother Brannan to full fel-lowship and confidence. We shall publish a notice of his restoration and he will return to our good f[aith,] fellowship and be[st w]ishes for his future success and prosperity.

Brother [Alexander] Badlam is here to ask council for himself.

We have instructed him to go to New York and go to work with his hands and take care of his family but not to go as an Elder to preach nor as a president of the seventies, but as a private member to labor for his fami-lies comfort as long as he has a mind to, or till further orders and when he wants to return with his family to Nauvoo, we have told him to do so. He will of course be under your direction and you can counsel him from time to time if you have a mind to.

WONDERFUL TALES ABOUT NAUVOO

Brigham Young now sent Brannan and Orson Spencer on a delicate political mission to the Illinois capital at Springfield. Spencer and Bran-nan met with Governor Thomas Ford in the state house, where they "held a familiar interview for several hours." Ford said that the people of Illinois had "rudely resisted" his efforts to plead the Mormon cause and warned Spencer of a possible "attack by the cooperation of steamboats upon our city." The governor cautioned that the LDS church's political influence "exasperated the people." Ford promised to protect the Saints as best he could, but admitted "large masses of people that might assemble for violent and tumultuous purposes could not be restrained by any law or government."[35] Brannan bemoaned his lack of writing skill, counseled moderation, advised Brigham Young to "exclude such doctrines" that would alienate potential allies—and again demonstrated his fondness for folk aphorisms.

---

[35]Roberts, ed., *History of the Church*, 7:423–24.

BRANNAN TO YOUNG, 2 JUNE 1845,
BRIGHAM YOUNG COLLECTION, LDS ARCHIVES.

Springfield, June 2, 1845

Elder Young Deer [*sic*] sir

I have just returned from an interview with the Editor of the State Register,[36] he informing me that the doctrines held forth in the Neighbor by
brother Taylor "That no civil process for debt ~~be etc shall not~~ from the United
States Marshall, shall ~~not~~ be served upon him, nor any other citizen of Nauvoo, until the General Government has Coerced the State of Illinois and Missouri has been the means of driving from the track.["] He says he has been our
friend from the begining, and will continue to be so as long as such doctrines
as the above are not set forth in the Neighbor. He says he replied to the article, but Br. Taylor did not receive it in the spirit that it was written but came
out against him, and joined the Warsaw Signal, but he says he is willing to
make allowances for Br. Taylor owing to the Carthage massacre.[37] He has let
his feelings get the better of his judgment but he says the Neighbor is looked
upon as an official organ, and the whole society will be considered responsible
for its doctrines, and if you wish him to advocate your cause, you must exclude
such doctrines, for the United States has no power to coerse this State or Missouri either. Now whether he be wright or wrong, a mild course on our part
will be sure to win us the battel [for] "there is more flies caught with molasses
than vinegar" the old Quaker woman said.

Since brother Spencer left I have had another interview with the Gov.
[Thomas Ford] and with Gov. Runnels [John Reynolds, Illinois governor,
1830–34] & Gov. Anderson, who is the United States Marshal, Judge
[Stephen A.] Douglas, Mr. Lambert and the Editor of the Register and they
are all professedly our friends, and you may rest assured that the power of
keeping down a mob is in our own hands. I wish I could only be with you
for one hour. I can talk much pla[i]ner than I can wright. They say that the
Carthagenians could not raise a mob of 500 men let them do their best.

Lambert tells me that the Laws Higbies and Robbinson[38] have told him
wonderful tales about Nauvoo, and the Wife system but he does not believe
them. He designs visiting Na[u]voo in a couple of weeks. Make friends with
the Register by all means—better have him speak for us than against us. He
is a smart fellow and very candid, and says he dont care a dam for public
opinion if we will only be careful and not publish such strong doctrine and
drive him from the tack. Take my word for it the political aspect of things

---

[36]William Walters and George R. Weber published the *Illinois State Register* from 1839 to 1855;
one of these men may have served as editor in 1845.

[37]Apostle John Taylor, editor of the *Nauvoo Neighbor*, which published this editorial, was wounded
during the murder of Joseph Smith.

[38]This referred to dissidents William and Wilson Law, Francis Higbee, and Ebenezer Robinson.

in this state could not be bettered in our behalf, considering the circumstances, and if we persue a mild and judicious course, the victory must be
ours. I leave this evening for St Louis. My love to the quorum, and may God
bless you all and I know he will.

I remain your obedient servant

S. Brannan

Excuse my bad writing, if I should write from now till dooms day I
should ~~write~~ wright no better, it is not because I am too lazy to learn, but as
the Hoosier said it is not in me.

As Brannan returned east, Parley P. Pratt despaired of Mormonism's
prospects in America, particularly in New York. Pratt felt that the few
devoted Saints in the East had answered the LDS church's call to gather
at Nauvoo, and all the church's political and religious influence could
not generate enough support to allow an elder "to work for nothing and
live on 'Sawdust pudding,' as doc Franklin said." Pratt doubted that the
New York church could continue to publish a newspaper at all. If the
Saints had "a dollar for spare it is handed in for tithing, or laid aside to
purchase arms, Clothing, Ammunition, etc, or to help them selves to
Emigrate and settle in the west." Pratt was convinced "I can do no good"
in New York. "The public are entirely indifferent, and will neither come
to meeting, hear, nor read the Truth." Only about fifty Saints attended
Sunday meetings, "and perhaps half a dozen Strangers come in and out,
to gaze and gape, and wander and perish." Since reaching the city in
December, mere subsistence had cost Pratt $150 more than he had
raised, despite the strictest economies. "I feel as if I was now done with
this City, and nearly with the Nation. My garments are Clean, if they all
perish." The eastern Saints cared "little for supporting papers, politics,
[preaching the] Gospel to the Gentiles, Elders or any thing else. They
want to Build the Temple—Gather to it—Get instruction and endowment. In short they want the Kingdom of God, and its righteousness,
and an end to everything else—and so do I."[39]

MY OPPRESSED CIRCUMSTANCES

Shortly after his return to New York, Brannan composed one of the

---

[39]P. P. Pratt to Young, 5 June 1845, Brigham Young Collection, LDS Archives. For an edited version of this letter, see Roberts, ed., *History of the Church*, 7:425–26.

most remarkable letters in his surviving correspondence. He complained about money problems; given his later financial success, the contempt he expressed for money is more than a little ironic. He noted that a missionary's remarks about polygamy had upset his wife—but exactly what Ann Eliza Brannan's "feelings and troubles" were remains a mystery.

The mention of Lansford W. Hastings reveals that Brannan had met and perhaps even traveled west with the young promoter before late May 1845, and indicates that Brannan had discussed Hastings' ambitious plans to seize California with the Mormon leaders while in Nauvoo. Brannan would forever after claim that the idea of sending a shipload of Mormons to California was his own. If he did make the initial proposal, he probably did so while in Nauvoo. After Lansford Hastings' plans matured in New York in early July, Hastings headed west, intending to visit Nauvoo to explain the details of his scheme to Brigham Young. Pressed for time, Hastings bypassed Nauvoo and went directly to Independence, but Brannan's proposal seems to have taken root. As the apostles defined their own plans, on 21 August 1845 Young informed Wilford Woodruff and the British Mission, "We trust within one year many of our brethren will be placed on the coast of the Pacific, or near by to receive their friends from the islands."[40]

BRANNAN TO YOUNG AND COUNCIL, 22 JULY 1845,
BRIGHAM YOUNG COLLECTION, LDS ARCHIVES.

New York, July 22, /45

Dear brethren

Day after day has passed away as I have been promising myself to write you a letter, and the occasion of my negligence, has been my oppressed circumstances. My mind ~~soul and~~ and body have been wracked day and knight ever since my return from the west—it seems that all the powers of Hell have arrayed themselves against me—or in other words God suffered it so to be to try me—for such we know is his manner of dealing. The forty dollars I borrowed from you has given me a great deal of pain, which I must confess to be the first pain I have ever received on the account of money—for I am no lover of money—neither was it for the love of it—but for the love of my word—that it should be forth coming as soon as I returned. Brother Taylor informed you I presume that I should send it as soon as the new postage law went into opperation. At that time, I was positive of doing it—as brother Shwack-

---

[40]"Latest from Nauvoo," *Millennial Star*, 1 October 1845, 124.

hamer[41] the one that I obtained a situation in the Custom House for, and is receiving eleven hundred dollars a year, pay [received] every month—promised to let me have the money when he drew his pay from the Government the first of July—but he failed to do it. [He] got a spirit of apostacy in him—and for what I care may go to the devil—all such men will let five hundred or a thousand dollars dam[n] them—Brother Pratt Has cursed him and so have I, with all my soul might, mind and strength, in the name of the Lord—in basket and stone, spiritually and Temporally, and ask you to do the same—I labored to raise him from a state of begary, and now he is judas. He promised when I started for the West to pay my expenses back—when I returned all the money that had been taken in had been paid out for the debts of the office—The paper stopping & stopped all business as many supposing that it would not start again withheld their subscriptions—so I had to start the paper again as I did at the first without a cent in my pocket—In order to get Br. Wm Smith exhonerated from 2000 dollar bonds when he was arrested in Philadelphia by B. Winchester—that he might go to the west with his family, I gave Winchester my note for three hundred dollars that Brother [Reuben] Hadlock was owing him in England for books, payable in four months from ~~date~~ the last of March, which I shall have to pay the last day of this month. The stoppage of the papers so long, ~~my expenses to the West~~ and my being called to the West, just as I was, ~~with to fouly~~ the money due you, and three hundred to Winchester and having to start the paper again all coming upon me at once, and then those ~~whom we you~~ I have depended on, ~~to~~ forsaking me—you may depend brethren it has been a great trial, no one kno[w]s it until they have experienced it—but I have not forgotten what you told me brother [Heber C.] Kimball, and I believe every word of it—as soon as God has tried me a little—I believe he will let me loose again. Perhaps you have received the money by this time for I wrote to Br. [Joseph] Ball that if he had it to go and give it to you and say I sent it to you. Perhaps he has done so, whether he has or not it will be forth coming before many days. I think I shall be able to send it by brother ~~Jarmin~~ [William?] Jarmen, or Br. [Ethan?] Pettit, who will start in a week or ten days—so brother Young you must forgive me this time for telling that lie unless Brother Ball has paid it or any one else. Brother Badlam has arrived, and him and his family are well.[42] Brother Pratt has located himself in

---

[41] *The Prophet*, 9 November 1844, reported that Elijah R. Schwackhamer addressed a Brooklyn congregation "on the authenticity of the Book of Mormon." The *New-York Messenger*, 12 July 1845, 14, referred to a "A Dutch gander by the name of Swhackhammer." On 2 August 1845, the paper reported that "E. R. Swackhammer" was disfellowshipped on 27 July in Philadelphia. He later served as one of Sidney Rigdon's apostles.

[42] Alexander Badlam presided over the LDS church's Boston branch from 1846 to 1848. Wilford Woodruff and his family visited "brother A. Badlam's house, in Cambridge Port, near Boston." See Jessee, ed., *The Papers of Joseph Smith*, 2:524; and "Letter from Elder W. Woodruff to Elder O. Spencer," *Millennial Star*, 15 October 1848, 317.

Boston, and will remain there until he goes west. A General peace and Union prevails throughout the Eastern churches. Adams is expected here before long with Little Joseph [Smith III] for a hobby horse, to ride on—but it will be the greatest failure that ever he made—Our City has been visited with an awful fire [with] 20 acres laid in ruins—upwards of four millions destroyed—340 horses burned—all men con til [?] nearby—by this time I presume you ~~had~~ have had a visit from Mr. Hastings. He is the one I was speaking to you about when I was there [in Nauvoo]—There is a greater spirit of gathering among the saints now than there ever was before, a great many will go in the fall to the west, so farewell may God be with you forever is the prayer of your unworthy brother S. Brannan.

My prospects for the paper are getting ~~a li~~ Brighter—I have quit preaching in New York, and spend my sabbaths in the country. I find it better for my health—being so confined to the city nearly wears me out, I am praying God night and day for deliverence but I wont budge one inch till he says so by the mouth of his Prophet.

Brother [Willard] Snow was not quite as wise as he might have been when he passed through New York, from what I learn in the office—My wife was present when he arrived—and his manner of throwing out his s[n]ide hints about myself and Br. Smith was very cutting to her—and very disgusting to ever body else in the office as they were acquainted with her feelings and troubles with what had taken place,—but he has injured himself more than he has any one else I have no [End of postscript]

Chapter 3

"For the Cause of God and the Truth"
The Plot to Conquer California

Upon his return to New York in June 1845, Brannan launched into a series of activities and schemes that would ultimately lead him to California. He also changed the name and style of his newspaper. An editorial claimed, "The 'Prophet' has been transformed into a 'Messenger' without any very great change except in name and form," but its content shifted from religious to secular subjects, such as western emigration. It informed "the saints that contemplate emigrating to the west this season" that Brannan had opened an "emigrating office in the city of New York at No. 7 Spruce street. We hope the Saints will give us their patronage, wee [sic] feel satisfied they will find it to their advantage."[1] The *Messenger* advertised Brannan's new travel agency on 19 July to "persons wishing to go to the western states," noting they could "obtain tickets, and correct information," at the paper's offices.[2] The paper soon reported the projected departure of "Saints in the East wishing to go to the West."[3]

Hurra for California!

The *Messenger* took up the theme: "Hurra for California!" the title of the poem that led off the second issue, echoing the sentiments of John Taylor's earlier song, "The Upper California, O! that's the land for me." The next story announced publication of extracts "from the late work, published in Cincinnatti, by Capt. Lansford W. Hastings." Hastings, son

---

[1]"To the Saints," *New-York Messenger*, 12 July 1845, 12.
[2]"Notice," *New-York Messenger*, 19 July 1845, 24.
[3]See *New-York Messenger*, 9 August 1845, 46.

of an Ohio doctor and legislator, was born in 1819, and read the law as
a young man. He seems to have abandoned his wife to travel overland to
Oregon with Elijah White in 1842. Unhappy with the country, he led a
party of similarly dissatisfied emigrants to California in 1843 and
returned to the United States via Mexico. In the spring of 1845, Hastings published his *Emigrants' Guide, to Oregon and California*, which promoted
California as a paradise and minimized the difficulty of overland travel.
His friend John Bidwell recalled that Hastings "desired to wrest the
country from Mexico" and "was ambitious to make California a republic
and to be its first president."[4] Hastings was in New York by May 1845
recruiting allies and touting his book. The *Messenger* informed its readers
that Hastings had "recently been lecturing in this city, upon the advantages of emigrating" to California. Hastings promised Mexican land
grants "not less than one square league nor over nine to every emigrant"
in a country whose "commercial advantages and natural recourses [*sic*] are
the greatest in the known world."[5] Early in August Brannan disingenu-
ously explained the Mormon paper's interest in California:

> Some of our readers may enquire why we have so much to say about Califor-
> nia. We would say that our religion is to acquire all the intelligence possible
> concerning every country. History is a matter of great interest to the elders
> that are called to go to the nations of the earth, and as California is a portion
> of the new world, so called, yea, a portion of that which God made choice
> above all others, we deem it sufficiently worthy of our attention.[6]

It was a long, hot summer in New York. In July the thermometer hit
"101 in the shade. Six fell dead in the street from the heat."[7] The men
who met in New York with Samuel Brannan to plot the American conquest of California were no idle collection of adventurers—they
included one of the most powerful men in the United States, former
postmaster general Amos Kendall; author Thomas Jefferson Farnham;
and two politically well-connected businessmen, Arthur W. and Alfred
G. Benson. No evidence connects Democratic editor John L. O'Sullivan

---

[4]Bidwell, "Life in California Before the Gold Discovery," 169, 176. For more, see Thomas F.
Andrews's thesis, "The Controversial Career of Lansford Warren Hastings." For a critical assessment
of Hastings, see Bagley, "Lansford W. Hastings: Scoundrel or Visionary?"

[5]"California," *New-York Messenger*, 12 July 1845, 9. The *Nauvoo Neighbor* reprinted this article without citation, leading some to assume that Lansford Hastings visited Nauvoo.

[6]"California," *New-York Messenger*, 2 August 1845, 37.

[7]*New-York Messenger*, 19 July 1845, 24.

with the group, but his editorials precisely outlined their political agenda—and that very July O'Sullivan would coin one of the enduring phrases of American history: Manifest Destiny.[8]

Mormon historian B. H. Roberts charged that Brannan was deeply involved in a "conspiracy to bond the Saints on the Pacific slope."[9] H. H. Bancroft outlined these events in 1886, noting that Brannan:

> discovered, or pretended to have discovered, that the government would probably take steps to prevent the Mormon migration, on the ground that they intended to take sides with either Mexico or England against the United States. But the shrewd Samuel also discovered a remedy for all prospective misfortune. He learned that Amos Kendall and certain influential associates, acting through one Benson as agent, and claiming President Polk as a "silent party" to the project, would undertake to prevent all interference if the Mormon leaders would sign an agreement "to transfer to A. G. Benson & Co. the odd numbers of all the lands and town lots they may acquire in the country where they may settle."[10]

Modern historians have seldom wrestled with this bizarre chain of events, but Dale Morgan searched for "definite information" about Brannan's association with Benson and Hastings. He hoped to "look into Benson quite thoroughly," but had "turned up just enough odds and ends to whet my curiosity." Morgan concluded, "There is a great deal more here than meets the eye."[11] Documenting any plot is a slippery business, for conspiracies by definition seldom leave a paper trail, but enough evidence of the Brannan-Benson-Hastings-Kendall-Farnham affair survives to indicate that they were involved in an 1840s-style covert operation whose aim was the conquest of California.

Arthur W. Benson and Alfred G. Benson were naval contractors and Pacific traders who had long-established trading contacts at the Hudson's Bay Company post at Fort Vancouver on the Columbia River.[12] F. W.

---

[8]For another look at these events, see Bagley, "'Every Thing Is Favourable! And God Is On Our Side': Samuel Brannan and the Conquest of California."

[9]Roberts, *Comprehensive History*, 3:33.

[10]Bancroft, *History of California*, 5:547–48

[11]Morgan to Virginia Sorensen, 29 December 1943, Morgan Papers.

[12]Nichols, *Advanced Agents of American Destiny*, 191, identified Arthur Benson as the son of A. G. Benson and his agent in the Pacific in 1856. Writing in 1854, however, A. G. Benson referred to "his two boys (16 and 18 years old)," one of whom may have been this Arthur. See Senate Report 397 (34–3), 1856, Serial 891, 264. The Arthur W. of the "Messrs. Benson" in the 1840s was perhaps A. G. Benson's brother.

Pettygrove went to Oregon as their agent and did "a good business for his employers."[13] Baptist missionary Ezra Fisher wrote on 27 February 1846 that "A. G. & A. W. Benson, No 19 Old Slip, New York, will probably send one vessel [to Oregon] each six months."[14] James Douglas of the Hudson's Bay Company reported that Pettygrove was "equipped by the House of Benson & Co. of New York." Pettygrove was "a sharp fellow, and deals very closely for cash only."[15]

The intrigue that began in 1841 was authorized in "a confidential letter from the then Secretary of the Navy" and by "a written statement, also confidentially put on file by President Tyler." This secret arrangement gave the Bensons the exclusive right to supply the navy's Pacific squadron in exchange for providing free transportation every year for fifty emigrants to Oregon.[16] In response to a congressional investigation, Tyler later described the United States government's first attempt to subsidize American emigration to the West.

PRESIDENT JOHN TYLER TO J. Y. MASON, 26 FEBRUARY 1845,
HOUSE DOCUMENT 161 (28–2), 21–22.

To the Secretary of the Navy:

I deem it proper, before retiring from office, to make the following statement, to be filed along with the letter of the Hon. Mr. Badger, under circumstances equally confidential, in your department, of the reasons that led me to direct the Secretary of the Navy to enter into the arrangement with the Messrs. Benson, referred to in his letter of the 10th September, 1841.[17]

Some short time after I came into office, a memorial was presented me by the Secretary of State, in full cabinet, from A. G. & A. W. Benson, for transportation of stores to the Pacific, for the use of the United States squadron at that station. The prominent inducement to granting the arrangement was, that the memorialists would bind themselves to convey, passage free, all the emigrants that might offer, of both sexes, (not exceed-

---

[13]Howison, "Report of Lieutenant Neil M. Howison on Oregon, 1846: A Reprint," 42.

[14]Henderson, eds., "Correspondence of the Reverend Ezra Fisher," 286.

[15]Douglas to Simpson, 18 March 1844, Hudson's Bay Company Archives, D.5/10, fo. 448.

[16]"Report to the Committee on Naval Affairs," 3 March 1851, Senate Document 319 (31–2), 1.

[17]Secretary of the Navy Mason wrote Tyler on 24 February 1845, "I have directed a diligent search to be made for the [Benson] memorial . . . which it appears was the basis of the arrangement . . . It cannot be found in this department, nor can it be found in the State Department. I regard it to be important if it can be found to be on file; but the search here has been unavailing." See "A Report from the Bureau of Construction &c., relative to contracts entered into with A. G. & A. W. Benson," 3 March 1845, House Exec. Doc. 161 (28–2), 21.

ing fifty at each shipment,) to the Oregon territory, as permanent settlers therein. The desire of the government to avail the United States of the benefit of the joint occupation stipulated for by treaty between the United States and Great Britain; and having presented to it a means, unaccompanied by charge of any sort, whereby emigrants (male and female—the latter the more important) might be transported thither, rendered the proposition of the Messrs. Benson highly acceptable. Those gentlemen were at that time unknown to me; but the endorsement of character which they brought left no room to doubt that they would faithfully execute the contract—as, it is believed, they have done. The cabinet looked upon the subject in the same light with myself; and Mr. Badger, the Secretary of the Navy, carried out the instructions. I regret that the memorial can be found neither in the State nor the Navy Department, as it would have saved the necessity of this statement. The prices allowed for the transportation of stores were regarded at the time as not exceeding a fair equivalent.[18] The Secretary of the Navy, as I understood, made an average of the prices paid for a consecutive number of years previous; to which was added demurrage previously paid, and the free passage of officers of the navy; from which was deduced the price for freight allowed the Messrs. Benson.

JOHN TYLER

Washington, *February 26*, 1845

Tyler's "arrangement" helped assemble the strange band of California promoters that met in New York in June 1845. Hastings lectured at Croton Hall and met Thomas Farnham, a fellow promoter. Farnham had traveled overland in 1839 and, despite his prejudices against the Mexican people, perhaps knew as much about California as anyone in the United States. Like Hastings, Farnham was a writer and lawyer with surprising Washington connections. No less an authority than Henry Wagner believed he conducted his western tour as a paid agent for the federal government.[19] Farnham had just republished his 1844 travelogue as *Travels in the Californias*. The Whig *New-York Tribune* of 21 May 1845 panned Farnham's *History of the Oregon Territory*, saying it was "fitted rather for a harangue in Tammany Hall than the discussion of a momentous

---

[18]The Bensons received three dollars per barrel shipped, fifty cents more than the standard rate.

[19]Wagner, *The Plains and the Rockies*, 48. Thomas Jefferson Farnham (1804–48) went overland to Oregon in 1839 and visited Hawaii and California. Returning east in 1840, he wrote several books, including *Travels in the Great Western Prairies* and *Travels in California and Scenes in the Pacific Ocean*. He died in San Francisco of "intermittent fever" 15 September 1848; his widow Eliza became one of California's first women writers. For the best current work on Farnham, see Churchill, *Adventurers and Prophets*, 219–42.

Historical and International question." The two men "fell in with a devious New York merchant, A. G. Benson, who had or professed to have access to high authority in Washington."[20]

The Bensons' political connections were extraordinary. Their most influential associate was a former cabinet officer. Amos Kendall had tutored the children of Henry Clay and was a most able editor, politician, and business promoter. As a "bosom friend" of Andrew Jackson, he served as U.S. postmaster general from 1834 to 1840. Many considered Kendall the smartest of Jackson's men, but one critic denounced him as Jackson's "*lying* machine" and called Kendall "a diabolical genius."[21] He had recently been imprisoned for debt after losing a lawsuit related to his government service and was attempting to recoup his fortunes as a lobbyist and entrepreneur.

Kendall's attempts to make money were diverse and imaginative. He proposed a bimonthly mail service to the Sandwich Islands and Oregon with ships running between New York, Panama, and the Columbia River, with a stop at the islands.[22] By March 1845 Kendall was managing inventor Samuel F. B. Morse's business interests. He persuaded Morse that the government would never fund the telegraph, but providing instant long-distance communication might make money as a business. Together they established the Magnetic Telegraph Company that would make both men rich.[23] Kendall also tried to secure his financial future by marketing his political connections—and while he may not have been America's first influence peddler, his career set "a model that was to endure."[24] For whatever motives, Kendall became embroiled in the Bensons' complicated affairs, and by late 1845 he was representing Mormon interests in the nation's capital.

UNAUTHORIZED BY LAW

Upon reviewing his department's papers, the new secretary of the navy, George Bancroft, abruptly canceled the Bensons' contract in March

[20]Morgan, ed., *Overland in 1846*, 1:26.

[21]McCormac, *James K. Polk*, 127.

[22]Camp, *San Francisco: Port of Gold*, 72.

[23]Sellers, *James K. Polk, Continentalist*, 272–73; and Thompson, *Wiring a Continent*, 38–40.

[24]DeVoto, *The Year of Decision*, 241.

1845. The Bensons asked Illinois Senator Sidney Breese to lobby the secretary to restore their lucrative agreement, but Bancroft refused to be moved by political pressure. He received Breese's request to continue the "contract made with the Messrs Benson of New York for conveying freight and passengers to the Columbia River, Oregon territory," but informed the senator he had determined that the contract was "unauthorized by law."[25] Bancroft was right, for the arrangement was clearly unconstitutional, since Congress had never appropriated money to subsidize emigration to Oregon.

Though the matter "terminated just as I expected," the senator was not pleased with Bancroft's laconic response. He complained, "If the Contract had been for the benefit of Boston or Cape Cod, it would not have been deemed so contrary to law and an end put to it." Since "it was a contract for the benefit of the west the subject was a disagreeable one to him & he dispatched it very promptly." On his return to Washington Breese intended to let the administration "know there is a *west* & possessed of important interests."[26]

When Senator Breese failed to save their profitable arrangement, the Bensons turned first to Amos Kendall, who worked his political connections, then to Lansford Hastings, who carried word of the scheme to the West Coast, and finally to Brannan, who had his flock start a letter-writing campaign to the president. Although Kendall claimed he had declined to represent the Bensons "in the way of business," he alerted the president to the political consequences of Bancroft's action in a confidential letter.

KENDALL TO POLK, 8 JUNE 1845,
JAMES K. POLK PAPERS, LIBRARY OF CONGRESS.
(Confidential)

New York June 8th 1845

My Dear Sir . . .

Now in a matter affecting the interests of the public and your administration upon which I have received information here which I think you ought to possess. Two weeks ago I was applied to in the way of business to endeavor to induce the Secretary of the Navy to recal[l] a letter to the

---

[25]Bancroft to Breese, 10 May 1845, James K. Polk Papers, Library of Congress.
[26]Breese to Col. E. D. Taylor, 18 May 1845, Ibid.

AMOS KENDALL.
One of the most powerful men
in America, Kendall played an
important role in the American
acquisition of California.
From Stickney, ed., *The Autobiog-*
raphy of Amos Kendall.

Messrs. Bensons of this city annulling an arrangement made with them by
[the late] Mr. Badger while Secretary of the Navy, for transporting supplies
to the Pacific Squadron and opening a trade with Oregon. I declined for reasons having nothing to do with the merits of the case. Indeed, my impres-
sions were strong, that in the present position of the Oregon question, it
was exceedingly unpolitic to disturb that arrangement, and inasmuch as the
order to annulment had not taken effect, it would be best silently to withdraw and cancel it. Since that time, a letter from Senator Breese has been
shown me inclosing a copy of one from the Secretary of the Navy, so significant in its character that I asked a copy to be transmitted to you. It is
herewith inclosed, together with an extract from the London Times which I
find in a New York paper, and the proceeding of a late Oregon meeting in
Illinois. The last resolution I presume has direct consequence to the arrangement in relation of which I understand our leading friends in the West have
long been apprized and have assured the emigrants that they would be able
to obtain axes, ploughs, hoes, and other farming utensils at the store of
Messrs. Bensons in Oregon.

You will mark the temper of Mr. Breese's letter: Rely upon it, the utmost
promptness is required to prevent a general outbreak of similar feeling

among the western friends of Oregon. It will not be wary to satisfy them that the ground on which the secretary bases his act is valid, after the arrangement has been for years in practical operation.

The same reasons which forbade my undertaking to operate on the Secretary in this matter as a business affair, induce me to request that you will not name me as having communicated with you on the object. On the present purity of his motives I have no doubt. Mr. Leonard, of the late House of Representatives, has determined to bring the matter fully before you; but not desiring it to appear in such a shape as unfortunately to create ill feeling between any member of your Cabinet and a Senator and deeming it proper at the same time, that you should know the facts as they are, I advised him to omit every thing which could be offensive to the Secretary, promising to put you in possession confidentially of the contents of Mr. Breese's letter. If, however, you do not wish it to be considered confidential, it may be dealt with as you think proper, except that I do not wish it so used as to create an impression of any unfriendliness towards the Secretary on my part, for the reverse is true. With the highest consideration, Your Friend

Amos Kendall

California-bound, Lansford Hastings left New York on 6 July 1845, carrying a letter from Thomas Farnham to Dr. John Marsh in the Mexican province. Farnham's letter expressed "the strongest desire of my heart, to wit, that the 'Republic of California' should arise." He even outlined a schedule for the conquest of California: "Neither Europe or the States are yet prepared for that event. The excitement consequent on the admission of Texas into the Union must have time to abate. The winter of 46 will do." Farnham wrote, "From 10 to 20 thousand emigrants will enter California next summer. There will then be population enough to *authorize* the step; & we shall have force enough for any contingency."[27]

Hastings had originally planned to return to the West Coast by sea, but decided instead to offer his vast experience to the large number of emigrants he imagined were gathered at Independence, to guide them "with entire safety, either to Oregon or California, and that too, in the short space of three months."[28] Hastings met with "the friends of Oregon and California" at the St. Louis court house on 25 July and finally led a pack-train party west from Independence on 15 August. Experi-

---

[27]L. W. Hastings to Marsh, 26 March 1846; and Farnham to Marsh, 6 July 1845, in Hawgood, ed., *First and Last Consul*, 24, 52.

[28]"Oregon and California," *New-York Daily Tribune*, 24 June 1844, 2/2.

enced frontiersmen recognized the folly of attempting an overland crossing so late in the season, and only nine men finally joined in this "foolhardy undertaking."[29] Along the way Hastings broadcast the Mormons' plans to go west in 1846, and Richard Grant's comments bring several Hastings schemes into focus. Hastings told Grant, the Hudson's Bay Company agent at Fort Hall, "that several thousands of Mormons were making great preparations in the States to steer their course [this] ensuing summer to the Promised Land which they say is Calefornia."[30] Grant supplied Hastings with provisions, and when later questioned about charges he had made loans to Americans, Grant roared:

> Rest assured that in whatever dealings I have with the Emigrants I am very Cautious, as to altercations with them, I am too well acquainted with the disposition & nature of these Animals to meet them on such grounds. Debt they get none in the present day. I have some years back given a pretty heavy debt to a Lawyer of the name of Hastings, but it was through the Instructions of John McLoughlin Esq. while in power.[31]

Hastings was one source of the rumors of an oncoming horde of Mormons that swept through California that winter. American Consul Thomas Larkin wrote, "There has been a report reached here, that the Mormons are breaking up in the States, for the purpose of removing to this Country, which has caused some excitement and fear among the natives."[32] Governor Pío Pico reported that "there were ten thousand American Mormons on the road, who claimed California to be the land promised them in the scriptures for an inheritance as the chosen people of God."[33]

Unable to deliver Farnham's message to Marsh in person before he headed east in April 1846, Hastings forwarded the letter, which contained "facts and statements which are not designed for the public eye."

---

[29]Morgan, ed., *Overland in 1846*, 1:30.

[30]Grant to Simpson, 2 January 1846, D.5/16 fo. 25, Hudson's Bay Company Archives. Grant understood that John McLoughlin planned to retire in California and commented that if the Mormons went there, "it will be a poor place for Catholics and our venerable Doctor had better not go to set himself down for Life."

[31]Grant to Simpson, 4 January 1849, D.5/24, fo. 227, Hudson's Bay Company Archives. John McLoughlin had befriended Hastings during his stay in Oregon and apparently hoped to use him to divert American emigration from Oregon to California.

[32]Larkin to Buchanan, 6 March 1846, in Hammond, *Larkin Papers*, 4:232.

[33]Hittell, *History of California*, 2:394, paraphrasing Pico letter in Cal. Archives, D.S.P. IX, 457–62.

Hastings reported, "Friend Farnham is doing everything in his power to increase the emigration to this far-famed region, and he is of the opinion that he will be able to bring at least three or four thousand from the State of New York alone." Hastings assured Marsh, "you can rely upon an accession of six or seven thousand human souls to our foreign population in California." He claimed that this was "the very least estimate that can be made" and believed "the universal excitement, which pervaded almost every portion of the Union" would "much more likely to amount to fifteen or twenty thousand." This was "only a prelude to what is to follow in succeeding years, for California is now looked upon, among a large majority of our people, as the *garden of the earth*."[34]

LIKE A GENERAL'S TRUMPET FROM THE TOP OF SOME PROMONTORY

As the LDS apostles struggled to define their long-term plans in the West, Brigham Young took time to write Brannan and assure him that he need not worry about the forty dollars he had borrowed, but to repay it as soon as possible. Young's reference to Brannan as his "friend and brother" indicates that warm relations existed between the two men after Brannan transferred his allegiance from William Smith. Yet Young remained wary of his mercurial protégé and soon sent Orson Pratt to replace his brother Parley as head of the LDS church in the East.[35] Pratt arrived in New York on 20 August, not long after his brother's departure for Nauvoo. Young wrote, "do not change the name of the Messenger or the Editor. But let it still be understood that brother Parley is the Editor, as he can conduct it here as well as there."[36]

YOUNG TO BRANNAN, 9 AUGUST 1845,
BRIGHAM YOUNG COLLECTION, LDS ARCHIVES.

Copyed   Nauvoo Aug 9th A.D. 1845
Brother Samuel Brannan:
    Dear Sir; I received your letter of the 22 ult. in due time and hasten to

---

[34]Morgan, ed., *Overland in 1846*, 1:39–41. Morgan estimated that 1,500 men, women, and children went overland to California in 1846.

[35]Orson Pratt, "News to England," *New-York Messenger*, 30 August 1845, 67; and "Message, To the Saints in the Eastern and Middle States," *New-York Messenger*, 30 August 1845, 70–71.

[36]Young to Orson Pratt, 20 August 1845, Brigham Young Collection, LDS Archives.

answer it, and I say unto you dear brother be not discouraged, or disheartened, but lift up your head and rejoice that you are accounted worthy to suffer for Christ's sake: and know that thou shalt obtain a victory over all your
trials and shalt arise above them and be made glad that you were bro't low,
and made to feel and see and realise the pains of necessity and hard strugles
and may the Lord bless you and ~~cause to~~ raise you above the present necessities: Amen—

   As to the money I loaned you give yourself no pain on that acco[u]nt,
but let me have it soon as you can and not distress yourself, as I borrowed
it—The Temple is going a head finely, the roof is nearly completed and the
inside work far advanced—The Nauvoo house also is progressing
rapidly[37]—health and peace prevail generaly among the Saints and their
crops are aboundant. The Lord blesses us on all sides and the Saints are continually gathering in from all parts, showing the powerful magnetism of the
word of God—

   This from your friend and brother

In the new covenant Amen [unsigned]

Brannan responded to Young's friendly note with a stirring essay on
the usefulness of the press in general and his own publication, the *Messenger*, in particular. He enclosed the forty dollars he owed the Mormon
leader and described his complicated financial condition. Brannan also
reported some of the first transactions in what would become his chosen career—real estate.

BRANNAN TO YOUNG, 29 AUGUST 1845,
BRIGHAM YOUNG COLLECTION, LDS ARCHIVES.

[Note on cover sheet: Recd Sept. 14.]

New York, August 29, 1845

Elder Young—

   Dear Sir—Through the blessing of a kind ~~providence~~ Parent, our heavenly father—I have advanced thus far, in the publication of the "Messenger" having issued the 9th number.[38] Br. O. Pratt gave me your council,
"That if it could not be restarted without getting into debt, that I had better discontinue it.["] My doctrine is, and has been, from the commencement
of this periodical, to follow council and break no covenants as much as in
my power so to do—And in regard to stopping the paper, ~~as far~~ to consult

---

[37]According to the Lord, the Nauvoo House was "my boarding house which I have commanded
you to build for the boarding of strangers" near Joseph Smith's Mansion House on the Mississippi
River. See *Doctrine and Covenants*, 124:56–61.

[38]This was the *Messenger* issue of 30 August 1845.

my own feelings; as far as the care and anxiety with the necessary labor to sustain [it] is concerned, there is nothing that would give me more pleasure. But when I see the necessity and the demand for a paper of some kind, to be published here in the Eastern Country, it swallows up every covetous feeling, to get clear of the concern, and "the still small voice whispers in my ear" "Go on *and overcome every obstacle that may present itself* and I am with you."

When We contemplate the many advantages within our reach, by the press, in this country; in tything gathering, organizing, the facilities for communicating speedily and generally to all the saints throughout the Eastern Country any important matter or movement, with what readiness the whole body may be brought into joint cooperation with the rest. The law of tything which only heretofore reached the large churches, now reaches every little town and hamlet, and that to[o] without the expense of travelling Elders to fetch it—and at the same time to give them a chimney corner sermon on the subject, before they could obtain it at that. All can now be performed through the press; and in case of any dificulty in the west, the press here like a General's trumpet from the top of some promontory, moves the whole army at once. In case all hell should come up and compass the camp of the saints round about, and the time hadn't come for the fire to come down out of heaven and destroy them; but [if] the Lord suffer us to be driven from Nauvoo, this then can be made use of to give a certain sound, and all move as on[e], and in a body together, and save the sheep from scattering. When Jackasses get to braying among the Churches—the Lion will have something to roar through, wicked men can soon be exposed and put to shame—and the evil checked in the bud. When a host of Elders are sent through this country, one of the Presidents can establish himself in New York, and through the Press can give the army the word of Command, heads up! front face! guarde right! and [the] retreat of the whole army can be beet up in double quick time! and all be in Zion again to defend her strong holds—I do really believe that the stopping of this paper would have a tendency to lesson the spirit of tything, gathering and building up; yet not withstanding all the views I may have on the subject, I am willing to abandon all at the word of command. God knows I am as sick as death of the concern, but I am willing to remain here until you see fit to put some one else in my place.

Brother P. P. Pratt's council was, before he went west, that it should be sustained, if it required a contribution in the end, to make up the loss it may sustain. Elders O. Hyde and O. Pratt since their arrival is of the same opinion. As for my opinion you know it.—I go for it neck and heels, or in other words, might mind and strength. I am now embarassed about one thousand dollars—which accrued in the first place by the bad council and manage-

ment, [which] George Leech[39] [made] in its commencement, which I had to
become responsible for, or it would have went down; in the next place there
was not subscribers enough at one dollar per year to pay the expenses, which
had to be paid before every thing else—I borrowed the money and pushed
it ahead lest it should loose its credit and character as a regular visitor, which
is one reason why it is so well liked; If I should abandon the concern now, I
know of no way at present that I could clear myself from my responsibili-
ties. Br. [Parley] Pratt has arrived in Nauvoo I presume ere this, and you have
had his views on the subject; Give him my love and everlasting respects—
and tell him that if he is'nt [sic] here his character is, his name is still at the
head of the paper to father all my miserable scribblings and I want him to
send along a regulator occasionally. Tell him I have his portrait, painted in
the first style, and if he should see it he would fall in love with himself. Tell
Br. William Smith I have his painted, and wish him much joy, and a happy
journey with his new bride.[40] All is well with him here, and every body else
connected with the twelve. I am having brothers O. Hyde and Pratts [por-
traits] taken, and if Brother [Joseph] Fielding that is here now going to England, would let me have Br. Richard's Dagerotype likeness, I would have his
taken, but he says it is seeled up in a tin box and he is afraid to take it out.
If Brother Young you have a Dagerotype likeness, of yourself, and will send
it to me by some one coming east, I will see that it is preserved, and returned
to you in safety or any of the rest of the Twelve they shall be taken good care
of and returned in safety. I think that if you should see those that are finished you would be pleased with them—However perhaps you had all rather
wait until you come east, which I would myself if I thought all of you would
ever get here.

   In this I send you the forty dollars that you accomodated me with—My
apology for its delay. I wrote you in my last, I obtained it by selling a lot of
land I bought of brother Layton. Brother Hyde is now east of hear. As you
will see by the papers, he is doing remarkably well. As for the document sent
me to raise the three hundred dollars I shall make no use of it, however I feel
grateful for your consideration of my situation. I have paid Winchester all
but 130 dollars [with] that some due next month, but God will open the
way some way or the other, he never has forsaken me yet. Tell Br. Kimball I

---

[39]In a New York conference Elder G. T. Leach first proposed "publishing a weekly paper for the
dispensation of our principles." As president of the Board of Control of the Society for the Diffu-
sion of Truth, Leach signed the paper's prospectus. See *The Prophet*, 18 May 1845.

[40]Smith married five women in 1845, but this is perhaps a reference to his 8 August 1845 sealing by Brigham Young to fourteen-year-old Henriette Rice. See Quinn, *The Mormon Hierarchy: Origins
of Power*, 221, 594. On 9 August, "Dinner to the Smith Family," *New-York Messenger*, 44, reported
William Smith attended with "Mary Jane [Rollins] Smith, Mary Jane [Jones] Smith, Caroline
Louise Smith"; Smith married both Rollins and Jones in 1845.

should not wonder if his prophesy was fulfilled yet, there is nothing like faith and works in my way of thinking, and if the Mormons ar'nt [sic] the people to produce, then I'd like to know where they are to be found. Give my love to all the Twelve and brother Kimball in particular. Tell him that brother Rodgers and me had a regular talk the other day about the washing of feet, and we almost thought he was present. Brother Walley carried my last letter to the post office that I sent to you and he neglected to pay the postage. I sent him back after it but he could not get it out it was to[o] late. I will make it up in sending the New York Heral[d] to you. Brother Wally is here and sends his love to you and Br Kimball. I have red this over, and have seen where I might make some corrections, but know you will find it out. Therefore I shall let it pass.

Mr. Daniel Meeker came in to see me last Tuesday and told me that you might have that track of Land that you wrote brother Pratt to Purchase for eight hundred dollars.[41] It seems that he has seen some person from Quincy Ill. that told him the Mormons were living on it, and that they were having difficulties there that has induced the old man to want to sell for the Price first agreed, so if you wish to purchase, let me know, for he has promised me to let no one have it, until I hear from you and let him know whether you will take it or not.

Yours truly in haste S. Brannan.

Orson Pratt soon advised Brigham Young about conditions in New York. Pratt had "drawn the reins pretty tight in relation to Covenanting and other illegal steps here in the east." He had decided "that it was highly necessary to take a firm and decided position in relation to those matters," indicating that he had made clear to local elders that they had no authority to perform marriages for eternity—especially plural marriages. Believing that the "press is a powerful engine," Pratt intended "to write and circulate through the columns of the Messenger all that I can," while leaving his brother as the titular editor. Brannan was "a very powerful preacher" and had circulated some twenty thousand handbills advertising "a course of lectures in this city which are well attended." Pratt's personal endorsement of Brannan's activities demonstrated the value he placed on the talents of this "go-a-head man."[42]

With a peculiarly Mormon perspective, the *Messenger* reflected the war

---

[41]This was probably land on Lake Superior, discussed in P. P. Pratt's 7 May 1845 letter to Brigham Young.

[42]Orson Pratt to Young, 4 September 1845, LDS Archives.

fever that swept the country that summer. "War between the United States and Mexico on this Texas question, in connection with California and Oregon," the paper announced, "may lead to a general war amongst the nations of the world, which may last for a half a century, and not terminate till an entirely new order of things be introduced in the governments of Europe."[43] The *Messenger* reported in August, "Plans are now secretly in operation to establish an independent government in Oregon."[44]

LDS church leaders had already announced in January 1845 that they were considering California as a haven for their people. In 1845 Mexico's claim to Alta California extended to the Rocky Mountains and included much of the Great Basin, making it difficult to determine exactly where in this vast territory the Mormons initially planned to settle. On 22 August Brigham Young wrote to Addison Pratt, a missionary in Polynesia, providing the first outline of his design for Mormonism's western migration. Young directed "the brethren of the islands [who] wish to emigrate to the continent" to go to "the mouth of Columbia river in Oregon, or the Gulph of Montery, or St. Francisco, as we shall have commence[d] forming a settlement in that region during next season." Young intended to "make arrangements with agents in each of those places" to direct and supply emigrants to the main Mormon settlement, which "will probably be in the neighborhood of Lake Tampanagos [Utah Lake] as that is represented as a most delightful district and [there is] no settlement near there."[45] The apostles decided on 28 August 1845 to send three thousand men and their families to California in 1846.[46] Parley P. Pratt outlined these plans in a letter to a friend in the East, revealing that the apostles had identified the Great Basin as their provisional destination.

> I write this letter mostly for the purpose of telling you of our council in regards to Callifornia. We have decided on sending from one to 3 thousand men to that place next spring. They will start from here with ox teams, cattle, cows, provisions, arms, tents, etc. the first of May. I expect to go also if I live and the Lord will. If so I shall Leave part of my family to keep house

---

[43]"War! War! War!" *New-York Messenger*, 23 August 1845, 61.
[44]*New-York Messenger*, 23 August 1845, 60.
[45]Young to Addison Pratt, 22 August 1845, Brigham Young Collection, LDS Archives.
[46]Journal History, 28 August 1845.

here, such as the old folks, others who are not able to go till preparations are commenced in that Country, and take the remainder with me. Our intention is to maintain and build up Nauvoo, and settle other places too. I expect we shall stop near the Rocky Mountains about 800 miles nearer than the coast, say 1,500 miles from here, and there to make a stand, until we are able to enlarge and to extend to the coast. . . .

When we arrive there we will have land without buying it. And we will have liberty without asking a set of corrupt office holders for it. Be sure to come, and be sure to save all you can, and bring it with you, it will cost a great deal to fit out. Keep all these things Still.[47]

The Saints hoped to maintain their city on the Mississippi, but after increasing pressure from Illinois officials, Brigham Young publicly announced on 24 September that the Mormons would leave the state as soon as grass grew.[48] Young's pledge would be formalized in a meeting with Governor Thomas Ford on 1 October. In the midst of this escalating crisis, Brigham Young wrote an optimistic letter from the "City of Joseph." As his letter made clear, he already had plans for Samuel Brannan.

YOUNG TO BRANNAN, 15 SEPTEMBER 1845,
BRIGHAM YOUNG COLLECTION, LDS ARCHIVES.

City of Joseph Sept 15th 1845

Dear Brother Samuel Brannon

Sir I have just received your favor of the 28th ult. I am glad to see you so willing to abide by our council and all I can say to you in regard to the office is do as you and brother Pratt think best, only do not think to sustain it from the tithing of the Church; and therefore I say do as you think proper about continuing the paper. You best know your circumstances and whether the subscription will warrant it and be assured that in as much as you are faithful you shall have the strength and benefit of our prayers and the Lord will bless and prosper you. We have troubles again around. The mob have commenced burning the brethren's houses in Morley Settlement, and have

---

[47]P. P. Pratt to Isaac Rogers, 6 September 1845, LDS Archives. Rogers took Pratt's advice, moved to Nauvoo, and started west in June 1847 "with 500 wagons for the Valley of the Great Salt Lake in California." The next summer he wrote from Fort Hall, "I start for the Bay of Francisco to-morrow or next day to get some goods I sent around by ship"—property shipped on the *Brooklyn*. He arrived in Sacramento about October 1848 and died at Sutter's Fort in April 1849. See I. Rogers to L. P. Rogers II, 11 July 1848; and I. Rogers to Son, ca. October 1848, LDS Archives. His widow, Mary M. Rogers, married Thomas Rhoades (or, as his Utah descendants spell it, Rhodes) in 1849 and bore him four children before she died at Great Salt Lake City in February 1853.

[48]Hallwas and Launius, eds., *Cultures in Conflict*, 302–04.

nearly burned the settlement out. The brethren have been obliged to come in here for safety. The Sherif has called on the militia to quell the mob and put a stop to such work but what his success will be is yet doubtful. The Sherif is not a mormon but is a friend to equal rights.[49]

The mob are holding meetings and soliciting help from other parts but I think they will not be able to do any more than burn a few houses, and some grain: although they threaten a great deal. But the Lord will make the wrath of man praise him and the remainder of wrath he will restrain—this has put the gathering spirit into the heart of the brethren in the affected part of the country and they will bring their grain and all their substance.

Since I last wrote you much has been done on the Temple and Nauvoo House. The atic store[y] and steeple are nearly complete and the first story of the Nauvoo House has gone up and a few days more [we] will put up the whole wall and they will get the roof on this fall.

I wish you together with your press paper and ten thousand of the brethren were now in California at the Bay of St. Francisco, and if you can clear yourself and go there do so and we will meet you there. We [end of letter]

B. Young

frm E M Greene clerk

So it was that Brigham Young suggested the expedition that would be the great adventure of Samuel Brannan's life—the first sea voyage of American emigrants to California. Yet Brannan was curiously reluctant to fulfill Young's wish to have "ten thousand of the brethren" on the shores of San Francisco Bay. "It will be out of my power to get off to California this winter," Brannan wrote, blaming his dismal financial condition. Something quickly changed his views after he received orders from the apostles to take a shipload of Saints to the West Coast. Somehow the young entrepreneur raised about $7,000 cash and acquired $30,000 worth of supplies, machinery, and farm equipment. He was soon ready to lead the first American emigrants around Cape Horn to California.[50]

To Get Off to California This Winter

Brannan's first letter to Brigham Young concerning what the Mor-

---

[49]This was Hancock County Sheriff Jacob B. Backenstos.

[50]See Coray to Richards, ca. 3 April 1848, in Chapter 8 for the possibility Brannan borrowed at least some of this money from his mother-in-law.

mons called their "Great Western Measure" flatly stated that his finances prevented him from undertaking the trip immediately, but this was perhaps a ploy to get church money to help him pay his debts.[51] Otherwise, the letter brimmed with significant gossip and conspiratorial allusions. The letter named unknown secret agents—Huinden and "Brother Learen"—and ended on a conspiratorial note: "Better have men looking out at St. Louis," revealing the plotter's "Counter Sign": *War in Mexico.*

BRANNAN TO YOUNG, 9 OCTOBER 1845, BRIGHAM YOUNG COLLECTION, LDS ARCHIVES.

New York, Oct. 9th 1845

Brother Young—I wrote a long letter, and then concluded not to send it—you might be engaged in a conflict, and if like me a long letter you would not read, and a short one you might glance over. All well in the east. Your trouble does not retarde emigration any; brethren are all an[x]ious to go that have got the true spirit—and myself among the rest. But when I leave here everything will tumble to the ground in the shape of printing. It will be out of my power to get off to California this winter. Therefore, I shall wait for further orders. I would like it well if I could get some one to by me out so that I could go ~~direct~~ immediately ~~up there~~. But I will trust in Heaven, "for there is nothing ~~surer than Heaven~~" sure but Heaven." The cause in this city is beginning to brighten. Some seven or eight [investigators] during my course of lectures avowed their belief in the doctrine who never heard Mormonism before ~~in their life~~. Br. Orson [Pratt] ~~and myself~~ is going to join me in the next course, Which will commence on the 9th of November, one month from to day. Between this and that time I shall have 20,000 handbills struck off and carried to the principl houses in this city. I am resolved this winter that not one soul shall be left with an excuse. I have heard that Br. William [Smith] has written several letters to the different branches in the east, that he should spend the winter in this country. Now I do not believe he will do so, by your willing council—and I would say to you, that if he comes into this country contrary ~~to it~~, he will have to go to work on the dock rolling molases or else starve. I have seen his letter to Peterboro and I do say unless he repents, and that sincerely too—I never shall do the work I have done for him over again—I am no traitor, neither will I be crucified for a traitor—let them go to their own place. We are happy to learn you have got possession of the country, and we say may God

---

[51]See "The Great Western Measure" in Bagley, ed., *The Pioneer Camp of the Saints,* for an overview of the Saints' emigration plans.

help you keep it until it is time to quit Egypt. I am to night we held a meeting (a pistol meeting) and you may depend, it was no fool of a one.[52] Br. Orson is now doing a good work. "In time of peace prepare for war" that is our motto, we shall give our best foot first. You will see by the Proclamation, what that is for the best, no infidelity here by not providing for our own household. Louse [Louis?] Huinden will starte on the 17th. Better have men looking out at St. Louis. The Counter Sign will be *War in Mexico.* Brother Learen will of this city will travel in cog. I shall write in advance of any good thing.

I remain your friend and brother
'til death
Spiritual or Temporally

Tell Br. [Parley] Pratt that his came safe to hand, and he will hear from me next week.   S.B.

THE TIME HAS NEARLY ARRIVED
FOR US TO ASSIST OURSELVES

Brannan had remarkable insights into President Polk's plans for Mexico. In late summer 1845 the *Messenger* marked out "the future course of the United States." The Polk administration would "send a commissioner to Mexico to lay down the boundary of the two countries. If Mexico refuses to receive the commissioner, and blindly turns away from a peac[e]able settlement, then her [U.S.] forces will immediately occupy the mouth and borders of the Rio Grande, and establish that as the boundary, whether or no."[53] American diplomatic relations with Mexico for the next nine months fulfilled this prophecy with striking precision.

Historians have never been able to document the involvement of any Mormon other than Samuel Brannan with the Benson-Kendall scheme, but Dale Morgan concluded that other "Mormon authorities" had to be involved.[54] Brannan had discussed Hastings with Brigham Young, and

---

[52]Orson Pratt received orders to purchase "six barrels of pistols for self defence (while journeying in western wilds)." Pratt thought he could "obtain several hundred dollars for that purpose." The "six inch barrel pistols" retailed for twelve dollars; "but by agreeing to take some 30 or 40 they can be obtained at nine & one half dollars." See Orson Pratt to Young, 21 October 1845, Brigham Young Collection, LDS Archives. This "pistol meeting" raised funds to buy the pepperbox revolvers that Brannan's followers later distributed in California.

[53]*New-York Messenger,* 20 September 1845, 92.

[54]Morgan, ed., *Overland in 1846,* 1:26.

Parley Pratt apparently carried a copy of Hastings' *Emigrants' Guide* and news of the Benson-Kendall "arrangement" to Nauvoo, but LDS sources are strangely silent on the subject.[55]

Orson Pratt's October report to Brigham Young described the difficulties he faced on the East Coast, noting especially the trouble made by William Smith. Pratt was trying to obtain "six barrels of pistols for self defence (while journeying in western wilds)" at wholesale prices. Tithing "comes in very slow," but the "recent troubles in the West have put a new life & zeal into the saints in the East; they are very anxious to assist all they can, & to gether westward ho!" He had heard that William Smith had left Nauvoo and was writing an exposé. Pratt forwarded his fellow apostles "a very black suspicious letter from Wm to J. C. Little" and another letter to Bro. David Rogers "written by the same apostate spirit" in which Smith "portrayed the corruption of his heart." Pratt promised to "take a decided stand against" Smith should he appear in New York. In the meantime an interesting cast of characters was turning up at the professor's door, including Thomas Jefferson Farnham and Utopian socialist Robert Owen.

> The celebrated Robert Owen has been to visit me several times, he calls almost every day. I have been endeavoring to persuade him to rent our houses and lands in Ill[inois], and he has quite a notion of so doing. He will let me know more about it in a few days, [and] he thinks some of visiting Nauvoo this fall. Mr. Farnham the Author of several works on Oregon, California, &c. has been to visit me a number of times. I have just this moment had an interview with him. He starts in about one week for California and apparently feels very anxious to have us locate in that country & professes to be willing to render us any assistance in his power.[56] But I thought in my heart that we have had enough of Gentile assistance & that the time has nearly arrived for us to assist ourselves.
>
> I have just had a letter from Phil[adelphia]. I expected they would raise several hundred dollars for pistols but what was my surprise when I found that 30 dollars was the amount they had raised. Bro. Brannan has just

---

[55]The minutes of the Council of Fifty undoubtedly contain information about LDS plans in the West. In response to a request for access to these documents, F. Michael Watson, Secretary to the First Presidency of the LDS church, wrote, "While your interest as explained in your request, is understandable, the information you seek does not happen to be available for use." Watson to Bagley, 29 January 1998, copy in editor's possession.

[56]Dale Morgan noted, "How and when Farnham reached California has not been established," so the comment on Farnham's plans is of interest. See Morgan, ed., *Overland in 1846*, 26.

returned from Boston. They had raised upwards of one hundred dollars for pistols there. Bro. [Jesse C.] Little of Peterboro writes me that he will use every exertion in N.H. to raise funds for that purpose. Bro. Brannan thinks it will be difficult to take his printing establishment and go to California unless he goes away dishonorably without paying debts. If he could sell he could pay his debts. He feels very anxious to go and is willing to do anything he is counseled. He says that the church perhaps would consider it wisdom to buy his establishment & still keep up the paper.[57]

I Cannot Think of Being Left Behind

Writing to Apostle Heber C. Kimball, Brannan detailed his financial problems and proposed some imaginative solutions. He spoke of going to California as if it were a foregone conclusion, but did not mention the sea venture that would soon change the course of his life. Instead, Brannan appeared determined to join the main body of the Saints on their journey overland. This letters vividly demonstrates Brannan's long devotion to Joseph Smith and the Mormon cause.

BRANNAN TO KIMBALL, NEW YORK, 31 OCTOBER 1845,
LDS ARCHIVES.

New York Oct. 31, 1845

Dear Br. Kimball—I have not forgotten the charge you gave me about writing, and the promise I made before I left the City of Nauvoo—I am happy to say that I have fully realised the truth of all your prediction[s], in regard to my money affairs; I have not been under the necessity of borrowing one dollar with the exception of 25 to get out the first number [of the *Messenger*], and 75 to pay the Winchester debt to clear William [Smith]—who I now understand is pouring out his vials of wrath against the church—May the God of Israel punish him severely, and if he comes east here he will do it—he will be certain to find there is no peace for the wicked.

I have labored unceasingly since the day of my first ordination—since I have been in the East—I have had to grapple seemingly with every thing—in the church and out of the church—I am very much involved in debt—not by consuming it upon my own lusts—but for the cause of God and the truth—And I want some council. The news of your moving has come very sudden upon me, and I [k]no[w] not which way to turn—I cannot think of

---

[57]Orson Pratt to Young, 21 October 1845, Brigham Young Collection, LDS Archives.

being left behind—and yet if I stop the paper, I have nothing but my finger in my mouth—either to go with [you] or pay my debts—An idea suggested itself to me this morning—and I will suggest it to you and your honourable body The Twelve—I think I could get out an edition of the Hymn Book of about 2000 copies struck off at this city on 60 days credit—I could sell enough [books] to pay for the binding—and the remainder I could turn out on my debts—and pay for the printing when I return from the Pacific, or California. If you are printing the Hymn Book there why I have nothing to say—If you should think it best to keep this paper in operation to help gather out next year what should be left behind—my choice would be—to have you council some one to take my place—and let me go free—I want to go over the mountains—When the Camp [of Zion] went out to Missouri in 1834 Brother Joseph Counciled me to remain and work in the printing office. I did so—those who went have not gon without their blessing for the sacrifice and willingness to obey him[58]—to tell you the truth Brother Kimball—I want you to tell the Brethren that I do not wish to be left behind—which I must be unless I can have your wise council—Br. Kimball—tell Br. Young I want to do wright—and act for for [sic] the best interest of the church—and I look to the Twelve and the President for dictation in what is best—Let me hear from you as soon as convenient—Tell Br. Pratt that Brother Rodgers the fisherman and Br. Walley will start for Nauvoo in two weeks.

Yours forever in the Bonds of

the Covenant

S Brannan

In the midst of these activities, Samuel L. Brannan, Jr., was born in New York, but no mention of the birth appears in his father's surviving correspondence.[59]

WILLIAM SMITH:
ROGUES RASCALS SCOUNDRELS COUNTERFEITERS

Brannan's letters make clear that by the summer of 1845 he had abandoned William Smith and cast his lot with Brigham Young and the

---

[58]As a teenager in 1834, Brannan wanted to accompany the paramilitary Camp of Zion on its march to Missouri. Although this attempt to avenge alleged injustices was a disaster, all of the original twelve apostles came from its ranks.

[59]Several sources gave the birth date as 17 November 1844 or 1845, but Ann Eliza Brannan provided the correct date of 17 October 1845, for she wrote of her son in September 1848, "he will be three years old the 17th of next month."

apostles. The apostles had removed Smith from the Council of Twelve and as church patriarch on 6 October 1845 for "general looseness and recklessness of character," and they excommunicated him on 19 October.[60] Smith subsequently wrote his former protégé an angry letter in which he denounced Brannan's disloyalty. In a "General Epistle" composed on the same day, Smith charged "that the apostate twelve" would "humbug the people and swindle the honist in heart out of their money." He alleged that they had set up a press to counterfeit "the coin of the Nation [with] Brigham Young being the principle head & leader by which means many are to Commit acts that deprive them of life or their liberty."[61]

WILLIAM SMITH TO BRANNAN, 14 NOVEMBER 1845,
WILLIAM SMITH LETTERS 1845, LDS ARCHIVES.

St Louis Nov. the 14, 1845

Mr Brannan,

Sir: the 14 No. of the New York Messenger dated Nov. 8 contains several lies or—more properly speaking humbug tales told by the apostate twelve. That Hypocritt Hide [Orson Hyde] [and] O[rson] Pratt &c the history of J. C. Benitt is still fresh in my memory. *So mote it be.* People that live in glass houses should not throw stones. The N Y prophet that was a glorious spirit that could apeal to the New York Saints [and] not one penny had been spent by *me* according to the Secretary. I wonder who he *was*, perhaps he never came to New York and got work in the office and by my influence afterwards came in charge of the paper without a single penny in pocket[62] and PPP could also come to N Y and enter into other mens Labours and trample me under foot and what is more than all you know it too (*thats all*) after I had Labourd hard for months through the [w]reck of Rigdonism [and] Journied traveled night and day [and had] the charge of the paper as Editor &c &c and by my justice and Exertion the paper was got up. A vote also was taken in Nauvoo by Josephs request before a Large meeting of the Saints that I Should take charge of the city of N Y [and] publish a paper &c &c. This notice too was published if I mistake not in the Nauvoo *Neighbor* and now it is Stated that I had nothing to do with the matter, fudge. Tell such tales till your Blind as a Bat and then I will tell the Honest in heart in N Y the truth in soberness and they are not to swallow down Evrey fals Statement that userping trators and Scoundrels make. It might be said truth is a *Jewel* but not many of them appear in the New

---

[60]Quinn, *The Mormon Hierarchy: Origins of Power*, 223.
[61]Smith, *General Epistle of Wm Smith*, LDS Archives.
[62]Apparently "the Secretary" referred to Brannan.

York Messenger of late: "what a Pitty that Wm Smith could not so Conduct himself as to keep in the Church" &c &c when these holy apostles treat him so well as to cheat him out of his office & sought his life [and] Surounded him by an armed police and so Charitable as to write letters & preach all summer to ruin *him*. Dont say it Mr. Brannan you will hear from me. See who has wrote the most letters. My *crime* is for writing letters to Elders &c &c not so mutch for writing the letters I supose as for the truths I have told on these apostate 12 puck [?] perhaps.

Some more of these truths will appear to light when a Mr. Turley the head Counterfieter of Nauvoo is sent to Alton *Penatenciary*. He is now in the hand of the officers of the Law at Springfield *Illenois*.[63] So look out for Brothers in you holey (12) userpers. They are on the road to hell as fast as they can go and all that follow them will soon find themselves in a bad *Box Penateciary* or some other Land of Callifornia with all the bea[u]ties and exalencies of the Law of *Moses*.[64] Go it then all that wants to follow these men and if you dont find them Powerless Rogues Rascals Scoundrels Counterfiters &c &c and further Brigham Young has no more Power than an old Shirt stufed with Straw for Joseph never appointed him to any [power]. I have no objection for you or all the gang of Rebbels to the original principles of mormenism to *follow* sutch men. I Know they are apostates from the true Church of Christ and in this point of light you may understand it. Now I supose some people will not think so mutch of me for writing this Leutanant. Thank god I ask no odds of them. What think you of the 12 [when] they have sent A Babbit to sell or rent the temple of god to the *Catholics*, the mother of *harlotts*. Will you go in for these measures, *outragious* I am Bold to say and will proclaim against it. But stop my way is hedged up [in the] East [by the] *Mesenger, Orson Hide*, O Pratt &c. What by Sutch men as *Hide*, who has three wives [and] O Pratt who is an apolijest for Sutch Scoundrels. Wall I g[u]ess the *river* is not frose nor the Canalls & railroads tere up yet so I will stand some chance to get over the Mountains if I live. G B Wallice this man I am Bold to say is a *liar*. [George B.] Adams was not with me at the time I saw him.

But all these things will be remembered in their turn. The Cut off Buisiness on my head was not don[e] write. I withdraw from these Leiers and

---

[63]Joseph Smith appointed gunsmith Theodore Turley as Nauvoo's official "weigher and sealer" on 8 March 1841. Turley had been "arrested at Alton on a charge of bogus-making" on 16 November 1845. See Roberts, ed., *History of the Church*, 7:532.

[64]Godfrey, "Crime and Punishment in Mormon Nauvoo," 219, citing *Niles' National Register*, 3 January 1846. A federal grand jury indicted twelve prominent Mormon leaders for counterfeiting United States coin. "This action was generally thought to be a ploy on the part of the government to make certain that the Saints would keep their promise to leave Nauvoo in the spring." LDS leaders issued a circular denying the counterfeiting charge.

Sink of Eniquity so you can hang your fiddle or make it your secret and prepare for the worst. If you have a mind to forsake an old and tried friend and
follow a set of the greatest Rascals that ever disgraced the footstool of god,
why go it, and the Blessing of god shall not rest on you head. So help me god.
Amen Amen

[Reversed at bottom of the page:] A general responce is murmered
throughout all the Eastern Churches on his being cut off. There all appear
willing to distroy the Last Remnant of the Smith familey. It is none but the
12, and a general response is to Beat them off & the work has Cammense &
down may go as Paith [to] Hel[l]. *Amen.*

Amen

Amen

Amen

INSTRUCTIONS FROM THE AUTHORITIES OF THE CHURCH

Despite the great significance of the LDS church's decision to send
colonists to California by sea, not a single document explicitly authorizing the enterprise survives in any of the major archives of Mormonism.[65] Brannan later claimed that "he conceived the idea of leading
a band of American pioneers to the shores of the Pacific," but the *Messenger* reported that Elder Brannan followed "instructions from the
authorities of the church directing him to go by water."[66] The evidence
indicates that by the second week of November, Brannan and Orson
Pratt had received official authorization to organize a sea-borne migration to California. One source claimed Parley Pratt sent the elusive
orders from Nauvoo on 1 November 1845.

[The apostles have] concluded that the Great Basin in the top of the Rocky
Mountains, where lies the Great Salt Lake, is the proper place for us . . . I
inclose to you a letter of instruction from the Apostles, authorizing you to
lead the group of Saints in its exodus from New York City and the Atlantic
seaboard. Brother Brigham is this day, sending a letter to my brother Orson
directing him to call a conference of all Saints in your mission to lay before
them the plan to emigrate by water.[67]

---

[65]Other historians, including Professor Richard Cowan of Brigham Young University, have also
been unable to locate such documentation.

[66]Soulé, *The Annals of San Francisco*, 749; and *Millennial Star*, 1 February 1846, 36.

[67]Quoted in Muir, *A Century of Mormon Activities in California*, 1:30. Muir cited no source for this
letter, and no letter from Young to Pratt containing these orders survives in LDS Archives.

The last numbers of the *New-York Messenger* provided much detail about Brannan's travels and the California plans of the Latter-day Saints. On 15 November Brannan announced he would preach in Philadelphia the next day and subsequently speak in New Jersey, Boston, and finally New Haven on 5 December. His schedule suggests that Brannan then visited Washington City. *The Messenger* reprinted some of the most useful pages from Lansford W. Hastings' *The Emigrants' Guide* in its last three issues. Brannan provided a brief introduction to this material for his readers who were "speculating" on "the comforts and pleasures" of a western journey.

"EQUIPMENTS, SUPPLIES, AND THE METHOD OF
TRAVELING OVER THE ROCKY MOUNTAINS,"
NEW-YORK MESSENGER, 1 NOVEMBER 1845.

We embrace the opportunity of laying before our readers this week, an interesting detail of practical facts, for the information of those who take pleasure in speculating, in their imagination, upon the comforts and pleasures of a journey across the Rocky Mountains. It is from the liberal pen of Capt. Lansford W. Hastings, leader of the Oregon and California Emigration, of 1842. We had the pleasure of his acquaintance, during his visit to this country; and he is now on his journey back to the country of his future home. He has published the following [guidebook] for the benefit of those wishing to emigrate.

Orson Pratt gave his New York congregation instructions from his fellow apostles and announced his departure for Nauvoo on 8 November 1845. Pratt encouraged all believers to follow his example and leave the United States. The Saints faced "the choice of DEATH or BANISHMENT," he said, and called on the Lord "to deliver us out of the hands of the blood-thirsty Christians." He welcomed exile "from this wicked nation; for we have received nothing but one continual scene of the most horrid and unrelenting persecutions at their hands for the last sixteen years." Pratt reported, "Elder S. Brannan has been counselled to go by sea. He will sail about the middle of January." All those who could afford an overland outfit should go to Nauvoo, but those who could not "must raise means to pay their passage by sea around Cape Horn." Pratt thought this would cost "but a trifle more, than our expenses from here to Nauvoo."

"Elder Samuel Brannan is hereby appointed to preside over, and take charge of the company that go by sea," Pratt announced, "and all who go with him will be required to give strict heed to his instruction and counsel." Brannan would "point out to you the necessary articles to be taken, whether for food or for raiment, together with farming utensils, mechanical instruments, and all kinds of garden seeds." Pratt thought "he will soon raise a company as large as can conveniently go in one vessel." Pratt and Brannan had devised a strategy to make the emigration possible. "If one hundred and fifty or two hundred passengers can be obtained," Brannan would "venture to charter a vessel for them." The Saints could "do almost anything, for our Father in Heaven will strengthen us."

"Judgment is at the door," the apostle warned. "Be determined to get out from this evil nation next spring. We do not want one Saint to be left in the United States after that time."[68] After Pratt finished speaking, "Elder Brannan laid before the congregation his instructions from the authorities of the church directing him to go by water, and calling upon all who wanted to accompany him, to come forward at the close of the meeting and put down their names."[69]

At a church conference four days later, Elder Brannan presented resolutions that denounced William Smith and urged the Saints in the East, "one and all," to move "west of the Rocky Mountains between this and next season."

"New York Conference,"
Times and Seasons, 15 November 1845, 1036–37.

The Church of Jesus Christ of Latter-day Saints met pursuant to appointment on the evening of the 12th of November, at the American Hall. Many of the brethren were present from Long Island, Connecticut, and New Jersey.

On motion, Elder O. Pratt was called to the chair, and G. T. Newell, Secretary.

After prayer and a dedication of the assembly to God by the president, and a song of Zion by the whole assembly, the President arose and laid

---

[68]"Farewell Message of Orson Pratt," *New-York Messenger*, copied in *Times and Seasons*, 1 December 1845, 6:1042–44; see also Roberts, ed., *History of the Church*, 7:515–19. Pratt's farewell vividly evoked the Mormon mindset on the eve of their departure for the West.

[69]*Millennial Star*, 1 February 1846, 36.

before the conference the present condition of the saints, and the necessity of all removing to the West. He exhorted them to a union of action for the benefit of the poor, that they might not be left behind. That as long as the church remained among the Gentiles, the fulness of the gospel could not be taken from them, and the Book of Mormon be fulfilled.

Elder Brannan then arose and presented the following preamble and resolutions, which were unanimously adopted by the whole assembly without a dissenting voice.

WHEREAS, we as a people have sought to obey the great commandment of the dispensation of the fulness of times, by gathering ourselves together; and as often as we have done so, we have been sorely persecuted by the Protestant Christian churches, our houses burned, and we disinherited of our possessions, and driven forth upon the charity of a cold hearted world, to seek protection and sustenance for ourselves and families.

And WHEREAS:—Inasmuch as the people and authorities of the United States have sanctioned such proceedings, without manifesting any disposition to sustain us in our constitutional rights, but have rejected our many petitions to judges, governors, and presidents for the last twelve years, having hardened their hearts like Pharaoh of old, against the cries of the fatherless and the widow, That we now cease our cries—wipe away our tears, and prepare ourselves to "enter into our chambers, and shut our doors about us for a little season until the indignation be overpast." Therefore,

Resolved, That we hail with joy the proclamation of our brethren from the City of Joseph [Nauvoo], to make preparations for our immediate departure, and give thanks and praise to our heavenly Father that the day of our deliverance is so near at hand.

Resolved, That we look upon the proclamation sent forth and published in the Warsaw Signal by our former brother, William Smith, as being actuated by purely selfish motives alone, for his own personal emolument and aggrandizement, at the sacrifice of the lives of his best friends, and the defamation of the character of the whole church; unchristianlike, even if true, because it brings persecution and affliction upon the innocent.

Resolved, That we most heartily sanction the proceedings of the council and Church at Nauvoo, in his excommunication; and that suffering innocence in this city by his hands, has demanded it long since. And in it we believe that prayers of the fatherless and widow have been answered. And further

Resolved, That we caution all the honest in heart among the Saints, where he has not visited in the East and elsewhere, that have not had an opportunity of proving his Apostleship as we have, to beware how they receive him into their houses, or bid him God speed, lest they bring condemnation upon themselves ignorantly.

Resolved, That during the mission and ministry of our brethren, the Twelve, among us, since the absence of William Smith, their conduct has been of the most exemplary character, both in practice and precept; which we are sorry we are not able to say of our former Brother William Smith. And

Resolved, That we advise him if he wishes to keep himself from trouble, shame, and disgrace—that if he has any feeling for the character of his family, and his martyred brethren, that he stay where he is, or go where he is not known. For we, the church in New York, have no desire to see him, unless he repent speedily, and go about making restitution for lifting his hand against the church and kingdom of God to destroy it.

Resolved, That the church in this city move, one and all, west of the Rocky Mountains, between this and next season, either by land or water; and that we most earnestly pray all our brethren in the eastern country to join with us in this determination, and carry it out effectually, to the delivery of the people of God from the daughters of Babylon, and not one left behind.

Resolved, That there are no apologies required of those who do not go, but old age, sickness, infirmities, and poverty; "For he that will not forsake father and mother, houses and lands, wives and children for me, and my name's sake, is not worthy of me."

Elder Brannan laid before the congregation his instructions from the authorities of the church directing him to go by water, and called upon all who wanted to accompany him, to come forward at the close of the meeting and put down their names. The conference was then dismissed by a benediction from the President.[70]

ORSON PRATT, Pres't.

G. T. Newell, Sec.

Samuel Brannan and his flock now began to prepare for a sea voyage to California.[71]

---

[70]See also Roberts, ed., *History of the Church*, 7:520–22.

[71]On 8 November, Brannan called on the New York Saints to "unanimously act upon the call" of church leaders to go West, and the next week announced that he "thought it expedient to issue one more number" of the paper "before bringing it to a close." Brannan admitted he still owed money he had borrowed to publish *The Prophet* and was "compelled to beg lenity a little farther." He asked, "Is there one that will cast any blame upon brother Brannan for not furnishing them the amount due on their subscription?" He answered, "No!" and promised to "make every satisfaction necessary" to his subscribers, hoping to "send back by the same ship that carries us out, several thousand copies; giving every information within our reach" in California. See *New-York Messenger*, 8 and 15 November 1845, 149/2, 156–57.

Chapter 4

"LOOK FOR FIRE AND SWORD"
THE KENDALL-BENSON SCHEME

Samuel Brannan promoted Mormon interests and his California project in Washington City throughout the fall of 1845, but it is difficult to determine when or how often he visited the capital. He tried to revive the Benson arrangement in the hope that Mormon emigrants could benefit from it. Years later Brannan gave a strange account of his political adventures that autumn. He claimed that the Mexican Consul threatened that if he sailed for California, his ship "would be sunk before it reached the island of Cuba." Brannan arrived in Washington after midnight and went directly "to the Executive Mansion, roused Mr. Polk, and related the Mexican Consul's statement to him." Brannan claimed the President "sent for the members of his Cabinet, who met at 2 oclock that night and discussed the situation. The Mexican Consul's statements were considered as a declaration of war on the part of Mexico." Brannan was told that if he rounded the Horn, the warship *Congress* and Commodore Robert Field Stockton would "accompany and protect him."[1]

This bizarre tale was filtered through a newspaper reporter and forty-two years of Brannan's brandy-soaked memory, and nothing in Polk's papers supports Brannan's memory of an emergency cabinet meeting. But the *Congress* and "Fighting Bob" Stockton left Hampton Roads, Virginia, for California on 25 October 1845 "with *sealed orders.*" Apparently Stockton was in no hurry to reach the Mexican province, for it would take the frigate nearly five months to travel from Rio de Janeiro to Valparaiso, and the *Congress* would only reach Hawaii in June.[2] Stockton, a wealthy capitalist and ardent expansionist, had spent the spring of 1845

---

[1]See "A Strange Career," *Sacramento Bee*, 21 January 1888, in Chapter 14.
[2][Bayard], *A Sketch of the Life of Com. Robert F. Stockton*, 95–97.

in the Gulf of Mexico. Anson Jones, president of the Republic of Texas, told his colleagues that the commodore "on the part of the United States, wishes me *to manufacture a war for them*."[3] Stockton wanted a Texan invasion of the disputed territory between the Nueces and Rio Grande rivers and informed George Bancroft that the Texas militia would "call out three thousand men & 'R. F. Stockton Esq' will supply them in a private way with provisions & ammunition." Texas declined Stockton's offer to start a war, and he had to be content to return to the United States with "the glad tidings of annexation."[4]

In Washington that fall, Amos Kendall met Samuel J. Hastings, a veteran seafarer. Kendall, "learning that he had been in California took him to see Mr Polk who kept him in talk some two hours."[5] The sea captain wrote Consul Thomas Larkin that a new flag would fly over California, and "it will be an American one or a new one & American Agents and American capital will be at the bottom of it." Hastings reported, "Our men of war are not ordered to California for nothing . . . Commodore Stockton is said to be the Presidents right hand man."[6] Larkin, who believed Stockton was "much in the confidence of Mr. Polk," asked an obvious question: "what object can you suppose a Commodore of Capt. Stockton's wealth rank and prospects had in leaving all, and coming to the North Pacific. Hardly to take charge of a squadron to see to Whalers and some merchants ships."[7]

S. J. Hastings sent a letter west with the *Brooklyn*. "California must belong to the Americans," he wrote Thomas Larkin. "So say the knowing ones at Washington & even Mr Polk thinks it must come to pass. Whether in his time or not he did not say. I was in company with him & he questioned me closely abt the Country."[8] There can be no question

---

[3] Price, *Origins of the Mexican War: The Polk-Stockton Intrigue*, 112.

[4] Stockton to Bancroft, 27 May 1845, quoted in Ibid., 122. Sellers, *James K. Polk*, 224–25, disputed the Stockton intrigue argument.

[5] Atherton to Larkin, 3 December 1846, in Hammond, ed., *Larkin Papers*, 5:290.

[6] S. J. Hastings to Larkin, 9 November 1845, in Ibid., 4:92.

[7] Larkin to Stearns, 24 May 1846, in Ibid., 4:392.

[8] S. J. Hastings to Larkin, 22 January 1846, in Ibid., 4:177. Hastings noted that "Here the people consider themselves well off to get rid of" the Mormons. Samuel J. Hastings visited Brigham Young in February 1846 and proposed to take LDS emigrants to California for "$150.00 including provisions." Roberts, ed., *History of the Church*, 7:598, mistakenly referred to him as the "Pathfinder of the West," an improbable honorific aimed at Lansford W. Hastings, who had no known relation to the sea captain.

that James K. Polk was powerfully committed to acquiring California during the single term he had promised to serve. Polk confided to George Bancroft that securing California was one of the four goals he had set for his administration.[9] On the same day he signed the declaration of war with Mexico, Polk exploded when Secretary of State James Buchanan proposed forswearing acquisition of California as a war aim: "I told him that before I took such a pledge, I would meet the war which either England or France or all the Powers of Christendom might wage, and that I would stand and fight until the last man among us fell in the conflict."[10] Brannan and the Mormons appear to have been one element of the president's multifaceted plan to achieve his goal.

STRIKE WHILE THE IRON IS HOT

With Orson Pratt's departure, Brannan again became presiding elder of the LDS church in the East, and at twenty-six he faced the daunting task of organizing an expedition to California. Brannan accompanied Pratt to Philadelphia, where William I. Appleby helped him promote the California expedition.

WILLIAM I. APPLEBY, AUTOBIOGRAPHY AND JOURNAL,
LDS ARCHIVES, 138.

[15 November 1845] Arrived this evening in Philadelphia, by way of Railroad in company with Elder Hale, there found Bro. O. Pratt, S. Brannan, and Willard Snow from New York, Elders Pratt and Snow on their way to Nauvoo.

16. Sabbath. Elder O Pratt addressed the Saints . . . in regard to the duties devolving upon them. . . . the Saints were determined, all that could go the following spring to go some to California Mexico—by water and some by land—and leave the Mobs and Gentiles to perish in their own abominations &c. In the afternoon and evening, Elder Brannan addressed the meeting. After which [a] considerable number of names were given to Elder Brannan for to go to California . . .

17. Elder Brannan went to Toms River N. J. I accompanied him as far as my residence . . . Elder Brannan returned again on Wednesday afternoon following. Several of the Saints having given their names to go by Sea to California, as Br. Brannan was about getting up a company and chartering a vessel or Ship for the purpose.

---

[9]Eisenhower, So Far from God: The U.S. War with Mexico, 1846–1848, 21.
[10]Quaife, ed., Diary of James K. Polk, 1:398.

Brannan apparently visited Washington, D.C., in early December 1845 to seek government money to finance his California expedition— and probably to confer with Amos Kendall. Excited reports in a *New-York Messenger Extra* reveal that plans for the California adventure had quickly coalesced.

"TO EMIGRANTS."
NEW-YORK MESSENGER EXTRA, 13 DECEMBER 1845. 1/1.

We have now on our books the names of about three hundred saints who wish to go by water, and it grieves us to say that only about sixty out of that number will have means sufficient to carry them through. If some of our wealthy brethren who are now dwelling at ease in the world, would but step forward, and plant this company of poor saints, (that have not the means, nor likely to have,) upon the western soil, how soon would it be before they would have it in their power to return four fold? And how sweet would be the reflections of that mind capable of performing such a noble act. Where is the magnanimity of God's people? Alas, it is in the poor and meek of the earth.

The passage for each person will be fifty dollars, children over five and under fourteen, half price. Each one will need from twenty to twenty-five dollars worth of provisions; the whole amount, seventy five dollars. If we obtain two hundred passengers, in all probability there will be a deduction.

We have been looking for assistance from another source. A merchant of this city who is now engaged in the Pacific trade [A. G. Benson], has made us the following proposition: that if he can obtain the government freight consisting of naval stores, to be carried into the Pacific, he will take two hundred of us at sixteen dollars per ton for the room we occupy and fifty more for nothing. As yet this arrangement has not been made, and it remains uncertain whether it will be.

We do not feel to place much dependence on it, lest we are unhappily disappointed. If the arrangement is affected the saints will receive timely notice.

We do not wish any persons to give us their names to go by water, and when the time comes for departure to be found missing; by doing so they will bring us into difficulty, and we shall have to be responsible and pay their passage as much as though they went. We have selected out all the names of those who have subscribed sufficient (at the rate of seventy five dollars) to take them through, and we shall depend on their going. And all who wish to join the company will send their names as soon as possible, so that we may know the exact number going and provide them with births [*sic*] two and three weeks previous to the day of sailing, we wish all to hold themselves in rediness to send in a part of their means to furnish all the outlays necessary to be made before sailing.

We have placed the names of some who fell short in subscription on the list of those going. And the amount short will be made up by others who have more than they need for. The following are their names: Wm. Stout, J. Joyce, J. Hairbaird, Wm. Mack, Wm. Atherton.

To his Excellency,

The President of the United States,
James K. Polk,

Dear Sir—Samuel Brannan, the agent of our company, consisting of between two and three hundred farmers and mechanics, had made a conditional arrangement with the Messres Benson of New York to take fifty of our number to Oregon for nothing, and the balance at very low rates; but we were informed by him that they have been disappointed in obtaining the freight from the government on which their offer was based. And the object of this is to make this matter known to you, and request that this or some other facility may be afforded, for it is evident that if that country is to be settled by americans, there must be a regular and cheap communication for the conveyance of emigrants, their furniture, impliments of husbandry, goods &c.

Respectfully yours.

We wish, that every place where there are two or three saints together east of the Alleghany, whether they wish to go or not, two [sic] write a letter similar to the above to the President, and as many sign it as can write their names. Brethren take our council and act on this matter as soon as it comes to hand. We shall visit Washington again before long, and your letters should reach there before us. Do not be slack for one moment.

We would advise all who go by water, to be well supplied with bags, that in case we should wish to move any distance from the sea shore when we arrive there, all baggage can be packed on horses.

The Globe of this city, a democratic paper, on Tuesday last, announced that there were from two to three hundred hardy and industrious men in this city, consisting of mechanics principally, who wish to emigrate to Oregon or the western coast of America, and that the government should take some prompt and efficient steps for their immediate removal. That meant us, we like the idea vary [sic] much. Brethren do'nt [sic] neglect your letter to the President, and that two [sic] in haste; strike while the iron is hot.

During our travels in the east, we found the saints united and animated with the idea and prospects of emigration in the spring. In Win[d]sor and Hartford we were not able to find any of the saints, and falling short of travelling expenses as well as our anxiety to reach home in order to get our paper to press, we passed through New Haven without stopping.

The saints in Nauvoo are all busily engaged in building wagons, and making preparations for moving in the spring; while apostates and the heathen are growling on the borders, and gnashing their teeth in despair, to terrify the flock; but as George Adams would say "the kingdom will move forward crushing to earth every opposing obstacle that presents itself,["] and so say we, and he had better be moving out of the way. The Warsaw Signal says that if Adams was not such a scamp himself he might give the saints some trouble.

Those going by land, who wish to send freight by water must report the quantity immediately on the reception of this. Price from 16 to 20 dollars per ton.

The President in his message has claimed the whole of the Oregon territory. If John Bull is stubborn, we may look for fire and sword.

Names are coming in briskley from every quarter, and the prospect bids fair of having a strong and able company. We shall report progress every week through the Messenger.

Brannan's call in "Come on Oh Israel" revealed how far his plans had developed and contained the first mention of the *Brooklyn*.[11]

"COME ON OH ISRAEL, IT IS TIME TO GO!"
NEW-YORK MESSENGER EXTRA, 13 DECEMBER 1845, 2/1–2.

Beloved Brethren—We are fully aware of the anxiety, that must necessarily rest on your minds at this time, in relation to our success in making up a company to go by water. And we feel happy to say, that the faith and energy of the saints in this matter has surpassed our expectations. Our company now numbers over one hundred who have means sufficient to fit themselves out handsomely and comfortably for the voyage. We would say to all who have any quantity of provisions on hand, such as beef or pork, to fetch it with them. They will also remember that they require no thick clothing on their arrival at the place of destination.[12] Every thing that is useful here is

---

[11]*Millennial Star*, 1 February 1846, 36–37; and *Times and Seasons*, 1 February 1846, 6:1112–13, reprinted this piece.

[12]Upon becoming familiar with the climate of San Francisco, Brannan corrected this advice in his letter "To the Saints in England and America" on 1 January 1847, when he advised emigrants "to provide themselves with thick clothing, instead of thin."

useful there, with the exception of thick clothing, stoves, &c. We want the company, on the reception of this, to commence sending in their monies. Where there is a large amount, it had better be sent by some responsible person; small amounts, such as two or three hundred dollars can be sent by the mail—one letter with the money or check on some bank in this city, and another giving the particulars. Persons having large sums of money, had better come to the city and assist in their investment and then there will be no cause for dissatisfaction hereafter.

We have chartered the ship Brooklyn, Captain Richardson, of four hundred and fifty tons, at twelve hundred dollars per month, and we pay the port charges; the money to be paid before sailing. She is a first class ship in the best of order for sea, and with all the rest a very fast sailor, which will facilitate our passage greatly. The between decks will be very neatly fitted up into one large cabin, with a row of state rooms on each side, so that every family will be provided with a state room, affording them places of retirement at their pleasure. She will be well lighted with sky-lights in the deck, with every other convenience to make a family equally as comfortable as by their own fireside in Babylon. She will be ready to receive freight on to-morrow, and all had better commence sending their things that they have no immediate use for, (well packed in barrels, boxes, or bags—marked,) and have them put on board the vessel, that when they come on they will have nothing to do but to "take up their bed and walk," and it will save much confusion prior to starting. This in particular should be observed by those at a great distance, and their things will be sure not to be left behind. Some of the females in delicate health had better come into the city as soon as they can; small rooms can be rented in the city very cheap, which would serve them until they get ready to go on board.[13] Bring all your beds and bedding, all your farming and mechanical tools, and your poultry, beef, pork, potatoes, and anything else that will sustain life. You had better pack your things in boxes with hinges to the cover, instead of barrels; the boards will serve for some useful purpose at your journey's end. Dont forget your pots and kettles, with your necessary cooking utensils, have them, with your crockery, packed snug, for you will not need them on the passage; the ship will be furnished with tin ware that will not break.

We have now but little better than four weeks to purchase our provisions and stores, also casks to hold our water, and get everything on board to serve us on the passage; to do this, we want your money before you can all get here, that the ship may not have anything to prevent her from sailing at the appointed time—time with us is money—also, to pay the charter money.

The ship will sail on the 24th of January, instead of the 26th: by doing so we shall gain two days, which would be otherwise lost by sailing on the latter, as all would have to lay in port over Sunday, when nothing could be

---

[13] The several *Brooklyn* passengers who gave birth on the voyage were in "delicate health."

done. All freight and letters to be addressed to S. Brannan, No. 7 Spruce St.

If any accident should happen to delay any one's arriving at the appointed time, we shall wait for them. It will be necessary for you to be in the city on the 20th or 21st.

All persons that can raise fifty dollars will be able to secure a passage on the ship. We believe we have said all that is necessary until you arrive here, which we hope you will not fail to do to a man. We have received our instructions from the Twelve at the West, which will be laid before the company on their arrival in the city.[14]

The captain and crew of our vessel are all temperance men. Capt. Richardson bears the reputation of being one of the most skillful seamen that has ever sailed from this port, and bears an excellent moral character.[15]

N.B.—Now brethren remember there must be no disappointment on the part of any individual that has joined this company, by doing so, it might be the means of stopping the whole company, and that man will be morally responsible for the injury done, and God will require it at his hands. We do not say this because we have any fears on the subject, but that none should have an appollogy for slackness, for we will accept of none. You would not accept it of me as your agent, neither can I accept it of you. When you find me off of my duty, bring me to judgement and make me feel the rod. Every man must be on the ground at the appointed time.

"A List of the Company Going by Water,"
New-York Messenger Extra, 13 December 1845, 2/2.

The following are the names of those we have selected, who have means sufficient to pay their expenses by water. We shall secure their passage on the ship and expect them to be in the city and all prepared to sail at the appointed time, *without fail*. On their failure, they will involve us in debt and difficulty.

Wm. C. Reamer and family, John Phillips, Wm. Stout, and family; Abraham Combs and family; Joseph Hicks and family; Stephen H. Pierce; John Joice and family; John Hairbaird and family; Mary Murry; Daniel P. Baldwin; Wm. Atherton and family; Susan A. Searls; Eliza Savage; Simeon Stanley and family; Darwin Richardson and family; Moses Mead and family; J. M. Farnsworth, and the names he has signed; Jonas Cook; Isaac Leigh and family; Manena [Marsena] Cannon and family; Thomas Tompkins and Family; Henry Roulam; Wm. Flint and family; Joseph Nichols and family;

---

[14]As with all other LDS documents allegedly authorizing the *Brooklyn* expedition, these "instructions from the Twelve" have not survived.

[15]The captain was Abel W. Richardson, who in November 1839 was listed as one of the ship's owners, with Stephen C. Burdett and Edward Richardson, his brother.

Newel Bullen and family; Ambrose T. Moses and family; Julius Austin and family; Isaac Adison and family; Silas Eldridge and family; Barton Morey and family; Isaac R. Robbins and family; John R. Robbins and family; James Embly and family; Jacob Hayse; Charles Russel and family; Alandus D. Ruckland and family; Wm. Glover and family; Robert Smith and family; John Eagar; Samuel Smith; Isabella Jones; James Light and family; Mary Hamond; Earl Marshall and family; Peter Pool and family; James Smith and family; Joseph France and family; John J. Sirrine and family; George W. Sirrine; S. Brannan and family.

There are some names that we have not published, as they from their own statement fell short in their subscription, but if they see their way clear, they can come on and go with us. And there will be still an opportunity for those who have not sent their names—let them write and come on, and they will be provided for. If we have neglected any names it must make no difference, come on and all will be made wright.

"GATHER OUT!"
NEW-YORK MESSENGER EXTRA, 13 DECEMBER 1845, 2/2.

The Lord has made a call for the saints to gather out, and has prepared the wao [way] before them to obtain a peac[e]able deliverance. And all who have it in their power, and neglect to do so, will find themselves falling short day by day, of the glory of God, until they are finally lost in the snares of the world, and at last bound in chains and fetters of apostacy. "Come out of her my people, and be not partakers of her sins lest ye receive of her plagues."

"SPECIAL INSTRUCTIONS,"
NEW-YORK MESSENGER EXTRA, 13 DECEMBER 1845, 2/2.

We wish every individual connected with our company on their arrival in this city to adopt the word Mr. instead of Brother. It will be impossible to prevent the people in New York from knowing [of] our departure, and place of destination. Public opinion will be in our favor if we keep our religious views to ourselves until we are gone. "Be wise as *serpents* and harmless as *doves*."

The last surviving issue of the *New-York Messenger* appeared on 15 December. It sketched Brannan's attempt to help revive the Bensons' government contract, but with atypical realism, Brannan recognized "we have little hopes of it being [implemented] soon enough to benefit our company."

"WASHINGTON."
NEW-YORK MESSENGER, 15 DECEMBER 1845, 1/3.

During our last visit to Washington, we were informed by the President, that a law would be passed by this Congress, under some general head (The Navy Department) affording facilities for the poor in the eastern countries to emigrate to Oregon or the North West Coast.—From the interest manifested by the Western members in Congress in favor of such a law, we have not the least doubt but what it will be done, and a "highway cast up for the deliverance of God's people". But we have lettle [sic] hopes of it being soon enough to benefit our company.—

We would advise the saints in the east after our departure to ralley to the standard—raise another company, and stand ready to embrace the first facilities that may be afforded by the Government. Let the elders in Israel not forsake the watch-towers—but coming to call on the name of the Lord day and night, and they will be delivered.[16]

Until We Strike Hands on the Shores of the Pacific

Brannan worked aggressively to recruit emigrants, including Oliver Cowdery, scribe for *The Book of Mormon*. "Samuel Brannan writes me strongly to come to New York and go with him by water," Cowdery noted, saying that if he chose to go west, he would prefer to take a sea voyage.[17]

As 1845 drew to a close, Brannan became obsessed with his great enterprise. Although apparently unaware of Brigham Young's instructions, he suggested that the English Saints consider California as a cheaper route to the new Zion in the West. In October Young had directed Wilford Woodruff of the British Mission to "send no more immigrants" to Nauvoo, "but let them wait in England until they can ship for the Pacific Ocean, say the Bay of St. Francisco."[18]

BRANNAN TO WOODRUFF, 26 DECEMBER 1845, LDS ARCHIVES.
New York Dec. 26th 1845

Dear Brother [Wilford] Woodruff—With a very bad pen and in great

---

[16]See also *Times and Seasons*, 6:1103, citing *New-York Messenger*. On the same page, the *Times and Seasons* reprinted "Good Council. Mind Your Own Business" from the *New-York Messenger*.

[17]Cowdery to Phinehas Young, 18 December 1845, in Gunn, *Oliver Cowdery*, 249.

[18]Young to Woodruff, 16 October 1845, cited in Hansen and Bringhurst, *Let This Be Zion*, 11.

haste, I imbrace the opportunity this evening to answer your kind letter, which very unexpectedly came to hand this morning. The Saints in the eastern country are all alive in the course of gathering across the mountains more so than they have been heretofore in gathering to Nauvoo. I have heard nothing by the Twelve concerning what course would be persued by the saints in England, neither of your stay or return, but I presume it will be much cheeper for the saints their to emigrate by water—for it is a great deal cheeper for the eastern saints to emigrate from here by water and of course it will be to[o] for you. I have chartered a Bark[19] of 450 tons for $6000. I shall take about 200 tons of freight for the Sandwich Islands at 16 dollars per ton which will reduce the expence to about 3800 say 4000 dollars.[20] I shall carry about 125 saints with me, which will be less than one half of the expense than going by land. Brother Sherrill was in here this evening having just arrived from Nauvoo. He says he heard Elder Kimball state on the public stand that after the endowment there would be fifty elders sent out on missions, and that he should go to England, from this you can draw your own conclusions. You have it as I received it. I suppose their object will be to gather up the remnant and bring them to Zion as a reserved guarde. Our Government contemplates establishing a mail every month by water between here and Oregon and California, that will you see, afford great facilities to those left behind to get information from Head Quarters. God is working with this nation in a marvellous manner. All things you see will work together for good to them that walk uprightly. Every man in Nauvoo the Twelve not excepted have striped off their jackets and gon to work making Waggons. Emma Smith has sent a letter and published [it] in the New York Sun. That she never for one moment believed in the revelations of Joseph— but it has no more effect upon the saints than water does upon oil.[21] It sinks to the bottom and the oil rises to the surface—their faith is not in the arm of flesh, nor to be poluted by a lying spirit. Wm Smith has not made his appearance yet in this country neither do I think he will until I am gone— which if the Lord will, will be on the first of February. I was in hopes until I received your letter that you would sail from England about the time I should and we should arrive together on the coast of California, but I see I shall have to try it alone, & my trust is in him that brought Israel out of Egypt which swallows up every fear.

I received the money sent by Brother Hadlock—and be assured that it was a welcome visiter. Winchester has been excommunicated from the Rig-

---

[19]The *Brooklyn* was a square-rigged ship, not a bark with a fore-and-aft rigged mizzen mast.

[20]Brannan's math was in error, for the payment for two hundred tons of freight would have been $3,200, leaving him to pay only $2,800 of the $6,000 charter fee.

[21]This letter, which appeared in the *New York Sun* on 9 December 1845, was a forgery. See Newell and Avery, *Mormon Enigma: Emma Hale Smith*, 222–26.

don ranks, and where he will go now to make a few shillings is hard to tell. Give my love to all the brethren with you and the same to you and sister Woodruff untill we strike hands on the shores of the Pacific. After my best wishes for your posterity, I subscribe myself your brother in the glorious Kingdom of the Last Days that will yet cause the earth to shake.

S. Brannan

Brother Woodruff I have writen all my lifetime and yet I can hardly read my own handwriting so you must excuse me.

By this time Brannan's erstwhile partner, Lansford W. Hastings, had arrived at Sutter's Fort. Before the year was out, his gracious host gave him "one half [square] mile of land lying in Sutterville," for Sacramento's first land records report that John Sutter "conveyed" the land "to Lansford W. Hastings some time in the year 1845."[22] Consul Thomas Larkin (still unaware that President Polk had appointed him a "confidential agent") reported that Hastings was "laying off a Town at New Helvetia for the Mormons." By 7 February, John Bidwell and Hastings had "finished laying out the town" on the Sutterville grant.[23]

John C. Frémont had reached Sutter's on 10 December, but departed three days later to find other members of his Third Expedition. Frémont returned to the fort on 15 January 1846, but Hastings was already claiming the explorer's recent discoveries as his own.[24] Jacob Leese informed Consul Larkin that Hastings "says he has found a road through the Stoney Mountains 400 miles shorter than has ever been traveled." Leese reported, "A Company has been formed in New York Called the Califa. Agriculturing Co/a. Two Shipps sailed in August last for this with all Kinds of cultavating implements & Seeds." Hastings had "come a head to enter the Shipps and make arrangements," and claimed "A Larg Emigration will be through this summer."[25]

In his own report to Larkin, Hastings asserted that the "tide of emigration" in 1846 would be "unparalleled in the annals of history." He predicted the summer's emigration "will not consist of less than *twenty*

---

[22]John A. Sutter, Deed to John A. Sutter, Jr., 18 November 1848, Book of Deeds A, Sacramento County Recorder's Office, 2.

[23]Sutter, *New Helvetia Diary*, 26; and Larkin to Buchanan, 2 April 1846, in Hammond, ed., *Larkin Papers*, 4:276. Who made Hastings an agent for the Mormon church is unclear.

[24]Sutter, *New Helvetia Diary*, 16–17, 19, 23.

[25]Leese to Larkin, 12 January 1846, in Hammond, ed., *Larkin Papers*, 4:161.

thousand souls," including "Our friend Farnham, and many other highly respectable and intelligent gentlemen." Hastings claimed to know "many wealthy gentlemen, and capitalists, who design to make large investments in California . . . The house of Benson & Co. is about to establish an extension commercial house, in some portion of this country." A Benson ship was due "in a few weeks, and another will arrive in the month of May or June," carrying trade goods. (Whether the first ship arrived is unknown, but Hastings approximately predicted the arrival of the *Brooklyn* that summer.) The Bensons planned to send two ships to California each year, "one in June, and another in November," and they would bring "thousands of emigrants," since "that house proposed to bring all emigrants to this country, and to Oregon, free of charge, they furnishing their own provisions." Hastings cautioned "that this latter arrangement is a confidential, governmental arrangement. The expense thus incured is not borne by that house, but by our government, for the promotion of what object, you will readily perceive."[26] The object, obviously, was the American acquisition of California.

A COVENANT WITH DEATH

Brannan's mysterious visits to Washington produced a dramatic response from the leaders of the LDS church. On 11 December 1845, Brigham Young

> called the Twelve and bishops together and informed them that he had received a letter from Brother Samuel Brannan, stating that he had been at Washington and had learned that the secretary of war and other members of the cabinet were laying plans and were determined to prevent the Saints from moving west, alleging that it was against the law for an armed body of men to go from the United States to any other government. They say it will not do to let the Mormons go to California nor Oregon, neither will it do to let them tarry in the states, and they must be obliterated from the face of the earth.[27]

No correspondence from November or December 1845 between Brannan and Young survives in Mormon archives, including the three

---

[26]L. W. Hastings to Larkin, 3 March 1846, in Ibid., 4:220–21. Hastings asked merchant William Leidesdorff to pay shipping charges and store the property he expected to arrive on the ships "of the house of Benson, of New York." See Morgan, ed., *Overland in 1846*, 35–36.

[27]Roberts, ed., *History of the Church*, 7:544.

letters Brannan wrote "from Boston, Washington and New York."[28] In this missing correspondence, Brannan proposed that he "become one of the Twelve to conduct the affairs [in California]"—a telling comment on his ambitions within the LDS church—but like others who lobbied to become apostles, his efforts went nowhere. Brigham Young paid close attention to the letters Brannan sent to Nauvoo during January, for Young's diary noted on 29 January 1846 Brannan's report "that [the] Govement [*sic*] intended to intercept our movements—by placing strong forces in the way to take from us all fire arms—on the grounds that we were going to another Nation." Brannan, wrote Young, said the trouble began with a James Arlington Bennet letter to the *New York Sun* that described the "Mormon empire now about to be established on the Pacific ocean!" To Young, this "was no more than what we expected—the fulness of the Gentiles could never have been brought in without the united [States] first rejected us as a People."[29] Although it did not mention Bennet, Brannan's surviving 12 January message to Brigham Young summarizes the dire warnings contained in his missing letters—and adds another mystery to the murky history of Mormon counterfeiting.

BRANNAN TO AGNES SMITH, 13 JANUARY 1846,
BRIGHAM YOUNG COLLECTION, LDS ARCHIVES.

New York Jan 13/46

Sister Agness[30]—After my respects and the respects of my wife and family—will you oblige me by handing the enclosed to Elder Young—I have sent it to you to prevent it from falling into wicked hands—let him have it as soon as possible—if the Lord will I hope to see you on the other side of the Mountains.

Yours respectfully
S. Brannan

---

[28]Several sources cite a 26 December 1845 letter from Young to Brannan that does not exist. The misleading letter Young wrote to E. D. Barnard of Chicago has been incorrectly identified.

[29]D. Michael Quinn, transcription of Brigham Young 1844–1846 Diary, 116–17, copy in editor's possession. Bennet claimed he had been offered "the first military command in the camp of the saints." See "The Mormons," *Times and Seasons*, 6:1051–52.

[30]Agnes Coolbrith Smith was the widow of both Joseph Smith and his brother, Don Carlos. See Compton, *In Sacred Loneliness*, 146–70. She may have accompanied Brannan and the Badlams on their 1833 trip to Kirtland. Brannan sponsored publication of a volume of poetry in 1865 that included works by Smith's daughter, Ina Coolbrith, who became California's first poet laureate.

BRANNAN TO YOUNG, 12 JANUARY 1846,
BRIGHAM YOUNG COLLECTION, LDS ARCHIVES.

[Cover sheet: Sam. Brannan to Prest. B Young in relation to agreement between Brannan and Amos Kendall. The Government proposing to disarm the Saints.[31]]

New York Jan 12th 46

Brother Young— I have writen you three letters of late, one from Boston, Washington and New York, and I fear they have been intercepted on the way[32]—and I have thought it prudent to direct this to some obscure individual that it may reach [you] in safety; I have received positive information that it is the intention of the Government, to disarm you, after you have taken up your line of march in the spring, on the grounds of the law of nations, or the treaty existing between the United States and Mexico— "That an armed force of men shall not be allowed to invade, the territory of a foreign nation"—Amos Kendall was in the city last week, and positively declared that that was the intention of the Government—and I thought it my duty to let you know that you might be on your guard—I declare to all that you are not going to California but Oregon and that my information is official—Kendall has also learned that we have chartered the ship Brooklyn and that Mormons are going in her, and it is thought that she will be searched for arms, and if found taken from us—and if not an order will be sent to Comadore Stockton on the Pacific by the Overland mail to search our vessel before we land—but we shall take all necessary steps to guard against being detected—Amos Kendall will be in the city next Thursday again and then an effort will be made to bring about a reconciliation. I will make you acquainted with the result before I leave. My company now numbers about 175—I charted the whole ship, put her in the market and have already obtained one thousand dollars worth of freight for the Sand Wich Islands and a good prospect for more. I now have it in my power to learn every movement of the Government in relation to us, which I shall make you acquainted with before I leave from time to time—God is at work in the east and so is the Devil—but Mose[s]'s rod will be too hard for him—I feel my weakness and inability, and desire your blessing and prayers, that I may be successful—my cares and labors way me down day and night—But trust in God that I shall soon have a happy deliverance.

Tell Brother Orson Pratt that I have Baptised the whol[e] family in Spring street, that [at]tended my lectures, and they are now selling out and

---

[31]This is the first of several notations on Brannan documents made in 1858 in the handwriting of clerk Robert L. Campbell of the LDS Historian's Office. Campbell's notes reveal the significance Brigham Young attached to the documents.

[32]At least one of these letters reached Nauvoo, but none survives in LDS Archives.

going with me in the ship. Tell him that the man that took the two counter-fit tens of him, made a great blow about it when the news reached here that he had been indicted for Counterfiting[33]—I also redeemed ten dollars that the pistol man took from him—and made [Quartus] Sparks take it back—If I do not see Winchester before I go I will leave the notes you sent me in the hands of Br. Newell who is going west in the Spring—he is a good man. I received last week a very pitiful letter from Wm Smith in Cincinnatti—and he closes it by declaring that I shall not have the blessing of Joseph—and that before many years I shall feel the effects of the Tyrant Brigham's Rod, and then I shall think of him—Silly man![34] That is the very thing I want to feel, and then I shall be good for something I hope. All the saints in the east are praying and crying for deliverence. But I must now close by sub-scribing myself—Your Brother in the everlasting [covenant].

S. Brannan

[On cover sheet:] Remember me to Brother O. Hyde, PP and O Pratt and to the rest of the Quorum.

December 4, 1858, This letter, correspondence and agreement con-nected therewith copied into Willard Richards Journal of 1845–6, by order of Prest. B. Young.

R. L. Campbell Clk

Brannan scrambled to raise cash until just days before the ship sailed. Massachusetts convert Henry Larkin Southworth wrote on 23 January that "16 Saints went to New York to day to start in a ship from there: money is not raised sufficient to take them there, and I expect they will have to wait." One of the brethren appealed "to get subscribers to buy a ship." At Sunday services two days later, Southworth noted that Jesse Lit-tle "preached in the afternoon quite powerfully." Little "said Br: Brannan had fell short $3000—by Brethren backing out—Br. Little came here to raise $1000."[35] Ever resourceful, Brannan overcame his financial problems, but was forced to borrow several thousand dollars from the LDS church. Addison Pratt claimed that in 1848 Brannan collected some "2 or 3,000 dollars" from *Brooklyn* veterans, "saying that he received that amount from an agent while the *Brooklyn* was fitting out at New York."[36] This may have been financial help sent to Brannan from Nauvoo, including funds from

---

[33]The man had apparently seen the report of Pratt's indictment "for counterfeiting the coin of the United States" in "The Mormons," *Niles' National Register*, 3 January 1846, 288/3.

[34]This indicates that William Smith wrote Brannan again after his 14 November 1845 letter.

[35]Henry Larkin Southworth, Journal, 23 and 25 January 1846, LDS Archives, 67–68.

[36]Ellsworth, *Journals of Addison Pratt*, 431.

"Bros Neff and Vancott . . . and Bro Barus of Boston," for they held his receipts in 1850.[37] John Neff "gave a considerable sum to start the ship 'Brooklyn' for California."[38] This money was a loan, apparently guaranteed against church tithing funds, which Brannan later repaid.

The best expert on the *Brooklyn* voyage, Lorin Hansen, counted 234 passengers, including 70 men, 63 women, and 101 children, including about 4 non-Mormons.[39] Although Brannan later claimed he financed the *Brooklyn* expedition out of his own pocket, if all of the 133 adults on the voyage paid $50 for their passage, Brannan raised $6,650 from the passage money, close to his expenses, not counting cash from the children's fares. Not all of the emigrants could pay their way, and wealthy members helped cover the expenses of the poor, following the example of the covenant of the Nauvoo Saints "to spend the last cent" to evacuate all faithful Mormons from the states. Brannan made additional money by taking on cargo from A. G. Benson and freight from Mormons such as Levi Riter and John Van Cott. Some of this cash was apparently spent stocking the ship with a remarkably complete set of supplies to outfit a colony, including "Agricultural and Mechanical tools," three grain mills, and a printing press.

Brigham Young sent Brannan a summary of his plans on 4 January 1846, and Brannan responded with a detailed report. Among the most significant of Brannan's papers, its most interesting comments were omitted from the version published in the official LDS history.[40] Brannan warned Young not to follow the advice of Thomas Farnham, who proposed "to annihilate the native Californians with the sword" and was now "blotted out of the books of Mr. Kendall and Benson." Brannan stressed his military preparations—his men would be "all armed to the teeth" with an arsenal that included fourteen cannon Benson had shipped to Hawaii. Aware that Young would not find the terms of the "contract I have made for our deliverance" appealing, Brannan urged the Mormon leader to sign it anyway— "and leave it for God to break."

---

[37] See Lyman to Young, 23 July 1850, in Chapter 10. In 1848 Brannan "collected 2000 Dollars of the Co. stating that he was oweing the Church the Same amt of tithing funds to bring off the Ship," perhaps the money borrowed from Van Cott and Neff. See Coray to Richards, 3 April 1848, in Ch. 8.

[38] Jenson, *Latter-day Saint Biographical Encyclopedia*, 2:786. For more, see Chapter 10.

[39] Hansen, "Voyage of the *Brooklyn*," 52, 69–72.

[40] See Roberts, ed., *History of the Church*, 7:588–89, for the edited version.

BRANNAN TO YOUNG, 26 JANUARY 1846,
BRIGHAM YOUNG COLLECTION, LDS ARCHIVES.

[Cover]

Sister Agnes—Excuse me for again troubling you with another letter to present to President Young.

Yours in haste S. Brannan
New York Jan 26th 46

Dear Brother Young—Your communication of the 4th has been duly received—and I haste[n] to lay before your honorabl[e] today the result of my movements since I wrote you last, which was from this city stating some of my discoveries in relation to the contemplated movements of the general government, in opposition to our removal. The day your letter reached here I had an interview with Amos Kendall in company with Mr. Benson, which resulted in a compromise, the conditions of which you will learn by reading the contract between them and us, which I shall forward by this mail. I shall also leave a copy of the same with Elder Appleby, who was present when it was signed—Kendall is now our friend—and will use his influence in our behalf in connection with 25 of the most prominent demagogues of the country. You will be permitted to pass out of the states unmolested—Their council is to go well armed, but keep them well secreted from the rabble—In your letter you suggested that you should stop and put in a crop before you reached California. Such a course I presume you considered policy for your safety—but I never should do it from the suggestion of Farnum—he is a man that is a friend to those who will serve him for power—I have learned that he is blotted out of the books of Mr. Kendall and Benson. They look upon him as a man of no stable principle—and have instructed me if he is troublesome to put him down and I shall do so. His doctrine is to annihilate the native Californians with the sword[41]—if he attempts to ~~carrie~~ carry it out on my arrival their I shall joine the oppressed, and if we can win the natives to our own side, all will go well—Hastings and Capt Sutter will go with me, and no mistake the country is ours. We shall have a strong and ruling party in this country that will back us, politically and commercially—I shall select the most suitable spot on the Bay of Francisco for the location of ~~a city~~ a Commercial City—Mr. Benson and other Merchants in this City are to open a trade with us—And the United States Mail will land at our own place— The project I wrote to you about to become one of the Twelve to conduct the affairs their—is now swallowed up in this new contract—which was brought about by their learning that I was a Mormon.

---

[41]For evidence that the "native Californians" Farnham proposed to exterminate were the province's Mexican citizens and not its Indians, see Churchill, *Adventurers and Prophets*, 238–40. David Weber credited Farnham with being largely "responsible for the spread of racist opinions about Mexicans." See Ibid., 224n10.

Beloved Brethren, I do not wish to council you—But I do belive and so does the company I have contracted with, that the main body cannot reach Francisco too soon—for before you reach their if it is the Lords will I shall have everything prepared for you. I shall meet you if possible at the South Pass and report progress. My company consists of a noble hearted set of men and they are all armed to the teeth and before they reach their, they will have learned how to use them—I shall have 14 pieces of cannon at my command, that Mr. Benson sent to the Sandwich Islands about four months ago—I shall take them with me from their, as I shall stop their to discharge about $1000 worth of freigh[t]. You must never admit you are going to California till you have reached the South Pass, and there you must rush right through—This is the council on the part of the Government—When I sail which will be next Saturday [31 January] at 1 o'clock—I shall hoist a Flag with Oregon on it— Immediately on the reception of this letter you must write to Messrs. A. G. Benson [and Co.] and let him know whether you are willing to coincide with the contract I have made for our deliverance. I am aware that it is a covenant with death but we know that God is able to break it—and will do it—the children of Israel from Egypt had to make Covenants for their safety—and leave it for God to break them—and the Prophet has said "as it was then, so shall it be in the last days." And I have been led by a remarkable train of circumstances to say, Amen—and I feel and hope you will do the same. Mr. Benson thinks the Twelve should leave and get out of the country first and avoid being arrested if it is a possible thing—but if you are arrested you will find a staunch friend in him and you will find friends and that a host too, to deliver you from their hands—if any of you are arrested, don't be tried west of the Alleghany Mountains—In the east you will find friends that you little think of.[42] It is the prayers of the Saints in the East day and night for your safety— and it is mine first [in] the morning and the last in the evening. I must now bring my letter to a close—Mr. Benson's Address is No. 39 South street—and the sooner you can give him an answer the better it will be for us—He will spend one month in Washington, to sustain you—and he will do it, no mistake. But Every thing must be kept as silent as death on our part—names of the parties in particular—I now commit this sheet to the Post—Praying that Israels God may prevent it from falling into the hands of wicked men. You will hear from me again on the day of sailing if it is the Lords will Amen.

Yours truly a friend and brother
in God's Kingdom
S. Brannan

If you could appoint Br. Appleby to raise another company and go from

---

[42]Brannan referred to the pending threat of arrest based on the January 1846 federal indictment of twelve LDS leaders, including Brigham Young, for counterfeiting.

here next August—it would be striking a mighty blow in our favor for safety
a[nd] security—I have left everything in such a shape in his and Brother Little's hands—that it would take them but a little time to raise a company—
In Boston there are a set of Ambicious numbsculls if I might so call them,
clubed together to purchase a vessel—but it cannot be done—on the principle they have started upon—therefore it must fall through—

December 7, 1858, Copied in Willard Richards Journal of 1845–6, with
the document connected therewith by order of Prest. B. Young.

R. L. Campbell

BRANNAN TO YOUNG, 27 JANUARY 1846,
BRIGHAM YOUNG COLLECTION, LDS ARCHIVES.

New York

27 January 1846

Brother Young Your letter confirming the contract I have made, which I
directed you to address to A. G. Benson, must be written to me and on the
out side and addressed to A. G. Benson—and all will go well—

Yours very respectfully in haste

S. Brannan

Brannan attached a draft of the remarkable contract "drawn up by
Kendall's own hand" that "covenanted" half the lands the Mormons
might settle in the West to Benson and "those whom by written contract
he may have associated with him." Interestingly, it was signed by the elusive Arthur W. Benson and not his better-known partner.

BENSON-KENDALL-BRANNAN CONTRACT, JANUARY 1846,
BRIGHAM YOUNG COLLECTION, LDS ARCHIVES.

Whereas the Latter Day Saints, generally known under the name of Mormons, though devotedly attached to the principles on Which the Government
of the United States and of the several States are founded, have become satisfied that, owing to the prejudices against them which designing men have created in the great mass of the community who do not appreciate their character
nor understand their designs, they cannot under the jurisdiction of any of the
present States, enjoy the privileges and security which their constitutions and
laws promise to all sects and creeds; and whereas they have resolved to seek for
liberty and security beyond the jurisdiction of the states and under the fostering care of the United States within their territories, not doubting that in
becoming a nucleus on the shores of the Pacific around which a new state shall
grow up, constituted of a people who, from their more intimate knowledge of

them will be free from those prejudices which now drive them into exile, thereby affording them peace & security, the only boons they ask at the hands of man; and whereas it is their earnest desire to depart in peace and reach their future homes without that molestation on their pilgrimage which the government of the United States, might under a misapprehension as to their designs, feel themselves called upon to offer; and whereas A. W. Benson [signature] states that he has it in his power to correct any misrepresentations which may be made to the President of the United States and prevent any authorized interference with them on their journey and also to extend to them facilities for emigration, especially by sea, and afford them great commercial facilities and advantages at their new homes: wherefore,

It is covenanted and agreed between A. W. Benson [signature] aforesaid on behalf of himself and such as he may hereafter associate with him on the one part and Saml. Brannan [signature] for and in behalf of the Latter Day Saints, by their principal men, duly authorized on the other part, that the said [blank] shall take the necessary steps to guard the said Latter Day Saints against the effects of misapprehension and prevent interference with them by the Office[r]s or Agents of the United States on their journey westward and shall as far as in his power facilitate trade with them in their new settlement, and promote emigration to strengthen them there; and on the part of the said [blank] for and on behalf of the Latter Day Saints aforesaid, it is covenanted and agreed that in case the said Saints shall be enabled to reach their new homes without molestation from the government of the United States and they or any of them shall acquire lands from the said United States, or from any other source then one half of the said lands shall belong and be conveyed to the said Benson [signature] and those whom by written contract he may have associated with him his and their, heirs and assigns, said lands if not surveyed to be held in common untill a survey shall be made when they shall be *ipso facto* divided by alternate sections, the odd numbers belonging to the said Latter Day Saints and the even numbers belonging to the said Benson [signature] and his associates, but if surveyed they shall be divided by sections, half sections, quarter sections or otherwise so as to carry into effect this agreement in its true nature and intent; and if the said Saints or any of them, or the said Brannan [signature] or any of his associates, assigns or heirs shall within ten years, lay off and establish any city or cities, Town or Towns on the lands acquired by them or any of them, each alternate lot in said cities and Towns, shall belong and be conveyed to the said [blank] and his associates and assigns as hereintofore stipulated in relation to lands acquired, or to the said Saints as the case may require; and it is further stipulated by the said Brannan that the said saints shall exert all their lawful authority and influence to prevent the imposition of any tax on the vacant lands held by said [blank] his associates and assigns, so long as they use due diligence to settle the same, or any higher tax upon vacant City and Town lots held by him and them, than shall be imposed on vacant lots held by resident citizens

And it is further stipulated & agreed by the said Brannan [signature] [on] behalf of said Latter Day Saints, that they shall not in any manner on their journey, or after their arrival in the west, violate the laws or constitution of the United States, it being hereby solemnly declared by him, that their dearest object, and most earnest desire is to enjoy, for themselves, their wives children & neighbors of whatever religion or political faith, the protection which that constitution and those laws promise to all men of whatever creed.

Witness our hands and seals at the City of New York. On the [blank] day of January 1846.

Saml Brannan   A W Benson

Witness
W. I. Appleby

[Postscript in Brannan's hand:]

This is only a copy of the Original which I have filled out—It is no gammon but will be carry [sic] through if you say Amen—it was drawn up by Kendall's own hand—but no person must be known but Mr. Benson.

Dec. 7, 1858, This letter or agreement copied into W. Richards Journal of the year 1845–6, by Prest. B. Y's order.

R. L. Campbell Clerk

B. H. Roberts published this contract in the official LDS church history with only minor editorial corrections.[43] Two other copies survive in LDS Archives, including a "True Copy" of a "Copy of Agreement" dated "24 Jany, 1846," with blanks inserted, apparently meant for Brigham Young's signature. Three sets of initials, A.I.W., B.G.A., and S.B., witnessed our hands and seals at the City of New York. On the 27th day of January 1846." (William I. Appleby and A. G. Benson apparently reversed the order of their initials when they signed as "Witness Present.") The third draft of the "Contract for Mormons to go & take California on share[s], A. G. Benson for A. Kendall" was in clerk Robert Campbell's hand.

Although the Kendall contract offerred to protect the Mormon leaders from federal power, Brannan's bargain did not impress Brigham Young.

---

[43]See Roberts, ed., *History of the Church*, 7:589–91.

The Mormon leadership "concluded that as our trust was in God, and that, as we looked to him for protection, we would not sign any such unjust and oppressive agreement." Young's manuscript history denounced the contract as "a plan of political demagogues to rob the Latter-day Saints of millions and compel them to submit to it, by threats of federal bayonets."[44] Despite this rejection, the Brannan-Benson-Kendall contract had an interesting legacy. Brigham Young believed that it was part of a diabolical conspiracy by Senator Thomas Hart Benton and Secretary of War William Marcy to exterminate the Mormons. In 1852 Young said William Appleby had shown him the Benson contract, and that "Capt. Hooper and Major Holman were astonished at the agreement and it being in existence."[45] As he compiled the official LDS church history in 1858, Wilford Woodruff read "the Article of agreement Between Mr Benson of New York & Samuel Brannan drawn up By Amos Kendel" to Young, who "said not [to] put it in [the] History But Copy it in a Book & seal it up stating on the outside of it what it is & let it lie untill we want it. It may be 20 years hence."[46]

Convinced that the Benson contract provided evidence of the government's perfidy, Young "let it lie" for eighteen years, when he released some of the material to his biographer, Edward Tullidge, whose book was the source for H. H. Bancroft's later account.[47] According to Tullidge, Benson identified Polk as a "silent party" in the affair, but nothing in the surviving Brannan-Young correspondence even hints at the president's direct involvement in the scheme. B. H. Roberts claimed to have seen a Brannan letter alleging "that even the president of the United States, James K. Polk, was 'a silent partner,' in this disgraceful effort to prey upon the fears of an exiled people," but if Roberts actually saw such a letter, it no longer survives at LDS Archives. Roberts acknowledged that Mormon writers "generally discredited" the charge that Polk was involved in this plot, but concluded that Brannan's "very questionable character" made it possible to suspect him of lying and "even of complicity in the schemes of the political sharpers at Washing-

[44]Ibid., 7:591.

[45]Journal History, 8 February 1852.

[46]Kenny, ed., *Wilford Woodruff's Journal*, 5:233–34.

[47]Tullidge, *Life of Brigham Young; or, Utah and Her Founders*, 20.

ton."[48] Roberts may have been right about Brannan's involvement, but the historical record does not link James K. Polk to any financial interest in the intrigue.

Young later claimed that "Poke [sic] wanted to give the Mormons a grant of Land some whare in the west." Secretary of War William Marcy opposed Polk "strongly & said if he did He would resign & do all he Could against him." Senator Benton "had prepared an Armey to destroy the Saints in the wilderness & Nothing saved us ownly our fitting out the Mormon Battalion to go to Mexico at the Call of the Government."[49] Young maintained that Polk had actually granted permission to call out the militias of Iowa, Illinois, and Missouri (and Kentucky, too, if necessary) to "raise a force strong enough to wipe this people out of existence" if the Mormons "refused to comply with the unjust demand on us for troops."[50]

H. H. Bancroft thought it "not at all unlikely" that Thomas Benton tried to turn Polk against the Mormons, but the evidence simply does not support Brigham Young's charge that James K. Polk made a devil's bargain with Benton and Marcy to exterminate the Saints.[51] Young's belief that "President Polk was at the Bottom of" such a plot probably began with misinformation Illinois Governor Thomas Ford disseminated in late December 1845 to hasten the departure of the Mormons from Illinois. Ford informed the Hancock County sheriff that he thought it likely that Polk would "order up a regiment or two of the regular army, and perhaps call on me for the militia" to "prevent the Mormons from going west of the Rocky Mountains."[52] Coupled with Brannan's rumors and the federal indictments of Mormon leaders, Ford's bluff worked and led Young to begin the evacuation of Nauvoo in the middle of winter.

The most compelling evidence against Young's conspiracy theory comes from Polk himself. The president met with Illinois Senator James

---

[48]Roberts, *Comprehensive History*, 3:33, 35.

[49]Kenny, ed., *Wilford Woodruff's Journal*, 5:233–34. In recounting a conversation with Thomas L. Kane in February 1858, Woodruff wrote that in 1846, "it was proposed to give us a part of Kansas Territory." See Ibid., 5:171.

[50]See Young's 1855 speech in Tyler, *A Concise History of the Mormon Battalion*, 352.

[51]Bancroft, *History of California*, 5:473.

[52]Kenny, ed., *Wilford Woodruff's Journal*, 5:233–34; and Roberts, *Comprehensive History*, 2:534.

Semple on 29 January 1846 "in relation to the intended emigration of
the Mormons." Polk said that he "possessed no power to prevent or
check their emigration; that the right of emigration or expatriation was
one which any citizen possessed. I told him I could not interfere with
them on the ground of their religious faith, however absurd it might be
considered to be; that if I could interfere with the Mormons, I could
with the Baptists, or any other religious sect; & that by the constitution
any citizen had a right to adopt his own religious faith."[53]

Brannan's contract would resonate through Mormon history as a
scandal. B. H. Roberts noted that the apostles "did not even deign to
reply to 'A. G. Benson, Kendall and Co.' or take further notice of the
incident; it was closed, so far as the twelve were concerned, and it is not
traceable further."[54] But the involvement of Benson and Kendall with
the affairs of the Mormon church was far from over.

Until We Meet in a Land of Freedom

On his last Sunday in New York, Brannan preached a farewell sermon
and wrote his final letters before the *Brooklyn* sailed. Only one survived,
written to Reuben Hedlock, the president of the British Mission who
would soon be excommunicated for embezzling church funds.

"News from America,"
Latter-day Saints' Millennial Star, 1 March 1846, 76–77.

New York, February 1st, 1846

Dear brother Hedlock,—Yours came to hand some time since, but I have
delayed writing till just before our setting sail for California, in order that I
might be more definite in relation to our departure.

The ship is now loaded, full to the hatchways, about five hundred barrels
of which we will leave at the Sandwich Islands, and the remainder is ours.
There are now in this city, and some on board the vessel, about 230 souls,
that will set sail next Wednesday at two o'clock; all happy and cheerful at the
prospect of deliverance. This afternoon I preached my farewell discourse at
the Hall, and the house was crowded. *I have made arrangements with the Government, that we are to pass out of this country to California, by sea and by land, unmolested.*
I received a letter from the West a few days ago, informing me that

---

[53]Quaife, ed., *The Diary of James K. Polk*, 1:205–06.
[54]Roberts, *Comprehensive History*, 3:36.

another man would be sent on as soon as I am gone, to raise another company; also that a large company was to leave Nauvoo about the 25th of last month, and travel westward until it was time to put in a crop, and then commence planting.

We have received intelligence that brother Woodruff was on his way home.

The reason I did not send you a Messenger, was, I thought that one of the ten was for you; but I have a very neat copy, bound, which I will shall keep for you until you come to California; if I had an opportunity, I would send it now.[55]

You need not forward any more money for Mr. Winchester; he is now in Pittsburgh, and has left the Rigdonites, and I should not be surprised if he went to the West, and crossed the mountains with the Saints.

The Saints in this country are very anxious to emigrate, and will do so as fast as they can procure the means.

A letter will reach me in California, by addressing it to the care of the American consul at Honolulu, on the Sandwich Islands.

I have many letters to write before I leave, and I shall be under the necessity of closing by bidding you farewell, until we meet in a land of freedom. Ask the Saints in England to remember us in their prayers, that we may have a safe passage.

Yours, as ever, in the gospel,
S. Brannan.

Three days later, Samuel Brannan was on his way to California.[56]

---

[55]The fate of this bound copy of the *New-York Messenger* is a mystery, but historians and collectors would obviously appreciate finding it.

[56]John Cumming has recently tracked reports of Lansford Hastings' movements in the spring of 1845. Hastings was traveling down the Ohio to St. Louis on 16 May—perhaps in company with Nauvoo-bound Samuel Brannan. Hastings told the editor of the *Pittsburgh Daily Gazette and Advertiser,* 22 May 1845, that Americans in California "had fully resolved to throw off the Mexican yoke, and that the independent government would be formed next fall in September or October" by a "bloodless revolution." Hastings planned to return to New York and "immediately embark, with a company of emigrants, mostly enterprising young men, who are going to sea. I strongly suspect that this vessel is to carry the means of overturning the Mexican government in California." See Cumming, "Lansford Hastings' Michigan Connection," 21–22. According to "Oregon and California," *New-York Daily Tribune,* 24 June 1844, 2/2, Hastings had changed his mind by late June, but his comments support the claim that Brannan conceived the idea of taking Mormon emigrants to California by sea.

Chapter 5

"To Go by Sea to California"
The *Brooklyn* Voyage

William I. Appleby left his home in New Jersey on 13 January 1846, "in company with a Mr. Levi Riter of Pennsylvania, to purchase articles to Ship by sea for California, for several of the Brethren, procuring Tents in New York &c for those going by land." Appleby and Riter arrived in the city that afternoon and visited the busy waterfront at the Old Slip on the East River, where they "went on Board the Ship 'Brooklyn' that Elder Brannan had chartered to convey the Brethren &c to California. A Splendid Ship she is too of 450 Tons Burthen, with State Rooms &c."[1]

WILLIAM I. APPLEBY:
A BEAUTIFUL SIGHT TO BEHOLD

Appleby wrote a vivid account of the *Brooklyn*'s departure on Wednesday afternoon, 4 February 1846—the same day Brigham Young sent the first wagons across the Mississippi to begin the LDS hegira to the West. On 7 February, Appleby published an extra of the *New-York Messenger*, apparently its last issue. No copies of the paper survive, but Appleby's article appeared in Nauvoo in the last number of *Times and Seasons*.

FROM THE *NEW-YORK MESSENGER EXTRA*.
"To Our Brethren and Friends Scattered Abroad,"
TIMES AND SEASONS, 15 FEBRUARY 1846, 6:1026–27.

We have thought proper to issue an Extra this morning, to inform our brethren and friends scattered abroad, of the ship Brooklyn leaving port last Wednesday, with about two hundred and thirty souls on board including

---

[1]Appleby, Autobiography and Journal, 1841–1856, LDS Archives, 143.

men, women and children, together with three or four passengers. As it regards the getting up of this company of emigrants, we desire to give a brief and correct statement, for the benefit of all concerned. Some two months since, Elder S. Brannan was counselled by President O. Pratt, of this city, before leaving for the west, to charter a vessel, and take out a company of the saints to Oregon or California, and as soon as an opportunity offered, others would follow and endeavor to get beyond the reach of persecution and oppression. Accordingly he obeyed the counsel. It is now about one month since he chartered the ship Brooklyn, Capt. Richardson, for twelve hundred dollars per month, besides paying the Port Charges. In this short space of time, by untiring assiduity, has he collected together the number heretofore stated, consisting of Farmers, Mechanics, &c., the greater part young and middle aged men and women.

The ship was expected to sail on the twenty-fourth or twenty-sixth of January, but in order to have all things in readiness, and complete to make them comfortable she did not get off until last Wednesday. At two o'clock, P.M. she left her moorings and swung around the Pier into the stream.

The Steamboat Sampson came along side, made fast to her, to pilot her down towards the narrows. As she left the wharf, it was a beautiful sight to behold. The noble ship with hundreds of ladies and gentlemen, lining her decks, friends, relations, &c., of the Emigrants. As she left the wharf, three hearty cheers were sent up, by the numerous crowd of Gentlemen upon the Pier, which was as heartily returned, or responded to by those on board the ship. The day was propitious, the bright luminary of the heavens, had passed the zenith of his meridian glory, and was retiring in his stately robes toward the chamber of the West! Yet his oblique rays, as the noble ship passed down the bay, glistened with a propitious smile upon the bosom of the waves, which were now being parted asunder by the bow of the gallant ship. The order at length was given, for all those who did not belong to the ship's company, to get on board the steamboat preparatory to her casting off. Then there was a scene, we feel ourselves inadequate to describe. There you could behold the father bidding adieu to his only son perhaps forever. In another quarter you could see the mother embracing a daughter, and bidding each other farewell. While tears of parental and filial affection, trickled warmly down each others cheeks there, you could also behold the young man and young woman, without Father, Mother, Brother or Sister, (except those of their brothers and sisters endeared to them by the Gospel of the Son of God) willing to leave all behind, sacrifising all the comforts and enjoyments of the scenes of their childhood, and former associations, for the faith which they have embraced, and which they know is true, and are willing to die for the same. They have borne reproach, defamation, obloquy, and scorn, they have been persecuted (or at least the church they belong to,) mobbed, plundered, robbed, driven and murdered, and now they go as exiles, banished from the land of their nativity, the land that gave them birth, the land that is called the "asylum of the oppressed," the liberty that was obtained by the sweat, blood and tears of their fathers, and bequeathed to them as the greatest legacy they could have, has taken its flight and gone, when it comes to be exercised in their behalf.

But to return from my digression after bidding a last farewell, the steamboat was disengaged, and as she rounded to return to the city, three hearty cheers were given by them on board, the steamboat consisting of ladies and gentlemen, (among whom were doctors, clergymen, merchants, ship owners, clerks, &c.,) which was immediately responded to, by three more, from those on board the ship; she then passed on in a beautiful and majestic style, with her topsails and jib spread to the breeze which was blowing directly from the N.N.W., amid the waving of handkerchiefs, hats, &c., until she was finally lost in the distance. Farewell our brethren and sisters in the Lord, we commit you to the care of him whose ye are, and whose name ye have confessed. You have our prayers and hearty wishes, that he who rules the destinies of Empires and Kingdoms, may send his Angel before you. Soothe the howling tempest, stay the rolling billows, vanquish the fell destroyer, and guide you safe to your destined haven. Go then noble ship, with thy noble crew, spread thy canvass to the winds of heaven, and bear them swiftly to their destined port, where no pious "christian" thirsts for gold nor seeks the blood of innocence. The prayers of the Saints of God shall be offered up, for those thou carriest, and that, ere long, thou mayest return and bear another company to the same desired spot. The ship is nearly new, of four hundred and fifty tons measurement; she is well loaded with Agricultural and Mechanical tools enough for eight hundred men, consisting of ploughs, hoes, forks, shovels, spades, plough irons, nails, sickles, nails, glass, Blacksmith's tools, Carpenters, d[itt]o. Millwrights, do. three Grain mills for grinding grain, turning lathes, saw mill irons, grindstones, one printing press and type, paper, stationary, school books consisting of spelling books, sequels, history, arithmetic, astronomy, grammar, Morse's Atlas and Geography, Hebrew Grammar and Lexicon, Slates, &c., &c. Also, dry goods, twine, &c., brass, copper, iron, tin and crockery ware, with provisions and water enough for a six or seven months voyage. They have also on board two new milch cows, forty or fifty pigs, besides fowls, &c. They have every thing on board to make them comfortable; there is thirty-two state rooms on board, with decent births [sic], where they can spread their mattress, and repose content.—They went off joyful and in high spirits; although they have a long journey before them, some fifteen thousand miles to perform, they purpose [propose] touching at the Sandwich Islands, and so on to Oregon or California.

The morning before the Ship's sailing, a gentlemen of Brooklyn, J. M.

Vancott, (a lawyer of great and noted celebrity I understand[2]) presented the emigrants through Mr. Brannan, with one hundred and seventy nine volumes of Harper's Family Library: may the Lord reward him for his kindness, towards a persecuted and oppressed, yet upright and virtuous people.—And not only him, but all those of our friends who have been kind in assisting us, and was not ashamed of us although as the Apostles were "every where spoken evil against," may our Heavenly Father bless such, as much as they do it with a desire to do good, and not from selfish motives is our desire.

A LIKELY LOAD OF YANKEES

Brigham Young instructed Jesse Little to "take the charge and preside" over the LDS church in the East "in the room and place of Elder Sam Brannan who is probably gone to the western coast." He directed Little "so soon as you can fit out another company to follow Elder Brannan, let them sail after him under your charge and presidency, and appoint a good man to succeed you in the East, or take them all along if possible."[3] William Appleby expected to charter a ship to take "another company of Saints to California, in May following, as several in Pennsylvania, New Jersey &c. were desirous of going." Events overtook these plans, and "war being declared between Mexico and the United States, the voyage for the present was abandoned." Jesse Little wrote, "as there was not means enough to warrant chartering a vessel, we did not send it." Appleby reported that Little had "received counsel from the authorities of the Church that no more Ships will go by Sea, from the United States to California. But for the emigrants to go by land, as fast as they can."[4]

Although the episode is fondly cherished in Mormon memory, the facts of the *Brooklyn* voyage are obscured in a haze of romance. The *Brooklyn* is remembered primarily for bringing some 230 Latter-day Saints to the West Coast a year before Brigham Young reached the Great

---

[2]This was Joshua M. Van Cott, a distant relative of John Van Cott; see Hansen, "Voyage of the *Brooklyn*," 51. Lorin Hansen's 1988 article in *Dialogue: A Journal of Mormon Thought* was a breakthrough in scholarship on the subject, and includes an excellent map of the *Brooklyn* voyage on page 56.

[3]Young to Little, 20 January 1846, LDS Archives.

[4]Appleby, Autobiography and Journal, 147–48; and Little, "Circular: Epistle to the Church." Jesse C. Little was president of the Eastern States Mission for 1846–47, but Appleby led the mission from March to November 1847 while Little was with the pioneer company.

Basin, but the true significance of the venture is that it brought the first shipload of American emigrants to California. Typically the Saints were prodigious record keepers, but few contemporary eyewitness accounts of the *Brooklyn* voyage survive—only a fragment of a single diary, three newspaper articles, and two personal letters.[5] Much of the story must be salvaged from the *Brooklyn* recollections. Most of these memoirs were written forty or fifty years after the event and were carefully crafted to reflect their authors' revised political beliefs. These accounts forgot the hostility the Saints felt toward the United States in 1846, although contemporary sources, both Mormon and non-Mormon, consistently described the pilgrims' bitterness toward the American government. The most colorful descriptions of the voyage were composed by passengers who were children in 1846. These tales often transposed and consolidated events, repeating misinformation from a variety of sources. Historians have drawn much vivid detail from the account of poetess Augusta Joyce Crocheron, but she was too young to have recalled any of the stirring incidents she described.[6]

The best published first-hand account of the voyage is the recollection "Twenty Years Ago" by Brannan's former apprentice and lifelong friend, Edward Cleveland Kemble.[7] Kemble did not tell all he knew about the Mormons' plans in California, but he was far more forthright than Brannan's "right-hand man," Scotsman William Glover, whose 1884 dictation is now in the Bancroft Library.[8] Glover's memoir included one of the few references to the communal organization adopted early in the *Brooklyn* voyage. The "people were called together and organized, and an agreement drawn up and signed by all of the men, 65 in number, that they would work together as a company to clear the debt of the ship and make all the preparations they could for the coming of the Church." Members of "S. Brannan & Co." promised to turn

---

[5]Caroline Joyce "kept a daily journal on the ship, *Brooklyn*, also [describing] the first five or six years in California." Her daughter, Augusta Joyce Crocheron, "considered this invaluable from the reliability and fullness of its historic matter and data, and after her demise I searched for it but it was gone." See Crocheron, *Representative Women of Deseret*, 103.

[6]Crocheron, "The Ship Brooklyn," 78–84. Crocheron was born on 9 October 1844.

[7]Originally published in the *Sacramento Daily Union* on 11 September 1866, Kendall's *Brooklyn* memoir is in Rogers, ed., *A Kemble Reader*, 7–25.

[8]See Glover, The Mormons in California, C-D 238, Bancroft Library; published as Bailey, ed., *The Mormons in California*.

"the proceeds of their labor for the next three years into a common fund from which all were to draw their living," instituting "a limited communism" for the company's "convenience and protection."[9] This agreement would lead to untold complications for Brannan and his followers.

Despite the passage of almost seventy years, James Skinner wrote one of the best recollections of the *Brooklyn* voyage in 1915. Although only four years old in 1846, Skinner recalled vivid details of the ship's daily life through a child's eyes, including a burial at sea.

> As I remember the corpse was placed in a sheet or shroud, then placed on a plank, one end resting on the side of the vessel, the other held by supports, the people standing around the corpse. After the service was over, one end of the plank was raised enough to let the corpse gently slide off, and disappear into the mighty and lonesome ocean, My Mother holding me tight in her arms, as if in fear that I, too, might find a watery grave. Some cattle that we had on board that were intended for beef were killed by the rolling and pitching of the vessel [and] were buried at sea. I well remember they were hoisted by block and tackle, swung over the ship's side, then dumped in the sea—food for sharks. I have heard it often said that sharks will follow a vessel for days if there is going to be a death, either man or beast.

Skinner called the *Brooklyn* "a good staunch tub," but noted that the passengers "were herded in like sheep in a pen" during the journey. "We suffered all the hard ships of a sea voyage, such as storms, close confinement, hardtack, sickness, etc., heat, etc., sea sickness." His account of the passage through the doldrums was especially graphic:

> We lay some three weeks becalmed under the burning sun of the Tropics, not a breeze. What air we had was as if it came out of a furnace. The seas were like molten glass. The Captain ordered an awning riged to protect the passengers from the excessive heat. There we would sit or lie panting like [a] lizard in Death Valley. At times a breeze would spring up perhaps half of a mile away, often further away, but none for us. At times a [breeze] would strike us and move the ship perhaps a few miles. O, how happy and refreshed the poor mortals [would] be after their terrible suffering. It was so hot that the pitch was drawn out of the ship's seams. Oh, how the people suffered! I will leave the readers to imagine our suffering.[10]

---

[9]Ibid., 15; and Crocheron, "The Ship Brooklyn," 83. Bailey, *Sam Brannan*, 62, claimed that if its members defaulted on the agreement, the organization's assets would revert to "First Elder" Samuel Brannan.

[10]James Skinner, Autobiography, LDS Archives. For Skinner's recollections of Yerba Buena, see Barker, ed., *San Francisco Memoirs, 1835–1851*, 110–15.

One intriguing record is a photographic fragment of a page of telegraphic descriptions from Daniel Stark's diary. Stark recorded crossing the equator in the night, and that when the ship rounded Cape Horn, the temperature was well below freezing. Although Stark's grandson had the journal in the 1950s, the family has lost track of the manuscript.

SAMUEL STARK,
LIFE AND TRAVELS OF DANIEL STARK AND HIS PEOPLE, 21.

Feb 4 [1846]	Ship Brooklyn sailed, towed out By steamer sampson at 2 pm
9	got in the gull stream [illegible—shipped sea below most all night?]
March 4	Crossed the equator in the night [illegible line]
April 10	Doubled cape horn. colder than 26° [?]
May 1	traded at Juan Fernandez for wood and water
8	Sailed from Juan—
June 20	[l]and at Ouhu & Islands
25	went to native Church
[Ju]ly 1	sailed from Islands [dates obscured by fold]
[3]1	arrived in francisco bay

Before departing New York, Brannan either printed or purchased a list of "Rules and Regulations for the Emigrants on Board the Ship."[11] These regulations governed the company's "daily duty," setting standards for conduct and cleanliness and the times for reveille, meals, and religious services.[12] Edward Kemble remembered that the ship's "camp discipline" was uneven and "for a few weeks every species of routine and system alike seemed unavailable." After crossing the equator, "better order was evoked, and the daily life on shipboard shaped itself to suit the necessities of the situation."[13]

A letter about the *Brooklyn's* voyage that was reprinted throughout the United States appeared in August 1846 in New York's *Journal of Commerce*. It described the pilgrims' progress to the island of Juan Fernandez, the legendary island of Robinson Crusoe, which in 1846 was an abandoned Chilean penal colony. The letter raises a basic question: who wrote it? Edward C. Kemble and John Eagar, former apprentices on the

---

[11]See *New-York Messenger Extra*, cited in *Times and Seasons*, 15 February 1846, 6:1127–28.

[12]For an example of the actual regulations, see the copy at the LDS Library, 82151-LIBR-88, on which someone has written "Brooklin." This may have been a standard form not original with the *Brooklyn*.

[13]Rogers, ed., *A Kemble Reader*, 20.

Messenger, have long been identified as possible authors, but neither man is its likely writer. Internal clues identify the author, who joined the captain on the quarterdeck; it seems likely that only the emigrants' leader, who shared Richardson's table, would be on such intimate terms with the captain.[14] The *Brooklyn* encountered much worse weather than the letter described, for Edward Kemble, George Sirrine, and James Skinner all recalled "intensely cold weather" in the southern latitudes. Whose interests were served by telling lies designed to promote emigration to California? Samuel Brannan. Finally, the letter's overblown style and cockeyed optimism are unmistakably Brannanesque.

"PROGRESS OF THE MORMON EMIGRANTS FROM THIS CITY,"
NEW-YORK TRIBUNE, 27 AUGUST 1846, I.

Last Winter a company of Mormon families left this city in the ship Brooklyn, Capt. Richardson, for California. So far as morality, enterprise, intelligence and habits of industry are concerned, they presented fair specimens of the universal Yankees, and seemed well fitted to lay the foundations of a great nation. The following extracts from a letter by one of their number give a favorable account of their progress:

ISLAND OF JUAN FERNANDEZ, MAY 8TH, 1846.

The second day we experienced a heavy sea, and on the following Tuesday laid to all day, in a heavy gale of wind, which occasioned a great deal of suffering among the passengers, from sea sickness, and being rolled from one side of the ship to the other, owing to their weakness; but they bore it without a murmur, or being in any way terrified of their danger, which was not a little.

Captain Richardson (God bless the man!) and myself stood watching those noble "sticks" that have since done us such a good service, with our hearts lifted up to the God of nations to spare them in his mercy. He did so, and the next day the ship flew before the wind like a thing of magic. We had a quick passage to Cape Horn, and found that the terrors of the passage round it, which had been depicted previous to our sailing, were all imaginary. Our little children were every day on deck, attending their schools, jumping rope, and engaged in all the other amusements resorted to pass off the time. We had no freezing weather, and at no time was the thermometer in our cabin below 50°. On the deck, at one time, it fell for a few hours as low as 36°, which was accounted for by Capt. R. by our passing near an iceberg. We ran

---

[14]George K. Winner, a master mariner, might have had access to the quarterdeck, but no samples of his writing survive to compare to the *Journal of Commerce* letter.

up to the Cape with a fair wind, then took a West wind and ran up to 60° South latitude in four days, then took a South wind till we had made our longitude West of the Cape, and then took a fair wind down the Pacific, which lasted till a few days ago. All was then life, joy and gladness, in the expectation of soon going ashore at Valparaiso. We dealt out fresh water for all to wash themselves and their clothes in. Capt. R. also scoured up the ship and anticipated the astonishment of the natives at such a likely load of Yankees; for they certainly look one hundred per cent. better than when they left New York, and since we started everything has gone on with harmony and peace. We experienced, however, a heavy gale from the South, and were unable to continue our course with safety; so we scud before the wind, until it hauled to the East, and we thought it best to land at this Island.

There are but two families living on the Island, and they are distant only 20 days' sail from Fuchywana on the coast above Valparaiso. We found excellent water, and very easy to be obtained, about two rods from the beach; and plenty of firewood on the east side of the left hand mountain as you enter the harbor. Goats, hares and pigs abound here. The first settlement on this Island was burnt by the Peruvians six years ago; the forts destroyed, the canoes sunk in the harbor, and the convicts carried away. The last settlement was abandoned four years ago, at the time of the earthquake at Valparaiso, when the Island sunk and rose about fifty feet. I have been informed that ships watering at Valparaiso have to pay one dollar for every thirty gallons from the water-boats. If that be the case, our ships had better water at this Island.

The harbor here is said to be much the safest in a gale from the North— it lying on the North-east side of the Island, which makes it easy for ships to put to sea, if they do not lie too near the shore. We took on board 18,000 gallons of water yesterday, and to-day we are getting our wood on board. and we expect to sail to-morrow. We came to anchor in the harbor on the fourth of May, at 1 o'clock P.M. The ship has proved herself to be better than she was represented, and our captain and first mate have been good and kind to our company. I believe every book in the little library has been read through.[15]

JOHN EAGAR: THE UNSETTLED STATE OF CALIFORNIA

Materials H. H. Bancroft gathered in the 1880s at the LDS church historian's office for his histories of Utah and California included a

---

[15]*Millennial Star*, 1 October 1846, 78–79, reprinted part of this letter from the *American Sun*. Through the newspapers, Mormon leaders monitored the *Brooklyn's* progress. Willard Richards at Winter Quarters noted, "We hear good news from Brother Brannon & those who sailed from New York for the West Coast. They were far on their journey in May." See Richards to T. Bullock, 8 October 1846, Henrietta Rushton Bullock Collection, LDS Archives.

short biographical statement by John Eagar. Eagar had died in Utah in 1864, but it seems the historian's office acquired his history about 1860.[16] Yet the sketch was filled with misinformation and misspelled Eagar's name, so perhaps the historian's office composed the version provided to Bancroft by combining the *Journal of Commerce* letter with information taken from Eagar or his family.[17]

JOHN EAGAR,
UNCLASSIFIED DOCUMENT, LDS ARCHIVES.

John Eager [*sic*] born Auburn, Cayahoga Co. N.Y. Feby 4, 1846 [*sic*]; gives the following statement pertaining to the ship Brooklyn.

The ship, Brooklyn, 450 tons burthen, was commanded by Captn. ~~Ritcheson~~ Richardson, and left New York February 4, 1846, having on board 236 passengers, all of whom were Mormons except Frank Ward. The company were well supplied with implements of husbandry and necessary tools for establishing a new settlement . . . [18]

May 9th, the Company left Juan Fernandez and reached the Sandwich islands on the 25th of June and anchored in the harbor of Honolulu; the island of Oahu the residence of King Kamehamaha; where the company remained eight days, to discharge cargo, and receive wood and water. ~~Our~~ Bro Winmer [George K. Winner] on going ashore was asked by a native, if he was a missionary to which he answered in the affirmative; the native informed him that his daughter was in the next room, and that he might visit her; bro. W. excused himself.

July 3; on leaving Honolulu Commodore Stockton ~~came~~ went a board and inspected the Brooklyn, and advised the passengers to procure arms on account of the unsettled state of California; the ships company accordingly bought condemned muskets at $3 and $4 each.

The ship Company celebrated the 4th of July, were inspected, and discharged their arms. There were fifty Allen's revolvers and each man had a military cap and suit of clothes. The company was drilled ~~by Cap.~~

July 29 [*sic*], arrived at in the harbor of San Francisco, ~~which at that t~~ and landed at Yerba Buena (which signifies a good herb) and which the

---

[16]The Eagar statement is in clerk Robert Campbell's handwriting, with the note, "This paper is inserted in History Nov. 30, [1859?]." Jones, "Ship *Brooklyn* Passenger Gravesite Location Search Project," provided Eagar's death date.

[17]The Bancroft Library's four-page manuscript copy of the memoir is available as Eagar, John, "Statement concerning the voyage of the ship, Brooklyn." The statement was "Copied from the original in the Church Historian's Office, Salt Lake City." The handwritten copy of the *Journal of Commerce* letter in the same collection, C-D 238:3, Bancroft Library, is attributed to "Kemble, Edward Cleveland?"

[18]Material derived from the *Journal of Commerce* letter is omitted.

Spainiards used as a tea—found twelve or fifteen spanish houses; Yerba Buena was subsequently named San Francisco. The company obtained a city lot and encamped thereon. There was one wind mill which tried to grind. ~~Captain Sutter who had bought out a Russian post, paid them Russian's yearly instalments of grain.~~

For their general benefit of the imigrants who arrived in the Brooklyn ~~company, they~~ formed themselves into a company under the name of S Brannan & Company. They branched out into the various mechanical & agricultural pursuits necessary for the purpose of building up a new settlement. They took up city lots and improved the same. When they landed they had three months provisions. The mechanics could get money for their labor. Eight ~~would procure~~ dollars bought a beef ox. There were fifteen or twenty white inhabitants, Americans and English who kept stores and bought the tallow and hide from the settlers. If any person rode into the country & killed a fat beef all the owner wished, was that such person would hang up the hide and tallow to be secure from the destruction of animals. A hide was considered a dollar, bank note.

Commodore Stockton arrived ~~at Yerba Buena~~ soon after and took possession of the country in the name of the United States, planting the American flag on the public square of Yerba Buena.

The First Expedition of its Kind by Water

On Sunday, 21 June 1846, the American frigate *Congress* lay anchored in Honolulu Roads. The ship's log reported, "Boarded American Ship Brooklyn. 140 days from New York. Bound for California." Commodore Robert Stockton visited the ship and reported that the United States was at war with Mexico. The next day, the supply ship *Erie* entered "the Harbor. the Emegrant ship Brooklyn also went in."[19]

Both Honolulu papers printed accounts of the ship's voyage derived from Brannan. The article in *The Polynesian* described the party's expectations and hopes, indicating that they were well informed about their destination and unconcerned about their reception by Mexican authorities. Brannan's tale contained particulars, such as the projected size of the 1846 overland emigration, that dovetail with the stories Lansford Hastings told on his arrival in California. The size of the company—178 emigrants—was perhaps given to shield Captain Richardson, for that is

---

[19]Log of the *Congress*, 16 September 1845–12 January 1849, RG 24, National Archives.

the number reported in the New York press, and also the number of passengers that the *Brooklyn* could legally accommodate.

"ARRIVAL OF THE BROOKLYN WITH EMIGRANTS FOR CALIFORNIA,"
THE POLYNESIAN, 27 JUNE 1846, 22/3.

The arrival of the Brooklyn, 136 days from New York, with 178 emigrants for California has created no little interest in our town. This being the first expedition of its kind by water to the El Dorado of the 19th century, we are induced to give our readers the following particulars obtained from Samuel Brannan, Esq., the principal of the company, and who appears to have been chiefly concerned in organizing the expedition. The company consists of 50 families, including some 70 men, 60 women and 48 children, some of whom are infants. They have on board about $30,000, invested in agricultural implements and the necessary articles for forming a settlement, with a stock of clothing for two years. The men are said to be supplied with rifles and know how to use them. Tents have been provided for habitations until houses can be erected. Their destination is the north side of the bay of San Francisco, where they design to establish a commercial town.

Attention will be given to agriculture and the lumber business in order to raise an export. It is in contemplation to load the Brooklyn immediately upon arrival with cedar logs direct for China. The ship will enter at Monterey. No real difficulties are apprehended in the way of landing by the Mexican authorities, though so numerous a party will undoubtedly be received with some jealousy. This company is but the forerunner of a large emigration to arrive this season overland, consisting, it is said, of 15000 individuals, mostly of the Mormon faith. Two thousand young men were despatched early in the year to a certain locality on the route to plant a crop, which would come forward in season for the main body, in case they should fall short of provisions. The body would spread themselves over the country, taking farms, &c., in the vicinity of the bay. From what we understand, they design to occupy the country and trust to future events as to their civil government. It may terminate in entire independence.

The friends of the emigrants in the United States and elsewhere will be gratified to learn that their voyage has been prosperous, and that the company have encountered but few of the hardships anticipated from sea life. The weather has been good, and so has their general health. Eleven deaths have taken place, which we report. A birth occurred in the Atlantic of a boy who was named after his birthplace; and the Pacific gave name to a girl born a few days before their arrival here.[20] An increase of several more is

---

[20]These children were John Atlantic Burr, whose career as a cattleman attached his name to the Burr Trail in southern Utah; and Georgiana Pacific Robbins, destined for "prominence in the musical life of early Salt Lake City." See Everett, "The Ship *Brooklyn,*" 236.

expected before arrival in California, and a number of marriages are to take place. The ship stopped 6 days at Juan Fernandez and took in 10,000 gallons of water. The weather off the cape was pleasant. Capt. Richardson speaks in the highest terms of the correct deportment and general harmony of his numerous passengers in every respect. Religious services and a school have been regularly held. They are well supplied with school books. Mr. Brannan has with him a press and intends establishing a paper to be called the California Star.—There are many practical farmers and master mechanics in the company, who all form, until well established in the country, a joint stock concern.—They will expend considerable money here for supplies. If their settlement flourish[es], as in that delightful climate it can scarcely fail of doing, it will create a new market for the produce of these islands, and we may speedily look for a comfortable exchange of commodities. We wish for our own part that some of the bone and sinew, industry and enterprise thus to be thrown upon the soil of California could be applied to our own vacant rich lands, which now literally encumber the kingdom. They will find owners and workers before long, we trust, even among the natives, who must be taught that potatoes are not the climax of agriculture.

The Brooklyn sails in a few days for the coast.

The Mormon pilgrims received a surprisingly cordial welcome from Protestant minister and newspaper publisher Samuel C. Damon.[21] His account is one of the best contemporary sources on the voyage of the *Brooklyn*. Damon's list accounted for 214 passengers, but despite omissions and misspellings, it is exceptionally useful. The listing of the ship's position when deaths occurred provides a rough map of the voyage. Damon's discussion of Mormon origins is omitted here, but his sympathetic view of the emigrants' political alliances and religious beliefs was derived directly from Samuel Brannan. He asserted that "all the Mormons in the U. S. are reputed to have voted for" James K. Polk, and boasted "that his election turned upon their vote." It would not take long, however, for Brannan to regret bragging about his intimacy with Joseph Smith. To show his appreciation, Brannan presented Damon with a load of Bibles and "three doubloons," a donation valued at forty-eight dollars.[22]

---

[21]Born in Massachusetts in 1815, Damon graduated from Amherst College and Princeton and Andover seminaries. He arrived in Honolulu with a new bride in October 1842, where he served as chaplain for the American Seaman's Friend Society. Damon founded *The Temperance Advocate and Seaman's Friend* in January 1843, but soon shortened the newspaper's name to *The Friend*.

[22]"Bibles! Bibles!"; and "For the Support of The Friend," *The Friend*, July 1, 1846, 103.

THE FRIEND, 1 JULY 1846, 100–02.

Joseph Smith, jr., Founder of "Church of Latter-Day-Saints," (or Mormons)—Origin—
Book of Mormons—History—Creed—present condition and prospective plans of the
Sect—California, &c., &c.

The arrival of the "Brooklyn," has brought to our shores a large company
of emigrants, on their passage from New York to California. Rumors are
afloat and numerous inquiries are made respecting the origin and sentiments
of those people, and the desire has been expressed that we should furnish for
the readers of the Friend, some information upon this subject. It cannot be
expected that an extended account would appear in our columns, but we offer
the following summary of information gathered from various sources . . .

Belief or Creed.—The following summary of their articles of belief, we
publish upon the authority of Mr. Brannan, who is the leader of the company now bound to California. We would remark in regard to Mr. Brannan,
that he is a young man, about 27 years of age,—a native of Saco, Me.—a
printer by trade—has resided for nearly three years in the family of Joseph
Smith, Jr.—been the editor of a weekly paper in New York city, called the
New York Messenger, and is intending to establish another paper on his
arrival in California . . .

As to the principles of this people upon other subjects—they profess to
advocate civil and religious liberty. During the election of President Polk, all
the Mormons in the U. S. are reputed to have voted for him, as the representative of the principles of democracy; and they assert that his election
turned upon their vote. In regard to slavery, they assert that whoever adopts
their views will be opposed to the system, and if he hold[s] slaves, that he
will very soon give them up.[23] The principle of total abstinence finds many
supporters among them; and as a body they would discountenance the use
of intoxicating liquors.

Their present Condition and Prospective plans.—As has been already stated, they
estimate their numbers by hundreds of thousands, very many of whom have
come off from other denominations. This is true of the company on board
the "Brooklyn."—Some have come from the Baptists, others from the
Methodists, a few from the Presbyterians, while almost every denomination
has its representative among them. So far as we are able to learn, California is
now to be their grand central rendezvous, while the beautiful region around
San Francisco Bay is the chosen spot where the latter-day-saints propose to
settle. Abating much from the highly colored descriptions which we have
always heard respecting that region, it must still be regarded as a most enchant-
ing spot, and the most desirable location for a colony to be found upon the
long line of the North and South American sea coast. The natural facilities of

---

[23]This reflected Brannan's personal beliefs, not LDS church policy.

the country and bay conspire to render it certain, that many years cannot elapse before flourishing cities and villages will diversify the scene. The watch-word of the Mormons now is "California." The few scores of emigrants on board the "Brooklyn" are but a fraction of the immense numbers already on their way thither. The difficulties in which these people found themselves at Nauvoo, and other parts of the states, have led to the resolution to "break up" and "be off" for California. From various reports, we conclude that about 25,000 have left Nauvoo and other parts of the states for California; while the report has reached us, that a vessel with Mormon emigrants has already left Liverpool, and that others will soon follow, all bound for California.

Whatever views different classes of christians and politicians, may form of the dogmas and tenets of this people; one thing is certain, that this gen-eral movement in the four quarters of the globe, and [their] rush for Cali-fornia, opens a new chapter in the colonizing and peopling of a sparsely inhabited and fruitful region of our globe. The influence which their arrival and settlement must have upon the present condition of California, is quite uncertain; but should the tide of emigration continue to flow in, (as it undoubtedly will) California must very soon become a very different coun-try from what it has been,—civily, socially, morally and religiously. We can-not but hope for a brighter day, and most certainly we are far from taking a dark view of the subject.

Before closing our remarks, we feel ourselves in duty bound to give pub-licity to the testimony of Capt. Richardson, master of the "Brooklyn" in regard to the general character of the emigrants as it has been developed during a long voyage round Cape Horn. Of their general behavior and char-acter, he speaks in the most favorable manner. They have lived in peace together, and uniformly appeared to be quiet and orderly. They are going with the full determination of making a settlement, and have brought ploughs, carts, scythes and all kinds of husbandry implements and tools for ship and house building. They have not lost sight of the means for promot-ing education and schools. Many of the emigrants coming from New Eng-land and the middle states, are inclined to transplant some of the noble institutions of their native region. Capt. R. informs us that during most of the passage they have maintained orderly and well conducted daily religious exercises, which still continue while lying in port.

During the passage of the "Brooklyn" there have occurred 10 deaths, (4 adults and 6 children,) and 2 births. A male child born before doubling the Cape, was called *Atlantic*, and a female born this side is called *Pacific*.

This numerous company of emigrants are soon to leave for their new home; may it prove more peaceful than the one they have left. So far as their minds may have been led to embrace error, may it be renounced. That we differ upon many essential points of doctrine and practice is clearly manifest, yet our best wishes and prayers go with them. May the fostering smiles of a kind and benignant Providence rest upon them. They are to lay the foundations of society, and institutions, social, civil and religious. O, may they be such that coming generations shall rise up and call them blessed.

☞The following is a list of deaths on board the ship Brooklyn:

February 14th: the infant of Joseph Nichols died with the diarrhoea after about two weeks illness, aged 2 yrs. and 18 days, and was buried the same day at 11 o'clock A.M. in 1st. 37 N. long. 50 W.

Friday, February 20th. Six o'clock in the evening, Mr. Elias Ensign died, after an illness of about three weeks, aged 59 years and 5 months. His body was consigned to the deep the next day at eleven o'clock, in lat. 19 30 N. long. 26 W.

Saturday, February 28th; the son of John R. Robbins died at 10 o'clock P.M. with the scarlet fever after an illness of three days, aged 5 years and 18 days, and was buried in lat. 3 16 N. long. 25 W.

March 6th; the son of Mr. John Fowler died with the diarrhoea, aged one year seven months and 28 days.

March 7th; six o'clock A.M., Miss Eliza Ensign died of the consumption, aged 20 years 8 months and 17 days. She had been confined to her bed about two weeks previous to her death. Lat. 3 S. long. 27 W.

Saturday, March 14th; ten o'clock A.M. the son of Mr John R. Robbins died of the consumption, aged 1 year 5 months and 16 days. Lat. 15 30 S. long. 32 W.

Tuesday March 17th; ten o'clock P.M. the son of Mr. Charles C. Burr died of the diarrhoea, age one year and five months.

Friday, March 26th; Edward Miles, one of the ship's crew died with the cramp in the stomach after eight days sickness.

Friday [sic], 27th March; two o'clock A.M. the daughter of Mr. George K. Winner died of the cankered sore throat, aged 6 months and 7 days.

Wednesday April 1st; two o'clock P.M. Mr. Silas Aldrich died of the dropsy in the stomach, aged 43 years 8 months and 20 days; and was consigned to the deep at ten o'clock A.M. the next day, in lat. 43 S. long. 47 W.

Wednesday, May 6th; Mrs. Laura Goodwin, wife of Mr. Isaac Goodwin, died aged 32 years 11 months and 23 days. Her death was occasioned by a fall which she received soon after we set sail from New York; she left seven children. Her remains were buried on the Island Juan Fernandez.

☞List of passengers on board the Brooklyn:

S. Brannan, Lady and child; Fanny M. Corwin; Robert Smith, Lady and two children; Wm. Atherton, and Lady; Q. S. Sparks, Lady and child; Mary

THE *BROOKLYN.*
From a print from the Hirschl & Adler Gallery Inc., New York.

Hamilton; J. M. Horner and Lady; E. Ward Poll, Lady and 2 children; Samuel Johnson; Cyrus Irea; Wm. Evans, Lady and four children; Jonathan Griffiths, Lady and two children; M. A. Meader, Lady and child; Peter Poole; Mary Poole; Elizabeth Poole; Jonathan Cade and Lady; Wm. Stout, Lady and child; Isaac Leigh and Lady; J. A. C. Austin, Lady and three children; Emaline A. Lane; Prudence Aldrich, son and daughter; Angeline M. Lovet; Lucy Nutting; Barton Morrey, Lady and two sons; Daniel Stark, Lady and two children; Mary Murrey; Isabella Jones; Joseph Nichols, Lady and child; Thomas Tompkins, Lady and two children; Henry Rowland and son; Wm. Kettleman, Lady and six children; George Kettleman; Richard Knowles and Lady; Robert Petch, Lady and two children; Elisha Hyatt, Lady and son; Jerusha Ensign and son; Jerusha H. Fowler and four children; John R. Robbins, Lady and two children; Sophia P. Clark; George R. Winner, Lady and six children; John Phillips; Newel Boylen, Lady and 3 children; John Joyce, Lady and child; Joseph Hicks; Eliza Savage; Zelnora S.

Snow; James Light, Lady and child; Jacob Hays; Earl Marshal, and Lady; Simeon Stivers; Caroline Warner and three children; H. A. Skinner, Lady and child; A. L. D. Buckland; Hannah D Buckland; Hannah T. Read and child; James Scott; Patrick McCue, Lady and four children; Isaac Goodwin and six children; Nathan Burr and Lady; Charles C. Burr, Lady and child; John Eager; George W. Sirrine; John Sirrine, Lady and child; Edwin Kemble; Abram Combs, Lady and three children; Mercy M. Narrowmore and child;[24] John Reed; Christiana Reed; Isaac Addison, Lady and daughter; Orrin Smith, Lady and six children; John Kettleman; Thomas Kettleman; Sarah Kettleman; Joseph R. Fisher; Mary Ann Fisher; Lucy Eagar and three children; Mary Eagar; George Still, Lady and three children; Wm. Glover, Lady and three children; Jessee A. Stringfellow; A. G. Haschal, Ambrose T. Moses, Lady and four children; Isaac Robbins, lady and two children.

EMELINE AMANDA LANE: A VERY GOOD VOYAGE SO FAR

Twenty-one-year-old Emeline Amanda Lane accompanied her married sister, Octavia Ann Austin, to California. The Lane family was from Suffield, Connecticut, and Emeline's letter was addressed to her father, Ashbel Lane, in Hartford County. She gave a short but vivid account of the voyage and described a few of the complex family relationships that connected the *Brooklyn* passengers. Her charming account of life in the Hawaiian Islands indicates that the "long letter" she proposed writing upon reaching California would have been equally interesting.

In California Emeline Lane married George Warren Sirrine, whose account of their courtship and wedding follows. She gave birth to a daughter, Sarah Ann, and, sadly, died about 1850.[25]

EMELINE LANE TO ASHBEL LANE, 29 JUNE 1846,
LDS ARCHIVES.

Honolula, Oahu
June 29th 1846

Dear parents and friends,

I joyfully embrace this opportunity of writing you a few lines knowing

---

[24]Mercy M. Naramore and her son Edwin stayed in Hawaii. See Jones, "Ship *Brooklyn* Passenger Gravesite Location Search Project."

[25]"The Brooklyn Saints," in Carter, ed., *Our Pioneer Heritage*, 3:517, 577. This compilation published an edited section of the Emeline Lane letter, attributing it to her sister.

that you are very anxious to hear from us and know whether we are dead or alive, well we are here at the Sandwich iselands and are all well as usual. Octavia has stood it remarkably well considering how feeble she was when she started from home. She has had one poor spell during the first warm we[a]ther of or about the time we crossed the line. The children have been well since they got over being seasick. I hardly know what to write about firste I have so many things to say, in fact a sheet of paper is a poor medium to my notion to communicate ones thoughts. Still there is no other recourse while [we are] as widely separated [and] we must gladly except of it. We have had a very good voyage so fare. We havent had but one severe gale on our long [*tear*] voyage[?]. We have come twenty thousand miles and are allmoste to our destined home I truste. We crossed the equator in 28 days after we started from Newyorke. We had a very good passage around Cape horn. The days were very shorte, there we could hardly get a glimps[e] at the sun for several days but we got around firste rate. We stopt at the Iseland of Juan fernandese to get wood and water which we did.

I presume you would like to heare something about this island we have read so much about. Well I have been on to it and spente several days. It is moste all mountains and [has] quite a gloomy appearance. I thinke the valyes are very narow but quite fertile and the plain land alonge the shore is allso fertile. The mountains are very steepe [with] the clouds allways resting upon them. Some of them are covered with trees. The Iseland is 9 miles long. There is onely 8 persons on the Iseland. There was formely more but there has been an earthquake and they all left the Iseland. Their is no buildings on it allthough there is the ru[i]ns of some. They said there was once quite a citty they say here once. This iseland is the first land we saw after we started from Newyorke. We talked of stopping at valperuso but did not on account of the wind which would make it very dificult and we thought it was the best plan to stop at Juan. We stayed at Juan 5 days [and] we have not had any rough wether [and] since we have been on the pacific it is quite smooth.

I will now tell you something about this Iseland [Hawaii] where we are. We come into this porte the 22 day of June and our shipe is lying at the wharf. The native[s] received us very kindly—there was hundreds it seemed waiting to see us land. We have been treated well by all classes. Since we have been here all the Americans were very glad to seey [*sic*] us. We have been invited to come and see them. The British Consul gave brother Brannan a letter of recomendation to the consul at Monterray. When we arrived here the American man of war was here and has now gone ahead to protect us. Their is a number of whaleships [that] are here in porte. The native[s] of the Iseland are very kind and friendly but they are very indolent. It is the greatest place for gossip I ever see. We have createed a good deal of excitement here among them but they think very well of us. I believe the mis[si]onaries treate us very well but I dont think they would care about us staying very long though brother Branon has preached once to them. I went to the native church laste Sunday and heard one of the mishonaries preach in the native tounge. He said a good deal about us I afterwards heard [but] I could not understand him. I donte think the mishonaries have done much good here. They degrade the nation while here. The white ladies are drawn around by the natives. I saw a greate many drawn to church by them and men to[o] which I think they would [have] looked better had they gone afoot. Many of the native[s] weare scarsely any clothing at all. They are rather darke complexion but not black. They have strate hare black eyes and are very large size very fleshy people. This Iseland is very fertile if it was onely cultivated. It is very beatiful up in the valies. I have spent one day their. Moste of the rich merchants live there.[26] I went to Mr. Lads[27] while I was there and took dinner with them—they was glad to see us. They told us the missonaries lived much better than the minesters do in the states. If they wanted any thing they could have it by just saying the word. They live in the greatest luxurry—they say they have the natives for theyr servants to come and go at there call. I went to the American hospitall. It is a beautfiull retired place. There is [illegible] beatifull plantation belonging to it. I saw coffe and sugar cane sweete potatoes growing there and various kinds of fruits. We had pineapples and grapes in abundance and all kinds of melons. The houses here are built of straw and sticks. They look very curious indeed [and] the walls and fences are made of mud. There is but a few fraimed houses and they are owned by the whites. A house as good as Juluses[28] was would coste four thousand dollars here. They cannot get wood to build houses of theire [tear] [own stra]w houses are very pretty though. I must now begin to draw my letter to a close as my space is getting small and you will please excuse all blunders as I have writen in a hury. I have made a greate many mistakes I dont know as you can read it. I am a going to write a long letter when I get to California. We have sent you a paper [from] which you will learn something of our voyage. I shall write when I get my mind composed all about our voyge and about our home. I cannot compose here or write at all. I want to have you write and send [mail at] every opportunity you can. I partly wrote a letter and sent [it] by a ship [but] I dont know as you will know what it means. I have wanted to see you very much but I have not wanted to go back and stay. I have enjoued myself first rate [and] have not regreted I come. We have a first rate company. O I wish you was all

[26]Nuuanu Valley was Honolulu's first suburb and is still home to many wealthy Hawaiians.

[27]William Ladd, whose Ladd & Company had been active in Honolulu since 1833 but was bankrupt in November 1844. See Nunis, The Journal of a Sea Captain's Wife, I, note 10, 16.

[28]This apparently referred to Emeline's brother-in-law, Julius Augustus Caesar Austin, husband of the fortuitously named Octavia.

going with us. O I wish you would come! Caroline [Augusta Perkins Joyce] and Julus [Austin] and Charles[?]. I want to see you and father and Mother. I must now close—give my love to all enquireing friends [and] tell them I want to have [them] write to us. I intend to write as often as I have an oppurtunity to send. I will now let Octavia write.

From your affectionate daughter, Emeline Lane

Dear Parents & Brothers & Sisters I have taken this time to write a few lines but one sheet of paper [is little] to communicate ones thoughts. If you knew my feelings for your eternal happiness I want to have [you] come where we are to live & die with the Saints of God.

Give my love to Sister King & enquiring Friends. One thing more we met with some relatives on board, Brother Nathan Burr married Chloe Clarke, grandchild of Thomas Pratt, grandmothers brother, she was acquainted with Aunt Stocking, has been to Uncle Stannerds house. They are first rate folks, she looks some like you mother. Julus sends his love

Octavia A. Austin, to you all.

G. W. SIRRINE:
ICE BURGHS AS LARGE AS THE SUPERSTITION MOUNTAINS

Although not an eyewitness account, Warren Leroy Sirrine's sketch of his father's adventures—including his romance with his first wife, Emeline Lane—is perhaps the most entertaining of all the *Brooklyn* narratives. The spelling and the facts in George Warren Sirrine's memoir are not perfect, but his son seems to have captured perfectly the voice of a wonderful storyteller.

WARREN LEROY SIRRINE,
A LITTLE SKETCH OF THE LIFE OF GEORGE WARREN SIRRINE,
LDS ARCHIVES, 5–7.

When G. W. Sirrine heard some Mormon Missionarys preaching he was very much interested in what they preached and when the meeting was over he went and had a long talk with them and got some of thear litature and read it and was soon baptised. And when he went and told his Mother and his only sister who was eight years older than George. She said George if you think no more of yourself and Mother and I than to join that class of people, go and stay with them for I never want to see you again nor hear from you as long as I live. So he bid them all goodbye and that he was going to sail on the old Ship Brooklin for California.

And when the old Ship Brooklin was about ready to sail Samuel Brannan who was Captain of the Mormon Emagrants called them all together and told them that theare was several of the Emegrants that did not have enough money to pay thear fare from N.Y.C. to California. And he wanted every one that could spare any money to let him have it for he did not want to leave any of them behind. So they raised money enough to pay for all of the tickets. On the fourth day of Febuary 1846 they sailed out of New York Harbor. They pased by the island of JoeAn Fernandies, the island that Robinson Crusoe was suposed to of been cast away on. And when they got to Honalula they stoped theare a few days to get fresh water, fruit, and fuel. Well everybody was eating fruit but George Sirrine. And Sam Brannan went up to him and asked what was the matter that he had seen every body eating fruit but him. Don't you like fruit? George said, "Branan, theare is a pretty good reason why I am not eating any fruit. When you called for everybody that had money to spare to give, so I gave you every dollar I had—never kept back a dime." Branan said, "I never expected you to give all you had. Here is $50.00 go and get some fruit."

George had charge of a warehouse in N.Y.C. and handled a great many ban[a]nas. So he knew how to buy. He bought one bunch that was nearly ripe and the rest of them was pretty green. So he had ban[a]nas untill he got to Yerba Beuna, California. You could get the largest bunches theare were for fifty cents.

While they were in Honulo several of the men took a big flat boat that would hold about five tons and went out fishing. You could catch a fish as fast as you could throw your line in and it wasn't but a short time untill they had all the boat would carry and one of the men caught a fish several feet long, when he went to take it off his hook it was so heavily charged with electricity that it knocked him down. Then another man tried it and he got a heavy shock and two or three other men tried it and they all got a shock. When G.W.S. tried it he only got a light shock.

For several days theare was a great storm and they were driven out of thear course and it got so bad they had to take down all of thear sails. And they were at the mercy of the wind. And they got Sixty two and a half degrees of South Lattitude. G.W.S. was raised near the Hudson River and some times it would freeze two and a half feet of ice. But he said he never had seen any cold weather untill then. And he could see the ice burghs as large as the Superstition Mountains. Captain Richardson called them all together and told them the condition they were in and that probely theare was only about one vessil out of 1000 (thousand) that ever lived to get out of theare. But that if every man would volenteer his servisies probely they could save the vesil, as the pasengers had all paid thear fare he could not compell them to work. At that all the sailors fell on thear knees and began to pray. But the Captain told them that there was no time for prayrs it was work or drown. Brannan, Sirrine and several of the saints stepped up to the Captain and said Captain we have done our praying, what shall we do. He said take those crow bars, hand spikes, cord wood, or anything they could strike the ropes with and go right around the vesil and for the other men to take shovels and through the ice overboard. It was so cold that you had to breathe through your nostrils. About five minutes was as long as any of them could work then thear nostrils would close up. Then you have to go down in the cabbin and get thawed out. G.W.S. was a very strong man and no matter how hard he worked it seemed as though the cold would go right through him. After about one and a half hours and they had throwed one hundred tons of ice, Captain Richardson called them all together and said Boys you have saved the vesil and the wind beginning to change and the sailors can take the sails and put them up. And it wont be but a short time untill we will be out of all danger.[29]

Just before they got to Yerba Buena, Cal. George crushed his left hand pretty badly while helping with the machinery on the boat. And when they got to Yerba Buena theare were three flags flying, the Mexican Flag, the Lone Starr Flag that was run up by Kernal Fremont, and the Stars and Stripes. Comodore Stockton had just got in with the American Man of War and he told Captain Richardson to stay out of the Bay for theare was liable to be some excitement theare, and when everything was o.k. he would signal for him to come in.

Comodore Stockton cut a figure eight in the Bay of Yerba Buena so the Mexicans could see those big guns on both sides and then Comodore Stockton anchored his vesil and told the Mexican Government to haul down the Mexican Flag or he would open fire on them. They soon pulled down the Mexican Flag. Then he told Kernal Fremont to pull down the Lone Starr Flag which he did. And Comodore Stockton put him in irons and put him in the hole of the vesil. And then he signaled for the old Ship Brooklin to come in and when they had landed Kernal Fremont had come to his senses. He was going to have a Lone State out of the State of California.[30]

G.W.S. had got pretty well acquainted with a young lady by the name of Emeline Lane. So before they got off the ship he told Emeline Lane that he wouldn't be able to work for several days and he thought it would be the best thing for them to do would be to get married. She said she thought that would be O.K. So G.W.S. called Samuel Brannan over and he married them. That was

---

[29]Sirrine's daughter told a similar story: The *Brooklyn* "had great difficulties and drifted so far south that the passengers had to work, desperately, for days keeping the ice off the ropes and decks." See Della Sirrine Hibbert, Biography of George Warren Sirrine, LDS Archives, 1.

[30]This fanciful recollection reflects the Mormons' general disdain for John C. Frémont. Montgomery of the *Portsmouth* actually captured Yerba Buena three weeks before the *Brooklyn's* arrival, while Frémont and Stockton were intermittent allies in their conflict with General Kearny.

the first marrage ceremony that was performed on the Pacific Coast in the English Language. Well as soon as they were married G.W.S. asked his wife how much money she had, she said she dident have a dollar nor even a cent. That they had been out of fresh fruit so long when they got to Hololula that she spent every cent she had then. She asked G.W.S. how much money he had, he told her that he had just the same amount that she had. She said then you haven't got a cent, we certanly are in a fine fix, neather of us has a cent and you with a cripled hand and in a strange country and didn't know a single person. G.W.S. told her that they would get a long all O.K. and for her to make out a bill of what they would have to have to start keeping house with. They then started up in town and G.W.S. went to the best looking merchentile house theare was in town and they went in and the clerks came to wait on them and George asked for the propritor and they told him he was back in the back part of the house. He went up to him and introduced himself and then his wife.[31] And George told him that they had just been married about an hour and that they were some of those notorious Mormons that you have heard about, and they had just come in on the old Ship Brooklin and that he was a millright by profession but he could build an engine and run it or [build] almost any kind of a house, but he had his hand crushed and would not be able to work for a few days and that he had to have a little assistance untill he got to work. He called his clerk up and told them to let them have any thing theare was in the house to fit the house with furniture, cooking utensils and provisions. She had run him in debt $10.00.[32]

Orson Hyde: We Shall Start en masse for California

A chatty letter from Apostle Orson Hyde in the fall of 1846 informed Brannan of the changing situation facing the LDS church. Hyde had picked up the details of the *Brooklyn* voyage from the newspapers, but he seemed to reply to a letter from Brannan written at Juan Fernandez. Hyde conveyed several critical points of information: the government had enlisted five hundred Mormons to fight in the Mexican War and had sent the Mormon Battalion to California under the command of General Stephen Watts Kearny. The main body of the Saints would camp on the Missouri River for the winter. (Hyde thought parties would winter on the Platte River, but they were recalled.) With the political situation in flux, he counseled Brannan to "espouse the American interest in Califor-

---

[31]The newlyweds probably met William Leidesdorff, Yerba Buena's leading merchant.

[32]For Sirrine's adventures with Brannan and the "Hounds," see Chapter 11.

nia." Hyde was unclear about the ultimate destination of the Saints, stating "we shall start en masse for California" and noting that the Mormon
Battalion would "be on the Pacific before we shall." Hyde, John Taylor,
and Parley Pratt were bound for England, where Pratt and Taylor would
investigate settling on Vancouver Island. Brigham Young was favoring the
Great Basin as the best site for the next stake of Zion, but he had not yet
determined the Saints' final destination.[33]

The single most telling sentence in the letter warned Brannan, "The
standard which you took with you, do not exhibit, till the council of the
church have approved of it." This was probably the flag of the Kingdom
of God that Brannan hoped to fly after conquering Yerba Buena for the
Saints. Having found the American conquest an established fact, Brannan had the good sense not to try to claim California for the Kingdom
of God.

There are several accounts of the appearance of the "standard" of the
Kingdom of God, and there may well have been several versions of the
flag.[34] An anonymous Brannan obituary, written by someone with
detailed knowledge of the Brooklyn's voyage, recalled:

> That they had a banner among them to float over a separate and indepen-
> dent government is a fact though unwritten in history. It was composed of
> white silk, and in the center was the Virgin and twelve stars. This standard
> was carefully put out of sight but it was manifestly designed by the leaders
> of the church which had dispatched this colony under the charge of Bran-
> nan to the Pacific to establish a civil eclesiastical government on this coast
> and to plant this banner on the soil of California.[35]

Literary forger Chauncey Canfield maintained that the flag "was
made on a white silk ground, the center bearing the figure of a virgin—
supposedly—the female surrounded by twelve stars in red, the virgin
typical of the purity of the Mormon church and the stars emblematic of
the twelve apostles." Canfield claimed Brannan kept the flag stored "in a

[33]The letter reached Brannan before April 1847, for Thomas Bullock recorded copying it in Salt
Lake Valley. See Bagley, ed., The Pioneer Camp of the Saints, 252.
[34]See Quinn, "The Flag of the Kingdom of God," 108, 113, for possible designs. For the flag's
history in Utah and its persistence, see Bigler, Forgotten Kingdom, 36–37.
[35]Anonymous obituary, State Library Collection, Box 3, California State Library, which also
claimed that on entering San Francisco Bay, the Brooklyn flew a "Mormon flag" at her masthead that
"bore the device of a woman crowned with stars."

THE FLAG OF THE KINGDOM OF GOD.
This image, reconstructed to remove the original headline, accompanied
Chauncey Canfield's 1909 newspaper article, "The Twelve Starred Flag
that Was to Wave Over California."

vault in his old office on Montgomery street" and was "wont to bring it forth, hang it over the table and expatiate on thwarted hopes and expectations." Rejecting Mormon offers to purchase the flag, Brannan later displayed it from a chandelier at his hotel in Calistoga, "and was never happier than when recalling his old dreams of empire and setting forth what might have been." The flag disappeared from the hotel's safe in 1870, "and although Brannan offered a big reward for its recovery, it has never been seen since that time. Sam always contended that the robbery was done at the instigation of the saints, but there was nothing to prove it, except they were the only ones who could have attached any value to it." Canfield concluded, "Possibly the virgin and the twelve stars are hidden away in some secret nook of the Tabernacle."[36]

---

[36]"The Twelve Starred Flag that Was to Wave Over California," *San Francisco Chronicle*, 17 January 1909, 2. Chauncey L. Canfield was the "editor" of *The Diary of a Forty-Niner*, "which is fictional," according to Dale Morgan, being "a made-up diary for one 'Alfred T. Jackson.'"

ORSON HYDE TO SAMUEL BRANNAN, 5 SEPTEMBER 1846,
LDS ARCHIVES.

New York, Septr. 5th 1846

Br. Brannan,

Having arrived in this city some three or four days since, in company
with Elders Taylor & Parley P Pratt, on our way to England, I have thought
best to give you a little idea of things as they exist in this country. We have
seen all the communications from the Brooklyn, up to her being at Juan Fernandez. We left the great Camp of Israel at Council Bluffs on the 1st day of
August last. Elders Young & Kimball were well, & all the rest of our quorum. There are between three and four thousand wagons on the way, with
cattle that cover a thousand hills, cattle, sheep, pigs, mules, horses, &c. &c.
without number. They are gone into Winter Quarters & are cutting grass to
keep their stock on. They will winter at Council Bluffs, & up on the Platte
River, & await until our strength gets collected up from different parts, & in
the spring, just as soon as grass shall start so as to sustain our teams, we shall
start en masse for California. We intend to return to our families in the
spring, in time to move on with the first that go.

We go to England on business to regulate the government & emigration
of the saints. The new citizens at Nauvoo have bought all our troubles, & are
at constant war with the antis. Our people are mostly gone from Nauvoo. We
have sent 500 men to California in the service of the United States.—They
go out under Col Kearny by way of Santa Fe. They will be on the Pacific
before we shall. We shall be highly pleased to meet you, or some one, in the
mountains, from your company about the 4th of July next, to report
progress, & tell us something of the best places for location.—You will of
course espouse the American interest in California, & use your press as a
faithful engine, to establish the pure principles of democracy, based upon the
constitution of our country, & inasmuch as your course cannot be
impeached, in truth, you will advance to an important station. I was sorry to
hear of [Quartus S.] Sparks' dissipation, & inclination to dissent, & also his
leaning too much on the side of the females. This is what we expected. Bro
Sparks must humble himself, or he will fall into the snare of the Devil, and
what I say to him I wish all to profit from. I think Elder Appleby has been
misrepresented to you; though he knows nothing of your sayings in your letter about him, yet he feels well towards you & does not show that he has had
any such feelings towards you or the ship that you represent.

The property that has been sent by you in the ship, & the owners here, or
gone by land, it will be for your interest to see that it is carefully preserved for
them when they come, as a thousand jealousies may have arisen about it, & no
doubt as unfounded as Rigdon's claims to the presidency of the church. But
be independent & take a straight forward course in all things, & that will carry

you beyond the reach of slander or jealousy. The standard which you took with you, do not exhibit, till the council of the church have approved of it.

I was sorry to hear of the deaths of our friends on the ship, but this is the lot of us all, a debt that we all have to pay. Be not troubled about money, whether it be much or little, that you may have taken. I could wish you had fifty thousand dollars. Only make a good use of the money you have & when you pay it away, make it tell in favor of Zion, that is all. You will probably have plenty of Mormons in California in the course of a year. If however you should need the property that was sent by you, or some portion of it, to get along with, of course you should use it & keep a proper account of the same. We are at Bro. Davids in Spring Street. They are all well & in good spirits. They wish to be kindly remembered to you, & to your good lady. They will probably write to you by this ship. Write all the good things you can, & as often as you can, for whatever you write will be published throughout the States, if given to the Editors. Let virtue be honored in all your little colony, & God acknowledged in all your proceedings, & the principles of good faith strictly maintained towards Jew & Gentile, & the Kingdom, the dominion will be thy portion, even when the Saints rest from their labors. Your brother in Christ, Orson Hyde

PS Brs. Pratt & Taylor join me in sending our best respects, our kind wishes, & pure love, to you & to your family, & to all the Saints under your charge. You have our prayers & our blessings, and what shall I say more? You will have ourselves probably in about a year. As before O.H.

MARY HOLLAND SPARKS: A BRIEF SKETCH OF OUR VOYAGE

Twenty-four-year-old Mary Sparks' charming "sketch" is one of the earliest and best sources on the *Brooklyn* voyage. Mary Holland Hamilton had married Quartus Strong Sparks in 1844 and the next year gave birth to her first son in Hartford, Connecticut. Her fifty-six-year-old mother, Mary Hamilton, also made the trip around the Horn. The Sparks letter provides a useful summary of the voyage and includes details, such as calling Yerba Buena "a beautiful village," that contradict later accounts.

MARY SPARKS TO MARIA AND HOLLY CLARK,
15 NOVEMBER 1846, LDS ARCHIVES.

Yerba Buena, Francisco Bay
15 November 1846

Dear Brothers and sisters and friends

Having an opportunity of sending a letter to New York, I with pleasure improve it, first giving a brief sketch of our voyage. We set sail from New York on the 4th of February. It was pleasant sailing for a few hours and then the wind began to blow. The ship began to roll and pitch. The sea broke over the sides of the ship. The water came down into the cabin in torrents some of the time. The Captain came down into the cabin and said that he had done all that he could. The sails were all taken in and no one at the helm. We were driven by the winds for about three days.[37] It happened that we were driven on our right course. We then hoisted our sails and sailed on very pleasantly for some weeks. Most all were seasick except myself and a few others. Mother was quite seasick. A few days after I was taken sick with the canker and was sick almost all the voyage. Little Quartus had two spells of sickness. The last time he was sick, it seemed as though we should have to give him up. All remedies seemed to fail until we got some tincture of rhubarb, which soon relieved him.[38]

But about the journey. The weather was very calm when we crossed the equater. The sea was very calm, and very cold around Cape Horn. We had good luck getting around the Cape, intending to stop at Valparaiso, but could not get in on account of a very bad storm of rain and wind. But sailed on until we came to the island of Juanfernandes, the former home of Robinson Cruiso, finding only eight inhabitants living in caves. Stopped there five days. Got a new recruit of wood and water. We then set sail for the Sandwich Islands, where we arrived in about four weeks, finding quite a city where the King resided. Mr. Brannan was invited to preach in one of the churches where we attended meeting. Was treated with great respect. Got almost all kinds of fruit such as watermelon, mushrooms, pineapples, grapes and bannanas also pure wine which suited me first rate. Stayed about two weeks. We then set sail for California. Was about five weeks from Sandwich Islands and then we came in sight of the shores of California. Sailed up the Francisco Bay until we came in sight of a beautiful village on the shore where we landed.

All things safe; nothing broke or injured much. Some of us found houses to move into and the rest pitched tents. I lived in our tent a few weeks. We then moved to a place called the mission—into the old castles we used to read of so much in the *Children of the Abby*.[39] It looks as though it had been a

---

[37]This is the earliest account of a faith-promoting story that became a classic element of *Brooklyn* memoirs, including those of John Horner, Joseph Skinner, and Augusta Joyce Crocheron. Sparks' version lacked the traditional point of the story—the faithful response of the passengers. Richardson "thought it was marvelous that any could sing while in such peril, and that we ought to be praying and preparing for death; but we felt and knew our Father was at the helm," recalled William Glover. "He stared at me when I told him I was going to California." See Bailey, ed., *The Mormons in California*, 14.

[38]The Sparks family suffered from scurvy.

[39]Regina Maria Roche's (1764?–1845) four-volume romance, *The Children of the Abbey*, went through multiple American editions, including the second, published in Philadelphia in 1800.

convent. There is no windows in the room except at the top of the doors—
although mother and I have two little rooms where we live very comfortable.
We live among the Spaniards. But they are very kind to us. They often send
us a quarter of beef at a time and milk and vegetables, fruit etc. They come
to see us—some of them—almost every day. I can talk with them some.
They call beef—carny, milk—leche, man—ombré, yes—si, cow—vaca. No more
Spanish this time. There is a Roman Catholic Church a few doors from
where we live.[40] They have an Indian priest that stays here part of the time.

The news has just come that the Mexicans have had a battle with the
Americans. Seven Americans killed and one hundred and ten Mexicans. The
battle was fought about six hundred miles from here.[41] We believe there is to
be wars and rumors of wars in order to fulfill prophecy and that peace is
taken from the earth for the present.

We believe in *Mormonism* yet, although we are poor samples of Mormonism. Mr. Sparks and some others have gone off taking up their lands,
sowing wheat, building houses, where we expect to move in the spring.[42] The
soil is very fertile. Beautiful fields—no stones, some hills and the climate is
very healthy. We never enjoyed better health than we do now and if you were
all here, we should be perfectly contented. No danger of starving here; if we
can work half as hard as we did in the states. Business is pretty lively here.
Most all kinds of wages are very high—money plenty. Mother has earned
four dollars per week some of the time. But goods and groceries are pretty
high on account of so many people emigrating here. Most all kinds of
goods are brought in; but we have not had to buy anything as yet. We
brought plenty with us for the present. Maria if I could only see you and the
children, Clarissa and her children, I could tell you more than I can write.
And I hope that we shall meet before many years but I cannot tell when or
where. We want to see you all so much.

I believe I will write how long we were on the water. Well, it was almost
six months. We arrived here on the very last day of July. There was ten
deaths in our middst during the voyage—only three that you know . . . Eliza
Ensign, her father and John Fowlers youngest boy. Mrs. Fowler and her

---

[40]Founded in 1776 about two and a half miles southwest of Yerba Buena Cove, the chapel of the
Mission San Francisco de Assisi was built in 1791 and was popularly known as Mission Dolores.
With secularization in 1834, the mission closed and fell into disrepair. It was used as a tavern and
dance hall until the chapel reopened in 1859 as a Catholic church. See Richards, *Historic San Francisco*,
31–32, 37.

[41]Sparks had heard an exaggerated account of Captain William Mervine's 8 October 1846
encounter near San Pedro with Mexican forces under José Carrillo. The Americans suffered four
dead and about an equal number of wounded, but apparently inflicted no casualties on the *Californios*. Commodore Stockton landed at San Pedro on 28 October with a powerful force, but a ruse
by Carrillo frightened off "Fighting Bob." See Harlow, *California Conquered*, 167–71.

[42]Quartus Sparks helped establish the settlement at New Hope on the Stanislaus River.

mother live a few yards from here and Mrs. Warner likewise.[43] Their husbands have not got here yet. We have heard from the company of Mormons
coming across the mountains.[44] We expect them every day. We are in hopes
that Coridon and his family will come here. I think he could get a good living here, as well as there or anywhere else. Wild horses and cattle are very
plentiful here. But if we are as smart as the Spaniards are, we can catch them
and tame them. Beef is very cheap here—only two cents a pound. We have
not starved yet. There is plenty of wheat here for 75 cents per bushel.
Mother cannot speak of you without crying. Her health has been remarkably good since we left home. She wants to tell Hugh, if she could see him
now that she could tell him plenty of stories about the bears and wolves and
Indians—for there are plenty here. Tell Adeline that Granny cannot forget
her baby. Tell Elizabeth that there is a little girl here that we love because she
looks just like her. Tell Dwight and Mary Jane that little Quartus can throw
the lasso and call mamy and papa and is as full of mischief as he can be—
running from place to place.

I must hurry and close my letter for it is most time to send it on board
ship. You must give our love to all our brothers and sisters, uncles and Aunts,
and Southworth and her husband. Tell her to write. There is ships coming
and going all the time from New York to Sandwich Islands and from Sandwich Islands here. You must take pains to send up a letter. We want to hear
from you so very very much. One more thing, I thought I would tell you the
name of the ship we came on is called the Brooklyn commanded by Capt
Pritchardson. Sophia Clark is here keeping house for Mr. [Isaac] Goodwin—his wife died on the ship. I have no time to write all this time but
intend to write every opportunity I have of sending to you. Mr. Sparks has
written once or twice and sent papers from the Sandwich Islands. Tell
Clarissa and Ely to write also. This is from your sister and mother.

Mary H. Sparks M.H.

[On a separate page:] to Maria and Holly Clark

When we arrived her[e] the American man-of-war called the Portsmouth
commanded by Capt. Montgomery lay at anchor in the harbor. They had
taken possession of the place about three weeks before we came. Had
hoisted the American flag before the barracks. Soon after the Congress
came in another man-of-war. They fired a gun salute, was immediately
answered by four canons from the Portsmough and four from the fort on
the hill, which made the ground tremble; which sounded like war. The
American officers were so pleased to see so many immigrants, only 240, that

---

[43]Like John Fowler, Caroline E. Warner's husband went overland to California, while she took
her three children around the Horn. See Hansen, "Voyage of the *Brooklyn*," 72.

[44]Brannan later complained he received no instructions in this period, so Sparks perhaps meant
the *Brooklyn* Saints had *not* heard from the main body of the church.

they gave a festival at the tavern. Invited us all to attend. A great number attended plenty of cakes and wines, music, and Spanish dancing. I wish you could see them dance what they called a Spandango. If you write you can send your letters to New York or Boston which will be sent in the first ship that goes out. Direct your letters to Yerba Buena, Francisco Bay, California. Give my love to all inquiring friends.

Yours MHS

> Yes my native land I love thee
> All thy scenes I love them well
> Friends, connections, happy country
> Can bid you all farewell
>   Can I leave thee
> For in distant lands to dwell

JOHN M. HORNER: INCIDENTS BY THE WAY

Sixty years after the voyage, Elder A. Milton Musser asked *Brooklyn* veteran John M. Horner, a wealthy farmer living in Pauilo, Hawaii, to recall his experiences in 1846. "I feel to thank you sincerely for your worthy thought of urging me to write up the incidents of the ship *Brooklyn* voyage," Horner replied.

> The importance of that voyage to the world was growing in my mind all the time, and I was honestly of the opinion that it had been carefully and ably written until receiving your letter. There were certainly able penmen on board. I was a youngster, more accustomed to handling farm tools than the pen, and never dreamed of trying to write it up until receiving your letter . . . The incidents written are as bright in my mind now, as though they had happened last week. I am pleased to know you are satisfied with it. It is to be regretted that the important subject has not been treated by an abler pen.

Horner's article captured several interesting details, including "a three-days' calm as we approached California." He was an admirer of Captain Richardson, who "proved himself an able navigator. He hit every thing he aimed at, and nothing which he did not want to hit."

JOHN M. HORNER, "VOYAGE OF THE SHIP 'BROOKLYN,'"
IMPROVEMENT ERA 9:10 (AUGUST 1906), 795–98.

I am requested to name the moving cause that sent the ship *Brooklyn*, loaded with "Mormons," from New York to California, by way of Cape

JOHN M. HORNER, CIRCA 1850.
From Horner's book, *National Finance and Public Money*, 246.
Courtesy, Lorin Hansen.

Horn, in 1846; what were the incidents by the way, and what has been the result . . .

After the prophet was massacred, and his mantle of leadership fell on the twelve apostles, with Brigham Young at their head, [and] the outlook for peace being gloomy, the people decided to emigrate and seek peace in the West. With that idea in view, the Twelve counseled the eastern Saints to charter a ship, get on board, and go around Cape Horn to upper California, find a place to settle, farm and raise crops, so that when the Church pioneers should arrive there the following year they would find sustenance.

This counsel was obeyed by the few eastern Saints taking the voyage, to the best of their ability. They chartered the ship *Brooklyn*, and 235 Saints—men, women and children,—and two other passengers—educated gentle men—the captain, mates, sailors, stewards and cooks, altogether 252 souls, got on board, and in due time arrived in California. The Saints did the work assigned them before they left New York . . .

We left New York, as above stated, with the promise of a prosperous voyage and the blessing of God to attend us. We received both with thanks.

Our captain proved himself an able navigator. He hit every thing he aimed at, and nothing which he did not want to hit. He was a Baptist in religious profession; held religious services on deck weekly, which the Saints attended. His mates and sailors, in morals appeared above the average. Unbecoming language was seldom heard on board. For the character of our company we copy from the *Friend*, the report of Captain Richardson to that paper, after his five months' acquaintance with us, during our long voyage from New York to this place, which report we copy and endorse.

The *Friend* announced our arrival at Honolulu on June 20, one hundred and thirty-six days from New York, which city we left on February 4, 1846. The paper further contains a six-column editorial on the history and doctrine of the Latter-day Saints . . . [45]

Our religious exercises were kept up until we anchored in front of Yerba Buena, now San Francisco. There has been no time since then when a "Mormon" Church did not exist in San Francisco. Now, active "Mormon" Churches are scattered over the state. Several of our company were elders. We were working men and working women, school teachers, preachers, carpenters, blacksmiths, masons, printers, etc. The first paper ever published in San Francisco—The *Alta California*, was printed by the ship *Brooklyn* company. War was raging in California when we arrived there, between Mexico and the United States, and some of our company enlisted and went down to the lower part of the territory with Colonel J. C. Fremont and helped finish up the war there.[46]

We left New York as above stated. Let me mention an incident. As we approached the Gulf Stream, a severe storm burst upon us. It was so severe that the sails were all taken in, except a small one that rested against the shrouds of the main mast; no one was safe on deck. The hatches were fastened down, except the one opening at the top of the steps leading down from the captain's cabin. The captain fearing his cabin would be swept off by the waves came down with a troubled countenance and announced to the passengers: "I have done all I can to save the ship. If any of you have not made your peace with God, you would better do it now, as the ship may go down any minute." Through faith in their promise of a "prosperous voyage," or through ignorance of their danger, none seemed alarmed but the captain. The storm passed without danger. Fortunately, it drove us on our journey. The captain, who was an old seafarer, was heard to say after the storm ceased, that it was the worst he had ever encountered.

We had a school on board for the children; and an ex-soldier, a brother who had spent years in the army, was required to drill the men of our company in the art of war during the fair weather, more for the benefit received

---

[45]Material from *The Friend* is omitted.

[46]Only two members of the company—Edward Kemble and Jesse A. Stringfellow—enlisted in Frémont's brigade. See Carter, ed., *Our Pioneer Heritage*, 3:557, 584.

from the exercise, than from any good we expected from learning the arts of war.

It was fine weather when we doubled Cape Horn. The women were making bread, pies, cakes, frying doughnuts, etc., and the children were playing and romping about the deck.

We were too far south to see the cape when we passed around it, in fact we saw no land after leaving New York until we sighted the island of Juan Fernandez, where we stopped a few days replenishing our wood and water, catching, eating and salting fish. While coming up the coast of South America, a hint was given that the captain did not know where he was. The captain, hearing of this, immediately pointed his ship toward the mainland and stated:

"If I am right, I will show you the highest points of the Andes, if this wind keeps up." Sure enough, we soon saw a small, black cloud arising out of the eastern horizon, which rapidly increased in height and length, and which, to us landsmen, looked like a thundercloud. By gazing through strong glasses, we saw the captain was right. He then again pointed his ship for the Hawaiian Islands, where we arrived as above stated.

Soon after leaving Honolulu, on the 4th of July we had a spirited celebration of that day. Flags were hoisted, guns fired, patriotic songs were sung, etc.

We encountered another storm coming up from the Horn, but it was not as severe as the one we had in the Atlantic. We had a three-days' calm as we approached California—one hundred miles or so out. Then a strong trade wind struck us and wafted us speedily and safely through the "Golden Gate," without a pilot, or halting, with all sails set, until we dropped anchor in front of Yerba Buena—now San Francisco—in the bay of San Francisco. We were all well, thankful and happy. We had truly a prosperous voyage, as we were promised before leaving New York.

When I look back and contemplate the voyage of the ship *Brooklyn* Saints, the distance traveled, time consumed, and purpose of the journey, and the incidents thereof, I now feel to rank it creditably with that of the Jaredites and Nephites in their voyage across the Pacific to America,[47] and with the voyage of the *Mayflower* pilgrims crossing the Atlantic from Europe to America. I am impressed further with the thought, that we were sent and protected by the Great Father, as were the pilgrims above mentioned, and to help forward a great work as did they. We performed the mission assigned, as we then understood it, not comprehending its importance, as it now more clearly appears. We had no prophets with us to guide and direct us, as did the Jaredites and Nephites, but we felt thankful upon being able to congratulate ourselves that

---

[47]The Jaredites and Nephites were *Book of Mormon* peoples.

we were blessed with a more complete and continued unity in our company during the entire voyage than the Nephite emigrants enjoyed. Neither were we chastised by the Great Father, as was the Brother of Jared because he had ceased calling upon him.

Although some of the *Brooklyn* Saints may have departed from the faith, yet I feel that the purpose for which they were sent was accomplished.

THERE'S THAT DAMNED AMERICAN FLAG

A persistent story about the *Brooklyn* tells that on entering San Francisco Bay, "one of the leaders was observed to shade his eyes and gaze anxiously ashore. Suddenly his countenance became ghastly, and, pointing to our national emblem, which floated over the plaza in all its beauty and glory, he exclaimed, '*By God! there is that damned American flag!*' "[48] Bancroft noted "it is even possible that the pious elder's first remark, as reported, was, 'There is that damned flag again!'"[49] Although anonymous and undated, this item from the Huntington Library may be one of the earliest versions of this tale.

SAMUEL BRANNAN, FRAGMENTARY REMARKS
RE: HIS EXPEDITION TO CALIFORNIA WITH THE MORMONS,
BRANNAN COLLECTION, HUNTINGTON LIBRARY.

Samuel Brannan—In the year 1845 he was editor of the "Prophet" a weekly Mormon paper published at No. 7 Spruce St. N.Y.

He was secretly instructed to fit out an expedition by sea for California. Chartered the ship Brooklyn 400 tons, Capt Richardson and called for volunteer families of Mormons.

Feb. 6, 1846 [*sic*], 238 pass. more than half of them women and children embarked. Sailed down N.Y. bay with flag hoisted bearing as a blind the word "Oregon."

Stopped at the island San Juan Fernandez for wood, water, &c. The Captain fearing a mutiny and capture [of] the ship ran over to Honolulu [*ink blot*] and decided for Cal. While at Honolulu the Brooklyn was visited by Commodore Stockton who reported war with Mexico and advised the emigrants to practice military drills, which they did during the voyage to S.F. Arrived at S.F. 31st July '46. As the ship passed the point (Ft. Pt.) all the

---

[48]Dunbar, *The Romance of the Age*, 44. Dunbar is the earliest printed source for this story, but his garbled account of 1846 events discounts his credibility.

[49]Bancroft, *History of California*, 5:550.

pass[engers] were ordered below that she might be taken for a hide drogher. Mr. B. at the sight of the U.S. flag flying on the plaza exclaimed, "By G—! There's that d[amned]. Am[erican] flag."

During the voyage 10 died, 4 adults and 6 children. Two children were born one boy named "Atlantic" and one girl, "Pacific."

Tents were pitched among the sand hills near the beach.

Disputes in the country soon sprang up. Trial, first by jury in Cal[ifornia], presided over by Brannan who was accused of various wrong acts as Pres[iden]t of the Association, but was exonerated. Some seceded however. Did not select land in company on account of their contentions. Many it is said joined Fremont's battalion as volunteers.

The *Brooklyn* company got its first view of California through a thick haze on the morning of 31 July. As the ship approached the narrow strait that John C. Frémont had recently named the Golden Gate, the passengers crowded on deck, only to be herded below with the sighting of the Castillo de San Joaquin, the decrepit fort that guarded the bay. The passengers were again permitted on deck as the masts of two whalers, several "hide droughers," and the U.S.S. *Portsmouth* came into view. Three weeks earlier, the *Portsmouth*'s crew had seized the bay for the United States. The stars and stripes flew from the mastheads of the ships at anchor and on the staff of the customs house in the village of Yerba Buena.

Portsmouth beat to quarters when lookouts sighted the strange sail, but stood down upon seeing women among the passengers. By three o'clock on one of the "bright, breezy afternoons peculiar to San Francisco at this season of the year," the *Brooklyn* had dropped anchor in Yerba Buena Cove.[50] Merchant William Heath Davis was the first to "welcome the newcomers to our embryo American town."[51] Seaman Joseph Downey of the *Portsmouth* recalled how "without signal or warning round the point came booming along a full-rigged ship, crowded with men, and bearing our flag at her peak. She came to anchor, [and] our boats boarded her."[52] Augusta Crocheron claimed, "In our sweet native tongue the officer in command, with head uncovered, courteously and confidently said in a loud tone, 'Ladies and Gentlemen, I have the honor to

[50]Rogers, ed., *A Kemble Reader*, 7, 25.
[51]Davis, *Seventy-five Years in California* (1967), 238.
[52]Rogers, ed., *Filings from an Old Saw*, 43.

inform you that you are in the United States of America.'" Crocheron probably invented the officer's speech—and she certainly manufactured the "three hearty cheers" she said greeted the announcement.[53]

Samuel Brannan had arrived in California.

---

[53]Crocheron, "The Ship Brooklyn," 83.

Chapter 6

"Very Largely a Mormon Town"
Yerba Buena, 1846

In the nine months following the arrival of the *Brooklyn*, Brannan and his hard-working pilgrims transformed the village on Yerba Buena Cove, which became "for a time very largely a Mormon town."[1] The company pitched tents below the sand hills of the "odd, uncouth" village and overwhelmed its every available living space.[2] Carpenters went to work building homes for the new arrivals and commercial buildings for local merchants; the millwrights set up a gristmill; the ship's military organization was established as a local—and sometimes comical—militia; the colonists organized a school to keep their many children busy; and the young printers limbered up their acorn press and produced San Francisco's first newspaper, the *California Star*. Their hard work diffused much of the suspicion about the newly arrived Mormons, but the communal arrangement established as Samuel Brannan & Co. generated so much bickering among the Saints that it soon resulted in one of California's first jury trials.

Commander John Berrian Montgomery of the United States sloop-of-war *Portsmouth* had seized Yerba Buena at eight o'clock on the morning of 9 July 1846. The navy hoisted the stars and stripes "in front of the custom-house, in the public square, with a salute of 21 guns from the ship, followed by three hearty cheers from on shore and on board."[3] Not only was there no opposition, there was not a single Mexican official present from whom to demand a surrender. With this easy victory the American conquest of Alta California appeared complete. Brannan's visions of glory were dashed against the navy's fulfillment of James K. Polk's standing orders of June 1845 to seize California's ports in the

---

[1]Bancroft, *History of California*, 5:551.   [2]Rogers, ed., *A Kemble Reader*, 9.
[3]Bancroft, *History of California*, 5:238.

event of war with Mexico. Brannan turned his energies to more practical matters, such as finding food and shelter for his followers.

Brannan had been so focused on creating an independent state on the West Coast that it had never occurred to him the United States government might have other plans. Edward Kemble reported that in his conversations with Commodore Stockton in Hawaii, Brannan "learned with blank dismay that the seizure of California was contemplated by the United States." This "obstruction of their plans of sovereignty" had "never been imagined," and there "were long faces and wrathful words, which in these days would have been counted as disloyal." Kemble thought that Brannan's men would gladly have fought "for any needful acquisitions under the banner of the church. But to help establish the authority of the United States again over them was a very wide departure from their original plans, if not in direct antagonism with their designs."[4]

Commander Montgomery "was a man equal to any emergency." After his ship's boats returned from their initial visit to the *Brooklyn*, "he at once decided on a plan to curb [the Mormons] if hostile, or to foster them if they came in peace." The *Portsmouth's* cutter delivered Brannan and "two or three of his coadjutors" to the warship. The elders were "ushered into the recesses of the private cabin of the Portsmouth, the views and plans of the new comers were at once explained, preliminaries arranged, the harmony so necessary to good government concerted, and the parties dispatched to their own ship again." The pious Montgomery invited the Saints to attend his "service of the Episcopal persuasion" the next day, where he read a printed sermon from the "copious supply" he kept on hand. The Mormon women naturally caught the attention of the *Portsmouth's* sailors and generated some surprise when they failed to match the reputation of this "wild, desperate people": "a dilapidated specimen of a Quarter-Gunner growled out, in no very sweet tone, 'D—mnation, why they are just like other women.'"[5] The *Portsmouth's* dour surgeon, Marius Duvall, simply noted, "Several of these people were on board today, to see the ship and attend church."[6]

B. H. Roberts relied on Augusta Joyce Crocheron's 1888 account to

---

[4]Rogers, ed., *A Kemble Reader*, 23–24. Writing in old age, Brannan reminded Jesse Little that Polk had upset their plans in 1846. See Brannan to Little, 5 February 1885.

[5]Rogers, ed., *Filings from an Old Saw*, 45–46.

[6]Rogers, ed., *A Navy Surgeon in California, 1846–1847*, 47.

stress the "joy of the colony on beholding the flag of their country" when they arrived in San Francisco Bay, but this reaction was as fictional as the salute Crocheron said the guns of the fort fired to honor the *Brooklyn*.[7] Marius Duvall gave a more forthright account of the Saints' reaction: "Some of the Mormons have pitched their tents on shore; they seem to be at a loss—it is said they were grieved when they found the United States Flag flying here." The put-upon Saints "had left that country, because its citizens had persecuted them. If the government of this country had not changed hands, they had proposed to land here with the permission of the Californians,—if that had been denied to them, to land by force of arms." Duvall wrote that "various reports have been circulated about Mr. Brannan the leader, and the whole party, much to the discredit of both—many are leaving the leader and engaging work wherever they can find it—it is melancholy to see the old men and women of the party—they have left comfortable homes for this 'Paradise' which they now see is dreariness itself."[8]

On the first of August, sea captain William Dane Phelps boarded the *Brooklyn* "to take a look at" the "50 Mormon families" on board. He noted:

> They appeared to belong to the middling class of people—mostly merchants and farmers. Their elder (Mr Brannon) who by the way is quite a young man and very much of a dandy—gave me a Sandwich Island newspaper containing an account which he furnished the Editor of that paper with, stating their views and objects in coming to California. It is there stated, that they are the pioneers of a large body of their sect who are on their way here. Two other ships are on their passage to this place, and 15000 are on their march a cross the mountains and are expected to arrive next month. The object of this party by sea was to found a town and establish themselves on the north side of the Bay of St Francisco, and expecting to find the Mexican flag flying they anticipated a little opposition from the people, but they were prepared to occupy by force of arms, whether or no. Every man of them is armed to the teeth with Rifles, six barrel pistols, and bowie knives.
>
> They profess to have a Revelation from Heaven, that the land is promised to them, and they have only to come and occupy it. That here they are to establish a great Republic of their own, extend their dominion over the shores of the Pacific and eventually spread their faith over the whole of India & China.

---

[7]John C. Frémont's men had spiked the decrepit cannons at the long-abandoned Castillo de San Joaquin on the first of July, and no contemporary source mentioned a salute fired by the battery Montgomery had erected at Yerba Buena.

[8]Duvall's 2 August 1846 journal entry, in Rogers, ed., *A Navy Surgeon in California*, 47–48.

I knew nothing of their origin, or of their doctrines, and being desirous of information I applied to a man of respectable appearance among them and desired to be enlightened—but the only answer I got was, "you must be baptised by one of our order, and then you will have a revelation."

They are sadly disappointed to find the flag of the U States waving here. They thought they were out of the jurisdiction of its laws, and find that tho the land was *promised* to them—'Uncle Sam' has *taken it*.

I have not seen enough of them to express an opinion yet—but I fear they will occasion trouble. Capt Montgomery told me that he should watch them sharp and should put them down if they committed trespass on the persons or property of the residents.[9]

At the request of Captain Richardson, on Monday morning the boats of the *Portsmouth* helped disembark "the Mormons and their plunder."[10] According to family lore, Letitia Dorsey Marshall supervised the unloading of the fine furniture she had brought around the Horn. One of the more zealous male passengers told her, "The world is coming to an end, and you won't need that furniture. Why don't you give it to me?" "If the world is coming to an end," said the skeptical Sister Marshall, "you won't need it either, thank you."[11]

To seaman Joseph Downey, "it seemed as if, like the ship of Noah, it contained a representative for every mortal thing the mind of man had ever conceived." At Honolulu the Saints had loaded at least three of the fourteen cannon A. G. Benson had shipped from New York the previous fall, for Downey watched them unload "three beautiful pieces of brass cannon, six pounders, mounted in the style of light artillery, with the necessary complement of powder and shot, round, fixed and grape," along with a large supply of ammunition. The cannon gave Downey's "reflective mind" pause, as he contemplated "what might have been done, had the flag of Mexico" been flying when the Mormons arrived. Later, "these cannon were pressed into the service of the United States."[12] The LDS church had no money to buy such weapons, so per-

---

[9]Busch, ed., *Frémont's Private Navy*, 43–44.   [10]Rogers, ed., *Filings from an Old Saw*, 47.

[11]Lilian H. Kelly to Will Bagley, 10 October 1996. Kelly, a descendant of Simeon Stivers, displayed Letitia Marshall's furniture at the San Francisco Maritime Museum during the *Brooklyn* sesquicentennial. She heard this story from her great aunt, Anna Maria Stivers.

[12]Rogers, ed., *Filings from an Old Saw*, 47. Malcolm E. Barker noted that Rogers' edition substituted "immediate" for "immense" in the phrase "immense supplies of ammunition" used in Downey's 1853 article in the *Golden Era*.

haps the Benson brothers purchased the artillery—or maybe it was paid for by the man who ultimately used it, Robert Field Stockton.

WASHINGTON A. BARTLETT: THEY ARE COMING TO CALIFORNIA LIKE A SWARM OF LOCUSTS

Rumors about Mormon plans for California had swept through the province after Lansford Hastings arrived at Sutter's Fort on Christmas Day 1845. The French consul reported that the Mormons were "to march towards California, which has been designated to them as the promised land where they are to develop their belief and multiply their posterity. This invasion, announced for the next summer, has thrown fear and anxiety into the minds of the Californians."[13] Reverend Walter Colton recorded that Californians considered calling someone a Mormon to be an "opprobrious" epithet.[14] The *Brooklyn's* arrival seemed to confirm the worst fears. From Yerba Buena Washington Bartlett wrote to Edward Kern, who had taken command of Sutter's Fort with the American conquest, that the Saints were coming "like a swarm of Locusts." Bartlett, an officer on the *Portsmouth*, described the *Brooklyn* pilgrims' first week in Yerba Buena and captured the suspicion with which local observers regarded the Mormons' intentions in general and their young leader in particular.

> The Mormons who came in the Brooklyn, number old and young 230!! instead of 178, as stated in the papers. There is no doubt but the grossest deception was used to induce them to emigrate [as] none but their leader has ever been at "Nauvoo." I have seen their paper, published in New York in Dec[embe]r. From the accounts in letters from "Nauvoo"—there can be little doubt, but they are coming to California like a swarm of Locusts; for my part I do not see how such a vast horde of people are to be supported here during the next year. Capt. [Stephen] Smith of Bodega told me this morning that about 30 of the company now here, go with him to his place in his employ—some on their own account others to pay their earnings into the company—I scarce know what to make of "Brennan" their leader—he seems a shrewd fellow of limited education (a practical printer)—but from certain things that are leaking out—I believe he is playing a deep game for his own benefit.—But we shall see anon. I am certain they could not have

[13]Nasatir, "The French Consulate in California, 1843–56," 355.
[14]Colton, *Three Years in California*, 24–25.

landed, had they arrived before our flag went up. I doubt very much whether it pleases the leader—although it does the people.[15]

The *Brooklyn* moved north and remained at Bodega Bay until the second half of September, loading her cargo of redwood prior to departing for Monterey, the Hawaiian Islands, and China.[16] William Heath Davis recalled (probably incorrectly) that he chartered the ship and sent her south with barley and other supplies for Commodore Stockton.[17] Despite the sorry descriptions of her in many memoirs, the *Brooklyn* continued to make significant voyages. *Niles' Register* reported in late 1848 that A. G. Benson & Co. had "established a line of Packet Ships between New York and San Francisco, California, to touch at Panama and intermediate ports. The first ship will be the Brooklyn, Capt. Richardson," scheduled to leave New York on 15 November.[18] The stout old tub made a notorious gold rush voyage: on 13 August 1849 at four o'clock in the afternoon, the *Brooklyn* again dropped anchor in San Francisco Bay, having "made the longest passage of any vessel that has arrived here from the states. No other vessel has had scurvy on board anything like the Brooklyn."[19] Dr. J. D. B. Stillman reported that six of the passengers died of scurvy, "and a dozen of them are buried in the sand on the shore up to their chins, a mode of treatment which the sailors think will cure them." On 14 August Stillman gave "evidence in a suit against the Captain of the ship *Brooklyn*." He reported that "Captain Richardson is tried by a Jury before the Alcalde, and I think he will have justice done him; but what justice can be rendered the poor men who are dead and buried in the desert sands of this far-off shore."[20] The *Brooklyn* was sold to the

---

[15]Bartlett to E. M. Kern, 6 August 1846, in Fort Sutter Papers, Huntington Library.

[16]Gleason, *Beloved Sister*, 135–36; and Hansen, "Voyage of the *Brooklyn*," 66.

[17]Rolle, *An American in California*, 51–52. Rolle wrote that Davis "bought from the Mormon, Sam Brannan, many scarce weapons which he later sold in the south to Stockton and to John C. Frémont."

[18]"Line of Packets to California," *Niles' National Register*, 25 October 1848, 257, quoted in Dale Morgan Transcripts, Utah State Hist. Soc. Joseph Richardson, who had served as first mate on the *Brooklyn's* 1846 voyage, replaced his uncle Abel W. as the ship's commander.

[19]Journal of Stephen L. and James E. Fowler, Society of California Pioneers Library, courtesy of Malcolm E. Barker.

[20]Johnson, *The Gold Rush Letters of J. D. B. Stillman*, 18–19. Stillman dated the *Brooklyn's* second arrival to 14 August 1849. "The Brooklyn Case," *Alta California*, 1 October 1849, 4/1–5, described several passengers' suit of Captain Joseph W. Richardson for $5,000 in damages. The passengers complained that the ship was badly ventilated, dirty, and overbooked, but Rush Green, who "came in second cabin," testified the *Brooklyn* "was a favorite ship in New York."

United States Mail Line in 1852, and by 1856 she had been sold again or scrapped.[21] In 1871 Edward Kemble recalled seeing her timbers on the east coast of Panama, "rotting on the beach at Aspinwall."[22]

TWELVE GOOD AND LAWFULL MEN

Almost immediately after landing, the *Brooklyn* company began a series of legal squabbles. As Washington Bartlett noted, the "limited communism" instituted on the ship quickly fractured. George Hyde, a lawyer who had come to California with Stockton and the *Congress*, filed a petition with Montgomery, who on 7 August assigned Bartlett—"loaded to the Brim with Gas and Law"—and surgeon Marius Duvall to conduct the hearing.[23] Montgomery did not describe the case, but on 12 August, he appointed Hyde alcalde of San Jose, indicating the trial—a hearing held before the naval commander and not a local authority—took place about 10 August. Historians have confused this case, which apparently investigated Hyde's charge of treason, with an action brought by Harry Harris in October, which resolved the contractual problems of "limited communism." Perhaps to avoid questions about the loyalties that brought him to the West Coast, Brannan orchestrated the confusion in his biographical statement to the authors of *The Annals of San Francisco*. Most accounts report that the charges were related to the financial covenant that bound the *Brooklyn* company "to remain banded together in the bonds of brotherly love for the space of three years," but Brannan wrote Brigham Young that Hyde had been his enemy "from our first landing here" and had brought "suit against me for 'high treason' in behalf of the government."[24] This first "trial" was actually Montgomery's inquiry into the Mormons' intentions, and Brannan succeeded in convincing the authorities of their loyalty.

Brannan's second—and best remembered—trial began in early October. Brannan blamed the dispute on *Brooklyn* Saints he had excommunicated—"about twenty males of our feeble number [who] have gone

[21]Everett, "The Ship *Brooklyn*," 233.

[22]Rogers, ed., *A Kemble Reader*, 27. Aspinwall is now Colón, Panama.

[23]Lamar, *Cruise of the Portsmouth*, 138; and Rogers, ed., *Filings from an Old Saw*, 50–51.

[24]Rogers, ed., *Filings from an Old Saw*, 50; and Brannan to Young, 2 April 1848, in Chapter 8.

astray after strange gods, serving their bellies and their own lusts." Sheriff Pell was among this number.

BARTLETT TO PELL, 2 OCTOBER 1846,
CALIFORNIA HISTORICAL SOCIETY.

Territory of California
District of San Francisco
To the Sheriff [E. Ward Pell] or either of his deputies in said district greeting.

In the name of the people of the Territory of California, you are hereby commanded to summon twelve good and lawfull men, in the town of Yerba Buena, qualified to serve as jurors, and not exempt from serving on juries in courts of record, who are in no wise of kin either to [Henry] Harris the plaintiff or to Saml. Brannan & Co the Defds [defendants], nor interested in this suit, to appear before me, the undersigned a justice for said district, at the court room in said town of Yerba Buena on this 2^d day of Octr. inst. at 10 Oclock in the forenoon, to make a jury for the trial of an action, now pending before me between the parties aforesaid, of a plea of breach of Covenant.—And have you then and there the names of the jurors and this precept.

Given under my hand at the town aforesaid, 2^d day of Octr. 1846.

Wash^n A. Bartlett
Justice

Seaman Joseph Downey acted as clerk of the court and recalled "there was no lack of business for a week, [as] Mormon after Mormon cited the immaculate Samuel and his councillors to answer; cords of evidence were taken and committed to paper, fact after fact was proven, but the fate of all was decided by the production of that same contract, and verdict for defendants was tacked to the tail of every case, until the plaintiffs in sheer despair, gave up the job."[25]

Amid these controversies, Brannan did not neglect his religious duties. He married George Sirrine and Emeline Lane shortly after the *Brooklyn* landed. Innkeeper John H. Brown credited Brannan with delivering the "first sermon delivered in the English language in Yerba Buena," which was "as good a sermon as any one could wish to hear." Brannan performed the marriage service, "according to the Mormon faith," for Lizzie Winner and Basil Hall. "There was a general invitation

---

[25]Rogers, ed., *Filings from an Old Saw*, 52.

extended to all, a large quantity of refreshments had been prepared, and as there was plenty of music and singing, we had lots of fun. The festivities were kept up until twelve o'clock." Brown remembered, "I never enjoyed myself, at any gathering, as I did there."[26]

JESSE C. LITTLE:
HE SHALL BE HAPPY TO HELP US AND DO IT FREELY

Several tantalizing intimations of Brannan's later relations with Amos Kendall and A. G. Benson survive in the documentary record. The contract they had drawn up with Brannan in January 1846 would long resonate through Mormon history as a scandal, but both men remained political allies of the beleaguered religion. In March 1846 Apostle Wilford Woodruff wrote Jesse C. Little, now president of the LDS church in the East, that he "Had a long interview with Mr. Benson yesterday and he exceedingly desires to do business with us he says if he does it for nothing. I was much pleased with my interview with him. He appears to me to be a gentleman. I think it will be well to keep upon good terms with him as far as possible . . . he apparently manifests much interest in our welfare."[27]

This connection soon yielded important benefits for the Saints. A. G. Benson gave Little a letter of introduction to Kendall on 11 May 1846. Twelve days later Kendall told Little he "thought arrangements could be made to assist our emigration by enlisting one thousand of our men, equipping and establishing them in California."[28] Kendall acted as a middleman between Polk and Little in the discussions that led to the authorization of the Mormon Battalion, whose payroll proved to be the financial salvation of the LDS church.[29]

Jesse Little mentioned Brannan by name in his 1 June 1846 letter to

---

[26]Sirrine, A Little Sketch of the Life of George Warren Sirrine, LDS Archives, 8; and Watson, ed., *Reminiscences and Incidents of Early Days of San Francisco*, 34. Warren Sirrine wrote that this was the first marriage "performed on the Pacific Coast in the English language," but Brown said the Hall-Winner marriage was the "first wedding which took place after this city was under the protection of the American flag." Like many Brannan "firsts," the facts are impossible to determine with any certainty.

[27]Woodruff to Little, 27 March 1846, Utah State Hist. Soc.

[28]Journal History, 6 July 1846.

[29]Luce, "The Mormon Battalion: A Historical Accident?" 30, 33.

President Polk: "I am not ignorant of your good feelings towards us, receiving my information from my friend, Mr. Samuel Brannan, who has gone to California, and also the Hon. Amos Kendall and others."[30] Little reported from Washington City in early October 1846.

> I have just called upon the President & find him well & finally haveing more confidence in our People than when I left him. I spoke to him concerning the Lands we might settle on provided California is retained. Of this he spoke well—I did not speak of this to you but presume you will be pleased with any thing that will do us good. I have also been to see the Indian Commissioner in relation to the document & permission to remain on the Indian Lands [at Winter Quarters]. Every thing will be right. The Commissioner will Transmit to me a copy of his instructions to [Thomas H.] Harvey the Indian agent at St. Louis and I will send a copy to you. I called upon Judge [John K.] Kane & he told me if I wanted to effect any thing at Washington he would assist me all in his pow[e]r. He wished me to say when I wrote to our people that his son [Thomas L. Kane] had Expressed his highest regard for you ...
>
> I have called with Bro. [Ezra Taft] Benson upon Mr Kendall who is here. He is friendly & says that if any time he can do us any good that he shall be happy to help us and do it freely and without Expecting any thing in return—I spoke of Land and I think that it is possible we can get ½ section for each family 360 [sic] Acres and for this reason I should [think] it would be wise to survey the Land we settle on & Let there be a House built & improvements made on Each ½ section and I have no doubt but what we can obtain it. I shall endeavour to Lay well the foundation for this through the influence of my friends.[31]

Kendall, of course, was manipulating the LDS church to support Polk's California policy. It was in a conversation with Kendall "about the Mormons" that ward-politician Jonathan Stevenson conceived the idea of sending a regiment of New York volunteers to counterbalance Mormon influence in California.[32] Kendall remained interested in the Saints, for John Bernhisel, Utah Territory's future representative in Congress, reported to Brigham Young in 1850 that Kendall wanted "to

---

[30]Golder, *The March of the Mormon Battalion*, 83.

[31]Little to Young, 6 October 1846, Brigham Young Collection, LDS Archives. Little began the letter with a description of his return from the Mormon camps on the Missouri River, where he had helped recruit the Mormon Battalion.

[32]Bancroft, *History of California*, 5:472, 501. For Polk's concern about flooding California with Mormons, see Quaife, ed., *The Diary of James K. Polk*, 1:449–50.

establish a line of Electro-Magnetic Telegraph to the City of the Saints." Bernhisel wished "Success to him."[33]

Brannan asked Jesse Little in 1847 to give his "kind respects" to Benson, Kendall, and President Polk, and asked Little to contact Benson to promote business for the *California Star*. Brannan said Benson was "General Agent" for the paper in the states. Brannan's relationship with Benson probably continued into the gold rush. Benson thought his standing with the Saints strong enough in 1849 to provide a letter of introduction for John Wilson, "Indian Agent for California."

> A. G. BENSON TO YOUNG, 5 APRIL 1849,
> BRIGHAM YOUNG COLLECTION, LDS ARCHIVES.

> Washington 5th April 1849
>
> To the Elders of the
> Mormon Nation
>
> Having served your people who went to California by water (wi[th] the Brooklyn) it now gives me great pleasure to give you another evidence of my good will in making you acquainted with Genl John Wilson Indian Agent for California and the personal friend of Genl [Zachary] Taylor. He is your friend and is connected with an administration which is disposed to do justice to all. I have talked your matters all over with him and I commend him to your confidence and hospitality and keen tho humble services. As ever your friend and Obt Svt
>
> A. G. Benson

A thorough investigation of the National Archives would probably shed more light on the relations between Amos Kendall, the Bensons, the federal government, and the Mormons. There certainly is much to be learned about the government's clandestine support of Manifest Destiny and the role of Samuel Brannan and the Latter-day Saints in this intriguing story.

R. F. PECKHAM: AN EVENTFUL LIFE

Edward Kemble recalled that "the main body" of *Brooklyn* Mormons formed "a Farming, Trading and Manufacturing company, elected a board of officers, and inaugurated their existence as a corporate body by taking

---

[33]Journal History, 24 May 1850.

a contract" to supply redwood logs to Stephen Smith's sawmill at Bodega. Between twenty and thirty members of this "new organization bought a ship's longboat, and sent her sloop-rigged up the San Joaquin, with a party on board to make the first venture in farming."[34] The men founded the first white settlement in the San Joaquin Valley and named it New Hope.

In September 1846 the company selected a site west of today's Caswell Memorial State Park, about a mile and a half up the Stanislaus River from its confluence with the San Joaquin, near the trapper's post called French Camp. Thomas Farnham's friend, Dr. John Marsh, a Harvard man who had established a "romantically situated" rancho at the foot of Mt. Diablo, described the Stanislaus as "a clear, rapid mountain stream, some forty or fifty yards wide, with a considerable depth of water in its lower portions."[35] Early travelers depicted the valley as a pastoral paradise abounding in elk and grizzly bears, and praised its limitless agricultural potential. What the settlers of New Hope recalled were the Indians, mosquitoes, malaria, floodwaters, politics, and bickering that bedeviled the short history of California's first commune.

Although by August 1845 the Mormon apostles had identified the Great Basin as their destination, Brigham Young did not make the council's plans clear to Brannan. Young himself did not commit to settling in the Salt Lake Valley until he had seen it for himself, and he had a variety of good reasons for not being totally forthright with the Saints in the East. Brannan certainly expected to see at least an advance party of Mormons come overland to the coast in 1846, and the Saints in California seemed convinced that they were preparing a home for the entire LDS church. Once in the country Brannan fell in love with California and its potential. Mountaineers may have told him that the Salt Lake country was too cold and dry to support an agricultural settlement, for the New Hope colony was preparing to raise enough grain to sustain an enormous emigration. Brannan selected William Stout to lead the colony, an unfortunate choice.

---

[34]Rogers, ed., *A Kemble Reader*, 41.

[35]Bryant, *What I Saw in California*, 303; and Agricola, "The Valley of the San Joaquin," *The California Star*, 17 April 1847, 57. Publisher John Howell made the early files of the first two California newspapers available in handsome facsimile reproductions edited by Fred Blackburn Rogers and George P. Hammond. The decision to print the second volume of the *Star* depended "on the reception given to the present publication." The reception was not good and no subsequent volumes were issued for either book, leaving generations of historians to endure the frustrations of microfilm. Page numbers refer to Rogers, ed., *The California Star*, while citations to the *Star's* 1848 numbers refer the issue's page and column number.

At Marsh's rancho on 16 September, journalist Edwin Bryant met two women and one man of the New Hope party who were "making a settlement for agricultural purposes." The three Mormons were "waiting for the return of the main party, which has gone up the river to explore and select a suitable site for the settlement. The women are young, neatly dressed, and one of them may be called good-looking."[36]

A young sailor, Robert F. Peckham, deserted the whaleship *Cabinet* at Yerba Buena in 1846 to find that about three-fourths of the town's population were Mormons "who had come in the ship Brooklyn and they were living in tents mostly on the block between Kearney and Montgomery, Clay and Sacramento streets." Brannan's house, he recalled, was on the opposite side of Washington Street, just above the Old Adobe.

Years later while living in San Jose, Judge Peckham recalled the grand days of the Saints' communal experiment at New Hope in a remarkable reminiscence printed in the *San Jose Pioneer* during June and July 1877, in the wake of John D. Lee's trials for his role in the 1857 massacre at Mountain Meadows and the subsequent national fascination with Mormonism. A great cast of early California characters peopled Peckham's recollections, which provide wonderful detail about New Hope's early days. The judge told the story in the third person, with the long perspective and wry humor of an old pioneer. He recalled how after hiding in the oak brush above Yerba Buena for several days, he stumbled out of the hills on Mission Creek, desperate and thirsty. He found "a small, undecked schooner," probably the ship's launch the Mormons had purchased and named *Comet*, "in the charge of two men who spoke English." They "proved to be Mormons who had come out on the ship Brooklyn."

R. F. PECKHAM, "AN EVENTFUL LIFE,"
SAN JOSE PIONEER, 16 JUNE 1877, 1/4–5.

One was named [Julius] Austin and the other was Q. L. Sparks now a lawyer of San Francisco. They were men of families and lived at Mission Dolores, in the old Mission building in which were quartered several other Mormon families. These men were engaged in freighting supplies in this schooner, round from Yerba Buena, instead of hauling them three miles through the sand.

In answer to their questions Peckham told them the whole truth. They told him that he could rely on them as friends, that they would befriend anyone

---

[36]Bryant, *What I Saw in California*, 304.

who ran away from a whaleship. Their subsequent conduct showed they meant what they said. They had plenty of fresh beef, the principle article of diet in the country, and some sea biscuit. A fire was made, some of the beef strung together on a stick and held before the fire until it could be eaten, and thus Peckham cooked and eat [sic] his first meal in California.

As darkness approached, Sparks took the sailor to his house and gave him a place to sleep. The next morning Sparks told him to remain there and he would go to Yerba Buena and see if the ship had gone. He went, and, coming back reported her still at her anchorage. Sparks then told Peckham that he could stay with him as long as he desired; that he should have a place to sleep and such as he had to eat. And, said he: "We are Mormons, we have some bad people among us but average as well as anybody. But, by having bad men among the Mormons, they, by their bad acts, have brought the whole Mormon people into trouble and disgrace. We are despised and persecuted because we are Mormons; but we have as much of the milk of human kindness and know how to practice Christian Charity as well as anybody." From thirty year's subsequent knowledge of Mormon character, the Judge, not believing in any of their religious theories, believes and openly defends the remarks of his friend, Sparks, as strictly true. Sparks was a man of above the average of intelligence, a good talker, was raised in Connecticut, had been a schoolmaster, and was then a preacher in the Mormon church.

Peckham accepted the situation and remained with Sparks a week or ten day, during which time each learned to respect the other as they both were Yankees and had both been schoolmasters. But, the old Cabinet not going to sea, Peckham determined to get into the interior where he hoped to find something at which he could make himself useful and not be entirely dependent on the charity of strangers . . .

R. F. PECKHAM, "AN EVENTFUL LIFE,"
SAN JOSE PIONEER, 23 JUNE 1877, 1/3–6.

While Peckham was at work [in Santa Clara], on the third day, he was surprised by hearing his name called from a distance and, turning round, saw his friend [Quartus] Sparks approaching, riding one mule and leading another. The meeting was of the most friendly character. The situation was talked over and Sparks informed him that about thirty of the Mormons had left Yerba Buena in a schooner bound up the San Joaquin river to found a settlement in the Valley of that name; that they were going to colonize that part of the country and that he had been sent round by land to get a yoke of oxen at [Robert] Livermore's Ranch and meet them at Marsh's Landing, where the town of Antioch now stands. He invited Peckham to go with him . . .

Sparks got his oxen and they started for Doctor Marsh's ranch, thirty miles distant. Sparks rode and Peckham went on foot and drove the oxen. They arrived at Marsh's about nine o'clock that night and found the Doctor at home, with John M. Horner and family living with him in the same house. They were Mormons and had come with Sparks in the ship Brooklyn. This fact secured the travelers a hearty welcome and a good supper. Stopping here, at that time was an old man by the name of [Ezekial] Merritt, who had spent his days among the Indians and who had trapped for beaver in nearly every stream from the Missouri river to the Pacific Ocean. Doctor Marsh was an American. He had come to California in an early day and had become wealthy. He was a man of great education and intellectual attainment. He was widely known but had a reputation for closeness in dealing that rendered him unpopular. Horner became one of the first large farmers in Alameda county, where he still resides and is considered a good as well as prominent citizen. His crop in 1850 is reported to have cleared him $100,000.

The next morning Peckham was furnished with a horse and saddle and the Doctor went with them to the Embarcadero where they found the schooner. She had about thirty Mormon passengers, all men, and armed with rifles and revolvers to defend themselves against any attack by Indians. The schooner was loaded with wheat, a wagon and implements necessary to put in a crop. They were under the control of one William Stout who had been appointed by Samuel Brannan, the leader of the Brooklyn Expedition.

From here, Sparks went by land with the oxen and Peckham went in the schooner. They were guided by a rude chart made for them by the trapper Merritt, and in about two days reached the head of navigation, where the Western Pacific Railroad now crosses the river. Here they disembarked and camped on the east side. This, so far as known, was the first sail vessel ever to ascend the San Joaquin River.

The next day the company proceeded to the location selected for the first settlement. This was a spot situated on the north bank of the Stanislaus river a mile and a half above its junction with the San Joaquin. They soon completed a log house after the western style, covered with oak shingles made on the ground, and Peckham, with one Cyrus Ira, erected a Pulgas Redwoods saw mill and sawed the boards from oak logs with which to lay the floor.

This was the first permanent settlement in the great San Joaquin Valley. A man by the name of Lindsay, had, two years before, built a hut where Stockton now stands, but the Indians turned hostile and killed him.

The Indians never troubled the Mormon Colony but the latter were always on the alert and a picket guard was kept around the house, nightly.

The valley was filled at this time with wild horses, elk and antelope, which went in droves by thousands. Deer were very plenty. The ground was covered by geese, the lakes and rivers with ducks and the willow swamps along the river banks were filled with grizzly bears . . . It was no more trouble for the colonists to get a bear than it was to get a deer or an elk and bear's oil was made to take the place of lard in the culinary department. Their flesh was also very palatable.

The only provisions sent up for the colony was unground wheat, sugar and coffee. All else had to be procured with the rifle; meat enough could be got in three hours by one man, to last the colony a week. To grind their wheat they had a mill with steel plates instead of burrs, driven by a crank by hand. The wheat was cut or ground up but not bolted. Every man had to grind his own wheat, make his own bread and coffee, and cook his own meat. But little washing or house cleaning was done.

As soon as the house was built they commenced plowing the ground and sowing wheat and fencing it in. By the middle of January, 1847, they had eighty acres sowed and enclosed. The fence was made by cutting down and cutting up oak trees, rolling the butts and large pieces into a line and covering them with the limbs. The native Californians made most of their fences, which were few, in the same manner.

There is something in the history of the Mormon settlement [in the West] that has never been written. California was a distant and unimportant province of Mexico, sparse in population, beautiful in climate, rich in climate and soil but illy prepared to subdue internal insurrection or resist the encroachment of a foreign foe. The Mormon Church, under the leadership of Brigham Young and the Mormon [Nauvoo] Legion, a well trained military force, sufficient to resist any force which could be brought against them by Mexico in California, came to the conclusion that they could no longer reside peacefully in Illinois. They broke up their settlement in Nauvoo and started for California. They crossed the State of Iowa, and spent the winter at a place they named Kanesville, now called Council Bluffs. Their intention was to take possession of California and, securing it from Mexico, establish in it a Theocratic Government of their own and so create for themselves a separate, independent national existence. With this object in view, in the latter part of 1845, the ship Brooklyn was chartered in New York to bring a company of Mormon emigrants California, as the advance guard of this great movement, while the main body came overland. Samuel Brannan was selected as the leader of this movement. She brought as passengers about three hundred men, women and children, mostly Americans from Maine, Rhode Island, Connecticut, New York, New Jersey, and Pennsylvania. She was freighted with seeds and agricultural implements to put in and harvest a very large crop. The men were all supplied with arms and ammunition sufficient to enable them to maintain themselves, and with provisions to last two years after their arrival in California. The object of this company was to establish a settlement, and make provisions for the reception and subsistence of the great body of Mormons when they should arrive overland, and it was for this purpose that the San Joaquin Valley was selected, this settlement made and the first crop of wheat in that valley was sown. It was at this time foreseen that the occupation California by the United States might interfere with Mormon independence for a while, but it was not doubted that it was destined to be the future home of the Mormon people and they quoted and believed a prophecy of Joseph Smith that a great and exterminating war was to come between the Northern and Southern portions of the United States and that they would then be able, not only to establish their independence and sovereignty, but should return and build up their New Jerusalem at Independence, Missouri, and eventually dominate over the whole United States with only one Government and that, the Mormon Church. This was certainly the understanding of the men engaged in the enterprise, and as proof that the same understanding existed on the part of Brigham Young and the other Mormons the fact existed that while they were at Kanesville, a call was made for volunteers to serve in the Mexican war. A regiment was raised by the Mormon authorities and tendered to the Government for service during the war with the express understanding and agreement that when their services were no longer needed, they would be transported by the Government to California. This was done. They arrived here [after their discharge in Los Angeles] in the Summer of 1848 [1847].

In the meantime the Mormon plan was changed and they settled finally in the Salt Lake Valley and most of the Mormon soldiers returned there overland. The majority of those who came in the Brooklyn remained in California, and quite a number of them still survive in different parts of the State.

While this settlement was being made and crops put in, the company became disillusioned with the leadership of Stout. He was unpopular. When the sowing had been done and fenced in, he essayed to make them a speech essentially as follows:

"Now boys we have got through putting in our crop and have got it fenced in, now go to work each of you and select a good farm of 160 acres, and make out the boundaries; we will go to work and put up houses, one at a time, so that by the time the crop is ready to harvest, you will all have your houses and farms. BUT I SELECT THIS PLACE; THIS HOUSE AND THIS FARM IS MINE." The latter part of this speech culminated the hostile feelings which had been growing against him and Samuel Brannan was sent for to hear their grievances. He came and held a church meeting at which a resolution was introduced and adopted with great unanimity setting apart and dedicating that house and farm to the use of the twelve Mormon Apostles. A few days afterward Stout abandoned the settlement and never returned . . .

The winters of 1846-7, were very wet and stormy. The river under the

influence of rain rose and fell very rapidly, eight feet an hour on the per-
pendicular was marked. About the middle of January, 1847, the river overflowed its banks and the whole country was under water for miles in every
direction. [Peckham] was again barefoot and almost destitute of clothing.
He became disgusted with the prospects of the San Joaquin and determined
to try his luck in the vicinity of Pueblo [San Jose] . . .

A visitor who called himself "Tule Rover" made "a noonday halt at
New Hope" in early April 1847 and found that the ten or twelve settlers
who had outlasted the winter floods "appear contented and energetic"
and had "three or four houses completed, and as many more under way."
He squashed a rumor that Indians had massacred the settlement, though
he encountered "a wild, wicked looking party of warriors, with horses
and arrows innumerable." Most of the "Tallalomes" in the area were
"actively employed in fishery, catching and drying vast quantities of
salmon."[37] John Marsh wrote that the Mormons had "built some two or
three houses near the mouth" of the Stanislaus.[38]

NANCY LAURA BUCKLAND: WE HAD QUITE A COMPANY

Almost sixty years after landing in San Francisco, *Brooklyn* pioneer
Nancy Laura Buckland recalled living at the mission and her husband
Alondus' involvement with the New Hope colony. Buckland's memory was
not perfect, but she remembered interesting details about the local Indians
who, according to her account, stole native children as well as horses.

NANCY BUCKLAND TO EDITH WEBB, 10 FEBRUARY 1904,
LDS ARCHIVES.

Copy   Bountiful, Daniel's, Utah
                                                    Feb. 10, 1904

Dear Grand[d]aughter Edith Webb
    I was much pleased to see the Old Mission Church. It looked natural and
nice. We lived thare Sept. 1846 till June 1847. The rainy season was soon
coming [and there were] no houses in San Francisco. I was married the 10.
of October [at the mission] in the long room divided by tents. 4 families of
us [lived] on the north side as we entered the door on the east or the same
side the Church was on. We had a fire place cut through in our room on the
wall towards the north. Alondus started [for New Hope on] Oct. 20. It

---

[37]Letter, *The California Star*, 17 April 1847, 59.
[38]Agricola, "The Valley of the San Joaquin," *The California Star*, 17 April 1847, 57.

commenced to rain when he was on the boat going up the river [and] it rained several days. They lay under a tarpolian. There was so many tularies growing in the river they could not go on shore. They were going to find a place to settle. Alondus came home [and] then went and built a house on his claim [and] harvested their wheat. We moved in July [1847] about the last. Everything went along very well until the last of August and the first of Sept. They most of them had the fever and Ague [malaria]. We had quite a company. Mother and Brother came down with it. She shook [and] he had the dumb [?] [and] died in February. They all left [except] one man and one family and us, left. I would not move. Your father was born there the 17th about 2 miles ½ up the river above the old Mormon Crossing where Willie was nearly drowned. Our nearest neighbor was an Indian tribe [who] often camp[ed] by us. [They] had been fighting [and] captured some young ones. They would howl and cry all night. Then he took his house down. We moved to Stockton in January. They all left there after Lafayette was born. Not a friend to be seen. I have been comfortable this winter. With kind regards to you and Husband.

Many thanks for your kindness

(signed) Nancy Laura Buckland

The *California Star*

Edward Kemble recalled that Brannan began preparing to publish "the pioneer newspaper of California" in New York, and even had the "name of the unrisen orb chosen, engraved, and stereotyped" and "type lines set up and packed" in December 1845.[39] Brannan missed his chance to publish California's first newspaper when Walter Colton, chaplain of the *Congress*, and Robert Semple, who had arrived with Hastings in 1845, issued the *Californian* in Monterey on 15 August. The paper's inaugural number noted the arrival of "La frigata Brooklyn" in both Spanish and English, miscounting the number of "mormon emigrants" and incorrectly dating the ship's arrival in California, but favorably reporting that the "emigrants are a plain industrious people, most of them mechanics and farmers."[40]

Brannan rented Nathan Spear's gristmill on the north side of today's Clay Street, "about the largest frame structure in town," and put a man to work grinding wheat. The mill produced a "a dirty mess of partially

[39]Kemble, *A History of California Newspapers*, 67.
[40]Hammond, ed., *The Californian*, 2, 3.

cracked wheat of a very inferior and damaged quality. That was our bread—very ill bread—of those times that tried men's teeth." Up the mill's "crazy staircase" Edward Kemble and John Eagar "lifted and pushed and dragged" the No. 4 Washington press "of Hoe & Co.'s make" and installed it on the second story. The press was set up by 6 September 1846 and the "first printing office in the Bay of San Francisco was ready for business."[41] Its first job was to print "Rules and Regulations, for the Trade of the Bay of San Francisco" in English and Spanish, for Washington Bartlett. The "Commander of the District of San Francisco, &c &c" had learned that "persons are engaged in stealing and killing cattle." He appointed an inspector general and imposed a long series of regulations, financed with a tax of three cents per hide and twenty-five cents "on each bag of tallow."[42] Brannan printed deeds, forms, programs, and proclamations for the conquerors of California, the most notable job being the "Order of the Day" printed on blue satin for Commodore Stockton's reception on 8 October.[43]

Dispatches from Zachary Taylor detailing American victories over Santa Ana arrived on 21 October. The information was already six months old, but it was news in Yerba Buena and prompted Brannan to issue "the first news sheet in what is now the City of San Francisco."[44] *An Extra in Advance of The California Star*, a single double-sided sheet, appeared on 24 October 1846, and besides gossip culled from the overland mail was devoted entirely to war news from the previous May. Just below the masthead, it listed S. Brannan, Printer, and "Price One Real."

The *Extra* was printed in the loft of the gristmill, but there still remained the business of starting a newspaper. Brannan set to work in December. Edward Kemble was suffering under John C. Frémont in southern California at the time, but he recalled that the printers and members of the Mormon joint-stock company erected an adobe build-

---

[41]Watson, "The Great Express of the *California Star*," 130; and Rogers, ed., *A Kemble Reader*, 42. The fate of the Brannan press has been a matter of much speculation ever since Brannan offered to pay "a handsome price" for it in the *Alta California*, 19 November 1859. Robert S. MacCollister, "What Became of the Brannan Press?" 1–7, did an excellent job tracking the artifact's history. He concluded that it is impossible to determine its fate, but an acorn press said to be the *Star*'s was displayed at the San Francisco Maritime Museum during the *Brooklyn* sesquicentennial.

[42]For reproductions of Brannan's early imprints, see Rogers, *Montgomery and the Portsmouth*, 77, 82.

[43]Kemble, *A History of California Newspapers*, 68; and Rogers, *Montgomery and the Portsmouth*, 82.

[44]Rogers, ed., *The California Star*, x; and Kemble, *A History of California Newspapers*, 69.

ing just behind the old Custom House, and the "typos took a part in the mixing of the clay and the moulding of the adobes."[45] Brannan told Brigham Young that he had found a man "who, with three men, would agree to make adobes for a 30 foot house and put a family in it in a week. His printing office was put up in 14 days and a paper printed."[46]

Before issuing its first official number, the *Star* printed another extra, no copies of which survive. Fortunately, the *Millennial Star* reprinted Brannan's informative letter, which described the contentions that plagued the *Brooklyn* voyage and contained a wealth of gossip. He reported the founding of the New Hope colony, expressed his conviction that California was the destination of the Saints, and gave a hint of his plans: "As soon as the snow is off the mountains we shall send a couple of men to meet the emigration by land, or perhaps go myself."

"TO THE SAINTS IN ENGLAND AND AMERICA,"
LATTER-DAY SAINTS' MILLENNIAL STAR, 15 OCTOBER 1847, 306–07.
(*From the California Star-Extra.*)
Yerba Buena, San Francisco, Jan 1 1847

Beloved Brethren,—Feeling sensible of the anxiety of your minds to become acquainted with the state of affairs in this country, induces me, at this late hour, to communicate to you this short and feeble epistle. Our passage from New York to this place was made in six months; since our arrival, the colony generally has enjoyed good health. In relation to the country and climate we have not been disappointed in our expectations; but, like all new countries, we found the accounts of it to be very much exaggerated; so much so, that we recommend to all emigrants hereafter to provide themselves with thick clothing, instead of thin. There has been no arrival in this country this fall, from those coming by land; but we are anxiously waiting for them next season. They will in all probability winter on the head waters of the Platt, where they can subsist upon Buffalo meat. We are now all busily engaged in putting in crops for them to subsist upon when they arrive; *I said all*, but I should have said all that love the brethren, for, about twenty males of our feeble number have gone astray after strange gods, serving their bellies and their own lusts, and refuse to assist in providing for the reception of their brethren by land. They shall have their reward. We have commenced a settlement on the river San Joaquin, a large and beautiful stream emptying into the Bay of San Francisco; but the families of the company are wintering in this place [Yerba Buena], where they find plenty of employment, and houses

---

[45]Kemble, *A History of California Newspapers*, 69.   [46]Journal History, 1 August 1847.

to live in; and about twenty of our number are up at the new settlement, which we call New Hope, ploughing and putting in wheat and other crops, and making preparations to move their families up in the spring, where they hope to meet the main body by land some time during the coming season. The Spaniards or natives of the country are kind and hospitable; but previous to our arrival they felt very much terrified from the reports that had been circulated among them by those who had emigrated from Missouri, which have proven to be false, and they have become our warmest friends. Governor Boggs is in this country, but without influence even among his own people that he emigrated with.[47] And during an interview I had with him a few days since, he expressed much dissatisfaction with the country, and spoke strongly of returning back in the spring. He says nothing about the Mormons, whether through fear or policy I am not able to say. As soon as the snow is off the mountains we shall send a couple of men to meet the emigration by land, or perhaps go myself. The feelings among the foreigners in the country are very friendly, and I have found, even among the emigration from Missouri some of the warmest friends. We shall commence publishing a paper next week, which will be the government organ by the sanction of Colonel Freemont, who is now our Governor, and is at the present time on a campaign to Lower California to subdue the Spaniards, who have lately taken up arms. We arrived here about three weeks after the United States' Flag was hoisted, and the country taken possession of by the Americans, which exempted us from paying a heavy bill of duties, which would have amounted to about twenty thousand dollars. Capt. Montgomery of the sloop of war Portsmouth, at that time held command over this district, and to whose gentlemanly attention we were under many obligations. A few of the passengers on our arrival endeavoured to make mischief and trouble, by complaints of the bad treatment they had received during the passage, which induced Capt. M. to institute a court of enquiry, before which the larger portion of the company were cited to appear, for private examination. But the truth was mighty and prevailed! and every effort that has yet been made to bring disgrace and reproach upon the cause, by cunning and wicked men, has been frustrated, and they learn that the warfare was useless. Four persons were excommunicated from the church during our passage, for their wicked and licentious conduct. Elder E. W. Pell, Orren Smith, A. T. Moses, and Mrs. Lucy Eagar.[48] The conduct of the above mentioned two, who were Elders, was of the most disgraceful character, and

---

[47]Lilburn Boggs, notorious for issuing his "extermination order" while governor of Missouri during the 1838 Mormon War, went overland in 1846 and settled in Sonoma.

[48]Edward Kemble recalled that "whatever their religion may have at that time taught on the subject of polygamy or the spiritual-wife doctrine . . . practically the system was ignored" on the voyage. See Rogers, ed., *A Kemble Reader*, 17. Yet the practice apparently motivated these excommunications.

could they have succeeded in carrying their sway, and successfully gained the ascendency of their doctrines, we must every soul of us have perished.

The captain of the ship became very much alarmed, and was continually urging some decided step to be taken in relation to them, which we delayed to do until we left the Sandwich Islands, when a council was called and the matter investigated, and a list of evidences given of the most disgusting character. And since our arrival three others have been excommunicated; Elisha Hyate, Jas. Scott, and Isaac Addison; the latter having returned to the United States, and others who deserved to share the same fate; but at the present our attention is more particularly called to temporal affairs, if we might so term it, than spiritual—by making every exertion in our power to provide for the arrival of our brethren over the mountains.

Provisions in the country are high, owing to the arrival of so many emigrants, and provisioning the Army and Navy; and without any doubt will be very scarce next season, from the unsettled state of affairs in the country, politically, which has had a very bad influence upon the agriculturists. Good mechanics are very much needed in the country, and in great demand. None of them need go idle for want of employment, and being well paid. Merchandise and groceries demand a heavy price, and emigrants coming to this country should come well supplied, which can be done only by coming by water. Wheat is now selling for one dollar per bushel, and flour for twenty dollars per hundred, owing to the scarcity of mills.

We have received no intelligence from our brethren at the Society Islands, and conclude that they have not yet learned of the warfare and pilgrimage of the Saints, or they would be wending their way to California. We are every day anxiously looking for the arrival of another ship load of emigrants. Two have been reported to have sailed—one from New York and the other from Boston.

We will now bring our epistle to a close by a few words of kindly advice to those wishing to emigrate to this Eldorado of the West, and that is, by all means come by water in preference to land, the advantage you will appreciate for years to come.

Yours truly, in the bonds of the everlasting Covenant,

S. BRANNAN, President

WE SHALL AT ALL TIMES SPEAK TRUTH

The *Star's* first issue appeared on 9 January 1847 and proclaimed that the weekly journal was "Dedicated to the Liberties and Interests of the People of California." Brannan had hired William H. Russell to edit the paper, but the Kentucky colonel was otherwise engaged. The "anxiety of the proprietor to commence publication of his paper" induced the colorful Elbert P. Jones to assume the position. Jones promised that "While on the editorial tripod, all private pique and editorial feeling and jealousy will be laid aside," and swore constant effort to make the paper "useful and interesting." In the prospectus, Brannan promised to support no "sectarian dogmas." He had "on hand paper enough to enable us to print about one thousand copies of each number for twelve months, and have made arrangements to be supplied from time to time."[49] Perhaps silently acknowledging a debt to Amos Kendall, the last article in the issue noted the completion of the telegraph from Washington to New York, but the piece may have simply been early evidence of Brannan's lifelong fascination with technology. The issue also named A. G. Benson & Co. as the paper's "General Agent for the United States."

"PROSPECTUS OF THE CALIFORNIA STAR,"
9 JANUARY 1847, 3.

The undersigned in common with the rest of the citizens of the United States, having experienced the good effects of the Press in diffusing early and accurate information on all important subjects, in advancing and defending the rights of every class of people, in detecting, exposing and opposing tyranny and oppression—and being anxious to secure to himself and the citizens of his adopted country, the benefits of a free, fearless and untrammalled Newspaper—Purchased and brought with him to California a press and all the materials necessary to effect that desirable object. Contrary to our original intention, but being fully convinced that the present crisis in the affairs of the country demands it, we have resolved to commence AT ONCE the publication of a paper to be styled "THE CALIFORNIA STAR".

The peculiar situation of our country, and the absence of all sinister motives forbid the idea of the intrusion into our colum[n]s of party politics—the bane of liberty, the usual door to licentiousness, and which defeat the true and noble objects of the press. It is our fixed purpose to advocate and defend to the utmost of our abilities the best interests of California; to which end we shall at all times speak truth of men and measures, regardless of the fame we may win or lose or how it may affect our individual enterprise.

We will endeavor to render the "STAR" pleasing and acceptable to all

---

[49]"Our Paper," *The California Star*, 23 January 1847, 10.

classes of readers by collecting and publishing the latest news from all parts of the world. It will communicate from time to time all the information that can be obtained, touching the commercial, agricultural, mechanical and mineral capabilities of the country; and will eschew with the greatest caution every thing that tends to the propagation of sectarian dogmas.

The STAR will be an independent paper uninfluenced by those in power or the fear of the abuse of power, or of patronage or favor.

The paper is designed to be permanent, and as soon as circumstances will permit will be enlarged, so as to be in point of size not inferior to most of the weekly papers in the United States.

It will be published weekly on a Royal sheet at six dollars per annum. As soon as a suitable person can be employed, all articles of general interest will be published in Spanish as well as English.

S. BRANNAN.

From Monterey the *Californian* took note of its new rival: "We have received the first two numbers of a new paper, just commenced at Yerba Buena. It is issued upon a small but very neat sheet, at six dollars per annum. It is published and owned by S. Brannan, the leader of the Mormons, who was brought up by Joe Smith himself, and is consequently well qualified to unfold and impress the tenets of his sect."[50] The *Star* soon denounced the *Californian* as "a dim, dirty, little, paper printed in Monterey on the worn out materials of one of the old California WAR PRESSES." It called Reverend Colton a "WHINING SYCOPHANT" and Robert Semple "AN OVERGROWN LICK-SPITTLE," and protested that a note on one of their papers to "please exchange" was a "bare-faced attempt to swindle us." The *Star's* editor gave his rival a free subscription, "to afford them some insight into the manner in which a Republican newspaper should be conducted."[51]

The *Star* engaged in a running battle with Washington Bartlett, alcalde of Yerba Buena. The paper's initial issue carried a commentary signed Yerba Buena, the pseudonym of C. E. "Philosopher" Pickett, that accused the alcalde of misappropriating funds. Later issues revisited the subject until an investigation exonerated Bartlett. The paper published Bartlett's proclamation renaming the village San Francisco on 23 January 1847, "to prevent confusion and mistakes in public documents," but

---

[50]"The Press," *The Californian*, 23 January 1847, 98.
[51]*The California Star*, 20 February 1847, 26.

the *Star* ran a full-page article on 30 January saying that some "old maps" used the name San Francisco, but it "is not known by that name here however."[52] The *Star* did not remove the name Yerba Buena from its masthead until its 20 March issue.

California learned of the Donner party disaster when the *Star* ran a short notice on 16 January about "Emigrants in the Mountains," reporting their "most distressing situation." Captain Sutter had sent them aid, but hoped "that our citizens will do something for the relief of these unfortunate people." Surveyor Jasper O'Farrell called a public meeting at Brown's Hotel to "take into consideration the best way for their release." John Brown recalled, "Samuel Brannan deserves much praise for the valuable assistance he rendered in raising a collection among the Mormons." The meeting collected $860.[53]

WE WILL GO TO THE MOUNTAINS AND SEE THE INDIANS

As the Saints' dreams of building the capital of a new Zion in California drowned under the floodwaters of the San Joaquin in January 1847, Samuel Brannan was already looking ahead to the prospect of a trip to the mountains to "make some new discoveries." He wrote the brethren at New Hope not to give up if the Lord destroyed their wheat crop. Like many of Brannan's comments from this time, irony pervaded the letter, for his advice not to be too "ravenous to make money and get rich, or you might forget God and die" would be personally prophetic. Isaac Goodwin's family preserved Brannan's letter for almost 150 years before donating it to the LDS church.

BRANNAN TO BRETHREN [AT NEW HOPE],
13 FEBRUARY 1847, LDS ARCHIVES.

Yerba Buena, Feb. 13, 1847

Beloved and respected

Brethren—I shall be up with you by the next launch without fail—and then we will all take a trip into the mountains—and make some new dis-

---

[52]"Yerba Buena and San Francisco Bay," *The California Star*, 30 January 1847, 14. Peter Browning located an article in the *San Francisco Call*, 8 September 1901, indicating Bartlett issued his proclamation changing the town's name on 19 January 1847.

[53]Watson, ed., *Early Days of San Francisco*, 62.

coveries. I hope you will not get discouraged, but press onward and trust in God, and that the strong will not be overcome by the faint-hearted—"He that sticks to the [w]reck will save his wages" and he that leaves it will loose it—for the ship is not going to sink—if she does let us go to the bottom together—but believe me—she is not—dont be to[o] ravenous to make money and get rich, or you might forget God and die—hang to the truth and your covenant and God will reward you if no body else dont—new things are springing up—things are working just right, and if the Lord wants to destroy our crop of wheat up their let his will be done not ours— he knows what is best, better than we—and he has the helm—and will do just what is right. Have your horses ready and we will go to the mountains and see the Indians without fail. Yours respectfully

S. Brannan

Samuel Brannan was now ready to cross the Snowy Mountains to find Brigham Young and the Pioneer Camp of the Saints.

Chapter 7

"ACROSS THE SNOWY MOUNTAINS"

Samuel Brannan left San Francisco on 4 April 1847 on the boldest venture of his audacious young life. With three companions, he set out to cross the Sierra Nevada and the Great Basin to find the long-lost "Camp of Israel." Brannan had heard nothing from the main body of the church for months. With no certain knowledge of the church's plans or its actual location, Brannan hoped to meet Brigham Young somewhere on the overland trail—and then guide the Pioneer Camp to California.

Brannan stopped at New Hope on his way to Sutter's Fort. Only ten or twelve settlers were left at the colony, but he seems to have gotten provisions and mules from the struggling community.[1] Brannan left Sutter's Fort on 26 April 1847 with Charles C. Smith, a distant relation of the Mormon prophet, and two other men. Little is known of Smith, but William Clayton remembered he had been involved with "the firm of Jackson, Heaton & Bonney, bogus makers of Nauvoo."[2] He traveled overland to Oregon in 1845 and he was probably the "Mr. C. Smith" whose arrival aboard the *Toulon* the *Star* noted on 27 January 1847. By February Smith was running a ferry service with Frank Ward, one of the non-Mormon *Brooklyn* passengers. The partners offered the services of their launch for the Donner rescue.[3]

Even less is known about Brannan's two other companions—and their identity remains a mystery. "Brannan's trip," Dale Morgan noted, "is one altogether too unsung in Mormon annals; and it is strange how both the trip and his companions have been neglected."[4] One likely can-

[1]Glover, *The Mormons in California*, 20.
[2]Smith, ed. *An Intimate Chronicle*, 353; and Bigler, ed., *The Gold Discovery Journal of Azariah Smith*, 100.
[3]Horace Whitney, Journal, 30 June 1847; and Morgan, ed., *Overland in 1846*, 701.
[4]Morgan to Korns, 20 September 1941, Dale L. Morgan Papers.

didate was *Brooklyn* pioneer Isaac Goodwin, who told a journalist in 1878 that he was

> the man who, with only one companion, travelled across the continent, successfully braving natural obstacles and hostile Indians, until they met Brigham Young on the eastern slope of the Rocky Mountains, and told him of the fertility of the soil of California. It was by his report Brigham was induced to act in accordance with his revelation [to settle in Utah], as the Mormons believe, but, as we are inclined to think, from the conviction that he would not be allowed to remain [in California].[5]

Goodwin's descendants preserve a strong family tradition that he made the trip with Brannan. His grandson, W. F. Butt, stated in a letter to the 14 August 1915 *Deseret News* that "Isaac Goodwin was one of those sent to report on California to Brigham Young, who was coming west overland." An 1870s photograph of Goodwin preserved by the family has a handwritten caption stating that he "came with Sam Brannan to Utah, 1847."[6] This would seem to solve the puzzle, but Goodwin's participation in the trip is problematic: none of the 1847 pioneer company journals named him, and his statement had errors of detail about Brannan's trip. Addison Pratt provided the best evidence against Goodwin's claim, for Pratt wrote that in June 1847 he accompanied "Brother Goodwin" to New Hope for the wheat harvest.[7] Circumstantial evidence—such as William Clayton's comment that Brannan's second comrade was a "young man"—also argues against the thirty-six-year-old Goodwin being Brannan's companion.

It seems certain that at least one of the unidentified men had traveled the California Trail and probable that the unnamed companions were non-Mormons.[8] Their identity, however, is impossible to determine with any certainty. As Dale Morgan commented, "It's damned unlucky

[5]Codman, *The Round Trip*, 198–201.

[6]Ricketts, "Isaac Goodwin—Noted Pioneer," 15, first identified Goodwin as Brannan's companion, but she no longer believes he was the man. Descendant Dale Goodwin provided his family's traditions.

[7]Ellsworth, ed., *The Journals of Addison Pratt*, 331, 543.

[8]Herbert Hamlin, in *The Pony Express*, July 1948, 5/1, wrote, "Sam Brannan, with Matt Harbin, Hunsaker and Smith, [rode] horse back through these regions in early 1847, looking for the lost Brigham Young and his hosts." The *New Helvetia Diary* put Matt Harbin at Sutter's Fort on 20 July, eliminating him as a candidate. The same source described the arrival of "Smith and Hundsaker" on 23 August 1847 "from the Emigration," but Dale Morgan eliminated Hunsaker as a candidate in a letter to Rod Korns, 14 December 1943. W. W. Riter, son of the Levi Riter who shipped goods on the *Brooklyn*, suggested in 1917 that mountaineer Joseph Chiles "had accompanied Brannan . . . to meet Brigham Young." See Carter, ed., *Heart Throbs*, 7:407.

that none of the Mormon diaries saw fit to inquire about these two men's names."[9]

THE SPANYARDS MAY TAKE THE COUNTRY AND BE DAMED!

Three days before heading east, Brannan wrote to E. P. Jones, editor of the *California Star*, to report the latest news from Sutter's Fort and to counter charges John Marsh had made in the *Star* against some of Sutter's Indian associates. Using a pen-name, Salem, Brannan recited the complaints of the veterans of Frémont's California Battalion, mourned the state of Sutter's finances, and denounced the government's California policy in general.[10]

Brannan's encounter with a "horse thief Indian" leader was a meeting of kindred spirits. Dale Morgan identified José Jesus as a Siyakum chief, and he is often identified as a Miwok, but he was probably a Northern Yokuts. His people had their main village at Las Casenno, now Knights Ferry, and controlled the land between French Camp Slough and the Stanislaus River, where New Hope was located. How the Mormons handled the tribe's land claim is not clear, but José Jesus had already made an arrangement with Charles Weber, recommending the town site upon which the German emigrant located the town of Stockton. The Indian leader even offered to provide warriors to defend Weber's settlement against his traditional enemies, the Mexicans.[11] José Jesus had succeeded Estanislao, the famous leader of the bands on the Stanislaus River who had learned the value of horses from Jedediah Smith's mountaineers in the winter of 1827. "Tall, well-proportioned, and possessed of remarkable ability," José Jesus had once been alcalde at San Jose, but "became offended" and "was ever after hostile to the Mexicans."[12] In 1845 Sutter sent José Jesus, who he called "Chief of the Chapeysimney," to catch other Indian raiders "in their holes." When war broke out the next year, Sutter persuaded the "old horse-thieves . . . now reformed under Jose Jesus, a christianized indian" to enlist in the California Bat-

---

[9]Morgan to Korns, 25 January 1944, Dale L. Morgan Papers.

[10]The pen-name "Salem" that Brannan used to sign this letter does not appear in the pages of the *Star*, which did not publish this report.

[11]Hammond and Morgan, eds., *Captain Charles W. Weber*, 5. I am indebted to California State Park Ranger José Rivera for information about José Jesus.

[12]Bancroft, *History of California*, 1:75–76.

talion. The Indians performed excellent service in Edwin Bryant's Company H, known to the *Californios* as "the forty thieves." Like the rest of Frémont's volunteers, they had trouble getting paid for their services.[13]

After José Jesus' meeting with Brannan, the New Helvetia diary recorded the arrival of "Jose Jesus, Felipe, Ra[y]mundo, Carlos & other Chief with their Alcaldes and people to work" on 7 August 1847. "I now have good prospects of getting the Wheat in," Sutter noted.[14] As Brannan reported, José Jesus had forsaken horse raiding. In 1848 he turned to slave trading, capturing Indians in the mountains and offering them as workers in San Jose, "as a token of his promise to give up horse raiding forever and be friendly to the government." (The Indians learned quickly that while rustling was a crime in the United States, slave trading was not.) During the gold rush he became a labor contractor—and business boomed. He sent twenty-five mounted men to Weber Creek, where they had astonishing success. By June Captain Weber had "gathered around him a thousand Indians" who worked for "the necessaries of life" and "little trinkets." After learning "the science of mining," these Indians discovered large lumps of pure gold in the Stanislaus, "the first gold found in what was known as the southern mines, and the first coarse gold found in California."[15] José Jesus adapted to white society and profited from the gold rush, but he appears to have been among its casualities, for he vanished from the historical record in the early 1850s.[16]

Brannan had left E. P. Jones in charge of the *Star* with instructions to "the boys"—John Eagar and Edward Kemble—to depose the rambunctious editor if he became too troublesome. The boys did so almost immediately (some say they rolled him down the hills of San Francisco in a barrel), breaking Jones' green spectacles when they threw him out of the office.[17] The *Star* printed another John Marsh letter on 1 May 1847 complaining about José Jesus and Filipe. Marsh seemed particularly

[13]Hurtado, *Indian Survival on the California Frontier*, 52, 81–82, 84.

[14]José Jesus left for two weeks on a borrowed horse on 10 August. On the 29th, "Jose Jesus, Felipe & Raymundo left with their people for the San Joaquin." See Sutter, *New Helvetia Diary*, 67, 68, 73, 112.

[15]Hammond and Morgan, eds., *Captain Charles W. Weber*, 18–19, citing E. Gould Buffum and George H. Tinkham.

[16]Hurtado, *Indian Survival on the California Frontier*, 99, 112, 123.

[17]Kemble, *A History of California Newspapers*, 76–77; and Rogers, ed., *A Kemble Reader*, vi, 116.

upset because the Indians were eating most of the horses they allegedly stole. He warned of an alliance between the "horse-thief Indians" and "a company of six white men" led by mountain man Miles Goodyear, who would drive a herd of wild (perhaps stolen) horses across the Great Basin the following summer. Jones must have passed Brannan's letter on to the new editors, for they had "indubitable proof" that the Indians who had served with Frémont had no part in "the thefts and outrages recently committed and complained of by our correspondent."[18]

Brannan's letter to Jones said much about local politics—noting especially the resentment felt by veterans of Frémont's campaign—but practically nothing about his planned trip, such as the names of his elusive companions. It revealed some of his limitations as a journalist, for he did not comment on the Donner party, many of whose survivors were recuperating at the fort. Still, his call for a humane policy for California's natives was enlightened and reflected his Mormon sympathies. Brannan's dark prophecy regarding their fate would not be precisely true, but he was largely right when he foresaw that "the cure" for California's Indians would leave them "doomed to one universal slaughter."

BRANNAN TO JONES, 18 APRIL 1847,
ELBERT P. JONES PAPERS, BANCROFT LIBRARY.

New Helvetia Fort Sacramento
April 18th 1847

Mr. E. P. Jones   Dear Sir

Capt. Sutter's Launch arrived at the Fort to-day, bringing me a full files [sic] of the Star, up to the 10th inst. Great complaints are made by the citizens of this District against the Government—for not paying them for their services in the last campagne under Col. Fremont and Com. Stockton—and the property that has been taken from them without any remuneration. Capt. Sutter has been supporting the families of those in the campagne during their absence some five or six months—his Indians that formerly labored for him ~~have also been~~ was inlisted and [have] since been in constant service. His fort, horses, and property have been rented during the war—his business retarded and some of his best mechanics taken into the service. The citizens in the surrounding country are now returning home, lean handed, leave footed, with scarcely a rag of clothes to cover their nakedness, all discharged with the heart-rendering intelligence that they will receive nothing for their services and property. They had no crops in the ground to support

___

18"Our Paper," *The California Star*, 1 May 1847, 66.

them [during] the coming season, no lands—no horses—no property but
perhaps an old sore-backed horse that has borne them from their field of
hunger and suffering of about six hundred miles—no employment for them
to engage in—as the season is past for agriculture. Is it *strange* that they
should complain? No! They are even driven to publicly declare, "let the consequence be what they may," they "will not take the field again, unless it
should be upon their own responsibility, the Spanyards may take the country and be damed!"

Many are getting discouraged and [are] turning their faces towards their
native country, without the means of reaching there unless obtained by
stelthe.—Is not this a horrid state of affairs—We are informed that ~~the
president wished to obta~~ our government has offered ~~to the~~ Mexican ~~Gov-
ernment~~ ten millions for the Territory of California. If she will ~~but~~ send but
half of that amount to those who have been fighting for her here, they will
give her a warrantee deed of it and defend it against the world.

The Statement of Agricola in of [*sic*] our 14 number, that "Jose Jesus and
Felipe are more daring and active than ever, since their return from the campaign to the south in military service," is incorrect.[19]—On my way to the
Sacramento I met with Jose Jesus going to San Francisco to see the Governor
in company with some eight or ten of his principle men—for the purpose of
having a proper understanding with the new government—and [to] obtain
some agricultural implements for farming—and obtain his children that are in
slavery among the Spanyards. ~~Felipe is at the fort.~~ He fell in with Capt. Tomp-
son[20] on the ~~east~~ west side of Joaquin—who the night previous had eight
horses stolen from his camp. Jose Jesus immediately volunteered with his men
to go in pursuit of them. I have since been informed by a party of volunteers
from the settlement on the Stanislaus—which by the by still survives the
flood—that he returned in five days with seven out of the ten horses that were
missing. Jose Jesus with proper treatment will make a useful man both fore the
people and goverment. Felipe, Jesus' interpreter, is here and will start in the
morning ~~for~~ to overtake him and request him to return. They both have been
at the fort nearly ever since they returned and could not have been among the
horse thieves in their late robberies.—As for the settlement on the Stanislaus
and Joaquin being broken up and the inhabitants murdered by the indians, [it]
is a false report without the slightest foundation. That there are horse thief

---

[19]Agricola was Dr. John Marsh. His 28 March 1847 letter on "the horse-thief Indians, that great
and particular scourge and curse of the whole country from Sonoma to San Diego," appeared in the *The
California Star*, 10 April 1847, 56. The section Brannan quoted actually read, "I recount the exploits in
both murder and robbery of the renowned Stanislaus and Diosculo, or their successors of the present
day, Jose Jesus, Simeon and Felipe, who are said to be more daring and active than ever . . . "

[20]Captain Bluford K. Thompson of the Pueblo volunteers was a veteran of the Battle of Salinas.
He later settled on the north side of the Stanislaus on the point "known as the Rancheria of José de
Jesús." See Hammond and Morgan, eds., *Captain Charles W. Weber*, 46.

Indians on the St. Joaquin we do not question, but when our government takes the proper steps to put their [tear] way to obtain an honest existence, and not [be] compelled to resort to horse stealing to keep from starvation, they will cease their depredations.

Salem

P.S. I shall start the last of this week across the mountains—give my respects to all enquiring friends—Kimbell [Kemble] can read my writing, but it may want some corrections, yours respectfully

S. Brannan

P.S. We have just learned by the arrival of Mr. [Henry] King by land— that the Government is about sending out a strong force to pursue the Indians or horse thieves—how will they make their distinctions or will there be none made, but all doomed to one universal slaughter. If such be the cure, we may ever expect to [be] troubled with the Indians, until they [are] all annihilated.

We Crossed the Snowy Mountains

The snows in the Sierra had not yet melted when Brannan and his three men left Sutter's Fort. They carried sixteen issues of the *California Star* and a surprising number of Mormon religious books. As they entered the mountains, Brannan's men encountered the last of the Donner relief parties led by W. O. Fallon.[21] Fallon's party included "the hindmost one of these unfortunate creatures making his way to the settlements. He was a German, and had lived upon human flesh for several weeks." (Brannan later employed "the notorious cannibal," Louis Keseberg, to run a brandy distillery in Calistoga.) Brannan's party then "passed directly over the camping ground where about 40 or 50 California emigrants had perished, and been eaten up by their fellow sufferers only a few days before. Their skulls, bones, and carcasses lay strewed in every direction."[22]

Brannan provided an account of his Great Basin crossing to G. T. Newell, a Mormon associate in New York.[23] Writing from the Hudson's Bay Company post at Fort Hall, Brannan's letter told the story of his remarkable journey. He commented that spring flood waters prevented

---

[21]Stewart, *Ordeal by Hunger*, 219.
[22]Orson Pratt's journal, 30 June 1847, quoted in Roberts, *Comprehensive History*, 3:202.
[23]*Millennial Star*, 1 February 1846, 35.

him from traveling "the regular route," indicating his men took the high ground above the regular wagon road. He lacked the time and paper to give a full "interesting account of the country and our travels throughout," but this letter captured Brannan's spirit and the restless possibilities of the West as well as anything he ever wrote.

"S. BRANNAN'S LETTER,"
LATTER-DAY SAINTS' MILLENNIAL STAR, 15 OCTOBER 1847, 305-06.
(*Transmitted by our kind Brother L. N. Scovil.*)
Fort Hall, June 18, 1847.

Brother Newell,—Once more I take up my pen to drop a few lines and let you know of my whereabouts. I left Capt. Sutter's post, in California, on the 26th of April last, and arrived here on the 9th inst. I am on my way to meet our emigration; I am now one thousand miles on my road, and I think I shall meet them in a couple of weeks. I shall start on my journey again in the morning with two of my men and part of my animals, and leave one man here and the rest of the horses to recruit until I return, and then it is my intention to reach California in twenty days from this post. We crossed the Snowy Mountains of California, a distance of forty miles, with eleven head of horses and mules, in one day and two hours, a thing that had never been done before in less than three days. We traveled on foot, and drove our animals before us, the snow from twenty to one hundred feet deep. When we arrived through, not one of us could scarcely stand on our feet. The people of California told us we could not cross them [in] under two months, there being more snow on the mountains than had ever been known before, but God knows best, and was kind enough to prepare the way before us. About a week before we entered the mountains it was extremely warm, which made the snow settle and work together, then it turned cool and there fell about 18 inches more of light snow, which kept the snow from melting during the heat of the day, and made travelling for our horses much better; we were enabled to get along much faster. During our journey, we have endured many hardships and fatigues in swimming rivers, and climbing mountains, not being able to travel the regular route owing to the high waters. Had I time and paper I might give you quite an interesting account of the country and our travels throughout. We past the cabins of those people that perished in the mountains, which by this time you have heard of. It was a heart-rending picture, and what is still worse it was the fruit of their idleness, covetousness, ugliness, and low-mindedness, that brought them to such a fate. Men shall reap the fruit of their folly and own labours. Some of the particulars you will find published in the STAR.

In relation to the company's affairs I can say but little. When I left, our crops were doing well; I think I have said something about it in my previous letter which will reach you the same time as this. A company arrived yesterday from Oregon, on their way to the States.[24] I forwarded by them; perhaps this letter will reach you before the other. Give my respects to brother Rodgers. I want you and him to write me a long letter and let me know all the little particulars—how things get along in church matters—what has become of [Sidney] Rigdon, [William] Smith, [George J.] Adams, and all the rest of the Big Guns. You need not be surprised if you see me in the States next year; I should think no more of travelling across the continent of America than I would of taking my breakfast. Oh! if you could but once have a taste of the keen appetite enjoyed in these mountain wilds, your city habitations could hold you no longer. I suppose you would not believe me if I should tell you I can sit down here and eat three or four pounds of roast beef at one meal; it is a fact. A man cannot know himself until he has travelled in these wild mountains. We killed a bullock this morning and we are now roasting one side—its ribs—for our dinner, four in number. It is most astonishing the amount of food the body demands in this region. But away with roast beef and let me come to our mental wants. Let me know how you all get along and enjoy yourselves. Remember me to Mr. Davids and family, and tell them I should have written to them half a dozen times before this, and so would Mrs. B., but we could not recollect Mr. David's given name and their number in the street. I know they must have thought very bad of us, especially after showing so much kindness before our departure, but I hope the day is not far distant when I shall make amends for all. You may hear from me again before I go home. There are none [some] coming on that are going into the States; and if anything important occurs I shall write again. Remember me to Mr. A. G. Benson and Co. and all the good saints in New York. May God and the angels guard you and bless you is the prayer of your unworthy brother.

As ever yours in love,

S. BRANNAN

THE CAMP WILL NOT GO TO THE WEST COAST

Despite Brannan's later complaints that the LDS church had forgotten him and his company, Brigham Young was curious about the fate of the California expedition. He paused on the evening of 6 June to sign a

---

[24]This party, led by Levi Scott and including Moses "Black" Harris, left Oregon City on 5 May 1847 and took the southern route to Fort Hall. Harris led eight men to South Pass, where they met the Mormon pioneer company on 26–27 June. One of these men, R. H. Holder, arrived in St. Joseph, Missouri, on 28 July 1847, perhaps bearing Brannan's letter. See Barry, *The Beginning of the West*, 707.

letter composed by Willard Richards that would inform the western-most element of the far-dispersed Mormon flock about the current progress of the Camp of Israel.[25] It gave an excellent summary of the status of all the elements of the LDS migration, including the complicated disposition of the Mormon Battalion, and even noted the Irish famine. Young clearly stated the reason the Pioneer Camp did not continue its journey to the Pacific: "they have not the means." Andrew Jenson wrote in the Journal History that this unsigned letter was never sent, but he included it for "its historical contents."

YOUNG TO BRANNAN, 6 JUNE 1847,
JOURNAL HISTORY.

Black Hills, Bitter Creek, 30 miles west of Ft. John or Laramie,
On Oregon & California route from the Platte,
In Camp of Israel's Pioneers. June 6th, 1847.

Mr. Samuel Brannan
    My dear Sir
    By my date you will discover my location, and as there is an Emigrating Company from the states camped about ¼ mile back this eve, some of whom, as I understand are destined for San Francisco, I improve a few moments to write to you. About the time you left New York, the first company of friends left Nauvoo for the West, and in June arrived at Council Bluffs, where they were invited by Prest. Polk, through Capt. J. Allen to enlist in the service of the U.S. and march to, and be discharged in California, in one year, from about the middle of July. Above 500 enlisted. Capt. Allen died at Fort Leavenworth, and was succeeded by others in command, & the Battalion was marched to Santa Fe, from whence some 150 were returned to Pueblo, on the Arkansas, as invalids, &c., and the remainder continued their route to Mexico or towards California by the South route.
    After the Battalion left Council Bluffs, the remainder of our camp settled on the West Bank of the Missouri, about 20 miles north of the Platte River, and threw up Log Cabins &c., so as to make themselves as comfortable as possible, and thus passed the Winter; with a tolerable degree of health, and much happiness; there was no more sickness than might very reasonably be expected.
    By the middle of September, Nauvoo was evacuated, and the City in possession of those who had chosen to go there for that purpose. Those who had left, came on to Winter Quarters, the village before mentioned on the Missouri, or stopped at intermediate places, which many did making two

[25]Bagley, ed., *The Pioneer Camp of the Saints*, 183.

large farms on Pottawatomie lands, while others who had no means went up or down the River to St. Louis, Galena, &c.

This camp which left Winter Quarters between the 6th and 14th of April consists of something less than 200 men—2 men to a waggon, accompanied by two thirds of the Council, and are in pursuit of a location for themselves and friends, which they expect will be West of the Rocky mountains.

We left upwards of 4000 Inhabitants at Winter Quarters and expect a large company [to] have since started, and are now en route, among whom will be as many of the families of the Battalion as can be fitted out, and if any of the Battalion are with you, or at your place, and want to find their families, they will do well to take the Road to the States, via the South Bank of Salt Lake, Fort Bridger, South Pass, &c. and watch the path or any turn of the Road till they find this camp.

If Mr. [Addison] Pratt should arrive from the Islands he will be as likely to find his wife at the location West of the mountains, perhaps in the Great Basin, as anywhere. She was well, and intended to come this season, if possible. Mrs. [Benjamin] Grouard was in Philadelphia at last accounts. Mr. John S. Fowler is in camp and wishes me to say to his wife Jerusha, who accompanied you, that he is well, has been well, is doing well and would be glad to meet her at the end of this route, where he expects to stop. The camp will not go to the West Coast or to your place at present, they have not the means.

Any among you who may choose to come over into the Basin or meet the Camp are at liberty to do so, and if they are doing well where they are, & choose to stay it is quite right.

One fourth of the Council had returned or were on their way from England, where they went last Summer and gave very cheering accounts of things in England, Scotland, &c, except Ireland which has suffered much from famine. The English Government were talking of making liberal offers to some of their good citizens to populate Vancouver's Island.

Two twenty-fourths of the council have been absent these two years, whereabouts unknown, as I understand.[26] Noah Rogers died in camp last summer and was buried at Mt. Pisgah, about midway between Winter Quarters and Nauvoo.[27] Mr. [Jesse C.] Little is in camp and lodges with me. Wooddrruuffee[28] is here.

The Papers report your safe arrival and that you have the only Printing Office in Upper California, but we do not know the name of your paper,

---

[26]This referred to dissident apostle Lyman Wight, who was in Texas.

[27]Rogers had served as president of the Society Islands Mission in 1844 and 1845. He died 31 May 1846.

[28]This spelling of Wilford Woodruff's name suggests an inside joke.

but hope to see [it] at the first opportunity, though I don't expect to see this scribble in type, it is only for your eye, and blunders are always excusable among old friends.

I would have mentioned that from information received at Ft. Laramie, it is expected that the command belonging to the Battalion at Pueblo is on their route toward California by the South Pass and will be at this point in a few days.

The Unexpected Arrival of Elder Samuel Brannan

The pioneers met Jim Bridger and two of his men on the Little Sandy on 28 June. The next day the saints proceeded to Green River, where they stopped to build rafts. Bridger, who was bound for Fort Laramie, sent one of his men back to his fort, presumably to prepare for the arrival of the Mormons. Brannan met this man and persuaded him to guide his men back to Young's camp. This French guide, Brannan, C. C. Smith, and their mysterious companion—unnamed in any of the camp's journals—arrived at the pioneer wagons, sheltered among the cotton-woods on the east side of the river, at three o'clock in the afternoon of 30 June. Almost every journalist recorded the event, but Horace Whitney noted, "we were all much surprised by the unexpected arrival." Brannan "was accompanied by 3 men, 2 of whom had come thro' with him from" California. Whitney was well acquainted with Smith, who "is I believe some distant relation of our prophet Joseph. He left Nauvoo (where I made his acquaintance) some 2 years since for Oregon." Smith told the pioneers "that in Oregon they had 2 seasons, *rust & dry*."[29]

Brannan gave the Saints a version of the Donner party disaster that served their bitter memories of the 1838 Mormon War. Many of the diarists (notably Orson Pratt) concluded that the disaster was God's vengeance against the church's Missouri persecutors, although only seven Donner party members could be described as Missourians.[30] Apostle George A. Smith reported Brannan's news to his father.

> Bro. Samuel Brannan arrived in our camp on June 30th, from California, accompanied by two men; he brought a file of the "California Star" pub-

---

[29]See Bagley, ed., *Frontiersman*, 53, for the full text of Whitney's journal.

[30]Donner party members who had lived in Missouri included members of the Foster and McCutchen families and Luke Halloran. Kristin Johnson, conversation with editor, 8 August 1998.

lished by himself at San Francisco. All is quiet in California; our battalion is there; most of our people in California are intending to settle in the San Joaquin country, rich and fertile, climate fine and healthy. The battalion is about 600 miles below San Francisco; Brannan has not seen any of them, nor any one who has, but it is reported that they came through quite destitute as to clothing and shoes, which would be a natural consequence . . . There was an unusual quantity of snow in the mountains last winter, and an emigrant company of 25 wagons, were overtaken by the snow, when within 100 or 150 miles of the Californian settlements, 45 out of 80 starved to death. The survivors, mostly women and children were packed into the settlements by the settlers, on snow shoes . . . Brannan represents Capt. Sutter as very friendly; he has about 1700 acres of wheat and expects to harvest 20,000 bushels.[31]

By the third of July, Brigham Young knew that the Mormon colony at New Hope was raising 150 acres of wheat, "besides potatoes, etc., etc., expecting us to help eat it, but our destination is the Great Basin, or Salt Lake for the present at least, to examine the country."[32] Historian B. H. Roberts concluded that Brannan's reception "was evidently not very cordial," but the sources do not describe any conflicts. Brannan spent much time in discussions with Young and the Mormon leaders.[33] He had much to explain—especially his endorsement of the Kendall-Benson contract—and Young subsequently sent him on a variety of odd errands, suggesting he was not particularly fond of Brannan's company, but there is no direct documentary evidence that relations between the two men were strained.

Brigham Young had sent Apostle Amasa Lyman south from Fort Laramie to rendezvous with the Mormon Battalion detachments that had wintered on the Arkansas River near today's Pueblo, Colorado. Lyman got lost and was reduced to eating seagulls, but the veterans marched north under the command of James Brown, perhaps the least able of the battalion captains Young had selected at Council Bluffs. After the detachments reached the Mormon Ferry on the North Platte, Sergeant Thomas Williams went ahead to track down some horse thieves, leaving forty-three wagons and two hundred men under Lyman and Brown.[34] On the Fourth of July, Williams' advance party of thirteen "battalion brethren" arrived at

[31]George A. Smith to Father, 3 July 1847, LDS Archives.
[32]Journal History, 3 July 1847.   [33]Roberts, *Comprehensive History*, 3:202.
[34]Jacob and Jacob, eds., *The Record of Norton Jacob*, 66.

Green River. Brigham Young led the welcoming hosannas. The apostles decided that "in as much as they have neither received their discharge nor their full pay, Brother Brannan shall tender them his services as pilot to conduct them to California." Young "counselled brother Brannan how to proceed in California, for the best."[35] The Mormon leader may have been tiring of Brannan's enthusiasms and perhaps saw an opportunity to send off several sources of potential trouble—Williams' dispute with moun- taineer Tim Goodale about stolen livestock threatened to explode into vio- lence. Brannan, Williams, and "and a few others" set out east from Fort Bridger on 9 July to guide the rest of the Mormon Battalion veterans into Salt Lake Valley. Horace Whitney noted that Brannan took the back trail "with his two comrades" from California.[36]

The letter Williams carried from Young to Lyman provides insight into the mind of the Mormon leader as he approached the Great Basin. It also outlined Young's plans for Brannan, who wanted to "discharge his men"—C. C. Smith and the enigmatic third man—but seemed to lack the fifty dollars needed to pay them off. Brannan met Lyman and the battalion detachments at South Pass about 13 July.[37]

YOUNG TO LYMAN, 8 JULY 1847,
BRIGHAM YOUNG COLLECTION, LDS ARCHIVES.

Bridger's Fort, 59 miles west of Green River Ford
July 8, 1847

Elder Amasa Lyman,

Thinking that you would like to hear from us again, we write you at this time, expecting to dispatch it in the morning by Sergeant Williams, who will probably meet you at the [Green River] ferry, ready to pilot you to this place.

We are very glad to hear the letter from Capt. Brown, that he is ready to follow council and desirous of obtaining it. Consequently, we expect he will be pleased that Sergeant Williams and the men of his command have been very obedient to council in doing as they have done; even if they have dis- obeyed [Brown's] orders, [and] we do not know that they have disobeyed orders; if they have, tell the captain he must not punish them till he catches them. And then, if we are not present, wait until we come up so that he can

---

[35]Roberts, *Comprehensive History*, 3:204; and Bagley, ed., *The Pioneer Camp of the Saints*, 219.
[36]Horace Kimball Whitney, Journal, 10 July 1847, LDS Archives.
[37]Beckwith, ed., "Extracts from the Journal of John Steele," 16, reported that Brannan "left us" on that date, but this is certainly an error.

have a full court. But enough of this, we have no doubt that Capt. Brown will be perfectly satisfied with our movements.

We believe he has followed out his instructions to the very letter, and inasmuch as they cannot well return on account of their [sic] soreness of the backs of their mules, and their being near worn out, they will continue their journey and as you will soon be with us, we expect it will be all right.

Elder Brannan direct from California, will accompany Sergeant Williams to your camp; his command will go on with us; and from time to time, some of them will return to you, to assist in piloting you thro' to our location in the Basin, and it is wisdom that you come on as fast as the nature of the case will admit.

We understand that the troops have not provisions sufficient to go on to the western coast, and their time of enlistment will expire about the time they get to our place; they will draw pay until duly discharged, if they continue to obey council; and there is no officer short of California, who is authorized to discharge them; therefore, when you come up with us, Capt. Brown can quarter his troops in our beautiful city (which we are about to build) either on parole, detached service, or some other important business, and we can have a good visit with them, while Capt. Brown with an escort of 15 or 20 mounted men and Elder Brannan for pilot, may gallop over to headquarters, get his pay, rations and discharge and learn the geography of the country.

If Capt. Brown approves of these suggestions, and will signify the same to Brother Brannan, he can discharge his men and remain in camp; otherwise he is anxious to go his own way. All the little particulars can be entered into when you come up. [We met the] battalion boys last Sunday; neither can we tell you how glad we will be to meet the remainder, but can tell them to come and see; tell them to cheer up their hearts, and not be overanxious about any thing. The clouds are frequently very heavy just before sun rise and we see that the day is beginning to dawn. "Its a long road that never turns" is an old maxim; and though this is a pretty long road, we expect that when we follow it a little further, it will so turn as to lead us directly east.[38]

The health of our camp is improving. There is not a very good chance to trade at this place. Col. Findley left here this morning for the States, direct from Oregon; doubtless you will see him.[39] It is 23 miles from the Green river to the first campground on Black's Fork; our next camp ground 18 ¼ miles, the next say noon halt about 10 miles. Last evening we arrived at this place, 7 ¾ miles.

Brother Brannan wishes to borrow fifty dollars in money from some one, and we say unto those who are able, lend it to him; he will secure you the

---

[38]Even as he contemplated founding "a stake of Zion" in the mountains, Young was predicting the return of the Saints to Independence, Missouri, where Mormons believe Christ will return.

[39]This was William Findley, an 1845 emigrant to Oregon.

repayment and send it back to whoever accommodates him by Capt. Brown on his return.

                                        and we remain your brethren in Christ.
                                        In behalf of the Council,
Willard Richards, clerk   Brigham Young, president

Brown loaned Brannan the money he needed, which probably went into the pocket of C. C. Smith or their guide. Paid or not, Smith immediately headed west, for on 19 July he met General Kearny and his eastbound Mormon Battalion "life guards" on Bear River, two days' travel east of Soda Springs. Smith gave the Mormons "much valuable information concerning the migrating Saints."[40] A little more than a month later, "Messrs. Smith & Hundsacker arrived from the Emigration" at Sutter's Fort.[41] The next day Jefferson Hunt carried Smith's report to the main body of battalion veterans approaching Sutter's Fort from Los Angeles at their camp on the Cosumnes River.[42] Robert S. Bliss noted that Hunt had "seen two men who went out with Bro Brannan to relieve the church they tell us that they have arived at bear valley & some 500 waggons are on their trail & will arrive soon at the same place."[43]

BRIGHAM YOUNG:
THE WEAKNESS AND FOLLY OF HUMAN NATURE

Amasa Lyman, Rodney Badger, Roswell Stevens, and Brannan reached the Salt Lake Valley at 8:30 A.M. on 27 July 1847, three days after Brigham Young arrived with the last element of the pioneer company and two days ahead of the battalion detachments. Brannan immediately joined Brigham Young, Wilford Woodruff, Orson Pratt, and eleven others on an "exploring expedition" to the Great Salt Lake. The scouts swam in the lake and extracted samples of salt, peered into Tooele Valley, and camped on the shore. Wilford Woodruff felt "that the great Salt lake ought to be added as the eighth wonder of the world."[44]

---

[40]Tyler, *Concise History of the Mormon Battalion*, 303.

[41]Sutter, *New Helvetia Diary*, 23 August 1847, 71. In his "Pioneer Register and Index," Bancroft identified "Hundsacker" as Daniel Hunsaker, an overlander from Missouri who brought "news of approaching immigration." Another candidate, Nicholas Hunsaker, was married to Lansford Hastings' sister Lois. See "The Family of Lansford Warren Hastings," 20.

[42]Bigler, ed., *The Gold Discovery Journal of Azariah Smith*, 100.

[43]Alter, ed., "The Journal of Robert S. Bliss," 118.

[44]Kenney, ed., *Wilford Woodruff's Journal*, 3:237.

Brannan returned to the main camp the next morning ahead of the explorers. At nightfall Brigham Young assembled the pioneers to express their feelings "pertaining to our locating here."[45] The meeting was held where Young at five o'clock had "struck his stick and said . . . that should be the site of the temple block."[46] He asked the assembly, "shall this be the spot or shall we look further? I want all to freely express their minds." Young knew that if he should give a revelation that this was the spot, his followers "would be entirely satisfied if it was on a barren rock."[47] The motion to "locate in this valley for the present, and lay out a city at this place" was "carried without a dissenting voice."[48]

Brannan was surely in the crowd, and perhaps Young called the meeting to resolve, once and for all, the questions Brannan continued to raise. Young outlined his plan to redeem the Lamanites and establish the Kingdom of God in the isolation of the Rocky Mountains. John Brown recalled that Young told Brannan, "We have no business at San Francisco; the Gentiles will be there pretty soon."[49]

The Mormon Battalion detachments marched into Salt Lake on 29 July to a great welcome. They had been caught in a flash flood in Emigration Canyon that "rose up to their wagon beds." Young used the flood and the outfit's broken wagons and failing teams to justify not marching the men to California for discharge.[50] On 4 August Young sent Brannan, Lt. Wesley Willis, Jesse C. Little, and "another man" on an exploring trip to Utah Lake. Brannan renewed his acquaintance with Little, a bond that lasted until Brannan's death. The four men returned the next evening, reporting that they had found the bodies of several Indians and a horse killed after a trading dispute between the Utes and Shoshonis on 31 July.[51]

Although it was now obvious that the Mormons had gone as far west as they could go in 1847, Brannan continued to argue that the LDS

[45]Egan, *Pioneering the West 1846 to 1878*, 111. See Bagley, ed., *The Pioneer Camp of the Saints*, 240–44, for Thomas Bullock's minutes of this remarkable meeting.

[46]Knecht and Crawley, eds., *History of Brigham Young*, 5–6.

[47]Jacob, *The Record of Norton Jacob*, 73.

[48]Egan, *Pioneering the West*, 111.

[49]Brown, "An Evidence of Inspiration," 269.

[50]Knecht and Crawley, eds., *History of Brigham Young*, 5–6.

[51]Journal History, 1 August 1847. Years later Brannan wrote Jesse Little, "Those Indians were 6 instead of three, they were killed on my account by the Utes for selling me a Stolen horse." See Brannan to Little, 13 January 1886, Folder 5, BYU Brannan Papers.

church should make California its ultimate destination. Ten years later, Young recalled that when he met "Brannan and a few others from California" at Green River, "they wanted us to go there." Young replied, "Let us go to California, and we cannot stay there over five years; but let us stay in the mountains, and we can raise our own potatoes, and eat them; and I calculate to stay here."[52] Wilford Woodruff remembered that Brannan "looked upon the desolation and barrenness, and tried with all the power he had to persuade President Young not to stop here, but to go on to California." But "President Young was inspired to come here," and Woodruff recalled seeing the Mormon leader strike the soil with his cane and answer Brannan, "No, sir; I am going to stop right here. I am going to build a city here. I am going to build a temple here, and I am going to build a country here."[53]

Willard Richards dictated two letters to Thomas Bullock on 7 August defining LDS church policy in California that Brigham Young signed two days later.[54] The first, to the "Saints in California under the presidency of Elder Samuel Brannan," summarized the trials of the Mormons but rejoiced at "the glorious prospect which is now before us." Young made clear that Salt Lake was to be the church's headquarters, but expressed his hope that eventually "the Pacific may be overlooked from the Temple of the Lord." He designated Brannan president of the church in California, but gave him a less-than-ringing endorsement. Young was "satisfied with the proceedings of Elder Brannan" and believed Brannan was "a good man." If he had made mistakes, they reflected humanity's imperfections. Young tentatively endorsed Brannan's "unitedly engaged" communalism, saying that the Saints did not believe in "having all things in common," but that it was quite right to unite their energies "in one common cause for a season." This carefully hedged endorsement of Brannan's leadership suggests that Young maintained reservations about his reliability. As for Brannan, he left Salt Lake convinced that the Mormons would be unable to survive in the Great Basin.[55]

[52]Brigham Young, 13 September 1857, *Journal of Discourses*, 5:231–32.
[53]Woodruff, *The Discourses of Wilford Woodruff*, 322–3.
[54]Bagley, ed., *The Pioneer Camp of the Saints*, 252–53.
[55]Tyler, *A Concise History of the Mormon Battalion*, 315.

BRIGHAM YOUNG, "TO THE SAINTS IN CALIFORNIA," 7 AUGUST 1847,
SPECIAL COLLECTIONS, BYU LIBRARY.
(Draft)

Camp of Israel, Pioneers,
August 7th–1847

An Epistle of the Council of the Twelve Apostles of the Church of Jesus
Christ of Latter-Day Saints to the Saints in California under the Presidency
of Elder Samuel Brannan. Greeting:

It is pleasing unto us, and also to the Holy Spirit, that we improve this,
the first convenient opportunity which we have had of writing to you, since
you left New York on the ship Brooklyn, by communicating as many incidents relative to the Church at large, as time will permit; Cheering your
hearts with the glorious prospect which is now before us; & giving you such
Counsel as Wisdom shall dictate.

About the same time that the Brooklyn ~~left~~ sailed from New York, we left
Nauvoo with a large emigrating Company of Saints, taking our course
Westward; yet, like Father Abraham, journeying we knew not whither; our
only object being to find a resting place, a place of peace & safety for ourselves, for our families, & our ~~kindred~~ friends; for we esteem all those our
friends, who are friendly to the Government of Heaven, keep the commandments of God, love righteousness, & desire to live in peace with all
men. After a tedious journey in which we had to encounter wind and snow
and hail and rain, & rivers, & floods & scarcity of provision & fodder, we
succeeded in making our way thro' a new country; where in many places,
there was not even an Indian trail to guide us; & arrived at the Missouri
River, near Council Bluffs, the latter part of June; having made two Settlements by the way on the Pottawattamie Lands, called Garden Grove &
Mount Pisgah; at which places some of our Company then stopped; and to
which many of the poor Saints have since gathered.

Soon after our arrival at the Missouri, we were called upon by the Prest.
of the U.S. thro' Capt. James Allen for a Battalion of 500 Volunteers to
march to California. Wisdom dictated that the request should be complied
with ~~as a matter of necessity on our part for the Salvation of Israel~~; & 500
of our brethren & friends enlisted agreeably to our Council, a few of whom
have died. About 150 are now with us, & the remainder marched to California by way of Santa Fe, whose situation you are more likely to be ~~better~~
acquainted with than ourselves.

After the departure of the Battalion from Council Bluffs, three of our
Council repaired to England, where they spent the Winter; & leaving the
Church in a very prosperous state on the British Islands, returned to the
Council Bluffs last Spring. One of the Council [Orson Hyde] visited the
Eastern States, setting in order the things of the Kingdom, while the major-

ity were attending to the affairs of the Church at home; such as locating the
Camp that was with us, & those who were coming to us continually; & sending Teams to Nauvoo to bring out those who had no other means of leaving the place.

Our principal location was on the west bank of the Missouri River,
about twenty miles North of the Platte, called "Winter Quarters," regularly
surveyed in City form, with Streets, Blocks, &c With very few men & boys
~~there were~~ & comparatively no means, having ~~all~~ most of our provision to
bring from Missouri, from 60 to 200 miles distant. We succeeded in building upwards of 700 houses, most of them more comfortable than are usually found on the borders of the Western States; & many of them are very
good, and most of this was accomplished in less than three months. We also
built a first rate flouring Mill, which cost several thousand dollars, & is
moved by Water Power, & thro' the Fall and Winter kept up ~~a conversation~~
communication by Express with the Battalion, with Nauvoo, & the Eastern
Cities & held correspondence with many parts of the Earth. Before we left
Nauvoo we completed the Temple & administered the ordinances therein to
many hundreds of the Saints.

After we left Nauvoo, the Saints continued to follow in our trail as fast
as their circumstances would permit. The Spirit of persecution which had
jeopardized our lives, & caused us to leave, continued to spread & prevail;
more especially after the former part of August [1846], until the 12 13 &
14 Septr, which days are memorable for successive battles with musketry &
cannon directly in the City; in which three of our brethren fell, & some of
the mob: Skirmishing continued until the 17th, when the ~~Saints agreed~~ mob
took possession of the city, & on the 18th drove out the remainder of the
Saints at the point of the Bayonet, many of whom were destitute of food,
clothing, or tents; & so sick as to need the best of nursing. Some went up
the River to Burlington, Galena, &c others down the River to St. Louis &
other places; while many were scattered abroad in Iowa, or came to our
Camp in the Wagons which we sent to their relief. But few houses, lots, or
farms [in Nauvoo] could be sold; ~~the few~~ those that were sold were for sums
merely nominal, consequently the Saints had but very little means to assist
them in their removal. Thus has another Stake of Zion been thrown down,
& another Temple of the Most High God been desecrated by the feet of
ungodly men; while the Sons & Daughters thereof have been left to wander
upon the Prairies & in the Wilderness; many of whom have suffered from
sickness occasioned by their exposure & hardships, even unto death; & their
bodies have returned to Earth again.

In the former part of last April we left Winter Quarters, a Pioneer Company of 143 men & 75 wagons & grain sufficient to sustain our teams a few
weeks, & made a new road up the north bank of the Platte to Fort Laramie,

or John, rising of 500 miles; thence took the Oregon trail to Fort Bridger; thence on the most Southerly route to this, the Valley of the Great Salt Lake, near 1100 miles from Winter Quarters. Most of our Camp arrived on the 22nd & 23 July, & that part of the Battalion with us, arrived on the ~~31st~~ 29th from Pueblo, where they wintered. No death has occurred in our Camp since we left home, or in the Command now here since they left their Winter Quarters. Elder Brannan met us on our route at Green River, & is still with us. Since our arrival at this place we have plowed, planted & sowed extensive fields of Corn, Potatoes, Buck Wheat, Peas, Beans, turnips, & a numberless variety of Garden seeds.

That portion of the Valley of the Great Salt Lake, where we are located, we will suppose, without measurement, to be 30 miles long & 20 wide. The Soil appears of an Excellent quality; abundantly watered by many streams of the Purest Water, & Timber in the mountains we believe sufficient for all necessary purposes until we can grow more. The Atmosphere is ~~pure~~ clear, the air salubrious, & thus far every appearance indicates perfect health to those who may live here long enough to recover from the remains of the Fevers, Agues, Chills, Rheumatisms, Poxes & Deaths to which they have been exposed in other climes.

We have selected a site for a city which for beauty & convenience we have never before seen equalled. It is on a gentle declivity, where every garden, house, lot, or room may be abundantly supplied with Cold Water from the mountains at pleasure; ~~a part of~~ the site is now under survey, 10 acres being reserved for a Temple lot; & four other 10 acre lots in various places will be reserved for public grounds. The streets are 8 rods wide & the lots ~~generally~~ 1 ¼ acre each & Blocks 10 acres. One side of the city borders upon the most beautiful bluffs, suitable for Summer houses, cottages &c; while the remainder is encircled by the richest meadows of choice grass & rush, & just ~~right~~ suitable for pasturage for the City. We now number at this point about 450 Souls, & anticipate the arrival of a large emigrating Co., in a week or two, direct from Winter Quarters.

Thus we have given you a very brief, though general idea of the events that have transpired relative to the Church, since you left New York; & Elder Brannan will be able to give you many particulars, which we have no time to write. & now, brethren & Sisters, we feel to say to you, that we are satisfied with your mission which you have taken to California, & that so far as we have been informed, we are satisfied with the proceedings of Elder Brannan. We believe that he is a good man & that it is his design to do right. No doubt he has been placed in very trying circumstances ~~in common~~ in connection & common with you, since your journey to California was first contemplated; & if he or you have erred in any thing, in the midst of your trials & troubles, it is nothing more than others have done before you, & nothing more than is expected of man while he is so imperfect as he now is. We do not say this because any charge has been preferred against him or you; but ~~because we~~ knowing the weakness & folly of human nature, we feel to exhort you at all times to cultivate the spirit of meekness, kindness, gentleness, compassion, love, forgiveness, forbearance, longsuffering, patience & Charity one towards another; & look upon others faults & follies as you want others to look upon yours; & forgive, as you want to be forgiven, & to deal justly, even as you want to be dealt by; & regard your brother's interest as your own; &, in all things, do as you would desire to be done by; & if you do these things the Holy Spirit will dwell with you, will abide in your hearts, & always be ready to whisper to you the way you should walk; & ~~always~~ withal remember the Sabbath day, & sanctify it, & attend to those ordinances that belong unto it, that you may be blessed in your labors the remainder of the week.

We do not desire much public preaching, or any noise or confusion concerning us, or our religion, in California at the present time; for the elements in which you live are in confusion, as it were, & the waters are troubled; therefore, be wise; meet together often; you who have the opportunity, in your still & quiet habitations; pray with & for each other; exhort each other; instruct each other; & do each other all the good you can, & forget not your Closet, whether it be a room in a house, a rock by the way side, a shubbery on the mountain, the grain in the field, or any thing else, it mattereth not, when necessity requireth it, let some secret place witness your devotions, your humiliation, & your prayers daily & many times in a day, that the God of Israel will arise to the exaltation of Zion, & the overthrow of the powers of darkness, & if ye do all these things, ye shall prosper.

And we feel to say to those who are unitedly engaged with brother Brannan in laboring unitedly for the good of the whole, that the poor, the widows, & the fatherless may not want; that you will be blest if you keep your contract to the end of the two years; & labor dilligently in your several occupations, & when that time shall expire, we hope you will be able to cancel all your obligations, & have enough to give each family an inheritance or stewardship, that he may commence, as it were, anew in the world, just as we are commencing here at this place. ~~We do not~~

We do not believe in having all things in common, & on general principles, as some have taught, both in the Church and out; but we believe that it is right for every man to have his Stewardship, according to the ability that God hath given him; yet, there are cases, situations & circumstances where it is quite right for the brethren to unite all their energies & labors in one common cause for a season; as, for illustration, we are now doing. Most of us, Pioneers, are expecting to return, immediately, to Winter Quarters; yet, since we have been in this Valley, we have united all our strength in plowing, planting, sewing, &c, & thereby have accomplished much. We shall leave it, & others will enjoy the benefits of our labor. We are also laboring unitedly to build a stockade of houses around a ten acre block; this also will doubtless be a greater blessing to others directly, than ourselves. We are engaged in other improvements here in like manner; but when we come here with our families & the inhabitants begin to spread abroad in the City, we expect that every family will have a lot on which they may build, plant &c.—also a farm, [with] as much land as they can till, & every man be a steward over his own. We understand that you are united in your labors for the time being for the good of the whole just as we are here. That is all right & we rejoice in it. We also understand that there are some of the Company who sailed with you from New York, have entered into business exclusively for themselves, & are laboring hard to get rich; & others who had entered into the original contract for two years, have broken that contract & are pursuing the same course; & though we approve not of breaking covenants yet to all such we would say, get rich, for the Lord designs that his should be the richest people on Earth; but remember, and get your riches honestly, & close not your ears, neither tie up your purse strings against the cries of the Widow, the Fatherless, the Poor, & especially of the household of faith; but let your charity be manifest to all that need them; otherwise you may expect that your riches will avail you nothing, but will rather prove a curse to you, be the means of your eternal overthrow.

We have been driven from the habitations of men, & hurled as it were like a stone from a sling, & we have lodged here in this goodly place, surrounded by a munition of rocks, just where the Lord wants his people to gather unto; and we say to you all, & to all the saints in California, you are in a goodly land; & if you choose to tarry where you are, you are at liberty so to do; & if you choose to come to this place, you are at liberty to come, & we shall be happy to receive you, & give you an inheritance in our midst; And if any emigrants should arrive upon the Western Shores, let no one discourage them from coming to this place, if they wish to so do; not that we wish to depopulate California of all the Saints, but that we wish to make this a Stronghold, a rallying point, a more immediate gathering place than any other; & from hence let the work go out, & in [the] process of time the Shores of the Pacific may be overlooked from the Temple of the Lord. It is desirable that there should be a stoping place, a resting place for the Saints on the west of the mountains, where those who arrive from the Western Ocean can locate if they chose, or stop awhile, & recruit, & prepare for their journey hither. We know not but your Settlement on the San Joaquin is the best location for this purpose that you can find, if so, it is the right place for you to labor upon to make a stronghold for the present.

Elder Brannan came up to meet us this Season, agreeably to our request,

& he also returns to you by our council. We want him to continue with you, & council you as hitherto, & continue to publish a Paper in California; & if you all live, so as to enjoy the Holy Spirit continually, you will rejoice in each others society, as you have hitherto done, & more abundantly.

If Elder Addison Pratt should arrive amongst you from the Western Islands, you will please inform him that his Wife was at Winter Quarters & well when we left, & no doubt will be at this place on the arrival of the next camp or, in two or three weeks, & here will wait for him.[56] Should Elder [Benjamin] Grouard arrive, say to him that his Wife was in Philadelphia & well the last fall.[57] Brother [John] Fowler goes to california, with Elder Brannan, to get his family & return to this place.

And now brethren we must close this our first letter to you. Wishing you peace & prosperity and the free enjoyment of the Holy Spirit we remain your brother in Christ.

In behalf of the Council

Willard Richards, Clerk   Brigham Young Prest

That same Saturday the pioneers dammed City Creek and in the evening performed baptisms and rebaptisms. The next day, despite considerable rain, the rite "was recommended and all who felt disposed were invited to come forward and receive the ordinance, which they did in great numbers."[58] Heber C. Kimball baptized Brannan, who was confirmed by Brigham Young, Wilford Woodruff, and Amasa Lyman.[59] Notwithstanding this apparent recommitment to the Mormon church, almost forty years later Brannan recalled that the "day before I left Salt Lake in 47" he denounced polygamy, telling "Brigham & Heber" that polygamy made women "a slave worse than the negro."[60]

Willard Richards dictated a second letter on 7 August 1847 containing instructions for Mormon Battalion veterans. Young did not object to the veterans staying in California, but he expressed a decided preference to have the men gather to Salt Lake. It seems that Young gave James

---

[56]Louisa Barnes Pratt would actually reach Salt Lake with the Brigham Young company in 1848. After a "cruel separation" of more than five years, Addison Pratt and his family were finally reunited in Utah on 28 September 1848. See Ellsworth, ed., *The Journals of Addison Pratt*, 358–59.

[57]Thomas Bullock's handwriting stopped here; Willard Richards appears to have completed, corrected, and signed the letter.

[58]Egan, *Pioneering the West*, 116.

[59]Samuel Brannan, Early Church Information. The ledger recording this event also listed baptisms of Abner Blackburn, J. S. Fowler, Lysander Woodworth, and James and Jesse Brown, but none for the elusive Isaac Goodwin. Most, if not all, of these ordinances were rebaptisms.

[60]See "Once an Able and Diligent Elder," in Chapter 14; and Brannan to Little, 24 December 1886, in Chapter 13.

Brown more explicit oral instructions, for Brown directed that those lacking supplies should return to California and earn money. The letter revealed a surprising grasp of western geography, probably acquired during the pioneers' many encounters with the mountaineers. It contained excellent advice, especially its council to avoid the Hastings Cutoff, and indicated that the Mormon leaders were already interested in developing a snow-free route from Salt Lake to southern California.

At 11 A.M. on Monday, 9 August, Brannan, Captain Brown, and "several others started for San Francisco." Jesse C. Little and John Brown went along to explore the Bear River and Cache Valley, while Tom Williams accompanied the party to Fort Hall to buy provisions for the battalion veterans. Edward Tullidge listed the men in James Brown's party as "'Sam' Brannan, Gilbert Hunt, John Fowler, Abner Blackburn, William Gribble, Lisander Woodworth, Henry Frank, and Jesse S. Brown."[61] Six of the men were battalion veterans, and Abner Blackburn left a colorful account of "the biggest torn fool errant ever is known." John S. Fowler was the husband of Jerusha Fowler, a *Brooklyn* pilgrim who had taken the couple's four children around Cape Horn; her father, her sister, and one of her children did not survive the voyage.[62] Henry Frank's identity is a mystery, for his name does not appear in any Mormon records of the emigration, although his widow was apparently rejected for a battalion pension. (Frank may be the "little German" Brannan later mentioned to Brigham Young.) As with any overland party, the Brannan-Brown company picked up and lost members along the way; Gilbert Hunt met his father in the Sierra and returned to Salt Lake. It seems the group added members at Fort Hall and at other stops along the trail.

Brown carried a power of attorney from each member of his command to get their official discharge and pay. Brannan resented being placed under Brown, for the captain had a well-deserved reputation as a martinet and quickly won Brannan's enduring hatred. Abner Blackburn recalled, "Brannan and Cap Brown could not agree on anny subject. Brannan thought he knew it all and Brown thought he knew his share of it. They felt snuffy at each other and kept apart." Tension between them

---

[61]Tullidge, "History of Ogden City," in *Tullidge's Histories*, 4. Tullidge's list of "nine others" besides Brown consisted of only eight names.

[62]Jones, "Ship *Brooklyn* Passenger Gravesite Location Search Project."

boiled over as the party crossed the Sierra, observed by Indians. One morning Brown wanted to get an early start, but "Brannan said he would eat breakfast first." Brown insisted on taking the horses "for they belonged to the gover[n]ment and were in his care." Both men "went for the horses and a fight commenced. They pounded each other with fists and clubs until they were sepperated. They both ran for their guns. We parted them again." The men left Brannan with his own horse, but he soon overtook and passed them. Blackburn concluded, "We thought the savages would get him certain."[63]

Brannan's encounters with the different parties of east-bound battalion veterans provides a good picture of their Sierra crossing. The advance company under Elisha Averett met Brannan east of Donner Lake early on 6 September. Henry W. Bigler recorded that "Brannan halted an hour to let his animals feed and to take a little refreshment himself."[64] He told the veterans that Captain Brown, carrying mail from Salt Lake, was only a short distance behind. The veterans returned to their camp near today's Truckee to wait for Brown and to let a slower group under Levi Hancock catch up. After an hour's rest, Brannan proceeded west with David P. Rainey, arriving at Hancock's camp "just at night," Azariah Smith noted, "to hur[ry] us on to [join] the rest of our company." The next day Hancock's men crossed "the back bone" of the Sierra to reach Averett's camp at 3 P.M.[65]

Daniel Tyler wrote that Brannan's description of the valley "was anything but encouraging." Brannan "considered it no place for an agricultural people" and had concluded that "the Saints could not possibly subsist in the Great Salt Lake Valley." The mountaineers reported that "it froze there every month of the year, and the ground was too dry to sprout seeds without irrigation." He "expressed his confidence that the Saints would emigrate to California the next spring." Brannan said Brigham Young had answered his objections to settling in Utah "with some rather insignificant remark," but once he "has fairly tried it, he will find that I was right and he was wrong, and will come to California."[66]

---

[63]Bagley, ed., *Frontiersman*, 65, 102, 112.

[64]Bigler, "Journal of Henry W. Bigler," 90–91. This version of Bigler's diary said Brannan "gave a fine account of the Salt Lake country but thought it no place to live."

[65]See Bigler, ed., *Azariah Smith*, 102, for Brannan's route on the sixth. Daniel Tyler, traveling with Hancock, garbled both dates and facts in *A Concise History of the Mormon Battalion*, 315.

[66]Ibid.

Brannan camped that night with Tyler's party. When Brown brought his men through the next morning, he gave the veterans Brigham Young's letter that encouraged those "who had no means" to stay in California through the winter. Samuel Miles recalled, "This word caused about half our company to return."[67] William Byram Pace reported that "Brown was on his way to California with a company of twelve or fifteen men," indicating that it had grown since leaving Salt Lake.[68]

THE GREAT EMPORIUM OF THE PACIFIC

Brannan arrived at Sutter's Fort on 10 September "in the Evening with one Man from the Mountains." His companion was John S. White, a battalion veteran and shoemaker. Sutter hired White the next day, and Brannan borrowed "the gray Mule (of Mr. McKinzie)" and left the fort, bound for the San Joaquin.[69] On 17 September 1847 Brannan arrived in San Francisco.[70]

"INTERESTING FROM THE EMIGRATION,"
THE CALIFORNIA STAR, 18 SEPTEMBER 1847, 148.

Mr. S. Brannan, publisher of this paper, after an absence of nearly six months, arrived at this place on Friday morning last, 28 days from Fort Hall.

By him we learn that the emigration to this county, this year will not exceed ninety wagons. An advance company of about twenty-five wagons, is supposed to be on Truckey's Lake,[71] while the most tardive [tardy], are in all probability at least 110 miles from the sink of Mary's River. The last named wagons, without brisk travel, may find their mountain road obstructed by snow, [and] fear is already entertained for their safe arrival.

Mr. Brannan informs us that the emigration to Oregon was still "rolling on;" that up to the 18th day of Aug., seven hundred and seventy wagons had passed Fort Hall, and before the expiration of the month, many more were expected.

Of the "Mormon emigration," there had arrived at the great Salt Lake, up to August 7th, 480 souls. This body, for the most part males, is but an

---

[67] Samuel Miles, Life History, 10.
[68] Bagley and Hoshide, eds., "The 1847 William and James Pace Trail Diaries," 5.
[69] Sutter, New Helvetia Diary, 77.
[70] For a map of Brannan's 1847 trip, see Fred Gowans, "Mormon Exploration and Settlement Routes," in Wahlquist and Christy, eds., Atlas of Utah, 88.
[71] This is the original name, if not spelling, of today's Donner Lake.

advance of an extensive emigration soon to follow, and there was expected in one week's time, an additional caravan, consisting of four or five hundred wagons.

Here they have laid off and commenced a town, planted large crops, which are described as being forward and flourishing, and have at hand eighteen months' provisions to be used in the event of a failure of crops.[72]

They contemplate opening an entire new road through to this country, in connection with the present rendezvous, and which completed, they move *en masse* to the valleys of California.

The "Mormon Battalion," of about 200 men, had been met in the mountains of California, many of whom were returning to winter here. Of this Battalion, 150 [of] whom sickness detained at Santa Fe, had joined the emigration at Salt Lake, their term of enlistment having expired; Col. Cook had been sent by Gen. Kearney to discharge them.

Mr. Brannan gives the general health of the emigration [as] good, few deaths having occurred throughout the travel.

Brannan immediately wrote to Jesse Little, who was still traveling east with the pioneer company. William Appleby would subsequently send a copy of this letter to Brigham Young from Boston. Brannan's relationship with A. G. Benson continued, but unfortunately his correspondence with the merchant does not survive. The growth of San Francisco during Brannan's six-month absence seemed "beyond all conception," but the transformation of the village on Yerba Buena Cove would soon exceed even his wildest visions.

BRANNAN TO LITTLE, 18 SEPTEMBER 1847,
BRIGHAM YOUNG COLLECTION, LDS ARCHIVES.

San Francisco. Sept 18th /47

J. C. Little Esq.

Dear Sir—I reached my home yesterday in good health. I left Capt Brown on the other side of the California Mountains and came on alone. The next day after I left him, I met a part of the Battalion about 200 men on their way to the Salt Lake. You may depend it was a happy meeting on both sides; they waited for Brown to come up, so they could get their letters, and then they would return to California again; and remain until spring, agreeable to council, not having provisions sufficient to winter at the Lake, four or five of them were determined to go on to the Bluffs this winter. With good animals they can do it. I found everything on the return better

---

[72]Brigham Young ordered all wagons going to the Great Basin to carry provisions for eighteen months, but few actually did. By late winter, the settlers at Salt Lake were reduced to eating roots and hides.

than my most sanguine expectations. Many little bits of interest you will learn by calling on Mr. Benson of New York, which will save me the trouble of writing over again; as I have just finished a letter to him and some things he might learn of you. The Battalion Boys have gained great credit in California, so much so that Gov. Mason has authorized Capt Hunt to raise 500 more. One company of young men enlisted for another year.[73] The Mormons are A. No. 1 in this Country. I forward you a file of the "Star"; In the last No. you will see the Election returns of this town. The head of the list Mr William Glover is the man that I left in charge during my absence this summer. It took place the day before my return.

Our friends in this country are increasing very fast. The predictions of Doct. Richards & President Young, have been truly verified in relation to my affairs on my return. I shall expect to hear from you by the first opportunity and particularly in relation to our business matters for that must go ahead. I want you to use your influence in connection with Mr. Benson, with our people, and every one else to obtain patronage for the *Star*. In this country it is very popular. Mr. Benson is the General Agent for the United States. By the Star being sustained "civil and religious" rights are retained in California, which is of great moment to us particularly. At this point will be one of the greatest cities of the present age. When I landed here with my little company there was but three families in the place, and now the improvements are beyond all conception, houses in every direction, business very brisk and money plenty. Here will be the great Emporium of the Pacific and eventually of the union. Here I shall make my headquarters and hope to receive the support of all good men, the bad I do not care for. My Journey this summer has been the astonishment to every body in the country. But for the life of me I cannot see anything in it so very astonishing. My most bitter enemies in this country have and are dwindling fast into insignificance, and "right" is *getting* to be *might*, so you see the old adage is reversed. If you visit the President give him my kind respects and also Mr. Benson and Kendall and your friend Col. Kane. Your friends are my friends, and my friends must be your friends, and it is hoped that the Ram will not return again to his thicket—if he does I shall make him another call. You must inform the twelve that you have heard from me and also the state of affairs in this country, which you will obtain from this [letter] and the one I have written to Mr. Benson. I would have written them one, but I did not know what point to direct it to, and it might fall into other hands. Give my kind leave to them all, and tell them that the people will go mad if they do not settle in this country, and that their manner of movements in relation to it is very popu-

---

[73]Seventy-nine discharged veterans and three boys re-enlisted for six months in the Mormon Volunteers under Captain Daniel C. Davis, but Young refused to support Mason's call for a second "volunteer battalion of 'Mormons.'" See Tyler, *Concise History of the Mormon Battalion*, 343, 345; and Ricketts, *The Mormon Battalion*, 261.

lar here with every one myself not excepted. Although it would be a great
pleasure to me to have their company here.

In haste I subscribe myself
Yours most Respectfully
S. Brannan

NB Notice for a duplicate
  P.S. Br. Young at the request of Elder Little I have copied Br. Brannans
  letter to him, and forward the same to you by Br. E. T. Benson.
      Your Br. &c
Boston March 9th 1848   W. I. Appleby

Chapter 8

"The Tongue of Slander"

Although legend tells that Samuel Brannan returned from the Rocky Mountains outraged with Brigham Young and disgusted with his church, the record paints a more complicated picture. Brannan remained excited about Mormonism's prospects and was pleased that Young had affirmed his authority over the Saints in California. Fearful of what James Brown would report, Brannan aggressively defended himself to Young, but Brown was not the only veteran who would give Brannan trouble. The Mormon Battalion had been discharged in Los Angeles the previous summer, and many of the men found their way to San Francisco, where they were not impressed with Brannan's leadership. Brannan increasingly spent more time on local politics and his business than he did on church affairs, and explosive news from the Sierra foothills would soon alter his life and California's history forever.

Treasurer and Banker of All the Mormons

Writing to an Iowa newspaper, an anonymous correspondent reported a revealing conversation with a Mormon shortly after Brannan's return from the Rocky Mountains. The letter is a compendium of misinformation (for example, the Mormons believed that the Garden of Eden was in Missouri, not California), but the report captured the distrust of the Saints in general and of Brannan in particular that prevailed among Americans in California in late 1847. The "many other visions and prophesies" that Brannan "put forth" on his return included his claim to be "Treasurer and Banker of all the Mormons in the promised land." With prophetic insight, the writer suspected that Brannan had his own motives—and that he would prove to be "among the missing" when he had accomplished those ends.

"LETTERS FROM CALIFORNIA,"
DAVENPORT GAZETTE, 17 MARCH 1848, I.[1]

Monterey, Upper Calif.
Oct. 1st 1847

Friends——; I received your letter dated Jan. 19th, this morning, and as the U. S. sloop of war Preble leaves tomorrow for Panama, with despatches, I hasten to write. You give me so little, and expect so much information, that I hardly know where to commence. *** I am in good health, and would be contented, if near home, where newspapers could be had; but here I am starved out, and not as much as a Dutch almanac in the whole country to get hold of. There are two newspapers in the Territory, both published at San Francisco Bay. In nationality, religion and politics they are of the "omniverous" species, although one, the "Star," is published by a Mr. Brannan, the leader of the New York Mormons, and advocates the Mormon doctrines.

The country is flooded with Mormons. Their regiment, under Col. Cook[e], has been disbanded, allowing each non-commissioned officer, musician and private to retain his arms and equipments—so they are a band of men, loafing about, some farming, some stealing, &c. ready to act for or against the United States [at] the first opportunity. As they are regularly "drilled," and some possess a large quantity of arms and equipments, it is generally supposed, they will join the Californians [and] help retake the country. I think it was a great oversight in General Kearney to allow them those privileges. Besides this, Mormon emigrants are arriving daily, by sea and land, from Europe and America—all bringing arms and ammunition to fight, as they say "the battles of the Lord and relieve their afflicted brethren from the persecutions and bondage of the Moobite [Mobite], and to build up an inheritance to the Lord in the wilderness." They have pitched upon the beautiful valley of the San Jookin and Sacramento as their future homes, and will shortly commence a city and a new temple, far superior in size, and magnificance [*sic*], to the one in Nauvoo. They pretend to have had a new prophecy through their leader, Samuel Brannan, which is, that San Francisco valley was the Garden of Eden; the "three great rivers," as mentioned in the Bible, are the Sacramento, San Joakin and Rio Delos Americanos; that they inherit this land from Adam, the ancient gardener himself, and that they and their forefathers have, up to this time, been compelled to wander through the world, suffering all manner of persecutions, to expiate the crimes of mother Eve; all of which sin is to be pardoned, or has been pardoned, as they have got possession of the "inheritance prepared for them from the foundation of the world." They say this war with Mexico was sent as to punish the U. States for the death of Joe Smith, and as a means to give them possession of the

---

[1]From *Galena Gazette*, in Morgan, *News Clippings from Iowa and Illinois, 1841–1849*, 202-b-202-d, a collection of Dale L. Morgan newspaper typescripts.

"promised land," which has been held in mortgage for sin for over four thousand years; reserved especially whereon the chosen are to build the New Jerusalem. They speak of many other visions and prophesies that Brannan has put forth; among them is one that he is to be Treasurer and Banker of all the Mormons in the promised land. But they are not unanimous, on that, as my informant says, "he might apostalize,"—a common word among them.

There are now more than *seven thousand* Mormons in, or on their way, to this Territory, and if report be true, there will be twice that number by next year. Their principal settlement is Bear Valley, above Sutor's Fort, where they have laid out a city and have commenced to build it; but their principal city, which is to be called the "City of the Prophets," will be built near Sacramento, on the San Joakin. There they intend building their "New Jerusalem," and burying the bones of their prophet, Jo Smith. Thus, step by step, this Brannan deludes the ignorant at every turn, until he gets his ends accomplished, after which he will be "among the missing."

A LITTLE FRAY WITH CAPT. BROWN

Brannan was a busy man in early October 1847. He sold a copy of *The Doctrine and Covenants* to battalion veteran John Borrowman, who had heard him preach the previous evening.[2] He helped the captain of the whaleship *Vesper* in a dispute with Brannan's bitter political enemy, Alcalde George Hyde, who had billed the captain for "12 or 14" of his men who had "been retained as prisoners in the guard house of this place." He supported construction of a schoolhouse, which was completed in December.[3] Reporting to Brigham Young, Brannan boasted of his cordial relations with Colonel Richard Mason, military governor of California, who was able to relax from the cares of his high office at a ball held in his honor on 30 September. Mason left San Francisco "highly grateful with the hospitality of our citizens."[4] The army was being especially solicitous of the Saints in the hope that Young would allow Jefferson Hunt, who had served as the senior LDS officer in the Mormon Battalion, to recruit another battalion of Mormons to help police California—but the project, despite Hunt's best efforts, came to naught. Mason was also interested in Brannan's "new road to Califor-

[2] John Borrowman, Journal, entries of 3 and 4 October 1847.
[3] *The California Star*, 16 October 1847, 165; and 4 December 1847, 192.
[4] *Californian*, 6 October 1847, 2; and 13 October 1847, 2.

nia," and Brannan reported that many of the *Brooklyn* pioneers already talked "of emigrating to the Salt Lake in the spring." Young wrote to Brannan from Ash Hollow on the overland trail on 6 October, but there is no evidence Brannan ever received this letter.[5]

Brannan sought to convince Brigham Young of his loyalty to the Kingdom of God—and to defuse negative reports about him that he knew would soon reach the Mormon leader. Brannan confessed he "might have been a little more prudent" in his relations with James Brown. He protested that he had no malice against the contentious captain, but Brannan accused Brown of forgery and defrauding the government. The charges were substantially correct and account for the hostile reception "this surly Nabal" accorded the Stansbury Expedition when it arrived in Utah in August 1849. Captain Howard Stansbury concluded that Brown "had some reason to expect and to dread a visit from the civil officers of the United States, on account of certain unsettled public accounts" from his California venture. Stansbury thought that Brown had mistaken his surveyors for "some such functionaries" sent to capture him, and subsequent experience "fully evinced the ungracious nature" of Brown to the topographical engineers.[6] In his report, Brannan justified his withdrawal from public preaching, commented on local politics, and noted the arrival of missionary Addison Pratt, returning from a long sojourn to the South Pacific that began in May 1843. Pratt would soon be caught in the struggle between Brannan's Mormon friends and enemies.[7]

BRANNAN TO YOUNG, 3 OCTOBER 1847,
BRIGHAM YOUNG PAPERS, LDS ARCHIVES.

San Francisco. Oct. 3rd 1847

Prst. B. Young

Dear Sir.—I embrace a convenient opportunity to forward you a few lines, by the way of Panama, the mail leaving here to-morrow morning—The feeling in this country towards our people has undergone a great revolution in our favor. General Kearny, from the last information I can obtain, has truly done us justice—he has publickly and privately given the Battalion the character of being the best men ever under his command. It has effectually silenced the

---

[5]For the text of this letter, see Bagley, ed., *The Pioneer Camp of the Saints*, 304.

[6]Stansbury, *Exploration and Survey of the Valley of the Great Salt Lake*, 83–84. Nabal was an inhospitable pastoral potentate whose fate was described in 1 Sam. 25.

[7]For Pratt's call and subsequent mission, see Ellsworth, ed., *The Journals of Addison Pratt*, 115, 121–300.

tongue of slander and arrayed among our supporters a powerful influence. The jealousy that heretofore existed against the "Star"—because of our religion has dissappeared—it is now read and sought after with interest and confidence by all classes—and since my return its circulation has increased greatly. If I can possibly sustain it for two years—I feel confident the Hydra headed monster will have to relinquish his footing in California.

Governor Mason left us yesterday after a weeks visit, during which he called and dined with me—and spoke in the most flattering terms of our people and the course they were pursuing—especially in relation to their policy of settlement at the Salt Lake and opening a new road to California—the project is also very popular with the people—but many say they would have rather seen you come in direct this season. I still keep up Two days before I reached home an election was held in this place for a town council—and Bro. Wm. Glover received the highest number of votes of those elected—he was the man I left in charge during my absence—I feel happy to acknowledge the truth of your prediction in relation to the state of affairs I should find on my return home—the paper has been conducted by the boys far better than by the former Editor Mr. Jones. I shall send you full files by this mail—I have also sent files to Br. Little—and Mr. Benson.

On my return home I had a little fray with capt Brown—which perhaps you have heard of by the return of some of the volunteers. I hope you will not decide on my head until you have heard both sides. I feel that I am able to vindicate my cause, though perhaps I might have been a little more prudent. There are two facts which I consider it my duty to mention—and I hope you will not look upon it as malice against him for I have none. Our difficulty arose through jealousy as far as I could learn from the boys in company with us. He came to the Quarter Master's Office here, which is the next door to my residence—and handed in a receipt for pilotage from the Salt Lake, for $70.00 in the name of a little German that travelled in company with me, and had never been in the country before, and drawed the money.[8] I spoke to him the evening before about my pilotage when he asked me for the money I borrowed of him in the mountains, he said he understood that Br. A. Lyman was to have it.[9] I told him that Br. A. Lyman told me that he refused to make any such arrangement &c and that the order from the Quarter Master to hire a pilot having been lost he did not expect to get his own [fee] but here I would and I would inform Br. Lyman that the Quarter Master here informed me that Capt. Brown produced the Order to the when it was called for, and paid his pilotage at the rate of 100 per month, amounting to 2,00 [$200] and some 8 or 10 dollars—he also pur-

---

[8]For the "little German," see the discussion of Henry Frank in Chapter 7.

[9]This was the fifty dollars mentioned in Brigham Young's 8 July 1847 letter to Amasa Lyman, but Brannan's explanation of the state of the debt is too confusing to untangle.

chased some horses at Capt Sutters of the manager of his place amounting to $150—and did not report them to the Quarter Master here with the rest of his horses—when the man called for his money of course the Quarter Master [k]new nothing about it—

These acts are now come before the public, one as fraud; and the other as a forgery, which you may be assured Pres. Young is no credit to our own cause and interest in this country. The conduct of one such a man will tear down more than 20 can build up again.

I have commenced public preaching in this place and have appointed Addison Pratt to preside in my absence. He is a fine man, as well as being wise and prudent.

Many of the saints here talk of emigrating to the Salt Lake in the spring, when the Battalion Brethren go—what brethren of the Battalion I have seen since I came home which has been a great portion of them, are strong in the faith—and conduct themselves with the greates[t] propriety. Some of our former troublesome brethren here made strong efforts during my absence to poison elder Pratts mind against me ~~during my absence~~ but I think to no purpose—I preached this evening to a crowded house and very attentive attendance. I do not preach often myself, as I do not think it prudent and wise in my position. My prayer to God all the day long is, that you will send ~~me~~ one good man to my assistance next year, and as many more as you see proper—eventually there will be a great field open in this country for the progress of truth—my policy will be to lay the foundation and by and by others to do the preaching—as it now has a tendency to create suspicion in the minds of some for a man to be preaching and at the same time standing at the head of a public journal—some times it makes me feel very awkward—but my motto is, to learn all things, and endure all things for the kingdom of heavens sake and do the best I can. In relation to brother [John S.] Fowlers course since his arrival, I feel sorry to say has been very indiscrete if reports are true. [Quartus] Sparks and him are in thick as they were before we left New York—I have many thoughts on my mind that I would like to write, but you see I have no room.

                    Yours most respectfully   S. Brannan

Unexpectedly Called to the North

On his return, Brannan lost little time mobilizing against his political foe George Hyde. Brannan sought allies for his vendetta with Alcalde Hyde, who stood accused of not selling lots to the first applicants and of altering the town map. Brannan's petition demanding Hyde's removal provides an accurate list of fifty-five of his political allies (including

John Sutter, several Mormon Battalion veterans, and at least twenty *Brooklyn* passengers) on 1 October 1847.

OFFICIAL DOCUMENTS RELATING TO EARLY SAN FRANCISCO, 1835–1857,
BANCROFT LIBRARY.

[Cover:] Petition of Citizens
of St Francisco. for
remove from office of Alcadae Hyde
Recd Oct 1, at Lt. F.
[Petition]
    We, the undersigned townspeople of San Francisco, humbly petition your Excellency that you may remove from office our present Alcalde George Hyde believing that his continuancy in office would be injurous to the best interests of our Town.

For His Excellency
Col. R. B. Mason
Governor of California

S. Brannan	C. L. Ross
Ed. C. Kemble	George M Evans
C. C. Smith	Simeon Stivers
John Eagar	John Borrowman
T. H. Rolfe	Arne [?] Stevens
William Glover	John Counel [?]
John Davis	John Read
Emmel Jewitt [?]	George Lathrop
Wm Smith	Hansel Twitchel
Charles Cody	David Clark
James Stuleysen [?]	Barton Mowrey
James Lee	Isaac R Robbins
H. Woods	Robert Petch
G. H. Johnson	Saml. G Ladd
V [?] Benett	John R. Robbins
L. Jones	Joseph Nichols
James Beauxly [?]	Richard Knowls
John Clancy	Daniel Stark
Robert Smith	Charles C Burr
Art Wilbur	Peter Pool
John Thompson [*sic*]	John Sirrine
W. C. Burnett	R. Mowrey
Jno. [?] McDongel	Seth S. Lincoln
Henry Booth	Wm McDonald
B Nollnet	Chauncey Spencer
James Ferguson	John Sutter
Julius A. C. Austin	John McLellan
C. Haines	J. M Lord

Governor Mason authorized an investigation of the charges, which "dawdled along" but ultimately exonerated Hyde.[10] Brannan had attacked his political nemesis since February 1847, when the *Star* accused Hyde of leading a clique of speculators attempting to appropriate waterfront lots. Ironically, as a member of San Francisco's city council, Brannan would later be accused of employing the same tactics to acquire valuable "water lots"—underwater property along the shallow margin of Yerba Buena Cove—that he had denounced Hyde for using. "As a member of a Committee selected to present His Excellency. Gov. Masson, with the petitions of many townsmen, praying the removal from office of George Hyde," Brannan asked the council on 7 October to delay hearing the issue "until the return of either absent committeeman." He was "very unexpectedly called to the North"— probably to Sutter's Fort to start C. C. Smith & Company, the trading firm that would lay the foundation of his fortune.[11]

The "Star" Takes a Bold Stand

In his second letter to Brigham Young in a month, Brannan recounted his recent triumphs and noted the demise of yet another attempt at Mormon communal economics. The *Star* had already announced that the "copartnership" of S. Brannan & Co. was dissolved on 27 September 1847. William Glover, Daniel Stark, and John Robbins offered the "effects of the late firm"—which included "a large quantity of wheat," all kinds of hardware, school books and the Harper's Family Library donated by the Van Cotts, and the launch *Comet*.[12] The termination of the firm also spelled the end of the farm at New Hope. Glover recalled that the "land, the oxen, the crop, the houses, tools and lounch [sic], all went into Brannan's hands, and the Company that did the work never got anything for their labor."[13]

---

[10]Mullen, *Let Justice Be Done*, 31, 34. For Hyde's statements and claim that he "triumphantly disproved" these "concocted" charges, see Davis, *Seventy-five Years in California* (1967), 298–300.

[11]Brannan to Town Council, 7 October 1847, in Morgan, *California Manuscripts*, 13–14, published as Eberstadt's Catalogue 159; and Sutter, *New Helvetia Diary*, 84.

[12]*The California Star*, 2 October 1847, 157.

[13]Glover, *The Mormons in California*, 21. Brannan was often accused of looting the funds of S. Brannan & Co., but Glover was involved in dissolving the company, so his charge must be regarded with suspicion.

Brannan asked Young to send an apostle to visit California, and noted he had dutifully followed his instructions not to praise the Salt Lake Valley too highly to outsiders. Brannan again tried to deflect the charges he expected James Brown to file against him. His repeated protestations of loyalty ring hollow—and inevitably raise the suspicion that, despite his denials, Brannan may well have told John Sutter that the Mormons "might go to hell." Yet Brannan would have much more to do with the Saints—and his note that Sutter had hired a number of battalion veterans was a portent of great events to come.

Brannan gave over the empty space in his letter to Addison Pratt, who wrote a simple but eloquent account of his missionary service. Pratt's comments on his long separation are touching and his calculations proved very accurate, for he would not be reunited with his family for another year.

BRANNAN TO YOUNG AND COUNCIL, 17 OCTOBER 1847,
LDS ARCHIVES.

San Francisco. Oct. 17th 1847

Prst. B. Young & the Council

Dear Sirs. Another opportunity presenting itself, to forward you a few lines by way of Panama, is my enducement at the present time for writing, feeling it my duty to inform you, as often as circumstances will permit, of the state of affairs in this country. I wrote you a letter a short time since; ~~by the same rout~~, upon the same subject, but for fear you will not receive it, I deem it prudent to embrace the present opportunity of forwarding another. The friendly feeling and confidence of the people and Government of this country still continues to grow stronger and stronger in our favor—since my return home, the subscription list of the "Star" has increased nearly doubled [*sic*]. (I forward you full files to this date.) My reception since my return by all classes has been with the warmest and kindest feelings—and those that were leagued together for our overthrow and distruction; have fallen back into obscurity—and stand ready on every hand to cry for peace. The "Star" takes a bold stand and a strait forward course, cutting to the line, and at the same time meeting with universal approbation.

On my return home I deemed it most prudent to dissolve our company association, from the fact that a great many were idle and indolent, and would try to live upon the hard earnings of the few—and at the same time it would leave me less incumbered to perform the duties involved upon me in sustaining the interest of the cause of Zion. I hope Brethren that you will not suffer your minds to be prejudiced, or doubt my loyalty from any

rumour or report that may be put in circulation by brethren or others—
Since my return home some of our good brethren here have put in circulation, that I told Capt. Sutter when I arrived at his place that the
"Mormons" "might go to hell, that I should have nothing more to do with
them." Men circulate stories sometimes against individuals through policy,
which has been very much the case with myself since I first engaged in the
cause of God. Brethren I want *your* confidence, faith and prayers—feeling
that I will discharge my duty under all circumstances, and then I am
happy—no undertaking will then be to[o] great—nor burthen too heavy—
I hope it may be counted wisdom by your council for one of your number
to visit us next fall after you reach the lake. My whole soul might mind and
strength is bent on labouring for you night and day—I look upon no one as
being judges of the fruits of my labor, but your honorable body—to them
I stand ready at any moment to render an account of my Stewardship. Capt
Brown while he was here done every thing in his power to destroy me—told
the brethren that I wanted him to join me to preach against the Salt Lake—
to prevent any one from going their—All I ever said to him was the council
I received from you as follows: Not to praise the Salt Lake in the paper or
tell the world that it was a very desirable place: The first company of emigrants that we overtook coming in, he began to prais[e] the country, which
made me say any thing concerning it, and I suggested the propriety of us
both telling the same story. I feel perfectly justified in the course I have pursued, and feel confident that it will meet with your approval when ~~the time
comes for~~ you become acquainted with the particulars. Capt Brown has left
this country—in a very improper manner, and brought disgrace upon the
people he represented by his acts while here—all I have to say [is] I hope he
will repent and make restitution—three or four more such men as him here
will wind up the success of our career on this coast and destroy all that has
been done.

There is about twenty of the Battalion working here in town and doing
well and about the same number at Capt. Sutter's, many more [at] different
parts of the bay, and as far as I can learn [they are] doing well.

Remember me to inquiring friends
Yours very respectfully,
S. Brannan

ADDISON PRATT: MY LONG BANISHMENT

Dear Brethren the Twelve

As Br Brannan has kindly offered a space in his letter, I readily improve
it. I arrived her[e] last June, from Tahiti. I left Br. Grouard on Ana, or Chain
Island, this is one of the Pau motu [Pahi Paumotu] group where he & I had

been labouring since February 1846.[14] There is a large branch of the Church there some 1100 members, when I left & the work is still progressing. Before I parted with Br Grouard, we called a Conference meeting of the brethren, took into consideration the work of the Lord among those Islands & of my leaving for home. Having never received any instructions from your honourable body (receiving but 3 letters from America since we left there, 2 from my wife, & one from Br Woodruff, all dated in the year 1844,) we knew not what to do, better than that I should leave for the body of the Church, find it where I might, report our proceedings & success, get instructions from you & wait your order, what ever it might be. The natives were very lo[a]th to part with me, but with the promise that I would come & get more Elders & return, they consented to it. The Lord has nearly overthrown that opposition that was arranged against us at our arrival among these Islands, & now there are many Elders wanted. With the blessings of God, I hope to meet you at Salt Lake next year. Then I hope I shall see my dear family also. This has been a long & grievous separation to me, but the Lord has thus far brought me through it, & I still live in hope of seeing them next year. Could I have met them this year at Salt Lake, it would have shortened by one year, this my long banishment. As my paper is used up I cannot say more—my best wishes to you all; & to my family & friends—I am &c. adieu

Addison Pratt

THE ALLUREMENTS OF THE WORLD

Despite his objections, the San Francisco branch elected Addison Pratt as its president on 2 December 1847. The reluctant missionary "could not get rid of acting" and accepted the office. He was immediately caught between "the two parties, one for Brannan, and the other against him." Pratt noted that as Mormon Battalion veterans drifted into town, they "were drawn in on either one side or the other, and the party feelings were fast growing, in spite of my best efforts to keep it down." Pratt tried to contain emotions by siding with the absent party, but found that this simply made "both parties to think I was against them." He eventually concluded that Brannan hoped to "rule through me, but when he found that I had some notions of my own . . . I became verry

---

[14]Pratt's name for the islands translates as "double canoe." His able missionary companion, Benjamin Franklin Grouard, had labored with astonishing success at Anaa Island in the Tuamotu Archipelago since May 1845. Grouard's son, born in 1850 to a Polynesian woman, became the noted Plains scout Frank Grouard. Pratt adopted Frank Grouard, who went to Utah with Pratt's wife, Louisa.

obnoxious to him." About the end of April 1848, Pratt resigned the office to go to Salt Lake and noted that Brannan managed to have his ally, convert Seth Lincoln, elected in his place.[15]

The battalion veterans brought word of revolutionary developments in Mormonism, specifically the institution of the "endowment," the temple ceremonies that ritualized Joseph Smith's polytheistic theology of immortal families and eternal progression. The endowment had been generally extended to faithful members with the opening of the Nauvoo Temple in December 1845. Brannan had already participated in William Smith's unauthorized sealings, and he probably learned more about the holy ordinances during his visit to the Pioneer Company, but his letter made clear that he was at a severe disadvantage trying to exert his authority as "President of the Saints in California" over the battalion veterans who had been initiated into the sacred and secret rites of the endowment.

Brannan continued to lobby Brigham Young to establish a Mormon presence in California, convinced that the "wealth and influence" of the country could fall under the church's control with the most modest effort. He pleaded for help resisting "the allurements of the world"— temptations that soon proved irresistible.

BRANNAN TO YOUNG, 5 DECEMBER 1847,
BRIGHAM YOUNG COLLECTION, LDS ARCHIVES.

San Francisco Dec 5th 1847

President Brigham Young and the Council—

To-morrow we have another opportunity of forwarding to you a few lines by the way of Panama—and I hasten to improve it—hoping that when this reaches you—it will find you in the injoyment of peace and prosperity—as it leaves us all at this place—The Volunteers that have been descharged—and all being at their labor and working [for] good wages— and will leave here in the spring for Salt Lake. Some also that came out in the Brooklyn will go up with them—We have organized a branch here, and brother Adison Pratt is acting as President of the branch—last Sabbath three were baptized—I am under the necessity of restraining myself from public preaching as much as possible—in order to guard against any jealousy on the part of those who might take an occasion "to make a man an

---

[15]Ellsworth, ed., *The Journals of Addison Pratt*, 336.

offender for a word." Could two or three hundred families of our people be thrown into this town—within a few years the wealth and influence of this place could be entirely received to our interest. I hope that this point you will take into consideration. I do not say with a view of dictating—but from my unceasing anxiety and interest for the formation of the course of Zion—unless it is done there is no use of my remaining here to publish a paper—and if it is, this place can never become a Carthage or a Warsaw—and our influence on this side of the mountains can never meet any opposition that will do us the least injury. I shall send up to you next spring, a full report of the affairs in this country, and how many things are going on with us. There is the greatest anxiety existing here for you to settle in the county—there are those no doubt, who would rather it would not be, but they fear to speak loud—the spirit of anti-mormonism is sinking lower and lower every day. The more contributed on our part to strengthen the "chain that binds the old Devil" the better it is for us—and by so doing adding to our own strength—in four years time the Gospel can be preached in every town and vilage of this country—without the least opposition—and the Kingdom be the Lords. My whole study is to effect the object of my mission—I feel the utmost confidence that I shall do it—but not without your assistance. The most trying opposition I have had to encounter with has been from false brethren—coming from a spirit of jealousy—the same as hinted by brother [Orson] Hyde in his letter—much is added to that spirit from the fact that I have not received my endowment—those who have presuming that a man who has not has neither the ability nor knowledge that they have—I was fortunate enough some time ago, to find out my ignorance, and I pray that I may not loose it—and if I never know any more—I hope to retain the little I have—if it remains only for a few fort[unate] to associate with "wise men"—and that is to "know that I am a fool"—and that for Christ's sake.

I hope it will be considered wisdom by your honorable body for one to visit this place next fall and spend the winter—I hope you will not forget my situation—I am surrounded by the allurements of the world and need your prayers and blessings that I stand faithful to my trust and never falter but go straight through—there is nothing more mortifying to me than to undertake a piece of work and not be able to go through with it—and as you have set me to work I hope you will not forget to help me through with it.

If we are not able to stay the Beast and False Prophet in this country—Heaven knows where he will be eleighen [alighting] throughout the world—The spirit and influence of the Kingdom of God, is taking such deep root in this country—that it will require a whole nation of Preests to root it up—we had a visit from one the other day—the first ever preached in this country—held forth in our school house—he could not get through without throwing a few stones—which put an end to his preaching in this place—the community were down on him at once—and that is the end of him—in this town sectarianism can do nothing and we wish to keep it so. Hoping this will find you all in the enjoyment of the blessings of health and prosperity I subscribe myself your obedient

Servant
S. Brannan

THE HIGH AND HOLY CAUSE

San Francisco society—such as it was—welcomed the new year of 1848 with a costume ball in Robert Parker's new City Hotel. According to legend, Mrs. Brannan went as Pocahontas and her husband—despite his expressed concern with "the allurements of the world"—attended dressed as Satan in a costume with a long tail that he switched back and forth.[16] The next day, "Brother Brannan" was back to his old ways, preaching to the Mormon congregation.[17]

As he had promised in December, Brannan sent Brigham Young a detailed account of affairs in California in the spring of 1848, which oddly failed to mention the discovery of gold in January. Brannan sent the letter east with an express mail party, mounted on muleback, that carried a special edition of the *California Star* to the states. Victor Fourgeaud was engaged to write the lead article, "The Prospects of California," and the *Star's* example would be a prototype of California promotional literature. Edward Kemble recalled that the special edition was prepared in late February and "set a good example which was unworthily followed." Brannan announced that the express would leave San Francisco on 1 April 1848 and offered to carry letters to the states for fifty cents. The issue praised California's agricultural and mineral prospects, containing "interesting and generally accurate" accounts of California's resources and prospects.[18]

---

[16]Scott, *Sam Brannan*, 204, citing *Oakland Tribune*, Knave Section, 28 February 1937. Scott's endnotes occasionally track to the cited sources, but this information could not be located on the microfilm of this issue at the California State Library.

[17]John Borrowman, Journal, 2 January 1848. Borrowman reported Brannan preached on the first two Sundays of February 1848.

[18]Rogers, ed., *A Kemble Reader*, 123. See Chapter 9 for Fourgeaud's "The Prospects of California."

NOTICE, *The CALIFORNIA STAR*,
8 APRIL 1848, 2/2.

Our office closed mail for the United States on Sunday last [2 April 1848], larger, probably, than were ever conveyed across land from the Northwest coast of America. Of the last number of our paper alone, 2000 copies were mailed, and letters and packages from every part of Upper California, with not a few from the Sandwich Islands.

It is idle to indulge in fears for the safe progress and despatch of this mail, huge as it is. Not a day will be delayed upon its arrival at the California mountain pass, but upon good animals, *hurried over the snow*, at a speed accelerated the more by fear of its melting.—Gen. Kearney and party crossed these mountains in June last over melting snows. Mr. S. Brannan, publisher of this paper, [crossed] in the month of April, and encountered little or no obstruction in the passage. Mr. B. accompanies the party to the base of the Sierra Nevada, to attend to its safe pilotage across.

About ten men made up the express, including battalion veterans William and Nathan Hawk, Sanford Jacobs, Richard Slater, Silas Harris, and Daniel Rawson. These men spent the week before their departure from Sutter's Fort prospecting at Mormon Island and carried the first news of the gold discovery to the eastern states. In his old age, Nathan Hawk recalled that the two thousand copies of the special edition weighed a ton. Brannan addressed packages to "every section of the Union" and directed the messengers to give single copies to the emigrants they encountered. One packet, "larger than the others, I remember was directed to the reading room of the National Library in the City of Washington." Hawk spent "quite a time" with Brigham Young after meeting the west-bound Mormon emigration of 1848 in the Black Hills of Wyoming. Hawk showed Young a sample of California gold and asked if he would go on to California. "No!" said the Mormon leader. "I hope they will never strike gold in the country where we located, for I do not want my people to go digging for their God."[19]

While Brannan's letters were filled with much old news and recapitulated his usual complaints, they were peppered with a surprising amount of new history. He described his conflicts with the leaders of the battalion veterans, who were now a substantial portion of his flock; his dis-

---

[19]Ricketts, *The California Star Express*, 3–19; and Ricketts, *The Mormon Battalion*, 188–90.

patching William Glover to the south on a trading expedition intended (at least in Brannan's telling) to raise money to supply the new settlement at Salt Lake; his continued scheming with Lansford W. Hastings, now aimed at monopolizing California's newspapers; and much cunning politics. Brannan again pleaded for a visit from an apostle and reported on his unsuccessful efforts to build a meeting house for his congregation. He demonstrated his passion for cryptic fraternal organizations when he told Young about the secret origins of "The United Order of Charitable Brothers." The brotherhood had "taken in" most of the respectable citizens in the country and Brannan expected that it would soon eclipse the Masons in influence. Despite his hopes, the organization vanished without another trace.

Brannan recounted his conflicts with former sergeants James Ferguson and William Coray, the leaders of the battalion veterans in San Francisco. They had received a letter from the High Council in Great Salt Lake City—probably composed by Parley P. Pratt—sent south with "our trusty and confidential brothers" Asahel Lathrop, Elijah Fuller, and Orrin Porter Rockwell, who Jefferson Hunt led to California to buy animals, grain, and seeds. Contradicting the orders Brannan had brought from Brigham Young in September, the letter directed battalion veterans not to re-enlist and to "repair to this place" as soon as circumstances permitted.[20] Brannan felt that the epistle—which the veterans refused to show him—undercut his authority, and he complained bitterly about the slight.

BRANNAN TO YOUNG, 29 MARCH 1848,
BRIGHAM YOUNG COLLECTION, LDS ARCHIVES.

[Cover:] Prest. B. Young
Salt Lake Valley
To be opend and read by Prest. P. P. Pratt and John Taylor at the Lake and then forwarded to B. Young by the express.
Copied by A. J. [Andrew Jenson]

San Francisco, March 29th/48

Pres. Young—Dear Sir It is a source of pleasure to me, to have another opportunity, of once more addressing you a few Lines. The wide distance that separates us at present and the peculiar circumstances under which I am

---

[20]Schindler, *Orrin Porter Rockwell*, 170–71.

at this time situated, occasions very peculiar feelings to rise in my heart, knowing fully the responsibility resting upon me, and my acts during my tarry here. That I am a man of errors, I most sincerely acknowledge. But with all of my errors, I hope and trust, they have not brought reproach upon the High and Holy cause which I have had the pleasure to represent in this country—That I have had my own troubles and difficulties to encounter, will appear evident, when once my course and policy in this country is fully understood by your honorable body, to whom I am most anxiously awaiting for the day to arrive, when I shall have the pleasure and happiness to submit the same for approval or disapproval. That I shall have many calumniators arising from *"jealousy"* and *"misrepresentation"* I am fully confident. But from my unbounded confidence, in the known integrity and disposition to give justice to all men, especially to the household of faith, in yourself and council, I do not give myself any alarm, putting my trust in the "God of Israel," the great architect and director of his kingdom on earth. I sincerely hope that another year will not pass away until I have the pleasure and happiness of receiving "One of the Twelve" in this place. I feel assured in saying, that the good results that would arise from it would pay a thousand fold to the cause and interest of Zion. For myself, I have labored under many disadvantages, from not receiving my endowment. Ambition on the part of those who have received it, disputing my Priesthood, and joining their influence with the slanderer, in order to strengthen their own influence and exalt themselves. This representation has appeared more fully on the part of Brother Corey and Ferguson, who are now in this place; much confusion has existed here from their teaching unmarried sisters the "spiritual wife doctrine" and making efforts to increase their kingdom, but in the latter I believe they have had very poor success as yet, the unmarried finding plenty [of] single men to suit their taste equally as well. Rather than be subject to such influences, I would prefer being reduced to the very lowest capacity in the "kingdom of God" and sit at the feet of all. And then I could be of some service to the cause without packing such characters on my back. Such ambition I pray God I may never be blessed with, for it certainly carries with it the seeds of its own destruction. They are as much greater men judging from their self importance, and professed [?] knowledge, with no small share of conceit, than the Twelve, than one can very consistently conceive. When Brother [Addison] Pratt took the Presidency of the branch, I was in hopes of receiving better results than I have; he is one day carried away with them and the next against them; and so it has been from the first three months. I do not say this with any feeling against Bro Pratt, for I have none; it arises from a want of natural stableness of purpose and firmness in decision and character.

Our care and interest is daily increasing in influence and strength, the tide of opposition that has heretofore existed against us under the recent control of [the] Alcolde [George Hyde] here, has received a successful defeat and the "Star" has become the representative of the commercial and influential portions of the community of the place, and is rapidly increasing in the surrounding country, after their using every effort in their power by colleaging with many enemies among our own people, to break and move me from the country, every effort failing, they have at last thrown down their weapons and taken our side of the question. Some of these were the most wealthy and influential in the country. In many questions of importance presented, they are glad to seek to us for council and assistance. The great trouble on our side was that they did not understand how to carry the common people with them and control the different interests that existed in the country. One fact I now communicate to you that never has been divulged to any living being with regard to its origin, from me, but to your trust, in as much as I communicate it to you upon the confidence that I entertain of your high character and standing, it will never be communicated to unworthy bosoms, that would make an ill use of it. I communicate it to you as a duty. Myself in connection with two other influential persons of this place have organized an order entitled "The United Order of Charitable Brothers." We three compose at present the only members of the Grand lodge and the Great Grant Lodges. A subordinate lodge has been organized in this place, entitled Samaritan Lodge No 1. We have taken in a majority of the most respectable citizens of this place. The order is advancing very rapidly, and we have applicants from all parts of the country to become members. It will, without doubt, become the most influential of any order in this county, and the two connected with me, both being Masons and Odd Fellows, will not give their influence any room for a charter. On this cord I intend to pull strong to sustain the good feeling that is now existing in this country towards our people to guard against any violent prejudices that may seek to take root among the people to our injury and discomforture, to sustain and uphold our character and to advance the cause when some good and wise men can be sent here to labor in the vineyard.

As for myself it will never answer (according to my judgment, though I may be incorrect) for me, to labor in open proclamation to the people, but others can do it with great success. I tried for a short time since to get the brethren to unite together to put up a small convenient little house to hold meetings in, in this place, that when anyone should come here, we would have a place for them to preach in. But those men that had been with the Twelve, so many years, and understood all of their plans and movement so much better than any body else, went from house to house preaching against it in secret, until we were all in confusion, and we thought it most prudent to let the matter rest for a season. There is no sectarianism in this place to contend against, and every one is anxious to attend our meetings, and in fact many have joined the church, and many more are believing; my object was to have a convenient little house and have regular preaching every Sabbath, which would have a great influence in this country by our numbers gradually increasing, but their main argument in opposition was, that I wished to do it in order to stop them from going to Salt Lake. Thus it has been from the time I returned; by Bro. Corey, Ferguson and Bariman [Borrowman] interfering and opposing me in every move I made for the good of the cause. If I have conversation with them on any subject, in 24 hours it is twisted into something else with different constructions put upon it, and scattered through the town; which has a tendency to create a strong party spirit, and of course no good can grow out of it to anyone. Brother Ferguson received a letter from Brother Hunter, Indian Agent at the Leward.[21] It was a letter from the High Council at the Salt Lake to the Battalion in California, requesting them all to return and not to enlist again, and what to bring with them. I have been informed by the brethren, for I have not seen it. He immediately called a meeting in town to learn the news from the Salt Lake. He sent an impertinent invitation to my house that if I wished to hear the letter, I must attend the meeting, for he would not let the letter go out of his hands. The letter commenced as follows: "To the Saints in California Greeting" and after reading it, he went on, (so I have been informed) with a long speech, calling upon every brother and sister to dispose of what they had, and go to the Salt Lake with them, for it was an express commandment of God.[22] Well says some I wonder if Brother Brannan is going? If this is the call, why did they not write to him something about it? Oh! They know Brannan—this was sent to me, because they had confidence in me—The Epistle that he brought with him from the Twelve, was written just to please him. When a man goes to them for council and at the same time tells them what kind of council he wishes them to give him, they always give it to him. I state this that you may have a small idea of the state of things here. Many are becoming disgusted with their conduct, and it also makes a very doubtful and bad impression upon the minds of many in reference to the character of the Head of the Church.

I long for the day to come when men will be made to know their own place and keep in it. And all understand and be governed by the people's

---

[21]Governor Mason appointed former Mormon Battalion Captain Jesse D. Hunter as Indian agent for the Southern Military District at San Luis Rey. See Ricketts, *The Mormon Battalion*, 263.

[22]This was the letter sent south from Utah on 16 November 1847 with Jefferson Hunt. For its contents, see Schindler, *Orrin Porter Rockwell*, 170–71.

influences, that every thing may move on in order and with effect. I have sent Brother Glover ~~below~~ down south with $2000 worth of goods to trade with the spanyards, which we obtained here on credit—if We realises 50 per cent on them and meet with good sale, he will then fit out immediately with more supplies ~~for you~~; and meet you at the Lake. You may rely upon my pushing every nerve to assist you and sustain you to the last—and when any man comes to you with his *fears* that Br. Brannan's carried away with the *world*, which no doubt there will be some, that I don't *preach* my business to [them] every night and morning. You will confer a great favor upon your unworthy friend; by informing them—that you ~~will~~ are fully able to look after him without their assistance—And if there is any one that goes up there growling about me and my horrible deeds, I hope you will make them put them into the shape of charges, and produce all the evidence ~~there is~~ they have against me; and whoever comes here, to bring the charges and evidence with them and let me meet them and be condemned or acquitted, and the tongue of slander cease.

I forward to you full files of the Star by the bearer. When you all get settled in the Salt Lake Valley, it would be a very good policy for a few to subscribe to the Californian our opposition paper here—it will have a good effect in "muzzling the Ox"—and bring them by interest somewhat under your influence. A few weeks ago it came very near falling into the hands of Capt. Hastings, which if it had one half of it, unbeknowing to the publick, would have belonged to me; if it is a possible thing to get hold of it, I shall do so and every other printing establishment that come into the country—that the control of public opinion may be in our hands, until the day of *Manhood* and *Independence*—There is a powerful party in this country that wishes you to come here and take possession of the valuable lands in this country. On this subject, though, I shall say no more; it is no perrogative of mine to dictate. The brethren here are alive to emigrate to the Lake; many will go this season—I shall be happy to receive a line from you by the first opportunity and any instructions you may see proper to give, I shall be most happy to obey. I wish to be kindly remembered to Bro. [Willard] Richards; I have not forgotten his kind hospitality, during my visit last Summer, in connection with many other kind friends that administered to my necessities. I hope the day is not distant when I shall have the pleasure to return it. You have my unceasing prayers for the onward process of the kingdom and the cause of God and my laborers abroad. You will hear from me again by the next party that goes out. Very respectfully, I remain your unworthy,

Brother in Christ
Samuel Brannan

Prest. B Young And Council

A GLORIOUS VICTORY

While earth-shaking news from the American River rippled through California, Samuel Brannan remained obsessed with personal and political rivalries that now seem trivial. Yet the political skullduggery that preoccupied San Franciscans in early 1848 had enduring consequences, as the campaign to remove Alcalde George Hyde demonstrated. Hyde, with support from the *Californian,* was the leader of those who wanted to develop Clark's Point rather than the waterfront of the old town favored by Brannan and his friends. Brannan coordinated a campaign that blamed Hyde for a crime wave, even though Brannan had engineered the appointment of Thomas Kittleman, a *Brooklyn* veteran, as constable. Hyde's position collapsed in March 1848 when he alienated an old ally, Councilman William Leidesdorff, who swore to remove Hyde and warned, "There is no law here but club law, and I mean to go armed and shoot anyone that offers to insult me." Hyde gave up and resigned.[23] The dramatic announcement of Hyde's removal revealed Brannan's political alliances with prominent non-Mormons such as Dr. John Townsend, who briefly replaced Hyde. Brannan's success in securing a virtual monopoly on government printing contracts in California perhaps mitigated his failure to gain control of all the presses in California.

> BRANNAN TO YOUNG, 2 APRIL 1848,
> BRIGHAM YOUNG COLLECTION, LDS ARCHIVES.

[Cover:] Prest. B. Young
Salt Lake Valley
To be opened and read by Elder PP Pratt, and John Taylor and forwarded, by Express

San Francisco April 2, 1848
Dear Sir—I hasten to inform you of our glorious success, the mail has just arrived from Monterey, with a document from the Gov. announcing the resignation of our former Alcalde Mr. Hyde (*the water here being to[o] hot for him*) and the appointment of Dr. J. Townsend, one of the members of our own Grand Lodge—he is a warm friend of mine, and of our people—You may depend this triumph is a great satisfaction to me—Hide [*sic*] has been our enemy from our first landing here but not openly but secretly—he is the man that carried on the suit against me for "*high treason*" in behalf of the gov-

---

[23]Mullen, *Let Justice Be Done,* 32. "Club law" was an early form of vigilantism.

ernment—and it has been my labor and prayer to get him removed. The Government took, also, the public printing away from the other office yesterday and gave it to us—and the Town Council not long since gave us the exclusive printing for the town for one year—Thanks be to the Most High for such a glorious victory.—My policy has been like the still small voice, but never shrink from responsibility, when a blow was needed—the coast is now clear, and the next is keep it so.

So fare well for the present.

very respectfully yours

in the bonds of the

Everlasting Covenant

S. Brannan

WILLIAM CORAY: IN THE MIDST OF A HEARTLESS PEOPLE

Sgt. William Coray of Company B, Mormon Battalion, brought his wife of three weeks, Melissa Burton, to California as one of the unit's official laundresses.[24] After his discharge, the Corays went north with Jefferson Hunt and stopped in Monterey, where a baby boy was born on 2 September 1847. Coray wrote to James Ferguson in San Francisco, "O James, I am the biggest man in all Israel. I have the greatest boy you [would] ever want anywhere, and I am coming up to show him to you just as soon as the woman gets well enough." Tragically, the infant died and was buried in Monterey.[25] Coray visited San Francisco, and "seeing there was plenty of money there, I concluded to move my effects there forthwith that I might gain some to myself." He met Brannan, who told him that Brigham Young had called "the Battalion all back, but not forthwith." Coray found the town to be a beautiful and healthy place, but felt "it was all speculation & money making both by the Mormons & the worldings & seemed to me that the Saints here were going to the Devil fast enough." Coray complained that Mormon girls were:

marrying sailors & drunkerds & he who should be their counselor [Brannan] was backing them up directly or indirectly, while at the same time he would play Billiards & drink grog with the greatest blacklegs in the place, saying it

---

[24]Ricketts, *The Mormon Battalion*, 29.
[25]Ricketts, *Melissa's Journey with the Mormon Battalion*, 81-82.

was policy to do so. Said he to me one time when he was some intoxicated, "Every act of my life is through policy."[26]

Coray was the first to accuse Brannan of appropriating LDS church funds for his own use. He denounced Brannan's efforts to build a meeting house, and charged that dissipation was "his only study." Coray's amazement that Brannan had advised him and other veterans to "purchase of lots 10 or 15 feet under water" led him to reject excellent economic advice, for the notorious water lots became one of the greatest California real-estate investments of all time. Coray complained that Brannan valued his business alliances with prominent Californians such as John Sutter more than his association with his brethren, for Brannan threatened to "have the scalps" of Mormon rustlers that he suspected had plans to rob him. The threat reflected an emerging violent rhetoric that would be transformed into action as Brannan became a power in California and a law unto himself.

CORAY TO RICHARDS, CA. 3 APRIL 1848,
BRIGHAM YOUNG COLLECTION, LDS ARCHIVES.

[3 April 1848]

Bro Willard Richards

I improve the opportunity of writing a few lines to you by S. Brannans express which starts in one hour from this for Independence in Mo via the Salt Lake.

My prolonged absence from my brethren & the church gives still stronger attachments for them & greater anxiety to meet them, & had I not my wife with me I should have been with you long before. The Batt. recd. a letter of instructions from the Presidency per Capt Brown from which I gleaned every thing in relation to my duty & I set myself about it ever since. I understand by the letter that it was my duty to return to the Church when I could provide myself with a plenty of Provisions clothing &c. From what Elder Brannan has stated we have a wrong conception of the letter altogether. But as we have some experience with Lyman White [Wight] Emit [James Emmett] & others who told flattering stories[27] and The Batt. Boys have thought it best to bear to the authorities a little longer, and have appointed the 16th of July as the day for a start back. As far as our means [permit we]

---

[26]Coray, Journal of Sgt. William Coray of the Mormon Battalion, 58.

[27]Apostle Lyman Wight and Council of Fifty member James Emmett unsuccessfully challenged Brigham Young's leadership of the LDS church.

will go. We should take young cows mares mules clothing provisions &c
seeds of every Kind that we can gather in the country & when we arrive there
I for one shall submit to any thing your wisdom dictates & I presume it is
the case with the rest of my brethren. We long to meet you & have a refresh-
ing time & hear your council. It would be better to me than daily food. We
live now in the midst of a heartless people. Our neighbours are made up of
Missourians & runaway Sailors, robers & horse theives. The Basest Gamblers
constitute the Aristocracy of the place. The brethren who came out in the
Brooklin with a few exceptions mingle with them & the Mormon girls some
of them are married to drunken Sailors & vagabonds.

Mr. Brannan has taught this to them by example & precept. Bro Richards
I do not state this expecting that it will amount to a charge because I dont
wish to be the person who prefers a charge against any of my brethren unless
duty drives me to it, but the facts you ought to know. He has collected 2000
Dollars of the Co. stating that he was oweing the Church the Same amt of
tithing funds to bring off the Ship. He has swindled them out of every
thing they have or could earn all of [which] he considers worth 7 thousand
Dollars. This he has mortgaged to his wives mother [Fanny Corwin].[28]
What his object is you may judge for your self. He has counseled his
brethren to stay her[e] to lay out their money in the purchase of lots 10 or
15 feet under water. This he advised me to do a while ago. He undertook to
build a meeting house worth 2 or 3000 dollars & wanted the Battalion to
subscribe as well as the others but they went against it & it was *no go*. I have
frequently heard him say in preaching to the Publick that the whole Kingdom of God was depending upon their or his movements in this place. I
thought to myself it stands upon a totering foundation for it is a fact he has
influence over but 2 or 3 of his own Co. Disipation [is] his only study. He
has gone in company with the C. C. Smith (that accompanied him to meet
you) in Keeping a store at the Sacramento where the most of our boys are at
work. The way they speculate off of the poor souldiers is a caution. [They]
purchase thing[s] at auction moth eaten & damaged & sell at 3 & 400 per
cent. Mr. Brannan stated to me that he believed sum of our men at Sooters
to be engaged with robbers & horse theives & that he mistrusted that one of
them wanted to break open his store. He said to me in great anger that he
would be on the mountains with a co[mpany] of gentiles & have the scalps
of 5 or 6 of them let them be Mormons or Gentiles if they took any horses
that did not belong to them. He was speaking of a co. that is supposed to
[be] gathering up horses to go over the mountains in the spring. He also said

---

[28]Coray's comment supports the conclusion that Brannan had applied $2,000 of LDS church
funds to underwrite the *Brooklyn* voyage. The figure of $7,000 approximates the expenses for the voy-
age, but the nature of the "mortgage" to Mrs. Corwin remains a mystery.

he has written to Capt Sooter (an old Gentile) informing him of the probability of their being men among us who were the worst of men & authorizing him if he saw any of our boys out of imployment to horse whip them off his premises & cry mad dog & run them out of the country. I told Elder Brannan I thought this to be doing our boys an unnecessary injury & cause them to be watched like theives. He said with an air of importance I am accountable now [to none] but the twelve. I am tired of mentioning a few of the many things which I could not sanction. Meanwhile I am sir your faithful friend & have the honor to be your brother,

In the bonds of the covenant,

Wm Coray a sevty

JAMES FERGUSON:
A BRIEF REPORT OF THE MOVEMENTS OF THE BOYS

Irishman James Ferguson was arguably the most literate enlisted man in the Mormon Battalion, as this "brief report" demonstrates. He subsequently served as a lawyer, actor, and editor, and during the Utah War of 1857–58 he was adjutant general of the Nauvoo Legion, Utah's territorial militia. The promising career of this "handsome, dashing, eloquent, and incisive" man was cut short, perhaps by drink, at age thirty-five in 1863.[29] His history of the Mormon Battalion, said to be the finest contemporary account of the venture, survived until 1900 but was apparently destroyed by the family.

Ferguson blamed the "discord and discontent" that wracked the *Brooklyn* pioneers on Brannan's unethical business practices. Like Coray, he complained about the demoralization present among the California Saints due to Brannan's "doctrine of amalgamation." Ferguson reported that the battalion veterans had already selected a date in mid-July to begin their journey to the Salt Lake Valley.

JAMES FERGUSON TO THE PRESIDENCY AND HIGH COUNCIL,
1 APRIL 1848, JOURNAL HISTORY.

San Francisco, Upper California, Apr. 1, 1848

To the Presidency and High Council of the Stake of Great Salt Lake City

Respected Brethren: By the request and decision of a meeting held last

---

[29]Jenson, *Latter-day Saint Biographical Encyclopedia*, 4:743.

evening by a few of the brethren of the Mormon Battalion, I beg to make a brief report of the movements of the Boys since their arrival in this town.

About twenty of them took up quarters in this place during the fall and were generally successful in obtaining business. Others found business in the Red Woods on either side [of] this bay and other[s] called a halt about the Rio Sacramento and the Pueblo de San Jose.

Those who remained here, of which I am one, found as a general thing a kindred feeling with the brethren and sisters who immigrated in the "Brooklyn," though among these latter discord and discontent prevailed too much. On tracing these feelings to the origin they found themselves, almost every instance at the organization of a firm (Samuel Brannan & Co.) in which the common stock principle was promulgated. They traced this from its organization to its dissolution and found that in every instance the many bereft and trodden upon, as they had always been, were the sufferers, and the few, who were the controllers and accountants of the firm, became rich and haughty.

In addition to these, more painfully still, they found that the doctrine of amalgamation had been promoted and taught and on its strength several daughters of the brethren here had sacrificed their virtue and honor in disgraceful wedlock to sailors and vagabonds; and the Saints were mingling the "Pasear" song and dance with whoever offered an invite. As far [as] the "Boys," without interfering in others business, could, they laid down mildly the principles opposite to this on which they had been instructed and their influence created a marked alteration in the aspect of affairs in this respect.

Many were established in the place and had made calculations on a long and protracted residence in this town and vicinity. The resolutions that the volunteers formed publicly to return home to the bosom of the Church created in many a spirit of gathering and desire to free themselves of the unholy influence that was increasing around them. This may likely have made them enemies in individuals who had previously made calculations on having companions to sustain them in their separate state from the Church.

From all the information I can obtain they have endeavored to carry out the instructions they received from the Twelve previous to leaving the Bluffs, as well citizens as soldiers, and have discharged the business they have been engaged in honestly and uprightly. They have hitherto stood aloof from the variety of ravengers who have become a terror to the whole Californian community, and have rested satisfied with the proceeds of their own work, this in spite of hints and unfounded suspicions which some have privately thrown out.

Your most instructive epistle of the 16th Nov., 1847, sent by Messrs [Asahel] Lathrop, [Elijah K.] Fuller, & [Orrin Porter] Rockwell, was forwarded to me by Lieut. [Robert] Clift and circulated among the brethren here.

The fact of the distance between this point and San Diego or the Pueblo de los Angeles being almost as great as between this and your city has prevented a communication in person between those [sent as] your commissioners and the brethren here. The counsel given by you, however, has been fairly digested and will have the most strict attention of all your obedient brethren, the volunteers. The purchase of cattle, mares and mules must be more limited here on account of the double value of animals in this district. Clothing and provisions may be obtained more advantageously here.

It has been concluded wise not to commence [our] march from here till about the 10th or 16th of July. The latter is the day appointed for a meeting at the Sacramento, from which point all will start en masse, or as wisdom may order it. The company from here it is expected will include a few families distinct from the Battalion boys.

With warm regards, I remain most obediently, your Brother,

James Ferguson

A Very Novel Incident

Samuel Brannan wrote the final chapter in the charges and countercharges that California Mormons sent to Brigham Young in the spring of 1848. His letter reveals that the express did not depart San Francisco on 1 April as long supposed, but probably left on the fourth. Brannan accompanied the messengers as far as New Helvetia, arriving on the *Dice mi Nana* on 7 April with "Mr Hawk the express Mail carrier and a few others." The express numbered perhaps ten men, mostly battalion veterans but including Virginian John B. Gray.[30]

BRANNAN TO YOUNG, 3 APRIL 1848,
BRIGHAM YOUNG COLLECTION, LDS ARCHIVES.

Prest. B. Young Esq
Salt Lake Valley
To be opened and read by P. P. Pratt, and John Taylor and then forwarded to the President.

San Francisco April 3rd/48
Dear Sir [Prest. B. Young Esq] While spending the evening with my fam-

---

[30]Sutter, *New Helvetia Diary*, 130; and Bigler, ed., *Azariah Smith*, 112. Henry Bigler, writing as Henele Pikale, "Recollections of the Past," 343, recalled that eight men left about 16 April.

ily at Brother Lincolns, from the Society Islands, He gave me the history of a very novel incident that transpired at a meeting called for the purpose of making some arrangement [for] how they should travel to Salt Lake—After the meeting being dismissed, ~~Mr Cory moved that~~ and all gone but Sixteen, Mr. Cory moved that Brother Ferguson write a letter of representation of the Battalion and the affairs in this country. And that Mr. Ferguson should write the letter, and just such a letter as he pleased—which was not to be read to the battalion or any one else here. I give you the names of all that voted on the letter out of the 16 that were in the house.

James Ferguson   Wm Cory
George Pickup   Timothy S. Hoyte
—— [Benjamin] Hawkins   Orlando F. Mead
John Fowler

I communicate this to you from the fact, that Brother Lincoln told me that every one understood that it was designed to represent me more than any one else in the country—Father Hawk I have been told was present at the meeting and can give you particulars.

Yours &c

S. Brannan

For all their internecine gossip, Brannan, Coray, and Ferguson did not mention the discussions that led to making the oft-mentioned "new road" to California a reality. With Brannan's encouragement, the battalion veterans declined to return to Donner Pass and that summer opened a new route across Carson Pass that soon became the main overland gateway through the Sierra Nevada. These letters to Brigham Young shared one singularly strange feature: they breathed not a word of the news that would soon shake the world. While testing the millrace of the sawmill he was building for John Sutter on 24 January 1848, James Marshall had discovered gold.

Chapter 9

"GOLD FROM THE AMERICAN RIVER!"

"Made a contract and entered in partnership with Marshall for a sawmill to be built on the Amer: fork," John Sutter noted on 27 August 1847. The next day the frontier entrepreneur hired Mormon Battalion veterans to help foreman James Marshall, a morose carpenter from New Jersey, build a lumber mill at Sawmill Seat on the American River's south fork. Sutter needed to supply his growing work force, and to fill that need Charles C. Smith "oppened his Store in the Baquero house" on 12 October.[1] Smith and his partner, Samuel Brannan, began stocking their mercantile operation as a general frontier emporium that George McKinstry called the "shirt-tail store."[2] By the spring of 1848, C. C. Smith & Co. offered a general assortment of hardware, clothing, and outfits for "parties wishing to cross the mountains with pack animals."[3]

Work on the sawmill in the Sierra foothills progressed slowly through the winter. Torrential January rains threatened to overwhelm the project, but the weather broke in the middle of the month. While inspecting the mill's tail race on Monday, 24 January 1848, "Mr. Marshall found some pieces of (as we all suppose) Gold."[4] Three days later Marshall arrived at Sutter's Fort "on very important business" and showed what he had found to Sutter. They consulted the *Encyclopedia Americana* and "proved the metal with aqua fortis," and a hammer, confirming it was gold.[5] Sutter journeyed to Coloma and told his workmen, "I would consider it a great favor if they would keep this discovery secret only for six weeks, so

---

[1]Sutter, *New Helvetia Diary*, 71–72, 74, 84. "General Sutter's Diary" noted "a small Store was established" in "one of the houses near the fort." See Owens, ed., *John Sutter and a Wider West*, 20.

[2]Bancroft, *California Inter Pocula*, 71. Sutter explained that the name came about because "every time I wanted a few things for my Indians, the proprietors exclaimed, 'O, you will break the assortment!'"—but why this made it a "shirt-tail" store remains a mystery.

[3]*California Star*, 1 April 1848, 6/4.

[4]Bigler, ed., *The Gold Discovery Journal of Azariah Smith*, 108.

[5]Paul, *The California Gold Discovery*, 126–27.

that I could finish my large flour mill."[6] He and Marshall immediately tried to secure title to the land. "All the Indians who owned the land was called in forth with and Marshall and Sutter leased a large scope of the surrounding country," paying for their worthless title with clothes, hats, "a little flour & peas," and promises.[7] Sutter recalled that despite the golden prospects, he returned home "very unhappy."[8] Even then he suspected that the secret would be impossible to keep—and the secret would destroy his frontier empire.

HE PICKED UP A PIECE OF GOLD

The reminiscences of later years that make up most of our accounts of the gold discovery were fraught with errors, and Samuel Brannan's 1872 version, written to correct "important mistakes," was no different. His brief story contained two errors worth noting: The contract to build the mill was drawn before Brannan established his store; and, following the lead of his old friend James Marshall, Brannan gave the wrong date for the discovery of gold. He noted that the Mormon miners paid a 10 percent assessment, not as tithing but based on the "right to the discovery." Yet Brannan's account is relatively early, and in it he staked his claim to having named Coloma and Natoma.

"CALIFORNIA GOLD DISCOVERY,"
DESERET NEWS, 5 JUNE 1872, 3/1.
When, Where and by Whom it was made.

I observe an article in your last week's paper, copied from the Oregon *Bulletin*, giving an account of the discovery of gold on the American River, California, in January, 1848, in which there are several important mistakes. The facts are as follows:

Captain Sutter made a contract with [James] Marshal, [Peter] Weimer & [Charles] Bennett to put up a saw-mill in the fall of 1847 on the south fork of the American River, where the town of Coloma now stands. Having a store at the fort at that time, I agreed to furnish them with all the necessary supplies on Sutter's account until the mill was in running order, otherwise

---

[6]Sutter, "The Discovery of Gold in California," 130. Sutter's flour mill at Natoma was never finished. Brannan and John Fowler later used its frame to build the first hotel in Sacramento.

[7]Henry Bigler, quoted in Paul, *The California Gold Discovery*, 130.

[8]Sutter, *New Helvetia Diary*; and Paul, *The California Gold Discovery*, 60–61, 130.

they would not have taken the contract. On the 19th of January, 1848, when Marshal let the water into the mill-race, and the water had run clear, he picked up a piece of gold—or what he supposed to be gold—at the bottom of the race, and gave it to the wife of Weimer, his partner, who was there cooking for the men, and it is still in her posse-sion [sic] at Santa Barbara, where she buried her husband a short time since.[9] A number of men from the Mormon Battalion were at work on the mill for Marshal & Co., all of whom left their work and commenced washing out gold, and that was the end of mill-building. Marshal, Weimer, Bennett, and Capt. Sutter claimed the right to the discovery, and charged every man who worked there ten per cent. of what they found. Some of the boys became dissatisfied and went prospecting down the river for themselves, and found good diggings about twenty-five miles below, on an island which has ever since been known as Mormon Island. I put up a store there, and called the place Natoma, after the name of the Indians who lived there. I also put up a store at the mill and called the place Coloma, after the name of the tribe there. [James] Queen, who is now living at San Francisco, had charge of the store at Natoma, and [Edward] Von Pfister, who is living at Benicia, had charge of the one at Coloma. Any other statement made in the article alluded to I deem it unnecessary to reply to. This is a true statement in brief, and there are many living witnesses to testify to its correctness.—Sam Brannan in the *Calistoga Tribune*, April 11.[10]

GOLD HAS BEEN DISCOVERED

Exactly when and how Brannan heard about the gold discovery is not clear. Sutter recalled that in mid-February teamster Jacob Wittmer tried to buy a bottle of brandy from C. C. Smith with raw gold. When Smith confronted him, Sutter confirmed that it was indeed gold and that night complained in his journal that Wittmer had "told every body of the Gold mines."[11] The secret was out, and a certain publisher would be among the first to hear it when Smith "sent word of it to his partner, Brannan."[12]

Charles Bennett, a veteran of the First Dragoons and a supervisor at the sawmill, left Sutter's Fort on 8 February for San Francisco. Bennett was sent to acquire title to the gold country for Sutter and Marshall

---

[9]W. W. Allen later purchased this nugget, now on display at the Bancroft Library, and wrote *The California Gold Book* to defend its authenticity.

[10]This issue of the *Calistoga Tribune* is not in the best collection of the state's newspapers, which is at the California State Library.

[11]Paul, *The California Gold Discovery*, 61, 130.

[12]Bancroft, *History of California*, 6:43.

from military governor Richard Mason.[13] In Benicia Bennett stopped at the store of Edward von Pfister (who had sailed on the *Brooklyn* from Hawaii) and exhibited several ounces of gold dust. He also showed his assay specimens "to Sam. Brannan, Mr. Hastings, and several others . . . and about the 1st of April, the story became public property."[14]

Readers of the *Californian* soon learned of the "secret." The paper reported on 15 March that "gold has been found in considerable quantities" in the raceway of Sutter's sawmill. The *Star* ran these stories about the discovery three days later.

NOTICES,
CALIFORNIA STAR, 18 MARCH 1848, 2/1–2.

We were informed a few days since, that a very valuable silver mine was situated above this place, and again, that its locality was known. Mines of quicksilver are being found all over the county. Gold has been discovered in the Northern Sacramento Districts, about forty miles above Sutter's Fort. Rich mines of copper are said to exist north of these Bays.

THE MINERAL MANIA—*all not Coal that glitters*—The Philosopher's Stone never called into the field, and away from honest labor such a host of diligent bodies, as have the recent discoveries in the mineral kingdom, in California. Gold—the veritable gold itself, has been dragged forth, and now that it has been turned from the earth without sowing, we would not be willing to risk a prediction where the excitement caused will cease.

Some silver-seeking 'uns, in the course of their researches, not many miles off, happened upon a shining substance, and *coal* at this particular juncture being preferable to suspense, or valueless black rock, coal it must be. Yes, coal had been brought to light! coal enough to provide the proposed line of Panama steamers with fuel!—Perhaps, though, it would be well to bring it to the light and heat of the furnace. Ah! there did exist a slight difference between this and the bona fide, lucklessly for the people. It did certainly look like coal and the scientific say it felt like coal! The only difference between this and *the* coal then, was, coal would burn and this would not!

THE MINES—We have purposely refrained a mere mention of our mineral wealth hitherto, being desirous of one day presenting a chapter or two,

---

[13]Mason rejected Bennett's appeal. For problems dating Bennett's trip to Monterey, see Gay, *James W. Marshall*, 473–74. The *New Helvetia Diary* noted that "Mr Bennet arrived from Monterey" on 13 March, indicating that the attempt to secure land rights was made at this time.

[14]Buffum, *Six Months in the Gold Mines*, 68. On this trip, Bennett met Isaac Humphrey, who had mined gold in Georgia. Humphrey returned to Coloma with Bennett and revolutionized mining methods.

from which there would be derived a fair estimate of its extent. In the course of the able review of the prospectus of California which we this week open, this will appear.

The *Star* reported on 25 March 1848, "So great a quantity of gold taken from the mine recently found at New Helvetia, that it is become an article of traffic in that vicinity."

DR. VICTOR FOURGEAUD: THE PROSPECTS OF CALIFORNIA

The promotional piece that Victor Fourgeaud wrote at Brannan's behest contained several noteworthy elements, including a prediction that the "gigantic prospect" of "a railroad from the states" would "ultimately be carried into execution." Fourgeaud extolled the country's climate and agricultural advantages, noting "the great wants of California—a liberal supply of industrious farmers and mechanics." The first page of the special edition did not even mention—let alone trumpet—California's mineral prospects, but focused on its fertility and agricultural potential, benign climate, fisheries, and strategic position for world trade. Ironically, the *Star's* amateur writers relegated the big story—the gold discovery—to its inside pages, but eastern journalists immediately seized upon the tantalizing allusions scattered throughout the issue when it reached the states. Douglas S. Watson demonstrated in 1931 that the *Star* was the source of the 19 August 1848 *New York Herald* article that first infected the eastern United States with gold fever.[15] These extracts from Fourgeaud's story contain the references to the gold discovery.

"PROSPECTS OF CALIFORNIA,"
CALIFORNIA STAR, 1 APRIL 1848, 2/1.

California is well known to be rich in mineral wealth:—Iron, copper, lead, sulphur, silver, quicksilver, gold, &c., are known to exist, and are believed to be abundant in quantity and rich in quality. Some of these mines are now in operation, and large amounts of capital will be invested in the business, and numerous laborers employed as soon as the necessary machinery can be obtained. It is known that the proprietors of the Santa Clara quicksilver mine only await the arrival of machinery to employ five hundred men in the prosecution of that enterprise alone. Similar undertakings in

---

[15]Watson, "Herald of the Gold Rush—Sam Brannan," 299.

other sections of the country will soon increase the wealth of California by calling out its mineral resources, and furnishing a market for its agricultural products . . .

It would be utterly impossible at present to make a correct estimate of the immense mineral wealth of California. Popular attention has been but lately directed to it. But the discoveries that have already been made will warrant us in the assertion, that California is one of the richest mineral countries in the world. Gold, silver, quicksilver, iron, copper, lead, sulphur, saltpetre, and other mines of great value, have already been found. We saw a few days ago, a beautiful specimen of gold from the mine newly discovered on the American Fork. From all accounts, the mine is immensely rich—and already, we learn, gold from it, collected at random and without any trouble, has become an article of trade at the upper settlements. This precious metal abounds in this country. We have heard of several other newly discovered mines of gold, but as these reports are not yet authenticated, we shall pass over them. However, it is well known that there is a placero of gold a few miles from the Ciudad de los Angelos, and another on the San Joaquin. Several silver mines, specimens of which we have seen, have lately been discovered. This metal, it is said, is abundant in the vicinity of Pueblo de San Jose, (now our most wealthy mineral district,) but it is said, also, to exist in many other sections of this country. Silver, as well as copper, we are informed, has been found near San Diego. Don Juan Bandini is the proprietor of a rich copper mine in that region. It is not yet in operation. We also learn that the country in the vicinity of Clear Lake is very richly provided with this ore. Sulphur abounds, especially in the Northern District, near Napa.[16]

The second page of the *Star's* special edition announced "one of the richest veins of mineral yet discovered" in an article titled "Another New Silver Mine." Four miles from San Jose, J. F. Reed (of Donner party fame) had found a vein of silver ore "which is, without doubt, the richest ever discovered in the Mexican Republic." The claim made in "Extracts from a private letter Bay and Town of San Francisco" that one man could pluck thirty dollars in "gold from the sand in one day" sounded extravagant, but it was a fact.

"SAN FRAN,"
CALIFORNIA STAR, 1 APRIL 1848, 4/2.

I pause before speaking of the mineral riches of California, and to pre-

---

[16]Fourgeaud devoted the rest of his article to Capt. J. L. Folsom's "report on *coal* and *asphaltam*" and the quicksilver mine at Almaden. It concluded that California "needs but one thing—men of industry and energy to develop its resources."

pare you, will remind you of the anecdote of the Irishman, who desired a person to write for him to his friends, "that in Ameriky he had beef three times a week." "But, Pat," said he, "you have beef every day." "Yes, faith, but they'll not believe the likes of that." Can you believe that the ore of one quicksilver mine at Santa Clara yields from 25 to 50 per cent? and that, too, with the most imperfect apparatus. Several other mines have been commenced at the same place, and with every prospect of success. A Silver mine has been discovered in the neighborhood of the Pueblo, a Coppermine in Napa, and Gold at Sutter's. A man positively picked $30 worth of gold from the sand in one day. This I have from an undoubted source.

"CALIFORNIA,"
CALIFORNIA STAR, 1 APRIL 1848, 4/3.

You will see plenty in the papers about the mines. Already, pickaxes, crucibles, and alembics are in requisition—quite an active interest and excitement being felt among us on the subject. And without allowing any *golden* hopes to puzzle my prophetic vision of the future, I would predict for California a Peruvian harvest of the precious metals, so soon as a sufficiency of miners, minerologists and metallogists find their way thither, and commence disimbouging her rich hidden treasures. Gold, and quicksilver will be the principle products of this soil, several mines of each having already been discovered.

"THE GREAT SACRAMENTO VALLEY,"
CALIFORNIA STAR, 1 APRIL 1848, 4/4.

. . . It has a mine of gold and a probable estimate of its magnitude cannot be derived from any information we have received. It was discovered December last,[17] on the south branch of the American Fork, in a range of hills forming the base of the Sierra Nevada distant 30 miles from New Helvetia. It is found at a depth of three feet below the surface, and in a strata of soft sand rock. Explorations southward [for] the distance of twelve miles, and to the north five miles, report the continuance of this strata, and the mineral equally abundant. The vein is from twelve to eighteen feet in thickness. Most advantageously to this mine, a stream of water flows in its imme-

---

[17]This early reference to the gold discovery taking place in December would appear to be a mistake, but historian Tom Mahach has noted circumstantial evidence suggesting that gold may have been found at the mill site in 1847. On 19 December Azariah Smith reported, "I missed a basin and knife off my shelf, stolen by someone." Smith wrote on 6 February, "what should I find on the shelf but my knife and basin," replaced by William Johnstun, who had returned from Sutter's on 2 February with Marshall. See Bigler, ed., *The Gold Discovery Journal of Azariah Smith,* 107, 110. Johnstun later claimed to have been present at the gold discovery, but he was not at the mill site on 24 January 1848—and the purloined knife and basin were exactly the type of tools battalion veterans used to extract gold from rock.

diate neighborhood, and the washing will be attended with comparative ease.

C. C. Smith & Co. published two advertisements in the special edition. The first touted the arrival "of a New and General Assortment of SUMMER CLOTHING," and both notices promoted its line of supplies "for parties wishing to cross the mountains" and "return to the States by overland." On his visit to Sutter's in April with the *California Star* express, Brannan spent only three days at the fort.[18] He met with the battalion veterans to discuss one of his favorite projects, opening a better overland road into California. Brannan had expressed his interest in finding a new road in an article that warned against "short cuts," meaning the Hastings Cutoff.[19] On 9 April, "pretty much all the boys came together to talk over matters and things in regard to making arrangements for going up to the Great Salt Lake and come to some understanding when we should make the start." Brannan advised the men to find an easier trail than the arduous Donner Pass route with its granite summits and many difficult crossings of the Truckee River. James S. Brown recalled, "We had become accustomed to pioneer life [and] thought we could find a better route."[20]

ANOTHER STILL MORE EXTENSIVE AND VALUABLE GOLD MINE

Many Californians still regarded news of the gold strike as mere speculation and rumor, but Brannan had better information about the discovery than anyone in San Francisco. In light of the mania that soon followed, the initial lackadaisical reaction to the discovery seems odd, but the consequences of this historic event were not immediately apparent even to those who witnessed it. Stories about gold had long been part of standard California lore. Francisco Lopez had found gold at Placeritas Canyon in 1842 and miners extracted more than fifty thousand dollars from its shallow placers over the next two years.[21] James Marshall was said to have long

[18]Sutter, *New Helvetia Diary*, 129.
[19]See "The Old Road," *California Star*, 1 April 1848, 3/4.
[20]Gudde, ed., *Bigler's Chronicle*, 106; and Brown, *Life of a Pioneer*, 107.
[21]Lavender, *California: Land of New Beginnings*, 121.

believed the province was rich in minerals. The discovery failed to impress the first to hear of it as being very consequential, and it took weeks for the discoverers themselves to realize the size and wealth of the gold field they had found.

Henry Bigler wrote to three former messmates about 21 February "and informed them that we had found gold at the saw mill, but to keep it to themselves unless it would be to someone who could keep a secret." The three men told fellow veterans Sidney Willes, Wilford Hudson, and Levi Fifield the news, and on the twenty-seventh they arrived at the sawmill "with their guns and blankets on their backs." James Marshall let Hudson prospect around the tailrace, where he found a nugget worth six dollars. Willes and Hudson returned to Sutter's flour mill on 2 March, prospecting along the river. In the evening, they shot a deer and made camp on a sandy flat of four or five acres "mostly overgrown with small shubbery." After supper enough light remained "to prospect the ground." They thought it a trifling prospect, but "Ephraim Green and Ira Willes, a brother to Sidney, kept coaxing and urging them to go back."[22] Returning several days later, they made the first major gold strike after Coloma at a site of legendary richness that became known as Mormon Island. A month later, Brannan's paper printed this notice.

"NOTICE,"
CALIFORNIA STAR, 22 APRIL 1848, 2/4.

☞ We have been informed, from unquestionable authority, that another still more extensive and valuable gold mine has been discovered towards the head of the American Fork, in the Sacramento Valley. We have seen several specimens taken from it, to the amount of eight or ten ounces, of pure, virgin gold.

Henry Bigler later wrote that the Willes brothers "met with Sam Brannan and let him in on the secret," which was soon a secret no longer. "Brannan told them," Bigler recalled, "he could secure the mine as church property and advised for all the Battalion boys to go to work in the mine and pay one-tenth to him and he would turn it over to the church as tithing." Bigler's recollection that Brannan collected tithing was a later interpretation. Brannan actually persuaded the discoverers to give

---

[22]Gudde, ed., *Bigler's Chronicle*, 101, 103–04; and *Grimshaw's Narrative*, 12.

him "a share with them" in return for his efforts (which failed) to secure title to the claim.[23]

THE BIGGEST SPECULATION IN THE WORLD

Elder Brannan gave his last sermon to the Mormon congregation in San Francisco on the last day of April 1848. Aggravated at the never-ending backbiting among the Saints, he "delivered a lecture on the dis-affection that existed in the branch and called for those that found fault with him to bring forth their charges."[24] As his realization of the poten-tial of the gold discovery increased, Brannan's interest in the bitter squabbles of his flock waned.

Brannan did not have time while at Sutter's in April to visit the mines, but the battalion veterans made clear the extent of their recent discover-ies and gave him a better appreciation of the potential of the "gold mines." At the same time, Edward Kemble, now officially editor of the *California Star*, visited Coloma to see for himself if there was anything to the golden rumors. Kemble reached Sutter's Fort on 17 April. Sutter himself accompanied Kemble, P. B. Reading, and George McKinstry to the sawmill/gold mine two days later. The "lumbering crew" told Kem-ble he could find gold "anywhere you're a mind to dig for it" down the river, but Kemble's personal experience convinced him that the rumors were a "humbug," the word he wrote in bold letters across the top of his notes. Reading spent several hours panning gold with an Indian basket and thought his efforts had not produced the price of a drink—about twelve cents. Kemble returned to San Francisco and honestly reported his observations, but he would spend the rest of his journalistic career explaining how he had missed "the greatest scoop in history."[25]

Historians have charged that Brannan ordered Kemble to keep the story quiet until he was in a position to maximize his profits. Sutter implied this in 1857 when he remembered that Smith reported the discovery to "Mr. Brannan, who came up immediately to get all possible information, when he returned and sent up large supplies of goods, leased a larger house from

[23]Gudde, ed., *Bigler's Chronicle*, 108.
[24]John Borrowman, Journal, 30 April 1848.
[25]Douglas S. Watson, quoted in Rogers, ed., *Kemble Reader*, vi–vii.

me, and commenced a very large and profitable business; soon he opened a branch house of business at Mormon Island."[26] This theory contradicts Kemble's account, which claimed he based his report on personal observation: what he had seen "justified him in proclaiming the gold discoveries to be a delusion and a snare."[27] Rather than falsifying his stories to suit Brannan's business interests, Kemble honestly expressed his skeptical reaction to gold fever.[28] As clever as Brannan may have been, the tradition that he delayed the release of the information that set off the gold rush overstates his cunning and foresight. Brannan made sure, however, that he was prepared to take advantage of any opportunity that might arise.

After delivering his farewell sermon on 30 April, Brannan left for New Helvetia, taking "a little sail-vessel" to Benicia. He stopped at Stephen Cooper's house for a horse. Brannan arrived at Sutter's Fort on 4 May and spent the next two days visiting "the Gold Mines"—Mormon Island—with C. C. Smith. What Brannan saw convinced him "there was more gold than all the people in California could take out in fifty years." With a new appreciation of the extent of the gold fields, on the seventh "Mr Brannan visited the new town where he intend[s] to build a Warehouse & a store." (The "new town" was the Embarcadero on the river front, which would soon take the river's name, Sacramento.) He had seen enough to appreciate that the gold deposits were greater than anyone dared to speculate, and he packed a sample of the metal into a quinine bottle. "Mr. Brannan left for San francsico" on 8 May.[29]

Stephen Cooper's recollection of these events provides important details:

> On the 4th of May, 1848, Sam Brannan, a Mormon, came to Benicia in a little sail-vessel. He came to my house, with his saddle on his back, and dunned me for a horse, saying that he had some horses at Sutter's Fort and wanted to collect them. I furnished him a good horse. When he was about to mount the horse, he told me he was not going after horses. He remarked, I know the biggest speculation in the world, and if there is anything in it, on my return I will let you into the secret; he was gone some four or five days.

[26]Paul, *The California Gold Discovery*, 130.

[27]Rogers, ed., *Kemble Reader*, 138.

[28]For Kemble's third-person explanation of these events, see Kemble, *A History of California Newspapers*, 78–79.

[29]Sutter, *New Helvetia Diary*, 133–34.

On his return my horse brought him to Knights Landing, on the Sacramento River. He had run him down; procured a fresh horse, which brought him to Vacaville; having also run that one down, another fresh one brought him on to Benicia. He told me he had stood over a man five minutes, and in that time had seen him wash out $8.00, and remarked that there was more gold than all the people in California could take out in fifty years. That was the first gold excitement that ever amounted to anything.[30]

Cooper reached Mormon Island by 14 May and in the next three days took out $980 in gold. Fifty-two years later Cooper's daughter Susan recalled that James Marshall had come through Benicia. He showed her the first gold discovered in California.

> Three days after that Sam Brandon [sic], a Mormon, came riding breathless into our place in Benicia and asked John Wolfskill, who was afterwards my husband, for a fresh horse. He said that gold had been discovered, and that he was going there to locate all the land he could and return to Monterey and file on it . . . But some time before that Brandon had been very unaccommodating to Mr. Wolfskill when he wanted horses to bring fruit trees from Los Angeles, so [Wolfskill] would not let Brandon have a horse. Brandon rode on urging his tired beast. He and Bidwell were going to locate [acquire] the whole gold bearing country, but Mr. Wolfskill told them it was placer mining, and that they could not hold it all.[31]

Brannan hurried to cross the bay, arriving at San Francisco on 10 May. He stepped from the ferry onto the beach, and "holding up a bottle of dust in one hand, and swinging his hat with the other, passed along the street shouting, 'Gold! Gold! Gold from the American River.'"[32] Battalion veteran Benjamin Hawkins was in San Francisco when Brannan arrived and "said Brannan took his hat off and swung it, shouting aloud in the streets that gold was found, etc. The inhabitants of the place seemed to be panic struck and in such a hurry to be off, that some of the mechanics left their work, not taking time even to take off their aprons, and he himself (Hawkins) struck out and bought up all the Indian baskets he could."[33] Brannan displayed the gold at his house that

---

[30]"Autobiography of Major Stephen Cooper, Written in 1888," in Rogers, *Colusa County*, 360.

[31]"The Foremothers Tell of Olden Times," *San Francisco Chronicle*, 11 September 1900, 27/3; and Tinkham, *California Men and Events*, 61. Wolfskill, of course, was right.

[32]Bancroft, *History of California*, 6:56.

[33]Gudde, ed., *Bigler's Chronicle*, 110–11. This summary was made much later when Bigler copied his journal for H. H. Bancroft.

"RESIDENCE OF SAMUEL BRANNAN, ESQ., IN 1847."
Stephen Smith of Bodega built this home for Brannan out of redwood. "In this
house were exhibited the first specimens of gold brought from the placeres."
From Soulé, *The Annals of San Francisco,* 347.

evening. John Borrowman noted, "Elder Brannan called a meeting and informed us of a gold mine being found by Brother Willis and gave his advice for all to go and work in it."[34] Brannan would never again meet with the Saints. Sutter noted his return to New Helvetia on 16 May, in company with "many passengers and some Goods" and a second "Launch close by."[35] Brannan was ready to profit from the frenzy he had created.

The Monday following Brannan's announcement, "fleets of launches" left the bay. As the disease he dubbed "gold fever" emptied San Francisco, Edward Kemble battled "the aggregated rumors, as Don Quixote charged the windmills."[36] Even after Brannan's dramatic announcement, Kemble maintained the mines were "all sham, a supurb

---

[34]Bancroft, *History of California,* 5:56, dated Brannan's dramatic announcement to 12 May, but the correct date is found in John Borrowman, Journal, 10 May 1848.

[35]Sutter, *New Helvetia Diary,* 136.

[36]Kemble, *A History of California Newspapers,* 78–79.

take-in, as was ever got up to guzzle the gullible."[37] He begged his vanishing subscribers on 27 May, "Pay up before you go—everybody
knows where. Papers can be forwarded to Sutter's Fort with all regular-
ity, but pay the printer." It was hopeless. The last number of the *California Star* appeared on 10 June 1848, and Kemble had to concede defeat.
The "conversion of San Francisco" to Brannan's golden gospel was now
a fact. By the middle of June, "the abandonment of San Francisco was
complete." Three-quarters of the male population had left for the
mines.[38]

As the town emptied, the *California Star* reported the results for the
city council election: "L. W. Hastings received 79 votes; C. L. Rose, 77;
W. H. Davis, 77; S. Brannan, 76; V. J. Fourgeaud, 75, and were declared
duly elected. The whole number of votes polled were 147."[39] Brannan
would soon find public service at least as profitable as his mercantile
operations. Some of his former disciples found other ways to wealth.
Before the discovery of gold, the Stivers and Marshall families of the
Brooklyn had established ranches on the contra costa. The men joined the
crowd seeking gold, leaving Letitia Marshall to manage the ranch. In a
story that would become typical of the gold rush experience, she made
"more money selling milk and eggs, than Simeon and Earl did mining
gold."[40]

Brannan probably tried to secure title to the gold country, but California's military government refused to cooperate. Governor Richard
Mason felt he had no power to grant land, a prerogative the Constitution reserved for Congress, and on 12 February he issued a proclamation
invalidating Mexican mining law, "preventing a few people from filing
on the best mining areas."[41] Mason's policy effectively forestalled the
plans of Marshall, Sutter, and Brannan to secure title to the gold fields,
but it left open the question of who owned California's gold. Mason visited the mining camps in June, hoping he "could secure to the government certain rents or fees" from the miners, "but upon considering the

[37]*California Star*, 20 May 1848, 2/4.
[38]Bancroft, *History of California*, 6:56–60.
[39]*California Star*, 20 May 1848, 2/4.
[40]Lilian H. Kelly to Will Bagley, 10 October 1996.
[41]Grivas, *Military Governments in California, 1846–1850*, 119.

large extent of the country, the character of the people involved, and the small scattered forces at my command, I resolved not to interfere." Mason suggested that the government should send out surveyors and issue mining licenses, but the "country is so great, and the gold so abundant, that for the present there is room and enough for all."[42]

Lieutenant William T. Sherman accompanied Mason on a tour of the gold fields in the summer of 1848. Years later he recalled "the scene as perfectly to-day as though it were yesterday." Sherman confused Brannan's "tax" on the miners for tithing, but his account enshrined one of the great legends of the early gold rush.

> As soon as the fame of the gold discovery spread through California, the Mormons naturally turned to Mormon Island, so that in July, 1848, we found about three hundred of them at work. Sam Brannan was on hand as the high-priest, collecting the tithes. Clark, of Clark's Point, one of the elders, was there also,[43] and nearly all the Mormons who had come out in the Brooklyn, or who had staid in California after the discharge of their battalion . . .
>
> I remember that Mr. Clark was in camp, talking to Colonel Mason about matters and things generally, when he inquired, "Governor, what business has Sam Brannan to collect the tithes here?" Clark admitted that Brannan was the head of the Mormon church in California, and he was simply questioning as to Brannan's right, as high-priest, to compel the Mormons to pay him the regular tithes. Colonel Mason answered, "Brannan has a perfect right to collect the tax, if you Mormons are fools enough to pay it." "Then," said Clark, "I for one won't pay it any longer." Colonel Mason added: "This is public land, and the gold is the property of the United States; all of you here are trespassers, but, as the Government is benefited by your getting out the gold, I do not intend to interfere." I understood, afterward, that from that time the payment of tithes ceased, but Brannan had already collected enough money wherewith to hire Sutter's hospital, and to open a store there, in which he made more money than any merchant in California, during that summer and fall. The understanding was, that the money collected by him as tithes was the foundation of his fortune, which is still very large in San Francisco.[44]

---

[42]"California and New Mexico," House Exec. Doc. 17 (31–1), 1850, Serial 573, 532.

[43]"Clark of Clark's Point" in San Francisco was William S. Clark, who was not LDS. Sherman perhaps met one of the several Clarks who had come to California with the Mormon Battalion.

[44]Sherman, *Memoirs of General William T. Sherman by Himself*, 52–53.

Most casual observers assumed that the money Brannan collected was tithing, and exactly how he separated the Mormon gold hunters from their money is confusing. Addison Pratt recalled that "the thirty per cent money he had collected of us" was made under "a pretence to buy cattle to send to Salt Lake, for the benefit of the church."[45] The journals of the men present provide a more accurate picture of these events. Azariah Smith called the money he paid to Brannan a "toll" that went "to Hudson and Willes, that discovered the mine, and Brannan who is securing it for them." John Borrowman described the thirty per cent of his findings that he paid to Brannan & Co. as "rent."[46] This tax was already in place at Mormon Island by early May, even before Brannan returned from San Francisco, for Stephen Cooper recalled "that ten Mormons on the island were washing gold, and claimed thirty per cent of all the gold for two miles up and two miles down the American River."[47]

R. F. Peckham: The Pioneer Store at Coloma

After his experiences at New Hope, Robert F. Peckham worked as a storekeeper at San Jose, where he met some of the survivors of the Donner disaster. Peckham believed that "in regard to the deprivations and hardships endured by that party, the truth has never been and never will be told."[48] With Brannan's announcement of the gold discovery, "The Alcalde left his records; the merchant his store; the carpenter his building unfinished; the farmer his crops half grown, and the ranchero his horses and cattle, and all flocked to the new El Dorado." While working as Brannan's chief clerk, Peckham witnessed the wonder of the gold fields in 1848 and watched the fight over where to build a city—a battle that Brannan won, but which soon had tremendous consequences for those who joined his settlement on the flood plain at the confluence of the American and Sacramento rivers.

---

[45]Ellsworth, *Journals of Addison Pratt*, 431. Pratt also charged that Brannan wanted "to put up an adobie Temple" on one of his San Francisco lots.

[46]John Borrowman, Journal, 30 May 1848. David L. Bigler first noted that Brannan's fee was for "undefined services," and that he was *not* excommunicated from the LDS "for extorting tithing gold or money" from California Mormons. See *The Gold Discovery Journal of Azariah Smith*, 115–16.

[47]"Autobiography of Major Stephen Cooper," in Rogers, *Colusa County*, 360.

[48]Peckham, An Eventful Life, 16.

R. F. PECKHAM, "AN EVENTFUL LIFE,"
SAN JOSE PIONEER, 14 JULY 1877, 1/6-7.

About the last of June some of the gold seekers returned [to San Jose] to look after their families and business, and brought the most astonishing stories of the new discoveries, and were able to verify them, by the gold they brought with them. They had found it. Some of those that had gone from San Jose had got four, some eight, some twelve and some as high as twenty thousand dollars.

Peckham could stand it no longer. The store of Cooke and Ruckel was permanently closed; and about the 4th of July, he started to the mines in company with Charles White and William Daniels. They went by way of Livermore Pass and Brewer Camp, it took about a week to make the journey. And they found most of the San Jose people in a place they had named Webber's Creek, about ten miles from Coloma and three from the present town of Placerville.

The stories that had come to San Jose were found to be no exaggerations. The people were at work up and down the creek for three miles with varying success. It was no object to work for less than sixteen [dollars per day] and some of them were making from two to four hundred dollars per day.

Charles M. Weber was then with John M. Murphy and Doctor Isabel. They had got in a lot of groceries and started a store; and were making a fortune rapidly. The Indians had learned what the gold was and how to collect it, but knew nothing of its real value: a dollar's worth of gold with them was the weight of a silver dollar, and the store of Weber and Co. did an extensive Indian trade.

There was no mining laws and no mining claims. If a man left his tools where he had been working, this was title to the hole in which they were found; outside of this any man dug where he pleased. Yet even at this time good places required a great deal of prospecting and patience to find. And this prospecting was very inexpensive but required perseverance. When a miner could not see gold by raking over the sand in the bottom of the creeks with the point of a knife, it was no place for him, and he pursued his hunt in search of a better locality.

Peckham prospected for a day or two without much success; left and went to Coloma. Here he found Samuel Brannan. Brannan had formed a mercantile partnership with William Stout, and they started a large wholesale store at Sutter's Fort. And he had come to Coloma to prospect the locality with a view to starting a branch and disposing of his goods at retail; he found a business already started by Stephen A. Wright and E. F. Van Pfister, [so] he purchased the store and left Peckham in charge of it, and returned to New Helvetia . . . At the time of this transfer, there was two other stores at Coloma. It was the centre of trade of a large and extensive mining section. In some localities yielding enormously; and the prices paid by miners for goods, is at this day deeply interesting. The same beef that was worth but four dollars a carcass in San Jose, six months before, was retailing at one dollar a pound. Crackers and flour, one dollar a pound; six quart tin pans, sixteen dollars a piece; pickels, sixteen dollars a quart; canned meats and sardines sixteen dollars a can or box; whiskey sixteen dollars a bottle and everything in proportion. The currency was gold dust as it was called, fine placer gold. And it was taken by weight, at sixteen dollars an ounce Troy. Though the native Californians, who must have coin to carry on their favorite game of monte would sell their gold for five dollars an ounce in silver coin.

Peckham stayed here but a few days boarding at the same house with J. W. Marshall, when he was relieved by Stout. From here he went to New Helvetia and as a salesman took charge of the wholesale establishment [S. Brannan & Co.] there. This was the largest and best assortment of stock in the country. It had a very extensive trade, averaging about four thousand dollars daily; from one-half to four-fifths of the amount sold was clear profit. Their shipments to San Francisco was about twenty-five thousand dollars weekly. The transportation between there and San Francisco was by schooner. They would go up [down] the river in about two days, and it took about six days to make the return voyage. The fare at the boarding house in New Helvetia was beef stake and sea biscuit with coffee and sugar three times a day, and the daily charge was twelve dollars.

The store was in Sutter's old hospital building outside the Fort. The Fort so called was on a little mound. It was a parallelogram about three hundred by one hundred and fifty feet. The outside walls were of adobe or sun dried bricks about twelve feet high and sixteen feet think, with a tower on each corner. A row of rooms was built around the walls on each side and ends; at the time of which we are writing these rooms was occupied principally as stores: on the north side was the residence of the proprietor, John A. Sutter . . .

The most of what is known as Sacramento city, was then a dense swamp. Wise gentlemen [John Sutter and Lansford Hastings], in the Fall of that year [1848], surveyed and mapped out a town on the high land, three miles below and called it Sutterville, and here is where the city should have been built. But Samuel Brannan decreed otherwise, and the low swamp at the junction of the Sacramento and American rivers was made the commercial emporium of the valley and the Sierras. Money enough has been spent to protect it from overflow, to have built another city, and yet the work is not done. About the first half of October, Stout closed out the store at Coloma and returned to Sacramento, and took charge of the wholesale establishment. An unkindly feeling existed between him and Peckham, and he soon left their service.

BRING ROUND GOLD IF YOU HAVE ANY

In a brief note Brannan invited Edward von Pfister to the opulent Fourth of July party he staged in Sacramento and reported that he had bought out Charles C. Smith. Smith had been the victim of an accident, having "got blown up by a powder flask."[49] After parting from Brannan, Smith may have gone into business with John Bensley as Smith, Bensley & Company, but he closed his California enterprises by the end of 1848 and sailed on the *Tepic* to Honolulu, taking his fortune back east and vanishing from the historical record.[50] The "good old Yankee style" Fourth of July celebration in a grove of trees proved "to be one of powder-smoke and liquor fumes." Samuel Damon opened with prayer and William Gwin made a few remarks about organizing a state government. Lieutenant Sherman attended the festivities with Governor Mason and thought "it cost the givers $1500 or $2000." The dinner "would have done credit in any frontier town," and there was "a liberal quantity of liquor disposed of."[51] Before the party ended, "Sutter was very tight and many others showed the effect of the *aguardiente*." Sutter recalled that he "was no more tight" than Sherman.[52]

BRANNAN TO EDWARD VON PFISTER, 27 JUNE 1848,
BANCROFT LIBRARY.

New Helvetia June 27th 48

Mr. VonPfister

Dear Sir, I received your letter a few days since and have had no opportunity of answering you until now. I appreciate your views, and as it is impossible for me to go up at present I should be happy to see you here. I have bought out Mr Smith and have the whole controll of the business Myself and have arrangements on hand that will give you regular supplies, to keep up your stock—yours respectfully S. Brannan

N.B A dinner will be given here at the fort on the fourth of July and a regular fourth of July celebration.

S.B.

come down

If your good[s] are gone bring round gold if you have any.

---

[49]Sterling to Larkin, 9 July 1848, in Hammond, ed., *Larkin Papers*, 7:314. C. B. Sterling reported the change of the company name from C. C. Smith & Co. to S. Brannan & Co.

[50]Kantor, ed., *Grimshaw's Narrative*, 47–48; and Bancroft, *History of California*, 5:722.

[51]Thorndike, ed., *The Sherman Letters*, 44.

[52]"The Fourth of July, 1849," *Sacramento Bee*, 26 September 1882, 1/2; and Zollinger, *Sutter*, 251–52.

John Borrowman: Brannan Had Seduced Her

Women—and his often notorious relationships with them—played a mysterious part in Samuel Brannan's life. Ironically, although gossip about his sexual escapades was common lore for thirty years in San Francisco, only scraps of these tales and general references to Brannan's legendary womanizing survive in the historical record. John Borrowman's tale of Brannan's relationship with a young *Brooklyn* passenger provided one of the few descriptions of his sexual exploits—and injects an interesting subject seldom encountered in documentary histories: sex.

Susan Eliza Savage was born about 1829 in Skowhegan, Maine, and worked in a factory to earn her passage on the *Brooklyn*. Despite her "deeply religious nature," she may have been infatuated with the handsome leader of the California Saints. Borrowman's account, however, identified the object of her affections as Miles Weaver, a thirty-two-year-old Mormon Battalion veteran. Borrowman painted an intense if ambiguous portrait of this young woman in crisis, though the "cause of her trouble" remains a mystery. A self-portrait probably painted in the 1850s shows her as an attractive woman with a long face and dark hair. Savage apparently did not go to the Salt Lake Valley with the Weaver brothers in the 1848 Ebenezer Brown company, but in Great Salt Lake City on 20 April 1851 Brigham Young sealed her to architect Truman Angell as a plural wife. She died 19 July 1893 in Logan, Utah, and was buried in the Salt Lake Cemetery.[53]

In addition to his charge that Brannan had seduced and was trying to abandon Savage, Borrowman provided a sample of Brannan's colorful language and described his predilection for violence, a trait that would emerge with growing force over the next decade.

JOHN BORROWMAN, DIARIES 1846–1853,
LDS ARCHIVES.

Sunday, 6th [August 1848] . . . This evening elder Brannan came into camp and told Miles Weaver that Eliza Savage had come up to the lower mines and wanted him to take her to Salt lake. They then started in com-

---

[53]Brown and Hathaway, *141 Years of Mormon Heritage*, 131, 133, 135; and Carter, *The Ship Brooklyn Saints*, 570; Truman Angell listed five children by Savage, but Carter credited the couple with six children. Savage's California crisis may have produced a baby daughter.

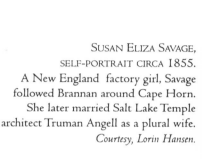

SUSAN ELIZA SAVAGE,
SELF-PORTRAIT CIRCA 1855.
A New England factory girl, Savage
followed Brannan around Cape Horn.
She later married Salt Lake Temple
architect Truman Angell as a plural wife.
Courtesy, Lorin Hansen.

pany with brother [John Rufus] Stoddard but in about an hour after one of
the brethren came in from Sutters and told us that he had heard Brannan
swear by the great Jehova that made him that he would drink a quart of
Miles Weavers blood. Then Franklin Weaver fearing for his brothers safety
got John Reid & James Ferguson and set off in pursuit of them and overtook them but did not let Brannan know their business only they watched
him closely. When they came to the mines they found Eliza out of her reason and anxous to go to the [Great Salt] lake and wanted Miles to take her
there and seemed to be in great distress and Brannan said that Miles had
sedused her and promised to take her to the lake and now was going to leave
her but this Miles denied & when they ask[ed] she said Miles never made
any promise to her and all she sent to him for was because she always loved
him and she wished to throw herself on his protection but as Miles had no
way prepared to take her he was compelled to leave her. Then she seamed to
be in great distress and when Franklin Weaver asked her what was the cause
of her trouble she told him she would not tell him now for he would hear it
soon enough. From this I believe that Brannan has seduced her and then
wanted to turn her off on Miles Weaver.

ANN ELIZA BRANNAN:
NOW IS THE TIME FOR MAKING MONEY

While Brannan was in the foothills of the Sierra, his wife "cleared five hundred dollars by making and getting made cheap clothing." Ann Eliza Brannan's letter to her sister-in-law, Mrs. John Brannan, is our single window into her world.

Legend tells that Ann Eliza Brannan (who by 1849 had already adopted "Lisa" as her middle name) was a snob who hated San Francisco. Her letter confirms that she had no intention of settling permanently in California, but a desire to get rich in the West and return to the comforts of the East was a common hope of early settlers. What role Ann Eliza Brannan played in the social life of Yerba Buena is only hinted at, though Joseph Downey noted, "The female portion of the emigration kept pace with the male, and the style of the town was fully sustained in the persons of Mrs. S. Brannan, Mrs. [Lucy] Eagar and her two lovely daughters [Mary and Arabella]."[54]

How she coped with her husband's legendary infidelity is impossible to know, but even Bancroft noted Brannan's "flaming devotion to the tender passion."[55] A newspaper commented late in his life that one of Brannan's costliest vices "was his passion for actresses. He lavished a fortune on Lola Montez when she was the rage in San Francisco."[56] Brannan was extravagant in his support of such women; in 1852 he paid $625 for the first ticket to a Kate Hayes concert at a benefit auction for the Firemen's Charitable Relief Fund.[57] A Victorian historian's typo accurately described the "great clod of marital infelicity" that characterized Brannan's conduct as a philandering husband.[58] From the evidence of her letter, Ann Eliza Brannan was a better wife than her husband deserved.

---

[54]Rogers, ed., *Filings from an Old Saw*, 140.

[55]Bancroft, *Popular Tribunals*, 2:115.

[56]"Sam Brannan," *San Francisco Examiner*, 15 January 1888. Brannan probably met Montez when they were both passengers on the Pacific mail ship *Northerner* in 1853, but none of her biographers describes an affair with Brannan. For example, see Varley, *Lola Montez*, 92, 94. Not deterred by this lack of documentation, Reva Scott devoted much space to a torrid description of an alleged liaison. See *Samuel Brannan and the Golden Fleece*, 334–50.

[57]Huntley, *California: Its Gold and Its Inhabitants*, 254–55.

[58]Palmer, *A History of Napa and Lake Counties*, California, 327.

THE BRANNAN FAMILY, CIRCA 1856.
These European miniatures were probably painted during Brannan's first visit to the
continent, showing Ann Eliza Brannan as an attractive young woman.
Courtesy, The Society of California Pioneers.

ANN ELIZA BRANNAN TO MARY [MRS. JOHN] BRANNAN,
2 SEPTEMBER 1848.[59]

San Francisco Sept 2 1848

Dear Mary

I now commence to write you a long letter, and you must excuse it if it
looks as though it had been wrote in a great hurry; for perhaps I shall be
three or four days at it just as I have time now and then. We received your
letter, and was happy to hear of the good health of you all. Also to know
that we had not passed entirely away from your minds. Our family are all

---

[59]From a copy in possession of Robert J. Chandler. A portion of the letter was originally published in Lewis, *Pioneers of California,* 85, 90, citing a copy in the Charles Hill Collection. Barker, ed.,
San Francisco Memoirs, 1835–1851, 123–24, first published the complete letter.

well and enjoying good health. Little Samuel has grown very much and is another S. Brannan over again. He is quite tall, but rather slender, he will be three years old the 17th of next month. He knows his letters and is beginning to spell quite rapidly.

We are living in one of the most healthy places in the world, and I am quite contented and happy for the time being; that is, untill we make our fortunes, but we would never think of setling here for life, and I rather think that too [sic] or three years will find us in *New York* or some wheres there abouts where we can enjoy life. That is, if we have good luck as at present: but now is the time for making money. Mary if you and John had come out hear when we did you would now of been independent for John could of made five dollars a day the year round, from the time we came here, and now it is much better; the Gold mines yeald abundance for all, and you by sewing could of made three times what John does now, besides doing your work. You will hardly believe me when I tell you that this summer that in little more than three months I have cleared five hundred dollars by making and getting made cheap clothing. Pants and shirts, such as you would get in N.Y. 25 cents for making I am given $1,50 cents and they have only one pocket in them as women can make five and six pair a day. Tis true I have a good cook and also have had a good girl which I brought from N.Y. with me but she has lately married and left, and I don't know but my cook will go to the Gold mines soon to work and then I shall be without help. I would like if you come out here that you would bring a girl for me and I will pay her expenses. If you come bring every garmant to last you a year or so that is clothing, and a plenty of dried fruit of every discription and I will buy all you don't want yourselves.

I send by Mr [Henry] Mellus three rings which we got made of the gold from the mines, one for your self, and one for Jane, Daniel [Brannan's] wife, and one for Mary Ann Badlam. You must deliver them with my love and best wishes for their welfair and hapiness. I should write to them both if I knew where to direct them. You must give Mr Mellus directions where Jane lives so that he can call and see her, and tell Jane I shall expect a letter from her with out fail if it is no more than three lines for she will have a good chance to send by the vessel that Mellus sends here from N.Y. And the same to Mary Ann if you see her. As for your self I shall say nothing for a word to the wise is suffiscent. Samuel says he wishes that Daniel was here with his family to[o]; and I wish you all was here for we have a pleasant place and good health also doing well and with these you could not fail to be contented for a year or too.

I think of you often and of N.Y. also for that is the place of my child hood and I look forward with a joyous heart to the time when I shall return.

There is many things I would like to write of if I had time. I will send a little of Samuels hair to you all. And I hope this will find you in the enjoyment of good health.

Yours with love and respect
A. L. Brannan

A flood of wealth engulfed the Brannan family in the fall of 1848, changing their lives forever. As new worlds opened before him, it remained for Samuel Brannan to extricate himself from the religious movement to which he had devoted his youth.

SAMUEL BRANNAN, CIRCA 1856.
This portrait appears to have been taken during the "20 years or
more" when Brannan "was rarely sober after noon."
Courtesy, LDS Archives.

Chapter 10

"He Forsakes Mormonism for Gold"

Few episodes in Samuel Brannan's life have come down in history as encrusted in myth as the story of his separation from Mormonism. Legend has it that Brannan built his fortune on tithes stolen from Mormon miners—money that he refused to deliver to Brigham Young without "a receipt signed by the Lord." The truth is even more intriguing. After his return from the Rocky Mountains in 1847, Brannan remained on intimate terms with his old Mormon friends and tried, unsuccessfully, to maintain his position and prove his loyalty to the LDS church. Brigham Young's failure to answer the many letters the young zealot sent from California left Brannan feeling betrayed, and early in 1848 he found a cause more rewarding than working for the Kingdom of God—exploiting a golden opportunity to build a personal fortune. By the time Young responded to his questions in 1849, Brannan had made his final break with Mormonism. Yet the record reveals that he accounted for the money he owed the Mormon church. When Brannan was finally disfellowshipped from the faith, it was for murder and apostasy, not theft.

WILFORD WOODRUFF: LIKE FIRE IN A DRY STUBBLE

Like many missionary members of the LDS hierarchy, Apostle Wilford Woodruff was dependent on the generosity of the devout for his livelihood. The fall of 1848 found Woodruff in Boston, staying with the Badlam family in the home of Brannan's sister. He sent "Brother Brannan" a summary of recent events, including comments on the effect of the news of the discovery of gold in California. Woodruff's discussion of cataclysmic fires and environmental disasters provides a fine example of his radical millennialism. It reveals that even the most senior

LDS leaders hoped to profit from the sudden rush of gold—and Woodruff's request for money was not the last Brannan would receive from an LDS leader.

WOODRUFF TO BRANNAN, 25 SEPTEMBER 1848,
LDS ARCHIVES.

Boston Sept 25 1848

Brother Brannan

Dear Sir

As their is a ship about to sail from New York to carry the mail to California I feel a disposition to improve it by dropping a few lines to you. To give you even a synopsis of every thing [that] transpired with me since I saw you & of the news of the country on a sheet of paper would require more skill than I possess. Yet I will say a few things.

We stopt in the [Salt Lake] valley about one month [and] put for home, met 600 wagons of Saints about the Mountain pass going on. While resting the last night with the last company the Indians stole 49 horses from us, & [in the] days after made an attack upon us in open day for more but only got one. We lived mostly on Buffalo Meat going Home without Bread. Arrived at Winter Quarters the fore part of Nov. [and] found our families generally well. And we all spent a good Winter, had good meetings & Councils & the Lord was with us, not a quarter as much sickness as the year before.

The folks all busy during the winter & spring getting ready to go either to the East or West. After I got ready with the rest to go West, it was decided that I should go to the Eastern States & preside over that part, and Canida, New Brunswick, Nova scotia, &c. I changed about & set my face for the East instead to West. I waited however to see the Springs Crops [planted and the] Camps start for the vally. I was with P[residents] Young & Kimball at the Horne [Elkhorn River] to see them start with their first company of 600 waggons. They made a grand looking Encampment. They were fitted out with provisions [for] one year & a half. They left about 25 May. W Richards & A Lyman left about the 25th of June with another company of over 300 waggon. Their were near 1000 waggons in all of the Saints went this spring. We had letters from them from Laramie & the Saints in the vally Date[d] 16 last of May, they were very well all [and in] good health [with a] prospect of good Crops ownly the Crickets had eat some of it. The camps at Laramie was getting along well. Had not seen an Indian on the same side of the river with them since they left the Horn. Winter Quarters was evacuated [and] all had gone on the Iowey side. They built a large log Tabernacle. They have a post office called Kane P.O. Kanesville Potawatomie Co Iowa. I think their is 15,000 Saints in that County. They are flowing in there from all parts making that their rendezvous to fit out for the vally. O Hyde, G. A. Smith & E T Benson stop & preach in that County. O Hyde came part of the way with me. [He] went to Washington [and] was sick there 4 weeks [and] came to Phila[delphia. He] got better & went home [and] is expecting to start a paper soon.[1]

I came to Boston via Nauvoo, St. Louis, Chicago, Buffalo & Albany. Brought my family with me & stopd for the time being with Alexander Bad-lam who is doing well in the varnish business & [has] made a home for many of the Saints. He treated me & my family kindly. His lady Your Sister is well. They received two letters from you of late but no papers, [and] they both wish [in] particular to be remembered to you. Sister Badlam says she will write to you soon. I expect to make my home with Br. Badlam or near him for a year or two until I go to the vally & I expect that will be when & ere [they] push the remainder of the Saints out of these eastern lands to the West. O Pratt sailed in July to England [and was] near 18 days on the way. The work is progressing like fire in a dry Stubble throughout that land. Thousands are coming into the Church in England, Wales Scotland &c. Capt Dan Jones has done wonders in Wales [and] has converted many thou-sands to the gospel, but has worn his lungs out at it. He is preparing to come to America with his Welch flock next season, Either to New Orleans or the Bay of San Francisco. We have sent many Elders to Europe & more are wanted.

As to the news in this Country I have ownly to say that the awful loss of life by burning & blowing up Ships Boats & Steamers at Sea, Lakes or the rivers &c, are running 50 per cent & fires in Cities [produce a death rate] more than that among the Mormons. Fires burnt last month one quarter of Albany NY & 200 Homes in Brooklin NY are in ashes. Pestilence of every kind is wasting away the people of New England & the States in General at the measure of 50 per cent. In the N[orth] the potatoes are roting. Clams are poisoning the people to death & the Eels are dying by cart loads sup-posed to be poisoned by eating clams. Politicks run High. VanBuren goes as the free soil Candidate, Taylor the Whigs, Cass the Dems. But I must leave these subjects for I want to say a few words about another.

The New England States are all Brought up sturdy like a rail car run off the street at the Astounding News that the Mormons have found ric[he]s which line beaches pure with gold to such a degree & extent that it has depopulated all the Towns in upper Calafornia [and] that men woman & Children are fleeing from their homes as they would from an Earthquake & making to the placers or American fork & Feather Rivers, Branches of the Sacramento, to dig for Gold which is found in such abundance that their is a prospect of having more gold than Bread. At first it was looked upon as a

---

[1] The first issue of Hyde's *Frontier Guardian* appeared at Kanesville on 7 February 1849.

Hoak but reports having been made from the Officers of the Navy confirming the Material that it is now generally credited. Ships are fitting out at New York with instruments & tools all kinds to supply the gold digers.

I now want Brother Brannan to write me a letter as soon as you get this (if you can leave the gold diggings long Enough) & give me all the news about it & Everything els[e] that will be of interest to me. Fill a sheet full & if you should get so much gold that you do not know what to do with it, if you will dispose of some of it & send me a check on any good bank it will come in but first rate good time & I can find [a] use for it to a good advantage, say any sum from 25 cts to $25000. Please direct to Wilford Woodruff Boston Mass and if I dont get the check I shall surely look for the Letter. Give my respects to all who know and inquire after me there. Yours Respectfully

W. Woodruff

That winter Woodruff noted that the *New York Herald* weekly of 27 January 1849 was "full of the Calafornia gold fever. It seems as though All the world was running stark mad to go to the gold mines of Calafornia on the Sacramento. Hundreds of ships And tens of thousand of men are preparing to go there."[2]

They Have Forsaken Me

No surviving document sheds more light on the end of Samuel Brannan's connection to Mormonism than the 1849 letter that Wilford Woodruff probably copied—not very legibly—and forwarded to Brigham Young. Brannan's bitterness was best expressed in his conclusion that he had been sent to California to get him out of the way—and to be killed. The letter provides Brannan's own assessment of his profits from the gold rush—and makes a veiled prediction that he would soon hear from the Mormon authorities.

BRANNAN TO ALEXANDER AND MARY ANN BADLAM, 13 MARCH 1849,
LDS ARCHIVES.

[Cover, perhaps in Wilford Woodruff's hand:] Copy of Samuel Brannan Letter to Mrs. Badlam

He forsakes Mormonism for gold

Sanfrancisco March 13th 1849

Dear Brother & Sister, I Embrace the opertunity for once and the Last Time till I Receive a Letter from you to drop you a few lines. My self & Fam-

---

[2]Kenny, ed., *Wilford Woodruff's Journal*, 3:412.

ily is in Good Health & Spirits. My Little Boy is upwards of Three years old and Speaks quite plain. He is a grate source of Happiness to me. I Think i shall goe to the States in a year from this time. I Hope you will Not Be alarmed But What i shall take pains to goe and See you. Any News you may have from this Country as a Golden one you Can Believe for you have not heard half the truth. With in the Last year I have Cleard over a Hundred Thousand Dollars and hope to [keep] This from the authorities of the Church. They have forsaken me. I Have Been Here three years and over and Received No acount only What i traveled Clear to the Salt Lake after. No one Ever thought Enough of Me During my Long Stay here to Wright to Me and in fact i am unable to See What i Was Sent here for unless it Was to Get me out of the Way Suposing it Being a Spanish Country i Would Be Kiled.

If So they mist a figure that this Brannin [*sic*] is Capable of undertaking a Sanjen Enterprises than Coming to California with a parcel of Women and Children and a few Men settlers. When the Lord finds out I have Got a Little Money He will Begin to feel after me. I would not have you think that I am making Light of My Creator, for i Still Entertain the Same feelings towards him that i Ever Did and He Has my prayers for Suport and Health & Strength.

I Remain your
Brother Most Truly
S Brannin

Brigham Young: A Hint to the Wise is Sufficient

Among the most entertaining documents in the Brigham Young papers is his April 1849 letter to Brannan, exhorting him to pay his tithing and asking for a substantial cash "present" to "help him in his labors." Mormon historian Eugene Campbell pondered Young's motives and acknowledged that a literal interpretation of the letter suggested that if Young used the Lord to entice money from Brannan, it would be "little different from Brannan's use of the same device to get gold from the miners." Campbell found no evidence "of such hypocritical, unethical practices" in the Mormon prophet's record and believed that Young was merely "putting Brannan to a severe test," but even he concluded that Young would not have "refused the money if Brannan had proved loyal."[3] Brigham Young's personal history said nothing about testing Brannan, but noted that the letter asked him "to forward, by Elder Amasa Lyman, his

---

[3]Campbell, "The Apostasy of Samuel Brannan," 166. Campbell's analysis relied on the edited versions of the Young and Lyman letters in the Journal History.

tithing and $20,000 dollars [*sic*] in gold for me and the same amount for my counsellors."[4] As a realist, he probably did not expect that Brannan would send the small fortune he requested, but Young clearly thought it was worth asking—and his "hint to the wise" (a favorite phrase) carried an implicit threat made more explicit in the concluding paragraph.

YOUNG TO BRANNAN, 5 APRIL 1849,
BRIGHAM YOUNG COLLECTION, LDS ARCHIVES.

[Cover:] April 5–1849
Brigham Young to Samuel Brannan asking for $50,000.
Copied, signed & sent TB [Thomas Bullock]
                    Copy
                              Gr Salt lake City, April 5th 1849
Brother Brannan,
    I have received your letters of Dec, 1847: of March 29, 1848, and others not before me, the dates of which I do not recollect, and think I can safely say all the subjects listed of by you, you will find answered in our general Epistle,[5] so far as is necessary at the present time, but if any thing has been overlooked, in my multiple cares and business, I will refer you to Bro Amasa Lyman, for an answer, and he will be ready to give you any information or council you may wish, though I will add that there has been no "legal complaints filed against you" as you have suggested. ~~and~~ The man who is always doing right has no occasion to fear any complaints that can be made against him, & I hope you have no occasion to fear.
    I am glad to hear you say that I "may rely upon your pushing every nerve to assist me, and sustain me to the last," for I doubt not you have been blest—abundantly and now have in your power to render most essential service. I shal[l] expect ten thousand dollars, at least, of your tithing, on return of Elder Lyman, and if you have accumulated a million to tithe, so as to send $100,000, so much the better, & may you get 2 millions next year.[6] If you want to continue to prosper do not forget the Lords Treasury, lest he forget you, and with the liberal the Lord is liberal; and when you have settled with the treasury, I want you to remember, that, Bro Brigham has long been destitute of a home, and suffered heavy loses & incurred great expenses in searching out a location & planting the church in this place, & he wants you to send him a present of twenty thousand dollars in gold dust to help him in his labors. This is but a trifle, when gold is so plenty, but it will do me much good at this time.

[4]Harwell, ed. *Manuscript History of Brigham Young, 1847–1850*, 180.
[5]For the First Presidency's 1849 "First General Epistle," see White, ed., *News of the Plains and the Rockies*, 3:195–208.
[6]Young asked for Brannan's personal tithing, not for money Brannan had collected from others.

~~I hope~~ Bro Brannan will remember that the revelation in the Doctrine & Covenants, refers to Josephs counsellers as being equal with him, which is all right in its true acceplaken [application]. But when you have complied with my request, my council will not be equal with me, unless you send 20.000 more to be divided between bros. Kimball & Richards,[7] who like myself are straitened, ~~and there~~ a hint to the wise is sufficient, & when this is accomplished you will have our united blessing, and our hearts will exclaim, God bless Bro Brannan & give him four fold, for all he has given us.

Now Bro Brannan if you will deal justly with your fellows, and deal out with [a] liberal heart and open hands, making a righteous use of all your money, the Lord is willing you should accumulete the rich treasures of the earth & the good things of time in abundance; but should you withhold when the Lord says give, your hopes & pleasing prospects will be blasted in an hour you think not of & no arm to save. But I am persuaded [of] better things of Bro Brannan. I expect all I have asked for when Bro. Lyman returns, and may God bless you to this end is the prayer[s] of your brethren in the New covenant. B.Y.

Some years later Young made a similar request to Brannan's fellow *Brooklyn* pioneer John Horner, who was for a time a California millionaire.

President Brigham Young wrote advising me to be cautious, as reverses frequently visited people doing large business, and suggested that I sent [*sic*] $30,000 to the Trustee-in-trust, as a precautionary measure that would serve a good purpose as a future help, if misfortune should overtake me. From ignorance, procrastination, or misfortune coming so quickly, the wise counsel was not acted upon.[8]

A Receipt Signed by the Lord

The most famous of all Brannan legends tells that he used "his Mormon authority over the horny-handed miners from his old [Mormon] Battalion, and took 'the Lord's tithes' of all their pannings." When Brigham Young sent an apostle to collect to "the Lord's money," Brannan replied, "You go back and tell Brigham that I'll give up the Lord's money when he sends me a receipt signed by the Lord, and no sooner!"[9] Although the tale captured the spirit of his conflict with Brigham

---

[7]Heber C. Kimball and Willard Richards were named Young's counselors in the First Presidency formed in December 1847.

[8]Carter, ed., *Our Pioneer Heritage*, 3:554. Young's letter to Horner cannot be found at LDS Archives.

[9]Scherer, *The First Forty-Niner*, 47–49.

Young, a look at its origins and evolution reveals a more interesting history—and indicates that the story originated with Brannan himself.

The legend was in the early stages of its evolution in 1881 when it first found its way into print in William Francis White's angry rebuttal to *The Annals of San Francisco.*

> It is further told of Sam that Brigham Young, on hearing of these collections [of tithing], sent to him for the proceeds; but Sam sent back word to Brigham that he had collected considerable sums of money from the Mormons in the name of the Lord, and that as soon as the Lord called on him for the money he would pay it over; but that he would hold on to it until the Lord did call.[10]

At the time of Brannan's death, historian John S. Hittell cast the most famous of all Brannan tales in its classic form. Hittell had heard it "reported that as head of the Mormons in California he collected tithes from the followers of his faith, and that when an agent of Brigham Young demanded 'the Lord's money,' Brannan offered to pay it over for a receipt signed by the Lord—and not otherwise." As a careful historian, Hittell noted that whether Brannan "made considerable collection, whether he failed to pay it over, and whether if so he had any good excuse, are questions about which no authentic information is accessible."

Chauncey L. Canfield told this version of the story in 1909:

> [Brannan] strenuously declined to render any accounting of the property he had accumulated as the representative of Zion. "It is all invested in the name of the Lord, with Sam Brannan [as] agent, and it will require the signature of the principal before any transfer can be made," answered Sam. "Brigham Young may think he is His earthly representative, but he will have to get a decision from the Supreme Court to that effect, and I doubt if that body will recognize his spiritual claims."[11]

The wide currency of the story suggests it was a standard part of Brannan's repertoire, designed to distance himself from Mormonism and support his assertion that his only interest in the religion was financial. Brannan's friend Asbury Harpending heard the tale during one of his "frequent interviews" with Brannan. In his 1913 memoirs, Harpending recalled:

---

[10]Grey, *A Picture of Pioneer Times in California*, 150.

[11]Canfield, "The Twelve Starred Flag," *San Francisco Chronicle*, 17 January 1909, 2/4.

"Sam" worked his [Mormon] companions on a per-diem basis and very soon accumulated a large fortune—certainly in excess of a million dollars, many well-informed people estimating it at two or three times as much. But while he settled promptly his labor bills, he was not so businesslike in squaring accounts with the Mormon Church, which claimed nearly all the profits. Finally, a trusted agent was dispatched from Salt Lake City with a peremptory order on Brannan to turn over the ecclesiastical share of the "dust" at once.

Brannan's reply was historic and to the point, even if a bit profane. The gold, he said, had been placed in his safe keeping on the Lord's account. He would surrender it upon the Lord's proper written order; otherwise not.[12]

A Calistoga neighbor with a complete contempt for Brannan provided one of the earliest versions of the story of how Brannan become "the only man that got ahead of Brigham."

JOHN M. MORRIS, AUTOBIOGRAPHY AND DIARIES, 1885–1906.
BANCROFT LIBRARY, 68–70.

There was no town at Calistoga then [ca. 1862], but a kind of Hotel building, owned by Samuel Brannan, then the richest man in San Francisco. And for fear we forget the Sagacity of this Business man, We will here give the comonly received reports of how Sam Brannan got his riches. He was sent out by Brigham Young as early as 1846 to the Pacific Coast as the Lord of the Pacific Coast Mormons. When the Gold was discovered many of the Mormons came and dug gold all of them being in Brannons Diocese. He was the Lord of all [the] Mormons in Cal[ifornia]. And said to be the only man that got ahead of Brigham of his many Lords to any considerable extent. Some say Brigham fitted out a vessel and sent [it] round the horn with Mormon passengers, but Sam [on] getting here sold the ship for Sixty Thousand Dollars [and] devoted the money to his own use. We never cared enough for the mormons or Sam Brannan to hunt up the facts. Be that as it may we are more familiar with the following story and believe there is something in the report for long years after we were acquainted with Brannan, he never came to Calistoda [sic] Springs from SF without having some one along they called his body guards. At any rate as reports have it These Mormon Gold Diggers when ever they got any considerable amounts of Gold would bring the treasure to Sam Brannan for safe keeping, Depositing it with the Lord as they called him. Brannan was then always careful to receipt in the name of the Lord. Soon the Mormons began to want to go to Salt Lake, or their several homes, and called on Sam for their money, bringing in

---

[12]Harpending, *The Great Diamond Hoax*, 119–20.

their receipts. Sam took them then looking at each one Says, This money is deposited in the name of the Lord. When you get an Order from the Lord I will pay over the money. Sam Kept the money. There must be something in this report for the Mormons threatened him and as stated before he in an early day always went with an escort heavily armed.

AMASA LYMAN: A WASTE OF PAPER AND TIME

A key element in the "receipt signed by the Lord" story is the persistent assumption that Brannan collected tithes from Mormon miners, a charge often repeated in recollections such as Sherman's memoir. But as the examination of the contemporary sources has demonstrated, the money Brannan collected in the mines was actually a finder's fee assessed by his partners; his 10 percent of the "toll" was to pay him for securing title to the land. What effort Brannan made to do this is unclear, but the operation was completely democratic, and he even "called a meting, to see who was willing to pay toll and who was not. The most of them agreed to pay the toll, and some would not."[13] John Borrowman confirmed that "Brannan & Co. requires thirty per cent" of the gold he had found, but on 30 May he recorded, "This day I have said against paying rent as I consider it an imposition."[14] Neither Smith nor Borrowman identified the "toll" or "rent" as tithing.

If Brannan was not collecting tithes from the miners as president of the Saints in California in 1848, who was? The answer appears to be, no one. After two parties of battalion and *Brooklyn* veterans reached Salt Lake in the fall of 1848, they deposited gold worth more than $6500 in the Brigham Young gold accounts.[15] Although some of this money was not tithing, Azariah Smith deposited $84.63 and recalled that he went "to Pres. Brigham Young, and paid my tithing, also donating

---

[13]Bigler, ed., *The Gold Discovery Journal of Azariah Smith*, 115–16.

[14]John Borrowman, Journal, 19 and 30 May 1848.

[15]Although this record is now off limits to scholars, J. Kenneth Davies listed "Deposits to Brigham Young's Daily Transactions in Gold Dust Accounts" for "likely [LDS] participants in the Gold Rush of 1848" from 10 December 1848 to 23 June 1849 in Appendix 3c, "Appendices for MORMON GOLD," 2. These deposits totaled $6531.15, plus an additional $492.26 deposited by *Brooklyn* Saints. This indicates that the Mormon miners extracted at least $70,000 from the California gold fields in 1848, and probably far more that was not tithed. Deposits from fall 1849 through winter 1850 totaled an additional $4,023; see Davies, *Mormon Gold*, 69.

Some for the poor and one dollar each to the twelve."[16] Clearly these men paid tithes on their golden windfall directly to Young, not to Samuel Brannan.

Although Brigham Young remained opposed to mining all his life, he could not ignore the wealth in California and its usefulness to his cash-starved colony. He worked hard to discourage loyal Saints from deserting Zion for El Dorado, but on 26 March 1849 "it was decided to send Elder Lyman and Orrin P. Rockwell to California with an epistle to the faithful Saints, and also to preach the Gospel and look after the interests of the Church and the Saints."[17] Lyman left Salt Lake on 13 April with at least twenty men and several families.[18] As his July 1850 report made clear, one of Lyman's main objectives was to collect funds for the LDS church.

Lyman carried Young's 5 April 1849 letter to California, but waited until winter set in to leave the "diggings" and deliver it. He did not visit Brannan until 8 January 1850: "This morning called on Mr branan [and] left with him a leter for Mr Squire."[19] Lyman's journal did not describe the conversation, but there is no hint of conflict. When he returned in June accompanied by fellow apostle Charles C. Rich, relations between Brannan and the two apostles were cordial—and financially advantageous for Lyman. Rich wrote on 28 June, "We paid Mr. Samuel Brannan a visit and learned from him that he stood alone and knew no one only himself and his family. He agreed to turn over some books."[20] Lyman recorded that they "spent the day in Francisco and we visited Samuel Brannan who made me a present of some $500,00 [$500] made an arrangement for the books in his possession." Brannan's "present" appears to have been a successful attempt to buy the support of his old friend, who never reported the gift to Brigham Young.[21] On the next Monday, Lyman "dined with Mr. Brannan to day [and] heard

[16]Bigler, ed., *The Gold Discovery Journal of Azariah Smith*, 146.

[17]Journal History, 26 March 1849.

[18]Davies, *Mormon Gold*, 110–11.

[19]Lyman, Journal, 8 January 1850, LDS Archives. Mormon Battalion veteran William Squires ran a saddle business and tavern in Sacramento; by the end of the year, he would be dead of cholera.

[20]Campbell, "Apostasy of Samuel Brannan," 166–67. These books were probably part of the *Brooklyn* library that Brannan had been unable to sell, despite advertisements in the *California Star*.

[21]This is also the conclusion of historian Edward Leo Lyman, an Amasa Lyman descendant.

of gold digins on the east side of the Siremavada Mts."[22] Addison Pratt
suspected that Brannan reminded Lyman that if Pratt had held his peace
in 1848 when Brannan proposed building a church in San Francisco, the
Mormons would now own real estate "worth from 25 to a 100,000 dollars." Pratt felt that if Brannan really wanted to help the LDS church,
"he would have long ago handed over to Br. Lyman the money that he
has already swindled off of the brethren"—but even Pratt was confused
about the details of the alleged deception.[23]

Amasa Lyman's report to Brigham Young provides the best account of
what actually happened. Brannan's final financial accounting to the apostle discussed only funds collected to finance the *Brooklyn* voyage, and the
two men resolved the church's claims against Brannan. Although Brannan "now disclaims any connection or interest with the Church" and
regarded "communications from the Brethren . . . rather as insults than
otherwise," this did not end his long-standing friendship with Lyman.
Beyond its wonderful detail on Brannan's apostasy, Lyman vividly
described the Mormon experience in gold-rush California and reported
about the search for a settlement site that resulted in the founding of the
San Bernardino colony Lyman and Charles C. Rich established in 1851.

LYMAN TO YOUNG, 23 JULY 1850,
BRIGHAM YOUNG COLLECTION, LDS ARCHIVES.

Upper California, July 23rd

Prest. B. Young and Councell,
    Beloved Brethren
    Your letter of April 23rd came duly to hand on the 17th of this month,
from Bro[s] [Hiram] Clark and [William D.] Huntington.[24] We were rejoiced
to hear of the prosperity of the Saints in the Valley notwithstanding the
severity of the winter, Indian difficultys and a little poverty. The mission for
the [Hawaiian] Islands with those accompanying them arrived in safty and
health after a journey of 68 days without any accident of importance.[25]

---

[22]Amasa Lyman, Journal, 28 June and 1 July, 1850, LDS Archives. On 22 June 1850, Lyman had
met "br Blackburn from Salt Lake" in Sacramento. His early reference to "gold digins on the east
side of the" Sierra supports Abner Blackburn's claim to be the first to discover gold in Gold Canyon,
which was later developed as the Comstock Lode. See Bagley, ed., *Frontiersman*, 172–73.

[23]Ellsworth, ed., *Journals of Addison Pratt*, 431–32.

[24]Clark and Huntington led the wagon party that left Salt Lake on 7 May 1850. See Davies,
Mormon Gold, 225.

[25]This party left Salt Lake on 8 October 1849 under Charles C. Rich. It overtook Jefferson
Hunt on the Sevier River to join in a difficult and legendary trip to California.

They are now making preparations for prosecuting their journey to their destination.

By the minutes of the conference we learn that the fall session is changed to the 6th of Sept which renders it impracticable for me (A Lyman) to be there. So we improve the oppertunity offered by the return of Bros [George H.] Foot & [E. L.] Barnard to communicate on paper ~~some of~~ what we would say if we were with you.

First. As to money matters as that is one thing to be considered, it is at a low ebb. When the drafts on myself and others (which by the by, all had the luck to fall into my hands) were presented by Messrs Butell & Pomroy [Francis Martin Pomeroy], I had not to exceed one hundred dollars in tithing on hand which was all that had been paid me after the departure of Capt [Thomas] Rhodes.[26] I however succeeded in borrowing funds to pay Bartell four hundred and fifty dollars and Pomroy the full amount of his draft, and have sense [sic] collected the tithing mostly from the brethren from the Lake and payed the loan having on hand Thirteen hundred and fifty one dollars 1351$ which amount from the presents prospects will not be much increased previous to the time of A Lymans leaving here for the Valley which we expect will be about the 15th August.

The amount of tithing may appear small compared with last year, but the tithing paid last year was readily obtained ~~from the men~~ for the men who paid the most of it had cashed their property and the money was on hand which has not been the case with those who have been left here since.

The Brethren of wealth in San Francisco have paid little or no thithing [sic]. Mr. Samuel Brannan has paid nothing and now disclaims any connection or interest with the Church and the communications from the Brethren are regarded rather as insults than otherwise, making drafts on him has amounted to a waste of paper and time haveing afforded him the chance to do good if he would but without effect. Those Brethren who would or say they would pay thithing have their money invested in real estate or loaned out and cannot *sell* or *collect* so in the midst of wealth they are poor.

It is an old maxim that the poor in spirit were blessed. If to have a little of the spirit of the Latterday work is to be poor then the above individuals are poor indeed, yet with enough of patience, watching and care by the shepherd of the flock ~~they~~ nearly all of them may be made to answer to some purpose.

The Brethren which arrived last winter brought with them a good spirit

---

[26]Thomas Rhoades, who came overland to California in 1846, left in the summer of 1849 with a personal fortune and the tithes Amasa Lyman had collected. Several *Brooklyn* veterans, including William Glover, joined the caravan. West-bound forty-niners James Pritchard and J. Goldsborough Bruff left reports of the fabulous wealth (said to amount to $30,000) that the Mormons had collected. See Davies, *Mormon Gold*, 146–49.

and continue to act as patterns for those who have lost the spirit and have strayed from the paths of righteousness. There are but few of them who have fallen in to the path of the Gambler or the Drunkard. They have little money at present but are anxiously waiting for the waters to fall and are in hopes of better luck.

To strike hands with a man haveing the spirit of God is a rare treat in California, and is like a fruitfull shower in a parched land.

Being aware that the most extravigent anticipations are entertained by some of our friends, it is time that the *bubble should burst* and the honest become sensible of the facts as they exist here, and we ardently wish we could make all our friends rich who ask us for help. But we assure you Brethren that we are not rich unless it should be in faith that when we have struggled long enough with poverty that our master will give us something better.

One example of the way we make money will suffice to illustrate our circumstances and how we obtain money for ourselves. We perform a jurney at an expense of 50$ of our own money and collect 11$ thithing for the church. To form some idea of our labour you can immagine the Cañons in the mountains from Little Salt Lake to the northern boundary of Deseret filled with gold and its hunters, in nearly all of which Salt Lake has its representatives. Then immagine yourselves commencing at one extremity of this region and finding the others not by travelling through extensive Valleys but by fording, ~~and~~ ferrying, and swimming the numerous streams that come rushing down from the mountains to find their resting place in the great Pacific and climbing the most rugged mountains, some parts of which are too steep for the sure footed mule and have consequently to try the surer foot of man, and this you know is somewhat tiresome when we have to carry from *180* to *200* weight.

We think that in the labour and toil of our present mission we have found a perfect antidote against the poison ~~and the care of the shining dust~~ of gold which consists in being taxed with the acquisition and care of the shining dust and still walk hand in hand with our old acquaintance poverty. We think we shall be satisfied if we can see our homes with enough to pay our debts, wood, school & other bills.

You will no doubt see by the above the total impracticability in our being able to carry out to the letter ~~of~~ your instructions in organizing and gathering the brethren togeather especially as they are continually moving as their diggins get worked out. Yet nevertheless we will act to your instructions as ~~far~~ near as we can, and no doubt will be satisfactory to you.

In relation to those matters which were left to us to determine vis: the expediancy or not of holding an influence in the country. We have thought, inquired, explored and prayed and we come to the conclusion that the interest of the church require a resting place in this region for the saints, and the portion of California described by Bro Rich in his letter to you, is the only place that is now open for settlement with all its advantages which are noted in the letter refered to.[27]

Acting upon the conclusion to which we have arrived at, we have sent Bro. J. D. Hunter (who has been confirmed in his former appointment as Indian Agent) to settle in the region, togeather with Bros. [Charles C.] Crisman & [Anthony] Blackburn to secure by settling on the same and looking out for the best points and direct and influence others who may settle there to do the same untill Bro. Rich shall be there to direct in person the settlement of those who may chose to make that country their home.

As to the right soil we have made no purchase considering it better to occupy the land than buy a doubtful title at present as it will require a few years to settle the question of titles. Here are missions and other unoccupied lands inviting the husbandman to make it his Inheritance and Home.

The members of the church generally, as well as those cutt off and many disaffected, are all anxious that a settlement should be made, and in order that it might not be composed of a major[ity] of the disaffected class we have not urged such to hasten to the lower country, hopeing that the foundation of society might be laid with better material than those who are so light that they have floated over the Sierra Nevada to the gold mines. And now Brethren if the conclusion to which we have come is right in your sight all is well, if not, the steps taken can produce no injury to individuals or the Church. If all is right and you should send an emmigration to the lower country by the south route this fall or any other time from the Lake or any other place ~~or time~~ by giving intimation of the same to Bro Rich they can be settled properly and profitably. From an advertisement is the St. Francisco papers it appears that a line of packets is about being established between the ports of Liverpool and Francisco. The advantages of this arrangement are obvious as the port of St. Diego is in the route.

In relation to the "California Star," Mr. Brannan had disposed of it previous to our arrival. He states it belonged to himself haveing purchased it in New York and paid for it ~~himself~~ with the exception of some 300$ which he expected to pay on his return to New York. The last conversation we had with M[r] Brannan he stated that he had borrowed or raised money for which he had given his receipts which money was to be credited to the individuals furnishing it as thithing. The money was expended for the company and by

---

[27]For extracts from this letter, see Arrington, *Charles C. Rich,* 154, 156–57.

them has been paid to Mr Brannan to the amount of 1700 dollars which money Mr Brannan says he is ready to pay on the presentation of his receipts which are in the hands of Bro^s Neff and Vancott of the Valley and Bro Barus of Boston by forwarding the receipts as early as possible to Bro Rich [so he] may secure the money previous to Mr Brannan's departure for the states this fall.[28]

We also wish to say that Bro^s [Parley P.] Pratt & [James S.] Brown started for the Islands about the 20th of April. The work is prospering in the Islands.

Just as we were closing this letter we received your communication and papers per M^r [Samuel G.] Chapin also a note on him which we will attend to.

In consequence of the uncertainty of letters arriving with saifty [sic] to us, we would suggest that they be directed to the A. A. Lathrope Mormon Tavern or Sacremento City Post Office.

We wish to say that if you want to get any information about this country we can refer you to Bros Bernard & Foot.

We must now conclude as the mail starts in a few moments praying our Heavenly Father to bless and prosper you, we remain Dear Brethren yours in the E. C.

Amasa Lyman
Charles C. Rich[29]

Brannan kept his word to Lyman and paid his debts to the Saints. Lyman wrote from San Bernardino in 1853:

> We have on hand of titheing funds four thousand seven hundred dollars & five cents, mostly paid in the last day of our conference and of this five hundred dollars we collected of Samuel Brannan on the receipt held by John Vancott to whose credit we suppose it has been placed in your City. If this is not so . . . the mat[t]er is subject to your correction.[30]

No one can know exactly what transpired during Lyman's meetings with Brannan, but in this discussion of receipts, it is not hard to see the genesis of the "receipt signed by the Lord" legend. The journals

---

[28]As noted, John Neff and John Van Cott made this loan in Nauvoo in late 1845, while "Bro Barus" also contributed. Brannan collected the $1,700 needed to cover the loan from the *Brooklyn* Saints in 1848; here he indicated his willingness to repay the men who had made the loan.

[29]Per LDS Archives policy, "a description of two men being cut off [from the LDS church] at the very end of the letter" was omitted from the copy provided to the editor. See archivist's note, 22 October 1990, Will Bagley File, LDS Archives.

[30]Lyman to Brigham Young and Council, 14 November 1853, LDS Archives.

and letters of Rich and Lyman provide additional clues that lead to a reasonable conclusion: Brannan himself created the receipt story from his recollection of his discussions with the apostles. It is easy to imagine an older Brannan in his cups, regaling his audience with the story of how he defied Brigham Young, a tale that grew more colorful over time. At Brannan's death, George E. Barnes told how Brannan was "custodian of all the gold" gathered at Mormon Bar, "which, as the story goes, they saw for the last time when it passed into his hands." When the authorities at Salt Lake demanded the gold, they "were refused by Brannan with a coarse joke, too common to be repeated here."[31] Barnes' delicacy suggests that the popular story about a receipt signed by the Lord was perhaps a sanitized rendition of a more obscene original.

It finally remained for his old colleague from *The Prophet*, Parley P. Pratt, to "cut off" Brannan from the Mormon church. At a meeting in Barton Mowrey's house (attended by Fanny Corwin, Brannan's devout mother-in-law) on the evening of I September 1851, "Fellowship was then withdrawn from Samuel Brannan by an unanimous vote for a general course of unchristianlike conduct, neglect of duty, and combining with lawless assemblies to commit murder and other crimes."[32] Pratt's indictment reveals Brannan was disfellowshipped for his personal sins, general apostasy, and involvement with the vigilantes. Pratt did not hesitate to call Brannan a murderer, but he said nothing about robbing the Saints—or the Lord. Pratt later regretted that his intervention in 1845 had saved Brannan's membership in the LDS church. He felt that Brannan

> was only to disgrace himself and the cause still more in a wider and more responsible career in California, where he, under our instruction, soon after repaired with a colony of Saints in the ship "Brooklyn." He was a corrupt and wicked man, and had the Church and myself been less long suffering and merciful, it would have saved the Church much loss, and, perhaps, saved some souls which were corrupted in California, and led astray and plun-

---

[31]Barnes, "Anent Samuel Brannan," *San Francisco Bulletin*, 12 October 1895, 9/1.

[32]Stanley and Camp, eds., "A Mormon Mission to California in 1851," 176. Pratt's language was not precise, but this action excommunicated rather than simply disciplined (or disfellowshipped) Brannan.

dered by him. I have always regretted having taken any measures to have him restored to fellowship after he was published in Nauvoo as cut off from the Church. However, if I erred, it was on the side of mercy.[33]

After settling his accounts with the Mormon church, Brannan encouraged the legend that he had defied Brigham Young—and apparently felt that his life was in danger. John Morris recalled that Brannan "always went with an escort heavily armed." But Asbury Harpending concluded that Brannan's fearlessness stood him in good stead.

> Brigham could not permit such a flagrant breach of church discipline to remain unpunished. Flock after flock of "destroying angels" took flight from Salt Lake City, duly commissioned to bring back Samuel's scalp or perish in the attempt. But their holy work was always a dismal failure. Brannan must have had some foreknowledge of their movement against the security of his person. Liking not to meet "angels" unawares of any kind, he arranged to encounter the "destroyers" halfway out in the trackless desert, or mountain fastnesses, with a competent group of exterminators he seemed to keep on hand for such occasions, and it was the "angels" who were always taken unawares. Some of them got back to Salt Lake minus tail feathers and otherwise damaged, but the majority of them never returned at all. At last the disciplining of Brannan became so manifestly an extra-hazardous risk that it was finally abandoned. How he defied the whole power of Mormonism and actually conducted a private and successful war against the church was one of the old romances of the Pacific Coast.[34]

Harpending recalled that Brannan "never forgot Salt Lake City or Utah," but concluded that his "life would not have been worth ten cents if he had once stepped within the territory of Brigham Young. But he always cast longing eyes at the scene of his early struggle. He knew Utah and its resources from end to end."[35] Legend told that "the fortunes of the Saints did not interest him nearly so much as the movements of Porter Rockwell and his Danites."[36] Except for Morris' account of the entourage of bodyguards, no credible details of his alleged "war against the church" survive, but Brannan enjoyed the notoriety such stories

---

[33]Pratt, Jr., ed., *The Autobiography of Parley Parker Pratt*, 338.

[34]Harpending, *The Great Diamond Hoax*, 120.

[35]Ibid., 120–21.

[36]Barnes, "Anent Samuel Brannan," *San Francisco Bulletin*, 12 October 1895, 9/1.

brought him and remained an implacable foe of Brigham Young's brand of Mormonism until the day he died.

Brannan's memories of the charismatic founding prophet of Mormonism seem to have influenced him throughout his life. In his old age, he called Joseph Smith "a fanatic," but Mormon friends recalled he "evidently had not lost all interest in the work begun under the ministry of Joseph the Seer," though "his head and heart were devoted first and last to worldly matters."[37] Brannan's determined attempts to become a Mason suggest that he wanted to participate in the rites that many believe Smith adapted from Freemasonry when he created the temple endowment. The Eureka Lodge of Auburn, California, rejected Brannan's petition for membership in January 1852.[38] Over the next three years Brannan applied to the California and Occidental lodges and was "rejected in both—presumably by the blackball of someone who disliked him," which left him "incensed." Not to be put off, Brannan joined Lafayette Lodge No. 64 while on a trip to New York. This was "not a rare procedure," but when he applied for recognition in the California orders, "the door of every lodge was firmly closed against him, and the brethren in New York were treated with strong letters of condemnation for their course in regard to the candidate from California." The Grand Lodge of California passed a resolution in May 1855 forbidding any "Masonic communication whatsoever" with him. The ban was withdrawn two years later, and by 1858 Brannan was a member of the Occidental Lodge in San Francisco. Although occasionally suspended for not paying his dues, his name appeared on the lodge's roster "till the day of his death."[39]

Other scraps of evidence suggest that Brannan never broke completely free of his ties to "primitive Mormonism." When Harry Patten tried to demolish the Winans family vault in Calistoga, he found "an iron casket of Mormon design containing the remains of Brannan's

---

[37]"Samuel Brannan," *The Saints' Herald*, 25 May 1889, 323/3. Joseph Smith III's personal correspondence with Brannan, not all of which survives, apparently led to this conclusion.

[38]Samuel J. Gower to the Worshipful Master, 16 January 1852, Brannan File, California State Library.

[39]Whitsell, *One Hundred Years of Freemasonry in California*, 3:984; and Barnes, "Anent Samuel Brannan," *San Francisco Bulletin*, 12 October 1895, 9/2.

infant son."[40] In old age, Brannan developed a rationalistic view of God and adopted a skeptical view of "prophets, or smart men as we call them." Yet he corresponded with Smith's son, Joseph Smith III, and he tried to recruit Mormons to people his last empire. Brannan repeatedly denounced Brigham Young in letters to Jesse Little, but he was kinder to Joseph Smith, the visionary martyr who had made such a profound and lasting impact on his life.

[40]Adams, *Memoirs and Anecdotes of Early Calistoga*, 27. The casket was adorned with sacred Mormon symbols resembling Masonic emblems.

Chapter 11

"The Hangman and the Laws"

By the fall of 1849, Samuel Brannan was a powder keg waiting to explode. The fires that drove him were always under the barest control, but after his separation from Mormonism they blazed with a vengeance. Whatever passions his faith had constrained, a sudden rush of fabulous wealth set free. He seemed tormented by personal demons that drove him to drink, sexual excess, and violence, but perhaps this overstates his psychological complexity. Like many of his contemporaries, Brannan simply may have enjoyed wine, women, and brawling. He channeled his remarkable energies into a series of enterprises, including an exploration of the northern coast of California, the acquisition of a real-estate empire in San Francisco and Sacramento, and a venture into the China trade. His most famous exploit was his leadership of the vigilante movement, a popular attempt to solve the problems of law and order in frontier California.

The classic telling of the vigilante legend celebrated the beleaguered businessmen who left their storefronts and counting rooms to subdue a tidal wave of lawlessness and discipline a corrupt bureaucracy. Yet modern scholarship finds no evidence of a crime wave in San Francisco in the spring of 1851.[1] While the local government was inept, the wonder was not that the city had a corrupt and incompetent administration, but that it had any government at all. The Americans who formed the core of the city's population by 1851 had established a complicated repre-

---

[1]Kevin J. Mullen's innovative *Let Justice Be Done: Crime and Politics in Early San Francisco* is the best account of the city's vigilante movement and Brannan's involvement in it. Much of my interpretation of these events relies on Mullen's keen analysis. He has demolished the notion that crime was endemic in early San Francisco, estimating that there was an average of one to two murders per month in the city, rather than the legendary hundred murders. Mullen counted thirty-two verifiable cases of criminal homicide between July 1849 and July 1851—discounting those murdered by the vigilantes themselves. See Mullen, *Let Justice Be Done*, 110, 177, 185.

sentative government and legal system, volunteer fire brigades, and two militia companies. The institutions of American popular democracy had taken root and grown up as quickly as the burgeoning metropolis itself—and the young city grew at an astounding rate. South of Market Street, a "Steam excavator" (dubbed the "Steam Paddy" in reference of the Irish laborers it replaced) inspired wonder in the population as it tore down the sandhills and filled in Yerba Buena Cove. Private subscriptions funded the installation of street lights on Montgomery and Merchant streets.[2] The city burned down almost as quickly as it could be built up, but it emerged Phoenix-like from these blazes, each time more resplendent than before.

Such explosive growth was not without cost. By its very nature, the gold rush attracted a disreputable population—farmers went to Oregon, Mormons went to Utah, and gamblers went to California. As early as 3 June 1848, the *California Star* predicted "the Gold Mines in the North will gather together as wild a class of unchristianized fellows as ever escaped the thralldom of honest law and broke loose upon barbarism." The paper complained that the country was already being harassed "by organized and practiced horse thieving marauders."

During the most colorful period of Brannan's life—the gold rush and the vigilante movement—his personal written record essentially vanished, not to reappear until the last decade of his life. In the midst of the gold-rush whirlwind Brannan created few documents, virtually none of which survive. As the editor of the papers of the first Committee of Vigilance complained, "Brannan was a wretched penman and an execrable speller, and few papers perpetuate his tenure as president."[3] This spotty record dictates that many of Brannan's remarkable exploits—founding the city of Sacramento and acquiring much of the Sutter empire, expanding his San Francisco real-estate fortune and driving the city's growth, his gambling and sexual escapades, and his wide-ranging commercial activities—must pass with only the briefest mention. Contemporary accounts of other events—Brannan's exploits with the "Hounds," his exploration of the northern California coast, his adven-

---

[2] Stewart, Jr., *Committee of Vigilance*, 65, 68.
[3] Williams, *History of the San Francisco Committee of Vigilance of 1851*, 261.

tures in Sacramento's "squatter war," and his comic-opera attempt to seize the throne of the Hawaiian Kingdom—tell these fantastic tales from period sources. The record also tells a more personal story—how Brannan gathered his brothers and sisters around him to enjoy his new wealth.

A Brother in Deed

The gold rush brought the extended Brannan family to California, where the family's youngest son shared his good fortune with his siblings. Most important for Samuel Brannan's affairs was the arrival of his seafaring half-brother. John Brannan sailed for El Dorado on the bark *Norwich* in May 1849 and described his voyage in letters to his wife, Mary.[4] The antics of the Reverend John H. Gihon, subsequently one of the compilers of *The Annals of San Francisco*, enlivened an otherwise tedious voyage. The passengers called Gihon "the black parson" for "going amongst the black prostitutes at Rio." Brannan found him "a perfect rouge" and complained "he behaved wors[e] on shore at Valperaso than he did at Rio. He was drunk and with bad women all the time." The preacher "quarrilled with everry pasenger on board [and] at last he began on me." Brannan gave the sinner "a beautiful pair of black eyes one morning of[f] Cape horn," and "every one on board was glad of it from the Capt to the Cook."[5] At Valparaiso Brannan spoke with a man who had seen his brother seven weeks earlier, who reported "the whole family are well. He says Samuel is worth about four hundred thousand dollars, he says he cannot conceive what he stays there for now."[6]

John Brannan received a warm welcome in San Francisco.

My dear Samuel has proved a brother to me in deed. He gave me every thing that I desired. After I had been here a fortnight he bot me the best vessel on the river and paid fourteen thousand dollars for her and told me to go where I plased with her. She is fore and aft Sch[oone]r Called the General Morgan 138 tons. [She] draws but a light draft of water and carreys a great cargo . . .

---

[4]John Brannan's material is taken from the originals in the Bancroft Library, cited as the John Brannan Papers; typescripts of these papers from BYU Library are cited as the Auerbach Collection.
[5]John Brannan to Mary F. Brannan, 20 August and 15 November 1849, John Brannan Papers.
[6]John Brannan to Mary F. Brannan, 28 September 1849, John Brannan Papers.

Samuel is very rich [and has] I suppose eight hundred thousand but he is the [same] Sam Brannan. Elisa is well and sends her love. By the by a few days after I arrived here Elisa had a fine daughter but no name yet.[7]

The Brannans operated their center-board schooner on shares, and Captain Brannan cleared $800 on her first voyage to Sacramento. "A lazy man will soon starve in this country," he wrote his wife, "and a smart one get rich."[8]

While in Rio de Janeiro on 27 July 1849, John Brannan reported that he had spoken with a Captain Doty who "saw my brother Daniel five days ago," but Daniel K. Brannan did not arrive in California until the next year. "Daniel & Jane arrived here. They came without a dollar to help themselves & they quarrel like cats & dogs," John Brannan wrote. "Jane made all the apollogy."[9] Brannan & Co. employed Daniel in 1851 as an agent at 43 Front Street, Sacramento.[10] John Brannan complained that Daniel was "half-crazsy," and there were hard feelings between Ann Eliza Brannan and the couple, for "Elisa would not have them in the house."[11]

Alexander Badlam caught gold fever and, with Wilford Woodruff's permission, left Boston on the *Corsair*, crossed Panama, took passage on the British whaler *Colloony*, and arrived in San Francisco on 30 June 1849. That winter he returned to the states by the same route, after first reporting to Brigham Young. Badlam complained that Brannan "says he will help Me yet he Leaves Me to Myself After Letting Me have a few hundred dollars & about 6 or 7 thousand dollars in Lots & Buildings which I have got to work out or fail in the Attempt."[12] John Brannan thought the ungrateful Badlam was "not fit for this country" and stated "we are glad to get rid of him."[13] "Badlam and his wife has wrote for money to fetch them acrost the plains but they will not get it from Samuel and you may be sure they will not from me," John Brannan wrote

[7]John Brannan to Mary F. Brannan, 15 January 1850, John Brannan Papers. This daughter was named Fanny Kemble Brannan.
[8]Ibid.; and Hesketh, "California in '50," *San Francisco Morning Call*, 9 November 1884, 1/1.
[9]John Brannan to Mary F. Brannan, 26 June 1850, John Brannan Papers.
[10]Ottley, ed., *John A. Sutter, Jr: Statement*, 119.
[11]John Brannan to Mary F. Brannan, 29 July 1850, John Brannan Papers.
[12]Badlam to Young, 16 September 1849, Brigham Young Collection, LDS Archives.
[13]John Brannan to Mary F. Brannan, 7 July 1850, Auerbach Collection, 109.

a year later. "I should think Badlam had enough of Calafornney while he was here."[14]

Badlam brought his family, including Brannan's sister, to Utah, where they stopped for the winter.[15] Brigham Young arranged for Badlam to accompany a missionary party to San Bernardino in 1852, and a year later the family was living in Sacramento, where they settled.[16] Unlike Samuel Brannan, Badlam remained loyal to the religion throughout his long life. Letters composed in the mid-1850s indicate he acted as an agent for Mormon interests in California.[17] His daughter, Sarah Adelaide Badlam, married Joseph Webb Winans, and Samuel Brannan had extensive (and some said scandalous) business and personal relations with the Winans.[18] In Brannan's declining years, his nephew, Alexander Badlam, Jr., became his business agent.

Alexander Badlam's letters to Joseph Smith's uncle and cousin sketched a colorful picture of life in California's "Cities of the wicked." Perhaps at the request of George A. Smith, Badlam made the "study of the Chinese" his "principle object," and Badlam provided Smith with a report (which referred to his "feeble testimony") on Chinese history and Mormon prospects in the country.[19] This early interest in Asia demonstrated the world wide vision of the LDS church, even as it struggled to survive in the Rocky Mountains.

---

[14]John Brannan to Mary F. Brannan, 31 May 1850, John Brannan Papers.

[15]Maude Badlam Pettus, untitled article in "Knave" section, *Oakland Tribune*; 20 September 1942; "By Covered Wagon," *Oakland Tribune*, 27 September 1943, from Maude Pettus Biographical Information File, California State Library; and John Brannan to Mary F. Brannan, 15 January 1850, John Brannan Papers. The Badlams were counted in the 1851 Utah Territory census. LDS temple records list ordinances for Alexander and Mary Ann Badlam, 9 April 1851, in the Endowment House.

[16]Cook and Harker, eds., *My Life's Review*, 127. Benjamin Johnson complained in 1894 that Badlam "never repaid one dollar" of a one-hundred-dollar loan. "Had he and his kindred been poor, I have no doubt they would have fulfilled their promise." Ibid., 130.

[17]As LDS church president, Wilford Woodruff often visited his old friend in California. Jenson, Alexander Badlam Biographical Encyclopedia form, LDS Archives, noted that Badlam "died faithful in the Church."

[18]For Joseph Winans, see Shuck, ed., *Representative and Leading Men of the Pacific Coast*, 248–55. Scott, *Samuel Brannan and the Golden Fleece*, 408–10, implied that to pay gambling debts, Sarah Winans blackmailed Brannan, her uncle, threatening to disclose their affair. Scott provided no evidence to support this surprising story.

[19]Badlam to Father John Smith, 3 April 1853; Badlam to George A. Smith, 12 January 1855; and Badlam to George A. Smith, 28 May 1855, LDS Archives. These letters are included in *Cites of the Wicked: Alexander Badlam Reports on Mormon Prospects in California and China in the 1850s*, the keepsake for the limited edition of this volume.

John Brannan's first project with his brother was an "exploring excursion" along the northern California coast. As early as March 1848, the *California Star* reported on a meeting to adopt "measures to raise and fit out a party to explore the region of Trinidad Bay . . . An interest has been felt for the last two years relative to this imperfectly known section of California."[20] Samuel Brannan proposed "fitting out an expedition to explore the country, either by land or water" and was appointed to a committee "to obtain all the important information relative to the country."[21] The lack of a port between San Francisco and the Columbia River inspired an 1850 search for a harbor "from which the many mining districts about to be established on the heads of the Trinity river and the streams adjacent might be supplied." Three participants, including remittance man Henry Hesketh, left accounts of the adventure, which offer a case study in how Sam Brannan built his fortune.[22]

General Morgan "beat out of the harbor with a stiff breeze and made a very close hug to the northern coast" on 30 March 1850. She "missed stays twice," and "had she missed a third time she would have tailed on the rocks," but by 4 April the schooner was anchored at the mouth of the Eel River—although other ships had beaten the *Morgan* to the scene. The next day the Brannan brothers crossed the bar and entered the stream, which they dubbed "the River Brannan." Samuel Brannan led two boats up the river until the local natives made a "hostile demonstration," which the explorers broke up with "a tremendous shout."[23] Unable to recross the bar due to heavy weather, the party carried their boats over Table Bluff and "discovered" Humboldt Bay, which they christened Mendocino Bay.[24] The men were unable to locate a proper townsite, and by the time they returned to the *Morgan*, a small fleet had

---

[20]"Exploring Expedition," *California Star*, 25 March 1848.

[21]"Public Meeting—Trinidad Bay," *California Star*, 1 April 1848, 4/3.

[22]The quote is from Dr. J. Henry Poett, "The General Morgan Exploration," *Alta California*, 24 April 1850, 3/1–2; Henry Hesketh's letter in *San Francisco Morning Call*, 9 November 1884, 1/1–2. is the best account. John Y. Young, *Facts of Early History in most of which I participated*, Biographical File Typescript, Society of California Pioneers, is an interesting reminiscence.

[23]Hesketh, "California in '50," 1/1. Henry Hesketh was the younger son of "a distinguished English family" who had been with Byron when the poet died in Greece. See Bancroft, *History of California*, 6:502, for the naming of the river and a summary of exploration of the Humboldt region.

[24]Carranco and Genzoli, "California Redwood Empire Place Names," 373.

assembled in the area. After "a whole day of wrangling and dispute," the party abandoned the project. On his return to San Francisco, Hesketh complained that the venture "was by no means managed with that science necessary that we considered Mr. B—n capable of." But the "sixty shares at $100 paid him well for the use of his schooner," so Brannan profited even from the failure of this "most boisterous, disagreeable, arduous and risky undertaking."[25] John Brannan would haul freight and passengers to the bay later in the year, recalling, "Samuel & my self has seen some hard times to gether on our upper co[a]st of Callaforney."[26]

BRANNON WALKED OFF WITH A PILE

The Humboldt expedition was only one of Samuel Brannan's unorthodox sources of income. Several tales recount his gambling adventures—in which he invariably seems to have been the winner. David Wharff recalled:

> I saw Sam Brannan put $10,000 in gold dust on one card at the corner of I street and the levee in Sacramento. The gambler's or dealer's hand shook as he drew the cards. Many crowded around the table. The tenth card he drew, Sam Brannan won. He had a man at the table with him. Took the gold dust and off he went.[27]

Miner Alonzo P. DeMilt worked in Sacramento at James Lundy's "eating house and gambling-saloon" and recalled:

> a Mormon of some note, Sam Brannon, came along one night, and cooly inquiring, at a roulette table, what the "limit," of the bank was, he was informed that it was $18,000. Brannon, without a word, produced that amount in dust and nuggets, and staked every dollar of it on one roll of the ball, putting his money on the red. This, of course, made a ripple in the large hall, where red-shirted and revolver-laden men from all parts of the habitable globe were congregated, drinking and gaming. The wheel was whirled, and the little ball started. When it stopped, Jim Lundy was a ruined man and Brannon walked off with a pile.[28]

[25]Hesketh, "California in '50," *San Francisco Morning Call*, 9 November 1884, 1/1–2.
[26]John Brannan to Mary F. Brannan, 31 May 1850, John Brannan Papers.
[27]David Wharff, Narrative of a California Pioneer of 1849, transcript from Sorenson Papers from an original in the California State Library.
[28]Fitch, *The Life, Travels and Adventures of an American Wanderer*, 57–58.

THE SQUATTER WAR

A close analysis of the complex schemes that made Samuel Brannan the largest landowner in the city of Sacramento is beyond the scope of this book, but river-front real estate on the Embarcadero of the town transformed Brannan from a merchant into a tycoon. He acquired the property in a series of questionable transactions with John Sutter and his son August. William Grimshaw observed, "It would be impossible to imagine two men more thoroughly unfit for business of any kind than the elder & younger Sutters," and Brannan exploited their incompetence.[29] He purchased the last large block of Sacramento real estate in 1850 for a pledge of $125,000, "but through artful stalling Brannan eventually forced the naive younger Sutter to settle for a few thousand dollars."[30] One Sutter biographer called this "one of the most flagrant, and one of the most brilliant, examples of confidancemanship" in California's history. Another claimed Brannan "publicly pillaged" the young Sutter and denounced him for wearing "the mask of Puritanism and patriotism to wage war upon the small-fry bandits," while being one of the "the wholesale robbers and despoilers of the law."[31] Acquiring the land was easy, however, compared to holding on to it.

During the summer of 1850, Brannan was a key player in "a fearful collision of hostile interests to grow out of the discussion of the question of land claims in Sacramento City." Although the treaty of Guadalupe Hidalgo specifically stated that Mexican land titles would be "inviolably respected," the respect was not shared by most of the Americans who poured into California in 1849. They felt that the land belonged to the United States by right of conquest, and they passionately believed that occupying and improving land established a more valid title than did Sutter's expansive grants from Governor Alvarado. The vagueness of the Mexican land grants and the "loose legal system of Alta California," which rested on different principles than American laws, complicated the situation.[32] The frontier experience had taught

[29]Kantor, ed., *Grimshaw's Narrative*, 18.

[30]Pisani, "Squatter Law in California, 1850–1858," 308. In the best current work on the subject, Pisani concluded Brannan "cheated both Sutter and his son."

[31]Dillon, *Fool's Gold*, 308; and Zollinger, *Sutter*, 307.

[32]Pisani, "Squatter Law in California, 1850–1858," 286.

white settlers that their right to claim vacant land (including Indian homelands) was "traditional and inalienable." They felt that "to be driven from their lots by speculators claiming under the Sutter title was unbearable."[33] Jean Voiget's inaccurate survey of the Sutter grant had set its southern boundary to the north of Sacramento—and to compound the problem, Sutter had "deeded away, not merely more land than he actually owned, but, if I mistake not, more land then even he himself had supposed himself to own."[34]

Always loyal to Brannan, the *Alta California* admitted it "had no sympathy with the squatter interests" and its columns decried the "ignorance and credulity" of the Sacramento City Settlers' Association. The association organized in Sacramento on 7 December 1849, and printed its motto on its receipts: "The public domain is free to all."[35] Reflecting the bias of the contemporary sources, traditional histories have largely ignored the squatter's perspective, but a modern analyst concluded that the "squatters blended greed and idealism, self-interest and a passionate devotion to natural rights," and called upon "time-worn legal principles" to justify their actions.[36] The press sided with Brannan's Law and Order Association and denounced the squatter party leaders as "corrupt, selfish and insidious" men, who were "crime-hardened conspirators against life and property" driven by a "base, hypocritical, money-serving scheme."[37]

Winter floods in 1849 helped spark the confrontation between the squatters and those who titles originated with Sutter—including, most prominently, Brannan. To escape the flood, the population camped out on the high ground near the fort and the river; when the water went down, the occupants refused to leave and it became difficult to land merchandise on the levee. Local bankers and merchants decided "to take matters into their own hands" and clear the levee. Brannan, "in a condition of frantic excitement, with a piece of manila rope around his waist, in which two revolvers were stuck," led the charge of the "regulators."

---

[33]Royce, "An Episode of Early California Life," 307; and Bancroft, *California Inter Pocula*, 410.

[34]Royce, "An Episode of Early California Life," 305.

[35]Ibid., 321; and Ottley, ed., *Thompson and West's History of Sacramento County*, 51.

[36]Pisani, "Squatter Law in California, 1850–1858," 277-78, 282-83.

[37]"Sacramento Squatters," *Alta California*, 27 June 1850, 2/1. David Broderick used the "Law and Order" name for his own group that opposed the Committee of Vigilance in 1851.

Squatter Charles Robinson had built a foundation near the foot of I Street that projected out into the river on pilings. Brannan's men ripped it up and moved on to a more substantial structure. Unable to dislodge a pole supporting the eaves, Brannan noticed a mounted rancher looking on with undisguised amusement. "Get down here, ——— you, and lend a hand!" roared Brannan. "Don't stand looking on!" The horseman threw Brannan a lasso, which he tied to the pole, and the rancher "started up the mustang, and down came the pole, roof, and one side of the house, amidst the shouts of the populace." Brannan moved down to J Street where a cabin owner confronted him with a shotgun. "Hold on, sir!" warned the man, "You touch this house at your peril! It's mine, and I am going to defend it." Brannan turned and "fairly screamed out: 'Warbass, cover that ——— scoundrel, and if he raises his gun shoot h—l out of him.'" The "belligerent Squatter" watched his house disappear, and by sunset Brannan and his "destroying angels" had cleared the levee amidst a "regular pandemonium."[38]

Violence erupted again on 22 June 1850, when a policeman "found Mr. Brannan breaking off boards from the front of a building" at four o'clock in the morning. Although it was little more than a drunken brawl, the *Alta* felt the subsequent battle was "productive of the least excitement yet the greatest possible amount of good for the city and her interests."[39] But the issue was not settled. In August, the squatter battles broke into open warfare that left the city's assessor, sheriff, and six residents dead.[40] Brannan's party won the war, but legal challenges to his land titles ultimately cost Brannan hundreds of thousands of dollars.

Brannan even had to contend with squatters in San Francisco. In 1851 he deeded the Odd Fellows land for a cemetery, but "by midsummer 1853 squatters swarmed on it."[41] Brannan's problems defending his vast properties aroused substantial popular resentment against him, as this item from an early San Francisco literary magazine demonstrated.

---

[38]Ottley, ed., *Thompson and West's History of Sacramento County*, 51. This local history supplied the colorful conversation and detail, but no date or source for these events.

[39]"Sacramento Squatters," *Alta California*, 27 June 1850, 2/1.

[40]Pisani, "Squatter Law in California, 1850–1858," 277.

[41]Bancroft, *California Inter Pocula*, 404.

GOLDEN ERA, 23 JULY 1853, 2/5.

While sauntering along the roadside leading to the Mission, a few days since, we picked up a 'shingle', on which were inscribed the following war-like lines:—

Thus far into the bowels of the land
I'll set my stakes; here I will pitch my tent
Even on *Brannan's* lots;
And while my "Colt" is loaded,
    and my nerves are firm,
The ground I'll hold; or bathe its face in blood.

Brannan's real-estate investments were not limited to urban development. He purchased four square miles of land on the west side of the Feather River from the Sutters, where he developed a luxurious ranch. He imported European sheep, French grape vines to develop a vineyard, and fine cattle. Brannan also bought stock from southern California businessman Abel Stearns, which perhaps led to Brannan's purchase of an interest in Stearns' estate in the late 1860s.[42]

G. W. SIRRINE:
THE ROUGHS AND TOUGHS OF SAN FRANCISCO

H. H. Bancroft thought that Brannan's work with the first Vigilance Committee marked "the brightest epoch of his eventful life," but the "cheerful recklessness" with which Brannan "threw his life and wealth into the scale" has not so enchanted modern historians.[43] Their view suggests he unleashed his own self-interest in a blaze of demagoguery and violence. Yet the classic image of the vigilantes as heroes still enjoys substantial popular support—and Brannan's cry for "Law and Order" evoked a slogan that subsequent generations of California politicians employed with repeated success.

Brannan's connection to citizen justice began in the fall of 1848, when he prosecuted Charles E. "Philosopher" Pickett for murder in a

---

[42]See *Alta California*, 23 November 1858, 3/1; and Brannan to Stearns, 5 December 1856 and 21 September 1867, Able Stearns Collection, Huntington Library.

[43]Bancroft, *Popular Tribunals*, 1:209. See Senkewicz, *Vigilantes in Gold Rush San Francisco*, 245–46, for the evolution of the historical interpretation of the vigilante movement.

farcical show trial.[44] After a band of drunken American veterans known as "the Hounds" rioted in the Chilean section of San Francisco on 15 July 1849, Brannan launched his first serious foray into impromptu law enforcement. Coming to the defense of the abused Chileans was an act of courage, but there is reason to suspect that Brannan had long supported the Hounds and now turned on them for political reasons.[45] These events created a pattern that Brannan repeated with increasingly dismal results: acting in the name of law and order but answering to no law but his own.

"Full of courage and bravado," Brannan rallied San Francisco to oppose the Hounds. He climbed atop a barrel at the corner of Clay and Montgomery streets and addressed the people, decrying the outrages against the Chileans. Brannan learned that the Hounds were threatening to burn his property, which made him "denounce the thieves [all] the stronger." Thoroughly aroused, he was "pale with anger and excitement." Threats came from the crowd "and presently pistols appeared with demonstrations of shooting." Undaunted, Brannan "hurled on them a torrent of his choicest invective, meanwhile baring his breast and daring them to fire."[46] This was his finest hour—whatever failings Brannan may have had, cowardice was not one of them. Brannan was "conspicuous among the Orators at the meeting on the Plaza" and his speech "was violent & passionate, possessing enough of the rude eloquence to produce in his hearers a reflection of the feelings it portrayed—One of those mixtures of stimulating ingredients which must be taken hot—As I listened to his fiery & somewhat blasphemous appeal I thought it fortunate for the Community that he was not a hound."[47]

Speaking "in his best auctioneer voice," Brannan insisted on justice for the Chileans. California "depended on Chile for flour, on her skilled artisans for laying bricks, on her bakers for bread."[48] He denounced the outrages of the Hounds and opened a subscription list "for relief of the sufferers by the riots of the previous evening." The meeting then spon-

[44]Bancroft, *California Inter Pocula*, 608–09; and Willis, *History of Sacramento County*, 60–61.
[45]Mullen, *Let Justice Be Done*, 65–66.
[46]Bancroft, *Popular Tribunals*, 1:97–98.
[47]Pomeroy, ed., "The Trial of the Hounds, 1849: A Witness's Account," 162.
[48]Monaghan, *Chile, Peru, and the California Gold Rush of 1849*, 168.

taneously organized itself into a volunteer police. By evening they had rounded up the most prominent Hounds and imprisoned them on the warship *Warren*. A grand jury indicted nineteen of the men on 17 July on "different charges of conspiracy, riot, robbery, and assault with intent to kill." A trial began the next day—"Prompt justice surely," noted the *Alta*. "All the usual judicial forms were observed." The jury convicted nine of the Hounds, sentencing their leader, Sam Roberts, and another man to ten years at hard labor, while the rest received shorter sentences, to be served "in whatever penitentiary the governor of California might direct." California had no prisons, so none of the men ever served their sentences, but some met rough justice in the mines "where several of them were unceremoniously hanged, at an hour's notice."[49] The miners "had a shorter path from murder to the gallows than the San Francisco merchants had yet found."[50]

That is the story that can be deduced from the traditional secondary accounts, but Kevin Mullen looked more closely at the scant primary sources and proposed an alternate interpretation. Noting that the Hounds were not even mentioned in the local press until the *Alta* printed the results of their trial on 2 August, Mullen suggested that "the Regulators," as they called themselves, were pawns in the power struggles that raged in San Francisco, with Brannan and his business associates "among the prominent men involved behind the scenes" who supported the criminal gang.[51] The scarcity of primary sources makes Mullen's case circumstantial, but it is compelling—and Brannan's character supports his suspicions.

A Mormon archive would seem an unlikely place to find an account of the Hounds episode, but George Sirrine's story of the battle makes up in color whatever it lacks in historical accuracy. As with the Sirrine account of the *Brooklyn* voyage, it is impossible to tell how accurately the son preserved his father's story, which itself had undoubtedly grown in the telling. The resulting tale is folklore, not history—but it is great

---

[49]*Alta California*, 2 August 1849; and Soulé, *Annals of San Francisco*, 558–60.

[50]Bancroft, *Popular Tribunals*, 1:100–01.

[51]Mullen, *Let Justice Be Done*, 64, 66. The 2 and 9 August 1849 issues of the *Alta* contained extensive but rambling reports on the Hounds. Mullen's study provides a good analysis of all the primary sources.

folklore, and while much of the memoir is wildly exaggerated, Sirrine recalled details that are only hinted at in other sources. Sirrine promoted Brannan to mayor and made Jack Powers leader of the Hounds, but his recollection contained elements of truth. John A. Powers was a veteran of Stevenson's regiment who became a gambler, "and later a robber and murderer known as 'Jack Powers.'" He was one of the Hounds indicted on 17 July 1849 and one of the few found not guilty. After a "career of crime" along the mid-California coast, vigilantes broke up his gang in 1856 and Powers "escaped to Sonora, where he was killed" in 1860.[52]

WARREN LEROY SIRRINE,
A LITTLE SKETCH OF THE LIFE OF GEORGE WARREN SIRRINE,
LDS ARCHIVES, 12–14.

During the great gold excitement in California, Samuel Branon was maror [mayor] of the city. George Sirrine was Special Police. The roughs and toughs of San Francisco got so bad and bold that they would kill a merchant and order all of the clerks out of the house and roll the entire stock of goods in the street and sell it at a public sale. Some of the time they would not ask for the second bid. They would kill from two to three of a day and from three to five of a night. George Sirrine saw a large crowd gathering in front of an old merchants store wheare he and Branon was doing thear trading—a fine old man. When George got theare he could not see the old man and he never saw him afterwards. He stayed theare some time and he was so mad he couldn't stand it any longer so he started for Branan's. When Branon see him a comeing he knew that he was mad and he asked him what was the matter. He told Branon what he had seen and he said Branon we have got to find out who is the strongest party—the cut throats or the good citizens or I am through with San Francisco. Branon said George I am in the same fix. Do you know of some good men that is true blue. George said Yes Sir. All right George you go one way and I will go the other and if you ever aproack [sic] a man and he refuses to come with you you put him in irons and lock him up for we don't want them roughs to know anything about what is going on. You and your men meet at my office in two hours. Well they had about 25 or 30 men and almost all of them knew of another man. So they went out and got several more. They had just 50 men and they didn't dare to go any further. So Samuel Branon made a talk to them and proposed that he give a lecture in the morning at 10 A.M. on the Porch of the American Council on general principals and when all of thease roughs will be theare to see if I am going to say any thing about them. We

[52] Alta California, 2 August 1849, 1/2 and 3/2; and Bancroft, History of California, 4:783.

GEORGE WARREN SIRRINE
This image of the *Brooklyn* veteran
captures him during his last
years as an Arizona pioneer.
Courtesy, Lorin Hansen.

all know who is the ring leader of thear gang—that is Jack Powers and he
would kill me as soon as he would a dog. But he said George Sirrine if you
will take care of Jack Powers, I will make the talk. George said Branon, I will
arrest him or kill him. O.K. said Branon. So they decided that every man
would get along side of one of thease hard cases and when George Sirrine
arrested Powers that would be the signal for every man to arrest his man.
They knew that Powers would resist.

So they had a lot of little pamphlets struck off and they scatter them all
over town telling about Branon making the talk. There was a big crowd gathered and of course all of thease cut throats were theare and George was following Jack Powers. Jack Powers elbowed his way right through the crowd
and got within about 30 feet of Branon. He was on an angle of about 45
[degrees] and George was right by his side. Samuel Branon was looking for
George and Jack Powers all over the crowd and when he see George Sirrine
right by the side of Jack Powers he sees George Sirrine wink at him to let
him know that he was ready. Then Branon began coming down on the way
that these roughs were killing people and robbing and plundering and we are
going to put a stop to it if theare is good citizens in San Francisco to do it.
At that Jack Powers drew a big revolver and was just coming down on Branon when George grabbed his gun with his left hand and put the musil of
his gun in Jack's breast and told him to drop that gun or you are a dead man.

He looked George in the eye and said, George give me some kind of a show with you. Drop that gun quick and he did. Then he told him to put up his hands high which he did. Then he told a man to unbuckle his belt and put his gun in the (holster) berth and then buckle them on George Sirrine. All of the roughs carried two revolvers and a Dirk. When Jack Powers revolver went off it cut a gash in George's hand and left a scar that he carried as long as he lived. I have seen it many times. When that revolver went off theare was 49 men under arrest, and disarmed and had the hand cuffs on.

Then they began to hunt for old Judge Levensworth.[53] His home and office was looked up and they were hunting for him and some men were passing by a livery stable hollering for Judge Levensworth. The Livery man run out and told them that Judge Levensworth had got the best horse theare was in the stable about an hour ago and was seen going south. Judge Levensworth weighed about two hundred and twelve pounds. So they got two light men and two of the best horses theare. And they run him nearly all day and just before sun down they over hauled him and disarmed him and put the irons on him and took him back to San Francisco. And they appointed two assiciate judges to sit with him and try those 49 men. George took Jack Powers out to his meals and he told him he was not going to put the hand cuffs on him but if ever he see him winking at a man or ofering to shake hands with him or get within several feet of him he would kill him. He said Sirrine I know when a man means business I will be good. Jack would order the best theare was on the market and enough for several men. Well these 49 men were sentenced to serve on board of an American Man of War for five years or run a plank. So the 49 men made up thear minds that they would not enlist and that they would not make them run a plank. So they put them all on board a big Man of War and went twenty-five or thirty miles out in the ocean and put up the plank and lined them all up and the first one close to the plank was asked what he would do—serve on board of an American Man of War or run a plank. He ripped out with an oath that he would not serve on board of an American Man of War, then step[ped] on that plank with two soldiers with bayonets on thear guns on each side and two at his back and they told him to march. He went overboard and the plank came back ready for the next man but all of the rest of the men enlisted.[54]

---

[53]Thaddeus M. Leavenworth was former chaplain of the New York Volunteers and had been San Francisco's alcalde since 1848. Along with William M. Gwin and J. C. Ward, Leavenworth presided at the trial of the Hounds. A San Francisco street bears his name.

[54]None of the standard sources reports that the convicted Hounds were pressed into the navy, but William Gwin recalled, "Commodore [Thomas ap C.] Jones kindly offered to take the exile[d Hounds] aboard his ship, the *Ohio*, and take them from the country, and I believe they became sailors on board the ship. This restored order in the city." See Ellison, ed., "Memoirs of Hon. William M. Gwin," 4.

Several months after that there was a big vesil coming in. He [George] wanted to see if thear were any one on board that he knew. He was sittin[g] on a big bale of goods when he see a large man and a meadiam sised lady holding to a man's arm and he was looking at him. He looked at her pretty close but he didn't recognize her and pretty soon he looked at her again and he see her pull on the man's arm and came over wheare he was and when she got within a few feet of him he see that she was Jack Powers dressed up in women's clothes. Then he said Jack what are you doing heare. I thought you was on board that American Man of War. Well, I was for several months. Then we landed on an island for fresh water and fuel and while we were gathering wood I told two other men now was the time for us to make our get a way. We were draging wood out in the clearing and others were chopping it up in cord wood and others were carr[y]ing it to the vesil. So we made our gettaway. They looked for us for several hours and we had got up on a high point wheare we could watch the vesil and finely they hoisted the anchor and put out to sea. After they had been gone some time we began looking around the island to see how we were going to live but we only found few berries and decided that we would starve to death if we stayed. So the next morning we started to make a raft. We cut strips of bark with our pocket knives and whipped those little poles together and got a small pole and took a white under shirt for a flag and put that on a pole and the wind was favorable and we pushed her out on the ocean. And we kept waving our flag. Finely the look out man on a big vesil sighted us with his glass and came and picked us up and we told them that we had been shipwrecked and all on board had been lost but us three men and we drifted ashore but found out that we couldn't exist on the island so we made that old raft. Well they treated us fine. Well in a short time the vesil landed and here I am. Now George for God's Sake don't give me away. All right Jack if you will go and never come back. All right George, you will never see me again. So they went to a hotell and got a room and registered as man and wife. And after supper they went to a livery stable and got a couple of the best horses theare was in the stable and showed the livery man the card that they had got from the hotel where they were staying and they wanted to ride about the town just for a short time. That was the last that was seen of them or the horses.

LYNCH 'EM: THE COMMITTEE OF VIGILANCE

Samuel Brannan played a key role in San Francisco's first Committee of Vigilance during 1851. In February a pair of "Sydney Ducks"— Australians (many of them former convicts) who had joined the gold rush—robbed C. J. Jansen's dry-goods store on Montgomery Street. In a daring attack and robbery, "English Jim" and an accomplice assaulted the proprietor with a "slung-shot" and escaped with some $1,586 and Jansen's watch. The police arrested a suspect, who gave his name as Thomas Burdue but maintained his innocence. "Certain clues" led the police to conclude that Burdue was actually a notorious criminal named James Stuart. They quickly apprehended Robert Wildred (or perhaps his name was William Windred) "while deep in the fascinations of a strap game on Commercial street."[55] The next day, Washington's birthday, Brannan helped organize one of California's first "Popular Tribunals," which was only prevented from hanging the two men by the Washington Guards, who "rushed in with fixed bayonets," and drove the crowd away among loud cries of "hang 'em," "lynch 'em," "bring 'em out." Brannan was a member of the committee assigned to hold the prisoners and strongly urged that they be hanged immediately.

> Mr. Brannan was very much surprised to hear people talk about grand juries, or recorders, or mayors. I'm tired of such talk. They are murderers, said he, as well as thieves, and I know it, and I will die or see them hung by the neck. I'm opposed to any farce in this business. We had enough of that eighteen months ago, when we allowed ourselves to be the tool of these judges, who sentenced convicts to be sent to the United State[s]. We are the mayor, and the recorder, the hangman and the laws. The law and the courts never yet hung a man in California; and every morning we are reading fresh accounts of murders and robberies. I want no technicalities. Such things are devised to shield the guilty.[56]

Both prisoners "cried like children, and protested their innocence," but Brannan moved "that the prisoners be hung at 10 o'clock on Monday morning."[57] His motion was voted down, but overnight he printed

---

[55]Bancroft, *Popular Tribunals*, 1:182. Bancroft spelled these names Wildred and Burdue, while Williams, *History of the San Francisco Committee of Vigilance of 1851*, 171, preferred Windred and Berdue. The spelling of names associated with the events of 1851 varies wildly; this chapter generally follows Bancroft and Soulé.

[56]"The Excitement Yesterday," *Alta California*, 23 February 1851, 2/3. Bancroft, *Popular Tribunals*, 1:184–85, paraphrased Brannan's call: "Why should we speak to juries, judges, or mayors?" cried Sam, in angry perspiration. "Have we not had enough of such doings in the last eighteen months? It is ourselves who must be mayor, judges, law, and executioners. These men are murderers and thieves; let us hang them!"

[57]"The Excitement Yesterday," *Alta California*, 23 February 1851, 2/3–4.

his minority report and distributed it as a handbill, which appeared on Monday in the *Alta California*.

"TO THE PEOPLE OF SAN FRANCISCO,"
ALTA CALIFORNIA, 24 FEBRUARY 1851, 2/2.

The undersigned, the minority of the committee appointed by you, report as follows: That the prisoners, Stuart and Wildred, are both deserving of immediate punishment, as there is no question as to their guiltiness of crime. The safety of life and property, as well as the name and credit of the city, demand prompt action on the part of the people.

Samuel Brannan, Wm. H. Jones, E. A. King, J. B. Huie.

The "trial" continued at a mass meeting at city hall on Sunday morning, 23 February 1851. It was after midnight when the tired but still murderous mob greeted the announcement of a hung jury with a mighty growl and cries of "Hang them anyway!" The crowd broke out the windows of the courtroom, rushed in, and began demolishing furniture, crying, "Hang the jury!" The jurors drew their sidearms and retreated "until the excitement had somewhat abated." The deflated mob dispersed and the prisoners—despite promises to hang them or set them free—were delivered to the county officers. The legal system eventually convicted but did not execute these men, who later proved to be innocent of the crime.[58]

Fire had been a constant threat to the wooden boomtown that was San Francisco. The fifth conflagration to sweep through the city since December 1849 destroyed some fifteen hundred buildings and "twelve millions of dollars" in ten hours on 4 May 1851. Brannan's home and office were spared, but the city "had never suffered such a blow."[59] The *Alta California*—the only paper to survive the blaze—reported it was "as if the God of Destruction had seated himself in our midst." The fire had started in a paint store near Portsmouth Plaza—a likely source of spontaneous combustion—but the public was in a mood to suspect that "the sad work was likely commenced by an incendiary." So on 3 June when it became known that Benjamin Lewis was being examined in the Recorder's Court on a charge of arson, a crowd assembled to watch the

---

[58]Bancroft, *Popular Tribunals*, 1:190–91.
[59]Soulé, *Annals of San Francisco*, 332, 610.

proceedings. Their mood was not improved when a cry of fire proved to be a false alarm. The assembly soon became a mob of some four thousand, "who began to get furious, continually uttering loud cries of '*Lynch the villain! Hang the fire-raising wretch! Bring him out—no mercy—no law delays! Hang him—hang him!*'" "Loud calls were made for 'Brannan,' to which that gentleman quickly responded." He calmed the mob "and advised that the prisoner should be given in charge of the 'volunteer police,' which had been recently formed." The real police had already secured the prisoner and the mob dispersed.[60]

Brannan's office on the northeast corner of Bush and Sansome streets was "up a narrow flight of stairs, in a little room partitioned off from the loft at the Bush Street end." The building stood just a block from the destruction of the 4 May fire on a spot that had been beach-front property until the filling of Yerba Buena Cove. Three stores on the bottom floor were empty and up for rent.[61] On the afternoon of Sunday, 8 June 1851, merchants James Neall and George Oakes met to discuss "the necessity of active measures." The men had probably read an editorial in the *Alta California* that proposed the creation of "a committee of vigilance" in each ward "to hunt out these hardened villains."[62] Oakes and Neall decided to talk to Brannan, and they found him in his office with his clerk, A. Wardwell. "As the fire licks lovingly new fuel," remarked Bancroft, "so the flame already blazing in his breast received the sentiments poured into it by his visitors." Wardwell drew up a list of reliable men to invite to a meeting the next day at the California Engine House.[63]

The noonday meeting was a success and reconvened that evening in Brannan's empty storefronts. The event was so well attended that the central room overflowed. To accommodate the crowd, Brannan cut passageways in the canvas that divided the building into rooms. The men drew up a constitution for the organization they spontaneously dubbed the Committee of Vigilance.[64] "Then and there," wrote Bancroft, "they

---

[60]Ibid., 330, 340. This reference to "volunteer police" indicates that some sort of vigilante force existed before the formal establishment of the Committee of Vigilance.

[61]Bancroft, *Popular Tribunals*, 1:206, 216.

[62]Stewart, *Committee of Vigilance*, 84–85.

[63]Bancroft, *Popular Tribunals*, 1:216.

[64]For the list of signers of the constitution and later members of the committee that eventually included some 716 names, see Garnett, ed., "Papers of the San Francisco Committee of Vigilance of 1851."

resolved to purge the city of crime at the hazard of their lives and fortunes." The committee was to preserve order and punish vice "through the regularly constituted courts, if that could be; by a more summary and direct process, if must be." That they proposed breaking the law themselves did not entirely escape the committee's attention, since a vow of "inviolable secrecy was laid on every member."[65]

"To secure at once secrecy, convert of action, and efficiency," the committee was organized into "passive and active parts." Selim Woodworth was the figurehead president of the "passive" general committee. Brannan the fire-brand headed the executive committee, "who should rule." Brannan enrolled as the second member (after Woodworth), and some two hundred more men signed the committee's constitution by Tuesday evening.[66] The vigilantes established a watchword and an assembly signal—three taps on the bell of the California Fire Company.

The committee dismissed, but many men lingered about Brannan's office. They were soon surprised to hear the agreed-upon alarm sound some twenty times. With extraordinarily bad timing, an Australian possibly named Simpton (but who called himself John Jenkins) executed a brazen theft just as the committee was signing its constitution. Jenkins, who kept a tavern called the Uncle Sam, had been watching the office of George Virgin on the Long Wharf for some time, with an eye to Virgin's safe. When Virgin left for the evening, Jenkins broke into the office, shoved the iron safe into a coffee sack, and hauled it down the stairs. Here Jenkins' luck took a very bad turn: he met Virgin. Jenkins pushed past and made his way to a dinghy moored at the end of the wharf, but not before Virgin raised the cry "Stop, thief!" Jenkins began rowing across the bay with his loot, but in minutes a dozen boats were in hot pursuit.[67]

John Sullivan was already on the water and headed off the dinghy before it could cross the half mile of water between the wharf and Sidneytown.[68] Jenkins dropped the safe overboard and was soon facing "twenty open-mouthed pistols, each thirsty for his life." The posse man-

[65]Bancroft, *Popular Tribunals*, 1:209–12.

[66]Ibid., 1:212, 215–19, 247. Members were usually identified in committee records by the number assigned to them when they joined the organization.

[67]Senkewicz, *Vigilantes in Gold Rush San Francisco*, 4; and Stewart, *Committee of Vigilance*, 98–99, 103–04. This account follows Stewart, whose version of Jenkins' capture is much more detailed than Bancroft's, which Stewart contradicted in many particulars.

[68]Ibid.

aged to dredge up the safe as Jenkins was hauled ashore. They proposed
to take him to the police, but George Schenck had just come from the
vigilante meeting and dragged Jenkins to Brannan's office to answer to
the "new tribunal of the people."[69]

The alarm increased the size of the crowd at Bush and Sansome.
Brannan organized the executive committee as a court, with himself as
chief judge and Schenck as prosecutor. The committee apparently did
not appoint a defense counsel. The impromptu court had no trouble
linking Jenkins to the theft, but broadened its inquiry to include past
crimes—and to organize another committee to find witnesses for Jenkins. When it appeared that the court's ardor was waning, William A.
Howard laid his revolver on the table. "Gentlemen," he said, "as I understand it, we are here to hang somebody!" The court set about doing just
that.

The "trial" ended about 11:00 P.M. and the jury quickly delivered a
guilty verdict. Jenkins gave a short response: "Bosh." Informed that he
was to die before daybreak, he simply said, "No, I am not." He requested
brandy and a cigar. After repeated assurances that his fate was sealed, the
prisoner agreed to see Flavel S. Mines, a minister. The reverend did not
share the committee's concern for promptness and talked to Jenkins for
about forty-five minutes. The vigilantes worried that Jenkins' friends
might try to free him, or, even worse, that the real law might rally around
politician David C. Broderick and seize the prisoner.

Broderick shared an Irish father and an involvement in New York
Democratic party politics with Brannan, but their similarities ended
there. Broderick came to California in 1849 and by 1851 was president
of the California State Senate, political boss of San Francisco, and
leader of the city's Empire Engine Company. In striking contrast to the
flamboyant Brannan, Broderick was an intellectual and something of a
puritan, and his determined—and politically unpopular—opposition
to the vigilantes seems to have been based on pure principle. "Without
this assumption," George Stewart concluded, "one is at a loss to discover
why Broderick opposed the Committee."[70]

As the prisoner's conversation with the minister dragged on, the will

[69]Bancroft, *Popular Tribunals*, 1:228–29; and Senkewicz, *Vigilantes in Gold Rush San Francisco*, 4.
[70]Stewart, *Committee of Vigilance*, 119.

of the committee began to weaken. William Coleman proposed that they hang their prisoner "by the light of day." G. W. Ryckman sent Brannan to "harangue the crowd while we make ready to move." Brannan—"a fit match for lighting the popular flame"—stepped into the moonlit street and "poured forth a torrent of words such as would drown a philippic of Demonthenes."[71] The committee, he reported, had convicted Jenkins and intended to hang him. In closing Brannan made a tactical error, shouting, "And now, tell me, does the action of the Committee meet with your approval?" Some in the crowd found the courage to shout "No!" and some asked, "Who is this man?" The "ayes" had enough of a majority to encourage the vigilantes to do what they did best—organize a committee. This time, Coleman, Schenck, and Captain Edgar "Ned" Wakeman were assigned to make arrangements for the lynching. They selected Portsmouth Plaza as the site.

At 1:30 A.M. the committee formed two lines two abreast, placed the bound prisoner between them, and began marching quickstep toward the plaza. The California Company's fire bell tolled a death knell. As the mob approached the square and the sound faded, the bell of the Monumental Company "struck clear and full upon the ear." At the corner of Kearny and Clay, police captain Benjamin Ray made a feeble attempt to rescue the prisoner and was easily turned away. Jenkins' friends—"desperadoes" as Bancroft called them—"were beaten back without much difficulty."

The lynch mob arrived at Portsmouth Plaza about 2:30 A.M. and would have run Jenkins up the liberty pole—a 110-foot Oregon fir that was a present from the citizens of Portland—but for objections that the act would desecrate the flag. From a cart, the fearless David Broderick appealed to the people to rescue the prisoner. Two equally brave police officers, J. P. Noyce and H. North, pushed into the vigilante phalanx and laid hands on Jenkins before Noyce felt someone jam a pistol into his chest and growl, "I'll blow your heart out, or let go of the man." The police retreated. The arrangements committee looped a manila rope over the high beam at the south end of the Old Adobe, ran it through a pulley on the railing, and tied a noose at its end.

Jenkins "was calm and courageous to the last. He marched to his death with firm step and fearless eye." Even as Ned Wakeman adjusted

---

[71]Bancroft, *Popular Tribunals*, 1:233.

SCOUNDREL'S TALE

the noose, Jenkins kept smoking. Perhaps the mob hesitated, for at this moment Brannan cried, "Every lover of liberty and good order lay hold!" Fifty hands seized the rope and jerked Jenkins into eternity, strangling him as he rose to the beam. He died with his cigar in his mouth. The vigilantes left the body hanging until daylight, when the city marshal cut him down. The $218 found in his pockets paid for his burial.[72]

The *Alta's* report of the lynching appeared within hours of the event.

"ARREST OF A ROBBER!"
ALTA CALIFORNIA, 11 JUNE 1851, 2/4.
TRIAL AND SENTENCE BY THE CITIZEN POLICE.
EXECUTION ON THE PLAZA!

Last evening about nine o'clock, a man came down to the Whitehall boat station with a bag containing some heavy article, which he placed in a boat and rowed off. A few moments afterward a gentleman who keeps a shipping office upon Central Wharf came along and stated that his office had just been robbed of his small iron safe, containing a large amount of money. Suspicion immediately fell upon the man with the bag, and some of the boatmen jumped into their boats and started in pursuit of the fellow. After a sharp race they overhauled him and as soon as he saw them gaining on him he threw his booty into the water. His pursuers succeeddd [*sic*] in capturing him and upon getting him on shore gave him a pretty severe drubbing and walked him off to the Station House. The bag was subsequently fished up and was found to contain the stolen safe. The thief is said to be a Sydney man of very powerful make, being nearly six feet tall. If the boatmen had followed up their drubbing with a little hydropathic treatment, by way of washing off the blood, they would not have been very severely condemned.

P.S.—Soon after the arrest of the person above mentioned, he was taken possession of by the committee of citizens, whose organization is noticed elsewhere, and by them was tried in the building on the corner of Sansome and Bush streets. The bell of the Monumental Engine House was rung to notify the members of the arrest of an offender, and people began to gather from all directions. A large crowd assembled around the building, where it was understood the trial was progressing, but nothing definite was known of the proceedings inside. About 12 o'clock it was reported that he had been convicted, and sentenced to be executed upon the Plaza. This statement was corroborated about an hour afterwards by Mr. Samuel Brannan, who

---

[72]Details of the hanging are from Bancroft, *Popular Tribunals*, 1:234–37; and Stewart, *Committee of Vigilance*, 112–15. "The Executed Man," *Alta California*, 12 June 1851, 2/4, reported Jenkins' "neck was not broken." Mullen, *Let Justice Be Done*, 161, noted that Jenkins was dragged by the neck for over a hundred feet "and was probably dead by the time he was hauled aloft."

addressed the populace, and informed them that the man had been fairly tried by a committee of citizens, and that no doubt of his guilt existed. He gave his name as John Jenkins. The crowd continued to mutate between the place of trial and the Plaza for a length of time; but there was little or no noise or confusion, although there were so many persons about.

At about 2 o'clock the prisoner was brought out pinioned, and accompanied by a strong guard, was conducted to the Plaza. There was much excitement on the Plaza, and a great deal of noise. Some persons cried out, "Don't hang him on the liberty pole," and a rope was rove through a block attached to a beam upon the end of the old Adobe building. The rope was placed about his neck by a dozen willing hands, and he was immediately run up, struggling furiously. His death occurred speedily. He denied most positively having committed the theft, and asked to be shot instead of hung. On the way to the Plaza he was perfectly composed and smoked a cigar. The Rev. Mr. Miner was sent for and prayed with the condemned man. As we close this article the cor[p]se of the doomed man is swinging in the night air, surrounded by a guard of the committee of citizens. What the result of this affair will be we cannot predict—we trust it will be salutary.

At daylight San Francisco found itself divided between the vigilantes and the Law-and-Order party—which included only "a few lawyers, two judges, some policemen, and David C. Broderick."[73] On the morning of 11 June, the coroner impaneled a jury for an inquest into the cause of Jenkins' death, which was hardly a secret to the crowds who viewed his body in the morgue. Brannan took the stand the next day, but did not "deem it prudent to tell all he knew." He admitted that the committee had arrested and tried Jenkins, but claimed he had heard threats against the lives and property of the committee members. Brannan asserted that the vigilantes had done nothing they would hide from the law, "under proper circumstances."[74]

The inquest concluded that Jenkins had died as a result "of a preconcerted action of an association of citizens, styling themselves a Committee of Vigilance," and listed Brannan among nine men "implicated by direct testimony."[75] No indictments ever followed, but Brannan published a card in the newspapers denying that he had claimed credit in

---

[73]Stewart, *Committee of Vigilance*, 119.

[74]Bancroft, *Popular Tribunals*, 1:238; see Soulé, *Annals of San Francisco*, 572–73, for Brannan's testimony, originally published as "The Coroner's Inquest," *Alta California*, 13 June 1851, 2/2.

[75]"Verdict of the Coroner's Jury in the Case of Jenkins," *Alta California*, 14 June 1851, 2/2.

the Union Hotel for hanging Jenkins. Brannan did not deny involvement in Jenkins' murder, but David Broderick was not impressed by this fine distinction and launched a telling assault on Brannan's character.

"COMMUNICATION FROM MR. BRANNAN,"
ALTA CALIFORNIA, 13 JUNE 1851, 2/4.

We have received the following communication for publication:

To the Editors of the Alta California:—

GENTLEMEN:—I have noticed in your paper this morning, in the evidence of David Broderick, before the Coroner's inquest on the body of John Jenkins, who was hung by the people on the 11th inst., at half past 2, A.M. the following statement: "I saw several persons at the Union, who appeared very anxious to have it known that they had participated in the affair, among these was Samuel Brannan, also Wm. H. Jones." In relation to the evidence referring to me, that part of his testimony I positively deny, and at any time when called upon, will refute, by the evidence of many respectable citizens, who stood by my side during the whole time I was there, which was but a few moments.

SAMUEL BRANNAN.

"COMMUNICATION FROM MR. BRODERICK,"
ALTA CALIFORNIA, 14 JUNE 1851, 2/4.

We publish, by request, the following communication:

Editors of the Alta California:—Having seen in your paper of this morning, a card signed by Mr. Samuel Brannan, respecting my evidence before the Coroner's Jury, I desire to say that I am surprised to find Mr. Brannan so studiously seeking to sherk [*sic*] the responsibility of an act, in the perpetration of which he was notoriously the prime mover. It is well known and easy of proof, that the man Jenkins was taken to the office of Mr. Brannan, and there tried by a self constituted jury, Mr. Brannan himself acting as judge; that Mr. Brannan, from the sand hill opposite his door, harangued the crowd assembled there, telling them that the prisoner would be hanged in one hour on the public Plaza; that there he was active in procuring his death; that after it was over, he was drinking at the bar of the Union, whilst the crowd were congratulating him upon the result of his work, evidently regarding him as the leader in the matter; and that he, by language, smiles, and gestures, congratulated them in return.

Of that gentleman it is unnecessary for me to say any thing further, notorious as he is for his violence and contempt of law. He is widely known as a turbulent man, ready to trample upon all laws that oppose his private opinions or private ends. I would, however, suggest to him the expediency of saving his "respectable witnesses," on whom he seems so much to rely, until he shall be arraigned for the crime of which, by the verdict of the Coroner's Jury, he stands accused.

D. C. BRODERICK.

Following Jenkins' lynching, the committee swelled to more than five hundred members, but it quickly lost momentum and focus. The papers credited the execution with a dramatic decrease in crime, and on 16 June the *Alta* reported "the pilferers, the slung-shot men, the lifters of safes" were quickly leaving town. Now the vigilantes faced an impossible task: how to transform a mob into a law-enforcement agency. It was easy to generate enthusiasm for lynching a criminal caught red-handed, but the tedious work of systematically enforcing the law lacked appeal to zealots like Brannan.

California celebrated a drunken and sullen Fourth of July with random acts of vigilantism. Brannan spent three hours in the committee chambers in the morning and examined a suspect from eight to midnight in the evening, but his devotion to the cause had already reached its limits. "Brannan was just the man to incite a revolution, but he was not the man to conduct one."[76] He had presided at the morning session on 2 July, but later in the day Stephen Payran was signing executive committee papers as president.[77] The official record states that Brannan "felt himself insulted" by the conduct of the sergeant at arms, A. J. McDuffee, but that day the committee passed a resolution "that in the future no spirituous liquor should be introduced into headquarters. Stimulants, if needed, were only to be served in the form of hot coffee."[78] This was a profound change in policy—in its first six weeks the committee had spent over $200 on liquor—and probably was a revolt by the teetotalers against the club-like atmosphere of the executive committee. This direct challenge to Brannan's leadership—and backhanded indictment

[76]Bancroft, *Popular Tribunals*, 1:245.

[77]Williams, *History of the San Francisco Committee of Vigilance of 1851*, 260.

[78]Brannan's conflict with McDuffee may have arisen when the sergeant at arms tried to enforce the ban on spirits. Ironically the committee censured McDuffee in early August, apparently for buying alcohol. See Ibid., 367. The two men resolved their differences, for that fall McDuffee joined Brannan's expedition to Hawaii.

of his drinking habits—apparently led to his resignation. Brannan's replacement by Payran may have been a move to placate the drinkers on the committee, since Payran was also a notorious drunk.

Brannan formally resigned on 5 July, and the committee immediately appointed three men to investigate. Stephen Payran issued an apology, and some felt Brannan should not "be sacrificed to his own irascibility."[79] Brannan "continued his work for a few days, but on the 8th finally withdrew from the Executive Committee, and gave up his position as president of the General Committee," marking the end of his active leadership of the Committee of Vigilance.[80] The general committee accepted his resignation on 9 July, gave him a vote of thanks, and elected Selim Woodworth in his place. At the same meeting, Brannan nominated W. C. Graham and G. W. Ryckman to fill the new vacancies on the executive committee.[81]

> WILLIAMS, ED., *PAPERS OF THE SAN FRANCISCO*
> *COMMITTEE OF VIGILANCE OF 1851*, 181.
>
> To the Vigilance Committee
> Gentlemen It is withe feelings of regret that I am compelled to offer my resignation as Presiding officer of your honorable body and also my membership in the Ex[ec]utive Committee, which has arisen from ve[r]y unpleasant circumstances   with feelings of grateful respect for your past confidence
>
> I remain yours respectfully
> S Brannan

Although he had little further involvement with the committee, Brannan arrested John Olligin and W. L. Harding on the afternoon of 19 August on suspicion of "their being connected with the murder of a man whose body was found on the road to the Mission."[82] The body belonged to Thomas Wheeler, a former servant of John C. Frémont. Brannan noticed two horsemen near the scene of the crime who dashed off into the brush to avoid his questions. With help, Brannan arrested them at gunpoint, though both men were ultimately discharged.[83]

---

[79]Bancroft, *Popular Tribunals*, 1:245.
[80]Williams, ed., "Papers of the San Francisco Committee of Vigilance of 1851," 181.
[81]Stewart, *Committee of Vigilance*, 189.
[82]Williams, ed., "Papers of the San Francisco Committee of Vigilance of 1851," 522.
[83]Williams, *History of the San Francisco Committee of Vigilance of 1851*, 318.

The vigilante movement was torn by an inherent contradiction: how could it both support and defy the law? After Brannan's resignation, the committee replaced the hellfire and brimstone of the original constitution with elaborate by-laws. The movement divided into conservative and radical factions, with the conservatives seeking an accommodation with the government. At a critical moment, Brannan appeared again as the executive committee met on 5 August to consider the fate of burglar George Adams. Six members voted to hand him over to the law, while six opposed the motion. The problem went to the general committee, which voted not to surrender Adams to the authorities. Brannan offered his own motion in its place: "That we now adjourn to meet tomorrow at 10 o'clock to meet at the sound of two bells"—the signal for an emergency meeting, whose purpose would be to try and hang Adams. The crowd that gathered to witness the "scene of fearful excitement" the next morning was to be disappointed. Sergeant at Arms McDuffee emerged from the committee rooms with the prisoner—and a deputy. A crowd followed the men through the streets, believing Adams was about to be hanged, but their trip ended at the jail. With the surrender of Adams, the conservatives triumphed and many believed the committee was finished.[84]

Chance again intervened, giving the committee one last shot at glory when it set about trying two notorious thugs, Sam Whittaker and Robert McKenzie. The committee spent a week interrogating its prisoners and a general meeting on 19 August approved hanging them the next morning. During the night Governor John McDougal roused Sheriff Jack Hays. Shortly after 3:00 A.M., in company with Mayor Blenham and a deputy, the officials walked into the committee rooms, walked out with the condemned prisoners, climbed into their waiting carriage, and drove to the city jail.[85] Alerted to the escape, vigilantes rang the Monumental Company's bell and a groggy crowd assembled long enough to vote to reconvene at 8:00 A.M. Motions were made to "rouse our City to Action, and show who has supremacy" and to march to the jail and seize the prisoners. Neither motion passed, but the committee appointed Brannan to chair a new committee to figure out what had happened.[86]

---

[84]Stewart, *Committee of Vigilance*, 238–40.

[85]Ibid., 243–46, 258–64. Brannan had "put forward" Hays as a candidate for sheriff. See Greer, *Colonel Jack Hays*, 257.   [86]Stewart, *Committee of Vigilance*, 268.

Of all the strange groups spawned by the Committee of Vigilance, none was more bizarre than Brannan's investigating committee. The chairman grilled the vigilante guard, while the governor, the mayor, and the sheriff all appeared before Brannan to explain how they had accomplished their feat. Brannan's report found vigilante police chief Jacob Van Bokkelen "guilty of gross neglect," but uncovered no evidence of treachery. At a general meeting, the vigilantes sustained the death sentences of Whittaker and McKenzie and voted to execute "the punishment due their crimes as the voice of the people demands it."[87] Seizing prisoners already in a jail promised to be no easy task, and the vigilantes spent four days planning the operation. On Sunday afternoon, thirty-six members of the Committee of Vigilance broke into the city jail and captured the prisoners just as the inmates' church service was ending. Before a quarter of an hour passed both men were hanging from two beams that projected from the "great hall" of the committee. An "excited multitude" of six thousand spectators gave a "tremendous shout of satisfaction" when the "struggling wretches were launched into eternity." Thirty minutes later, Brannan addressed the crowd. He assured them the prisoners had confessed and had claimed they would not have committed their crimes but for the corruption of the authorities—civic-minded thoughts for the men who would not live through what the *Alta* called "A Day of Terror!" Brannan assured the mob that the committee was aware of its fearful responsibility, but the first law of nature—self-preservation—forced them to take action. He promised that the committee took no pleasure in its gruesome duty and that no innocent man need fear—though if Thomas Burdue were in the throng, he might have had his doubts. Brannan swore the vigilantes would not take a life unless the proof of guilt was beyond cavil.[88]

Brannan's call to hang Burdue and Wildred in February and this speech bracket his career as "the hangman and the laws." The lynching of Whittaker and McKenzie proved to be the last act of the first Committee of Vigilance. By the end of the summer, the movement lost momen-

---

[87]Ibid., 270–72.

[88]Soulé, *Annals of San Francisco*, 584–85; and Williams, *History of the San Francisco Committee of Vigilance of 1851*, 301, 302. Williams paraphrased Brannan's speech, but cited no source.

tum and collapsed. In mid-September the committee indefinitely suspended "farther operations regarding crime and criminals in the city."[89] The excitement had lasted exactly one hundred days.

One of Brannan's last acts of vigilantism took place in November 1855 after Charles Cora shot Marshall William Richardson in "as cold-blooded a murder as has ever taken place in San Francisco." Once again the Monumental Bell rang and the old Committee of Vigilance rallied to its call. Hearing that Brannan had tried to incite a crowd at the Oriental Hotel to seize Cora, the sheriff arrested him "as a general precaution against a public outbreak." Brannan was quickly released, explaining he "was merely talking to one or two acquaintances inside the hotel."[90] Such assurances did not fool the police, who knew exactly the man to arrest when they decided to round up the usual suspects.[91]

WHO'S THE KING? IS IT YOU?

Among the devotees of Manifest Destiny in California, it was only natural that the Hawaiian Islands would rank high on their list of prospective American acquisitions. Both the British and the French had already seized and then returned the islands to the dissolute Hawaiian king. Kamehameha III had started his reign in 1825 as a capable ruler, but by 1851 alcoholism had weakened his hold on his dominion. Threats from the French led his government to "have it in contemplation to take down the Hawaiian flag, and run up that of the United States."[92] Half the naturalized foreigners in Hawaii were former Americans who resented being ruled by "a set of ignorant, indolent savages or their bigoted quondam-missionary rulers."[93] Rumors of filibusters

---

[89]Soulé, Annals of San Francisco, 350.

[90]Williams, History of the San Francisco Committee of Vigilance of 1851, 397; and Higgens, ed., Continuation of the Annals, 82–83.

[91]A 21 May 1856 letter attributed to Brannan about the Cora episode is in Folder 12, Auerbach Collection. It says, "I think the Vigilens will hang a Bout 5 or 6 more of th[ese] Rascals. I have been on duty, for 6 days   I think Cory and Casey will be hung to Night." Neither the handwriting nor the signature, however, matches Brannan's.

[92]U.S. Commissioner to Hawaii Luther Severance to Daniel Webster, March 1851, in Shewmaker and Stevens, eds., The Papers of Daniel Webster, 259.

[93]Bringhurst, "Sam Brannan's 1851 Hawaiian Filibustering Expedition,'" 22.

"about to descend upon the islands from the California coast" were current as early as 1849.[94] The *Alta California* reflected the prevailing sentiment in April 1851: "The native population are fast fading away, the foreign fast increasing. The inevitable destiny of the islands is to pass into the possession of another power . . . The pear is nearly ripe; we have scarcely to shake the tree in order to bring the luscious fruit readily into our lap."[95] When Californian José Maria Osio warned Hawaiian foreign minister Robert Wyllie of the schemes, Wyllie thanked Osio but said that the plots were not news to him.[96]

Brannan went to Hawaii "with the idea that his Majesty Kamehameha III was so hampered by the missionaries that he would gladly give up his kingdom and crown, and retire on an annuity for life, with his chiefs, who were also to be provided for." Brannan "was to be Governor-General of the Islands; and the lesser offices, such as governor of the different islands, were to be appointed among his party."[97] He might have had more personal reasons to embark on this bizarre venture, for Mormon missionaries had been active in Hawaii since 1850. Perhaps Brannan saw seizing the islands as a way of challenging Brigham Young on yet another front to ease whatever sting his recent separation from the church still carried. Characteristically, Brannan may have "wanted a little Kingdom of his own and he thought that wish might be easily accomplished in Hawaii."[98]

Dismal economic conditions in the islands encouraged the plot. "Business is more restricted," reported *The Polynesian*, "than it has been for many years, if not more than it ever has been." Published on the very day Brannan arrived in Hawaii, the editorial reported "the islands are passing a crisis, such as they have never before been subjected to; and the result, we fear, will prove disastrous to many."[99] Disillusioned Hawaiian officials seem to have come to the same conclusion and may have helped draw Brannan into

[94]Kuykendall, *The Hawaiian Kingdom, 1778–1854*, 291.

[95]"Acquisition of the Sandwich Islands," *Alta California*, 22 April 1851, 2/2; reprinted in *The Polynesian*, 17 May 1851.

[96]Dillon, "Filibuster in Paradise," 4. Richard Dillon researched this story in the Hawaiian archives.

[97]Parke, *Personal Reminiscences*, 27.

[98]Rolle, "California Filibustering," 260; and Bringhurst, "Sam Brannan's 1851 Hawaiian Filibustering Expedition," 23.

[99]"Stagnation of Trade," *The Polynesian*, 15 November 1851, 126/1.

the scheme. He "had long and confidential conversations" in California with Elisha Allen, the king's commissioner and minister of finance, and with John S. Spence, the king's consul. Spence even agreed to act as agent for Brannan's expedition.[100] These men encouraged Brannan's belief that Kamehameha would trade the cares of government for a steady pension. Spence sold Brannan the steam brig *Fremont*, which was supposed to accompany the expedition and transport 150 armed men. Brannan instead chartered the clipper *Game Cock* and had her fitted up with gaming tables to entertain his twenty-four companions on their passage to the islands.[101] The California papers printed denials that the adventurers planned to use force to conquer the islands; Brannan apparently anticipated a peaceful conquest.

The over confident Americans had not counted on the formidable opposition of William Cooper Parke, a Scot who took his commission as marshal of the Hawaiian Islands seriously. Parke had considerable experience dealing with "disappointed gold hunters" from California, many of whom he found to be "of the lowest and most desperate character." While Parke had brought new discipline and pride to the police force, he relied on guile to foil Brannan's sweeping plans. His wry account is the single best description of this comic-opera filibuster. Parke arrested one of Brannan's men for "furious riding" the day the *Game Cock* arrived, and when Brannan tried to bail him out, Parke "told him that the object of his mission was known, and that he had been misinformed as to the condition of affairs. I also advised Mr. Brannan to be careful of his actions, as he and the rest of his party were being watched." Parke kept a close eye on the Americans and frustrated their attempts to meet with the king.[102]

The schemers had ruined their chances of enlisting the support of Hawaii's American population when it looted their mail, destroying let-

---

[100]Bringhurst, "Sam Brannan's 1851 Hawaiian Filibustering Expedition," 22; and Rolle, "California Filibustering," 255–56. Elisha Allen had served as American consul in Hawaii.

[101]Bringhurst, "Sam Brannan's 1851 Hawaiian Filibustering Expedition," 22; and Dillon, "Filibuster in Paradise," 4. "The Steamer," *The Polynesian*, 27 December 1851, 130/2, reported, "The steamer Fremont, Capt. W. A. Howard, was advertised in the California papers to sail for these islands on December 6th. But from private advices we learn that such would not be the case."

[102]Parke, *Personal Reminiscences*, 27–31.

ters bound for whaling ships in the islands.[103] *The Polynesian* published a letter on 6 March 1852 charging the "passengers in the celebrated Game Cock" had "broke open the Mailbag, rummaged its contents, broke open letters and destroyed such as did not suit their notions." The purloined mail described "the plans, purposes and desires of said passengers, in regard to upsetting this government, and setting up themselves" in its place. The "act charged has been admitted by several of the said passengers," and the editor could see no difference between violating the mail and ordinary theft.[104] Whatever hopes Brannan may have had of local support went overboard with the mail bag. James Tanner's March 1852 affidavit provided the most accurate—and humorous—picture of Brannan's looting of the U.S. Mail.

"TO THE PUBLIC,"

BROADSIDE, BANCROFT LIBRARY.

JAMES HENRY TANNER, Passenger by the ship Game-Cock, being duly sworn, deposeth, and says;

THAT one night at about twelve o'clock during the passage of the Game Cock from San Francisco, I accompanied Samuel Brannan into the ship's cabin. After being seated, Mr. Samuel Brannan showed me copies of letters purporting to be from the American Commission at Honolulu, and from the Honorable Daniel Webster at Washington City. He then told me that it was his intention to break open the MAIL BAG which was in the mate's room in the possession of Mr. Baldwin, but that the thing must be done without the knowledge of Mr. Baldwin, as he thought it possible that he, Mr. Baldwin, would object to it. Mr. Brannan requested me to say nothing of the affair, and at the same time inquired if I had any sealed letters for the Sandwich Islands; I told him I had one which was directed to Messrs. Starkey, Janion & Co.; I then left Mr. Brannan and retired to bed. The next day I was told by Mr. Petrovits that they had got possession of the Mail Bag, and that it was then in the State-room occupied by Mr. Brannan and Mr. Hanna, and that he, Mr. Petrovits, together with Mr. Hanna had opened and read all the letters, and that there was one or two of them that spoke in low terms of Mr. Brannan and the whole party—one of these he said was addressed to a Catholic priest, and the other to General Miller, and were written by a Frenchman.

He, Mr. Petrovits, said there was one letter in particular that contained a

[103]Bringhurst, "Sam Brannan's 1851 Hawaiian Filibustering Expedition," 21.

[104]"Violating the Mail," *The Polynesian*, 6 March 1852.

draft for some money, and that he did not know how to dispose of the letters as they were all broken open. I advised him to reseal the letters, and if necessary on our arrival at Honolulu to detain them for some time, but not to destroy them.—He said that it was their intention, that is, Mr. Brannan, Mr. Hanna, and Mr. Petrovits, to throw the letters overboard, reseal the letter bag, and replace it to the state-room from which it was taken.

On the same day, Mr. Hanna came to me and asked me if I had any sealed letters, saying if I had, I should open them, and read the contents, as they had found in the mail bag which had been broken open, many things derogatory to the parties on board the ship and that they had destroyed them. On the same day that the letters were opened, I went to the state room occupied by Mr. Brannan and Mr. Hanna, and was about to go in, when I was accosted by Mr. Petrovits and told that I must not go in, as the state-room was then private. I had however opened the door and saw a large quantity of opened letters and papers. I then closed the door and retired. The letter which I had in my possession addressed to Starkey, Janion, & Co., I delivered to them on my arrival, sealed as I received it in San Francisco.

So far as my knowledge extends, I do not believe that any other passengers on board of the ship were knowing to or had any hand in the breaking open of the mail bag with the exception of the parties already named in this affidavit. I make this my affidavit to the truth of the circumstances so far as my knowledge extends for the purpose of showing that the passengers on board of the ship, with the exception of Mr. Brannan, Mr. Hanna, and Mr. Petrovits, are, in my belief, innocent of any charge of violating or being cognizant of the violation of the mail the ship "Game Cock."

JAMES H. TANNER

Subscribed and sworn before me this 15th day of March A. D., 1852, Honolulu, Island of Oahu, H. I.

C. C. HARRIS,
Police District Magistrate of Honolulu

As the scheme collapsed, a placard appeared that distributed the kingdom's offices among the filibusters, listing "Brannan as Governor-General, down to one of them as Tax Collector of Honolulu." Brannan's men "accused one of their number, a Pole by birth and a portrait painter, of having made the placard," and attacked Paul Petrovits in the bar of the French Hotel, abusing him "in a shameful manner." Parke's men arrested four or five of the attackers, and Parke knew "that the Pole had no hand in the placard, for I saw it printed and posted up myself." The Scot's wily opposition "put a decisive check on their adventure," but Brannan had already "left in disgust," and "in a short time they had all left the Kingdom wiser men than when they came here, with the exception of one or two. And so ended the 'Game-Cock' fiasco."[105]

The Americans, of course, told a different story. They claimed that after Parke arrested some of his men, Brannan "formed up the rest of his force in a column of fours" and "marched into the fort where the prisoners were being held." Although the Americans were armed only with revolvers, Vi Turner ("the courageous cripple") "disdainfully swept aside the muskets of the two sentries at the gate" and "Brannan found himself in control." Parke sued for peace and released Brannan's drunken men. The Americans also claimed that Kamehameha visited Brannan's bungalow "to be initiated into the mysteries of monte and draw poker."[106] They failed to persuade the king to trade his throne for a pension, and Brannan was left to disguise his failure by claiming he had gone to Hawaii to invest in real estate.

Brannan probably left the islands on "the fast-sailing schooner" *Golden Rule*, which was scheduled to sail on 16 December. Henry Heap, who accompanied Brannan on his return to San Francisco, reported the ridicule that awaited the unsuccessful conqueror on his return to California in a letter to minister Wyllie. A crowd on the docks greeted Brannan's arrival with biting sarcasm: "Well, have you taken the Islands? Who's the King? Is it you?"[107]

---

[105]Parke, *Personal Reminiscences*, 30–31. Petrovits, a likely refugee from Europe's revolutions, had been active in the vigilante movement.

[106]Dillon, "Filibuster in Paradise," 4.

[107]Rolle, "California Filibustering," 260. Some report Brannan returned aboard the *Baltimore*.

Chapter 12

"The Richest Man in California"

As Samuel Brannan blazed through the 1850s, his legend continued to grow in California. The decade found him at the height of his wealth and power. The instability of California's early economy, with its wild swings between boom and bust, encouraged Brannan's speculations and both helped and challenged his business career. Prices fluctuated chaotically due to eastern merchants consigning goods bound for the state without any knowledge of what was in demand or what the competition was shipping, which led to massive surpluses or shortages. During the first decade after the gold rush, California went through four major business cycles, "all quite independent of the national economy." The first boom ended in January 1850, and except for the months between May 1852 and December 1853, until 1858 the state's economy was in recession or—for most of the time—in depression.[1] Brannan's opportunistic business style was perfectly suited to these conditions, but the chaos meant that he built his enormous fortune on a precarious foundation. The scope of his many and varied enterprises—including railroad promotion, business and agricultural pursuits, and an erratic political career—defies simple summary, so these pages only sketch Brannan's frenetic adventures and provide a few insights into how he became "the richest man in California."

Samuel Brannan's wealth was legendary—and often exaggerated. An 1851 work aptly titled *A Pile* ranked six hundred Californians by wealth, crediting Brannan with a fortune of $275,000, a substantially smaller "pile" than that of Swiss banker Felix Argenti, who had accumulated $500,000, and less than Brannan's friends W. D. M. Howard ($375,000) and Jonathan Stevenson ($350,000).[2] Still, Brannan was widely heralded

---

[1]Decker, *Fortunes and Failures,* 34.

[2]Williams, *History of the San Francisco Committee of Vigilance of 1851,* 188n3.

"Samuel Brannan, in the Regalia of President of the Society of California Pioneers. (From a painting in the Society Rooms.)" From John Hittell, "The Discovery of Gold in California," *Century Magazine* (February 1891), 531. The original oil portrait was destroyed in the San Francisco earthquake of 1906.

as the richest man in California, and probably had a valid claim to the title during much of the 1850s and 1860s.

A BAND OF BROTHERS

When word reached California of the death of Zachary Taylor in August 1850, Brannan led the "Pioneers of California" in a procession to honor the dead president. The event led to the formation of the Society of California Pioneers.[3] Brannan remained active in the organization all his life and in 1853 served as its second leader, which enabled him to wear "The Regalia of the President," consisting of "a gold tinsel scarf trimmed with silver bullion, with first class Rosette and cross Mallets of silver." Serving with him was treasurer William T. Sherman.[4] Brannan's eloquent annual address in 1854 described the goals of the society, which still survives in San Francisco. He recounted "the stirring and startling incidents" of California's "still astounding" youth, which would beguile "the fancy-weaving brain of the wildest dreamer." The

---

[3]Johnson, *Gleanings from the* Picayune, 33.
[4]*Constitution and By-Laws of the Society of California Pioneers*, 2.

"SAM BRANNAN ON HORSEBACK."
The Society of California Pioneers believes this equestrian portrait by Thomas
J. Donnelly shows the Society's second president in Masonic regalia, but the
bearded figure bears little resemblance to Samuel Brannan.
Courtesy, The Society of California Pioneers.

pioneers "dared the dangers of trackless oceans and deserts, scaled mountains and miasma-breathing latitudes, to make a home and build an empire [that] bids fair to civilize the world." Brannan promised the society "would collect and preserve facts" for historians. "We are a band of brothers," he orated, "useful to the world as a fountain where philosophers, history, poetry, and painting may quaff their purest inspirations in after years."[5]

The Ablest Business Man in California

One pragmatic historian reasoned that Sam Brannan "was unquestionably the ablest business man in California, as he was the richest."[6] A closer study of Brannan's financial operations suggests that he was the luckiest capitalist in California, not the most capable. Historian John Hittell aptly summarized Brannan's failings as a businessman: "He lacked prudence, close calculation, attention to details, knowledge of men, and tact." Brannan was at heart a "plunger"—a wild-eyed gambler in the parlance of the times, with an eye for the main chance.

Early in his career, Brannan managed his own affairs, taking an active role in the raucous trade of San Francisco and Sacramento. Bancroft recalled, "Sam delighted in auctions. Never was he so happy as when perched on a high box smoking a long cheroot, and sinking the small blade of his sharp knife into the soft pine."[7] He formed any number of temporary alliances, including an 1849 partnership with J. W. Osborn that engaged briefly in the China trade. By 1851 Brannan had a small office on the corner of Bush and Sansome streets, where he apparently left the paperwork to a mysterious clerk, A. Wardwell. By the mid-1850s Brannan had moved into impressive quarters in his building at 420 Montgomery Street. He transferred much of the responsibility for the day-to-day management of his affairs to John Brannan. His brother's death on a voyage to China in 1862 contributed to the decline of Brannan's fortunes during the 1860s. Alexander Badlam, Jr., took over management of his uncle's affairs, but Badlam's financial talent was no match

[5] "Society of California Pioneers," *Daily California Chronicle*, 9 January 1854. Transcription from Norma Ricketts Brannan Collection.

[6] Eldredge, *History of California*, 5:431   [7] Bancroft, *California Inter Pocula*, 346.

for Brannan's recklessness.[8] Litigation involving his land deeds, assaults, railroad lawsuits, and divorce supported a legion of attorneys for more than two decades.

William Heath Davis painted the most telling picture of Brannan's "confiding disposition and carelessness in business." Davis recalled how Brannan decided to buy two or three mines from Mexicans he had met at the offices of Ferdinand Vassault. Brannan invited Vassault to join in the investment, but when Vassault arrived at his office, "Brannan informed him that he had already agreed upon the price to be paid for the mines, namely $200,000, of which $10,000 was to be paid down to bind the bargain." On the table "were several samples of beautiful ore," said to come from the mines. Vassault recognized the gold ore and took Brannan aside to ask him "to let the matter rest until the next day," but Brannan declined, saying he had drawn the check and "wished to close the business that afternoon." Vassault explained that the specimens were his and had been stolen from his office. Brannan threw the men out of his office, "and thus ended the attempted swindle. Vassault saved Brannan from a loss of at least $10,000."[9]

Davis, who never had a bad word for anyone, had much good to say about his old friend. "Samuel Brannan, when himself, was liked by everyone who knew him. He was kindhearted, confiding and generous to a fault, and was always ready to open his purse for the relief of the needy." When asked for help, "Brannan had a sort of bluntness towards poor people," and would question them closely, but he invariably gave them "a generous gift and the remark: 'Come again if there is further need of my assistance.'"[10]

Brannan returned to the East Coast early in 1852 on business, the first of many such trips over the next decade. John Brannan oversaw the construction of his brother's brick buildings on Montgomery Street and wrote that "he is now going to New York after materials for buildin[g]s which wil be fire Proof." Brannan did not intend to stay in New York "over 2 or 3 weeks." Before he left, Ann Eliza threw "a party or ball at

---

[8]John Brannan to Mary Brannan, 11 December 1861, and letters of sympathy dated April 1862 in the Auerbach Collection, 151–55; Stellman, *Sam Brannan, Builder of San Francisco*, 173–74; and Scott, *Samuel Brannan and the Golden Fleece*, 388.

[9]Davis, *Seventy-five Years in California* (1929), 215–16.   [10]Ibid., 216.

the house in consequence of Samuels going away."[11] Brannan secured the needed materials, for on 1 July 1853, construction started on the fireproof Armory Hall, an "elegant structure" that was completed by the middle of November at a cost of $225,000. He rented "a splendid hall" on the fourth floor to local militia units for $500 a month.[12] While the armory was being built, Brannan started work on his Express Building at the northeast corner of Montgomery and California streets, which became home to Wells, Fargo & Co. and the Society of California Pioneers.[13] His offices were in this building, also known as the Brannan Building, at 420 Montgomery Street, which became a social center noted for the "gentleman's saloon" of Barry and Patten. "The walls were hung with chaste oil paintings. The wines and liquors were of the finest. The free lunch of the best." Gambling was prohibited, but the "upstairs was fitted [as] an elaborate billiard parlor."[14]

San Francisco elected Brannan a state senator on 7 September 1853, but he resigned before even being sworn into office. He had returned to the city from another visit to the East Coast on 21 May 1853, having arranged low-interest loans in New York and lobbied in support of Senator William Gwin's land bill.[15] The trip that led to his resignation may have been to help John Brannan bring his family to San Francisco.

"RESIGNATION OF MR. BRANNAN,"
SACRAMENTO UNION, 7 DECEMBER 1853, 2/3.

The causes assigned by Samuel K. Brannan. Esq., for his resignation as State Senator, will be found in the following letter addressed to Gov. Bigler:
SAN FRANCISCO, Dec. 3d, 1853.

SIR—The indisposition of some of the members of my family, now in New York, after an absence of ten months upon a visit, renders it necessary that I should join them at as early a day as possible, and accompany them home when sufficiently recovered to travel. I am, therefore, compelled to resign my office as one of the Senators of the Fifth Senatorial District of

---

[11]Brannan left for New York on 14 February 1852. See John Brannan to Mary F. Brannan, 10, 13, and 17 February 1852, John Brannan Papers.

[12]Soulé, *Annals of San Francisco*, 707–08. A picture on page 702 reveals that part of the ground floor was occupied by the "Cheap Book Store."

[13]Soulé, *Annals of San Francisco*, 513–14. The corporate headquarters of Wells Fargo are still at 420 Montgomery.

[14]Jacobsen, "A Fire-Defying Landmark," *San Francisco Bulletin*, 4 May 1912.

[15]Stellman, *Sam Brannan, Builder of San Francisco*, 142–43.

the State of California; and do so at the earliest moment after being impressed with the necessity which requires it, but not without a due sense of my obligations for the honor conferred by a constituency with whom I have been so long associated, and am directly interested in all the relations of a permanent citizen of California.

Very truly, your ob't servant,
S. BRANNAN.

To his Excellency, JOHN BIGLER, Governor of the State of California.[16]

Brannan perhaps made a voyage to Europe in 1854, but by 1856 he had moved his family to the continent. Ann Eliza Brannan had never been happy in the gold rush metropolis, and her husband's legendary escapades probably did not contribute to domestic bliss. During the summer of 1856 Brannan wrote from Geneva, informing his brother that he would leave for Hamburg in two days and would sail from Liverpool on 12 July, hoping to "be home as fast as possible. Lisa and the family are beautifully located and Sammy is perfectly delighted with his school and so are we all. I bless the day I took this journey for my children's sake if nothing more." The Masonic Lodge at Geneva had given Brannan "a handsome reception," even though "I could not speak a word of French or German."[17] With his family settled in Europe, Samuel Brannan returned to California for all intents and purposes a bachelor, free from one of the last restraining influences on his excesses.

AT THE HEIGHT OF HIS GLORY

Volunteer fire companies formed the basic political organization of many nineteenth-century American cities, and when the forty-niners came to San Francisco, they brought their fire companies with them. Firemen from Boston organized the Howard Engine Company, best known as Social Three, in 1850. The fire stations became neighborhood social and political centers.[18] The Howard company boasted a glee club, a piano, and "the best clam chowder anywhere" at its headquarters on

---

[16]This letter, the only source to use K as Brannan's middle initial, suggests that his middle name was perhaps Knox, in recognition of his relation to America's first secretary of war.

[17]Samuel Brannan to John Brannan, ca. June 1856, from Stellman, *Sam Brannan, Builder of San Francisco*, 155. Stellman described "several well-preserved letters in granduncle's handwriting" in Sophie Brannan's possession; these letter do not seem to have survived. See Ibid., 244.

[18]Mullen, *Let Justice Be Done*, 85.

Merchant Street between Montgomery and Sansome. Repentant fire-men allegedly started the city's first temperance society at the Howard Engine House "after an exciting debauch during the Stanford Warehouse Fire."[19] San Francisco's companies—the Monumental, the Empire, the California—each had its patrons. A man as powerful and ambitious as Samuel Brannan quite naturally had to sponsor his own organization, for "no local politician had any chance of being elected unless he was connected to one of the fire companies."[20] The story of the engine he purchased reveals much about his flamboyant style, for he spared no expense to make sure his fire company had nothing but the best.

On 3 January 1857, the "new Engine belonging to the Brannan Fire Association" arrived in San Francisco on the clipper *Bostonian* after a voyage of 141 days. A reporter got a look at the engine while it was still in "the Bonded Warehouse on Market street, below the Oriental Hotel." Hunneman & Co. of Boston, "whose reputation as engine builders is world-wide," had taken more than three years to build the fabulous contraption. From his "hurried view," the journalist attempted a detailed description of the machine, "to convey to our readers a satisfactory idea of its elaborate finish and workmanship."

"THE BRANNAN ENGINE,"
ALTA CALIFORNIA, 13 JANUARY 1857, 2/2.

. . . The Engine is one of the most complete and beautiful pieces of mechanism we have ever seen. Every portion of the steel and iron work is richly and heavily plated with silver, and at the first glance, it would appear too brilliant, too elegant, for common service or efficiency; but on closer inspection, there is nothing gaudy or superfluous about it—nothing but what is substantial and serviceable; and imposing as the *tout ensemble* is, yet in detail, all is plain and in perfect taste. There are but three colors of paint upon the wood work—green and gold, and the richest shade of carmine, and these are so happily blended as to harmonize with the silver work of the remainder, and produce a charming effect.

The weight will probably be about 5,000 pounds. There are two cylinders of 8 and 10-inch capacity, and the stroke varies from 14 to 18-inch. The scroll work is graceful in design and perfect in finish. The levers or

---

[19]Jacobson, "California's First Millionaire," *San Francisco Bulletin*, 20 May 1916.
[20]Mullen, *Let Justice Be Done*, 85.

brakes are twenty feet in length, and capable of manning with ease 44 men. There is an extra set of levers accompanying the machine. The beams and arms are one solid piece of iron, the forging of which is said to have caused the necessity of the maker procuring entire new machinery. The beam is not straight like ordinary engines, but curves gracefully to correspond with the goose-necks, and adds greatly to the symmetry of the whole. There are two silver-plated pipes, six feet in length, with extra nozzles of every necessary capacity. The pipes are supported upon either side by spring shackles of new and improved patent. There are also four lengths of suction pipe, seven feet each, capable of drafting water a distance of 28 feet. The branch arms which hold the suction pipes in front, and the standards which support them in the rear, are elaborately finished; even the suction hose-couplings are silver-plated. There is a bell upon each side of the Engine, above the pipes; and surmounting the whole is a richly figured cut glass lantern, made to order expressly for the Engine, in Birmingham, England. The front wheels are 3 ft. 5 inches in diameter; those in the rear are 4 feet. The tongue is a beautiful piece of workmanship, with all the iron work heavily plated, and having a spring near the end, by which the rope on the reel may be let out at pleasure while running. It has also a swivel chain to raise or lower the tongue, which is a great improvement. Another improvement which we noticed is, that the gates of the outlets are on the inside, instead of the out-side, as in the old style, and they work with a screw instead of a key. The suction gate works with three cog-wheels instead of a lever, as in other engines. The woodwork of the box is of the best mahogany; in the rear, on each side of the coupling, is a griffin's head finely carved and gilded.

On the left side of the box is a landscape painting, with horses, trees and a lake with a boating party; above it on the same side of the air chamber is an exquisite painting upon copper, said to have been copied from an old English engraving, for which Mr. Hunneman paid $50. We were not quite satisfied as to what the painting was intended to represent. There are four female figures in the fore ground, dancing to the music of old Father Time, who sits playing upon a harp; his scythe lying at his feet, and a child beside him with an hour glass; beyond the dancers is a monument with carved busts upon it, wreathed with ivy; and above, on a cloud, in his golden char-iot, sits Phoebus, reigning the bold coursers of the sun. On the right side of the box is a beautifully correct view of Niagara Falls from the Canada side; above, on the same side, is a painting copied from a French picture and rep-resenting three females at the bath, one of whom is dallying with a swan upon the stream. To complete the beauty and symmetry of the engine there are four richly painted fire buckets hanging upon the scroll work, one at each corner. The paintings upon them represent the four seasons, and are beauti-ful in conception and execution. Accompanying the Engine is a Tender or

Hose Carriage, finished to correspond, and having a thousand feet of double riveted hose of extra capacity, being 3 ½ inches. The Engine and Tender are said to have cost, when landed here, and put up, $10,000. The silver needed upon it, in plating, cost $3,500; the plating work was done at New Haven, Connecticut. Take the whole machine together [and] it entirely exceeds in beauty, strength and finish, anything of the kind ever made before. The Brannan Fire Association may well be proud of their machine. We understand they propose giving a public Ball on or about the 22nd of February, and will parade with their new engine on the day following, when the public will have an opportunity of seeing it and judging of its beauty.

"The Brannan machine" had a brief but troubled career. The engine was damaged in October 1858 "by the fall off the bank on the corner of Lombard and DuPont streets to the extent of $450." Brannan restored the engine, but "it was never quite the same."[21]

Brannan's leap into "the banking system" in 1857 captured the essence of his business abilities: "Far sighted, clear headed, and energetic, he was quick to see the necessity for a change . . . and to take advantage of the opportunity."[22] It also revealed the more reckless aspects of Brannan's style. A banking panic in 1855 had shaken California's already convulsive economy, and the industry would not recover until the next decade. Brannan, however, had made much money borrowing at low rates in New York and lending in California, where interest could be as high as 5 percent per month. Brannan gambled that he could master the economy's booms and busts, which even as astute an observer as banker William T. Sherman found to be a "complete mystery."[23] In the fall of 1857, as financial panic swept the Midwest and East Coast, Brannan launched his own bank, just as Sherman's was failing. There were irregularities in the bank's finances, for Brannan pledged securities belonging to his wife without her permission, and he had to send to Europe to get it.[24] Editor Thomas S. King led a chorus of critics who denounced Brannan's "shin-plaster" paper currency, an unpopular financial medium in the land of gold.[25]

---

[21] *Alta California*, 10 October 1858, 2/2. According to Bailey, *Sam Brannan and the California Mormons*, 216, it "took another slice of Sam's money to put the shining beauty back into action." The Sam Brannan Chapter of E Clampus Vitus is trying to locate the machine.

[22] Eldredge, *History of California*, 5:431.

[23] Lavender, *California: Land of New Beginnings*, 205; and Bean, *California*, 217–18.

[24] "Brannan's Bank," *Sacramento Bee*, 16 November 1857, 2/1.

[25] "Brannan's Paper Currency," *San Francisco Evening Bulletin*, 16 November 1857, 2/1.

Brannan launched a more successful banking enterprise six years later. Along with former California governor Peter Burnett and Joseph Winans, Brannan founded the Pacific Accumulation Loan Company in February 1863 with a capital of five million dollars divided into fifty thousand shares of stock. The promoters faced a hard struggle selling the stock, but once it became known "that Mr. Brannan had positively declared that the enterprise *must* and *should* succeed, and had largely increased his subscription," stock sales raised $700,000 although the bank opened in October with less than $20,000 in capital "paid in." Brannan resigned the presidency in June in favor of Burnett, his former associate in Sacramento land speculation. Burnett fought with his directors, refusing to pay unjustifiable dividends, but he eventually established the business on a sound footing as the Pacific Bank. He recalled, "It is but simple justice to Samuel Brannan to state that he is the father of the bank . . . With all his faults, he has many noble qualities, and has done much for California."[26]

Merchant Samuel H. Auerbach joined his brother in the gold fields in 1862. He described Brannan at this time.

> When I knew him, Brannan was at the height of his glory. He was a very handsome man, tall and well built. He had large, alert brown eyes and strong, handsome features. He wore sideburns and a Vandyke beard and had very thick, wavy black hair. He was always dressed in the finest clothes that could be made—the best imported fabrics and the most painstaking tailoring, made in the height of fashion. He was the darling of the ladies of San Francisco, and achieved much notoriety for his numerous and scandalous affairs with the most famous of the girls whose moral standards were not as noticeable as their beauty and extravagance. He was always in the gayest humor and he spent lavishly on past and present favorites, and on friends among the fashionable and wealthy of the city.[27]

CASES OF ASSAULT AND BATTERY

Even as a man of great wealth and social prominence, Samuel Bran-

---

[26]Burnett, *An Old California Pioneer*, 246–27. Burnett wrote his account of the Pacific Bank on 26 September 1878. He noted, "In no city on earth is it so difficult to ascertain the true financial condition of men as in San Francisco." Ibid., 246–47, 249.

[27]"Sam Brannan," Auerbach Collection, 203. Herbert Auerbach may have actually written this sketch.

nan never lost his taste for street fighting. Over the years, California's newspapers frequently recounted his exploits as a brawler, often noting that intoxication contributed to Brannan's misdeeds.

Samuel and John Brannan exchanged harsh words with Mr. J. Garvitt in 1856. "Mr. S. Brannan finally threw off his coat, and struck and kicked Mr. G. several times," while Garvitt protested "he would not fight Mr. Samuel Brannan, and made no resistance."[28] A "difficulty occurred in Sacramento" in 1857 between Brannan and Ed McGowan "about the vigilance question. Brannan asked McGowan to drink, the latter refused and called Brannan a strangler. Brannan then put his hand on his pistol, when McGowan seized him, threw him down and took the weapon from him. The parties were examined the next day by the Recorder and discharged."[29] Earlier that year, Brannan "was fined $50 by Recorder Price for being drunk and disorderly, and on Monday evening he was severely caned by his own brother."[30] A confrontation a year later perhaps inspired a trip to Europe after "cross cases of assault and battery" were filed in San Francisco's police court between Brannan, Benjamin Moulton, and Dr. G. G. Hayden. On a Saturday night, 3 April 1858, a "partly intoxicated" Brannan assaulted Moulton "in the stairway of the Express Building." When Brannan's assault and battery case came before the court, "The defendant, having left in the John L. Stephens, en route for Europe, will, of course, not appear," and Brannan forfeited bail of fifty dollars.[31]

Brannan even battled the police. About 1859, "Sam Brannan was fined $70 for his assault on officer Jacobs. His preceding visit to the city had added only $50 to the police fund, and the press spoke discouragingly of the outlook for the future, if the high-rolling millionaire was to be let off so easy."[32] Not all his confrontations ended in violence. Shortly after Brannan's return from Europe in 1856, "a little difficulty" took place with Billy Mulligan in the reading room of New York's Metropolitan Hotel. Mulligan and "a dozen or so of his rowdy friends"

[28]"An Affray," *San Francisco Evening Bulletin*, 14 March 1856, 3/1.

[29]"Vigilante Fight," *Nevada Democrat*, 12 August 1857, 2/2.

[30]"In Bad Luck," *Sacramento Daily Bee*, 12 March 1857, in B49.3, Sorensen Papers.

[31]"The Affray between Brannan and Moulton," *Alta California*, 7 April 1858, 2/3.

[32]Carroll D. Hall to Frederick Sorensen, 3 October 1942, Sorensen Papers. Hall cited a *Sacramento Record-Union* "Thirty Years Ago" clipping from "apparently, 1889."

approached Brannan, who "returned the salutation rather distantly. 'I suppose,' said Mulligan, 'it is lucky for me that you were not in San Francisco. Had you been there, I reckon the Committee would have hung, instead of banishing me!'" Brannan "made some general reply, and turning away from him, continued the conversation." Mulligan "fiercely said" that Brannan "was a d–d s–n of a b–tch." Mulligan's "horde of ruffians closed in, ready for and expecting a row; but Mr. Brannan and his friends disdaining to take notice of such rascals, withdrew."[33]

Brannan's most admirable moral stand was his devotion to abolitionism. The conflict over slavery caught Brannan in its web of violence in 1860 in the bar of New York's St. Nicholas Hotel, when he "came near having a serious encounter" with "Capt. Farnham of the slaver *Wanderer* notoriety," who had recently been "liberated by his friends" from jail in Savannah. The cause of the trouble was unclear, "but from brandy punches and politics the belligerents came to blows. Pistols were quickly drawn, and a general melee seemed inevitable," when a policeman "rushed into the saloon and put a stop to the difficulty." After "considerable trouble," the officer arrested Brannan and a man named Reed, who had to "give bonds in the sum of $500 to keep the peace for the next six months." Farnham escaped when he "was taken off in a carriage by some of his friends." The affair "caused a good deal of excitement among the guests at the hotel."[34]

WE MUST DRAW THE SWORD

Brannan made several attempts to revive his political career. With the approach of the Civil War, he abandoned his long alliance with the Democrats. "Untrammelled by party," he ran a losing campaign for the California State Senate in 1856, leading the People's Reform ticket.[35] His devotion to the Republican party began with Lincoln's 1860 presidential campaign. Brannan was in Washington on 5 May 1860 and dined with California Senator Milton Latham—and it seems safe to assume he joined in the "little bender" Latham mentioned in his jour-

[33]"Billy Mulligan and Samuel Brannan, Esq.," *Sacramento Union,* 1 September 1856, 1/5–6.
[34]*Alta California,* 16 October 1860, 1/5.
[35]*Golden Era,* 21 September 1856, 4/5; and 26 October 1856, 5/1.
[36]Robinson, "The Day Journal of Milton S. Latham," 18.

nal.[36] Brannan became a strong supporter of California's Union party, an alliance of Republicans and Union Democrats. At the party's convention in Sacramento at the end of August 1864, Brannan was nominated to be a presidential elector at large. He thanked the delegates for the honor in a fiery acceptance speech.

"SPEECH OF SAMUEL BRANNAN,"
SACRAMENTO UNION, 1 SEPTEMBER 1864.

MR. BRANNAN came forward in response to calls and said—Mr. President and gentlemen of the Convention: I thank you for the high honor which you have conferred upon me this day. I do not know that I have the power of language to express my thanks for the very high compliment you have paid to me personally as a loyal citizen of the State of California. It is a crisis with our country and with every individual citizen, and it is, on your part, the mark of confidence placed in me at such a crisis which makes me feel proud of the position I occupy. (Applause.) To cast the vote of this State—the great Western State of our Union—is an honor that every loyal citizen should feel proud of. He that loves his country should feel proud of the people he represents when that country is in danger. (Applause.) We are somewhat isolated from the heart of our country; our land is filled with rebellious arms and rebellious spirits, and we wish to sustain that Union that was handed down to us by our sires—by those who passed through the fiery furnace before us. We have both intestine and external enemies, and we have, in such a crisis, to make a selection of such men as we deem that we can trust in the hour when the enemy are seeking to overthrow the citadel of our liberty. The vote of this State must go for the Union, and if the State cannot be carried for the Union by its vote, then we must draw the sword. (Applause.) There never should be a faction existing in the Union ranks of our State; and none should be tolerated who would ever tarnish our glorious flag. There should be no personal feeling at this time carried into counties, sections, townships or neighborhoods, that should ever permit that flag to be torn down, but everywhere let it float to the breeze from the mast of every ship and the steeple of every church. (Applause.) Gentlemen, I do not wish to intrude upon your time, which is valuable, in making a speech. My platform is in my heart, thank God. It was born with me. (Cheers.) Your trust will never be betrayed by me under any circumstances. My all is with you and your all is me, and I shall never betray you. (Applause.) I thank you for the kind confidence that you have bestowed. (Applause.)[37]

The delegates greeted Brannan's speech with such thunderous

---

[37]Thanks to Malcolm E. Barker for providing his transcription and copy of the original.

applause and stomping that the ceiling below the hall began to fall, prompting the chair to ask members to limit their response to clapping their hands. Brannan campaigned for Lincoln across northern California, visiting Horsetown, Oroville, Red Bluff, Marysville, Woodland, Folsom, Nicolaus, Forest Hill, and Weaverville, in addition to giving speeches in San Francisco and Sacramento. In late October residents of You Bet, Red Dog, and Little York heard Brannan crusade for the Union at "a grand mass meeting and torchlight procession."[38]

As the Civil War drew to its close, news reached California of the fall of the key Confederate strongholds at Charleston and Wilmington. Samuel Brannan sponsored a wild celebration that shattered glass throughout San Francisco.[39] Unfortunately the news turned out to be premature, and Brannan had to pay for damages.

GENEROUS TO AN EXTRAVAGANT DEGREE

As much as for sharp practice, Brannan was known for his philanthropy. "Without fear of contradiction," wrote his old friend, William Heath Davis, "I may say that Samuel Brannan was one of the most public-spirited men in San Francisco and that his hand and heart in the early days were in every enterprise for the promotion of education and the general prosperity of the state of his adoption."[40]

Bret Harte edited and published the first collection of California poems, *Outcroppings*, in time for Christmas of 1865—and then wrote an anonymous editorial saying that the West had yet to produce a first-rate poet. Harte's critics charged that *Outcroppings* slighted the "he-men among Pacific Coast poets" in favor of "slight effeminate fellows who had never toted a gun." A "mob of poets, consisting of 1100 persons of various ages and colors, and of both sexes," besieged the publisher's book store, while "three or four hundred more" descended the Sacramento River in a "fine phrensy." The volume drew especially bad reviews from the Comstock, where it was derided as a "feeble collection of drivel" and "hog-wash ladled from a slop bucket."[41]

---

[38]*Sacramento Union*, 22 October 1864 and 1 September 1864, in Barker, "When Sam Brannan Stumped for President Lincoln."   [39]*Alta California*, 26 February 1865, 1/2.

[40]Davis, *Seventy-five Years in California* (1967), 167.

[41]Walker, *San Francisco's Literary Frontier*, 214–16.

Perhaps to deflect the sarcasm of local literary elite (including *Golden Era* columnist Charles Henry Webb, who once called him "a thing of booty and a bore forever"), Brannan jumped into the controversy with an offer to sponsor a "genuine collection" of western poetry.[42] Harte's friends in the literati greeted the proposal with hoots of derision. Undeterred, Brannan arranged for May Wentworth to edit and H. H. Bancroft to publish *The Poetry of the Pacific* with the avowed purpose of answering the "vexed question of who are the California poets, or whether we have any poets, by giving everyone a fair chance to show up his Pegasus." The book appeared early in 1866, "its financial solvency assured, for Sam Brannan gave it liberal support, although he probably never got around to reading the poems." The book was "mediocre in quality and repetitious in theme," most notable for the poets' failure to use the American West as either subject or setting for their poetry.[43]

Although he was a generous contributor to charities such as the San Francisco Musical Fund Society, Brannan had a hard time earning the respect of artists. Louis Moreau Gottschalk left a comical account of his interview with "one of the Croesuses of San Francisco, whose fortune, it is said, is incalculable." The pianist was unimpressed with the uncultured Brannan, who greeted him slouched in his office chair, "amourously caressing the big toe of his bare foot with the index finger and thumb of his right hand." "Gottschalk! Gottschalk!" drawled Brannan, "without letting go his big toe. 'I know that name. Ain't you one of them opera singers? What do you sing, bass or tenor?'" The experience convinced Gottschalk that both California and Brannan were hopelessly barbarous. "He has," the musician noted, "renounced the doctrine of polygamy, but he drinks a great deal."[44]

Not all of Brannan's patronage of the arts went so unappreciated. In 1855 he subscribed a benefit to help musician Stephan C. Massett recover from a "recent financial disaster." The concert at the Metropolitan Theatre was a great success and enabled Massett to launch a concert tour.[45] On the thirtieth anniversary of his arrival in California, the San

---

[42]Ibid., 134. Walker credited Webb's "Things" column in the *Golden Era* as the source of this famous pun.

[43]Ibid., 217–19.   [44]Gottschalk, *Notes of a Pianist*, 297–98.

[45]Shumate, *The California of George Gordon*, 139.

Francisco Musical Fund Society saluted its long-time patron. The orchestra played some thirty-five pieces, beginning with the "Sam Brannan March." Speakers praised Brannan as "benevolent and generous to an extravagant degree," and did not mention his scandalous connection with Mormonism. Judge Hall urged the crowd to "drink heartily" and "raise a rousing cheer for our honored guest," and they responded with three cheers and a "tiger." The old pioneer himself recalled that when "he sailed from New York he had a faint idea that somewhere in the mysterious West there was a port called Yerba Buena. Exactly where it was he did not know."[46]

THE CALISTOGA OF SARIFORNIA

In April 1847 the *California Star* marveled at Napa Valley farmer George Yount's fourteen-inch radish and his one hundred peach trees. The place took center stage in Brannan's dreams when he fell in love with Napa Valley and pondered the commercial possibilities of its hot springs. Brannan may have visited Napa in 1852 with James S. Estell, a comrade on the Hawaiian expedition. He began seriously acquiring real estate in 1857 from the old Rancho Carne Humana.[47] Here, for the first time, Brannan's extravagance outran his fortune.

Legend has it that too much brandy fueled Brannan's speech at the dedication of his resort, and he proclaimed, "This will be the Calistoga of Sarifornia!"—a garbled reference to the famous New York spa, and a confused echo of Brannan's slogan for his new watering place: "the Saratoga of the Pacific."[48] The story of how Calistoga got its name was once so famous that H. H. Bancroft, pondering the origins of the word

---

[46]"Samuel Brannan: Celebrating the Thirtieth Anniversary of His Arrival on this Coast," *Alta California*, 1 August 1876, 1/1.

[47]Abstract of Titles of John McFarling, copy from Carolyn McDonald in possession of the editor. The first deed in the abstract is a transfer from "Martha H. Ritchie (widow of A. A. Ritchie, deceased,) to Samuel Brannan," dated 6 April 1857. A second deed book at the Sharpsteen Museum in Calistoga confirms the April 1857 date.

[48]There are differing accounts of the origin of the name. "The name of Calistoga was given to the place in the fall of 1867, by Mr. Brannan . . . he just spliced the names [Saratoga and California] and called it Cal(is)toga, the middle syllable being inserted for euphony." See Palmer, *History of Napa and Lake Counties, California*, 329. Robert Louis Stevenson wrote that the name "was invented at a supper-party by the man who found the springs." See Stevenson, *The Silverado Squatters*, 206.

California, wondered what "brilliant etymological theories might be drawn out by the name Calistoga, if it were not known how Samuel Brannan built the word from California and Saratoga."[49]

Brannan ultimately purchased a square mile of property from the Fowler and Hargrave families, creating an empire of two thousand acres for his Calistoga Hot Springs Resort. "Mr. Brannan has spared no efforts to make the whole upper part of the country prosperous," and he poured not less than half a million or as much as five million dollars into improving the place. Brannan estimated he spent "about $200,000" developing the resort, which included a telegraph office, "a large hotel, a swimming pool, a bath-house, a skating-rink, a dance pavilion, a nice fish pond, a grotto which represented a Druidical temple and other buildings also."[50] In 1859 Brannan built a large stable and carriage barn on today's Grant Avenue. He called the small hill above the resort Mt. Lincoln and gave Indian words and the names of Republican presidents to the resort's streets, along which Brannan built some twenty cottages that had palm and fir trees planted in front of them. For his family, he created a country-style "Mansion House" at the foot of Mt. Lincoln.

When his brother returned to San Francisco from Europe in the fall of 1858, John Brannan wrote that he "brot some sheep with him."[51] At "immense expense," Brannan ultimately imported "nearly a thousand head of invaluable French and Spanish merino sheep."[52] The animals did not win Brannan friends among his Napa Valley neighbors, since he let them run at large. The sheep ruined pastures, and when local farmers objected, Brannan "shrugged his shoulders and said, 'Build yourselves some fences.'" The locals "got together one night and drove the sheep over a cliff and the band was exterminated. Mr. Brannan never did anything about it."[53]

Brannan "spared no expense or pains in improving and beautifying" Calistoga. The dynamic entrepreneur worked relentlessly to make his

[49]Bancroft, *History of California*, 1:67.

[50]Adams, *Memoirs and Anecdotes of Early Calistoga*, 14. For Brannan's estimate, which perhaps dropped a zero, see the Bancroft dictation, "The Hon. Samuel Brannan," in Chapter 1.

[51]John Brannan to Mary F. Brannan, 16 September 1858, John Brannan Papers.

[52]"Letter from Calistoga," *Alta California*, 11 May 1868, 1/5.

[53]Adams, *Memoirs and Anecdotes of Early Calistoga*, 12–13.

BRANNAN'S CALISTOGA RESORT ABOUT 1865.
Courtesy, I. C. Adams Collection, Sharpsteen Museum Assoc.

"magnificent tract of land, embracing 2,200 acres of valley and 800 acres of hill land" profitable. As a "man of liberal ideas and cultivated taste," Brannan imported Japanese gardeners to tend a tea plantation and kept "a large band of horses, some seven or eight hundred in number, the most of them American stock, and among them many animals of superior blood." He built "an immense distillery, for making brandy from grapes," that in 1869 consumed some 2,500 tons of grapes, paying "$25 per ton for the ordinary California variety" from which "some 90,000 gallons of brandy will be made." Brannan hired Donner party survivor Louis Keseberg as "manager of the works, being an adept at the business." Although most of his other Napa Valley enterprises floundered, the wine industry he helped establish continues to enrich "the vintagers throughout the entire section of the country."[54]

[54]"Calistoga and Its Surroundings," *Alta California*, 3 November 1869, 1/5.

In its heyday, Brannan's resort entertained San Francisco journalists in addition to the wealthy and powerful. One of their reports vividly evokes the place, providing a tour of the resort. It was probably written by Frederick Marriott, an 1850 California pioneer and editor of both the *San Francisco Newsletter* and the *Mail Bag*, which was allied with Central Pacific Railroad interests in promoting California to an American public reluctant to pay the high cost of riding the recently completed transcontinental railroad.[55]

"CALISTOGA."

CALIFORNIA MAIL BAG, JUNE 1871, 19–20.

CALIFORNIA STATE LIBRARY.

Every season we have longed to go to Calistoga, and eventually our longing has been satisfied. It is so easy to go there: *New World* steamer at four o'clock, with a bright hour and a half's sail to Vallejo, and two hours' rail and we are at the gates of the Springs . . . Five or six years ago a plain of some hundred acres in area, walled in by pine-clad mountains, dotted with wooded knolls and teeming with hot springs of various medicinal qualities, was enclosed by Mr. Brannan for the purpose of laying it out with proper walks and baths and building a hotel for the accommodation of visitors. To-day you pass under an archway and sweep up to the covered entrance in front of the hotel, or rather that portion of the intended structure already finished. The grounds proper, apportioned to the hotel and baths, embrace about a hundred acres, and with the exception of Mounts Washington and Lincoln, are perfectly level. A carriage-drive sweeps the outer boundaries of this oblong part, and an inner circle is surrounded by some of the neatest and prettiest cottages imaginable. To us they appear the most attractive portion of the establishment. Fancy a *cottage ornée* with deep balcony, a sitting-room extending along the front and three bedrooms in the rear. Every one of these cottages is precisely alike—so alike indeed that they might have been made from the same mold. Each has a date palm and fir tree in front of it, and attached to each is a summer-house with small table and other convenience—the *fac simile* of its neighbor. There can be no bickerings or jealousy among the guests, for there is no difference even in the chairs, the only inconvenience that might arise would be that some belated or bemused visitor might find it difficult to decide which was his own domicile. Each house has either a classical, historical or local name, such as Neptune, Ralston or St. Helena, and they are very pretty, very clean, and very comfortable. Apropos of St. Helena, the great hill looks down upon the

---

[55]For other contemporary accounts of Calistoga, see *Pacific Mining Journal*, 6 August 1864; and *Alta California*, 20 September 1866, 1/5.

Springs in cold grandeur. The hotel grounds are well laid out with ornamental shrubs and shade trees. These require time, but in a few years will add much to the beauty of the place. At the east end of the inner or home circle, adjoining the large swimming bath, a spacious skating rink has been finished. The floor is as smooth as a billiard-table; and the hall will do admirably for a ball-room, or in case of necessity as a dormitory when the Springs are over-crowded. It is intended to paint the walls of the rink with frescoes representing scenes from the Arctic regions, or sleighing in Siberia, etc. This building will be a great feature of the Springs. Of the springs themselves we could write columns, for their names are legion and they run about every where asking you to test their medicinal virtues. Immediately in front of the hotel is an arbor, with a tank of cold water containing goldfish. Immediately by its side is an artesian well, the water of which is 175 degrees, where eggs are boiled in three minutes . . . In front of the hotel is a grotto composed entirely of fragments of the petrified forest in the neighborhood. The forest is about five miles from the springs, and is one of the many wonders of Calistoga . . . We could say even more about Calistoga, about Mr. Badlam, who has created such order and beauty out of chaos and brought Art to adorn Nature; we might expatiate on the Geysers which are close by, . . . on the White Sulphur Springs, the native wines, Mr. Brannan's model farm, merino sheep and agricultural school, but we are not writing a guide book, only a just tribute to a very pleasant few days spent at the Springs, and we leave it to visitors to find the health and pleasure we experienced there. Of one thing travellers may rest assured; they will find the kindest attention and information from the genial captain of the *New World*, and every facility of transport at the hands of the General Superintendent of the C.P.R.R.

Brannan narrowly escaped death in a gun fight at Calistoga in April 1868. He arrived one evening, apparently drunk, and led several men to his sawmill, whose tenants were contesting their eviction. At Brannan's approach, someone called, "Give it to the son-of-a-bitch!" Firing began suddenly with "two or three shots" and ended with a fusillade of thirty rounds from shotguns and revolvers. Brannan retreated, cried "I am shot," and collapsed. His companions dragged his unconscious body to the roadside as he bled profusely from eight wounds. The most serious damaged his trachea and esophagus, while one bullet "passed obliquely through his right arm about four inches above the elbow." Another struck "close down to the hip, passed from the rear and right to the left of the spine."[56] Brannan's embittered neighbor, John Morris, recalled:

---

[56]"The Shooting Affray at Calistoga," *Alta California*, 26 April 1868, 1/1.

They put seven bullet holes through the old Emissary and any one it were said was sufficient to kill any Ordinary man. The best Surgeon in SF was sent for and stopped eight or ten days charging Brannan One Thousand Dollars per day it was said. On being asked his Opinion, He replied 'Well if it was any other man but Sam Brannan I know it would kill him. But I don't think anything will kill Sam Brannan.'"[57]

After "a tedious and critical sickness, during which his life was more than once despaired of," Brannan was "pronounced out of danger, although some balls from the cowardly fusillade are still lodged in his body." By May Brannan was "busily engaged in his mulberry nursery and vineyard, directing his numerous workmen, and looking like anything but a candidate for the graveyard, although considerably reduced by loss of blood."[58]

Brannan's railroad interests should have insured his fortune forever. He built California's second railroad from Sacramento to Folsom, and in 1864 he invested $20,000 in the Central Pacific Railroad, which gave him fifty more shares in the transcontinental railroad than each of the notorious Big Four. Brannan later claimed, "I helped [Leland Stanford] when he commenced the Central Pacific. Every one knows he would not have built it only for my help."[59] Always adept at harnessing politics to his economic interests, Brannan persuaded the California legislature to authorize Napa County to issue $225,000 in bonds to finance a railroad to his resort, a plan that the electorate narrowly endorsed in May 1864. The Napa Valley Railroad was organized with the legislator who introduced the bill, Chancellor Hartson, as president, Brannan as treasurer, and his nephew Alexander Badlam, Jr., as secretary. By January 1865, four and a half miles of track had been laid from the bay north to Napa City. Rolling stock consisting of two cars and a pony engine were imported from England, and Brannan purchased the locomotive "Napa City" for $9,000. Brannan and Badlam put together a shady scheme to fund the extension of the road to Calistoga, but their proposal to have all of the 1864 bonds donated to the railroad was defeated by two votes. The railroad refused to release the initial bonds and the issue—like many of Brannan's enterprises—wound up

[57]Morris, Autobiography and Diaries, 1885–1906, Bancroft Library, 73.
[58]"Letter from Calistoga," Alta California, 11 May 1868, 1/5.
[59]Brannan to Little, 6 March 1885, Folder 2, BYU Brannan Papers.

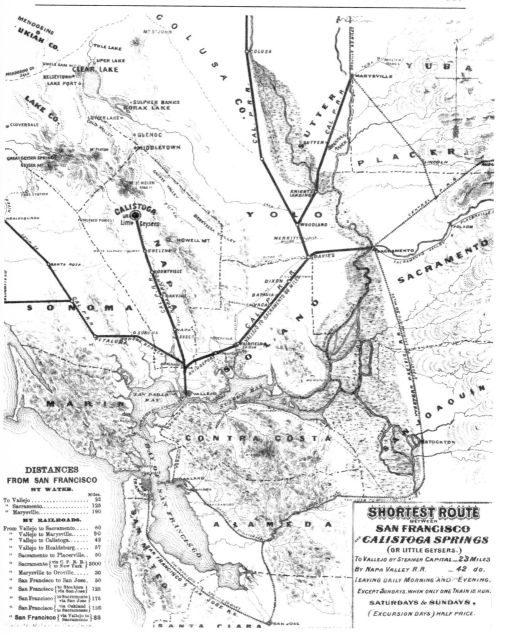

BRANNAN COUNTRY, 1871.
This map from the *Hand Book of Calistoga Springs* shows the "shortest route"
to Calistoga Springs. Note Brannan's Ranch south of Marysville.
Image courtesy of Brandon R. McArthur, Digital Lab, Harold B. Lee Library, Brigham Young University.

in court. The California Supreme Court found in his favor, and by August 1868 Patterson & Gray had laid more than twenty-six miles of track to connect Calistoga with Napa. A later generation considered the railroad "of the greatest ultimate benefit to the valley," but at the time it was regarded as "a gigantic 'steal,' engineered by that prince of scheme and adventure, the famous Sam Brannan." When the railroad was finished, an excursion train "brought three thousand people into the place, and Mr. Brannan tendered the visitors a grand reception."[60] The triumph was short-lived. Although it was popular, Brannan's resort was too small to finance his extravagance and did not generate the land boom he had anticipated. The Napa Valley Railroad failed to meet the interest on its construction loans and was sold at foreclosure to contractors.[61] The line, "which the county paid for but does not own," was ultimately absorbed into the Southern Pacific system.[62]

Brannan tried to salvage his Calistoga interests in 1872 with the help of Alex Badlam, Jr. They organized the Calistoga Water Company and established the Calistoga Hotel Company to manage the Calistoga Springs Hotel.[63] Their efforts came to naught, and as his fortune collapsed, Brannan was forced to sell his resort. This undated advertisement, posted at the Sharpsteen Museum in Calistoga, provides an accurate description of Brannan's shattered dream.

FOR SALE! CALISTOGA HOT SULPHUR SPRINGS. FOR SALE!

The property consists of 600 acres of highly improved fertile land. It includes the Hot Sulphur Springs, with swimming and private baths; the Hotel and it's [sic] numerous cottages—37 buildings in all—and 900 village lots, unsold; two large uncovered water reservoirs; a good steam mill site; a fully equipped distillery and refinery; with a cooper shop annexed; 40 acres of bearing grape vines. There is a race course, and several miles of carriage drives.

About 1,400 acres of rich adjacent lands can also be bought, with two orchards, a vineyard, and 9,000 mulberry trees of choice variety, adapted to silk culture. The price of the estates will be quite moderate.

Leland Stanford purchased the property, briefly considering it as the location for a university, but the resort languished under bad management.

[60]Palmer, *History of Napa and Lake Counties, California*, 329.
[61]"Napa Valley Railroad," in Neelands, *About Sam Brannan*, 4–5.
[62]Anonymous, *Memorial and Biographical History of Northern California*, 166.
[63]Menefee, *A Historical and Descriptive Sketch Book of Napa, Sonoma, Lake and Mendocino*, 109, 111.

In its decline, Calistoga attracted the honeymooning Robert Louis Stevenson, who described the "system of little five-roomed cottages, each with a
veranda and weedy palm before the door."[64] By the turn of the century
even the ruins of Brannan's resort had disappeared, but today visitors can
again take the waters at the site of his Hot Springs Hotel.

THE DESTRUCTION OF HIS PROPERTY

For all his erratic business practices, Brannan might well have died
rich had not his wife insisted that he provide a cash divorce settlement
instead of merely dividing their property. The liquidation of Brannan's
empire in the dismal financial conditions that existed in California in
1870 proved disastrous for both parties, but any Gilded Age tycoon
would have been hard pressed to convert a paper fortune into hard
money. Mrs. Brannan later proved unable to invest her settlement safely.
   Alleging that her husband was "addicted to open and notorious
intemperance," Ann Eliza Brannan brought suit on 18 May 1870 for a
divorce that was granted without contest on 11 November. A supplemental decree—apparently necessitated by some questionable property
transfers and 45,000 gallons of brandy worth $101,250 found on the
docks in New York, which had been overlooked in the original settlement—itemized an astonishing fortune, including two hundred shares
of Central Pacific Railroad stock, $134,000 in Pacific Bank stock, and
vast properties in Sacramento, San Francisco, and Calistoga.[65] Early on
Brannan had filed an affidavit that minimized his wealth but painted an
accurate picture of the precarious nature of his fortune.

"LAW INTELLIGENCE,"
ALTA CALIFORNIA, 10 JUNE 1870, 2/3.

Thursday, June 9th, 1870.
Fourth District Court—Morrison, J.
   Ann Liza Brannan vs. Samuel Brannan—The defendant in this case has
filed an affidavit in which he declares "that the whole amount of the alleged
property of defendant is worth six hundred thousand dollars; that his

---

[64]Stevenson, *The Silverado Squatters*, 208. Stevenson visited the resort in 1880.
   [65]Stellman, *Sam Brannan*, 198; and Copy of Supplemental Decree, District Court, Fourth Judicial
District, San Francisco, Calif., in Book C, Miscellaneous Records, Napa County, 223, copy in possession of the editor. Other original records were destroyed in the San Francisco earthquake of 1906.

income amounts to the sum of five thousand dollars per month, or there-abouts; that his indebtedness amounts to over four hundred thousand dol-lars, the greater part of which is secured by mortgages upon his real estate, and his said income is absorbed in the payment of the interest thereon; that the moneys which he has supplied to the plaintiff for her support were obtained from his business profits in outside operations, or by borrowing; that if the injunction prayed for by the plaintiff should be granted, it would cause a total cessation of his business and the destruction of his property, and his whole estate would be involved in ruin, as his creditors would enforce the payment of their respective claims, many of which are now due, but which they are willing to delay; and deponent would be deprived of all means for his own support or that of the plaintiff. That the said mortgage would necessarily be at once foreclosed, and in that event the said property would sell for little, if anything, more than the amount of indebtedness thereon at the present value of real and personal estate, which, owing to the depressed condition of business and trade, are very low. That in all proba-bility, the result of such a course would be to throw deponent into bank-ruptcy which would swallow up his whole estate."

On this affidavit, the defendant's attorneys moved to dissolve or vacate, or otherwise modify the injunction heretofore issued in this case, to prevent him from disposing of his property, and for such other relief as may be just.

Judge Morrison has issued an order, fixing this day for hearing the motion, and that until the further order of the Court, said injunction be so modified as to allow [the] defendant to so use the said alleged common property to carry on his ordinary business operations therewith.

Shortly after filing this affidavit, Brannan initiated a lawsuit against the Central Pacific Railroad, charging that the Big Four had never paid for the stock issued to them.[66] The charge was true, and Edwin Bosqui, who printed "a voluminous brief in the case," recalled that the suit was settled out of court, with Brannan receiving $250,000, one-fifth of which went to his lawyer.[67] Like the rest of Brannan's wealth, this money vanished. The divorce settlement forced him to sell his railroad stock when it was worth only a fraction of its ultimate value.

Brannan's fortunes had sunk so low by 1875 that he ran for Congress on a platform that was pro-labor and anti-Chinese. Nothing does Samuel Brannan less credit than his racism, but ironically Brannan's overall record on racial issues had many bright spots. He had been a committed aboli-tionist and after the Civil War outfitted a militia unit, the Brannan Guard,

---

[66]"Suit Against the Central Pacific Railroad Company," *Sacramento Union*, 4 July 1870, 1/2–7.
[67]Holmes, ed., *Memoirs of Edward Bosqui*, 48–49.

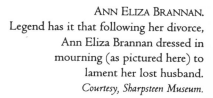

ANN ELIZA BRANNAN.
Legend has it that following her divorce,
Ann Eliza Brannan dressed in
mourning (as pictured here) to
lament her lost husband.
Courtesy, Sharpsteen Museum.

"the first successful military organization of Blacks in San Francisco."[68] Despite his good works on the part of African-Americans, he shared the general prejudices of his time, including anti-Semitism. His racism was curiously selective—he always had good relations with California's Chicanos and even married a Mexican woman, but he declared "in favor of the people rising en masse and declaring that no more Chinese shall come to these shores." His hatred of Asians was particularly vicious, and he proposed that if the fight to end Chinese immigration "was not made now in the ballot box, it would some time have to be made with the bayonet."[69] His belief that the Chinese controlled California's economy was absurd, but such bigotry was a driving force in the state's politics for decades.

ZION'S PRODIGAL SON

The *Salt Lake Daily Tribune* shared Brannan's anti-Mormon sentiments in the 1870s, but his old connection to the LDS church meant he could not escape being ridiculed in its pages.

---

[68]The unit existed from 1866 to 1874 and in 1869 had forty-five members. See Parker and Abajian, *A Walking Tour of the Black Presence in San Francisco*, 1.

[69]"Citizens' Independent Nominating Convention," *Alta California*, 11 August 1875, 1/3.

"SAMUEL BRANNAN,"
SALT LAKE DAILY TRIBUNE, 24 MARCH 1877, 4/2.

A few days ago THE TRIBUNE correspondent saw on the streets one of early Zion's prodigal son's, Sam Brannan. More than twenty years ago he was a full-fledged, orthodox Saint, enjoying the full confidence of Brother Brigham, respected by the Church brethren and feasted and courted by the polygamous sisters. For Samuel was a sly old boy, and lusted after the fair maidens, matrons, or even widows of Zion. San Francisco was the base of supplies for Utah in everything except women—they were imported from the regions where they were more verdant. In an over confiding hour Brother Brigham entrusted Brother Brannan with $50,000, with which to come to San Francisco and purchase provisions, farming implements, grain, blue-grass whiskey, etc., for the Saints. He came; but he fell from grace and never returned—neither did he return that $50,000, but invested it in corner lots and outside lands. Whereat Brother Brigham waxed wroth exceedingly, exalted his horn, and cried aloud in the wilderness of Zion against the perverse generation of Brannans, in general, and especially Samuel. But Samuel grew fat in the land of Gomorrah, and in the hours of his prosperity became filled with the spirit—not of the Holy Ghost, but the spirits of Bourbon. Since he quit worshipping at the foot of Brigham and Belial, he has fallen down and worshipped at the shrine of Bacchus with more than ordinary zeal. This incompatabilty [*sic*] of temperament drove his wife to institute a suit for divorce. She got it, and an equal division of property, amounting to $200,000 or $300,000, followed, whereas Samuel waxed wroth. But Gentile Judges and courts have a way of making heartless husbands provide for their mistreated wives, and not let them adopt the Mormon plan of sending their wives adrift in poverty and old age, after the fashion of turning out an old and useless horse, to starve and die. Samuel now seeks consolation by looking upon the wine when it is red—or otherwise.

Brannan had now hit bottom. By 1877 his farms and commercial properties were gone and his Calistoga wounds still pained him. He became a "penniless drunkard . . . finally reduced to sleeping in back rooms of saloons."[70] It was said that men who owed their start in business to Brannan crossed the street rather than meet him. Artist Charles Robinson recalled that Brannan visited his studio "one cold rainy day, wet, bedraggled and under the influence of liquor. His clothes were threadbare and his shoes torn. He wept as they talked together of the old happy days."[71] Samuel Brannan was down, but he was not yet out.

---

[70]Scott, *Samuel Brannan and the Golden Fleece*, 428; and Bailey, *Sam Brannan and the California Mormons*, 228.
[71]Jacobsen, "California's First Millionaire," *San Francisco Bulletin*, 20 May 1916.

Chapter 13

"An Empire of Our Own"

Despite the loss of his reputation and the collapse of his fortune in the 1870s, Brannan remained confidant that he could rise again from the ruins. His campaign to regain his riches during the last decade of his life generated a flood of correspondence that ended the thirty-year gap in his papers. His letters to family members and his old Mormon colleague Jesse C. Little could fill a volume of their own, but the complete reproduction of this correspondence would be tedious and, at best, only marginally useful. The picture these letters paint of Brannan's last years is depressing and pathetic. This volume summarizes the material to sketch Samuel Brannan's last days, focusing on the comments related to Mormonism.

Brannan's hopes to revive his fortune centered on a loan to the Mexican government made in 1865 to support Benito Juarez' war with Maximilian. Brannan invested some $30,000 in gold to prepare ten million dollars in bonds for sale. When the bonds appeared in August 1865, their sponsor, General Gaspar Sanchez Ochoa, found that no one would buy securities from a government with poor prospects of surviving long enough to redeem them. To protect his investment, Brannan negotiated an agreement "hypothecating the entire issue of ten million dollars as a guarantee for the thirty thousand in gold." Brannan took possession of the bonds "with the understanding that if the debt were not paid in sixty days he might do with them as he saw fit." Ochoa and Brannan sent an agent to New York to sell the bonds, but the Mexican government already had a parallel fund-raising effort underway in the city. The affair became hopelessly complicated when John C. Frémont joined in, hoping to secure rights to build a railroad through Sonora. In November the Mexican government learned that Brannan intended to foreclose his mortgage and auction the bonds in New York. Brannan did not foreclose, but hired Peter Burnett, his old partner in the Sutter land deals, "to care for his interests."[1] Burnett offered to return the bonds if Brannan's initial investment—with interest worth some $57,508 by May 1867—was paid back. Desperately poor, the Mexican government paid $8,447 to redeem three-twentieths of the bonds. Over the years the payments continued, but in 1878 the Mexican government reported that Brannan still held bonds worth $500,000.[2] This debt formed the basis for Brannan's subsequent land grants.

Besides these bond transactions, Brannan subsidized the American Legion of Honor, a company that was popularly known as the Brannan contingent or brigade. He supplied the outfit with uniforms, horses, wagons, sabers, Henry rifles, Colt pistols, ammunition, and medical supplies.[3] He filed a bill of $19,376 in 1876 for his "services and pecuniary advances as a recruiting agent in California," but the claim was dismissed.[4] Brannan solicited payment of $16,695.87 from the Mexican government in September 1880 for "the expenses attending the organization of a Co[mpany] of 25 men with the respective officers armed and provisioned by you with all necessary [equipment] to make the Campaign in 1865 fighting against the French intervention." The government rejected this claim, too, noting that Brannan's witnesses, Harvey Lake and Alexander Badlam, were his employees, and that Lake, captain of the company, had already accepted $3,000 for his services.[5]

Bad faith corrupted Brannan's dealings with Mexico. His support for her struggle against European empire-building was perhaps a selfless act of patriotism, but Brannan ruthlessly exploited the Mexican government—and his dealings in Sonora were duplicitous from the start. He courted the regime with promises to develop his land grant, but privately he reverted to his worst filibustering traditions, plotting to annex Sonora to the United States. Ultimately Brannan would spend years enmeshed in his scheme to colonize and conquer Sonora.

---

[1]Frazer, "The Ochoa Bond Negotiations of 1865–1867," 398–400, 412.

[2]Luce, "Samuel Brannan: Speculator in Mexican Lands," 40.

[3]Miller, "The American Legion of Honor in Mexico," 233.

[4]Frazer, "The Ochoa Bond Negotiations of 1865–1867," 398–400; and Luce, "Samuel Brannan: Speculator in Mexican Lands," 35, 40–41.

[5]Secretary of State for War and Navy, Mexico, to Brannan, 28 October 1880, Typescript, Sorensen Papers.

Indomitable Perseverance and Yankee Pluck

Brannan spent the fall of 1879 in New York promoting his Sonoran land project, staying at the Astor, one of the city's best hotels. He founded four companies, beginning with the Sonoran Colonization Association of California in 1879. He launched its New York counterpart a year later, with his old friend Edward Kemble as president.[6] Brannan formed the Hidalgo City Company in 1880 to promote establishing a city at the confluence of the Yaqui and Verde rivers, and in 1881 he started the Sonora Land and Mining Company and Colonization Association, which would survive until at least 1900.[7]

Kemble was not the only old ally Brannan recruited. Manuel Castro, commander of Mexican forces in California before the Bear Flag Revolt, accompanied Brannan to Mexico in 1881 and provided key political support to secure his grants. The following letter to Castro and newspaper article provide insight into Brannan's operations.

BRANNAN TO MANUEL CASTRO, 6 SEPTEMBER 1879,
TYPESCRIPT, JOHN HOWELL COLLECTION, BANCROFT LIBRARY.

ASTOR HOUSE

Broadway and Vasey Street
New York, Sept. 6th, 1879

Friend Castro

I wrote to you on the 3rd—Since then every thing has gon[e] all well, I am in possession of the Bonds—$13,000 principal and interest—Will have every thing arranged so as to leave here by the fore part of next month. Send on your business as soon as possible—I will remain here a week longer if you should come on and make a visit. You will be delighted with [the] trip.—Plenty of People here wish to join the association for Senora.

I wish you would see [the] man that keeps the Comstock Exchange No 28 Leidesdorff [Street] between California and Pine street [in San Francisco] and tell him I forgot to pay him before I left but will settle on my return, also 350 that I did not pay Mr. [John] Ricketson for making the copy of the constitution and names to the same. Get all the signatures to our Coloney you can. I have written to Virginia City [to] push up their roll

---

[6]Kemble probably wrote the association's ambitious 1880 prospectus, "Sonora Colonization Enterprise: Its History, Objects and Plans Explained." See the copy in Folder 15, BYU Brannan Papers.

[7]Bringhurst, "Samuel Brannan and His Forgotten Final Years," 149; and Luce, "Samuel Brannan: Speculator in Mexican Lands," 117–18.

as fast as possible—we cannot have too many, and the time now is growing short and every one should do his best to increase the roll.

Remember me to all

Yours truly

S. Brannan.

"BRANNAN'S BONANZA,"

NEW YORK TIMES, 3 FEBRUARY 1880, 8/2.

A YANKEE'S PAY FOR AIDING THE FUGITIVE, JUAREZ, IN MEXICO.

A chattel mortgage was recently recorded in the Register's office in this City, given by Gen. Ochos Sanchez, individually and as agent for the Republic of Mexico, to Samuel Brannan, of San Francisco. The instrument was made in September, 1865, in consideration of a loan of 43,478 [and] 26 cents, and is a lien upon $10,000,000 of bonds of the Government of Mexico, which, it is stated, are deposited in the Bank of Commerce.

The San Francisco Call of Jan. 24 throws the following light on this transaction, which it calls "Brannan's Bonanza:"

"When Maximilian landed at Vera Cruz, in May, 1864, he found the Royalist party in possession of the Government, the Republican troops were scattered, and Juarez and his immediate followers were fugitives. In the following Spring, Samuel Brannan was a passenger on one of the Pacific Mail steamers, on his way from Panama to this city. At one of the Central American ports Gen. Juarez, with Ochoa and several other officers of the Republican Party, came on board of the steamer on their way to the Gulf States, at one of the ports of which they were landed. It was in Northern Mexico that Juarez gathered about him a handful of followers, which was gradually augmented, until the army was formed which succeeded in overpowering the imperial forces, and captured and shot the Emperor Maximilian two years afterwards. While on the steamer, Brannan made the acquaintance of Juarez, and a friendship sprang up between them. Brannan was in possession of considerable ready capital at that time, and having become an enthusiastic supporter of the Republican cause, offered to aid it with money and men, relying upon the future success of the movement to be reimbursed. This financial support was doubly welcome to Juarez in this hour of his failing fortunes, and he accepted the proffered assistance with alacrity. Immediately upon his arrival here Brannan sent a sum of ready money to Juarez, and set about raising a company of men to go to his support. Soon afterward Gen. Gaspar Sanchez Ochoa arrived in this city, and arrangements were perfected by which a detachment of men and a supply of arms were soon afterward dispatched to Juarez. They succeeded in joining him and aided materially in his future success. It is not believed by friends of Brannan in this City, that any funds were given him at this time, but the

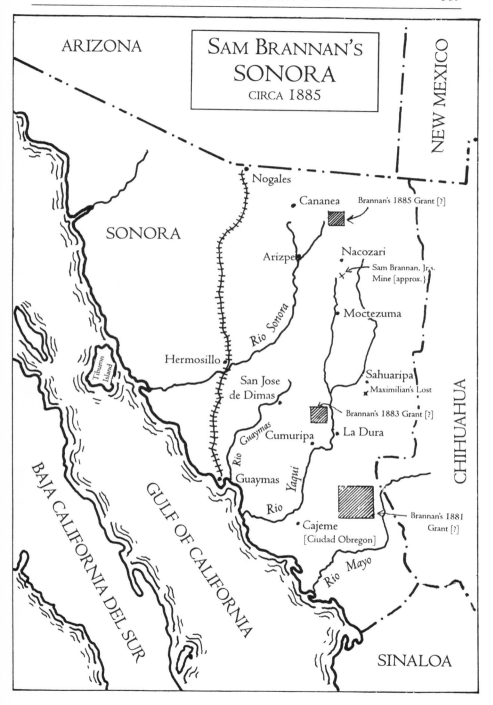

SAM BRANNAN'S
SONORA
CIRCA 1885

ARIZONA

NEW MEXICO

Nogales

Cananea   Brannan's 1885 Grant [?]

SONORA

Arizpe   Nacozari
                        Sam Brannan, Jr.'s.
                        Mine [approx.]

Rio Sonora

Moctezuma

Tiburon Island

Hermosillo

San Jose
de Dimas   Sahuaripa
                        × Maximilian's Lost

                        Brannan's 1883 Grant [?]

Guaymas   Cumuripa   La Dura

Rio

Yaqui

BAJA CALIFORNIA DEL SUR

GULF OF CALIFORNIA

Guaymas

Rio   Brannan's 1881
                                     Grant [?]

Cajeme
[Ciudad Obregon]

Rio Mayo

CHIHUAHUA

SINALOA

Republic always recognized the justice of his claim, and promised pecuniary reimbursement. The well-known want of funds, which is a characteristic of the Mexican Treasury, has, however, up to this time, not resulted to the financial benefit of Brannan. When that gentleman left here several months ago, he visited the City of Mexico, and it is reported that the Government gave him a large grant of land, in lieu of cash."

It will be 34 years to-morrow since the same adventurous person set sail from this port with the first ship-load of emigrants that ever embarked from these shores for California. That State was then a province of Mexico, and war had not been declared by the United States. Brannan took with him a printing-press, all the improved machinery for mills and agricultural work, and a hundred muskets to arm his associates in case they were attacked, and their purpose was to settle peaceably on the shores of San Francisco Bay. San Francisco as a city or even a town, had not then an existence. It is a curious illustration of indomitable perseverance and Yankee pluck to find this same man now in this City organizing a colony to plant on the land said to have been assured for him in Sonora.

About this time Brannan contacted Jesse C. Little, his "old friend before the Mexican war, 45 years standing and never broak friend ship."[8] Little had been a prominent and loyal Latter-day Saint until the mid-1870s, when he apparently had a falling out with Brigham Young. The cause of his breach was a mystery even to Brannan, who told his friend, "I know the mormons are down on you for Something but say nothing [and] when I inquire after you they shake their head!"[9] Little further distanced himself from Mormonism when Apostle George Q. Cannon married Emily Hoagland, one of Little's former polygamous wives, who had, in total, produced thirty-two children. He told Brannan in 1886, "I am not and have not been Living in Polygamy for more than five years."[10] He commented bitterly that the LDS church was "gathering up Money

---

[8]Brannan to William A. Scott, Jr., Letter of Introduction for J. C. Little, Folder 12, BYU Brannan Papers. Jesse C. Little's granddaughter, Mrs. Franklin Walton, donated his papers to Brigham Young University in 1966. See Redding, Sr., "Historical Letters," 1. Although Little's papers form the collection, they are designated the Brannan Papers, Vault MSS 37, Special Collections, BYU Library (cited as BYU Brannan Papers). They include maps, circulars, stock certificates, newspaper articles, broadsides, and samples and summaries of Little's correspondence. W. Ray Luce's 1968 master thesis provided the first analysis of the Little-Brannan letters and remains an excellent summary, although Luce omitted some of the more provocative material

[9]Brannan to Little, 5 February 1885, Folder 2, BYU Brannan Papers. If Little explained what caused the headshaking, the letter does not survive in his papers.

[10]Little to Brannan, 1 March 1886, Folder 10, BYU Brannan Papers.

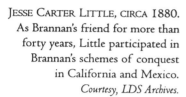

JESSE CARTER LITTLE, CIRCA 1880.
As Brannan's friend for more than
forty years, Little participated in
Brannan's schemes of conquest
in California and Mexico.
Courtesy, LDS Archives.

among the people to pay the Bonds men $45,000.00" to free Cannon, but "they would not give me 45 cents."[11] Little became Brannan's key associate in Utah, where the two hoped to recruit Mormons dissatisfied with the society Brigham Young had created.

The earliest surviving letters in the revived Brannan-Little correspondence indicate that the two men had communicated earlier and perhaps had met to discuss the Mexican land project. Brannan explained the "considerable embroilments" that surrounded his attempts to secure his Sonoran land grants.

BRANNAN TO LITTLE, 14 JUNE 1880,
FOLDER 1, BYU BRANNAN PAPERS.

Gen Agent
Mexico, June 14 1880

My Dear Friend Little
Your favor of May 24 I received last evening on my return from Pachuca the Great Mining City of Mexico. Twenty thousand inhabitants—The mail leaves for New York this evening and I have many letters to answer—so you

---

[11]Little to Brannan, 20 March 1886, Folder 10, BYU Brannan Papers. For Cannon's legal entanglements, see Bigler, *Forgotten Kingdom*, 329–30.

must excuse the brevity. Your communication in the Ogden Junction is to the point. Rifles and Belt Pistols are the best, blankets from two to five—

My affairs here are going slowly along. The Mexicans are not a fast people. Gov. clerks only work four hours a day—I have three claims that have to go through separately all the departments, I may be here three months yet—The Surveying party will be paid by me—Price will be fixed when I see you—We will have three hundred miners from Virginia City. Fifty have already gon[e] to Arizona to wait for the rear gu[a]rd, or on my return and further orders. The President is now very busy making the Contracts for the different R. Roads, and may keep me here two or three months—but I think I shall know in a Couple of weeks the time I can leave—Dont have any drones in your Command—all must be *able* bodied men—A few Boys will be useful—Hoping this will find you quite recovered. I remain your sincere friend   Saml. Brannan.

BRANNAN TO LITTLE, 27 JULY 1880,
FOLDER I, BYU BRANNAN PAPERS.

City of Mexico, July 27th 1880

My Dear Sir

From my long absence and detention here, you no doubt feel anxious to know how I am progressing and when I expect to return; all I can say at present [is] everything is progressing slowly but very satisfactorily with the prospect of closing everything up within the next six or eight weeks. There are three different claims and each one has to go through the Departments separately. All governments you must understand move slow. On my arrival here the railroad bills were before Congress with considerable embroilments. The Presidential and Congressional elections were approaching during which little or nothing could be done in the State Departments, but now those obstacles have all been removed and the election is over and my matters are progressing as well as I could wish. During its progress, if anything should take place you will be advised.

After I obtain my grant I shall apply for a railroad franchise from Hidalgo City to the Guaymas Railroad, the power to grant was confirmed upon the President by the last Congress. The Guaymas Railroad Company will afford all the assistance they can, and becomes the feeder or contributor to their road. I shall also apply for the right of establishing a gold and silver refinery at the City of Hidalgo.

Dr Ord President of the Sonora Colonization Association is now at Fort Grant, Arizona, near the line of Sonora and writes very encouraging news. He will return to San Francisco, when the land concession is made.

Yours very respectfully
Saml. Brannan

Brannan made three trips to Mexico City between 1879 and 1881. He met with President Porfirio Diaz in 1880 and spent almost a year lobbying the Mexican Congress for a land grant. The new president, Manuel Gonzales, early in 1881 granted Brannan's company some 242 square miles of land located between the Yaqui and Mayo rivers in central Sonora on the western edge of the Sierra Madre.[12] It was the homeland of determined Indians who had resisted white occupation for centuries and remains remote to this day. Brannan trumpeted his grant in a glowing broadside, but failed to describe the many conditions attached to it.[13] He had to survey the entire property, start the job within three months, and lure five hundred to a thousand settlers to the land. The grant was not issued directly to Brannan, but was assigned to Manuel Castro, who was to transfer title to the American if he met the grant's terms.[14] Brannan failed to meet the conditions and the grant reverted to the Mexican government in July 1881.[15] A Mormon paper noted the demise of the scheme and ridiculed the old apostate.

SALT LAKE DAILY HERALD, 29 JULY 1881.

SAM BRANNAN'S Sonora colonization scheme has all the appearance of drifting into a failure. At any rate it seems to be in the nature of fraud on the part of the promoter, which is not strange, when we take into consideration Brannan's past career. He is now in Guaymas, trying to settle the business of the alleged land grant, and get possession of the territory that he claims belongs to him; but he has little prospect of success. In the first place the land he says was originally allotted to him, is occupied by the Indians who are in open rebellion against the state, and if they were not they would dispute the right of anybody to dispose of their country without consulting them. But the federal court at Guaymas does not recognize Sam's claim, and has refused permission to his engineers to make surveys of the tract. It seems that the alleged grant was made without authority, and further, that had it been valid, Brannan has failed to comply with the conditions imposed, and hence forfeited whatever rights he might have acquired. The people of Sonora are madly opposed to Brannan's occupation of the claimed territory, and some of them in their newspapers, talk boldly of

---

[12]Bringhurst, "Samuel Brannan and His Forgotten Final Years," 148–49; West, *Sonora: Its Geographical Personality*, 1, 70–79

[13]"The Sonora Land and Mining Company and Colonization Association," Broadside, Folder 19, BYU Brannan Papers.

[14]Luce, "Samuel Brannan: Speculator in Mexican Lands," 51–52.

[15]Bringhurst, "Samuel Brannan and His Forgotten Final Years," 150.

employing force to keep him and his colony out, should the government acknowledge his title to the tract . . .

Sam had better return to his wallowing in San Francisco. He will find little difficulty in obtaining what whiskey he can drink during the few remaining years of his earthly sojourn, and as drunk seems to be his happiest if not his normal condition, he ought to surrender himself to this state and let big schemes and big frauds alone hereafter.

A Yaqui revolt prevented Brannan from starting the survey on time. By August the grant was "dead, without hope of resurrection. It never had any chance of being operative. It covered the valuable land that has been held by the Yaqui."[16] This report discounted the old promoter's resilience. Brannan owned a map drawn by one of Maximilian's engineers that allegedly showed the location of twenty-eight "Old gold and silver mines" that "was worked by the *old* Jesuit Padres, who were all massacreed."[17] With two companions he launched a month-long mule trip into the hills of Sonora to locate the mines. His letter to the widow of his brother John marked the start of this adventure.

BRANNAN TO MARY F. BRANNAN, 28 AUGUST 1881,
G. RALPH BAILEY COLLECTION.

Guaymas, Mexico
August 28th 1881

Mrs. Mary F. Brannan
  San Francisco
Dear Sister,

I have been here since the 1st of July, owing to floods and rains, there has been no mail and I was unable to communicate to you before. I leave in the morning for the headwaters of the Yaqui river and the Sierra Madre Mountains, some 300 miles E[ast] of here. I expect to be gone from four to five weeks. You will hear from me again on my return. The mails are now in running order. Everything is going on very satisfactorily and I hope to hear in another year that your family is well settled in Sonora.

My love and kind regards to all the family and children. My address will be Guaymas, Sonora, Mexico, c/o U.S. Consul, postage five cents. I shall be happy to hear that you are all well.

I remain, Your dear brother,
Saml. Brannan

---

[16]"Editorial Notices," *Daily Alta California*, 10 August 1881, 2/3.
[17]Brannan to Little, 26 February 1885, Folder 2, BYU Brannan Papers.

The journey revived Brannan's hopes, and as reports of his failures appeared in the newspapers, he was actually deep in Mexico's back country. A letter to John Ricketson, his business associate, marked the end of the sixty-two-year-old adventurer's month-long trek into the heart of Sonora.

"LETTER FROM SAM. BRANNAN—HIS SONORAN ENTERPRISE,"
DAILY ALTA CALIFORNIA, 11 OCTOBER 1881, 1/3.

The ALTA is permitted to publish the following from Sam. Brannan to Col. John Ricketson, Pioneer Hall, San Francisco:

COMORIPA, YAQUI RIVER, September 28th, 1881.—I arrived yesterday from Eglisia and Mullatus. I was in the saddle one month and twenty days. I will go to Guaymas on the 6th proximo. This communication is sent this morning by one of my men to the railway station. I have travelled with only two men and a guide, and I had no weapon on my person. There are worse Indians in San Francisco than in Sonora. I wish that you had been with me as a companion. The citizens of Guaymas thought we would never return. I will forward you full details of our explorations from Guaymas. Yours truly,
SAM'L. BRANNAN

There might have been "worse Indians in San Francisco," but Sonora's native peoples insured the failure of Brannan's plans. The Yaqui had been fighting white encroachment since 1553, when their resistance to a slave raid prompted a Spanish soldier to write that nowhere in the New World had he seen such bravery in battle. Juan Banderas led a revolt in 1825 that drove all the white settlers out of Yaqui and Mayo territory; in 1827 the Mexican government recognized him as captain-general of the Yaqui pueblos. Banderas was deposed and executed in 1833, but he left behind a tradition of resistance that flared up in 1857 and 1875 and was still alive when the Mexican government deeded Yaqui territory to Brannan. Under the leadership of Jose Maria Leyva, known to Brannan by his Indian name, Cajeme, "He Who Does not Drink," fourteen thousand Yaquis offered bitter resistance to white encroachment that would continue even after their defeat at Buatachive in 1886 and the execution of Cajeme in April 1887.[18] When Geronimo led a small band of Apaches into Sonora in May 1885, it helped kill whatever chances Bran-

---

[18]Spicer, Cycles of Conquest, 46, 61, 65, 67–74. Cajeme had long experience with men such as Brannan, having visited the California gold fields in 1849 with his father. See Smith, Emilio Kosterlitzky, 58.

nan's plans might have had. The old dreamer continually discounted the Indian threat to his proposed settlements, but he admitted it was "hard work to get good men to face the Apaches." Brannan finally confessed he had "given up all hopes of their being subdued."[19] He later recalled that his 1881 journey:

> nearly cost me my life. I crost the Yaqui river at Duro twice, which was highe[r] than it had been in 20 years. The map I found correct, and when I returned to Guaymas, the people would hardly believe it was me, they never expected to see me again. [They thought] I would be killed by the Apaches sure, that year they killed a great many all around me. I was gon[e] three months. I had one Mexican and one Englishman and never let them know what I went for.[20]

Romance again found Brannan in Mexico. After the failure of his first land grant, Brannan settled in the port of Guaymas, where he married the "handsome, intelligent and wealthy" widow Carmelita Carmen de Llaguno in March 1882. Writing to Alexander Badlam, Jr., Brannan expressed his affection for his new wife. He asked Badlam to purchase thick cotton socks and an ice pitcher inscribed "Carmelita B. del Brannan" for his bride. The marriage, however, received dour notice in the Mormon press.

SALT LAKE DAILY HERALD, 9 APRIL 1882, 4/2.

> SAM BRANNAN, who, as our readers are aware, has for some years been trying to get possession of an alleged land grant in Mexico with the view of settling thereon of a large American colony, has gotten possession of a handsome, intelligent, and wealthy Mexican lady, to whom he was married at Guaymas, on March 25th. If Sam is punishing as much whiskey as he used to in San Francisco, and is anything like as much of a physical wreck as he was a few years ago, marriageable men must be scarce in Mexico or else the tastes of the Castilian ladies are peculiar.

The *Napa Register* reported on 20 January 1883 that Sam Brannan "was paralyzed about one month ago on one side of his face, and is in a very precarious condition. His face is all drawn on one side, nevertheless he continues in his former style of life, and is daily seen in his old

---

[19]Brannan to Little, 31 March 1886 and 2 June 1886, Folder 5, BYU Brannan Papers.
[20]Brannan to Little, 11 February 1885, Folder 2, BYU Brannan Papers.

haunts." Brannan described the precarious state of his health to Jesse Little in March: "I was struck by paralissis at the Cathedral while listening to their music on my right side and fell to the floor and was carried home in a carriage where I have been confined to my Room for over three months. But now am able to walk out and attend to my Bussiness. I have not the use of my right arm and cannot write and have lost the hearing in my right ear."[21] This period of ill-health left Brannan despondent, and he later wrote Little that he had been "struck with the Paralesis Oct. 10th [1882] and the following Summer I had the Yellow fever, and then my agent sent me the 2nd grant and I sent him word I probably would die and I hope[d] so any how and I did not want it."[22]

A PITIABLE SPECTACLE TO BEHOLD

As federal prosecution of polygamy in Utah Territory intensified during the 1880s, LDS leaders cast about for a new refuge and sent missionaries to survey the prospects of Mexico. Inevitably they met Sam Brannan, whose connection with Mormonism proved inescapable even in Mexico. A short notice in Utah's Deseret News set off a bitter exchange between the old apostate and his former associates.

"AN INTERESTING TRIP. ANCIENT RUINS—SAM BRANNAN,"
DESERET EVENING NEWS, 27 FEBRUARY 1883, 2/2.

[Joseph Phelps and John Cozzens] took the railroad to Guaymas, on the coast of [the Gulf of] California. There they met a character known to a number of our citizens—the notorious Sam Brannan. He is partially paralyzed, in the depths of poverty, residing in a little shanty, friendless, and living in the most groveling forms of vice. When the visitors saw him he was half naked and filthy, a pitiable spectacle to behold. His great Yaqui land scheme had fallen through, and he admitted to his visitors that he did not own a foot of land. The travelers learned that the Yaqui Indians in Sonora are at deadly enmity with the Mexicans and are determined fighters. They are reported as capable of placing 10,000 fighting men on the war path inside of twenty-four hours. They are a high spirited, energetic, independent race, kind and hospitable to friends, but revengeful to those who seek to impose upon them.

---

[21]Brannan to Little, 21 March 1883, Folder 1, BYU Brannan Papers.
[22]Brannan to Little, 11 February 1885, Folder 2, BYU Brannan Papers.

The missionaries agreed with Brannan on one point—Sonora's land was "exceedingly rich." One Saint saw their report on the decrepit Brannan as confirmation of prophecy.

"PROPHESY FULFILLED,"
DESERET EVENING NEWS, 8 MARCH 1883, 3/2.

A short time since, as our readers are aware, we published an account of a visit paid to Sam Brannan, by Brothers Phelps and Cozzens, of Montpelier, who found the former millionaire at Guaymas, in the most squalid penury and wretchedness. B. M. Pratt, of Fillmore, Millard County, having read the statement, forwards the following as showing the fulfillment of a prediction made concerning Brannan, by the late Parley P. Pratt:

"In the winter of 1844 and until the fall of 1845, he assisted Parley P. Pratt in publishing in New York City a paper in the interest of the Latter-day Saints. He subsequently took a company of Saints around Cape Horn to San Francisco, which was then but thinly settled, and he became rich through speculating, etc., and forsook his religion. In 1854, while the late Parley P. Pratt was on a mission on the Pacific Coast, he was informed that Mr. Brannan, then a millionaire, was very much afraid some one would kill him for his money. Parley P. Pratt said: 'Go, tell Sam Brannan from me that he shall not die till he is in want of ten cents to buy a loaf of bread.' It seems the word of the Prophet has been fulfilled."

When Brannan saw these articles, the old war-horse answered the call to battle. Salt Lake's fiery anti-Mormon press was glad to print Brannan's rebuttal, which described his continuing effort to acquire Mexican land and railroad grants.

"SAM BRANNAN," *SALT LAKE DAILY TRIBUNE*, 31 MAY 1883, 3/2.

He Tells What He Knows About the New Gold Fields,

And Denounces the Mormons as Base Liars.

A gentleman of this city has received the following private letter from Sam Brannan, date Guaymas, Sonora, May 20th:

I hasten to drop you a few lines, knowing that you will feel an interest to learning some particulars of the gold excitement now existing in Lower California.

All that you have read in the newspapers concerning the wonderful placer deposits there is true, and much more. The gold that has been taken out resembles the placer gold of California in 1849. The largest lump yet found weighed eighteen ounces. It came from Molly Hay, the name of one of the districts. It was taken out by a friend of mine who was there from San Francisco to purchase a copper mine. He left to-day, with his rich nugget and other proofs of the marvelous wealth of that region, for San Francisco.

The nearest placer is thirty to forty miles from here across the gulf—a short trip by steamer. The extent of the gold-bearing surface is some 300 miles in length by 100 miles in width. The gold is in abundance, but there is no water; and men going there should have an artesian apparatus and a pump; the pump similar to that used on the Harlem River or hights near New York City, costing about $35. It throws water from 100 feet to 300 feet in height—a late invention. None need come here for gold unless they bring with them the artesian apparatus and pumps.

We need here a few good tailors, shoemakers, butchers, bakers, a watch maker, and a heavy stock of blankets and groceries; also a tinner who knows how to make pans and mining tools; also a big stock of picks and shovels.

Lumber is selling here at $60 per M. for dressed, and $50 per M. for undressed. A saw mill has been put up here by Messrs. Hooper & Co. They also make rockers for the miners.

With regards to the prophesy of Parley P. Pratt, as printed in the *Deseret News* sometime since, that I would die a pauper—I don't believe he ever uttered it. If so, he must have been drunk or crazy. I never saw him in San Francisco, or in any other place, except in New York, and that was many years ago—about 1848 or 1849. The whole yarn is a pure fabrication of their own.

I can hardly consider my circumstances extremely desperate; not withstanding they reported I was living in a "dug out." I own ten lots and two houses here, all rented at good rates. My wife also owns a large double house and lot from which she derives a nice little revenue; and we board with her daughter.

I hold two claims against the Mexican government—one for land, the other a railroad franchise to the headwaters of the Yaqui river, near the foot hills, over which there is no dispute with the Indians. These claims require only the confirmation of the Mexican Congress. They have already received the signature of the President. My attorney is now in the City of Mexico attending to the matter, assisted by a Congressman from this State.

These claims I have accepted in consideration of $500,000 [in] bonds I hold from the Mexican government, drawing ten per cent interest per annum from July, 1865, the payment of which is guaranteed by one-half the revenues of Mazatlan, Manzanillo and Guaymas. The claims will no doubt be confirmed by the present Congress or the next.

It is my intention to make a liberal donation of land to the actual settler. A dam will be built on or near the projected town of Hidalgo, on the Yaqui River, which will afford water enough for irrigation on both sides of the river, and for all the mills and machine shops, including [a] quartz mill, that may be built. The survey will probably be commenced this fall. The location is in the best mining region in this State, and for agriculture and health, it cannot be surpassed anywhere.

My health is improving rapidly, but I am not yet able to write much, though I am able to walk my two and four miles a day. You will hear from me again.

Yours Respectfully,
SAMUEL BRANNAN.

Frederick K. Sorensen transcribed six of the original twenty-six articles of Brannan's June 1883 contract with Secretary of Public Works General Carlos Pacheco for the "Survey and Colonization of Public Lands in the State of Sonora." They reveal that Brannan's agent, Manuel Peniche, succeeded in making a second agreement with the Mexican government, but the contract was even more restrictive than the first. Brannan was authorized "to survey (provided no other party has a better right thereto) up to seventy-five thousand *hectares* of public lands, situated to the west of the river Yaqui, between Comoripa and Sahuaripa, in the State of Sonora." He would pay all expenses and had to begin the survey within three months or the contract would be null and void. Within five years Brannan had to have five hundred families on the land, "at least three-fourths thereof to be of Spanish origin," and he agreed to have at least fifty families settled within two years. Brannan was to "provide to poor colonists provisions for one year, tools and other implements that may be necessary," which would be repaid in ten annual installments.[23] The conditions attached to his second grant were difficult, but a bout with ill-health made them impossible. "I had the Paralesis and the Yellow Fever," Brannan later wrote, "and that went up the *flume*."[24]

"NEVER SAY DIE": BRANNAN IN NOGALES

The paralyzing stroke and subsequent bout with yellow fever had left a mere 120 pounds on the six-foot frame of Samuel Brannan by the spring of 1884. At sixty-five, the old pioneer "fled" his home in Sonora on 24

---

[23]Contract, 7 June 1883, Typescript, Sorensen Papers.
[24]Brannan to Little, 27 January 1885, Folder 2, BYU Brannan Papers.

May, leaving behind his Mexican wife and property. He spruced up his graying hair with Hall's Hair Restorer and Bachelor's Hair Dye and moved to Nogales, Arizona Territory, where he made his home until the fall of 1887.[25] Barely two years old, Nogales was a tough frontier town of one thousand even tougher inhabitants. Brannan selected the place because it was hard on the border with Sonora and provided a good spot to oversee his Mexican enterprises. He built a two-room house with a windmill for his well and planned to add a fish pond and garden. Within eight months of his arrival, he had gained fifty pounds and felt he would last another thirty years. The old pioneer spent much time living in the past and dreaming about an unlikely future. He continually recalled the two great villains of his life: James K. Polk and Brigham Young.

A persistent tradition claims Brannan gave up "steady drinking" while living in Mexico.[26] If so, his erratic handwriting did not reflect it, but perhaps this was an effect of his paralysis. Alexander Badlam's accounts indicate that he shipped five gallons of cider, two quarts of spirits (perhaps "for samples"), and five gallons of "cologne spirits" to his uncle in the summer of 1884.[27] Brannan seems to have come to terms with his alcoholism before he visited San Francisco in 1887, but some stories suggest that he continued to take an occasional drink.

Always the promoter, Brannan waxed lyrical about the attractions of Nogales. During his first summer in the territory he composed a promotional letter "that would do justice to a chamber of commerce president."[28] Brannan praised the town's climate, industries, farms, and especially "the richest mines in the world—gold, silver copper, lead, coal, and iron" that surrounded it. He assured readers that local Indian troubles had "disappeared utterly and forever." Parts of the letter appeared in San Francisco even before they were published in Nogales. A version appeared in the *Nogales Express* on 15 August 1884 and was reprinted separately as a pamphlet.[29]

For the next two years, Brannan tried to raise capital to develop his

[25]Ibid.; and Luce, "Samuel Brannan: Speculator in Mexican Lands," 63. The hair products are listed in the Brannan-Badlam Accounts, Box 3, California State Library Collection.

[26]Stellman, *Sam Brannan*, 227–28; and Scott, *Samuel Brannan and the Golden Fleece*, 435.

[27]Brannan-Badlam Accounts, Box 3, California State Library Collection.

[28]Luce, "Samuel Brannan: Speculator in Mexican Lands," 65.

[29]See *San Francisco Examiner*, 11 August 1884, 1/9. For the edited offprint, see "Communicated," *Nogales Express*, 20 September 1884, BYU Library.

Sonoran mines. His letters outlined his expansionist agenda, described his religious beliefs, and revealed his increasing attachment to the past as he stormed about LDS colonization in Mexico. Brannan's renewed interest in Mormonism produced an article, now lost, attacking polygamy. He feared it would "raise to[o] much stink, for my use at present, although there is nothing offensive to the Mormons in it but to the Contrary." Brannan asked Little, "Excuse my writing my hand is cold and I have to write with my door open for light. I can't write as well as [I] use too—nor you either from the looks of your last letter."[30] To revive his fortunes, Brannan planned to draw on his traditional sources of wealth—real estate, trade, mines, and transportation. He hoped to open railroads in Sonora and Arizona with Leland Stanford's support.

Missionary Benjamin F. Johnson set out in November 1884 with Brigham Young, Jr., on a mission to the Yaqui Indians. At Nogales he met "my old schoolmate, the once great Samuel Brannon, the millionaire, now living in great poverty with a Mexican woman, in a poor Mexican hut, decrepid [sic] with palsy." Johnson summed up the Mormon perspective on Brannan's condition: "To die in poverty while waiting on the Mexican government! Poor Sam! To have worked for the Lord would have paid you better!"[31]

Brannan received a third conditional land grant from the Mexican government early in 1885 that totaled about two hundred thousand acres.[32] Again, his attempt to secure title to the property proved difficult. His letter to John Taylor, who succeeded Brigham Young as president of the Mormon church, reveals how broadly Brannan cast about for people to settle his land grant. Mormon leaders did seek to colonize polygamous havens in Mexico, but they had no interest in using Sam Brannan as their agent. Taylor never answered Brannan's letter.

BRANNAN TO JOHN TAYLOR, 16 OCTOBER 1884,
JOHN TAYLOR PAPERS, LDS ARCHIVES.

Nogales Oct 16 1884

President J. Taylor
Dear Sir
    The Mexican Gov. made me a grant last year of 200,000 acres of Land

---

[30]Brannan to Little, 12 February 1885, Folder 2, BYU Brannan Papers.
[31]Cook and Harker, eds., My Life's Review, 268–69.
[32]Luce, "Samuel Brannan: Speculator in Mexican Lands," 70.

and I was unable to make the Survey according to law (in 6 months) having been struck with the Peralisis and not able to ride and from Sickness, it went by defolt [*sic*]. My attorne[y] in Mexico proposes to apply for a renewal or another grant, when Dies [Porfirio Diaz] takes his Seat on Dec. next, and take it between here and the Yaqui River—it is a beautiful Country. I propose to give you one half of the same for settlement and you give me $1000 for past expenses.

I will meet any one you may send me at Calabasas ten miles from here. The Stage runs there da[i]ly from Tucson. You can have the Balance of the Land at almost your own terms. I know you will be delighted with the country.

Inclosed I send you a printed letter. Yours truly

Saml Brannan

P.S. 4 months ago I was unable to write, Please answer and oblidge.

yours, S. B.

After an eighteen-month hiatus, Brannan resumed his extensive correspondence with Jesse Little early in 1885. His letters were written with a purple pencil until mid-1886, when he switched to black ink. "Wet this letter with your Tongue and it will turn to dark," he advised Little. "I am not well yet. I write to[o] much but cant help it."[33] Brannan thought his "Dear Old Friend" was "dead or very sick." He was glad to find Little "alive and well, never say *die* is my *motto*." He sent Little a map (lacking the key, of course) of the twenty-eight mines and "mountain of silver" he claimed to have located in the Sierra Madre in 1881. Brannan wrote that he had found his first grant "infested with the Yaqui" and had rejected it, but he now had a grant of two hundred thousand acres "About 2 days ride from here into Sonora." He wanted Little to recruit "a hundred Brave young men with $200 each" to go with him to Mexico to survey the land and build houses. He wanted "no *Polygamy*," but promised "There will be no tithing business," and told Little, "I want liberal Mormons as was on the Brookly[n]."[34] So began a burst of letters in which Brannan recalled their shared past and outlined their glorious prospects.

It is 39 years ago yesterday at 2 O'Clock, that I sailed from N.Y. for Cal. the Industry of which is now controled by Chinamen, and the *free white* man, is being run out that can get away. You will not think [it] strange if I tell you,

---

[33]Brannan to Little, 5 February 1885, Folder 2, BYU Brannan Papers.
[34]Brannan to Little, 27 January 1885, Folder 2, BYU Brannan Papers.

I am going to make an assylam for them or a *Paradise*, for it is truly intitle [entitled] to that name if there is such a thing *on earth*, and I want you to come along, and help me, and no James K. Polk to turn you off the track. What do you think of it?

I shall locate and survey my 200 000 acres track next month, 3 days ride from here South by east, and in that vicinity is over 1 000 000 acres of public land, and your hundred young men are intitled to one League each, and as many more as you can [survey], in case they settle there. Now is your chance to establish yourself in your declining years. "*Taylor*" I think will have no objections and if he *does*, you dont care. You must keep your own council at any rate till I get Located. Those [should] do the same that go with you, and join the *gang*. I have written to the City of Mexico, to my agent there to get me a pass to pass the Custome house free for whoever goes there. There should not be a rush but two or three teams travel together, and create no excitement, and keep every thing out of the N[ew]s Papers.

It is at the head of the west fork of the Yaqui River and the head of the San Padro not far from Nocasari, [with] a beautiful climate, water, grass, tilable land, and Springs and Rivers enough, and more rain than is here, and that is useless. Gold, Silver and Copper mines plenty and on the East side of the Yaqui is the Sirra Madre Mountains full of Mineral Wealth, grass and Timber. I must say it is the richest part of the whole earth, and I am veine enough to think it has been reserved for me and my friend, for I am a libberal of the most *liberal kind!*[35]

Little "must be the head man in Utah at all hazards and your Old days be your happyest days and many of them." The two old pioneers deserved it, for "You crost the Continent, and I Plowed the Ocean and Land." Brannan felt he was "good for 30 years yet, if I have braved the Indians, the yellow fever, and Peralesis."[36]

BRANNAN TO LITTLE, 14 FEBRUARY 1885,
FOLDER 2, BYU BRANNAN PAPERS.

Nogales, A. T. Febr 14th 1885

Dear Col.

I have read the balance of your letter and concur with the Spirit of it, but not with the part that alludes to you and *me* going east again. If they want *saving* let them come to us in the "*South west*" and you will agree with me, after you have read my 3d letters. As for their money we dont [want] it or need it. Send along your Gentiles, Mormons, Catholics, Infidels, and other reli-

---

[35]Brannan to Little, 5 February 1885, Folder 2, BYU Brannan Papers.
[36]Brannan to Little, 11 February 1885, Folder 2, BYU Brannan Papers.

gions, they are all welcome, and make all the money they can, and be rich, for here is the wealth of the world in this country and Let John Taylor and his Revelation take the mouth of the Yaqui river with all his mortgage title. I would not take it as a gift. The Yellow fever will slaughter them as fast as they go there. I have been there and got enough and told young Brigham so, but I did not tell him where I was a going to. I have two houses and some lots in Guaymas that cost me about five thousand dollars, and them I shall sell if I can, if not I shall abandon them to their fate, for [if] the yellow fever is once there it will be there every summer as it is in Verra Cruise, for there is no frost there nor 30 miles south of there on the Yaqui river. The Indians had it there as bad as they did in Guaymas, and I told Brigham's crowd so. One of them [Benjamin Johnson] I knew in Kirtland, Ohio when he was a boy 16 years old, ~~and~~ he came to see me and invited me to his camp close to town when they passed through here with 8 waggons and 20 men, and good looking men they were, too good to be used up by the Yellow fever in that cursed hole, for it is nothing else, and next summer they will have the yellow fever, Collery and Small Pox there, that will try the virtue of their Medicine and healing pow[er] of their souls. Thank God I dont want to go back into Egypt, but I will go down by and by and bring up my wife for it is 9 months since I left there. Then I waid 120 lbs and now I way 170 lbs and can walk and write which I could not do when I left there. I commenced getting better from the first day I arrived here and still am growing better, and will be able soon to run a foot race with you. I am writing by candle light and no fire in the house this winter so you will have to Excuse my bad writing. I will finish in the morning the 15ᵗʰ. I may get a letter from you. I got 5 this morning [and] answered them.

This morning the 15ᵗʰ no letter from you. I have 4 letters to write, when you get the maps answer it by all means. I have but one besides that. And I want you to send me a map of Utah with the Counties on it if you can, so good by, I think I shall get a letter from you tomorrow,

Yours truly
Saml Brannan

Wet this letter with your tongue and it will turn to ink, I cannot use a pen yet! I use a pencil.

Brannan boasted that he could "get plenty of men here in Sonora, Arizona and New Mexico, but I prefer to give the Chance to your men, for when I once get to Surveying that country I shall take the whole of it. And President Diaz would rather I would have it than Any one else— he knows me and likes me and my politics."[37] Brannan did not say why

[37]Brannan to Little, 6 March 1885, Folder 2, BYU Brannan Papers.

he wanted Mormons for his colony, but he later explained, "we want none but good Substancial Men & Woman [sic] such people as doubled Cape Horn with me in 1846."[38] He asked Little:

> How many men do you think you could send if I should send for them? They must keep a secret, and all that follow them, and no back[ing] down. This is to be a rich Kingdom, not like John Taylor's a poor man's home. To hell with poverty. I go for riches, as I went to California an[d] told Brigh Young in Salt Lake in (47) forty-seven, Now is the time to strike, when everything is favorable! and God is on our side.[39]

Brannan shared his theological musings with his business partner. He promised Little that if he visited Sonora:

> you will know what John Taylor with all his *wisdom* never dreamed off [sic], and furthermore never will, till it is too late. His god is a little god, my God is of the whole Earth and people, and has the same respect for *Mormon Catholic, Mahometon* or *Methodist* all alike. All Sects have little gods of their own, which is quite right, and proper (they never went round Cape Horn). The laws of the God of the World has *no* respect to *Sects*, however foolish, and cares less; He as lives [sic] destr[o]y by Earth quacke or Thunder & Lightning a City, Church, or a Corrall of Cattle as you or me; We must all look out and obey his laws; *If we know how!*
>
> And That is the Great Wisdom of This World! Know God's Laws and Live up to them If You Can; But old Age is bound to fetch you finally.
>
> The Priest of the Mormon, Protestant, Catholic and the Great Egyptian Proffit Is all the same to *Him!*
>
> Now You Know my Religion! *God!!* But I keep my little god in my room, and will show him to you when you come here and the big *God* too! He is quite harmless when you know how to handle him.[40]
>
> I see by your letter you have children enough for me. I have some and dont want to make any more—I'll try and help you take care of yours if they are good for anything, and I suppose you think so any how, and that is according to the Big Gods Laws. The little god is selfish but the big *God* is all life and *Soul* and all men have him, and when he leaves *Man, He is dead!* "*So Mote it be.*" . . .
>
> If you see any of the Brooklyn boys tell them to come along. They were first rate men & women you bet, but they like the little god, but that is

[38]Brannan to Little, 31 May 1885, Folder 2, BYU Brannan Papers.

[39]Brannan to Little, 6 March 1885, Folder 2, BYU Brannan Papers.

[40]This statement suggests that Brannan had taken up idol worship, but may reflect his fascination with technology. His "little god" was perhaps an electrical device.

wright. I got a letter from little Jo Smith in Iowa a short time since.[41] He is
a very good little god man, but small Caliber, like Taylor.[42]

I Have Got the World by the Cahonies

Brannan traveled to Guaymas in March 1885 to persuade his wife to
return with him to the United States and to close his Sonoran business
ventures. He was unsuccessful on both counts. Yellow fever convinced
him to abandon his property, and his wife did not join him in Nogales.[43]
He claimed he had received confirmation of his grant and soon had even
better news. An old business associate, William H. A. Brown, offered as
much as ten million dollars to complete the survey. Brown visited Brannan and brought with him John A. Kruse, a Chicago engineer and businessman, who was to travel to Mexico City to make arrangements for
the survey.[44] Brannan invited Jesse Little to visit in disguise and sometime during May, Little came to see Nogales. He returned to Salt Lake
to find considerable enthusiasm for the project. "You can hardly imagine," he wrote, "how I am Thronged and Button Holed."[45]

Brannan reported to Alexander Badlam, Jr., that his agent in Mexico
City, Manuel Peniche, had arranged for him to survey "about 4 to 6 million of acres" in return for part of the land "direct from the government
instead of from second hands," but he had to begin the survey "within
90 days as the President has no right to make an Extention of time
without a Special act of Congress."[46] Brannan believed he did not need
Leland Stanford's help, for he had investors "in Chicago that are ready
to put up all the funds I may need."[47]

Samuel Brannan, Jr., had been educated as a mining engineer in

---

[41]See Joseph Smith III to Brannan; and Smith III to D. S. Mills, 17 July 1883, RLDS Library-
Archives.

[42]Brannan to Little, 8 March 1885, Folder 2, BYU Brannan Papers.

[43]Luce, "Samuel Brannan: Speculator in Mexican Lands," 73–74. Luce cited a 14 March 1884
letter that is no longer in the BYU Brannan Papers.

[44]Ibid., 77. Brannan would have a long and tempestuous relationship with Kruse.

[45]Brannan to Little, 8 March 1885, Folder 2; and Little to Brannan, 21 May 1885, Folder 10,
BYU Brannan Papers.

[46]"Mexico's Old Bonanzas," *New York Times*, 29 April 1887, 5/2, listed Manuel Perriche as a
member of the Sonora Land Company of Chicago, but Mexican sources give the correct spelling as
Peniche.

[47]Brannan to Badlam, 30 and 31 March 1885 and 6 April 1885, Typescripts, Sorensen Papers.

Europe and now put his schooling to good use.[48] Brannan reported that
his son was "getting out very rich oar from his mine at the head of the
Yaque," but complained that Sam Jr. was "drinking too much muscall
for me." Brannan also explained his relationship with Little:

> I have a man in Utah to bring the anti-poligamist Mormons here, that was
> to follow me around Cape Horn. His name is Col J. C. Little of Littleton,
> Morgan Co., Utah, who will come here as soon as he sells his property. The
> reason he did not follow me, Brigham Young and James K. Po[l]k stoped
> him to rais[e] the Mormon Battallion and it got too late in the season. He
> said he will give me all the population I want for the *new Town*. Let them
> come. Mormonism has got its death blow now; it carries the seeds of its
> own destruction with it. Salt Lake will soone be a gentile City. It will soon
> be my day.

Brannan could even comment on his poverty with humor:

> Blessed be nothing! What a pleasure it is to be poor; you ought to see my
> *den*; one room 12x12, one door, ½ window, dirt floor, 2 tables, 4 trunks and
> 2 chairs and the walls are adobe with a dirt roof [and] when it rains I get the
> benefit. Office and bedroom in one, no fire all winter, and yet I am as happy
> as a Clam in a crow's nest, for I have got the world by the Cahonies and don't
> care a D——m for nada![49]

Brannan asked Badlam to tell Leland Stanford "that he ought to be in
my fix about a month for fun." His next letter to Jesse Little described
his memories, feelings, and predictions about Mormonism.

BRANNAN TO LITTLE, 16 APRIL 1885,
FOLDER 2, BYU BRANNAN PAPERS.

Nogales, A. T. April 16th 1885
Dear Little—It is now drawing close to the time for my papers to arrive from
Mexico and I commence the work at once. I cannot wait for an answer from
you much long[er]. I feel that this is my last letter to you. I wrote you March
21, 22 and April 6, 11, 13 and no answer yet. The conference I see is held in
Morgan near your place and the heads of the Church are absent, *they had better
be*. The days of Polygamy are numbered in this world. The English Government is at war against it, in the person of the Prophet 2 & Mardi in Egypt[50]

---

[48]Stellman, *Sam Brannan, Builder of San Francisco*, 180.

[49]Brannan to Badlam, 17 April 1885, Typescript, Sorensen Papers.

[50]The Mahdi, Sudanese leader Muhammad Ahmad, besieged the British outpost at Khartoum
for ten months during 1884–85. This action ended with the massacre of the Anglo-Egyptian gar-
rison and its commander, Charles George Gordon.

and the U.S. against the Last Prophet (Taylor) on the American Continent. I will live to see it closed up and Polygamy no more in the U.S. My opinion of Prophesy is that all men with well balanced minds is endowed with the spirit of prophesy at times regardless of what religion, and an unbalanced mind is a fanatic, Such was Joseph Smith & Brigham Young the latter better balanced of the two. All men [are] subject to animal passions and a few with a love of money (the miser for instance). Man is not at *falt* for what he *is*! All religions are from the hand of the Greate Creator and has its share of inspiration and all men are his instruments, great and *Small* according to their geographical position and are of the Great Chess board of the world, Nationally, Socially, [and] Individually, with the advantages of climate and soil and riches & poverty.

Such was my situation in 1846 & 1847 and such at present only I have more at my command than I had then. I told Brigham at Salt Lake so. And Kimball asked me how many *wives I had?* I replied *One* and d——d hard work to support her. Taylor was present at the time.[51] Next day I started for California and he [Brigham Young] stayed and sacrificed the Mormons for his lust, when he could have made them a rich and happy people and not been a miser, which he was! And if Taylor dont mind his Ps and Qs he will go under. Now I will tell you a Secret (not for the press, for it is not my turn to speak yet). I wrote a letter to John Taylor offering him one half of my 200,000 acre track in the Northern part of Sonora for nothing for his people to settle upon, and he never answered my letter. After that his party with young Brigham went through this place on their way to the Yaqui river. I mentioned nothing to them about it. Taylor in my opinion will make a fool of the whole buisness [*sic*].

San Francisco and Chicago has offered* me all the money I want on my [land grant] papers when I get them, which will be in a few days more.

I offered you one half [of what] I made and you do the business there and I do the business here, & get all the Mormon boys that is worth a d——n and let the fenatical part follow John Taylor. Our party will have good homes and be a rich community. I have 4 letters to write before the mail leaves so A Dios.

Samuel Brannan

*[At top of page:] As did Brigham Young in 1847, stoping at Salt Lake [and] building a City for other people to injoy. If the Lord is at the head of such conduct he is a *shit ass* that is all I have to say, I dont want any of him.

Brannan's speculative plans were further complicated when Geronimo and his followers left Fort Apache, Arizona, heading for their old homelands in Sonora—which were uncomfortably close to Brannan's new

---

[51]John Taylor was actually on the overland trail in August 1847.

land grant. Brannan believed the army would quickly stop Geronimo, but it would take seventeen months and two generals to persuade the Apaches to surrender. Such problems did not deter the old promoter, and he continued to urge Little to support his schemes. "The advance of Empire is South instead of West," Brannan wrote. Sonora "will be the cradle of wealth . . . We commenced the work in 46 and we will live to see it consummated." Sonora would soon be "intirely shut" of the Apaches, and the Yaqui War "will be for our benefit, they will all flock to us for employment, and are truly my friends, so there need [not] be any alarm on that account, but our main stay for *labor* and *help* which will help make it '*The Paridice of America*.'" Pioneers were "the making of a country and should not be kept poor, for instance the Brooklyn party in 1846. How much would they be worth to day if they had held on to their property and not went to Salt Lake? Millions upon millions!" Brannan was even convinced "I shall want a Historian writer in a couple of years or less."[52]

Jesse Little fell victim to Brannan's siren song and offered to send him $1,000 to launch the survey.[53] Brannan received two postal orders totaling $400 on 2 July and wrote the next day, "You can form no idea how that $400 brought me out." He noted that "Kruse has not paid any thing yet, but has telegraphed to Chicago for the money," and "the Survey is commenced and every thing is all right."[54] John Kruse arrived in Nogales on 30 June and reported that he had engaged President Diaz' father-in-law to work for the company in exchange for one-fortieth of the land it acquired.[55]

"So you see," Brannan wrote, "everything is fixed, which will give us a good slice of Sonora (which will be in the U. S. before the next President is elected)." In Mexico Kruse "has had a very hard time of it," and "to tell you the Gods truth since you left here and while Kruse was in Chicago and Mexico I have passed through the most severe ordeal of my whole life," Brannan recounted. "After this I think I can stand most any

---

[52]Brannan to Little, 27 May 1885, Folder 5, BYU Brannan Papers. "I forgot to tell you," Brannan added. "I am a Mason in good Standing in San Francisco and have my card with me."

[53]Luce, "Samuel Brannan: Speculator in Mexican Lands," 80.

[54]Brannan to Little, 2 and 3 July 1885, Folder 2, BYU Brannan Papers.

[55]Diaz' father-in-law was Senator Romero Rubio, who had close relations with the Torres family that long ruled Sonora. See Beals, *Porfirio Diaz, Dictator of Mexico*, 250, 374.

thing that turns up.— '*Doubt and suspence*' is a hard thing to indure but it is over thank God. I hope hereafter there will be nothing but plain sailing." His health was also improving. "Since you left here, I have been gradually gaining and can walk about almost as well as ever. I have every thing to inspire me." Brannan reported, "One party of surveyors is already in the field and another goes next Friday if I can get them off." He assured Little, "We shall have no trouble with the Apaches," but he soon had to confess that the survey was "Suspended at present for Apaches."[56]

By early September the Mexican government had allowed more time to meet the conditions of the grant "on account of the Indian raid," and Kruse had restarted the survey.[57] "Everything is going on well," Brannan wrote. "Kruse means business. He has been gone with 15 men 4 days and will return in a dozen days more." Two weeks later Brannan had to report that one of the surveying parties was "discharged, all drunk." Kruse had purchased a house to use as an office and hired a mining engineer named Henderson from Rapid City, Dakota Territory, presumably the man who told Brannan in August that he had "500 men [who] are ready to come when wanted."[58] Brannan proposed opening "a Big Store" at Nogales and a smelter that would "Command the whole trade of Sonora and Smugling." Commenting on recent politically provocative actions by the Mormons, Brannan observed that they "seem to be putting their foot in it continually."[59] Yet he was happy to learn that the "Mormons in Chiuawawa have struck it rich," finding "immensly rich" mines. The news rekindled his interest in his mining prospects and those of his son.[60]

> My son Junior is at the San Pascal and St. Paul mines and has the centre of them as you will see on my map of Sonora a little Square Marked Nicosari in the Moctezuma district. He owns part of them & Lives there for the last 4 years, and will make me a visit in a couple of weeks and if I wish will go to the mines with me.[61]

---

[56]Brannan to Little, 14 July and 2 August 1885, Folder 3, BYU Brannan Papers.
[57]Brannan to Little, 3 September 1885, Folder 3, BYU Brannan Papers.
[58]Brannan to Little, 14 and 17 September 1885, Folder 3, BYU Brannan Papers.
[59]Brannan to Little, 19 August 1885, Folder 3, BYU Brannan Papers.
[60]Brannan to Little, 7 September 1885, Folder 3, BYU Brannan Papers.
[61]Brannan to Little, 11 September 1885, Folder 3, BYU Brannan Papers.

The younger Brannan could read and write Spanish, and his father hoped they would explore the country together. Samuel Brannan, Jr., must have learned something from his European education as a mining engineer, for Nacozari became a cornerstone in the Phelps Dodge mining empire and would help "put the mining industry of Sonora on the map."[62] Relations between father and son warmed, and during his son's long absences, Brannan often expressed concern that Apaches had killed him.

Brannan remained certain that everything "will come out for the best for all of us." John Taylor's "position with the Govt. I fear will create mischief," but "conflict withe Taylor & the Govt. seems inevitable, by Taylor wishing to denounce all Mormons, that dont agree with his views. The Mormons, as a people, have not a bad reputation among the masses of the people of the Teritries, which is more than can be said of Taylor, and the Polygamists."[63] "Sometimes we think we know it all, because we wish it," Brannan wrote. "So it Proved with John Taylor. And he has got himself now where he has got to go damd slow."[64]

THE YAQUIS WILL CLEAN OUT
ALL THE MEXICANS IN SONORA

As 1885 began Brannan promised "My Dear Friend" that "we will have a Kingdom of our own without going to heaven for it, and we will send our Representatives to the City of Mexico, or go it alone on our own hook—'Dam the odds.'"[65] Brannan's filibustering instincts had revived. "We will have an Empire of our own," Brannan pledged.[66] The empire included Sonora, where he hoped to raise the flag of an independent state and repeat his triumph in California: "I will have a Big Store here to Supply the Colony and Northern Mexico when the 'Loan Star' or 'Bear Flag' floats."[67] An 1880 circular promoting his Sonoran venture claimed that Mexico knew "that neither he nor his colonists are tainted with any filibustering

[62]Ruiz, The People of Sonora and Yankee Capitalists, 38–39.
[63]Brannan to Little, 25 October 1885, Folder 4, BYU Brannan Papers.
[64]Brannan to Little, 14 September 1885, Folder 3, BYU Brannan Papers.
[65]Brannan to Little, 26 February 1885, Folder 2, BYU Brannan Papers.
[66]Brannan to Little, 24 November 1885, Folder 4, BYU Brannan Papers.
[67]Brannan to Little, 28 September 1885, Folder 3, BYU Brannan Papers.

designs, or even dream of annexation of foreign territories or peoples."[68] Brannan had written, "Annexation is not in the interests of the people; [the Mexican] constitution and laws are better than ours." He made the strange assertion that "No Indian wars are required for the purpose of robbing the people or government," but the old leopard could not change his spots.[69] Brannan had a dark vision of using the Indians to seize the border state—he would arm the Yaquis and with one battle "Sonora would be ours." He shared his new scheme with Little. Having learned from General Patea that "another war is to be made by the State of Sonora against the Yaquis," Brannan suggested a remarkable alliance:

> Now I propose, if you can get me a dynamite Bohm or gun, we will make a short war of it, and the Yaquis will clean out all the Mexicans in Sonora. We furnish the Indians withe the means, and two or three men to handle it.
>
> I am acquainted with the second chiefs, Neiphfue [nephew] of Caheme the old Chief, and will make all arrangements here and end the war in 30 days and we will take one half of their land (the Yaquis) in payment. It is 90 miles on the Gulf south of the Yaqui river and 50 miles inland, from the river South. It is a very feasable proposition and can be carried out.
>
> The Sub Chief offered all the Yaquis I wanted to Settle up the River when I wanted them. They are better workers than the Mexicans.
>
> You might have some difficulty at first in getting the proper person to handle the Dynamite, but with a little inquiry, I think you can do it, and there would be but one battle with the Mexicans, and Sonora would be ours, all they wish is to get the land of the Yaquis, and instead of that, the Yaquis would get the whole State (or we would).[70]

Here Brannan set a new standard for duplicity, but his ruthless plans were also pathetically naive: the Yaquis had been dealing with Europeans for more than three centuries and were not about to exchange Mexican for American domination. Nothing came of his plot.

Technology intrigued Brannan, who predicted "One year more and Dynamite will be Prophet and King of the whole world. These little Pretenders will be no whare."[71] He dreamed of using dynamite and electricity to rebuild his shattered empire, and both technologies would

---

[68]"Sonora Colonization Enterprise: Its History, Objects and Plans Explained," 1.

[69]Brannan, "Get a Farm in Mexico: A Land of Peace and Plenty, " Folder 15, BYU Brannan Papers.

[70]Brannan to Little, 3 November 1885, Folder 4, BYU Brannan Papers.

[71]Brannan to Little, 14 September 1885, Folder 3, BYU Brannan Papers.

revolutionize the mining industry in the twentieth century. Dynamite for blasting and "the separation of gold by Electricity" would be "the great feature of the age, the overthrowing of Priest Craft, and the separation of Church & State." Less credibly Brannan found that his "electric jacket" was doing wonders for his health. He told Little, "Electricity has cured me." It could perform miracle cures and had "most certainly demonstrated itself on me. Since you were here I am another man, altogether." Electricity would "soon be running all the R.R.'s in the world, in fact is working an entire revolution in the Medical and Physical World and why not the Mineral. It will overthrow all the Kings and Priests on Earth."[72] Despite these expansive dreams, the land-grant survey dragged on, but Brannan had abiding faith that his plans would bear fruit. He worked on his new home and even contemplated visiting Utah.

Early in 1886 Jesse Little "opened an office in Salt Lake City for the purpose of settling up portions of our land."[73] There was considerable interest in Utah about the prospect of Mexico becoming a safe haven for polygamy, but Brannan knew that the Mormons lacked political support. "One of your correspondents Speaks of buying for $5000 some land in Sonora, and also [of] parties from Salt Lake being in Mexico negotiating with the Govmt," he wrote Little. "They will do nothing there, it is no use for them to try. Diaz dare not do it, he told me so. The Catholics are opposed to it and so are the Masons, and he is 'one.' As for my negotiating with the Church Authorities you know better. It is all Bosh."[74]

Perhaps to avoid discussing difficult business questions, Brannan's letters often returned to the past. He told Little that he planned to write a history. "You will here the history of the whole when I write the History of California next year and a good many other things," he claimed. "I am the only man living that can write it correctly."[75]

He also tried his hand at prophesy. Brannan's racism found its ulti-

[72]Brannan to Little, 16 November 1885 and 13 January 1886, Folders 4 and 5, BYU Brannan Papers.

[73]Little to A. J. Stewart, 29 November 1892, Folder 16, BYU Brannan Papers.

[74]Brannan to Little, 16 November 1885, Folder 4, BYU Brannan Papers. Brannan was wrong about the Mormons' chances. Their colonies in northern Mexico survived until the revolution of 1910.

[75]Brannan to Little, 13 January 1886, Folder 5, BYU Brannan Papers.

mate expression in his perverse vision of a final world war that would result in the extermination of all but his own kind. His apocalyptic vision evoked the prophecies of Daniel: "the Little '*stone*' will never stop rolling until Dynamite & Electricity, is King & Bos[s], and rule the earth through the people (white people). Such is Manifest Destiny and all will have to submit to it."[76] In letters that are quintessential Brannan, he predicted a universal race war in one paragraph, extolled motherhood, and interspersed the lot with comments on polygamy, labor, and Indian wars. His long campaign to restore his fortune had finally brought him a measure of realism, for he now acknowledged that it would take at least two years and perhaps the rest of his life to secure his land grant.

> You must *brace* up Old boy, you are not used to handleing big things. This is one of the bigest things out, and requires patience, and *I have got it*. I expect to be two years at it yet, *if not my whole life*. My Organization cannot be beat in no part of the world. *John Taylor* cant beat it, and all the "*hosts of hell*"! The man that gets in the way of our crowd, after the Indians are gone, will will [*sic*] have to git. What you have done, will do no harm. All will go well yet, we must expect some obstacles, the whole world has them . . .
>
> Polygamy Must fall with Slavery, and next will come the war of darke races of all the whole world.
>
> Degrade the Mothers and you degrad[e] the nation, such has been the History of the world. All great men had great *Mothers* so with Nations, their greatnes[s] is dependent on the Mothers of the People. Inslave woman to the lust of man and that people must fall and nations too. Such was our revolutionary Mothers. The Chines[e] must go, and the Women must be elevated, such is the law of Destiny, and the *will* of Educated white men, "That is the Law of God."[77]

A bitter attack on polygamy dominated Brannan's correspondence as 1886 drew to a close. Brannan's critique of Joseph Smith's marriage system used an odd combination of feminism and racism that contained not the slightest hint that Brannan himself had participated in "spiritual wifery." He noted that "Uncle Sam is going to build a Penitentiary in Salt Lake. It will make it very convenient for the Polygamists." It was "a strange fanaticism that a few people can suppose they can establish a branch of Paganism and Mohometanism at this age of the world, after

[76]Brannan to Little, 3 November 1885, Folder 4, BYU Brannan Papers.
[77]Brannan to Little, 31 March 1886, Folder 5, BYU Brannan Papers.

witnessing the overthrow of Slavery & the gradual down fall of Caniballism." The scandal was "enough to make humanity blush," but once polygamy was destroyed, it would "never make it appearance on this continent again. Slavery in its fall cost a great deal of Blood & Money, but thank God Poligamy will be a little" matter. Brannan even envisioned Utopia at the end of the struggle: "As the people grow inteligent fanaticism drops out of all creads, and knowledge comes to the surface, and when cap[i]tal and labor strikes hands together, there will be no Political & Religious strife and the World will be at peace."[78]

Brannan hoped to get "away for the mountains or mines" as 1887 approached, but his unnamed companion fell ill. He again expressed concern for Jesse Little's welfare, but boasted that his own "health was never better in thirty years."[79] He soon returned to his critique of polygamy.

BRANNAN TO LITTLE, 24 DECEMBER 1886,
FOLDER 5, BYU BRANNAN PAPERS.

Nogales, Arizona. Ter. Dec. 24th 1886

Dear Col.

The Tribune of to day you sent me, is correct in his quotations from the Pratts, Taylor and Brigham are correct. They are mistaken about God's Government, it is the U. States instead of the Mormon Church, for God's Gov. is a government of the the the [sic] People as Uncle Sam as it was demonstrated in the Last War against Slavery and so it will be against Polygamy, both Pagan institutions, and must be put down and will be as sure as there is a God in heaven.

No institution that makes a slave of Woman, can prosper under a government of the people, and that is God's government, Brigham Young not with standing. Pagan principles must cease to govern man kind, and all nations, that tolerate it, will be reorganized and have a Constitutional and a representative gov. and that within a few years, and in view of that all Europe and the world will soon be involved in war, but Uncle Sam and she will furnish the material to carry it on. Uncle Sam has fought her battle and won with out any assistance, and now she is going to look on.

Why should the Mormons be allowed to practi[ce] Polygamy or commit a Crime, and you and [the others be] punished for the same. The practice of Polygamy will be the overth[row] of all Nations, that uphold it. As History

---

[78]Brannan to Little, 15 November 1886, Folder 5, BYU Brannan Papers.
[79]Brannan to Little, 22 December 1886, Folder 5, BYU Brannan Papers.

has proven Women are the mothers of great men & Nations, and should be looked up at instead of down, and so I told Brigham & Heber that day before I left Salt Lake in 47 and have never changed my mind. I think I will see it annihilated before I step out.[80]

I am sorry that Brigham has any children that tryes to defend it. They will yet be sorry. It is wors[e] than Slavery, as it in [en]slaves the white woman and exalts the man, when she was made for his helpmate, and companion in life.

It is one of the great abominations in the social life and [as bad] a curse to good government as Paganism and Mahomitamism. I am Glad to hear you you [sic] were out of it.

I think that Electricity will entirely cure me of Paralesis. I never was so well in my life.

> Yours till death
> Saml Brannan

"Your views in regard to Polygamy I concur with heartily," Brannan told Jesse Little on the last day of 1886, and he again outlined his views on God, civilization, and the apocalypse. The history of the twentieth century would be darker than anything Brannan could imagine, but from a modern perspective, Brannan's vision is bigoted nonsense. Yet it very much reflected the prevailing racial attitudes of his time, and deep thinkers such as H. G. Wells would subsequently popularize the same type of racist predictions.

The men that try to establish [polygamy], will come to nough[t], and will have [only] their labor for their pains. They will fall before the hand of civilization, as fell Slavery; Kings & Priest Craft with all its attachments will be overthrown, if it takes the blood & money of 50 million of people. It has become a part and parcel of mormonism and it will have to go with it, it has sown its own seeds of disolution. There is no Government can exist within a government of the people, no matter how wiley and cunning they may be. It has to fall as sure as mahometanism falls with all the collored race[s] of the world. Civilization needs them no longer and by degrees they will disappear and machienery will be substituted in their place for labor. Their day of usefulness is past and in 500 or a 1000 years from now there will be nothing but a white race on earth and isms will be no more. They are the inventive race of the world, and their inventions will be the means of annihilating in *wars*, all that are not needed, and room for. The old Jewish almanac, the bible if I might call it so, will have outlived its usefulness, and have a decent burial.

---

[80]Brannan died a year before his old comrade Wilford Woodruff issued the Manifesto that publicly renounced the practice of polygamy in the United States.

Mankind is at work for this great result, but they are not allowed to see it, no more than to see after death. "Man Proposes and God disposes." "The Great I am," is not the Small personage we picture to ourselves he is. His ways are not our ways; He is the creator and the destroyer of all living things and we are not confided with any of his movements, further than is developed from the Laws of Nature and the advancement of [the] white race who are the predominant race of the world. From Plymouth Rock we take our advancement, our Laws, protecting the same.[81]

As the old speculator pondered the fate of the world, age and the "Laws of Nature" brought him closer to his own fate, but not before he made one last run at fortune.

---

[81]Brannan to Little, 31 December 1886, Folder 5, BYU Brannan Papers.

Chapter 14

"Over for Eden"

Wanderlust struck Samuel Brannan again in 1887. The former tycoon sold pencils door-to-door in Nogales to finance a trip to San Francisco, where he spent a humiliating November in the city he helped build and had ruled for so long. He decided to move to San Diego to join in "the next big Boom," but he did so with a growing awareness of his own mortality: "I can't live for ever, we all have to travel 'Over For Eden.'"[1] In December he retreated to northern San Diego County, where he tried his hand at fruit ranching until his death on 5 May 1889. Brannan's extensive correspondence and newspaper articles produced as a result of his San Francisco visit paint a detailed picture of the old pioneer's last days.

As it approached its end, Sam Brannan's life again traced the trajectory of California's history. The farmers won the long war between hydraulic mining and agriculture in 1884, when Judge Lorenzo Sawyer enjoined miners from dumping "tailings, bowlders [sic], cobble stones, gravel sand, clay, debris or refuse matter" into the Yuba River. The decision marked the triumph of pastoral California over the boomer mentality of the gold rush that Brannan had long personified.[2] Now Brannan himself had retired to the backcountry and adopted a bucolic rural vision of California's future. Like many gold rush veterans, he spent his old age mired in poverty. Perhaps he shared their wonder at how it all came to pass. The former dandy now dressed "in the light pajama-fashioned cotton clothing of the ordinary Mexican paisano, and wore a large sombrero."[3] His appearance struck one young reporter as

[1]Brannan to Little, 6 June 1887, Folder 6, BYU Brannan Papers.
[2]Kelley, *Gold vs. Grain*, 239–44. J. S. Holliday alerted the editor to this conflict in a 19 December 1997 letter.
[3]Barnes, "Anent Samuel Brannan," *San Francisco Evening Bulletin*, 12 October 1895, 9/3.

"no more interesting than that of any old farmer whose world is his ranch." The "old farmer" maintained his interest in politics, land development, Mormons, "Electricity, Dynamite and War," Mexican mining, and his past, but he spent his days cultivating his garden.

A Bigger Fortune Than Ever

Brannan wrote to Jesse Little from Nogales in mid-1887 that the Sonoran survey was at last finished. John Kruse was in Mexico to secure its "approval, acceptance & division." Brannan's lawyer believed the arrangement could be completed by the next fall. "I shall then apply for my (200 000 acres) to be set apart," he assured Little, "and then one will want settlers."[4] But again, the endless process dragged on. Reduced to selling pencils, Brannan pondered relocating to the coast and dreamed of making "a biger fortune than ever."

BRANNAN TO BADLAM, 5 JUNE 1887,
TYPESCRIPT, SORENSEN PAPERS.

Nogales, Arizona, June 5, 1887

Dear Alex,

The Pencils have arrived. They are splendid—Everybody wants them Sam Brannan buyes them![5]

The more I think of it, the more I want to go to San Diego. I think I can make a biger fortune than ever, if the climate suits me and Stanford carries out his project, to build the road from there to Fort Euma [Yuma] and connect with the S[outhern] P[acific]. I want to get there as soon as I can. What do you know about the road being built? And who is down there that I know?

I heard that Henry Edgerton was there. Stanford had better bought property there than Calistoga. I have written to Chicago to sell me out and see if the Company will not buy me out it is for their interest . . .

Kind love to all,
Saml Brannan

[P.S.] I can write like a race horse with these pencils.

---

[4]Brannan to Little, 17 May 1887, Folder 6, BYU Brannan Papers.

[5]Here Brannan confirmed an old legend that a pie vendor "attested in the old days when he plied his wares at the corner of Sacramento and Montgomery streets: 'Mince pies, apple pies, cheese pies. Everybody buys 'em. Sam Brannan buys 'em.'" See Jacobsen, "California's First Millionaire," *San Francisco Bulletin*, 20 May 1916.

Brannan repeated his apocalyptic vision once again for Jesse Little, recounting his contradictory mix of racism, feminism, and theology, but including the hopeful note that "Truth will triumph over bigotry and fanaticism."

It is a glorious world but the fools are not all dead yet. But Europe dare not go to war, they have got afraid of each other until they can get the Dynamite and the inventive power out of the hands of the people (which the[y] never will do) and Mormonism destroys the United States and sets up a Kingdom with a "*fools Cap*" for a crown. Revolutions never go backward, the mass of the People gains in every fight. And the result will be all rulers will be elected by elected by [*sic*] the Mass of the people *not* by the fanatical minority. The nation that leads in public Schools, will stand at the head of the world, for they will stand at the head of the Patent Beauro. The "Old Jew Bible" that they palmed on to the Christians through the Catholics, will have to take a back seat. Truth will triumph over bigotry and fanaticism, and facts will take its place and mankind will be forced by *reason* to become enlightened. Old fashioned Christianity has filled its mission, Soc[ial]ism has gone by the board, and Polygamy, the last link of Paganism, and the enslavor of Women, ("*the Mother of Nations*") has received its last ipsidicses[?]. "So wags the world." Nature is purifying it by Earthquakes, Thunder and Lightening, Electricity, Dynamite and War. Universal peace will be brought about through the instant fear of Death by man Kings and Nations and the will of the People being obeyed which is the will of God and he is the "*Great I am*" for ever and ever.[6]

A flash flood struck Nogales in August 1887 and Brannan's "house was washed down." Some say he lost his papers and the draft of his history of California in the deluge.[7] The disaster perhaps prompted him to abandon Nogales, but shortly before leaving, Brannan wrote to an old friend, D. S. Mills, a leader of the Reorganized Church of Jesus Christ of Latter Day Saints church in California. The official RLDS newspaper published this summary of the letter.

---

[6]Brannan to Little, 6 June 1887, Folder 6, BYU Brannan Papers.

[7]Citing no source, Reva Scott claimed historian H. H. Bancroft visited Brannan on his last day in San Francisco and offered to pay him to write a personal history. See *Samuel Brannan and the Golden Fleece*, 439–40. Scott was unaware of the autobiographical sketch now in the Bancroft Library and again speculated far beyond the evidence. She claimed Brannan wrote his history "in a cheap little tent house on the edge of a creek" in San Diego that was destroyed in a deluge, but Brannan to Little, 13 March 1888, dated the flood to August 1887, while Brannan was still living in Nogales.

"ONCE AN ABLE AND DILIGENT ELDER,"
SAINTS' HERALD, 3 SEPTEMBER 1887, 34:572–73.

MR. SAMUEL BRANNAN, once an able and diligent elder in the church, one of those who engaged in the emigration of the Saints from New York to California round Cape Horn, in 1846, in a late letter to Bro. D. S. Mills, of Santa Ana, California, which letter Bro. Mills has kindly sent us, expresses himself as follows:

"Mormonism in Salt Lake is a curse to the earth. Polygamy is a limb of Paganism, and has to fall as slavery fell with war and blood, which will wipe out a people who sustains it; but it has its role to perform, like slavery, to illustrate to the world (civilized) its criminality.

"Polygamy destroys women (who is the mother of nations) and makes her a slave worse than the negro; and this has been the cause of the decay of every nation that sustained it, and eventually of its downfall.

"Women is the mother of nations, and her degradation is the downfall of that nation that fosters it; and so I told Brigham Young when I left him in Salt Lake camp there, to return to California in August, 1847, and now his people witness its fulfillment.

"I heard Joseph Smith preach a sermon against polygamy, as being one of the causes of the overthrow of nations, when I was a boy in Kirtland, Ohio; and his theory was correct, and it will soon be illustrated in the United States, and polygamy will go under."

Mr. Brannan was one of the editors of the *Prophet*, published in New York City, and was afterwards connected with the development of the city of San Francisco, California. He has of late been engaged in an effort to colonize a grant of land from the Mexican Government at, or near Guaymas, in Sonora. He was known as a man of energy, experience and brains in his vigorous days. Bro. Mills is personally acquainted with him and has great friendship for him.

One of the most surprising items in the Brannan papers is from West Point's first black graduate, Henry Ossian Flipper. After serving in the 10th Cavalry from 1877, Flipper was court-martialed and dismissed from the army in 1882 for a shortage in his commissary records. He was not a good accountant, but Flipper maintained his innocence and blamed prejudice for his dismissal; he was posthumously granted an honorable discharge in 1976. Appreciating his talent as a mining engineer, Kruse took Flipper to Mexico City in 1887 and gave him his "first experience" of being "treated by Americans and other foreigners on an absolute equality." He recalled that Kruse "hurried back to Chicago" after learning that his brother had shot himself in the foot.[8] Flipper "spent a year surveying and looking up lands" for the Sonora Land Company "with the determination of trying to solve the mystery of the lost mines" of Maximilian.[9] Flipper sent good news to Brannan: at long last, the Mexican government had *almost* approved his Sonoran land grants.

FLIPPER TO BRANNAN, 25 OCTOBER 1887,
TYPESCRIPT, SORENSEN PAPERS.

Mexico, Oct. 25th, 1887

Samuel Brannan, Esq.
Nogales, Arizona.
Dear Sir:—

Mr. Kruse directs me to say to you that his business will be concluded within two or three days and that we will leave Saturday or Sunday of this week. The maps and reports have been approved and we only await the President's signature to the titles. A very advantageous location has been secured, one large tract in Arizpe, and Moctezuma and we have been permitted to take about Two Hundred (200,000) acres in that part of Moctezuma which was cut out. To do this it has been necessary to distribute about Five Thousand (5,000) Dollars among various persons. Within the Company's lines there are only a very few private tracts. The following shows how the lands are distributed.

The Company gets in	
Arizpe	206,604.6 Acres.
Moctezuma	1,111,721.0 [Acres]
All in one tract and in	
Sahuaripa	290,340.3 [Acres]
Total	1,608,705.9 [Acres]

We were allowed to include in our calculations only a part of the *sobrantes* [grants]. We believe we have a perfect title free from all gravamens. Every question has been fully ventilated and a decision given, and for this reason we believe the title [is] as good as any the government ever issued.

With best regards for self and friends from Mr. Kruse, Penniche, and myself, I am,

Very sincerely,
Henry O. Flipper

---

[8]Thrapp, *Encyclopedia of Frontier Biography*, 1:501; and Harris, ed., *Black Frontiersman*, 6, 65.

[9]"A Mexican Bonanza," *Nogales Record*, 26 May 1887, 2/2. This article claimed that Flipper actually located the mines.

About All I Know of the Mormons

On the last day of October 1887, Sam Brannan arrived in San Francisco from Mexico on the *Newbern*.[10] The visit (and a later encounter with a reporter in San Diego) produced several newspaper stories that worked "the rich mine of his memory" of old California. Much of this historical ore was salted with questionable claims, but these articles demonstrate how creatively the old pioneer could reconstruct his past. His involvement with Mormonism was now simply "poppycock," and the *Brooklyn* voyage a mere "business venture."

"OLD LANDMARKS,"
SAN FRANCISCO MORNING CALL, 12 NOVEMBER 1887, 5/7.

Some Reminiscenses [*sic*] of Ancient Pioneer Buildings

Fifteen Dollars for a Fifty-Vara Lot on Stockton and
Washington Streets—High-Toned Dwellings of the Past

Recently there has been removed from the corner of Dupont and Clay streets a building which had occupied the position of a landmark and time-register to many old-timers. The building was no less than the old Lefan House, which was placed in position as far back as 1851. It was a zinc building and formed part of the cargo of forty-two of the same description which were brought by ship in 1850, at great expense, from New York.

Old Sam Brannan, one of the earliest California pioneers, in conversation lately with a CALL reporter on the subject, drew from the rich mine of his memory many interesting details of the old building. "Ay," he said, "I can remember well when that cargo of two-storied zinc affairs came in. They called them English fire-proof buildings. I believe the one you speak of is the last of the lot extant in the State. The others were terribly tested as to their fire-proof qualities in the two fires we had soon after their arrival. The Lefan House was put up after a second fire and has stood till now. Out of six or eight shiploads [of houses] I don't believe there is another [standing] to-day.

WHERE THE SHIP STRANDED.

"I can see the old place now as it was then. But you must not suppose it was spoken of lightly in those days. By no means, it was decidedly aristocratic as houses went then.

"You must remember that we had no place—half of us—to put our heads under, much less our things, our grub and that. Folks were glad to get hold of

---

[10]*Sacramento Union*, 2 November 1887, 2/4.

a bit of canvas and stretch themselves under a makeshift tent. And it was located close to the water front. You know the old Niantic Building on Clay and Sansome?—well a ship stranded where that now stands. I remember—"[11]

The reporter hastened to bring back the speaker's train of thoughts to the house in question by asking:

"Did Lefan let his building?"

"That house—yes. He divided it up into rooms and rented the rooms. It was mostly lawyers and miners with luck that frequented it. It was very high toned. I think Lefan came from New York. He died quite twenty years ago. You know that house close by it, in the middle of the block above the Plaza? Well, B. Davidson built that. He was the Rothchilds' California agent. Yes, it was a toney neighborhood."

BEFORE THE FIFTIES

Captain Samuel Brannan[12] built for himself the old house on the corner of Washington and Stockton streets, which is shortly to disappear. The house was built in 1847, the timber for it being sawn out the same year. It was constructed of redwood throughout, and the lumber came from the redwoods at the back of the bay, in Oakland. He hired a man named [Stephen] Smith to saw out the lumber by hand.[13]

The land on which it stood was granted by Bartlett. He paid 15.62^1/_2$ for the 50-vara lot, 137 feet square. There were no houses anywhere round and the lot was covered with scrub oaks, which they had to cut down to make room to build. He made a contact with a man named [Seth S.] Lincoln, a carpenter from the Society Islands, to build it. It was a frame house, one and a half stories high. He lived in it from 1847 until 1852, when he rented it to a Mr. Gregory Yale, the eminent lawyer, who afterward bought it and the surrounding property.

Cribbing much information from Bancroft, another reporter found Brannan "broken in strength," needing a cane to get about. Yet "his spirit has survived the decay of the body." Brannan remained "as full of ambition as a man in his prime."

---

[11]The remains of the *Niantic* still lie near the intersection of Battery and Clay streets in San Francisco's business district. See Richards, *Historic San Francisco,* 74–75.

[12]According to Barnes, "Anent Samuel Brannan," *San Francisco Evening Bulletin,* 12 October 1895, 9/3, in 1867 Brannan was a captain in the First California Light Guard, which "owed its existence to Brannan."

[13]This house, located facing Washington Street at its intersection with Stockton, "was among the first residences of any pretention [*sic*] of the pioneer days of San Francisco." Although Soulé, *The Annals of San Francisco,* 347, reported that it had burned, Charles G. Yale recalled that his father bought the house from Brannan in 1851. It survived the fires of 1851 but was later moved and was finally destroyed in the 1906 earthquake. See Yale to Cushing, 14 February 1926, Society of California Pioneers.

"Sam Brannan,"

San Francisco Examiner, 15 January 1888, 10/7.

[San Francisco Correspondent of the N.Y. Tribune.]

The Adventurous Life of a Noted California Pioneer

A Vigilante Leader

Of fine Business Ability, and Once the Wealthiest Man in the State

Samuel Brannan was a born speculator, who made a princely fortune in ten years, lost it in another decade, and now in his old age is sanguine of wrestling a second fortune from a huge land grant in Sonora. Brannan came from Maine, and in Ohio learned the printer's trade. When he was 19 he bought up his time and plunged into real-estate speculation, coming out with no more cash than he went in, but learning valuable lessons in business experience. Then he strolled about the country as a journeyman printer. In this way he came in contact with the Mormons, and, being struck with their creed, joined them, and for three years in New York City published their organ, the New York *Messenger*. It was in 1846 that he conceived the plan of forming a Mormon colony in California, then Mexican territory. He secured the approval of Brigham Young, chartered the ship Brooklyn, fitted her up for passengers, stocked her with food and all manner of agricultural implements and tools, not forgetting printing press and paper, secured 236 passengers, mostly Mormons, and then set sail for the new Western land. It was five months before the party reached the Sandwich Islands, where they made a brief stay. Then they were transferred to San Francisco. Some stayed in the city, but the majority went into the country, settling at a place called Mormon Island, on the Sacramento river.

Brannan showed great administrative ability in his management of this party, but when he got all the colonists well settled he was intensely disgusted to learn that Brigham Young had decided not to move the headquarters of the Latter-Day Saints to the Pacific Coast. Brannan made a trip to Salt Lake City to see Young, and being unable to shake his decision he returned to San Francisco with his Mormon enthusiasm greatly cooled. In the following year he wound up the concerns of the Mormon enterprise and began business on his own account. He erected two flour mills in San Francisco, established the *Star*, the first newspaper published on the Coast, started a country store at Sutter's Fort on the Sacramento River, and speculated in town lots. The discovery of gold proved the first step in Brannan's great fortune. When he learned the news of Marshall's discovery in the millrace on Sutter's farm, he at once bought large quantities of goods in San Francisco and shipped them to his store near the fort. When the gold rush came a few months afterward he did an enormous business, his sales amounting to $150,000 a month, on which the profit was fully three-quarters.

The city of Sacramento, afterward the capital of the State, grew up around Brannan's store. He made thousands by selling off town lots, but he soon found Sacramento too cramped for his speculative ability. He carried on mining at Mormon Island, went into the China trade in San Francisco and bought heavily of real estate in the young and growing city. He improved everything that he purchased, built fine business blocks, opened up streets and took a lively interest in the municipal governments. He was President of the first Vigilance Committee, and one of the Vice-Presidents of the great Vigilance Committee of 1856. As early as 1857 he was recognized as the richest man in California, and he occupied this position until as late as 1864. His energy appeared inexhaustible. Now he was developing the resources of sugar and fruit plantations in the Sandwich Islands, and now opening new mines in Nevada and Utah. Every one with a scheme for developing the country went to Brannan for aid in those years, just as they went ten years later to [banker William] Ralston.

For fifteen years Brannan was the leading citizen of San Francisco. He was a man of immense force of character and great originality and independence. In every public enterprise he was foremost, and his liberality kept pace with his fortune. In an unlucky hour he purchased the Calistoga estate, in the upper Napa valley, and started to make it a great public resort. He built a costly railroad to the place, and spent hundreds of thousands trying to beautify what was naturally a sterile and mountainous spot. He lost not less than five millions by this venture. Then one after another his mining schemes failed. Like most of the Argonauts who lived at high pressure and made fortunes in a month, he drank a great deal, and as his fortunes began to decline he was seldom sober after midday. Thus the man who was noted as an organizer, and whose shrewdness was proof against all tricks, fell an easy victim to swindlers. He had his vices also, and one of the costliest was his passion for actresses. He lavished a fortune on Lola Montez when she was the rage in San Francisco. His charities kept pace with his extravagances, and it was soon seen that Brannan's prestige and wealth were both on the wane.

It took fewer years to scatter than to gather his imperial fortune. Almost before the public was aware of it Brannan had dropped out of prominence. The new generation that had come from the East elbowed him aside, although in his wreck he was superior to them in ability and enterprise. He soon lost his grip entirely, and he would have been left stranded without money or friends had it not been for one of his acts of enterprise years before, which now bore fruit in his dark days. He had always been in favor of the Mexican people, and when Maximilian tried to capture the throne, and a large number of Americans, headed by "Duke" Gwin,[14] were schem-

---

[14]Former California Senator William Gwin's support of the Confederacy in Mexico during the Civil War won him the nickname "Duke of Sonora." See Thrapp, *Encyclopedia of Frontier Biography*, 2:601.

ing to aid the foreign usurper, Brannan gave money and equipped a regiment of troops to aid the Republican cause. Republics are proverbially ungrateful, but Mexico is somewhat of an exception. She voted Brannan a large sum of money, something over $100,000, and a grant of land in Sonora. He obtained $25,000 in 1880, and went to Guaymas to push his scheme for establishing an American colony on his land.

The old speculative instinct seemed for the time to get the better of his dissolute habits, and he entered actively into the scheme of colonization, but when he came to survey his lands he found that the greater part of the grant was ranged over by the Yaqui Indians, and he has been patiently waiting for a settlement of the troubles with this tribe, as fierce and warlike as the Apaches. A few weeks ago he returned to this city on a brief trip, but as was said before, his arrival was almost unnoticed, and he received scant attention from the men who ought to hold him in regard. I can remember well how proudly Brannan used to walk the streets of San Francisco about 1859. Everyone was eager to offer him deference, for he represented millions. He was handsome then, with strong features, a broad forehead and a brilliant eye. He dressed very richly and paid unusual attention to his personal appearance. Now he is old, gray, broken in strength, able only to get about with the aid of a cane. The old keenness of eye alone shows that his spirit has survived the decay of the body, and in fact Brannan is as sanguine and as full of ambition as a man in his prime. Considering the success of the Ensenada colony on Todas Santos Bay, in Lower California, there is no good reason why Brannan, if he lives ten years longer, should not make his Sonora grant worth a million. If he should round out his life with a second fortune his career would be as remarkable as that of Harry Meigs, who fled from San Francisco to escape his creditors, and who closed his life one of the richest of Peruvian railroad builders.

"A STRANGE CAREER,"
SACRAMENTO BEE, 21 JANUARY 1888, 1/1–2.
[Reprinted from San Diego Union]

Pages from the Life of Sam Brannan, the Pioneer

Bringing Mormons Around the Horn

How the Once Richest Man in California Lost His Fortune

An old man, upon whose steel-gray hairs and bent form the finger-marks of a long lifetime were deeply impressed, walked up F street a few days ago and seated himself in a chair in front of the St. James. His step was slow and feeble. A large silk handkerchief encircled his neck, partly covering a woolen shirt, and with an old stiff hat and ordinary clothes, his appearance was no more interesting than that of any old farmer whose world is his ranch.

"That old man sitting there is one of the most remarkable men in the history of California," said a gentleman who sat near by. "It is old Sam Brannan, a man well-known by every pioneer in the State."

"Yes sir; why certainly I'll tell you the history of my life," cordially replied Mr. Brannan to a *Union* reporter. "A great deal has been said about me in the papers, but no reporter has ever come to me and asked me to give him something about my life for publication."

He then proceeded with the narrative of his life's history, stating that he was born in Saco, Maine, sixty-six years ago and that he learned the printer's trade at Painesville, Ohio. During several years succeeding 1841 he published a literary journal at New Orleans, a paper called the *Gazette* at Indianapolis, and the *Messenger* at New York.

THE FIRST NEWSPAPER

Early in the forties he went to New York and a year or so later commenced the publication of the *Prophet*, which was, Mr. Brannan said, purely a literary journal. About this time Mr. Brannan entered into the undertaking that made him famous. According to his story he realized that the Mormons were oppressed in the East, and he accordingly conceived the idea that it would be a money-making investment to charter a ship and convey the Mormons to a country where they could do as they pleased. With this determination, he chartered the ship Brooklyn, a vessel of 400 tons burden and commanded by a Captain Richardson. In a very short time 238 Mormon emigrants, consisting of seventy men, sixty-eight women and 100 children, were obtained, the fare for adults being $50, with $25 additional for sustenance. The ship was loaded with flouring mills, the printing outfit of the *Prophet* office, besides arms, ammunition and general merchandise.

As the ship was ready to sail a difficulty came in the way, which, for a time, made it look as though the expedition would never start. Just before the breaking of the Mexican war the relations of the two countries were greatly strained, and the Mexican Consul told Mr. Brannan that if the vessel ever sailed, it would be sunk before it reached the island of Cuba. Hearing this Mr. Brannan went direct to Washington, arriving after midnight. He direct went to the Executive Mansion, roused Mr. Polk, and related the Mexican Consul's statement to him. The President thereupon sent for the members of his Cabinet, who met at 2 o'clock that night and discussed the situation. The Mexican Consul's statements were considered as a declaration of war on the part of Mexico, and Mr. Brannan was told that if he should decide to take his vessel around the Horn, the United States ship Congress, under Commodore Stockton, should accompany and protect him. Accordingly, the Brooklyn sailed from New York on February 4th 1846, destined for San Francisco via Honolulu.

Brannan and the Mormons

The Congress did not sail until three weeks later, but when the Brooklyn arrived at Honolulu the Congress was there waiting for her.[15] Stockton had found it necessary to arm his men with rifles, and accordingly all the firearms, powder and bullets on the Brooklyn were transferred to the Congress, but these were not enough, and Stockton, Mr. Brannan says, induced him to smuggle 300 stands of arms on board his vessel for the Congress. This was done at night, and a day or two after the ship sailed from Honolulu for California. Commodore Stockton proceeded in the Congress to Monterey, where the American flag was raised on July 9, 1846, but the Brooklyn went direct to San Francisco, arriving there on the last day of the month. Nothing unusual occurred on the voyage and no objection was made at San Francisco to the Mormons landing there. They proved to be sober, industrious and fine workers, Mr. Brannan said, "but right here," he continued, "I want to say that all these stories about my being a Mormon, and about my bringing a boatload of Mormons here for colonization purposes are simply 'poppycock.' I chartered the ship and brought them out here only as a business venture and not for religious purposes. After the gold mines had been discovered and the Mormons had made themselves rich in them, Brigham Young ordered them all back to Salt Lake and fleeced them. That's about all I know of the Mormons."

The Richest Man in California

Soon after he arrived in San Francisco, Mr. Brannan started the *Yerba Buena Star*, which, after a year's existence, was changed to the *Alta California*. The *Star* was a small weekly paper, printed with the materials of the *Prophet* office, which was brought out on the Brooklyn. Mr. Brannan's next venture was a general merchandise store, and before the expiration of a year, he had large branch stores at Sutter's Fort, now Sacramento, Stockton, Coloma, and at other points along the Sacramento and San Joaquin rivers. When gold was discovered these stores did an immense business at enormous profits, and Mr. Brannan's wealth increased until he became the richest man in California. He was a leader in all the public improvements in the earlier days of San Francisco, took an active part in the old vigilance committee work, and was a member of the Town Council under General Geary, who was the last Alcalde and first Mayor of San Francisco. He was also a member of the Sacramento Town Council in the early fifties. During that time General Sherman, then Lieutenant Sherman, was camped there, and as the matter of naming streets had been left in Mr. Brannan's hands, he wished to honor the young Lieutenant by calling the principal thoroughfare Sherman street.

---

[15]Commodore Richard Stockton and the *Congress* actually left Norfolk on 25 October 1845.

Sherman objected, however, stating it would be better to designate the streets by letters of the alphabet and by numbers. Acting upon Lieutenant Sherman's suggestion, the streets were so named. The principal streets of San Francisco were located during Mr. Brannan's incumbency in the Town Council and one of these thoroughfares bears his name.

A WRECK PHYSICALLY AND FINANCIALLY

In 1858 Mr. Brannan purchased the famous Calistoga estate, upon which he erected the largest distillery on the coast, and ten years later, in protecting the property from a mob that endeavored to capture it, he was shot eight times, but the remarkable man's life was spared. Early in the '60s, Mr. Brannan took to drink, and it has been said that for twenty years he was rarely sober after the hour of noon. Gradually his vast estates were divided and his immense riches melted away, until he found himself a physical and financial wreck. The whole right side of his body, his tongue, arm and face became paralyzed, but he stopped drinking, his paralysis wore away, and now, although he appears aged, his mind is as bright and it seems as full of vigor as it ever was. In the days of his prosperity he had liberally supported Mexico against Maximilian and the French invasion, and to repay him in a measure for the services rendered, in 1879 the Mexican Government granted him nearly 2,000,000 acres of land in the State of Sonora. Three or four years later he moved from San Francisco to Guaymas, where he has since resided and endeavored, with considerable success, to work up colonization schemes. He is still in the Mexican land business, but says he is tired of Guaymas and for that reason has located in Old San Diego.

BLOOD AND "BIG MONEY," OR, WHAT THE YANKEES CAN DO

Brannan had settled at Escondido in rural San Diego County by late December 1887. He considered the area the "coming country" and purchased a "little fruit farm" of some one hundred acres, now "the only home of one whose landed property had once been measured by provinces."[16] His new letterhead advertised "Office of Samuel Brannan, Dealer In REAL ESTATE." An Escondido pioneer recalled Brannan was "white haired, walked with a cane, was never known to indulge in liquor, and was afflicted with epileptic seizures."[17] With his business at a standstill, Brannan again outlined his vision of the future for Jesse Little.

---

[16]Brannan to Badlam, 13 May 1888, Box 3, California State Library; and "The Pioneer at Rest," *San Francisco Examiner*, 7 May 1889, 1/3.

[17]"Mr. Bradbury," in Samuel Brannan—Appearance, Paul Bailey Papers, Utah State Hist. Soc.

BRANNAN TO LITTLE, 24 DECEMBER 1887,
FOLDER 6, BYU BRANNAN PAPERS.

North San Diego, Dec. 24ᵗʰ 1887

Friend Little, I have carefully read your long letter. I agree with you, but that prophet you speak of, I think has already raised, and [is] now being educated, & that is the government of the *United States*, and it will lead a foolish people not God's people, out of the bondage of the Human Mind which is the bullwork of Paganism the twin Sister of Slavery. I mean that damnable doctrine of Polygamy, and that too with blood as the North did the South with her institution of Slavery. They boath are crimes that the World can never get rid of without *blood* and *"big Money."*

God is God of the whole World [and] the mormons are but a small figure in camp, but he will use them for his purposes nevertheless, and Uncle Sam as his big prophet and the "Boys in Blue" for his fighting men until Polygamy, Slavery and Idolitry, are exterminated from the whole earth; All Christian Isms will be drawn into that battle, and will be made to fight for or against it. Until the world is rid of the Plague.

Then will commence the reign of peace and not before. The battle of Gog and Ma Gog must be fought first, and that *is*, *"Polygamy"* and *"Slavery,"* must go first, and then *Idolitry* to wind it up. This will take some hundred years, and eventually there will be no other, but a white race, coming from the Collage and School House with no forts or navies or Soldiers, & all [will] earn their bread by industries of various kinds, according to their capacity. By that time they will know the use of wine and Spirits, and a tolerable fair knowledge of other Worlds, and God to[o] if he dont keep out of sight. That old bundle of Jewish Manuscripts, called the *Bible* has got a few true sayings in it, but [is] principlly made up of old yarns and fiction and a History of a very wicked peopl[e], guilty of the most horible crimes.

The world has been full of prophets, good & bad since it was m[a]de, but in the present age, it is getting innundated with the prophets, or smart men as we call them.

Nothing to report on business, but will soon. My health is improving wonderfully. I have hopes of getting well, and strike a 100 years before I hand in my checks.

This is a great country and shows what the Yankees can do when they start in. There is not Steam Boats & R.R.'s enough for freight and passengers.

Yours very truly Saml Brannan

Through the first half of 1888, Brannan's business ventures were gridlocked. He tried to exchange some of his Mexican land claims for cash, but he was unable to finance a trip to Mexico City on what would probably have been a fool's errand. Even as he regaled Little with tales of his new El Dorado and his apocalyptic visions, Brannan could never let go of the past—or his long-standing grudge against Brigham Young. Yet in the face of his poverty and limited prospects, Brannan's relentless optimism remained undimmed: "My Star was never on the wain from birth."

BRANNAN TO LITTLE, 6 FEBRUARY 1888,
FOLDER 7, BYU BRANNAN PAPERS.

North San Diego, Feb. 6th 1888

My dear friend Little,

Yours of the 29th at hand. I shall go to the City of Mexico by rail & return immediately, & then I hope to inform you what our prospects are, and the outlook.

With regard to Brigham I have nothing to say, but that he did not keep his word, and my trip into the mountains in 47 was for nothing, and his people has been the suffer[ers] for it, and the whole world benefited. He evidently showed himself a coward in not coming to San Francisco or here or some important point on the coast. Now he has ruined his whole Organization, & like the Jews they well be scattered among the whole world where they belong, & will do some good instead of harme. The gods placed it in their power to be the richest people in the world and [sic] as well as useful, but they trusted too much on God fighting for them in the Clouds for their Imaginary wrongs, and became a body of cunning avaricious distinktive [peo]ple, like the Jews only more so, thinking they were the chosen people of God; as you say they drive all well meaning and thinking people from among them, and tried to make a Basterd of Masonry, and spoilt the whole job, by substituting cunning for wisdom, & showed their shirt tails. Brighams greed for money in calling it "Church Property" when he intended it *all* for himself has develloped into a disolution and will scatter the whole fraternity. The patriot sentiment of the whole U.S. is aroused and the Oath of a mormon to suport the church before the state will be nev[er] allowed, by 60,000000 million of people, no quicker than slavery was; when Mormonism tries to engraft itself on Mahometanism, Paganism and Judahism, and a few Lamanites that are being annihilated it shows that it is come to its last teather and has showed the lowest stage of weakness, while asking for Power in the *"name of God."*

The man that married the little Saco, Me. girl (Woodruff)[18] will find his match in his old days, to put up the bars after Brigham & Taylor; I pitty the

---

[18]Wilford Woodruff married Phoebe Carter, a native of Maine, in 1837.

people that have been fooled, some will do well and some will go to the Dogs. I would like to see you out of it and here in this place, it has a great future; from San Francisco South, I can see the big work that I commenced, and Brigham & Taylor in their graves, with poor Woodruff to save the wreck and I alive and everything going a head, and good for 30 years yet.

Brigham & Taylor's Mormonism is like a mushroom, *come & gone.* Congress hated to tackle Slavery but she had to do it, & so she does Mormonism, but she is compeled to do it. Now it is mormonism they have to fight, not Poly[g]amy, and it will result in the death of Woodruff.

The gathering business is played out and the Josephites will find it out so when they hold their Conference next april at Independence, Jackson Co Mo. God uses *all* men for his purposes, Not the Mormons *alone, isms* run into fanaticism, then its greatness is gon[e]. God is progression in itselfe, men are tools.

I wrote this because I had a little spare time and I hope this finds you and yours all well. We have to wait for the waggon and go slow, but this is a past I would have not forgot.

I am in the best of health.

Yours very truly
Saml. Brannan

Brannan sent Little yet another "map of my mines, in the Siera Madra Mountains," but not the key that would make the map usable. The largest mines "are Bonanzers, and immensely rich in Gold & Silver. There is a mountain of Horn Silver & Low Grade Oar near there." The mines "were Originalley owned & worked 100 years ago by the Jesuit Priests, who were all massacred by the Comanches & Apaches." The map was only a copy of one "once in the possession of Maximillian before he was Shot," which Brannan "obtained from his mining Engineer who is now dead."[19] Brannan wanted Little to find someone to furnish money to open the mines in the fall. He reported that anti-polygamy lecturer Kate Field was "here interviewing me for a book she is going to publish."[20] Brannan continued to fulminate against polygamy. "Russia

---

[19]Brannan to Little, 26 February 1888, Folder 7, BYU Brannan Papers. Of the several maps Brannan sent to Little, this description best matches the one now in Folder 17, BYU Brannan Papers.

[20]Mary Katherine Keemle Field (1838–1896), or "That vixen, Kate Field," as Joseph F. Smith called her, was an early feminist, actress, and writer who lectured and lobbied on "the Mormon problem" after a short stay in Utah. See Arrington, *Kate Field and J. H. Beadle,* 1–12. Her book was never published. Despite a long search, the editor has been unable to locate the "3 photos" (which would presumably be the only known portraits of Brannan in old age) mentioned in Brannan's 22 March 1888 letter. Field's letters have been collected in Moss, ed., *Kate Field: Selected Letters.*

will destroy Mahomedon Poligamy," he predicted, "and America will destroy Mormon Polygamy as they did Slavery, and so wags the World." The new prophet, Brannan's old friend, Wilford Woodruff, "will be the last Mormon King, *you bet!*"[21]

During the summer of 1888 Brannan expressed a growing awareness of his mortality. The long struggle to profit from his Mexican land claims was finally wearing him down. His letters indicate that Brannan maintained relations with his Mexican wife much longer than previously thought, and comments about his mother and father contradict the standard stories of his early life. Brannan also described his complicated finances. The Odd Fellows had started an effort to help out the old pioneer, but Brannan felt they "should have done it long ago."[22] William Brown had advanced him twenty-five dollars a month to live on during his stay in Nogales, so Brannan's interest in the Sonora Land and Mining Company and his other land ventures were now encumbered with an $850 debt to Brown and other obligations.[23]

Brannan continued his agricultural pursuits, raising oranges and investigating "Smirney fig trees and Malaga grape vines." He must have had some success, for he was "not Orange hungry or Lemon thirsty."[24] Brannan had come to depend on Alexander Badlam, Jr., for much of his financial support, and he even asked his nephew to get him a tricycle to ride to his orchards. His May 1888 letter to Badlam provides a good example of their correspondence and includes much personal information and arcane detail about his complicated business ventures.

BRANNAN TO BADLAM, 24 MAY 1888,
CALIFORNIA STATE LIBRARY COLLECTION.

North San Diego, May 24th, 1888

Dear Alex,

Yours of the 21st received. I do not wish to divide the Sonora Land, it will sell better and [be] worth more undivided, and I would not travel over that Land to divide it, for the whole of it, as much as I need money, [for] it

---

[21]Brannan to Little, 22 March 1888, Folder 7, BYU Brannan Papers.
[22]*San Francisco Call*, 5 May 1888, 8/5; and Brannan to Badlam, 13 May 1888, Box 3, California State Library Collection.
[23]Luce, "Samuel Brannan: Speculator in Mexican Lands," 109, 114.
[24]Brannan to Badlam, 11 May, 15 and 20 October 1888, Box 3, California State Library Collection.

would take 2 months and then be the death of me. I would rather give it to [Adolph] Sutro. No more Peralesis has for me.

The Certificates of it Stock will be issued any time [for] what is due the Co. I already hold the Secretary's certificit [sic] to that effect for three years.

I have written to Brown yesterday to let 40,000 acres go for $8000 which I dont believe he will get. The whole of it would bring from 1 to $3 if Waterman's road was finished, [for] there is a French & German Cindy-cate, that would take the whole 1,670,000 acres at a dollar [an acre], so you see the importance of my finding out first when it [the railroad] will be finished.

Brown is trying to make some thing off the sale, or get one 40th (40,000 acres) for him self. He has an order for one 40th as security for the money he has advanced ($25) every month for me to live on and pay rent, and come here.

Mrs. B. went to the City of Mexico for her health on the 19th inst. I here nothing from the boy, he wrote me that he had the Lung Fever[25] last March. A gent wrote me yesterday from El Paso that he saw him in Tombstone in March in good health; I guess he is a chip of[f] his mother.

[Francis T.] Wheeler's Brother Wm left Nogales for Chicago on the 20th inst, we will then here his report on Kruse, who is in the Sierra Mountains, hunting for my mines. I hope he will have a good time and find something *rich*. He is within 40 miles of one and going from one. Brown thinks he is a great rogue, but I think there is wors[e]; but he will go for all that is in sight.

If you negotiate a lone for me why not let the Co. issue the Stock to them in trust for me, till the amount is paid, and they pay off my debt to them.

I hold 4 shares, one of 40th each, 40,217 acres, in all 4 times that amount. I had 5 but I gave Frisbie one as attorney's fees, which Kruse or the Co. owes me for, and Wheeler promised to protect me.[26]

If you can make that arrangement, I will come up to S.F. when needed.

I was going into to [sic] New Town to make some arrangements there, but I was waiting to here from Brown, but there is no show with him, in fact he wants to buy it himself if he can sell his property and he cant; and I know it. His ideas are *way up*.

I go out in the morning to the cole mine (dont think it costs me any thing) and back in the evening on the rail 18 miles. There may be something in it. The Equarian statue quo [?]

The Tin Mine is sold in N.Y. for England if it passes examination and my party can put up the security in case it is a failure, for expences.

[25]Pneumonia.
[26]Francis T. Wheeler of San Francisco was trying to sell land for the Sonora Land and Mining Company.

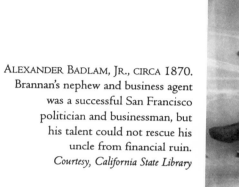

ALEXANDER BADLAM, JR., CIRCA 1870.
Brannan's nephew and business agent
was a successful San Francisco
politician and businessman, but
his talent could not rescue his
uncle from financial ruin.
Courtesy, California State Library

I have arrangements made for the sale of any good mine that will pass muster at a good big price; My friend has just returned from Rome and all Europe to New York and established a regular buisness for cash sales on legitimate [mines] in America of any kind.

Fathers Painting from Memory was sent to me at N. York when I returned from Mexico by my last school teacher, that went to school with your mother & [is] about her age. Charles Granger [was] a splendid Portrait Painter;[27] as I passed through S.F. I left it with your mother to take care of. Will you see if you can find it for me; I wrote to Mary C. twice about it and received no answer; he [Thomas Brannan, Sr.] is taken standing and dressed for winter coming out of the house (it is as I saw him) and as near perfection as need be, you will see his history when I have passed away; he was natures nobleman and his wife also. She was a Knox all over and died a marter to your mother in the far west, Heaven Bless her!

Love to all
Uncle

---

[27]Charles Henry Grainger was a Maine artist; his picture of "an old-time muster" included a "small, bent, old man . . . peddling eggs and pie" that was "said to be Tommy Brannan." See Dunlap, "Samuel Brannan," 2. Reva Scott reproduced this image and a portrait similar to the one described here in *Samuel Brannan and the Golden Fleece*, opposite 116.

Brannan attended the Society of California Pioneers meeting in September 1888 as the oldest surviving "Ex President." An old legend tells that Brannan used $49,000 he extracted from the Mexican government to pay all his old debts during his last visit to San Francisco.[28] Like many such charming Brannan tales, there is not a shred of evidence to support it. Jesse Little wrote to ask him about his long silence and Brannan's reply demonstrates that he was too poor to buy a ticket to San Francisco. This letter was the last in his correspondence with Little.

BRANNAN TO LITTLE, 25 SEPTEMBER 1888,
FOLDER 7, BYU BRANNAN PAPERS.

Escondido, Sept. 25th 1888

Col J. C. Little
My dear Sir
Your letter is at hand, and glad to here you are among the living yet. When I received the map from you and no letter I felt there was something wrong and then none since then, I thought some one intercepted our letters, and think so still. One letter I wrote you, you could not otherwise than be answered [sic]. But never mind they found out but little.

I had to go to San Francisco to attend the Pioneers. I am the Oldest Ex President and one of the founders of the Society. The Old Ones are passing away. The steamer gave me a Complimentry Passage or I would not have gone.

After my arrival in San Diego The Mexican Gov. made arrangements for a $60 Million Loan with the Berlin Bankers in Germany in case there was no war in Europe by the first of May fowling [sic]. I then made up my mind to take money instead of land, if they got it, and wrote to N.Y. and to you the same before I went to S. F. and remain in the same mind still, if so it would be necessary for me to go there, and that would take more money than I could rais[e], until the Chicago matter is settled and that I learn will not be till next January.

I am satisfied the land would be of no use to me, it will bring no money, and will be of no benefit to us. My people in New York were in Europe at the time, and they have agreed to it, since their return.

The American People are opposed to any Govt. but the Stars and Stripes, unless it is the "Mormons" and "Solid South" and you know they are no good to themselves or any one else; They are Rebels yet, and want a solid North and they will get it, this or [the] next Presidential Election sure! and another war if they want it. Cleveland's dog is dead this time, his game can't win any more.

---

[28]Stellman, *Sam Brannan, Builder of San Francisco*, 236.

I shall remain here for the future. This is "*the place*," the Climate is delightful, Summer & Winter, and the scenery grand, and I have commenced
preparing the Ground for an Orange Nursery to pay expenses.

Brown thinks of coming here. He is not in the employment of the Co.
and Kruse is in Nogales sick with the fever; lost his wife sister and 2 brothers; he has not treated me well, and he had better look out or he will loose
himself. I shall go to Mexico as soon as I can rais[e] the means and make a
final settlement. I think it is the best that I did not take the land from the
Mexicans, I hope so at any rate, what is your views, on things [in] general.

Polygamy is on the down hill grade, and China Slavery too. Let them
slide they are not needed. I am within 4 miles of where the Mexicans
whipped Gen. Carney.[29]

Your true friend   yours
Saml Brannan

The Blues—I Never Had Them

As 1888 drew to a close, Brannan developed serious health problems
that he accepted philosophically. He was unable to swallow solid food,
and "it is d—d inconvenient when I go to eat, but I must not expect to
have everything my way." After a visit from his nephew, he made a
remarkable confession: "The morning you left I felt very bad, perhaps
you would call that the blues. I never had them."[30]

His financial situation had gone beyond embarrassment. Brannan
wrote to the Society of California Pioneers to try to recover part of his
book collection and become the beneficiary of his past charities, which
had apparently been embezzled by the society's secretary, the same Ferdinand Vassault who had once saved him from being swindled. Brannan
concluded that "All cannot die rich" and seems to have accepted that he
would be included in that number.[31]

The last of Samuel Brannan's surviving papers is a letter to John Dart,
a friend of his son, that was composed on the eve of his seventieth birthday. Department store heir Herbert S. Auerbach, whose father had
known Brannan in the gold rush, later interviewed Dart. Auerbach was

---

[29]Mounted Californians killed twenty-two of General Stephen W. Kearny's one hundred dragoons at San Pasqual on 8 December 1846.

[30]Brannan to Badlam, 16 November 1888, Box 3, California State Library Collection.

[31]Brannan to H. F. Graves, 16 January 1889, Society of California Pioneers.

working on a never-finished biography of Brannan, and acquired this letter from Dart.

BRANNAN TO JOHN N. DART, 1 MARCH 1889,
AUERBACH COLLECTION, BRIGHAM YOUNG UNIVERSITY.

Escondido, March 1ˢᵗ 1889

John N. Dart, Esq.
 Tombstone, A.T.
  Dear Sir

  Your favor of the 25th & Check with a letter from Saml [Samuel Brannan, Jr.], is at hand, and [is a] great relief to my mind, supposing Saml was sick or dead; he never writes, by and by he will be glad to; Mr. W. W. Thomas, is at San Diego arranging for another R.R. to come here from the East to San Diego, (I think he will win). When he returns, I will arrange about your Taxes.

  If Thomas succeeds, your land will be worth $1000 per acre, some parties has applied for it already. I sent you a paper on taxes, and a letter for Saml.

  My health is much better. [I am] 70 years old tomorrow; Saml & Me was on the Coast of Africa in sight of Cape De Verd Islands, 42 years ago to day; write, before you le[a]ve when you will be back; The Dam & Floom will be commenced in a few days; and the street from Depot to Hotel is being graded.

Yours truly
Saml Brannan

How is Saml Doing, is he steady, he should write.

PEACE TO HIS ASHES

The fall before he died, Brannan wrote his nephew, "I am rooming over the Confectionary, and boarding there, on the main street to the Hotel opposite the Bank and Post Office." Legend has it that Brannan spent his last days in Escondido at the boarding house of Magdalena Moraga, relying on her care as his health failed.[32] A bowel ailment laid him low in April 1889 and he fought a two-week battle with death. The elders of the Reorganized Church of Jesus Christ of Latter Day Saints—including perhaps Joseph Smith III himself—visited Brannan

---

[32]Bailey, *Sam Brannan and the California Mormons*, 247; Scott, *Samuel Brannan and the Golden Fleece*, 441; and Brannan to Badlam, 9 October 1888, Typescript, Sorensen Papers.

"on his deathbed, but too late for a satisfactory interview."[33] The old pioneer died on Sunday evening, 5 May 1889.[34] One biographer claimed that Brannan asked for his pants shortly before he died and removed a twenty-dollar gold piece. "Parley Pratt, the Mormon elder, said I'd die without a dime," he said. "I fooled him."[35]

Brannan's obituaries recalled his days of glory, and most repeated the many legends that already obscured the facts of his life. A fair example of the mythic recounting of his life appeared in the *San Francisco Examiner*.

"THE PIONEER AT REST,"
SAN FRANCISCO EXAMINER, 7 MAY 1889, 1/3-4.
Sam Brannan Dies at Escondido, Aged Seventy Years.

His Singular Life.

Reminiscences of One of the Strangest and Most Remarkable of Men.

Was He Ever a Mormon?

On Sunday evening at Escondido, near San Diego, died Samuel Brannan, after being confined to his house for two weeks in consequences of an aggravated attack of inflammation of the bowels. With his death passes away the bearer of one more of the pioneer names which will always hold a familiar place in the memories of Californians.

He died on the little fruit farm of about one hundred acres, which had, in his last years, become the only home of one whose landed property had once been measured by provinces.

Samuel Brannan—or, to give him a name which has far more historical significance, "Sam" Brannan—was a native of Saco, Me, the son of Thomas Brannan of that place. He was born on the 2d of March, 1819, and was consequently seventy years, two months, and three days old at his death. He lived a long life, and one which almost from infancy was a succession of scenes of the most enterprising labor and effort.

When fourteen years of age he located in Lake county, Ohio, where he became a printer's apprentice. After serving three years, however, though but seventeen years of age, he pined for a freer field for his energies, bought the remainder of his time and launched into real estate speculation. He soon

---

[33]Smith, III, *The History of the Reorganized Church*, 3:194. Joseph Smith III was in California at this time, but his surviving correspondence does not mention visiting Brannan.

[34]The date of Brannan's death is often given as 6, 7,10, or 14 1889 May, but reports of his death on Sunday evening establish the date as 5 May.

[35]Stellman, *Sam Brannan, Builder of San Francisco*, 239. Alone among Brannan's biographers, Stellman correctly dated Brannan's death, but he provided no source for this wonderful but unlikely tale.

discovered that this was not all it was "cracked up" to be, however, and resumed work as a journeyman printer, travelling as such over a great portion of the Union. From 1842 to 1844 he was the printer and proprietor of the *New-York Messenger*, a weekly political journal published in the eastern metropolis.

AN EARLY ARGONAUT.

But a year or two later, having in the mean time become interested, to a certain extent at least, in Mormonism, he determined on a yet bolder flight than any he had adventured upon, and in the first weeks of 1846 he was found organizing a company of "Saints" for an expedition to the then almost totally unknown territory of California. No obstacle was offered to interfere with the enterprise, and on the 4th of February, in the good ship Brooklyn, which had been chartered for the purpose, the party left New York, 230 souls in all. On the last day of July in the same year the ship dropped anchor in the bay of San Francisco.

There has always been some difference of opinion regarding the precise nature of Brannan's early connection with the Mormon movement, though by some authorities the assertion is pointedly made that he was an earnest convert to the faith and had brought his shipload of immigrants at this early day to the California coast with an idea of getting at once and forever entirely beyond the jurisdiction of the United States. If this were true the sight of the American flag proudly dominating the entire territory when the Brooklyn first entered the bay must have been rather startling at first, and a comical story, doubtless manufactured to fit the occasion, is told of the manner in which the pilgrim commander expressed his feelings at the sight; "Well I'm blessed!" he is quoted as saying; "there's that d——d flag again!"

But this story, though amusing, is generally discredited, doubtless with reason, for certainly Sam Brannan did good service for his new State later on, and proved himself in every sense an American.

At all events he accepted the situation immediately, entered heartily into the work that was to be done, and became at once, as young as he was, a man of work in the infant community. Two flour mills, erected on about what is now the line of Clay street, were among the first evidences of his enterprises.

THE FIRST NEWSPAPER.

But his old printer's trade still had attractions for him, and in January, 1847, he brought out the initial number of the California *Star*, which came within about one of being the first English newspaper published on the Pacific Coast. The single exception was the *Californian*, a $5 weekly published at Monterey by Colton & Semple, who brought out their first number August 15, 1846. In May of the following year however the *Californian* removed to San Francisco, and a month later consolidated with the *Star*, so honors were easy.

It was the *Californian*, by the way, the first issues of which were printed with the famous font of Spanish type containing no w's, instead of which double v's had to be utilized. The printer actually printed a paragraph of explanation in regard to this until the matter was remedied, the effect of the constantly recurring v's being rather more bewildering in the explanation than anywhere else in the paper.

In May, 1848, Brannan, in a measure, came to grief with the *Star*. Not from any loss of business popularity, but from the simple circumstance that everybody in the office except himself—printers, foremen, devil and all, dropped rule and composing stick and rushed away to the mines. Calmly Brannan took the bull by the horns, suspended publication—he could, indeed, do nothing else—and quietly slipped away to the mines to see for himself what was in the glittering tales. What conclusion he came to was evident.

SAM BRANNAN EXCITED.

Through the main streets of San Francisco one day late in May walked, or rather, rushed Sam Brannan, excited then if never excited before in his life. In one hand he held on high a bottle full of the shining "dust," while, as he wildly swung his hat in the other, he shouted again and again:

"Gold, gold, gold! from the American River!"

It was enough. The last doubt of the most dubious in San Francisco was removed. Sam Brannan had spoken, and Sam Brannan never made a mistake on subjects such as this.

This statement is no exaggeration, though perhaps it had a little more force at a later date. It was, indeed, some years later when, all over the Pacific Coast, wherever, at least, the paint brush of the pictorial advertiser had gone, were seen such signs as—"Buy 'Pinole.' Everybody buys 'Pinole.' Sam Brannan buys it." Certainly, everybody wanted to buy what Sam Brannan did, though not so many succeeded.

In September of the year of the gold discovery Brannan sold out his printing "plant" to E. C. Kemble, who out of the *Star* and *Californian* created the *Alta*. But while engaged in his publishing business, Mr. Brannan had not neglected other interests, but constantly seized such opportunities as arose to acquire desirably situated real estate, both in San Francisco and the interior, the wisdom of which became apparent later when he was known as one of the richest men on the Pacific Coast. He also engaged largely in commercial enterprises, late in 1847 starting, in connection with C. C. Smith, a store at Sutter's Fort, the first in the Sacramento valley. In the following year he bought out his partner, and conducted the business personally, removing thither for the purpose immediately after disposing of his newspaper.

How He Arrested a Philosopher

It was during his stay at Sutter's Fort Brannan first figured as an Alcalde, and had his encounter with "Philosopher" Pickett, an incident which illustrates both his courage and general convivial qualities. Pickett had killed a man, and though it turned out to be a case of self-defense, it was felt that a proper legal investigation must be held.

Alcalde Bates was directed to arrest Pickett and bring him before a jury of his peers for trial. Alcalde Bates respectfully declined. Pickett had already killed one man and the Alcalde was not ambitious of figuring second in the list. Rather than undertake the arrest, he quietly resigned his office.

But this did not suit the majority of the residents and it did not suit Brannan. The latter called a public meeting, where the matter was considered at length and which resulted in Brannan himself being chose the new Alcalde, and directed to arrest Pickett. Brannan quietly hunted the philosopher up, told him to come along and the philosopher came. But his belt was bristling with weapons and Alcalde Brannan told him to lay them on the table before the Court. Pickett laid them on the table. Then the trial proceeded, resulting in everybody, Judge, jury and prisoner, imbibing freely of whiskey and water until a recess was taken until the next day, the defendant being kindly furnished with his weapon again and allowed to go until morning. The ultimate result of the case was, and quite properly, an acquittal.[36]

A Transaction in Tea

Returning to San Francisco in 1849, Mr. Brannan invested in the China tea trade with a partner, the firm name being Osborn & Brannan, and the business which they did was said to have been something almost phenomenal. Brannan never missed a chance, and many were the shrewd moves with which he was credited. It sometimes happened that cargoes of tea were sold out on the street at public auction, and one such occasion the "trade" had occasion to remember.

Gillespie, the famous old-time auctioneer, was officiating. "Gentlemen, give me a bid," he said. "Ten chests, with the privilege of as many more as you want. Give me a bid."

Thirty-five cents a pound was offered as a starter, and the figures ran up, 5 cents at a time, to 60 cents a pound. There they stopped, and while Brannan, who had not yet opened his mouth, still sat on a dry-goods box whittling a stick, the tea seemed about to be knocked down for 60 cents a pound.

"Going, going, go——" said the auctioneer.

"Sixty-one cents," interrupted Brannan, and the auctioneer took the usual second wind.

---

[36]This story was taken from Bancroft, *California Inter Pocula*, 608–09.

Now there was a consultation. The tea was worth in the market all the way from $1.50 to $4 a pound, perhaps even more, but it wouldn't do to run it up any higher. It would be better to let Brannan get his 50 cases or so out of the 500 which there were in all, even at his own price, that the other buyers might secure their's equally low. There was tea enough there to supply the State it would seem. So the bidding stopped and Brannan's bid won.

"How much do you take Mr. Brannan?" inquired Gillespie. "Twenty cases? Thirty? Fifty?"

"The whole — concern!" exclaimed Brannan, getting down from his box and walking off amid the disgusted looks of his late companions.[37]

ELECTED TO OFFICE

In August, 1849, Brannan was elected a member of the Town Council. Two years later he attained to another position of magisterial dignity, though [of] somewhat irregular authorization, being chosen President of the Vigilance Committee. The "Hounds" and other outlaws of the day had no sterner, braver, more implacable foe than Sam Brannan.

In the winter of 1851 Mr. Brannan visited the Sandwich Islands, as a matter of course investing while there in real estate, and with his usual good judgment.

He took a great deal of interest in the organization of the California Pioneers, and in the years 1853 and 1854 served as President of the Society. In 1853 he was elected State Senator, and in 1861 was Presidential Elector on the Republican ticket.

Previous to the latter date, in November, 1856, Brannan brought himself prominently into notice in connection with the killing of United States Marshal Richardson by Charles Cora, the Italian gambler. Cora shot down his man about 6:30 o'clock on the evening of the 17th. Then he delivered himself up to the officers of the law, feeling as confident, perhaps, as did the mass of the indignant populace, that thus he secured his ultimate safety. But the bells began to ring and the crowds to gather, and above the throng at the Oriental Hotel was seen the form of Sam Brannan, his voice ringing out over the turmoil, urging the instant execution of Cora. The Sheriff commanded him to desist, but he refused. Then the official arrested him and started with him to the Station-house. A howling and hooting mob followed the two, and a rescue was about to be immediately effected. But Brannan restrained his friends, and at the Station-house the officials made a virtue of necessity and released him on his own recognizance.

BRANNAN'S LIBERALITY

The first school in San Francisco was made a success largely through

---

[37]See Ibid., 346–47 for the source of this story.

Brannan's liberality, and, in this connection, some further mention should certainly be made of that exceeding generosity of disposition which was ever one of his most distinguishing characteristics. Among all the many liberal California givers to the fund raised for the Sanitary Commission during the war, none equaled the extent of Brannan's donations, and the same might also be said to be true of his part in the furtherance of every other charitable and worthy object.

Later in the "sixties" reverses began to come upon him. He had advanced a large amount of money to the Republican party of Mexico to assist in the war against Maximilian, the American legion in the patriotic army being known as "Brannan's contingent." The honor, however, scarcely supplied the place of hard coin just when it was most needed. His wife, too, obtained a divorce from him about this time, and in the settlement between them he deeded her and her four children a great amount of property. A period of financial stagnation supervening, he soon found himself terribly embarrassed.

Applying to the Mexican Government for compensation for what he had formerly done in its behalf, he obtained a grant of 2,000,000 acres of wild land, cumbered with burdensome conditions, and—more serious still—nearly all in the actual possession of warlike Indians. Subsequently, however, he secured what seemed to be a more advantageous concession, in the State of Sonora, which it was necessary that he should have surveyed in order to secure entire possession of. He had the work done, but it consumed $100,000, and when it was completed he found his great domain had melted from his grasp. For two years past his home has been in the modest cottage on the fruit farm in Escondido, where he died.

John S. Hittell's obituary was the most thoughtful contemporary summary of Brannan's life.[38] Hittell made only a few minor errors, producing an effort worthy of the man many consider the best of California's nineteenth-century historians.

JOHN S. HITTELL, "SAMUEL BRANNAN,"
OVERLAND MONTHLY (JUNE 1889), 648–50.

We have no direct knowledge of the plans of the Mormon leaders in sending a colony to San Francisco early in 1846; but circumstances indicate that they intended to establish the sacred city of their faith in California.

They had been driven by popular persecution from their homes in Ohio, then in Missouri, and again in Illinois. There was evidently no peace nor

---

[38]For other obituaries, see *Sacramento Union*, 7 May 1889, 2/2; *New York Times*, 7 May 1889, 4/5; *San Francisco Morning Call*, 8 May 1889, 4/3; and *The Saints' Herald*, 25 May 1889, 323/2–3.

safety for them in the settled portions of the United States. They must seek a refuge elsewhere. In Missouri they heard of the sunny region on the shore of the Pacific, where fertility of soil, geniality of climate, and cheapness of land and cattle offered attractions greater than those of Palestine in the time of the Hebrew patriarchs. The scantiness of the Mexican population and their lazy mode of life were guarantees of security. It was the land of promise.

Nothing but an American conquest and a large American settlement were to be feared, and they seemed remote. Before their occurrence a Mormon community might grow up with strength enough to defend itself against aggression, and perhaps to declare and maintain its independence. Brigham Young and his associates did not know that the American cabinet had for years been scheming to get possession of California, had given orders to their fleet on the western coast of North America to be ready to take possession of the coveted territory at the first outbreak of hostilities, and looked forward, at the close of 1845, to war with Mexico as one of the events of the near future.

Undoubtedly the Mormon leaders regarded the conquest of California by the Americans as a not remote probability—as something that might occur within ten or twenty years—but they could not anticipate that it would be followed promptly by a wonderful gold discovery and a great migration across the continent. There was still [in 1846] abundant room for settlers in Iowa, Missouri, Dakota, Wisconsin, Minnesota, Arkansas, Texas, Kansas, and Nebraska; and the remote California might be left for many years to the Latter Day Saints.

Concentration of forces has ever been the policy of the Mormon Church. They have sent their missionaries to distant lands, but urge all converts to gather about their chief place of worship. It was so in Ohio, so in Missouri, so in Illinois, and it is so in Utah. They presumably intended that the California colony should be the nucleus of their new Zion, to be soon founded somewhere. If the pioneers sent favorable reports, all the others would soon follow. Such must have been the ideas with which the Mormons of the ship Brooklyn, under the leadership of Samuel Brannan, set sail, ostensibly for Oregon, in February, 1846, from the harbor of New York.

The party numbered about two hundred and forty, nearly all Mormons. The few Christians among them had been employed by the Mormons, and were regarded as prospective Mormon converts. The immigrants consisted mostly of families. The men were skillful, industrious, and honest mechanics or farmers, men of average intelligence and more than average moral character, as they proved afterwards by their lives in California. They were generally good citizens and good neighbors.

Brannan, then only twenty-seven years of age, was a native of Maine. He had been converted to the faith of Joseph Smith in Ohio, and had published a Mormon journal in New York city. He had all the mental and physical activity, all the enterprise, courage, and decision of character required for leadership in such an enterprise.

The voyage was made without disaster, and after being at sea nearly six months, the immigrants sailed into San Francisco Bay, where, to their astonishment and dismay, they found themselves under the American, not the Mexican, flag. The situation was one for which they were not prepared, but from which they saw no escape. They settled themselves in the village of Yerba Buena, soon to become San Francisco, went to work, bought lots, built houses, and were a valuable and harmonious addition to the American population.

Brannan had brought his press and a young type-setter, Edward C. Kemble, one of the few who were not Mormons. With Kemble's aid, Brannan's printing office was soon open for job work, issuing handbills, placards, and official blanks. In October, a sheet of news was printed; in January, 1847, the weekly California "Star" made its appearance; and in April, 1848, a special edition of the paper was issued for circulation in the Mississippi valley, containing an excellent essay, six columns long, by Dr. Victor Fourgeaud, on the resources of California. Two thousand copies of this issue of the "Star" were sent overland by express, for the purpose of attracting immigrants, with a promise that another paper with useful information for immigrants should be published and dispatched by the 1st of June. But that promise was not kept. Before June the importance of the gold discovery—which had been made on the 24th of January[39]—had so impressed itself on the public mind that nobody wanted to make any effort to attract immigrants. So Brannan's April "Star" for distribution in the Mississippi valley was the first publication of its kind, and indicated as much enterprise and public spirit as anything since printed to boom California.

Besides owning the printing office, Brannan was partner in a store at Sutter's Fort. There the miners went for supplies in the summer of 1848, and as prices were very high, Brannan made immense profits for a time—rumor said more than $100,000 a month. He became the owner of many lots in the new town of Sacramento, and sold them at a great advance. He chartered ships to go to distant ports for provisions. He erected a number of buildings, including some of the most substantial and elegant of the early business houses in San Francisco. The oldest house, except some at the Mission, now standing in San Francisco, was built by him, in 1847, at what is now 30 Washington Alley, near the corner of Jackson and Dupont streets.

He was noted for his public spirit. He gave money liberally to the Vol-

---

[39]Using Henry Bigler's journal, Hittell had established the correct date of the gold discovery.

unteer Fire Department, and to various charities. He was an active member of the Vigilance Committees of 1851 and 1856. Between those years, he was generally regarded as the richest man in the State, and one of the most widely known in San Francisco. He was always full of business, and of bold enterprises, but he undertook too much. He lacked prudence, close calculation, attention to details, knowledge of men, and tact.

Fires and floods in Sacramento, fires in San Francisco, and the failure of his scheme to make a great pleasure resort of Calistoga, were causes of serious loss to him. Before 1865 many other men had become more prominent than he in the business of the State; and before 1870 [sic] he had gone to Mexico in the hope of making another great fortune there. During the French invasion, Brannan had given liberal pecuniary aid to the Mexican republicans, and the government in return gave him a huge grant of land; but after spending many years attempting to convert it into cash, he had the mortification of seeing all his efforts there end in failure.

His character as a whole was not lovable. His intellectual fibre was coarse. He had scanty education, no refinement of manner, and little delicacy of feeling. His temper was high; his speech often coarse. He never was a polished gentleman, and when under the influence of strong drink, as he frequently was, he could be extremely rude and boisterous. But he had many admirable qualities. He was generous, bold, frank, and prompt. His wealth did not make him vain. He had no affectation or false dignity. While very rich he was cordial to those who had been his associates when poor. He was always ready to help those whom he liked and who needed his assistance. He was generally considered honest.

It was reported that as head of the Mormons in California he collected tithes from the followers of his faith, and that when an agent of Brigham Young demanded "the Lord's money," Brannan offered to pay it over for a receipt signed by the Lord—and not otherwise. Whether he made considerable collection, whether he failed to pay it over, and whether if so he had any good excuse, are questions about which no authentic information is accessible. Soon after the gold discovery, Brannan withdrew from the Mormon church; and he never joined any other.

When he died, on the 6th of May, 1889, in San Diego County, he had long ceased to be a familiar figure in the streets of San Francisco, and a prominent man in the business of California. He was no longer a leader in public subscriptions, in popular excitements, in building railroads, or in erecting costly homes. But his memory will long remain as that of a man of strong character and much influence in the early development of our State, a man whose career and its close deserve mention in a magazine which strives to make the history of California familiar to its people, and especially to its younger generation and newcomers who have no direct knowledge of the events that occurred in the first ten years after the American conquest. During that period, Mr. Brannan was one of the leading Californians, in some respects second to none. Peace to his ashes.

John S. Hittell.

The official newspaper of the Mormon church bid Brannan a surprisingly sympathetic farewell.

"SAM BRANNAN GONE,"
DESERET EVENING NEWS, 9 MAY 1889, 2/1.

Sam Brannan, the California pioneer, is dead. He breathed his last in Sonora, on the 6th inst., having suffered agonies for two weeks from inflammation of the bowels. His name and career are familiar to the people of Utah. He was once a "Mormon" and obtained some prominence in early times, as he took a company by water from New York to San Francisco and wanted our people to settle on the coast. His course and habits were not consistent with the life of a Latter-day Saint, and so he was disconnected with the Church and plunged into the speculations and excitements of pioneer Californian experience. He was at one time quite wealthy but finally drifted into poverty. He hoped to recuperate by the sale of land which he acquired by a Mexican grant in Sonora, but never realized his expectations. He had some redeeming qualities and it is to be hoped that these will outweigh the faults which were manifested in his adventurous and eventful life. Poor Sam! will be the general expression over the news of his departure to another sphere.

Brannan's estate consisted of deeds and mortgages for land in Escondido, a "Cloth House" or tent, a large number of second-hand books, garden tools, a silver watch, 2,900 shares in the Sonora City and Improvement Company, and two trunks containing "articles of no value."[40] In an early draft of his will, Brannan bequeathed a single dollar to each of his children, explaining that he had settled half a million dollars on their mother after their divorce, and "she took charge of the children and ali[e]nated them from me, and I since learned that she has squandered it away in gambling in Mining Stocks, which I am sorry to hear." Brannan revised this will in 1884, leaving his son, his oldest daughter, Adelaide Vischer, and her sister, Fanny Schuyler, an additional

---

[40]Inventory of Property of Samuel Brannan Deceased, Box 3, California State Library Collection. The "articles of no value" were perhaps Brannan's personal papers.

dollar. He granted "Lizzie," Alisa, his youngest daughter, one hundred of his elusive acres in Sonora. The "residue of my property" went to Alexander Badlam, Jr.[41] Badlam's legacy consisted mainly of claims against his uncle's estate. Jesse Little tried to track down Brannan's son to inquire about what had happened to his half interest in 200,000 acres in Sonora and the four hundred dollars he had lent to Brannan in June 1885.[42]

Alexander Badlam, Jr., was in Alaska when his uncle died. In January 1890 the law firm of Collier, Hammack & Mulford notified him that Brannan's body was stored in a vault in San Diego, with ninety-five dollars due for embalming. On 26 September 1890, Badlam bought lot 7 in section 2, division 4 at Mount Hope Cemetery in San Diego for fifteen dollars, and on 1 October was billed thirty-one dollars for burial expenses.[43] Brannan lay in an unmarked grave until an admirer, J. Harvey McCarthy of Los Angeles, erected a headstone on 30 May 1926.[44] It was inscribed:

SAM BRANNAN
1819–1889
CALIFORNIA PIONEER OF '46
—DREAMER—LEADER—
AND
EMPIRE–BUILDER

Brannan's daughters Adelaide and Fanny left California and vanished from history. Their younger sister, Alisa Gjessing, died at seventy-five in San Francisco on 21 February 1931 and was buried following an Episcopalian service.[45] Samuel Brannan, Jr., spent his old age in San Diego, supported by the Society of California Pioneers. He died on 3 December 1931 and was buried next to his father.[46] His mother, Ann Eliza

---

[41]Frederick Sorensen Notes 843 and 844, Sorensen Papers.

[42]Little to A. J. Stewart, 29 November 1892, BYU Brannan Papers.

[43]Business Papers regarding funeral expenses, estate, etc. of Samuel Brannan, Box 3, California State Library Collection.

[44]John Davidson to Don M. Stewart, 17 May 1944, Norma B. Ricketts Brannan Collection, copy in the possession of the editor.

[45]*San Francisco Chronicle*, 24 February 1931, 7/5; Typescript, Brannan File, California State Library.

[46]Brannan, Memorabilia, 1924–1979, LDS Archives.

Brannan, had died at ninety-three on 7 December 1916 in San Francisco.[47] No one ever seems to have asked what she remembered of her adventurous life in early California.

A friend remembered visiting Brannan shortly before his death. He found the old pioneer paralyzed on his right side and looking "gaunt and haggard, but there was something of the old nerve and spirit that had carried him through his long and arduous career in California still remaining." Brannan invited him to share a drink of mescal. "Come, amigo," he said. "We will drink to the memory of old times in California. I did the state some service when I lived there, you cannot deny that." His friend later told the story in a subdued voice. "And to think that I knew the poor fellow in the flush times of San Francisco, when his income often reached $1,000 a day. Lord! Lord! What fools of fate we are."[48]

---

[47]*San Francisco Examiner*, 12 December 1916, 17/7; Typescript, Brannan File, California State Library.

[48]Barnes, "Anent Samuel Brannan," *San Francisco Evening Bulletin*, 12 October 1895, 9/3.

"White Roses on the Grave"

History has a strange way of picking its heroes—how else to account for the enduring fame of such celebrated losers as Davy Crockett, John C. Frémont, George Armstrong Custer, Billy the Kid, and Emperor Norton? Sam Brannan's legend did not die with him, but he never achieved the undying celebrity that the public conferred on many of his less-noteworthy contemporaries. Brannan and his friends tried to attach his name to a river and a county in California, but only a street in San Francisco and an island in the Sacramento River commemorate his memory. Yet given the characters enshrined in the pantheon of Western history, Brannan had all the qualities needed for enduring historical renown. His stock rose steadily during the first half of the twentieth century as his story fascinated Mormon scholars and California history buffs. During World War II, a Liberty ship was named for him. Journalists could not resist the lure of his charismatic legend, which was widely told in California papers and pulp publications. His colorful life provided grist for the popular histories of the thirties and forties that celebrated Manifest Destiny, but Brannan did not fare well in subsequent decades as the general public lost interest in history and the vision of historians expanded. Today he is largely forgotten.

Brannan's biographers did not serve him well. The first attempt by James Scherer in 1925, *The First Forty-Niner and the Story of the Golden Tea-Caddy*, indiscriminately recounted practically every legend about its subject. Marred by countless mistakes, Scherer's story propagated a wealth of misinformation about Brannan. He described "the incredible career of one of those hardy adventurers who wrought the Golden Age of California . . . an age of coarse gold: primitive, raw, unrefined, but dramatic, heroic, Homeric." Dale Morgan concluded Scherer's book "could not well have less information about a man and still purport to be a biography of him."

As historian Malcolm E. Barker noted, the invented dialogue in all the fictionalized Brannan biographies was obviously scripted for Clark Gable. Despite the mighty efforts of his biographers, no movie was ever made of Brannan's life, and his legend suffered.

Hollywood studios rejected Paul Bailey's scripts for a movie about Brannan, but he produced a series of articles on the apostate's life for the *Improvement Era*, the official magazine of the LDS church. Bailey carefully tailored the resulting biography, *Sam Brannan and the California Mormons*, for his Mormon audience, and in 1943 it became the first publication of his Westernlore Press. The book went through multiple editions, but it also failed to please Dale Morgan, who found it "slipshod romantic history with pseudo-scientific paraphernalia in the shape of footnotes." He complained to Juanita Brooks that Bailey's book gave him "a more discouraged feeling about Mormon scholarship than I've had for a long time. For hell's sake, Juanita, what is the matter with these young Mormon scholars? Are they all imbeciles, or just what is wrong?" Bailey had "bowdlerized some original sources, misquoted others, badly misinterpreted others, didn't even trouble himself about others, and emerged with a pseudo-documented rehash that was a disgrace even to the pages of the Improvement Era." Bailey published a novel, *The Gay Saint*, based on Brannan's life that Morgan simply called "terrible."[1]

Reva Scott's *Samuel Brannan and the Golden Fleece* sold well enough to go through several printings. The *Sacramento Union* called it "a Walter Winchell expose of the intimate life of one of California's early financial pirates," praising it as "one of the most vivid, powerful and best books of early California to be written in recent years."[2] Miriam DeFord thought Scott's book "definitive, and there is nothing left for later biographers to discover," but a more discerning critic noted that "fictionalized biography is less likely to be biography than fiction. It is apparent that Mrs. Scott often let fancy reign when facts were few."[3] The book's title page proclaimed it a biography of "San Francisco's Forgotten

---

[1]Morgan to Virginia Sorensen, 1 November 1941, Morgan Papers; and Walker, ed., *Dale Morgan on Early Mormonism*, 51.

[2]*Sacramento Union*, 11 June 1944, 16.

[3]DeFord, *Sacramento Bee*, 10 June 1944; and Wayne B. Selliek, *San Francisco Chronicle*, 18 June 1944; copies in Brannan File, California State Library.

Jason," but Scott's experiment with the techniques of fiction did not produce a happy result. Better could have been expected of Reva Holdaway Stanley Scott, a scion of Parley P. Pratt who had studied at the University of California and published credible history with Charles Camp. The footnotes Scott haphazardly inserted occasionally lead to her sources but reveal that she often misinterpreted or simply misrepresented them. When Scott lacked reliable information, she turned her imagination loose and invented it.[4] Her papers have vanished, so there is no way to validate some of her stranger conclusions. Relying heavily on interviews with one of Brannan's nieces, Scott produced a bounty of interesting gossip and much bad history. In her acknowledgments, she credited "Sophie Brannan Haight, a woman of remarkable memory who died a short time ago in her eighty-fifth year." Scott derived most of her bizarre information about Brannan's personal life from Haight, but a cousin, Maude Pettus, questioned Haight's reliability. "I wonder just how much was the truth that she told and how much was the embroidery of her fancies," Pettus wrote. Regarding Haight's tales about Brannan's divorce, Pettus warned they "should not be taken as the actual truth, for Cousin Sophie was a more or less embittered woman and she undoubtedly did not like her uncle's wife."[5]

Louis J. Stellman produced a biography, *Sam Brannan, Builder of San Francisco*, that might be called the best of a bad lot, but Stellman also believed much of the nonsense he picked up from Sophie Haight. He identified Haight as his source for many of his "extraordinarily dramatic" stories about Brannan, including the otherwise-undocumented marriage to Harriet Hatch.[6] Stellman's book was reissued in 1996 by publisher James Stevenson with a preface by Al Shumate, an introduction by California State Librarian Kevin Starr, and an excellent new selection of photographs.

Two more discerning researchers, Frederick and Virginia Sorensen,

---

[4]For example, Scott's invention of detail included reporting a conversation with a half-brother, Rufus, who died thirteen years before Brannan was born.

[5]Pettus to Virginia Sorensen, 9 and 13 July 1942, Sorensen Papers.

[6]Stellman, *Sam Brannan, Builder of San Francisco*, 244. Stellman also spoke to a second Sophie Brannan, granddaughter of John Brannan. She provided him with letters from John Brannan's papers, genealogy, and newspaper clippings, but does not seem to have supported Sophie Haight's stories.

left hundreds of pages of Brannan research notes, apparently for a formal life history and what Fawn Brodie described as a "fictionalized biography." Scott's work may have led the couple to abandon the project, but the Sorensens' interest provided Brodie, a very talented writer, with "at least one good reason why I could not work on [Brannan's] biography," for she and Mrs. Sorensen shared publishers.[7] Alfred Knopf rejected a biography by a very credible historian, Douglas S. Watson, because it was "hum drum and lacked zip."[8] Several less talented men, including tycoon Herbert Auerbach and publisher Herbert Hamlin, also tried to tell Brannan's story.

More disturbing than the amateurish works about Brannan is the blind acceptance of such questionable evidence by authorities who should know better. One noted historian chose to look no further than the legend to assert that Brannan built his fortune "on money diverted from church property and tithes to his personal profit, a practice not far from the robbing of almsboxes." For Walter Bean, the remorse that Brannan never felt for a crime he did not commit explained his role in the vigilante movement: "Clearly, Brannan was subconsciously seeking freedom from his own guilt in arrogating to himself the punishment of others."[9] Even in the face of such questionable insights, the significance of Brannan's archetypal life outshines his fading memory.

Although consigned to obscurity, Brannan was never entirely forgotten, particularly among the Latter-day Saints, who could point to his sad example as "the 'classic Mormon apostate' who paid the ultimate price for his apostasy." A religion professor at Brigham Young University found him "a good example of the steps of apostasy" and used Brannan's case to demonstrate that "the fruits of apostasy are always bitter."[10] On a brighter note, E Clampus Vitus, California's "fun-loving historical society," has practically adopted Brannan as its patron saint. (In 1861 Brannan allegedly presented ECV's Downieville Lodge with "a magnificent sword as a mark of his esteem for the liberality of the lodge in reimbursing him

    [7]Brodie to Young, 12 January 1945, Special Collections, BYU Library.
    [8]Watson to Virginia Sorensen, 9 July 1942, Sorensen Papers.
    [9]Bean, *California: An Interpretive History*, 137.
    [10]Daniel H. Ludlow, quoted in Bringhurst, Samuel Brannan: From Devout Latter-day Saint to Disillusioned Dissident, 2.

for the loss of sheep by the high water in Napa County two years ago."[11]) Their Yerba Buena chapter installed a plaque commemorating "the Prince of Californiacs" on the site of Brannan's Calistoga resort in 1954. The Clampers' Sam Brannan Chapter now keeps his memory evergreen.

In contrast to his bad repute among the Saints, Brannan's legacy shines brightly in the Napa Valley town he named and loved. Calistoga maintains the bucolic and boisterous traditions of his Hot Springs resort, and the wonderful Sharpsteen Museum is a shrine to Brannan's memory. The creation of one of Walt Disney's legendary animators, Ben Sharpsteen, the museum includes a diorama of Brannan's resort that brings its rustic charm to life. In early 1959 Jule Ashworth of the Calistoga Chamber of Commerce requested information from Mt. Hope Cemetery officials about transferring Brannan's bones to his spiritual home. Don Driese, president of the San Diego Historical Society, promised to "never tolerate the proposal and would fight it with every means at his disposal."[12] Brannan's bones stayed in San Diego, but his soul lives on in Calistoga.

Samuel Brannan has always found admirers even among devout Latter-day Saints, and for the religion's many dissenters he is an inspiration as a man who fought against the worst aspects of its authoritarian system. Whether one considers Mormonism's second leader a tyrant or a prophet, who can help but admire a man willing to defy a powerhouse like Brigham Young? Nothing evokes the contradictory heritage Samuel Brannan left to Mormonism better than the begrudging admiration and enduring affection expressed by many of those who followed him to California in 1846. Let us end this study of his life with the story an old bishop told seventy-two years after sailing around Cape Horn with Sam Brannan.

EDWIN L. AUSTIN, DICTATION, 11 APRIL 1918,
LDS ARCHIVES.

Bishop Edwin N. Austin [was] one of the passengers who made the famous voyage from New York to California in the Ship "Brooklyn" in 1846. Shortly after his visit [in 1905] he wrote the following:

---

[11]"Clamper Sam Brannan at Downieville 1861," *The Pony Express*, February 1951, 5.

[12]"Sam Brannan's Bones Stir Up 2-City Feud," *Los Angeles Times*, 2 February 1959.

On Tuesday, May 30, 1905 I visited the Mount Hope Cemetery at San Diego, Cal., for the purpose of seeking the last resting place of the renowned Samuel Brannan who led a company of Latter-day Saints from New York to California in 1846 and who subsequently figured prominently in the early history of California being at that time a very wealthy and prosperous citizen. I had previously been told that his remains had been interred in the Mount Hope Cemetery. This being decoration day I and some friends who accompanied me took flowers with us with a view of decorating the graves in the cemetery. I first went to the Sexton's Office, and made inquiries of Mr. Smith, the Sexton, as to the location of the grave of the late Samuel Brannan. The section [sic] told me that owing to the large crowd which needed his attention his time would not permit him to assist me in looking through the records but he gave me the privilege to peruse the books myself. I accepted his offer and after examining the records I found information to the following effect:

Samuel Brannan died May 14, 1889, at the city of San Diego, Cal., in great poverty. Some acquaintance furnished a casket for his remains. As he had no money to buy a lot in the cemetery, his body lay in the receiving vault of San Diego City for something over a year, when Alexander Bledon [Badlam] bought a lot in the Mount Hope Cemetery, to which his remains were removed in 1890. He was buried in Division 4, section 2, lot 7. A 2x2x7-inch stake is the only mark at the grave. I decorated the spot by strewing a number of beautiful white roses on the grave.

Edwin N. Austin

A Calendar of
Samuel Brannan Letters

This appendix lists all Samuel Brannan correspondence located but not reproduced in full in this collection of his papers.

Brannan to Bidwell, 15 March 1851, Frederick Sorensen Typescript, Virginia Sorensen Papers, Boston Univ.

Brannan to Price, 31 August 1852, The Rodman M. Price Papers, 1843–1892, C-B 455, Box 1, Bancroft Library.

Brannan to Warren, 22 January 1856, James L. Warren Papers, 1846–1889, C-A 418, Box 2, Folder 208, Bancroft Library.

Brannan to John Brannan, ca. June 1856, in Stellman, *Sam Brannan, Builder of San Francisco,* 155.

Brannan to Stearns, 5 December 1856, SG Box 11, Folder 5, Abel Stearns Collection, Huntington Library.

Brannan to Grayson, 1 August 1859, Andrew Jackson Grayson Papers, 1844–1901, C-B 514, Bancroft Library.

Brannan to Stearns, 21 September 1867, Abel Stearns Collection, SG Box 11, Folder 6, Huntington Library.

Brannan to C. F. McGlashan, 26 April 1879, McGlashan Papers, C-B 570, Folder 68, Bancroft Library.

Brannan to C. F. McGlashan, 30 May 1879, McGlashan Papers, C-B 570, Folder 68, Bancroft Library.

Brannan to Little, 27 July 1880, Folder 1, BYU Brannan Papers.

Brannan to Little, 1 June 1880, Folder 1, BYU Brannan Papers. Damaged copy with missing text.

Brannan to Little, 9 February 1881, Folder 1, BYU Brannan Papers.

T. B. H. Stenhouse to Little, 27 June 1881, Folder 8, BYU Brannan Papers.

Brannan to Badlam, 18 August 1882, Box 3, California State Library Collection.

Brannan to Badlam, 19 August 1882, Box 3, California State Library Collection.

Brannan to Little, 21 March 1883, Folder 1, BYU Brannan Papers.

Joseph Smith III to Brannan; and Smith III to Mills, 17 July 1883, P6, Manuscript Typescript, JS LB #4, RLDS Library-Archives, Independence, Missouri.

"Communicated," *Nogales Express*, 20 September 1884, AC 901.Al #624, BYU Library.

Brannan to Little, 27 January 1885, Folder 2, BYU Brannan Papers.

Brannan to Little, 5 February 1885, Folder 2, BYU Brannan Papers.

Brannan to Little, 11 February 1885, Folder 2, BYU Brannan Papers.

Brannan to Little, 12 February 1885, Folder 2, BYU Brannan Papers.

Brannan to Little, 26 February 1885, Folder 2, BYU Brannan Papers.

Brannan to Little, 6 March 1885, Folder 2, BYU Brannan Papers.

Brannan to Little, 8 March 1885, Folder 2, BYU Brannan Papers.

Brannan to William A. Scott, Jr., 8 March 1885. Letter of Introduction for J. C. Little, Folder 12, BYU Brannan Papers.

Brannan to Little, 21 March 1885, Folder 2, BYU Brannan Papers.

Brannan to Little, 6 April 1885, Folder 2, BYU Brannan Papers.

Brannan to Little, 10 April 1885, Folder 2, BYU Brannan Papers.

Brannan to Little, 11 April 1885, Folder 2, BYU Brannan Papers.

Brannan to Little, 17 April 1885, Folder 2, BYU Brannan Papers.

Brannan to Little, 20 May 1885, Folder 2, BYU Brannan Papers.

Brannan to Little, 27 May 1885, Folder 2, BYU Brannan Papers.

Brannan to Little, 31 May 1885, Folder 2, BYU Brannan Papers.

Brannan to Little, 4 June 1885, Folder 2, BYU Brannan Papers.

Brannan to Little, 12 June 1885, Folder 2, BYU Brannan Papers.

Brannan to Little, 15 June 1885, Folder 2, BYU Brannan Papers.

Brannan to Little, 18 June 1885, Folder 2, BYU Brannan Papers.

Brannan to Little, 19 June 1885, Folder 2, BYU Brannan Papers.

Brannan to Little, 20 June 1885, Folder 2, BYU Brannan Papers.

Brannan to Little, 21 June 1885, Folder 2, BYU Brannan Papers.

Brannan to Little, 24 June 1885, Folder 2, BYU Brannan Papers.

Brannan to Little, 26 June 1885, Folder 2, BYU Brannan Papers.

Brannan to Little, 30 June 1885, Folder 2, BYU Brannan Papers.

Brannan to Little, 2 July 1885, Folder 3, BYU Brannan Papers.

Brannan to Little, 3 July 1885, Folder 3, BYU Brannan Papers.

Brannan to Little, 8 July 1885, Folder 3, BYU Brannan Papers.

Brannan to Little, 14 July 1885, Folder 3, BYU Brannan Papers. Two letters, one describing Arizona pioneer Charles Poston.

Brannan to Little, 23 July 1885, Folder 3, BYU Brannan Papers.

Brannan to Little, 28 July 1885, Folder 3, BYU Brannan Papers.

Brannan to Little, 29 July 1885, Folder 3, BYU Brannan Papers.

Brannan to Little, 2 August 1885, Folder 3, BYU Brannan Papers.

Brannan to Little, 7 August 1885, Folder 3, BYU Brannan Papers.
Brannan to Little, 17 August 1885, Folder 3, BYU Brannan Papers.
Brannan to Little, 19 August 1885, Folder 3, BYU Brannan Papers.
Brannan to Little, 22 August 1885, Folder 3, BYU Brannan Papers.
Brannan to Little, 27 August 1885, Folder 3, BYU Brannan Papers.
Brannan to Little, 3 September 1885, Folder 3, BYU Brannan Papers.
Brannan to Little, 7 September 1885, Folder 3, BYU Brannan Papers.
Brannan to Little, 11 September 1885, Folder 3, BYU Brannan Papers.
Brannan to Little, 14 September 1885, Folder 3, BYU Brannan Papers.
Brannan to Little, 17 September 1885, Folder 3, BYU Brannan Papers.
Brannan to Little, 22 September 1885, Folder 3, BYU Brannan Papers.
Brannan to Little, 27 September 1885, Folder 3, BYU Brannan Papers.
Brannan to Little, 2 October 1885, Folder 4, BYU Brannan Papers.
Brannan to Little, 14 October 1885, Folder 4, BYU Brannan Papers.
Brannan to Little, 25 October 1885, Folder 4, BYU Brannan Papers.
Brannan to Little, 3 November 1885, Folder 4, BYU Brannan Papers.
Brannan to Little, 16 November 1885, Folder 4, BYU Brannan Papers.
Brannan to Little, 18 November 1885, Folder 4, BYU Brannan Papers.
Brannan to Little, 24 November 1885, Folder 4, BYU Brannan Papers.
Brannan to Little, 26 November 1885, Folder 4, BYU Brannan Papers.
Brannan to Little, 1 December 1885, Folder 4, BYU Brannan Papers.
Brannan to Little, 10 December 1885, Folder 4, BYU Brannan Papers.
Brannan to Little, 27 December 1885, Folder 4, BYU Brannan Papers.
Brannan to Little, 7 January 1886, Folder 5, BYU Brannan Papers.
Brannan to Little, 13 January 1886, Folder 5, BYU Brannan Papers.
Brannan to Little, 15 January 1886, Folder 5, BYU Brannan Papers.
Brannan to Little, 26 January 1886, Folder 5, BYU Brannan Papers.
Brannan to Little, 27 January 1886, Folder 5, BYU Brannan Papers.
Brannan to Little, 29 January 1886, Folder 5, BYU Brannan Papers.
Brannan to Little, 24 February 1886, Folder 5, BYU Brannan Papers.
Brannan to Little, 27 February 1886, Folder 5, BYU Brannan Papers.
Brannan to Little, 31 March 1886, Folder 5, BYU Brannan Papers.
Brannan to Little, 26 April 1886, Folder 5, BYU Brannan Papers.
Brannan to Little, 7 May 1886, Folder 5, BYU Brannan Papers.
Brannan to Little, 27 May 1886, Folder 5, BYU Brannan Papers.
Brannan to Little, 2 June 1886, Folder 5, BYU Brannan Papers.
Brannan to Little, 20 June 1886, Folder 5, BYU Brannan Papers.
Brannan to Little, 19 July 1886, Folder 5, BYU Brannan Papers.
Brannan to Little, 29 August 1886, Folder 5, BYU Brannan Papers.

Brannan to Little, 15 November 1886, Folder 5, BYU Brannan Papers.

Brannan to Little, 22 December 1886, Folder 5, BYU Brannan Papers.

Brannan to Warren, 23 December 1886, James L. Warren Papers, 1846–1889, Box 2, Folder 208, Bancroft Library.

Brannan to Little, 31 December 1886, Folder 5, BYU Brannan Papers.

Brannan to Little, 17 May 1887, Folder 6, BYU Brannan Papers.

Brannan to Badlam, 5 June 1887, Typescript, Sorensen Papers, Boston Univ.

Brannan to Little, 6 June 1887, Folder 6, BYU Brannan Papers.

Brannan to Little, 4 November 1887, Folder 6, BYU Brannan Papers.

Brannan to Warren, 7 January 1888, James L. Warren Papers, 1846–1889, Box 2, Folder 208, Bancroft Library.

Brannan to Little, 23 January 1888, Folder 7, BYU Brannan Papers.

Brannan to Little, 26 February 1888, Folder 7, BYU Brannan Papers.

Brannan to Little, 13 March 1888, Folder 7, BYU Brannan Papers.

Brannan to Little, 22 March 1888, Folder 7, BYU Brannan Papers.

Brannan to Badlam, 11 May 1888, Box 3, California State Library Collection.

Brannan to Badlam, 13 May 1888, Box 3, California State Library Collection.

Brannan to William Heath Davis, 5 October 1888; copy in Davis, *Seventy-five Years in California* (1929), 211; original at Huntington Library.

Brannan to Badlam, 9 October 1888, Typescript, Virginia Sorensen Papers, Boston Univ.

Brannan to Badlam, 15 October 1888, Box 3, California State Library Collection.

Brannan to Badlam, 19 October 1888, Box 3, California State Library Collection.

Brannan to Badlam, 20 October 1888, Box 3, California State Library Collection.

Brannan to Badlam, 11 November 1888, Box 3, California State Library Collection.

Brannan to Badlam, 16 November 1888, Box 3, California State Library Collection.

Brannan to Society of California Pioneers, 22 December 1888, Society of California Pioneers.

Brannan to H. F. Graves, 4 January 1889, Society of California Pioneers.

Brannan to H. F. Graves, 16 January 1889, Society of California Pioneers.

BIBLIOGRAPHY

This bibliography lists all works cited in the text and many, if not all, of the secondary sources consulted about the life of Samuel Brannan. Abbreviations used here are described in the "Sources" section of the preface.

BOOKS

Adams, Ira C. *Memoirs and Anecdotes of Early Calistoga.* Calistoga, Calif: Sharpsteen Museum Assoc., ca. 1996.

Alexander, Thomas G. *Things in Heaven and Earth: The Life and Times of Wilford Woodruff, a Mormon Prophet.* S.L.C: Signature Books, 1991.

Allen, W. W. and R. B. Avery. *The California Gold Book: Its Discovery and Discoverers.* S.F: Donohue & Henneberry, 1893.

Anonymous. *Hand Book of Calistoga Springs, Or, Little Geysers: its mineral waters, climate, amusements, baths, drives, scenery, the celebrated Great Geysers and Petrified Forest, and the Clear Lake Country.* S.F: Alta California Book and Job Printing House, 1871.

Anonymous. *Memorial and Biographical History of Northern California.* Chicago: The Lewis Publishing Co., 1891.

Archuleta, Kay. *The Brannan Saga: Early Calistoga.* St. Helena, Calif: Illuminations Press, 1977.

Arrington, Leonard J. *Kate Field and J. H. Beadle: Manipulators of the Mormon Past.* S.L.C: Center for Studies of the American West, 1971.

————. *Charles C. Rich: Mormon General and Western Frontiersman.* Provo: Brigham Young Univ. Press, 1974.

Backman, Milton V., Jr. *A Profile of Latter-day Saints of Kirtland, Ohio, and Members of Zion's Camp, 1830–1839.* Provo, Utah: Dept. of Church History and Doctrine, 1982.

Badlam, Alexander, Jr. *The Wonders of Alaska.* S.F: The Bancroft Co., 1890.

Bagley, Will, ed. *A Road from El Dorado: The 1848 Trail Journal of Ephraim Green.* S.L.C: The Prairie Dog Press, 1991.

————. *Frontiersman: Abner Blackburn's Narrative.* S.L.C: Univ. of Utah Press, 1992.

————. *The Pioneer Camp of the Saints: The 1846 and 1847 Mormon Trail Journals of Thomas Bullock.* Spokane, Wash: The Arthur H. Clark Co., 1997.

Bailey, Paul. *Sam Brannan and the California Mormons.* Los Angeles: Westernlore Press, 1943. 3d ed., 1959.

————. *The Mormons in California, by William Glover.* Los Angeles: Glen Dawson, 1954.

Bancroft, Hubert Howe. *History of California,* 7 vols. S.F: The History Co., 1886–1890.

————. *Popular Tribunals,* 2 vols. S.F: The History Co., 1887.

————. *California Inter Pocula.* S.F: The History Co., 1888.

————. *History of Utah, 1540–1886.* S.F: The History Co., 1889.

Barker, Malcolm E., "When Sam Brannan Stumped for President Lincoln," in *California and the Civil War 1861–1865.* Edited by Robert J. Chandler. S.F: The Book Club of Calif., 1992.

————. *Samuel Brannan: San Francisco's Pioneer Printer.* S.F: Book Arts, 1991.

————. *San Francisco Memoirs, 1835–1851: Eyewitness Accounts of the Birth of a City.* S.F: Londonborn Publications, 1994.

Barry, Louise. *The Beginning of the West: Annals of the Kansas Gateway to the American West, 1540–1854.* Topeka: Kansas State Hist. Soc., 1972.

Barry, T. A. and B. A. Patten. *Men and Memories of San Francisco in the Spring of '50.* S.F: A. L. Bancroft & Co., 1873.

Bayard, Samuel John. *A Sketch of the Life of Com. Robert F. Stockton.* N.Y: Derby & Jackson, 1856.

Beals, Carleton. *Porfirio Diaz, Dictator of Mexico.* Philadelphia: J. B. Lippincott Co., 1932.

Bean, Walton E. *California: An Interpretive History.* N.Y: McGraw-Hill Book Co., 1973.

Beilharz, Edwin and Carlos Lopez. *We Were '49ers: Chilean Accounts of the California Gold Rush.* Los Angeles: Ward Ritchie Press, 1976.

Bergeron, Paul H. *The Presidency of James K. Polk.* Lawrence: Univ. of Kansas Press, 1987.

Bidwell, John. *In California Before the Gold Rush.* Los Angeles: The Ward Ritchie Press, 1948.

Bigler, David L., ed. *The Gold Discovery Journal of Azariah Smith.* S.L.C: Univ. of Utah Press, 1990.

————. *Forgotten Kingdom: The Mormon Theocracy in the American West, 1847–1896.* Spokane, Wash: The Arthur H. Clark Co., 1998.

Bronson, William. *Still Flying and Nailed to the Mast: The First Hundred Years of the Fireman's Fund Insurance Company.* Garden City, N.Y: Doubleday, 1963.

Brown, Archie Leon and Charlene L. Hathaway. *141 years of Mormon Heritage: Rawsons, Browns, Angells—Pioneers.* Oakland, Calif: Archie Leon Brown, 1973.

Brown, James S. *Life of a Pioneer, Being the Autobiography of James S. Brown.* S.L.C: Geo. Q. Cannon & Sons, Printers, 1900.

Browning, Peter. *To the Golden Shore: America Goes to California—1849.* Lafayette, Calif: Great West Books, 1995.

Bryant, Edwin. *What I Saw in California.* N.Y: D. Appleton & Co., 1848. Reprinted Palo Alto, Calif: Lewis Osborne, 1967.

Buffum, E. Gould. *Six Months in the Gold Mines.* Philadelphia: Lea and Blanchard, 1850. Reprinted Los Angeles: The Ward Ritchie Press, 1959.

Burnett, Peter Hardeman. *Recollections and Opinions of An Old Pioneer.* N.Y: Appleton, 1880. Reprinted as Peter H. Burnett, *An Old California Pioneer.* Oakland, Calif: Biobooks, 1946.

Busch, Brinton Cooper, ed. *Frémont's Private Navy: The 1846 Journal of Captain William Dane Phelps.* Glendale, Calif: The Arthur H. Clark Co., 1987.

Camp, William Martin. *San Francisco: Port of Gold.* Garden City, N.Y: Doubleday & Co., 1948.

Carter, Kate B., ed. *Heart Throbs of the West*, 12 vols. S.L.C: Daughters of Utah Pioneers, 1939–51.

————. *Treasures of Pioneer History*, 6 vols. S.L.C: Daughters of Utah Pioneers, 1952–57.

————. *Our Pioneer Heritage*, 20 vols. S.L.C: Daughters of Utah Pioneers, 1958–77.

Caughey, John Walton. *Hubert Howe Bancroft: Historian of the West*. Berkeley: Univ. of Calif. Press, 1946.

Chandler, Robert J. *California and the Civil War 1861–1865*. S.F: The Book Club of Calif., 1992.

Churchill, Charles B. *Adventurers and Prophets: American Autobiographers in Mexican California, 1827–1947*. Spokane, Wash: The Arthur H. Clark Co., 1995.

Clark, Harry. *A Venture in History: The Production, Publication, and Sale of the Works of Hubert Howe Bancroft*. Berkeley: Univ. of Calif. Press, 1973.

Cleland, Robert Glass. *The Cattle on a Thousand Hills: Southern California, 1850–1880*. San Marino, Calif: The Huntington Library, 1941. 2d ed., 1951.

Coblentz, Stanton A. *Villains and Vigilantes: The Story of James King of William and Pioneer Justice in California*. N.Y: Wilson-Erickson, 1936.

Codman, John. *The Round Trip*. N.Y: G. P. Putnam's Sons, 1879.

Colton, Walter. *Three Years in California*. N.Y: A. S. Barnes, 1850.

Compton, Todd. *In Sacred Loneliness: The Plural Wives of Joseph Smith*. S.L.C: Signature Books, 1997.

Cook, Lyndon W. and Kevin V. Harker, eds. *My Life's Review: The Autobiography of Benjamin F. Johnson*. Provo, Utah: Grandin Book Co., 1997.

Coray, William. *Journal of Sgt. William Coray of the Mormon Battalion*. Typescript in possession of editor.

Cowan, Richard O. and William E. Homer. *California Saints: A 150-Year Legacy in the Golden State*. Provo, Utah: Religious Studies Center, Brigham Young Univ., 1996.

Craig, Donald, ed. [*William R. Garner's*] *Letters from California, 1846–1847*. Berkeley: Univ. of Calif. Press, 1970.

Crocheron, Augusta Joyce. *Representative Women of Deseret*. S.L.C: J. C. Graham & Co., 1884.

Davies, J. Kenneth. *Mormon Gold: The Story of California's Mormon Argonauts*. S.L.C: Olympus Publishing Co., 1984. With separate "Appendices for MORMON GOLD."

Davis, William Heath. *Seventy-five Years in California*. S.F: John Howell, 1929. 2d ed., 1967.

Decker, Peter R. *Fortunes and Failures: White-Collar Mobility in Nineteenth-Century San Francisco*. Cambridge, Mass: Harvard Univ. Press, 1978.

Deering, Frank C. *The Proprietors of Saco and a Brief Sketch of the Years following the First Settlement of the Town also a Little about an Old Bank in Saco, Maine*. Saco, Maine: York National Bank, 1931.

DeFord, Miriam Allen. *They Were San Franciscans*. Caldwell, Idaho: The Caxton Printers, Ltd., 1947.

DeVoto, Bernard. *The Year of Decision, 1846*. N.Y: Houghton–Mifflin Co., 1943.

Dillon, Richard. *Embarcadero*. N.Y: Coward-McCann, Inc., 1959.

————. *Fool's Gold: The Decline and Fall of Captain John Sutter of California*. New York: Coward McCann, 1967. Reprinted Santa Cruz, Calif: Western Tanager, 1981.

Dunbar, Edward H. *The Romance of the Age; or, the Discovery of Gold in California*. N.Y: D. Appleton and Co., 1867.

Egan, Howard. *Pioneering the West, 1846 to 1878*. Ed. and comp. by William M. Egan. Richmond, Utah: privately printed, 1917.

Eldredge, Zoeth S. *The Beginnings of San Francisco*. S.F: Zoeth S. Eldredge, 1912.

————. *History of California*, 5 vols. N.Y: The Century History Co., 1915.

Elliot, Russell R. *History of Nevada*. Lincoln: Univ. of Nebraska Press, 1973.

Ellsworth, S. George, ed. *The Journals of Addison Pratt*. S.L.C: Univ. of Utah Press, 1990.

Faulring, Scott H., ed. *An American Prophet's Record: The Diaries and Journals of Joseph Smith*. S.L.C: Signature Books, 1989.

Ferlinghetti, Lawrence and Nancy J. Peters. *Literary San Francisco*. S.F: City Lights Books and Harper & Row, Publishers, 1980.

Fitch, Franklin Y. *The Life, Travels and Adventures of an American Wanderer: A Truthful Narrative of Events in the Life of Alonzo P. DeMilt*. N. Y: John W. Lovell Co., 1883.

Garnett, Porter, ed. "Papers of the San Francisco Committee of Vigilance of 1851," in *Publications of the Academy of Pacific Coast History*, 2 vols. Berkeley: Univ. of Calif. Press, 1910 and 1911.

Gay, Theresa. *James W. Marshall, the Discoverer of California Gold: A Biography*. Georgetown, Calif: The Talisman Press, 1967.

Gottschalk, Louis Moreau. *Notes of a Pianist*. Philadelphia: J. B. Lippincott & Co., 1881. Republished as Jeanne Behrend, ed. *Notes of a Pianist*. N.Y: Alfred A. Knopf, 1964.

Graebner, Norman A. *Empire on the Pacific: A Study in American Continental Expansion*. N.Y: The Ronald Press Co., 1955.

————. *Manifest Destiny*. Indianapolis: Bobbs-Merrill Co., 1968.

Gray, Wallace F. *They Brought Their Faith: History of the Escondido California Stakes, The Church of Jesus Christ of Latter-day Saints*. Escondido, Calif: Escondido Calif. South Stakes, 1993.

Greer, James Kimmins. *Colonel Jack Hays: Texas Frontier Leader and California Builder*. N.Y: E. P. Dutton & Co., Inc., 1952.

Grey, William [William Francis White]. *A Picture of Pioneer Times in California*. S.F: W. M. Hinton, 1881.

Grivas, Theodore. *Military Governments in California, 1846–1850*. Glendale, Calif: The Arthur H. Clark Co., 1963.

Gudde, Erwin G., ed. *Sutter's Own Story: The Life of General John Augustus Sutter and the History of New Helvetia in the Sacramento Valley*. N.Y: G. P. Putnam's Sons, 1936.

————. *Bigler's Chronicle of the West: The Conquest of California, Discovery of Gold, and Mormon Settlement as Reflected in Henry William Bigler's Diaries*. Berkeley: Univ. of Calif. Press, 1962.

————. *California Place Names*. Berkeley: Univ. of Calif. Press, 1969.

Gunn, Stanley R. *Oliver Cowdery, Second Elder and Scribe*. S.L.C: Bookcraft, 1962.

Hallwas, John E. and Roger Launius, eds. *Cultures in Conflict: A Documentary History of the Mormon War in Illinois*. Logan: Utah State Univ. Press, 1995.

Hammond, George P., ed. *The Larkin Papers: Personal, Business, and Official Correspondence of Thomas Oliver Larkin, Merchant and United States Consul in California*, 10 vols. Berkeley: Univ. of Calif. Press, 1951–68.

————. *The Californian: Volume One, Facsimile Reproductions of Thirty-eight Numbers, a Prospectus, and Various Extras and Proclamations, Printed at Monterey between August 15, 1846 and May 6, 1847.* S.F: John Howell Books, 1971.

———— and Dale L. Morgan, eds. *Captain Charles W. Weber, Pioneer of the San Joaquin and Founder of Stockton, California.* Berkeley, Calif: Friends of the Bancroft Library, 1966.

Hansen, Lorin K. and Lila J. Bringhurst. *Let This Be Zion: Mormon Pioneers and Modern Saints in South Alameda County.* S.L.C: Publisher's Press, 1996.

Hanson, Klaus J. *Quest for Empire: The Political Kingdom of God and the Council of Fifty in Mormon History.* East Lansing: Mich. State Univ. Press, 1967.

Harlow, Neal. *California Conquered: War and Peace on the Pacific 1846–1850.* Berkeley: Univ. of Calif. Press, 1982.

Harpending, Asbury. *The Great Diamond Hoax.* S.F: James H. Barry Co., 1915. Reprinted Norman: Univ. of Okla. Press, 1958.

Harris, Theodore D., ed. *Black Frontiersman: The Memoirs of Henry O. Flipper, First Black Graduate of West Point.* Fort Worth: Texas Christian Univ. Press, 1997.

Harwell, William S., ed. *Manuscript History of Brigham Young, 1847–1850.* SLC: Collier's Publishing Co., 1997.

Hastings, Lansford W. *The Emigrants' Guide, to Oregon and California.* Cincinnati: George Conclin, 1845.

Hawgood, John A., ed. *First and Last Consul: Thomas Oliver Larkin and the Americanization of California.* Palo Alto, Calif: Pacific Books, 1970.

Hayward, John. *Hayward's Gazetteer of Maine.* Portland, Maine: S. H. Colesworthy, 1843.

Hietala, Thomas R. *Manifest Design: Anxious Aggrandizement in Late Jacksonian America.* Ithaca, N.Y: Cornell Univ. Press, 1985.

Higgens, Dorothy H., ed. *The Annals of San Francisco by Frank Soule, John H. Gihon, M.D., and James Nisbet. Together with the Continuation, through 1855.* Palo Alto, Calif: Lewis Osborne, 1966.

History of Humboldt County. N.P. Wallace W. Elliott & Co., 1881.

History of York County, Maine, with Illustrations and Biographical Sketches of Its Prominent Men and Pioneers. Philadelphia: Everts & Peck, 1880.

Hittell, Theodore H. *History of California,* 4 vols. S.F: N. J. Stone & Co., 1897.

Holmes, Harold C., ed. *Memoirs of Edward Bosqui.* Oakland, Calif: The Holmes Book Co., 1952.

Horner, John. *National Finance and Public Money.* Honolulu: Hawaiian Gazette Co. Printers, 1898.

Hu-DeHart, Evelyn. *Yaqui Resistance and Survival: The Struggle for Land and Autonomy, 1821–1910.* Madison: Univ. of Wisc. Press, 1984.

Huff, Sharon. *Hannah Daggett Buckland, 1802–1881.* N.P., 1993.

Huntley, Henry Veel. *California: Its Gold and Its Inhabitants.* London: T. C. Newby, 1856.

Hurtado, Albert L. *Indian Survival on the California Frontier.* New Haven, Conn: Yale Univ. Press, 1988.

Hussey, John Adam, ed. and Louis C. Butshcer, trans. *Early Sacramento: Glimpses of John Augustus Sutter, the Hock Farm and Neighboring Indian Tribes form the Journals of Prince Paul, H.R.H. Duke Paul Wilhelm of Württemberg.* Sacramento: The Sacramento Book Collectors Club, 1973.

Jackson, Donald Dale. *Gold Dust.* N.Y: Alfred A. Knopf, 1980.

Jacob, Edward and Ruth S., eds. *The Record of Norton Jacob.* S.L.C: The Norton Jacob Family Assoc., 1949.

Jenson, Andrew. *Latter-day Saint Biographical Encyclopedia.* 4 vols. S.L.C: Andrew Jenson History Co., 1901.

Jessee, Dean C. *The Papers of Joseph Smith,* 2 vols. S.L.C: Deseret Book, 1989, 1992.

Johnson, Allen and Dumas Malone, eds. *Dictionary of American Biography,* 20 vols. N.Y: Charles Scribner's Sons, 1928–36.

Johnson, Clark V. *Mormon Redress Petitions: Documents of the 1833–1838 Missouri Conflict.* Provo, Utah: Bookcraft, 1992.

Johnson, J. E. *Johnson's Original Comic Songs.* S.F: Presho & Appleton, 1858.

Johnson, Kenneth M. *Gleanings from the* Picayune. Georgetown, Calif: The Talisman Press, 1964.

————. *The Gold Rush Letters of J. D. B. Stillman.* Palo Alto, Calif: Lewis Osborne, 1967.

Journal of Discourses, 26 vols. London: Latter-Day Saints Book Depot, 1854–1886.

Kelley, Robert L. *Gold vs. Grain: The Hydraulic Mining Controversy in California's Sacramento Valley, A Chapter in the Decline of the Concept of Laissez Faire.* Glendale, Calif: The Arthur H. Clark Co., 1959.

Kemble, Edward C. *A History of California Newspapers, 1846–1858: Reprinted from the Supplement to the Sacramento* Union *of December 25, 1858,* Edited by Helen Harding Bretnor. Los Gatos, Calif: The Talisman Press, 1962.

Kemble, John Haskell, ed. *To California and the South Seas: The Diary of Albert G. Osbun.* San Marino, Calif: The Huntington Library, 1966.

Kenny, Scott G., ed. *Wilford Woodruff's Journal,* 10 vols. Midvale, Utah: Signature Books, 1983.

Knecht, William L. and Peter L. Crawley, eds. *History of Brigham Young.* Berkeley, Calif: Mass-Cal Associates, 1964.

Korns, J. Roderic and Dale L. Morgan, eds. *West from Fort Bridger: The Pioneering of Immigrant Trails across Utah, 1846–1850.* Revised and updated by Will Bagley and Harold Schindler. Logan, Utah: Utah State Univ. Press, 1994.

Kurutz, Gary F., ed. *The California Gold Rush: A Descriptive Bibliography of Books and Pamphlets Covering the Years 1848–1853.* S.F: The Book Club of Calif., 1997.

Kuykendall, Ralph S. *The Hawaiian Kingdom, 1778–1854.* Honolulu: Univ. of Hawaii Press, 1938.

Lamar, Howard R., ed. *The Cruise of the Portsmouth, 1845–1847: A Sailor's View of the Naval Conquest of California by Joseph T. Downey, Ordinary Seaman.* New Haven, Conn: Yale Univ. Library, 1958.

Larson, Carl V. *A Data Base of the Mormon Battalion.* Providence, Utah: Kieth W. Watkins and Sons Printing, Inc., 1987.

Lavender, David. *California: Land of New Beginnings.* N.Y: Harper & Row, Publishers, 1972.

Lewis, Donovan. *Pioneers of California: True Stories of Early Settlers in the Golden State.* S.F: Scottwall Associates, 1993.

Lotchin, Roger. *San Francisco, 1846–1856: From Hamlet to City.* N.Y: Oxford Univ. Press, 1974.

McCormac, Eugene Irving. *James K. Polk: A Political Biography.* Berkeley: Univ. of Calif. Press, 1922.

McGlashan, C. F. *The History of the Donner Party: A Tragedy of the Sierra.* Stanford, Calif: Stanford Univ. Press, 1947.

Menefee, Campbell A. *A Historical and Descriptive Sketch Book of Napa, Sonoma, Lake and Mendocino, comprising sketches of their Topography, Productions, History, Scenery, and Peculiar Attractions.* Napa, Calif: Reporter Publishing House, 1873.

Merk, Frederick. *Manifest Destiny and Mission in American History: A Reinterpretation.* N.Y: Alfred A. Knopf, 1963.

Mitchell, S. Augustus. *Texas, Oregon and California.* Oakland, Calif: Biobooks, 1948. The frontispiece is a color reproduction of the Brannan family miniatures.

Monaghan, Jay. *Australians and the Gold Rush: Californians and Down Under, 1849–1854.* Berkeley: Univ. of Calif. Press, 1966.

———. *Chile, Peru, and the California Gold Rush of 1849.* Berkeley: Univ. of Calif. Press, 1973.

Morgan, Dale L., ed. *California Manuscripts: Being a Collection of Important, Unpublished & Unknown Original Historical Sources.* N.Y: Edward Eberstadt & Sons, 1962. Published as Eberstadt's Catalogue 159.

———. *Overland in 1846,* 2 vols. Georgetown, Calif: The Talisman Press, 1963.

———. *In Pursuit of the Golden Dream: Reminiscences of San Francisco and the Northern and Southern Mines, 1849–1857 by Howard Gardner.* Stoughton, Mass: Western Hemisphere Inc., 1970.

———. *News Clippings from Iowa and Illinois, 1841–1849.* Burlington, Wisc: John J. Hajicek, 1992.

——— and James R. Scobie, eds. *Three Years in California: William Perkins' Journal of Life at Sonora, 1849–1852.* Berkeley: Univ. of Calif. Press, 1964.

Moss, Carolyn J., ed. *Kate Field: Selected Letters.* Carbondale: Southern Ill. Univ. Press, 1996.

Muir, Leo. *A Century of Mormon Activities in California,* 2 vols. S.L.C: Deseret News Press, 1951–52.

Mullen, Kevin J. *Let Justice Be Done: Crime and Politics in Early San Francisco.* Reno: Univ. of Nev. Press, 1989.

Myers, John M. *San Francisco's Reign of Terror.* Garden City, N.Y: Doubleday & Co., 1996.

Neelands, Barbara. *About Sam Brannan.* Calistoga, Calif: Sharpsteen Museum Reprints, 1990.

Nelson, Anna Kasten. *Secret Agents: President Polk and the Search for Peace with Mexico.* N.Y: Garland Publishing, 1988.

Newell, Linda King and Valeen Tippitts Avery. *Mormon Enigma: Emma Hale Smith.* Garden City, N.Y: Doubleday and Co., 1984.

Nichols, Roy. *Advanced Agents of American Destiny.* Philadelphia: Univ. of Pa. Press, 1956.

Nunis, Doyce B., Jr., ed. *Josiah Belden, 1841 California Overland Pioneer: His Memoir and Early Letters.* Georgetown, Calif: The Talisman Press, 1962.

Ogden, Annegret S., ed. *Frontier Reminiscences of Eveline Brooks Auerbach*. Berkeley, Calif: Friends of the Bancroft Library, 1994.

Ottley, Allan R., ed. *John A. Sutter, Jr., Statement Regarding Early California Experiences*. Sacramento: Sacramento Book Collectors Club, 1943.

—————. *Reproduction of Thompson and West's History of Sacramento County, California with Illustrations,*. Berkeley, Calif: Howell-North, 1960; reprint of 1880 edition.

Owens, Kenneth N., ed. *John Sutter and a Wider West*. Lincoln: Univ. of Nebr. Press, 1994.

[Palmer, Lyman A.] *History of Napa and Lake Counties, California, Comprising their Geography, Geology, Topography, Climatography, Springs, and Timber*. S.F: Slocum, Bowen & Co., 1881.

Parke, William C. *Personal Reminiscences of William Cooper Parke, Marshall of the Hawaiian Islands from 1850 to 1884*. Cambridge, Mass: The Univ. Press, for the author, 1891.

Parker, Elizabeth L. and James Abajian. *A Walking Tour of the Black Presence in San Francisco during the Nineteenth Century*. S.F: San Francisco African American Hist. and Cultural Soc., 1974.

Parker, Michelle. *The San Francisco Mormon History Walking Tour*. N.P., The Church of Jesus Christ of Latter-day Saints, 1996.

Patton, Annaleone D. *California Mormons by Sail and Trail*. S.L.C: Deseret Book Co., 1961.

Paul, Rodman W. *The California Gold Discovery: Sources, Documents, Accounts and Memoirs Relating to the Discovery of Gold at Sutter's Mill*. Georgetown, Calif: The Talisman Press, 1966.

Phillips, Catherine Coffin. *Portsmouth Plaza: The Cradle of San Francisco*. S.F: John Henry Nash, 1932.

Powell, Lawrence Clark. *Philosopher Pickett*. Berkeley: Univ. of Calif. Press, 1942.

Pratt, Parley P., Jr., ed. *The Autobiography of Parley Parker Pratt*. N.Y: Russell Brothers, 1874. Reprinted S.L.C: Deseret Book Co., 1938.

Price, Glenn W. *Origins of the Mexican War: The Polk-Stockton Intrigue*. Austin: Univ. of Tex. Press, 1967.

Quaife, Milo Milton, ed. *The Diary of James K. Polk During His Presidency, 1845 to 1849*, 4 vols. Chicago: A. C. McClurg & Co., 1910.

Quinn, D. Michael. *The Mormon Hierarchy: Origins of Power*. S.L.C: Signature Books, 1994.

—————. *The Mormon Hierarchy: Extensions of Power*. S.L.C: Signature Books, 1997.

Record Book of the Town of Saco. Saco, Maine: Committee on Public Property, 1895.

Richards, Rand. *Historic San Francisco: A Concise History and Guide*. S.F: Heritage House Publishers, 1995.

Ricketts, Norma B. *The California Star Express*. Sacramento: Sacramento County Hist. Soc., 1982.

—————. *Melissa's Journey with the Mormon Battalion—The Western Odyssey of Melissa Burton Coray: 1846–1848* (S.L.C: Daughters of Utah Pioneers, 1994).

—————. *The Mormon Battalion: U.S. Army of the West, 1846–1848*. Logan: Utah State Univ. Press, 1996.

Roberts, Brigham H. *A Comprehensive History of The Church of Jesus Christ of Latter-day Saints*, 6 vols. S.L.C: Deseret News Press, 1930.

—————, *History of the Church of Jesus Christ of Latter-day Saints. Period 2. Apostolic Interregnum. From the Manuscript History of Brigham Young and Other Original Documents*, vol. 7. S.L.C: Deseret News, 1932.

Rogers, Fred Blackburn, ed. *Filings from an Old Saw: Reminiscences of San Francisco and California's Conquest by "Filings"—Joseph T. Downey.* S.F: John Howell, 1956.

————, ed. *A Navy Surgeon in California, 1846–1847: The Journal of Marius Duvall.* S.F: John Howell, 1957.

————. *Montgomery and the Portsmouth.* S.F: John Howell, 1958.

————, *A Kemble Reader: Stories of California, 1846–1848 by Edward Cleveland Kemble, Early California Journalist.* S.F: The Calif. Hist. Soc., 1963.

————. *The California Star. Yerba Buena and San Francisco, Volume I, 1847–1848: A Reproduction in Facsimile.* Berkeley, Calif: Howell-North Books, 1965.

Rogers, Justus H. *Colusa County: Its History Traced from a State of Nature through the Early Period of Settlement and Development, to the Present Day.* Orland, Calif: N.P., 1891.

Rolle, Andrew F. *An American in California: The Biography of William Heath Davis, 1822–1909.* San Marino, Calif: The Huntington Library, 1956.

Rosales, Vicente Pérez. *Recuerdos Del Pasado*, trans. as *California Adventure*, Edwin S. Morby and Arturo Torres-Rioseco. S.F: The Book Club of Calif., 1947.

Royce, Josiah. "An Episode of Early California Life: The Squatter Riot of 1850 in Sacramento," in *Studies of Good and Evil: A Series of Essays upon Problems of Philosophy and of Life.* N.Y: D. Appleton and Co., 1910; reprinted from *Overland Monthly* (September 1885).

————. *California.* N.Y: Houghton, Mifflin and Co., 1886. Reprinted Santa Barbara, Calif: Peregrine Publishers, Inc., 1970.

Ruiz, Ramon Eduardo. *The People of Sonora and Yankee Capitalists.* Tucson: Univ. of Ariz. Press, 1988.

Salas, Miguel Tinker. *In the Shadow of Eagles: Sonora and the Transformation of the Border during the Porfiriato.* Berkeley: Univ. of Calif. Press, 1997.

Saxton, Alexander. *The Indispensable Enemy: Labor and the Anti-Chinese Movement in California.* Berkeley: Univ. of Calif. Press, 1971.

Scherer, James A. B. *The First Forty-Niner and the Story of the Golden Tea-Caddy.* N.Y: Minton, Balch & Co., 1925.

Schindler, Harold. *Orrin Porter Rockwell: Man of God, Son of Thunder.* S.L.C: Univ. of Utah Press, 1966. 2d ed., 1983.

Scott, Reva. *Samuel Brannan and the Golden Fleece.* N.Y: The Macmillan Co., 1944.

Sellers, Charles. *James K. Polk, Continentalist, 1843–46.* Princeton, N.J: Princeton Univ. Press, 1966.

Senkewicz, Robert M. *Vigilantes in Gold Rush San Francisco.* Stanford, Calif: Stanford Univ. Press, 1985.

Sessions, Gene A. *Mormon Thunder: A Documentary History of Jedediah Morgan Grant.* Urbana: Univ. of Ill. Press, 1982.

Sherman, William T. *Memoirs of General William T. Sherman*, 2 vols. N.Y: D. Appleton and Co., 1876.

Shields, Steven L. *Divergent Paths of the Restoration: A History of the Latter Day Saint Movement.* Los Angeles: Restoration Research, 1990.

Shewmaker, Kenneth E. and Kenneth R. Stevens, eds. *The Papers of Daniel Webster: Diplomatic Papers, Volume 2, 1850–1852.* Hanover, N.H: The Univ. Press of New England, 1987.

Shuck, Oscar T., ed. *Representative and Leading Men of the Pacific Coast.* S.F: Bacon and Co., Printers and Publishers, 1870. Includes William V. Wells' "Samuel Brannan," 454–59.

Shumate, Albert. *The California of George Gordon and the 1849 Sea Voyages of his California Association.* Glendale, Calif: The Arthur H. Clark Co., 1976.

Sirna, Anthony and Allison, eds. *The Wanderings of Edward Ely.* N.Y: Hastings House, 1954.

Smiles, Samuel. *The Autobiography of Samuel Smiles.* N.Y: E. P. Dutton and Co., 1905.

Smith, Cornelius C. *Emilio Kosterlitzky, Eagle of Sonora and the Southwest Border.* Glendale, Calif: The Arthur H. Clark Co., 1970.

Smith, George D., ed. *An Intimate Chronicle: The Journals of William Clayton.* S.L.C: Signature Books, 1991.

Smith, Joseph, Jr. *History of the Church,* ed. by Brigham H. Roberts, 7 vols. S.L.C: Deseret News, 1932. 2d ed. 1950.

Smith, Joseph, III. *The History of the Reorganized Church of Jesus Christ of Latter Day Saints,* 7 vols. Independence, Mo: Herald House, 1967.

Society of California Pioneers. *Constitution and By-Laws of the Society of California Pioneers.* S.F: C. Bartlett, 1853.

Sonne, Conway B. *Ships, Saints, and Mariners: A Maritime Encyclopedia of Mormon Migration 1830–1890.* S.L.C: Univ. of Utah Press, 1987.

Soulé, Frank, John H. Gihon, and James Nisbet, *The Annals of San Francisco; Containing a Summary of the History of the First Discovery, Settlement, Progress and Present Condition of California, and a Complete History of All the Important Events Connected with Its Great City: To Which Are Added, Biographical Memoirs of Some Prominent Citizens.* N. Y. and S.F: D. Appleton & Co., 1854.

Spence, Mary Lee and Donald Jackson, eds. *The Expeditions of John Charles Frémont,* 3 vols. Urbana: Univ. of Ill. Press, 1970–1984.

Spicer, Edward. *Cycles of Conquest: The Impact of Spain, Mexico, and the United States on the Indians of the Southwest, 1533–1960.* Tucson: Univ. of Ariz. Press, 1962.

Stansbury, Howard. *Exploration and Survey of the Valley of the Great Salt Lake.* Philadelphia: Lippincott, Grambo & Co., 1852.

Stark, Samuel. *Life and Travels of Daniel Stark and His People.* S.L.C: By the Author, 1955.

Stegner, Wallace. *The Gathering of Zion.* N.Y: McGraw Hill Book Co., 1964.

Stellman, Louis J. *Sam Brannan, Builder of San Francisco.* N.Y: Exposition Press, 1953. Reprinted Fairfield, Calif: James Stevenson Publisher, 1996, with a preface by Albert Shumate and an introduction by Kevin Starr.

Stevens, Sylvester K. *American Expansion in Hawaii, 1842–1898.* N.Y: Russell & Russell, 1945.

Stevenson, Robert Louis. *The Silverado Squatters.* S.F: Grabhorn Press, 1952.

Stewart, George R., Jr. *Committee of Vigilance: Revolution in San Francisco, 1851.* Boston: Houghton Mifflin Co., 1964.

Stickney, William, ed. *The Autobiography of Amos Kendall.* Boston: Lee and Shepard, 1872.

Sutter, John A. et al., *New Helvetia Diary.* S.F: The Grabhorn Press, 1939.

Swasey, William F. *Early Days and Men of California.* N.P. Oakland, Calif: 1891.

Thompson, Robert Luther. *Wiring a Continent: The History of The Telegraph Industry in the United States, 1832–1866.* Princeton, N.J: Princeton Univ. Press, 1947.

Thorndike, Rachel Sherman, ed. *The Sherman Letters: Correspondence between General Sherman and Senator Sherman from 1837 to 1891.* N.Y: Charles Scribners Sons, 1894. Reprinted N.Y: Da Capo Press, 1969.

Thrapp, Dan L. *Encyclopedia of Frontier Biography,* 4 vols. Glendale, Calif. and Spokane, Wash: The Arthur H. Clark Co., 1988, 1993.

Tinkham, George H. *California Men and Events.* Stockton, Calif: Record Publishing Co., 1915.

Tullidge, Edward W. *Life of Brigham Young; or, Utah and Her Founders.* N.Y: Tullidge & Crandall, 1876.

———. *Tullidge's Histories, [of Utah].* Volume II: *Containing the History of all the Northern, Eastern and Western Counties of Utah; Also the Counties of Southern Idaho.* S.L.C: The Press of the Juvenile Instructor, 1889.

Tuthill, Frank. *The History of California.* S.F: H. H. Bancroft & Co., 1866.

Tyler, Daniel. *A Concise History of the Mormon Battalion in the Mexican War, 1846–1847.* S.L.C: 1881. Reprinted Glorieta, N.M: The Rio Grande Press, Inc., 1980.

Unruh, John D., Jr. *The Plains Across: The Overland Emigrants and the Trans-Mississippi West, 1840–1860.* Urbana: Univ. of Ill. Press, 1979.

Van Wagoner, Richard. *Sidney Rigdon: A Portrait of Religious Excess.* S.L.C: Signature Books, 1994.

——— and Stephen C. Walker. *A Book of Mormons.* S.L.C: Signature Books, 1982.

Varley, James F. *Lola Montez: The California Adventures of Europe's Notorious Courtesan.* Spokane, Wash: The Arthur H. Clark Co., 1996.

Wagner, Henry R. *The Plains and the Rockies: A Bibliography of Original Narratives of Travel and Adventure, 1800–1865.* S.F: John Howell, 1921. 2d ed., with Charles L. Camp, Columbus, Ohio: Long's College Book Co., 1953.

Walker, Franklin. *San Francisco's Literary Frontier.* N.Y: Alfred A. Knopf, 1939.

Walker, John Phillip, ed. *Dale Morgan on Early Mormonism: Correspondence and a New History.* S.L.C: Signature Books, 1986.

Wahlquist, Wayne L. and Howard A. Christy, eds., *Atlas of Utah.* Provo, Utah: Brigham Young Univ. Press, 1981.

Watson, Douglas S., ed. *Reminiscences and Incidents of Early Days of San Francisco. 1845–50 by John Henry Brown.* S.F: The Grabhorn Press, 1933.

Werner, M. R. *Brigham Young.* N.Y: Harcourt, Brace and Co., 1925.

West, Robert C. *Sonora: Its Geographical Personality.* Austin: Univ. of Texas Press, 1993.

Wheat, Carl I. *Pioneers: The Engaging Tale of Three Early California Printing Presses and Their Strange Adventures.* Los Angeles, Calif: N.P., 1945.

———. *Mapping the Transmississippi West,* 5 vols. S.F: The Grabhorn Press (vol. I) and The Institute of Hist. Cartography, 1957–63.

White, David A., ed. *News of the Plains and the Rockies, 1803–1865,* vol. 3, *Missionaries, Mormons, 1821–1864; Indian Agents, Captives, 1832–1865.* Spokane, Wash: The Arthur H. Clark Co., 1997.

Whiting, Lilian. *Kate Field: A Record.* Boston: Little, Brown, and Co., 1899.

Whitsell, Leon O. *One Hundred Years of Freemasonry in California,* 4 vols. S.F: The Grand Lodge, Free and Accepted Masons of Calif., ca. 1950.

Williams, Mary Floyd. "Papers of the San Francisco Committee of Vigilance of 1851," in *Publications of the Academy of Pacific Coast History,* vol. 4. Berkeley: Univ. of Calif. Press, 1919.

——————, ed. *History of the San Francisco Committee of Vigilance of 1851: A Study of Social Control on the California Frontier in the Days of the Gold Rush.* Berkeley: Univ. of Calif. Press, 1921.

Willis, William L. *History of Sacramento County, California, with Biographical Sketches of the Leading Men and Women of the County Who Have Been Identified With Its Growth and Development From the Early Days to the Present.* Los Angeles: Historic Record Co., 1913.

Wiltsee, Ernest A. *The Truth about Frémont: an Inquiry.* S.F: John Henry Nash, 1936.

Woodruff, Wilford. *The Discourses of Wilford Woodruff.* S.L.C: Bookcraft, 1969.

Young, Bob and Jan. *Empire Builder, Sam Brannan.* N.Y: Julian Messner, 1967.

Young, John P. *Journalism in California.* S.F: Chronicle Publishing Co., 1915.

Zollinger, James Peter. *Sutter: The Man and His Empire.* N.Y: Oxford Univ. Press, 1939.

PERIODICALS

Alter, J. Cecil, ed. "The Journal of Robert S. Bliss, with the Mormon Battalion." *Utah Historical Quar.* 4 (July, October 1931).

Andrews, Thomas F. "The Controversial Hastings Overland Guide: A Reassessment." *Pacific Hist. Review* 36 (February 1968).

——————. "The Ambitions of Lansford W. Hastings: A Study in Western Myth-Making." *Pacific Hist. Review* 39 (November 1970).

Bagley, Will. "Lansford W. Hastings: Scoundrel or Visionary?" *Overland Journal* 12 (Spring 1994).

——————. "'Every Thing Is Favourable! And God Is On Our Side': Samuel Brannan and the Conquest of California." *Journal of Mormon History* 23 (Fall 1997).

Beckwith, Frank, ed. "Extracts from the Journal of John Steele." *Utah Hist. Quar.* 6 (January 1933).

Bidwell, John. "Echoes of the Past about California." *Century Magazine* 41 (December 1890).

——————. "Fremont in the Conquest of California." *Century Magazine* 41 (February 1891).

Bieber, Ralph W. "California Gold Mania." *Mississippi Valley Hist. Review* 35 (June 1948).

[Bigler, Henry W.], "Henele Pikale." "Recollections of the Past." *Juvenile Instructor* 21 (1 and 15 December 1886).

Bigler, Henry W. "Diary of H. W. Bigler 1847 and 1848." *Overland Monthly* 10 (September 1887).

——————. "Extracts from the Journal of Henry W. Bigler." *Utah Hist. Quar.* 5 (April, July, October 1932).

Bringhurst, Newell G. "Sam Brannan's 1851 Hawaiian Filibustering Expedition: A 'Paradise Postponed.'" *The Californians* (September/October 1987).

—————. "Samuel Brannan and His Forgotten Final Years." *So. Calif. Quar.* 79 (Summer 1997).

Brown, John. "An Evidence of Inspiration." *Juvenile Instructor* 16 (1881).

Campbell, Eugene E. "The Apostasy of Samuel Brannan." *Utah Hist. Quar.* 27 (April 1959).

Carr, James. "The California Letters of James Carr." *Quar. of the Calif. Hist. Soc.* 9 (June 1932).

Carranco, Lynwood and Andrew Genzoli. "California Redwood Empire Place Names." *Journal of the West* 7 (July 1968).

Christian, Lewis Clark. "Mormon Foreknowledge of the West." *Brigham Young University Studies* 21 (Fall 1981).

Coleman, William C. "San Francisco Vigilance Committees." *Century Magazine* 43 (February 1892).

Crocheron, Augusta Joyce. "California Memories." *Contributor* 6 (May 1885).

—————. "The Ship *Brooklyn*." *Western Galaxy* (March 1888).

Cumming, John. "Lansford Hastings' Michigan Connection." *Overland Journal* 16 (Fall 1998).

Dillon, Richard H. "Filibuster in Paradise." *Hawaiian Life Week-End Magazine* (26 November 1955).

Ellison, William Henry, ed. "Memoirs of Hon. William M. Gwin." *Calif. Hist. Soc. Quar.* 19 (March 1940).

Esplin, Ronald K. "'A Place Prepared': Joseph, Brigham and the Quest for Promised Refuge in the West." *Journal of Mormon History* 9 (1982).

Everett, Amelia D. "The Ship *Brooklyn*." *Calif. Hist. Soc. Quar.* 37 (September 1958).

"The Family of Lansford Warren Hastings." *Nugget: A Publication of the Calif. Genealogical Soc.* 2 (Winter 1991).

Fifield, Allen. "Wagons East Across the Sierra." *Hist. Soc. of So. Calif. Quar.* 43 (September 1961).

Fitch, George Hamilton. "How California Came into the Union." *Century Magazine* 40 (September 1890).

Frazer, Robert W. "The Ochoa Bond Negotiations of 1865–1867." *Pacific Hist. Review* 9 (December 1942).

Godfrey, Kenneth W. "Crime and Punishment in Mormon Nauvoo, 1839–1846." *BYU Studies* 32 (Winter 1992).

Hall, Carroll D. "Sam Brannan's Press." *Book Club of California Quar. News-Letter* 13 (Winter 1947).

Hansen, Lorin. "Voyage of the *Brooklyn*." *Dialogue: A Journal of Mormon Thought* 21 (Autumn 1988).

Hawgood, John A. "The Pattern of Yankee Infiltration in Mexican Alta California, 1821–1846." *Pacific Hist. Review* 27 (February 1958).

Henderson, Sarah Fisher, Nellie Edith Latourette, and Kenneth Scott Latourette, eds. "Correspondence of the Reverend Ezra Fisher, Pioneer Missionary of the American

Baptist Home Mission Society in Indiana, Illinois, Iowa and Oregon." *Quar. of the Oregon Hist. Soc.* 16 (September 1915).

Hittell, John S. "The Discovery of Gold in California." *Century Magazine* 41 (February 1891).

————. "Samuel Brannan." *Overland Monthly* 13 (June 1889).

Horner, John M. "Voyage of the Ship 'Brooklyn.'" *Improvement Era* 9 (August and September 1906).

Jones, Lu. "Ship *Brooklyn* Passenger Gravesite Location Search Project." *The Ship* Brooklyn *Assoc. Newsletter* 2 (Fall 1997).

Kemble, E. C. "Confirming the Gold Discovery." *Century Magazine* 41 (February 1891).

Luce, W. Ray. "The Mormon Battalion: A Historical Accident?" *Utah Hist. Quar.* 42 (Winter 1974).

Lund, A. William. "The Ship Brooklyn." *The Improvement Era* (October 1951).

Lyman, George D. "Victor J. Fourgeaud, M.D., Second Physician and Surgeon in San Francisco, Writer of California's First Promotion Literature." *Calif. Hist. Soc. Quarterly* 9 (June 1932).

MacCollister, Robert S. "What Became of the Brannan Press?" *Kemble Occasional* 20 (October 1978).

Miller, Robert Ryal. "The American Legion of Honor in Mexico." *Pacific Hist. Review* 30 (August 1961).

Nasatir, A. P. "The French Consulate in California, 1843–56." *Calif. Hist. Soc. Quar.* 9 (December 1932).

Nunis, Doyce B., Jr. "Six New Larkin Letters." *So. Calif. Quar.* 49 (March 1967).

Palmer, John Williamson. "Pioneer Days in San Francisco." *Century Magazine* 43 (February 1892).

Pierce, Norman C. "A Curse upon His Head." *Old West* 4 (Fall 1967).

Pisani, Donald J. "Squatter Law in California, 1850–1858." *Western Hist. Quar.* 25 (Autumn 1994).

Pomeroy, Earl S., ed. "The Trial of the Hounds, 1849: A Witness's Account." *Calif. Hist. Soc. Quar.* 29 (June 1950).

Posner, Russell M. "A British Consular Agent in California: The Reports of James A. Forbes, 1843–1846." *So. Calif. Quar.* 53 (June 1971).

Quinn, D. Michael. "The Flag of the Kingdom of God." *BYU Studies* 14 (Autumn 1973).

————. "The Council of Fifty and Its Members, 1844 to 1945." *BYU Studies* 20 (Winter 1980).

Richards, Sherman L. and George M. Blackburn. "The Sydney Ducks: A Demographic Analysis." *Pacific Hist. Review* 42 (February 1973).

Ricketts, Norma B. "Isaac Goodwin—Noted Pioneer." *The Pioneer* (Sept.–Oct. 1966).

Robinson, Ebenezer. "Items of Personal History of the Editor." *The Return* 1 (July 1889).

Robinson, Edgar Eugene. "The Day Journal of Milton S. Latham." *Quar. of the Calif. Hist. Soc.* 11 (March 1932).

Rolle, Andrew F. "California Filibustering and the Hawaiian Kingdom." *Pacific Hist. Review* 19 (August 1950).

Royce, Josiah. "Light on the Seizure of California." *Century Magazine* 40 (September 1890).

Stanley, Reva Holdaway. "Sutter's Mormon Workmen at Natoma and Coloma in 1848." *Calif. Hist. Soc. Quar.* 14 (September 1935).

————— and Charles L. Camp. "A Mormon Mission to California in 1851: From the Diary of Parley Parker Pratt." *Calif. Hist. Soc. Quar.* 14 (March and June 1935).

Stenberg, Richard R. "The Failure of Polk's Mexican War Intrigue of 1845." *Pacific Hist. Review* 4 (March 1935).

—————. "Polk and Frémont, 1845–1846." *Pacific Hist. Review* 7 (1938).

Sutter, John A. "The Discovery of Gold in California." *Hutchings' Illustrated California Magazine* 2 (November 1857).

Taylor, Samuel. "The Gold Baron of California." *Coronet* (January 1960).

Van Alstyne, R. W. "Great Britain, the United States and Hawaiian Independence, 1850–1855." *Pacific Hist. Review* 4 (March 1935).

Watson, Douglas S. "Herald of the Gold Rush—Sam Brannan." *Calif. Hist. Soc. Quar.* 10 (September 1931).

—————. "The Great Express Extra of the *California Star* of April 1, 1848." *Calif. Hist. Soc. Quar.* 11 (June 1932).

Whittaker, David J. "East of Nauvoo: Benjamin Winchester and the Early Mormon Church." *Journal of Mormon History* 21 (Fall 1995).

Wiltsee, Ernest A. "The British Vice-Consul in California and the Events of 1846." *Calif. Hist. Soc. Quar.* 10 (June 1931).

—————. "Double Springs, the First County Seat of Calaveras County." *Quar. of the Calif. Hist. Soc.* 11 (June 1932).

Yurtinus, John F. "Images of Early California: Mormon Battalion Soldiers' Reflections During the War with Mexico." *Hist. Soc. of So. Calif. Quar.* 53 (Spring 1981).

Zobell, Albert L. Jr. "Sam Brannan and the Sea Saints." *Improvement Era* 71 (August 1968).

NEWSPAPERS

Alta California, San Francisco, California.

Anderson, Mary Audentia Smith, ed. "The Memoirs of President Joseph Smith (1832–1914)." *Saints' Herald*, 6 November 1934.

Austin, Edwin N. "Historic Trip of the Good Ship Brooklyn." *Deseret Evening News*, 6 April 1918.

Barnes, George E. "Anent Samuel Brannan." *San Francisco Bulletin*, 12 October 1895, 9/1–3.

"Brannan's Bonanza." *New York Times*, 3 February 1880, 8/2.

"The Brooklyn Case." *Alta California*, 1 October 1849, 4/1–5.

Canfield, Chauncey L. "The Twelve Starred Flag that Was to Wave Over California." *San Francisco Chronicle*, 17 January 1909, 2/1–5.

"Communicated." *Nogales Express*, 20 September 1884, AC 901.Al #624, BYU Library.

Cook, John. "Sam Brannan Epic Integral Part of Migration to West." *Sacramento Union*, 20 February 1961, 9.

[Damon, Samuel C.] "Joseph Smith, Jr., Founder of 'Church of Later-Day-Saints,' (or Mormons) . . ." *Honolulu Friend*, 1 July 1846, 100–02.

"The Foremothers Tell of Olden Times." *San Francisco Chronicle*, 11 September 1900, 36–27.

"The Fourth of July, 1849." *Sacramento Bee*, 26 September 1882, 1/2.

Hesketh, Henry, "California in '50: History of the Famous Trinidad Bay Expedition." *San Francisco Morning Call*, 9 November 1884, 1/1–2.

Jacobsen, Pauline. "A Fire-Defying Landmark." *San Francisco Bulletin*, 4 May 1912.

————. "California's First Millionaire." *San Francisco Bulletin*, 20 May 1916.

Lattin, Dan. "S.F.'s Devilish Mormon Finally Gets His Due." *San Francisco Chronicle*, 26 July 1996, A1, A13/1–2.

Lyman, Amasa to J. H. Flanigan, 11 April 1850, in *Millennial Star* 12, 214–15.

"A Mexican Bonanza." *Nogales Record*, 26 May 1887, 2/2–3. Copy in Folder 13, BYU Brannan Papers.

Niles' National Register. Typescripts in Dale L. Morgan Transcripts, Utah State Hist. Soc.

Peckham, Robert F. "An Eventful Life." *San Jose Pioneer*, 16 June 1877–4 August 1877.

Poett, Dr. J. Henry. "A Report of the Progress and Discoveries of the General Morgan Exploring Party to Mendocino Bay." *Alta California*, 24 April 1850, 2/1-2.

Pony Express Courier, 1935–May 1944.

Pony Express, June 1944–June 1978.

"Primitive Mormonism: A Personal Narrative of it by Mr. Benjamin Winchester." *Salt Lake Tribune*, 22 September 1889.

Redding, Ned Sr. "Historical Letters." *California Intermountain News*, 30 June 1966, 1.

Salt Lake Herald, 9 April 1882.

"Samuel Brannan." *Saints' Herald*, 25 May 1889, 323/2–3.

San Francisco Daily Herald.

The Ship Brooklyn *Assoc. Newsletters*, (1996–98).

Stanley, Don. "The Calistoga of Sarifornia." *Sacramento Bee*, 26 November 1981, D1.

Times and Seasons, Nauvoo, Ill., 6 vols. (Independence: Independence Press, 1986).

"Voyage of Historic Ship 'Brooklyn' New York to Yerba Buena 70 Years Ago." *Deseret Evening News*, 29 July 1916.

Theses, Dissertations, and Papers

Andrews, Thomas F. "The Controversial Career of Lansford Warren Hastings: Pioneer California Promoter and Emigrant Guide." Ph.D. diss., Univ. of So. Calif., 1970.

Baldridge, Kenneth Wayne. "A History of the Mormon Settlement of Central California with Emphasis on New Hope and San Francisco, 1846–1857, and Modesto, 1926–1954." M.A. thesis, College of the Pacific, 1955.

Christian, Lewis Clark. "A Study of Mormon Knowledge of the Far West Prior to the Exodus." M.A. thesis, Brigham Young Univ., 1972.

———. "A Study of Mormon Westward Migration Between February 1846 and July 1847 with an Emphasis and Evaluation of the Factors that Led to the Mormons' Choice of the Salt Lake Valley as the Site of Their Initial Colony." Ph.D. diss., Brigham Young Univ., 1976.

Dunlap, Florence McClure. "Samuel Brannan." M.A. thesis, Univ. of Calif. at Berkeley, 1928.

Luce, W. Ray. "Samuel Brannan: Speculator in Mexican Lands." M.A. thesis, Brigham Young Univ., 1968.

McCready, Clint. "New Hope: A Mormon Colony in Central California." M.A. thesis, Brigham Young Univ., 1973.

Rudd, Calvin P. "William Smith: Brother of the Prophet Joseph Smith." M.A. thesis, Brigham Young Univ., 1973.

Shoptaugh, Terry L. "Amos Kendall: A Political Biography." Ph.D. diss., Univ. of N.H., 1984.

Volkman, John Duncan. "Samuel Brannan: An Annotated Bibliography." M.A. research paper, San Jose State Univ., 1975.

Yurtinus, John F. "A Ram in the Thicket: The Mormon Battalion in the Mexican War." Ph.D. diss., Brigham Young Univ., 1975.

Pamphlets and Documents

Ancestral File, LDS Family History Library.

[Benson, Alfred G.] "A Report from the Bureau of Construction &c., relative to contracts entered into with A. G. & A. W. Benson," 3 March 1845, House Exec. Doc. 161 (28–2), 1851.

[Benson, Alfred G.] Senate Report 397 (34–3), 1856, Serial 891.

"Brannan: A Local Character Song," Broadsheet, Calif. State Library.

Brannan, Samuel. "Get a Farm in Mexico: A Land of Peace and Plenty." Broadside, ca. 1883. Folder 15, Samuel Brannan Papers, Mss 37, BYU Library.

Brannan, Samuel. Early Church Information File, LDS Family History Library, Record # re bap. 1808 2.

"California and New Mexico," House Exec. Doc. 17 (31–1), 1850, Serial 573.

Hardy, John. "History of the Trials of Elder John Hardy, before the Church of Latter Day Saints in Boston, for Slander in Saying that G. J. Adams, S. Brannan and Wm. Smith, were licentious characters." (Boston: 1844).

Hittell, Theodore H. "In the Supreme Court of the State of California, Charles L. Wilson, Appellant, vs. Samuel Brannan, Respondent: Reply to Respondent's Brief." S.F: Towne & Bacon, 1864.

[Kemble, Edward C.?] "Sonora Colonization Enterprise: Its History, Objects and Plans Explained." The Sonora Colonization Association of New York, 4 February 1880. Copy in Samuel Brannan Papers, Folder 15, Brigham Young Univ.

Little, Jesse C. "Circular: Epistle to the Church of Jesus Christ of Latter Day Saints, in the Eastern States." Copy in LDS Library.

Log of the *Congress*, 16 September 1845–12 January 1849, Record Group 24, National Archives.

[Pratt, Parley.] "Proclamation of the Twelve Apostles of the Church of Jesus Christ of Latter-day Saints to All the Kings of the World, to the President of the United States of America; to the Governors of the Several States, and to the Rules and People of All Nations." N.Y: Pratt and Brannan, 1845.

"Report to the Committee on Naval Affairs," 3 March 1851, Senate Document 319 (31–2).

Statement of Kamehameha III, in "Hawaiian Islands." Sen. Doc., No. 77, 88–89, Serial 3062.

Sutter, John A., Deed to John A. Sutter, Jr., 18 November 1848, Book of Deeds A, Sacramento County Recorder's Office.

Tanner, James Henry. "TO THE PUBLIC." Broadside xf F865.B82 T3, 1852, Bancroft Library.

MANUSCRIPTS

Appleby, William I. Autobiography and Journal 1841–1856. MS 2737, Box 2, LDS Archives.

Arrington Leonard J. Papers, Charles C. Rich Research Files. MS 4212, LDS Archives.

Auerbach, Herbert S. Collection. A88–259, BYU Library. Elements of Auerbach's collection, which was sold following his death, are owned by Dr. G. Ralph Bailey of Bountiful, Utah.

Badlam, Alexander to Father John Smith, 3 April 1853, LDS Archives

———— to George A. Smith, 12 January 1855 and 28 May 1855. MS 1322, LDS Archives.

Badlam, Alexander, Jr./Maude Pettus. Papers, Box Three, Calif. State Library Collection.

Bailey, Paul Dayton. Papers. MS B 414, Utah State Hist. Soc.

Bartlett, Washington to Elijah Ward Pell, 2 October 1846. Vault MS 105, Calif. Hist. Soc.

Benson, A. G. to Brigham Young, 5 April 1849. Brigham Young Collection, MS 1234, Box 21, Folder 15, LDS Archives.

Book of Deeds A. Sacramento County Recorder's Office.

The Book of Pioneers. Utah State Hist. Soc.

Borrowman, John. Diaries 1846–1853; 1856; 1859–1860. MS 1495, LDS Archives.

Brannan, John. Letters and other family papers, 1839–1890. BANC MSS 92/755 c, Bancroft Library.

Brannan, Samuel. Brannan to Brethren, 13 February 1847. MS 4721, LDS Archives.

————. Collection. HM 4089, Huntington Library.

————. File. Calif. State Library.

————. Papers. Vault MSS 37, Division of Archives and Manuscripts, BYU Library.

————. Memorabilia, 1924–1979. MS 13674, LDS Archives.

—————. to Wilford Woodruff, 26 December 1845, MS 1352, Box 6, Folder 13 #2, LDS Archives.

Brannan, S. Letter to [Edward] von Pfister, 27 June 1848. C-Y 70, Bancroft Library.

Bringhurst, Newell G. Samuel Brannan: From Devout Latter-day Saint to Disillusioned Dissident. Paper in possession of editor.

—————. Samuel Brannan and Virginia Sorensen: An Aborted Literary Encounter. Paper in possession of editor.

—————. Samuel Brannan and His 1851 Hawaiian Filibustering Expedition: A Closer Look. Paper in possession of editor.

Brodie, Fawn M. to Gordon Ray Young, 12 January 1945. MSS 935, Special Collections, BYU Library.

Buckland, Nancy to Edith Webb, 10 February 1904. MS 13665, LDS Archives.

Bullock, Henrietta Rushton. Collection, 1836–1914. MS 5404:2, LDS Archives.

Bullock, Thomas. Papers. MS 1385, LDS Archives.

Eagar, John. Statement concerning the voyage of the ship, Brooklyn. MS C-D 238:2, Bancroft Library.

Fort Sutter Papers. Manuscript 26, Huntington Library.

Gower, Samuel J. to the Worshipful Master, Wardens, & Brethren, 16 January 1852. Brannan File, Calif. State Library.

Hastings, Lansford Warren. Instructions, 1847. MS 1385, Folder 5, LDS Archives.

Hibbert, Della Sirrine. Biography of George Warren Sirrine. LDS Archives.

Honorable Sam Brannan: A Biographical Sketch. CD 805, Bancroft Library, 2.

Horner, John to Brigham Young, 28 April 1853. Brigham Young Collection, MS 1234, LDS Archives.

Huff, Sharon. Hannah Daggett Buckland, 1802–1881. Based on the research of Cora Prescott Lewis, copy in editor's possession.

Hyde, Orson. Journal, 1832. MS d 1386 fd 1, LDS Archives.

Jenson, Andrew. Alexander Badlam Biographical Encyclopedia form. MS d 4029, Box 13, Folder 3, LDS Archives.

—————. Manuscript History of Kirtland, Ohio. MS 4029, LDS Archives.

Jones, Elbert P. Papers. C-B 464, Bancroft Library.

Journal History of the Church of Jesus Christ of Latter-day Saints. LDS Library-Archives.

Kirtland High Council Minutes, 1832–1837. MS 3432, LDS Archives.

Kirtland, Ohio, Township Record, 1817–1846. MS 3427, LDS Archives.

Lane, Emeline to Ashbel Lane, 29 June 1846. MS 2422, Photostat of manuscript, LDS Archives.

Lyman, Amasa. Journal. Typescript, MS 2757, LDS Archives.

————— and Charles C. Rich to Brigham Young, 23 July 1850. Brigham Young Collection, MS 1234, LDS Archives.

————— to Brigham Young and Council, 14 November 1853. MS d 4212, Box 4, Folder 2, LDS Archives.

Manuscript History of Kirtland, Ohio, MS 4029, LDS Archives.

McFarling, John. Abstract of Titles [Calistoga land records]. Personal collection of Carolyn McDonald, copy in possession of the editor.

Memorandum of Agreement 1840. MS 2983, LDS Archives.

Miles, Samuel. Life History. Reel 920 #1, BYU Library.

Morgan, Dale L. Collection. MSS B-40, Utah State Hist. Soc.

————— Papers. Bancroft Library. Microfilm copy at Special Collections, Marriott Library Univ. of Utah.

Morris, John M. Autobiography and Diaries, 1885–1906. C-D 5209, Bancroft Library.

Nunis, Doyce B., Jr., ed. The Journal of a Sea Captain's Wife during a Passage and Sojourn in Hawaii and of a Trading Voyage to California and Oregon, 1841–1845, by Lydia Rider Nye.

Official Documents Relating to Early San Francisco, 1835–1857. C-A 370, Box 2, Folder 208, Bancroft Library.

Peckham, R. F. An Eventful Life, 1877. In Documents relating to the history of Calif., MSS C-E 107, Bancroft Library.

Pettus, Maude. Biographical Information File. Calif. State Library

Polk, James K. Papers. Library of Congress.

Pratt, Orson to Brigham Young, 4 September 1845. MS d4768, LDS Archives.

Pratt, Parley P. to Isaac Rogers, 6 September 1845. MS 4657, LDS Archives.

Quinn, D. Michael. Transcription of Brigham Young 1844–1846 Diary, 116–17; and transcription of Minutes of Quorum of Twelve Apostles, 24 May 1845, in Samuel Brannan Index Cards, 1–4. D. Michael Quinn Papers, Yale Collection of Western Americana. Copies in possession of the editor.

Records of Members 1836–1970. CR 375/8/Reel 6109, LDS Archives.

Rich, Charles C. Journal. MS 889, LDS Archives.

—————. Letters, 1855–[1868]. MS 5338/3, LDS Archives.

Richards, Willard. Journal, 5, 23, and 24 May 1845. MS 1490, LDS Archives.

Ricketts, Norma B. Brannan Collection, in possession of the editor.

Robertson, Boyd Leslie. Samuel Brannan: Benefactor or Opportunist? Paper presented at Mormon Hist. Assoc., Logan, Utah, May 1988.

Rogers, Isaac to L. P. Rogers II, 11 July 1848; and I. Rogers to Son, letter ca. October 1848. MS 3987, LDS Archives.

Simpson, George. Incoming Correspondence. Hudson's Bay Company Archives, Provincial Archives of Manitoba, Canada.

Sirrine, Warren LeRoy. A Little Sketch of the Life of George Warren Sirrine. MS 13771, LDS Archives.

Skeen, Joseph. Reminiscences and Diary, 1846 July–1847 May. MS 1551, LDS Archives.

Skinner, James. Autobiography. MS 6587, LDS Archives.

Smith, Joseph III to Brannan; and Smith III to D. S. Mills, 17 July 1883. P6, Typescript, JS LB #4, RLDS Library-Archives, Independence, Missouri.

Smith, Samuel Harrison. Diary 1832 Feb.–1833 May. MS 4213, LDS Archives.

Smith, William. Letters 1845. MS 601, LDS Archives.

Sorensen, Virginia. Papers. Mugar Memorial Library, Boston Univ.

Southworth, Henry Larkin. Journal, 1843 Jan.–1846 Mar. MS 1708, LDS Archives.

Sparks, Mary to Maria and Holly Clark, 15 November 1846. MS 7519, LDS Archives.

Stearns, Abel. Collection. Huntington Library.

Taylor, John. Papers. LDS Archives.

Woodruff, Wilford to Jesse C. Little, 27 March 1846. A662, Utah State Hist. Soc.

Woodruff, Wilford to O. Pratt and S. Brannan, 17 October 1845. MS 1352, Box 6, Folder 3 #12, LDS Archives.

Wyatt, Stewart R. The Life and Times of Alondus De LaFayette Buckland, 1824 to 1854. Copy in possession of editor.

Yale, Charles G. to Charles S. Cushing, 14 February 1926. Brannan File, Soc. of Calif. Pioneers.

Young, Brigham. Collection. MS 1234, LDS Archives (available by special permission).

Young, Brigham to P. P. Pratt, 26 May 1845. Vault Mss 76, #77, Box 1, Folder 35, Special Collections, BYU Library.

Young, Brigham to J. C. Little, 20 January 1846. MS 14691, LDS Archives.

Young, Brigham. "To the Saints in California," 7 August 1847. MSS SC 468, Special Collections and Manuscripts, BYU Library. Original at LDS Archives.

Young, John Y. Facts of Early History in most of which I participated, Biographical File Typescript, Soc. of Calif. Pioneers, S.F., Calif.

INDEX

THE EDITOR

Will Bagley is a historian and writer who lives in Salt Lake City with his wife and two children. He edited *A Road from El Dorado: The 1848 Trail Journal of Ephraim Green* and *Frontiersman: Abner Blackburn's Narrative*, which Utah State University awarded the 1991 Evans Manuscript Prize. With Harold Schindler, he revised and updated Dale L. Morgan's classic *West from Fort Bridger*. During the centennial of Utah's statehood, he published *This is the Place: A Crossroads of Utah's Past*, a children's book, with his brother, cartoonist Pat Bagley. *The Pioneer Camp of the Saints: The 1846–1847 Mormon Trail Journals of Thomas Bullock*, the first volume of the Arthur H. Clark Company series KINGDOM IN THE WEST: *The Mormons and the American Frontier*, won the 1997 Stephen F. Christensen Award for Best Documentary from the Mormon History Association. That year Mr. Bagley was awarded the Association's T. Edgar Lyon Award for the Best Article of the Year in Mormon History for "'Every Thing Is Favourable! And God Is On Our Side': Samuel Brannan and the Conquest of California"

Mr. Bagley believes he has what Samuel Brannan considered the "QUALIFICATIONS FOR AN EDITOR.—'He must possess the constitution of a horse, obstinacy of a mule, independence of a wood sawyer, endurance of a starving anaconda, impudence of a beggar, spunk of a chicken cock, pertinacity of a dun, and entire resignation to the most confounded of all earthly treadmills.'"—*New-York Messenger*, Saturday, 15 November 1845, 156/1.